CHRYSLER

CARAVAN A[...]
1984-94 REPAIR [...]

CHILTON'S

BEECH GROVE PUBLIC LIBRARY

President, Chilton Enterprises	David S. Loewith
Senior Vice President	Ronald A. Hoxter
Publisher & Editor-In-Chief	Kerry A. Freeman, S.A.E.
Managing Editors	Peter M. Conti, Jr., W. Calvin Settle, Jr., S.A.E.
Assistant Managing Editor	Nick D'Andrea
Senior Editors	Debra Gaffney, Ken Grabowski, A.S.E., S.A.E.
	Michael L. Grady, Richard J. Rivele, S.A.E.
	Richard T. Smith, Jim Taylor
	Ron Webb
Project Managers	Martin J. Gunther, Jeffrey M. Hoffman
Production Manager	Andrea Steiger
Director of Manufacturing	Mike D'Imperio
Editor	Martin J. Gunther

CHILTON BOOK COMPANY

ONE OF THE **DIVERSIFIED PUBLISHING COMPANIES,**
A PART OF **CAPITAL CITIES/ABC,INC.**

Manufactured in USA
© 1994 Chilton Book Company
Chilton Way, Radnor, PA 19089
ISBN 0-8019-8561-7
Library of Congress Catalog Card No. 94-071966
2345678901   4321098765

Contents

Contents

SAFETY NOTICE

Proper service and repair procedures are vital to the safe, reliable operation of all motor vehicles, as well as the personal safety of those performing repairs. This manual outlines procedures for servicing and repairing vehicles using safe, effective methods. The procedures contain many NOTES, CAUTIONS, and WARNINGS which should be followed along with standard procedures to eliminate the possibility of personal injury or improper service which could damage the vehicle or compromise its safety.

It is important to note that the repair procedures and techniques, tools and parts for servicing motor vehicles, as well as the skill and experience of the individual performing the work vary widely. It is not possible to anticipate all of the conceivable ways or conditions under which vehicles may be serviced, or to provide cautions as to all of the possible hazards that may result. Standard and accepted safety precautions and equipment should be used when handling toxic or flammable fluids, and safety goggles or other protection should be used during cutting, grinding, chiseling, prying,or any other process that can cause material removal or projectiles.

Some procedures require the use of tools specially designed for a specific purpose. Before substituting another tool or procedure, you must be completely satisfied that neither your personal safety, nor the performance of the vehicle will be endangered.

Although information in this manual is based on industry sources and is complete as possible at the time of publication, the possibility exists that some car manufacturers made later changes which could not be included here. While striving for total accuracy, Chilton Book Company cannot assume responsibility for any errors, changes or omissions that may occur in the compilation of this data.

PART NUMBERS

Part numbers listed in this reference are not recommendation by Chilton for any product by brand name. They are references that can be used with interchange manuals and aftermarket supplier catalogs to locate each brand supplier's discrete part number.

SPECIAL TOOLS

Special tools are recommended by the vehicle manufacturer to perform their specific job. Use has been kept to a minimum, but where absolutely necessary, they are referred to in the text by the part number of the tool manufacturer. These tools can be purchased, under the appropriate part number, from your dealer or regional distributor, or an equivalent tool can be purchased locally from a tool supplier or parts outlet. Before substituting any tool for the one recommended, read the SAFETY NOTICE at the top of this page.

ACKNOWLEDGMENTS

The Chilton Book Company expresses appreciation to Chrysler Corporation for their generous assistance.

No part of this publication may be reproduced, transmitted or stored in any form or by any means, electronic or mechanical, including photocopy, recording, or by information storage or retrieval system without prior written permission from the publisher.

1

GENERAL INFORMATION AND MAINTENANCE

HOW TO USE THIS BOOK

Chilton's Total Car Care Manual for the Dodge Caravan/Plymouth Voyager is intended to teach you about the inner workings of your van and save you money on its upkeep.

The first two Sections will be the most used, since they contain maintenance, tune-up information and service procedures. Studies have shown that a properly tuned and maintained vehicle will get better gas mileage (which translates into lower operating costs) and periodic maintenance will catch minor problems before they turn into major repair bills. The other Sections deal with the more complex systems of your car. Operating systems from engine through brakes are covered. It will give you the detailed instructions to help you change your own brake pads and shoes, tune-up the engine, replace spark plugs and filters, and do many more jobs that will save you money, give you personal satisfaction and help you avoid expensive problems.

Before attempting any repairs or service on your vehicle, read through the entire procedure outlined in the appropriate section. This will give you the overall view of what tools and supplies will be required. Many times a description of the system function and operation is given, helping you to understand what repairs must be done.

Two basic mechanic's rules should be mentioned here. First, whenever the LEFT side of the car or engine is referred to, it is meant to specify the DRIVER'S side of the car. Conversely, the RIGHT side of the car means the PASSENGER'S side. Second, all screws and bolts are removed by turning counterclockwise, and tightened by turning clockwise (unless otherwise noted).

Safety is always the most important rule. Constantly be aware of the dangers involved in working on or around an automobile, and take proper precautions to avoid the risk of personal injury or damage to the vehicle. See the section, Servicing Your Vehicle Safely, and the SAFETY NOTICE on the acknowledgment page before attempting any service procedures. Pay special attention to the instructions provided.

There are 3 common mistakes in mechanical work:

1. Incorrect order of assembly, disassembly or adjustment. When taking something apart or putting it together, doing things in the wrong order usually just costs you extra time; however, it CAN break something. Read the entire procedure before beginning disassembly. Do everything in the order in which the instructions say you should do it, even if you can't immediately see a reason for it. When you're taking apart something that is very intricate (for example a carburetor), you might want to draw a picture of how it looks when assembled at one point in order to make sure you get everything back in its proper position. We will supply exploded views whenever possible, but sometimes the job requires more attention to detail than an illustration provides. When making adjustments (especially tune-up adjustments), do them in order. One adjustment often affects another, and you cannot expect satisfactory results unless each adjustment is made in accordance with its sequence.

2. Overtorquing (or undertorquing) nuts and bolts. While it is more common for overtorquing to cause damage, undertorquing can cause a fastener to vibrate loose and cause serious damage, especially when dealing with aluminum parts. Pay attention to torque specifications and utilize a torque wrench in assembly. If a torque figure is not available remember that, if you are using the right tool to do the job, you will probably not have to strain yourself to get a fastener tight enough. The pitch of most threads is so slight that the tension you put on the wrench will be multiplied many times in actual force on what you are tightening. A good example of how critical torque is can be seen in the case of spark plug installation, especially where you are putting the plug into an aluminum cylinder head. Too little torque can fail to crush the gasket, causing leakage of combustion gases, and consequent overheating of the plug and engine parts. Too much torque can damage the threads or distort the plug, which changes the spark gap. Since more and more manufacturers are using aluminum in their engine and chassis parts to save weight, a torque wrench should be in any serious do-it-yourselfer's tool box.

➡️**There are many commercial chemical products available for ensuring that fasteners won't come loose, even if they are not torqued just right (a very common brand is Loctite®). If you're worried about getting something together tight enough to hold, but loose enough to avoid mechanical damage during assembly, one of these products might offer substantial insurance. Read the label on the package and make sure the product is compatible with the materials, fluids, etc. involved before choosing one.**

3. Cross Threading. This occurs when a part such as a bolt is screwed into a nut or casting at the wrong angle and forced, causing the threads to become damaged. Crossthreading is more likely to occur if access is difficult. It helps to clean and lubricate fasteners, and to start threading with the part to be installed going straight in, using your fingers. If you encounter resistance, unscrew the part and start over again at a different angle until it can be inserted and turned several times without much effort. Keep in mind that many parts, especially spark plugs, use tapered threads so that gentle turning will automatically bring the part you're threading to the proper angle if you don't force it or resist a change in angle. Don't put a wrench on the part until it's been turned in a couple of times by hand. If you suddenly encounter resistance and the part has not seated fully, don't force it. Pull it back out and make sure it's clean and threading properly.

Always take your time and be patient; once you have some experience, working on your car will become an enjoyable hobby.

TOOLS AND EQUIPMENT

▶ **See Figures 1, 2, 3, 4, 5, 6, 7, 8, 9, 10, 11, 12 and 13**

Naturally, without the proper tools and equipment it is impossible to properly service your vehicle. It would be impossible to catalog each tool that you would need to perform each or every operation in this book. It would also be unwise for the amateur to rush out and buy an expensive set of tools, on the theory that he may need one or more of them at sometime.

The best approach is to proceed slowly, gathering together a good quality set of those tools that are used most frequently. Don't be misled by the low cost of bargain tools. It is far better to spend a little more for better quality. Forged wrenches, 6- or 12-point sockets and fine tooth ratchets are by far preferable to their less expensive counterparts. As any good mechanic can tell you, there are few worse experiences than trying to work on a car with bad tools. Your monetary savings will be far outweighed by frustration and mangled knuckles.

Begin accumulating those tools that are used most frequently; those associated with routine maintenance and tune-up.

In addition to the normal assortment of screwdrivers and pliers you should have the following tools for routine maintenance jobs:

1. SAE/Metric wrenches, sockets and combination open end/box end wrenches in sizes from ⅛ in. (3mm) to ¾ in. (19mm), and a spark plug socket (¹³⁄₁₆ in. or ⅝ in.). If possible, buy various length socket drive extensions. One break in this department is that the metric sockets available in the U.S. will all fit the ratchet handles and extensions you may already have (¼, ⅜, and ½ in. drive).
2. Jackstands for support.
3. Oil filter wrench.
4. Oil filler spout or funnel.
5. Grease gun for chassis lubrication.
6. Hydrometer for checking the battery.
7. A low flat pan for draining oil.
8. Lots of rags for wiping up the inevitable mess.

In addition to the above items there are several others that are not absolutely necessary, but handy to have around. These include oil-dry, a transmission fluid funnel and the usual supply of lubricants, antifreeze and fluids, although these can be purchased as needed. This is a basic list for routine maintenance, but only your personal needs and desires can accurately determine your list of necessary tools.

The second list of tools is for tune-ups. While the tools involved here are slightly more sophisticated, they need not be outrageously expensive. A basic list of tune-up equipment could include:

9. Tachometer
10. Spark plug wrench
11. Timing light
12. Wire spark plug gauge/adjusting tools

In addition to these basic tools, there are several other tools and gauges you may find useful. These include:

13. A compression gauge. The screw-in type is slower to use, but eliminates the possibility of a faulty reading due to escaping pressure
14. A manifold vacuum gauge

15. A test light
16. An induction meter. This is used for determining whether or not there is current in a wire. These are handy for use if a wire is broken somewhere in a wiring harness.

As a final note, you will probably find a torque wrench necessary for all but the most basic work. The beam type models are perfectly adequate, although the newer click (breakaway) type are more precise, and you don't have to crane your neck to see a torque reading in awkward situations. The breakaway torque wrenches are more expensive and should be recalibrated periodically.

Torque specification for each fastener will be given in the procedure in any case that a specific torque value is required. If no torque specifications are given, use the following values as a guide, based upon fastener size:

Bolts marked 6T
- 6mm bolt/nut: 5-7 ft. lbs.
- 8mm bolt/nut: 12-17 ft. lbs.
- 10mm bolt/nut: 23-34 ft. lbs.
- 12mm bolt/nut: 41-59 ft. lbs.
- 14mm bolt/nut: 56-76 ft. lbs.

Bolts marked 8T
- 6mm bolt/nut: 6-9 ft. lbs.
- 8mm bolt/nut: 13-20 ft. lbs.
- 10mm bolt/nut: 27-40 ft. lbs.
- 12mm bolt/nut: 46-69 ft. lbs.
- 14mm bolt/nut: 75-101 ft. lbs.

Special Tools

Normally, the use of special factory tools is avoided for repair procedures, since these are not readily available for the do-it-yourselfer mechanic. When it is possible to perform the job with more commonly available tools, it will be pointed out, but occasionally, a special tool was designed to perform a specific function and should be used. Before substituting another tool, you should be convinced that neither your safety nor the performance of the vehicle will be compromised.

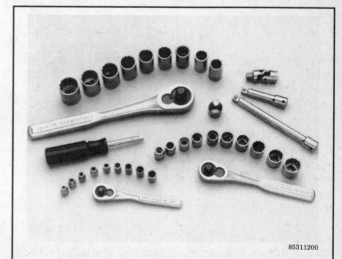

85311200

Fig. 1 ¼, ⅜ and ½ inch drive rachets and extensions with both Standard and Metric size sockets.

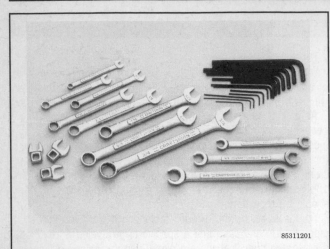

85311201

Fig. 2 You should have a set of box and open end wrenches and crows feet in both Standard and Metric sizes and a set of allen wrenches

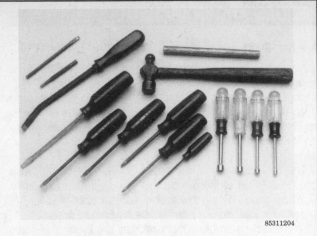

85311204

Fig. 5 An assortment of both slotted and phillip screwdrivers, chisels, nutdrivers, hammer and drive bar are shown

85311202

Fig. 3 Use a good jack and jackstands when you are working under your car

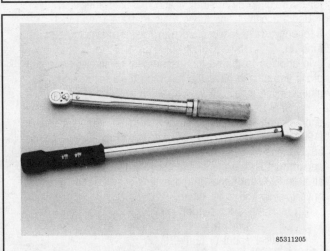

85311205

Fig. 6 Clicker type torque wrenches are available in both ⅜ and ½ inch drives, and measure foot or inch lbs.

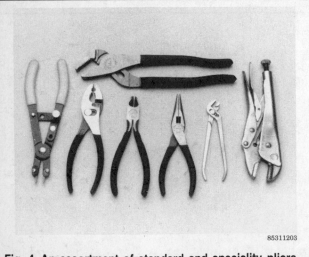

85311203

Fig. 4 An assortment of standard and speciality pliers are needed when working on your car

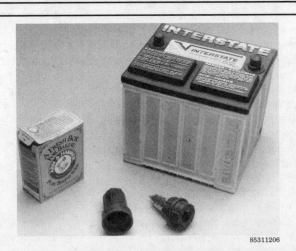

85311206

Fig. 7 Battey terminal cleaning brushes along with a baking soda and water solution do an excellent job of cleaning the battery off

85311207

Fig. 8 The brush shown is for cleaning batteries posts. Special cleaning brushes are also available for batteries with side terminals

85311210

Fig. 11 The items shown are necessary when performing engine oil changes and chassis lubrication

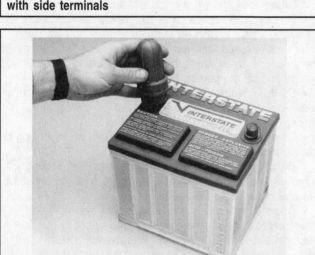

85311208

Fig. 9 To clean the terminals positon the brush over the post as shown and twist back and forth

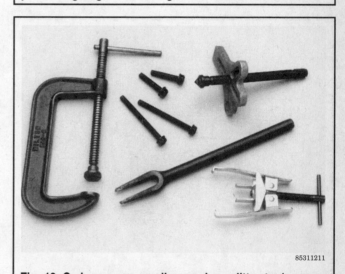

85311211

Fig. 12 C-clamps, gear pullers and a splitter tool are necessary when performing certain jobs.

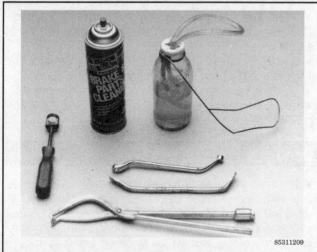

85311209

Fig. 10 This assortment of tools will make brake jobs easier

85311212

Fig. 13 These tools will help when you are removing spark plugs or adjusting valves

Some special tools are available commercially from major tool manufacturers. Others can be purchased from Miller Spe-cial Tools; Division of Utica Tool Company, 32615 Park Lane, Garden City, Michigan 48135.

SERVICING YOUR VEHICLE SAFELY

▶ **See Figures 14 and 15**

It is virtually impossible to anticipate all of the hazards in-volved with automotive maintenance and service but care and common sense will prevent most accidents.

The rules of safety for mechanics range from 'don't smoke around gasoline', to 'use the proper tool for the job.' The trick to avoiding injuries is to develop safe work habits and take every possible precaution.

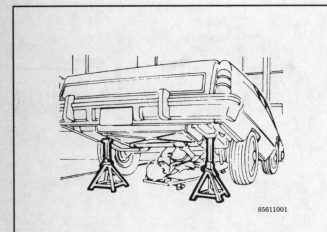

Fig. 14 Always use jackstands when working under the vehicle.

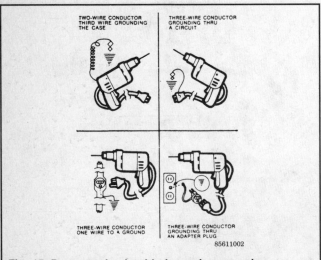

Fig. 15 Power tools should always be properly grounded.

Do's

• Do keep a fire extinguisher and first aid kit within easy reach.
• Do wear safety glasses or goggles when cutting, drilling, grinding or prying. If you wear glasses for the sake of vision, then they should be made of hardened glass that can serve also as safety glasses, or wear safety goggles over your regu-lar glasses.
• Do shield your eyes whenever you work around the bat-tery. Batteries contain sulfuric acid. In case of contact with the eyes or skin, flush the area with water or a mixture of water and baking soda and get medical attention immediately.
• Do use safety stands for any under-car service. Jacks are for raising vehicles; safety stands are for making sure the vehicle stays raised until you want it to come down. Whenever the vehicle is raised, block the wheels remaining on the ground and set the parking brake.
• Do use adequate ventilation when working with any chem-icals. Asbestos dust resulting from brake lining wear cause cancer.
• Do disconnect the negative battery cable when working on the electrical system.
• Do follow manufacturer's directions whenever working with potentially hazardous materials. Both brake fluid and antifreeze are poisonous if taken internally.
• Do properly maintain your tools. Loose hammerheads, mushroomed punches and chisels, frayed or poorly grounded electrical cords, excessively worn screwdrivers, spread wrenches (open end), cracked sockets, slipping ratchets, or faulty droplight sockets can cause accidents.
• Do use the proper size and type of tool for the job being done.
• Do when possible, pull on a wrench handle rather than push on it, and adjust you stance to prevent a fall.
• Do be sure that adjustable wrenches are tightly adjusted on the nut or bolt and pulled so that the face is on the side of the fixed jaw.
• Do select a wrench or socket that fits the nut or bolt. The wrench or socket should sit straight, not cocked.
• Do strike squarely with a hammer. avoid glancing blows.
• Do set the parking brake and block the wheels if the work requires that the engine be running.

Don'ts

• Don't run an engine in a garage or anywhere else without proper ventilation — EVER! Carbon monoxide is poisonous. It is absorbed by the body 400 times faster than oxygen. It takes a long time to leave the human body and you can build up a deadly supply of it in your system by simply breathing in a little every day. You may not realize you are slowly poisoning yourself. Always use power vents, windows, fans or open the garage doors.

• Don't work around moving parts while wearing a necktie or other loose clothing. Short sleeves are much safer than long, loose sleeves. Hard-toed shoes with neoprene soles protect your toes and give a better grip on slippery surfaces. Jewelry such as watches, fancy belt buckles, beads, or body adornment of any kind is not safe while working around a car. Long hair should be hidden under a hat or cap.

• Don't use pockets for toolboxes. A fall or bump can drive a screwdriver deep into you body. Even a wiping cloth hanging from the back pocket can wrap around a spinning shaft or fan.

• Don't smoke when working around gasoline, cleaning solvent or other flammable material.

• Don't smoke when working around the battery. When the battery is being charged, it gives off explosive hydrogen gas.

• Don't use gasoline to wash your hands. There are excellent soaps available. Gasoline may contain lead, and lead can enter the body through a cut, accumulating in the body until you are very ill. Gasoline also removes all the natural oils from the skin so that bone dry hands will suck up oil and grease.

• Don't service the air conditioning system unless you are equipped with the necessary tools and training. The refrigerant, R-12, is extremely cold and when exposed to the air, will instantly freeze any surface it comes in contact with, including your eyes. Although the refrigerant is normally non-toxic, R-12 becomes a deadly poisonous gas in the presence of an open flame. One good whiff of the vapors from burning refrigerant can be fatal.

➡ **The Dodge and Plymouth vehicles described in this manual are metric-specified. While some inch-standard parts are used, body panels, fasteners, drivetrain components, and tires are all specified according to the Metric System. Dimensions and performance data are also expressed in metric units.**

MODEL IDENTIFICATION

The Caravan and Voyager models covered in this manual have remained much the same since their introduction. There are a few variations on the basic model, these include the Mini Ram Van, the 1991 Chrysler Town & Country and the Plymouth Grand Voyager. All of these models are still based on the Caravan and Voyager, and are only different in trim configurations.

For 1991 Chrysler is offering both anti-lock brakes and All Wheel Drive (AWD) as an option on the entire Caravan and Voyager line.

SERIAL NUMBER IDENTIFICATION

Vehicle Identification Number (V.I.N.)

▶ See Figures 16 and 17

The vehicle identification number (VIN) consists of seventeen numbers and letters embossed on a plate, located on the upper left corner of the instrument panel, near the windshield.

Engine Identification Number (E.I.N.)

▶ See Figures 18, 19, 20, 21 and 22

All engine assemblies carry an engine identification number (E.I.N.). On 2.2 liter and 2.5 liter engines, the E.I.N. is located on the face of the engine block, directly under the cylinder head (left side of vehicle).

On 1984-90 2.6 liter, 3.0 liter and 3.3 liter engines, the E.I.N. is located on the left side of the engine block between the core plug and the rear face of the block (radiator side of vehicle). On the 1991-94 3.0 liter, 3.3 liter and 3.8 liter engines, the engine serial number (E.I.N) is located on the rear face of the engine block, directly below the cylinder head.

Engine Serial Number

In addition to the previously covered E.I.N., on 1984-90 models, each engine assembly carries an engine serial number

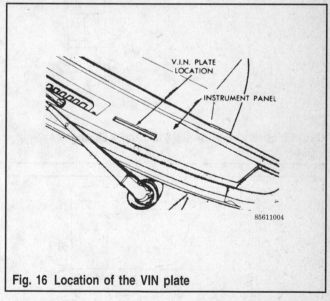

Fig. 16 Location of the VIN plate

which must be referenced when ordering engine replacement parts.

On the 2.2 liter, and 2.5 liter engines, the engine serial number is located on the rear face of the engine block, directly below the cylinder head (below the E.I.N.). On the 1984-90 2.6 liter, and 3.0 liter engines, the engine serial number is located on the exhaust manifold stud (dash panel side of vehicle).

Fig. 17 Example of a VIN plate

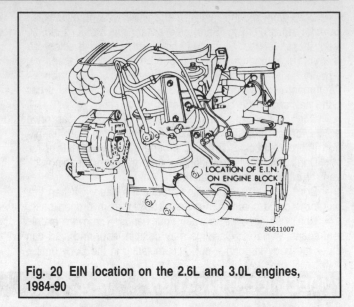

Fig. 20 EIN location on the 2.6L and 3.0L engines, 1984-90

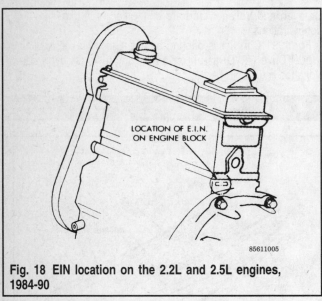

Fig. 18 EIN location on the 2.2L and 2.5L engines, 1984-90

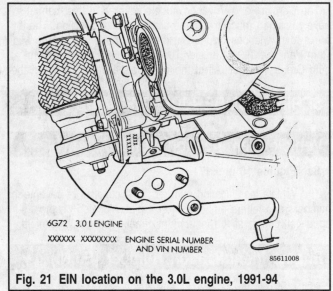

Fig. 21 EIN location on the 3.0L engine, 1991-94

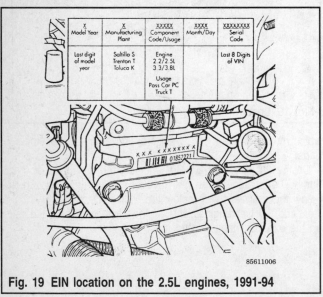

Fig. 19 EIN location on the 2.5L engines, 1991-94

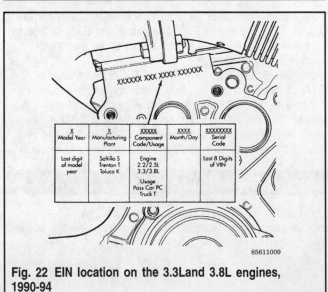

Fig. 22 EIN location on the 3.3Land 3.8L engines, 1990-94

Transaxle

▶ **See Figure 23**

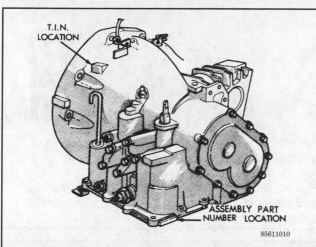

Fig. 23 Location of the Transaxle Identification Number (T.I.N.) on the automatic transaxle and assembly part number location

The transaxle identification number (T.I.N.) is stamped on a boss that is located on the left upper transaxle housing.

In addition to the T.I.N., each transaxle carries an assembly part number. On manual transaxles, the assembly part number is located on a metal tag at the front of the transaxle. On automatic transaxles, the assembly part number is located just above the oil pan at the rear of the assembly.

ROUTINE MAINTENANCE

Air Cleaner

The air cleaner element on vehicles equipped with 2.2 liter engine should be replaced every 52,000 miles. Vehicles equipped with 2.5L, 2.6L, 3.0L, 3.3L and 3.8L engines should be replaced every 30,000 miles. However, if the vehicle is operated frequently through dusty areas; it will require periodic inspection at least every 15,000 miles.

REMOVAL & INSTALLATION

2.2L Engine
▶ **See Figures 24, 25, 26, 27, 28, 29 and 30**

1. Unfasten the three hold down clips and remove the three wing nuts that retain the top of the air cleaner housing.

2. Remove the top of the air cleaner housing and position out of the way with the breather hose attached.

3. Remove the air cleaner element from the housing.

4. Clean the inside of the housing but take care not to allow the dirt to enter the carburetor air intake.

5. Install a new air cleaner element with the screen side up into the plastic housing.

6. Position the steel top cover so that the hold down clips and support bracket studs are aligned.

➡**The procedures in the next steps should be followed as stated to prevent loosening and air leaks.**

7. Install the wing nuts on both carburetor studs and tighten them to 14 inch lbs. Install the wing nut that attaches the air cleaner tab to the support bracket and tighten to 14 inch lbs.

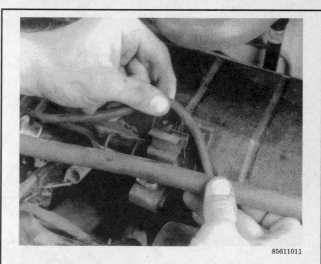

Fig. 24 Before removing the air cleaner housing, disconnect the hoses from the housing retaining clips

8. Fasten the hold down clips.

2.5L, 2.6L, 3.0L, 3.3L and 3.8L Engines
▶ **See Figures 31, 32, 33, 34 and 35**

1. Unfasten the hold down clips that retain the air cleaner cover.

2. Remove the air cleaner housing cover with intake hose attached and position out of the way.

3. Remove the air cleaner element from the housing.

4. Clean the inside of the air cleaner housing.

5. Install a new cleaner element and position the cover on the air cleaner housing. Secure the hold down clips.

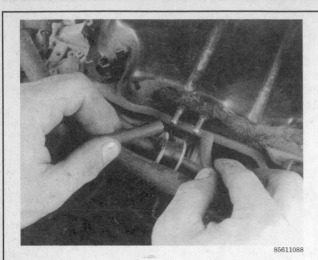

Fig. 25 Although not necessary, the hoses may be disconnected from the housing connectors

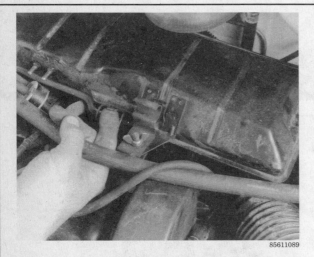

Fig. 26 Unsnap the spring clips from the air cleaner housing

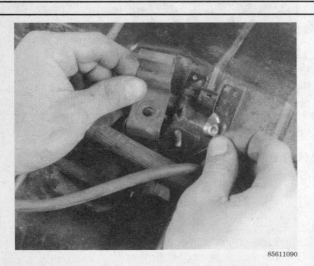

Fig. 27 When removing the housing, remove this wingnut first. Install this wingnut last during installation

Fig. 28 When removing the housing, remove the two end wingnuts last. Install these wingnuts first during installation

Fig. 29 After unsnaping the spring clips and removing the wingnuts the air cleaner housing cover can be removed

Fig. 30 With the air cleaner housing cover removed the air filter element can easily be replaced

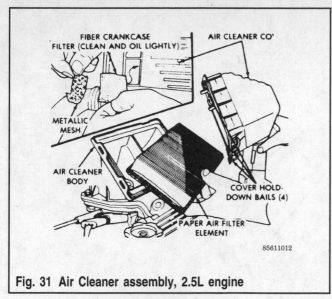

Fig. 31 Air Cleaner assembly, 2.5L engine

Fig. 32 Air Cleaner assembly, 2.6L engine

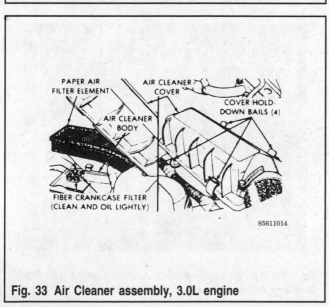

Fig. 33 Air Cleaner assembly, 3.0L engine

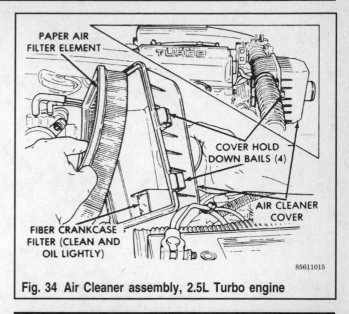

Fig. 34 Air Cleaner assembly, 2.5L Turbo engine

Fuel Filter

✳✳CAUTION

Don't smoke when working around gasoline, cleaning solvent or other flammable material. The hoses used on fuel injected vehicles are of a special construction due to the possibility contaminated fuel in the system. If it is necessary to replace these hoses, only hoses marked EFM/EFI may be used. The hose clamps used on fuel injected vehicles are of a special rolled edge construction to prevent the edge of the clamp from cutting into the hose, resulting in a high pressure fuel leak.

The fuel system on all vehicles incorporate two fuel filters. One is part of the fuel gauge unit; located inside the fuel tank at the fuel suction tube. Routine servicing of this filter is not necessary. However, if limited vehicle speed or hard starting is exhibited, it should be inspected.

The second filter is located in the fuel line between the fuel pump and the carburetor or fuel injector rail. Replacement of this filter is recommended every 52,000 miles.

REMOVAL & INSTALLATION

2.2L and 2.6L Engines
▶ See Figures 36, 37, 38 and 39

1. Clean the area at the filter and clamps with a suitable solvent
2. Loosen the clamps on both ends of filter.
3. Wrap a shop towel or clean rag around the hoses to absorb fuel.
4. Remove the hoses from the filter, and discard the clamps and filter.
5. Install the new filter between the fuel lines and clamp.
6. Tighten the clamps to 1 Nm (10 inch lbs.)

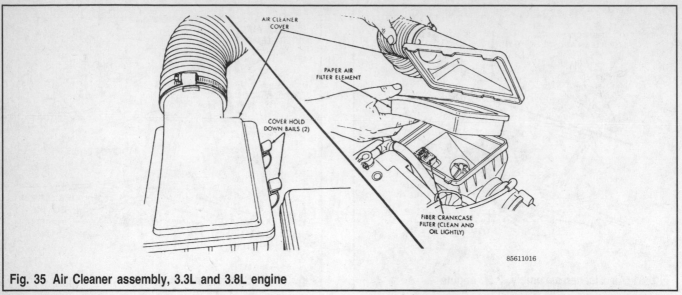

Fig. 35 Air Cleaner assembly, 3.3L and 3.8L engine

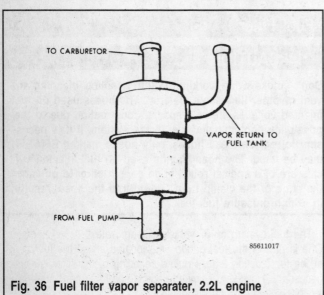

Fig. 36 Fuel filter vapor separater, 2.2L engine

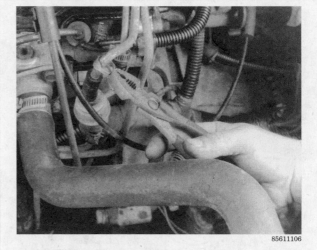

Fig. 38 Squeeze open the other hose retaining clamps with a suitable pair of pliers

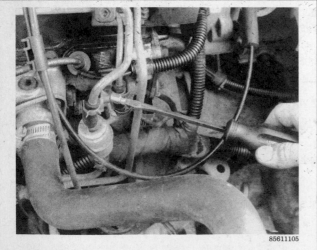

Fig. 37 Place a shop rag under the fuel filter and unscrew the hose retaining clamp at the fual line

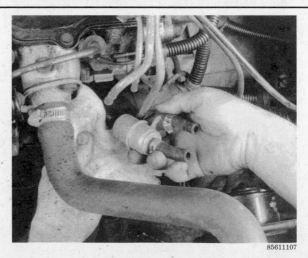

Fig. 39 After the loosing the retaining clamps pull the filter and hoses from the fuel pipes

2.5L, 3.0L and 3.3L Engines Except All Wheel Drive
▶ See Figure 40

The fuel filter on these vehicles is located along the chassis, mounted just ahead of the fuel tank. To remove the filter, the vehicle will have to be raised slightly.

❋❋CAUTION

Before servicing any components within the fuel system, the system pressure must first be released.

1. Release the fuel system pressure. Refer to the procedure below.
2. Raise the vehicle slightly and safely support it. Remove the retaining screw and filter assembly from the chassis rail.
3. Loosen the clamps on both ends of the fuel filter.
4. Wrap a shop towel or clean rag around the hoses to absorb fuel
5. Remove the hoses from the filter, and discard clamps and filter.
6. Remove the filter retaining screw and remove the filter from the rail.
7. Install the new filter between the hoses and clamp.
8. Tighten the clamps to 1 Nm (10 inch lbs.).
9. Position the filter assembly on the chassis rail.
10. Tighten the mounting screw to 8 Nm (75 inch lbs.)

All Wheel Drive Vehicles
▶ See Figures 41 and 42

❋❋CAUTION

Before servicing any components within the fuel system, the system pressure must first be released.

1. Release the fuel system pressure. Refer to the procedure below.

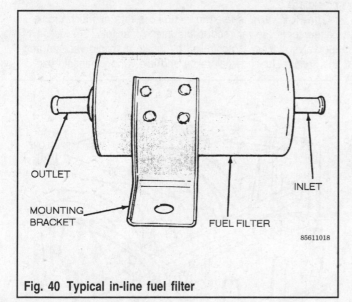

Fig. 40 Typical in-line fuel filter

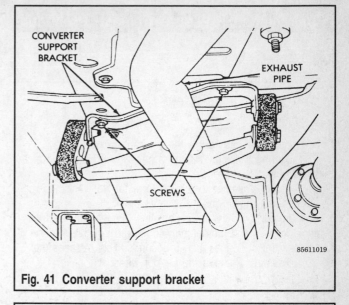

Fig. 41 Converter support bracket

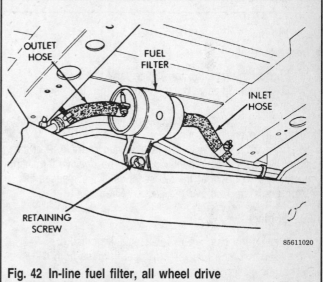

Fig. 42 In-line fuel filter, all wheel drive

2. Raise the vehicle slightly and safely support it. Remove the retaining screw and filter assembly from the chassis rail.
3. Remove the converter support bracket.
4. Remove the exhaust pipe heat shield.
5. Loosen the clamps on both ends of the fuel filter.
6. Wrap a shop towel or clean rag around the hoses to absorb fuel
7. Remove the hoses from the filter, and discard clamps and filter.
8. Remove the filter retaining screw and remove the filter from the rail.
9. Install the new filter between the hoses and clamp.
10. Tighten the clamps to 1 Nm (10 inch lbs.).
11. Position the filter assembly on the chassis rail.
12. Tighten the mounting screw to 8 Nm (75 inch lbs.)
13. Install the exhaust pipe heat shield.
14. Install the converter support bracket.

Fuel System Pressure Release Procedure

1987-92

2.5L, 3.0L and 3.3L Engines
▶ **See Figure 43**

1. Loosen the gas cap to release tank pressure.
2. Disconnect injector wiring harness from the engine or main harness.
3. Connect a jumper to ground terminal No. 1 of the injector harness to engine ground.
4. Connect a jumper to the positive terminal No. 2 of the injector harness and momentarily touch the positive terminal of the battery for no longer than 5 seconds. This releases the system pressure. Remove the jumper wires.

1993-94

2.5L Engine
▶ **See Figure 43**

1. Loosen the gas cap to release tank pressure.
2. Disconnect injector wiring harness from the engine or main harness.
3. Connect a jumper to ground terminal No. 1 of the injector harness to engine ground.
4. Connect a jumper to the positive terminal No. 2 of the injector harness and momentarily touch the positive terminal of the battery for no longer than 5 seconds. This releases the system pressure. Remove the jumper wires.

3.0L Engine

1. Loosen the gas cap to release tank pressure.
2. Disconnect the fuel rail electrical harness from the engine harness.
3. Connect one end of a jumper wire to the A142 circuit terminal of the fuel rail harness connector.

4. Connect the other end of the jumper wire to a good ground source.
5. Momentarily ground one of the injectors by connecting the other end of the jumper wire to an injector terminal in the harness connector. Repeat the procedure for 2 or 3 injectors.

3.3L and 3.8L Engine
▶ **See Figure 44**

1. Disconnect the negative battery cable.
2. Loosen the gas cap to release tank pressure.
3. Remove the protective cap from the fuel pressure test port on the fuel rail.
4. Place the open end of fuel pressure release hose, tool No. C-4799-1, into an approved gasoline container. Connect the other end of hose C-4799-1 to the fuel pressure test port. Fuel pressure will bleed off through the hose into the gasoline container.

➡ **Fuel gauge C-4799-A contains hose C-4799-1**

PCV Valve

▶ **See Figures 45, 46, 47 and 48**

OPERATION

2.2L, 2.5L, 3.0L and 3.3L Engines

Crankcase vapors and piston blow-by are removed from the engine by intake manifold vacuum. The emissions are drawn through the PCV valve (usually located in the top of the engine valve cover) into the intake manifold where they become part of the air/fuel mixture. Crankcase vapors are then burned and pass through the exhaust system. When there are not enough vapors or blow-by pressure in the engine, air is drawn from the air cleaner. With this system no outside air enters the crankcase.

The PCV valve is used to control the rate at which crankcase vapors are returned to the intake manifold. The action of the valve plunger is controlled by intake manifold vacuum and the spring. During deceleration and idle, when manifold vac-

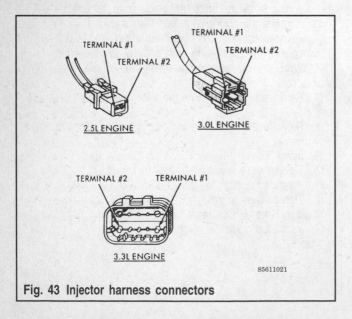

Fig. 43 Injector harness connectors

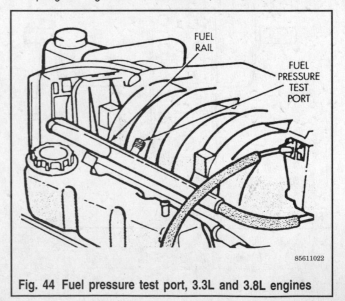

Fig. 44 Fuel pressure test port, 3.3L and 3.8L engines

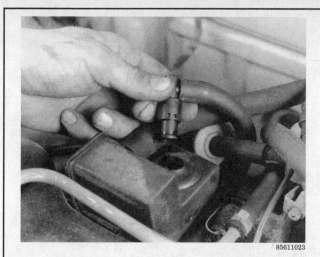

Fig. 45 Removing the PCV valve from the crankcase vent module

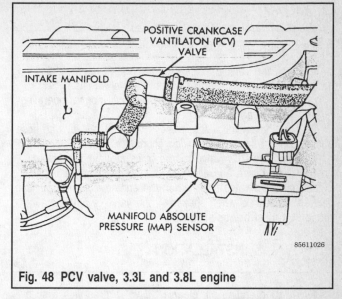

Fig. 48 PCV valve, 3.3L and 3.8L engine

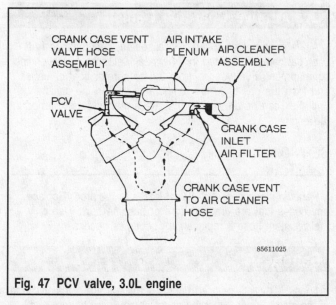

Fig. 47 PCV valve, 3.0L engine

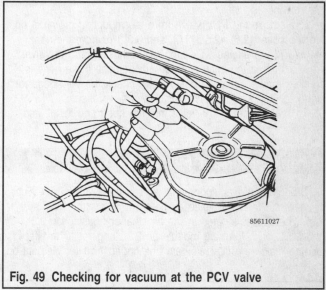

Fig. 49 Checking for vacuum at the PCV valve

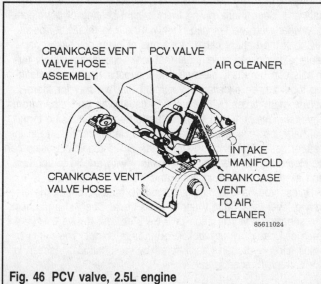

Fig. 46 PCV valve, 2.5L engine

uum is high, it overcomes the tension of the valve spring and the plunger bottoms in the manifold end of the valve housing. Because of the valve construction, it reduces, but does not stop, the passage of vapors to the intake manifold. When the engine is lightly accelerated or operated at constant speed, spring tension matches intake manifold vacuum pull and the plunger takes a mid-position in the valve body, allowing more vapors to flow into the manifold.

2.6L Engine

Intake manifold vacuum draws air from the air cleaner through the valve cover into the engine, the outside air is mixed with crankcase vapors and piston blow-by and drawn through the PCV valve (located in the top end of the engine cover) and into the intake manifold where it becomes part of the air/fuel mixture. The vapors are burned and expelled with exhaust gases.

TESTING

▶ **See Figures 49 and 50**

1. Place the vehicle in Park, or Neutral (if manual transaxle). Set the parking brake and block the wheels.
2. Start the engine and allow to idle until normal operating temperature is reached.
3. With the engine idling, remove the PCV valve, with hose attached, from its rubber molded connector.
4. When the PCV valve is free of its mounting, a hissing noise will be heard and a strong vacuum felt when a finger is placed over the valve inlet. When the engine is turned off, the valve should rattle when shaken. If the valve is not operating properly it must be replaced.

REMOVAL & INSTALLATION

1. With the engine off, clean PCV valve area with a suitable solvent.
2. Remove the PCV valve from the mounting grommet on the top cover (2.6L, 2.5L, 3.0L and 3.3L) or from the vent module (2.2L) engines. Disconnect the hose from the valve.
3. Examine the vacuum hose and replace if the hose is cracked, broken or dried out. Always check the vent hose for clogging. If clogged, replace or clean as necessary.
4. Install a new PCV valve into the hose and install into mounting grommet.

Crankcase Vent Filter

All engines are equipped with a crankcase vent filter which is used to filter the outside air before it enters the PCV system. The filter is located in the air cleaner housing on 2.6L and 2.5L, or in the vent module on 2.2L engines. The filter is located inside the filter element box under the filter element on 3.0L engines and the filter element is located in the bottom of the filter element box on the 3.3L and the 3.8L engines. Replacement should be performed every 50,000-60,000 miles.

VENT FILTER SERVICE

1. On models equipped with the 2.2L engine, remove the PCV valve from the vent module and remove the vent module from the engine cover. Wash the module thoroughly in kerosene or safe solvent.
2. Lubricate or wet the filter with SAE 30 weight oil. Reinstall the module, PCV valve and hose.
3. On models equipped with the 2.5L and 2.6L engine, remove the vent filter from the air cleaner housing. Replace with a new element. Wet the new element slightly with SAE 30 weight oil before installation.
4. Models equipped with the 3.0L, 3.3L and 3.8L engines, remove the filter from the filter element box. Renew filter.

Evaporative Charcoal Canister

All vehicles are equipped with a sealed, maintenance free charcoal canister, located in the wheel well area of the engine compartment. Fuel vapors, from the carburetor float chamber and from the gas tank, are temporarily held in the canister until they can be drawn into the intake manifold and burned in the engine.

SERVICING

Periodic inspection of the vent hoses is required. Replace any hoses that are cracked, torn or become hard. Use only fuel resistant hose if replacement becomes necessary.

Battery

Loose, dirty, or corroded battery terminals are a major cause of 'no-start.' Every 3 months or so, remove the battery terminals and clean them, giving them a light coating of petroleum jelly when you are finished. This will help to retard corrosion.

Check the battery cables for signs of wear or chafing and replace any cable or terminal that looks marginal. Battery terminals can be easily cleaned and inexpensive terminal cleaning tools are an excellent investment that will pay for themselves many times over. They can usually be purchased from any well-equipped auto store or parts department. Side terminal batteries require a different tool to clean the threads in the battery case. The accumulated white powder and corrosion can be cleaned from the top of the battery with an old toothbrush and a solution of baking soda and water.

Unless you have a maintenance-free battery, check the electrolyte level (see Battery under Fluid Level Checks) and check the specific gravity of each cell. Be sure that the vent holes in each cell cap are not blocked by grease or dirt. The vent holes allow hydrogen gas, formed by the chemical reaction in the battery, to escape safely.

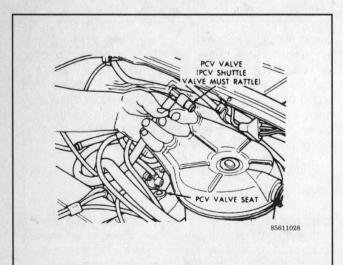

85611028

Fig. 50 To be considered servicable, the PCV valve must rattle when shaken

MAINTENANCE FREE BATTERIES

◗ **See Figure 51**

All models are factory equipped with a maintenance free battery. Maintenance free batteries are as the name implies, totally free of maintenance as far as adding water is concerned. The battery is generally completely sealed except for some small vent holes that allow gases, produced in the battery, to escape. Battery terminal and cable end connector maintenance is required. Also, the cables should be disconnected, and the terminals and clamps cleaned at least once a year.

The factory installed battery contains a visual test indicator which signals when an adequate charge level exists. The test indicator is a built-in hydrometer that is equipped with a sight glass and is permanently installed in the battery cover. The sight glass indicator will show green when the battery has from a 75% to full charge. The glass will appear dark if the battery needs recharging and show yellow when replacement may be needed.

✳✳CAUTION

Batteries contain electrolyte, a mixture of sulfuric acid and distilled water. The use of adequate eye protection, and a suitable pair of rubber gloves is strongly recommended when working with batteries. In any event, if battery acid comes in contact with the skin or eyes, flush the affected area with plenty of clear water, and seek medical attention.

REPLACEMENT BATTERIES EXCEPT MAINTENANCE FREE

If a replacement battery of the non-maintenance free type has been installed in your vehicle, be sure to check the fluid level at least once a month. During warm weather or during periods of extended service, more frequent checking is necessary.

The fluid level can be checked through the case on translucent polypropylene batteries. The cell caps must be removed on other styles. The fluid (electrolyte) level should be kept filled to the split ring inside each cell filler opening, or to the line marked or molded on the outside of the battery case.

If the fluid level is low, add water (distilled water only) through the top openings until the correct level is reached. Each cell is separated and must be checked and filled individually.

If water is added in freezing weather, the vehicle should be driven several miles to allow the water to mix with the electrolyte.

Specific Gravity (except maintenance free batteries)

At least once a year, check the specific gravity of the battery. It should be between 1.20 in. Hg and 1.26 in. Hg at room temperature.

The specific gravity can be check with the use of a hydrometer, an inexpensive instrument available from many sources, including auto parts stores. The hydrometer has a squeeze bulb at one end and a nozzle at the other. Battery electrolyte is sucked into the hydrometer until the float is lifted from its seat. The specific gravity is then read by noting the position of the float. Generally, if after charging, the specific gravity between any two cells varies more than 50 points (0.50), the battery is bad and should be replaced.

It is not possible to check the specific gravity in this manner on sealed (maintenance free) batteries. Instead, the indicator built into the top of the case must be relied on to display any signs of battery deterioration. Refer to section marked 'MAINTENANCE FREE BATTERIES'.

CABLES AND CLAMPS

◗ **See Figures 52, 53 and 54**

Once a year, the battery terminals and the cable clamps should be cleaned. Loosen the clamps and remove the cables, negative cable first. On batteries with posts on top, the use of a puller specially made for the purpose is recommended.

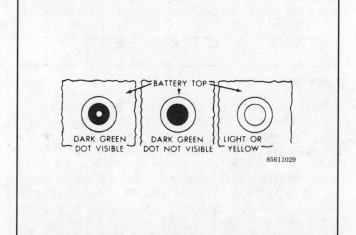

Fig. 51 The battery is equipped with a built in test indicator

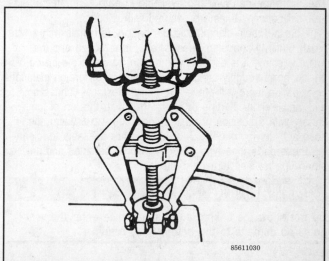

Fig. 52 A small puller will easily remove the cable from the terminals

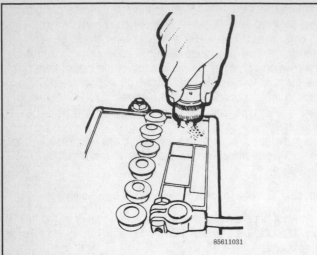

Fig. 53 An enexpensive tool easily cleans the battery terminal post

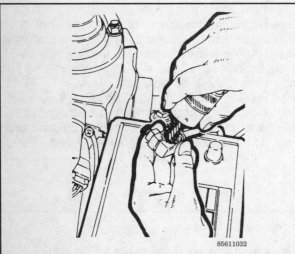

Fig. 54 Clean the inside of the battery cable end connectors

These are inexpensive, and available in auto parts stores. Side terminal battery cables are secured with a bolt.

Clean the cable clamps and the battery terminals with a wire brush, until all corrosion, grease, etc., is removed and the metal is shiny. It is especially important to clean the inside of the clamp thoroughly, since a small deposit of foreign material or oxidation there will prevent a sound electrical connection and inhibit either starting or charging. Clean the top of the battery with a solution of baking soda and warm water, then rinse and dry thoroughly. Special tools are available for cleaning these parts, one type for conventional batteries and another type for side terminal batteries.

✳✳WARNING

Do not allow the baking soda solution to enter the vent holes as damage to the battery may result.

Before installing the cables, loosen the battery hold down clamp or strap, remove the battery and check the battery tray. Clear it of any debris, and check it for soundness. Rust should be wire brushed away, and the metal given a coat of anti-rust paint. Replace the battery and tighten the hold down clamp or strap securely, but be careful not to over tighten, which will crack the battery case.

After the clamps and terminals are clean, reinstall the cables, negative cable last; do not hammer on the clamps to install. Tighten the clamps securely, but do not distort them. Give the clamps and terminals a thin external coat of grease after installation, to retard corrosion.

Check the cables at the same time that the terminals are cleaned. If the cable insulation is cracked or broken, or if the ends are frayed, the cable should be replaced with a new cable of the same length and gauge.

✳✳CAUTION

Keep flame or sparks away from the battery; it gives off explosive hydrogen gas. Battery electrolyte contains sulfuric acid. If you should splash any on your skin or in your eyes, flush the affected area with plenty of clear water. If it lands in your eyes, get medical help immediately.

Drive Belts

INSPECTION

Check the condition and tension of all drive belts every 12,000 miles, or at least once a year. Loose drive belts can lead to poor engine cooling and diminished alternator, power steering pump, air conditioning compressor, or emission air pump output. A belt that is too tight places a strain on the bearings in the driven component.

Replace any drive belt that is glazed, worn, cracked, or stretched to the point where correct adjustment tension is impossible. If two belts are used to drive a component, always replace both belts when replacement is necessary. After installing a new belt, run the engine for ten minutes, shut off the engine and recheck the belt tension. Readjust if necessary.

CHECKING DRIVE BELT ADJUSTMENT

▶ See Figures 55, 56, 57, 58 and 59

Two popular methods of checking drive belt adjustment are; the Belt Tension Gauge Method and the Belt Deflection Method. The former requires a special gauge and the latter requires a straight edge and scale or just a good eye for measurement. The deflection method will be used in the following belt replacement instructions. A rule of thumb for checking belt tension by the deflection method is to determine the midpoint between two pulleys of the drive belt and press down at that point with moderate thumb pressure. The belt should deflect to the measurement indicated in the following installation procedures. Adjustment is necessary if the belt is either too loose or too tight.

Accessory Drive Belt		Gauge	Deflection	Torque
Air Conditioning Compressor	New	105 lb.	8mm (5/16 in.)	54 N·m (40 ft. lbs.)
	Used	80 lb.	9mm (7/16 in.)	41 N·m (30 ft. lbs.)
Air Pump	New	—	5mm (3/16 in.)	61 N·m (45 ft. lbs.)
	Used	—	6mm (1/4 in.)	47 N·m (35 ft. lbs.)
Alternator/Water Pump "V" Belt and Poly "V"	New	115 lb.	3mm (1/8 in.)	149 N·m (110 ft. lbs.)
	Used	80 lb.	6mm (1/4 in.)	108 N·m (80 ft. lbs.)
Power Steering Pump	New	105 lb.	6mm (1/4 in.)	102 N·m (75 ft. lbs.)
	Used	80 lb.	11mm (7/16 in.)	75 N·m (55 ft. lbs.)

85611043

Fig. 55 Engine belt tension chart, 2.2L engine

Accessory Drive Belt		Gauge	Deflection	Torque
Air Conditioning Compressor	New	105 lb.	8mm (5/16 in.)	54 N·m (40 ft. lbs.)
	Used	80 lb.	11mm (7/16 in.)	41 N·m (30 ft. lbs.)
Alternator/Water Pump Poly "V"	New	115 lb.	3mm (1/8 in.)	149 N·m (110 ft. lbs.)
	Used	80 lb.	6mm (1/4 in.)	108 N·m (80 ft. lbs.)
Power Steering Pump	New	105 lb.	6mm (1/4 in.)	102 N·m (75 ft. lbs.)
	Used	80 lb.	11mm (7/16 in.)	75 N·m (55 ft. lbs.)

85611044

Fig. 56 Engine belt tension chart, 1987-89 2.5L engine

Accessory Drive Belt		Gauge	Deflection	Torque
Power Steering Pump	New	95 lb.	6mm (1/4 in.)	149 N·m (110 ft. lbs.)
	Used	80 lb	9mm (3/8 in.)	102 N·m (75 ft. lbs.)
Alternator	New	115 lb	4mm (3/16 in.)	—
	Used	80 lb.	6mm (1/4 in.)	—
Alternator/Air Conditioning Compressor	New	115 lb.	6mm (1/4 in.)	—
	Used	80 lb.	8mm (5/16 in.)	—
Water Pump	New	—	8mm (5/16 in.)	—
	Used	—	9mm (3/8 in.)	—

85611045

Fig. 57 Engine belt tension chart, 2.6L engine

BELT TENSION CHART

ACCESSORY DRIVE BELT		GAUGE	TORQUE
2.5L ENGINE			
AIR CONDITIONING COMPRESSOR	NEW	125 LB.	47 N•M (35 FT. LBS.)
	USED	80 LB.	27 N•M (20 FT. LBS.)
ALTERNATOR/WATER PUMP POLY "V"	NEW	130 LB.	
	USED	80 LB.	
POWER STEERING PUMP	NEW	105 LB.	58 N•M (43 FT. LBS.)
	USED	80 LB.	43 N•M (32 FT. LBS.)
3.0L ENGINE			
AIR CONDITIONING COMPRESSOR	NEW	125 LB.	
	USED	80 LB.	
ALTERNATOR/WATER PUMP/POWER STEERING PUMP	NEW	DYNAMIC TENSIONER	
	USED		
3.3L ENGINE			
AIR CONDITIONING COMPRESSOR	NEW	DYNAMIC TENSIONER	
ALTERNATOR/WATER PUMP/POWER STEERING PUMP	USED		

85611046

Fig. 58 Engine belt tension chart, 1990-93

BELT TENSION CHART

ACCESSORY DRIVE BELT		GAUGE	TORQUE
2.5L ENGINE			
AIR CONDITIONING COMPRESSOR	NEW	135 LB.	47 N·m (35 FT. LBS.)
	USED	80 LB.	27 N·m (20 FT. LBS.)
GENERATOR/WATER PUMP POLY "V"	NEW	135 LB.	
	USED	80 LB.	
POWER STEERING PUMP	NEW	105 LB.	58 N·m (43 FT. LBS.)
	USED	80 LB.	43 N·m (32 FT. LBS.)
3.0L ENGINE			
AIR CONDITIONING COMPRESSOR	NEW	125 LB.	
	USED	80 LB.	
GENERATOR/WATER PUMP/POWER STEERING PUMP	NEW	DYNAMIC TENSIONER	
	USED		
3.3L AND 3.8L ENGINE			
AIR CONDITIONING COMPRESSOR	NEW	DYNAMIC TENSIONER	
GENERATOR/WATER PUMP/POWER STEERING PUMP	USED		

85611047

Fig. 59 Engine belt tension chart, 1994

REMOVAL & INSTALLATION

▶ See Figure 60

➡Jack up the front of the vehicle, support on jack stands and remove the lower splash shield if access is hampered due to space limitations when changing drive belts.

A/C Compressor Drive Belt — 2.2L Engine

▶ See Figures 61, 62 and 63

1. Loosen the idler pulley bracket pivot screw and the locking screw.
2. Remove the belt and install replacement.
3. Using a breaker bar and socket apply torque to welded nut provided on the mounted bracket to obtain proper tension.
4. Tighten the locking screw first, followed by pivot screw. Tighten to 40 ft. lbs.

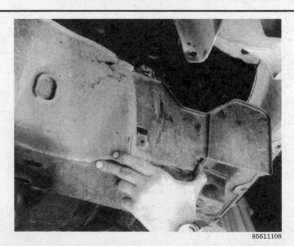

85611108

Fig. 60 With the vehicle properly supported, remove the lower right side splash shield for access to the drive belts

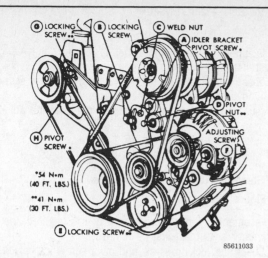

Fig. 61 A/C compressor drive belt adjusting points, 2.2L engine

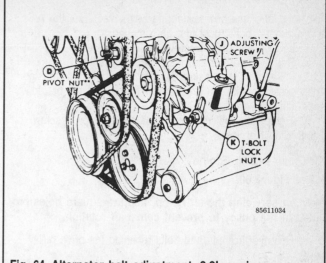

Fig. 64 Alternator belt adjustment, 2.2L engine

Fig. 62 Loosening the locking screws for A/C compressor drive belt removal

Fig. 65 Loosening the locking screw for alternator drive belt removal

Alternator Drive Belt — 2.2L Engines (Chrysler Type)

▶ See Figures 64 and 65

If removal of the alternator belt is required, the A/C belt must first be removed.

1. Loosen the pivot nut, locking screw, and the adjusting screw.
2. Remove the belt and install replacement.
3. Adjust to specification by tightening the adjusting screw.
4. Tighten the locking screw to 25 ft. lbs.
5. Tighten the pivot nut to 30 ft. lbs.

Alternator Belt — 2.2L Engines (Bosch Type)

If removal of the alternator belt is required, the A/C belt must first be removed.

1. Loosen the pivot nut, locking nut, and adjusting screw.
2. Remove the belt and install replacement.
3. Adjust to specification by tightening the adjusting screw.
4. Tighten the locking nut to 25 ft. lbs.
5. Tighten the pivot nut to 30 ft. lbs.

Fig. 63 Removing the A/C compressor drive belt from under the vehicle

Power Steering Belt 2.2L — Engine

If removal of the power steering belt is required, the A/C and alternator belts must first be removed.

1. Loosen the locking screw, and pivot screw.
2. Remove the belt and install replacement.
3. Install a ½ in. breaker bar into the pump bracket slot, apply pressure with the breaker bar and adjust the belt to specification.
4. Tighten the locking screw first, then the pivot screw. Tighten to 40 ft. lbs.

Air Pump — 2.2L Engine

▶ See Figure 66

➡ **When servicing the air pump, use the square holes provided in the pulley to prevent camshaft rotation.**

1. Remove the nuts and bolts retaining the drive pulley cover.
2. Remove the locking bolt and pivot bolt from the pump bracket, and remove the pump.
3. Remove the belt and install replacement.
4. Position the pump, and install the locking bolt and pivot bolt finger tight.
5. Install a ½ in. breaker bar into the bracket assembly (block the drive pulley to prevent camshaft rotation), and adjust the belt to specification.
6. Tighten locking bolt and pivot bolt to 25 ft. lbs.

Air Conditioning Compressor — 2.5L Engine

▶ See Figure 67

1. Loosen the idler bracket pivot screw and the locking screws to replace, or adjust belt.
2. Remove the belt and install replacement.
3. Adjust the belt to specification by applying torque to weld nut on the idler bracket.
4. Tighten locking screw first, followed by the pivot screw. Tighten to 40 ft. lbs.

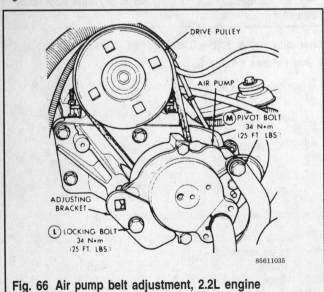

Fig. 66 Air pump belt adjustment, 2.2L engine

Alternator Belt — 2.5L Engine

▶ See Figure 67

If replacement of the alternator belt is required, the A/C drive belt must first be removed.

1. Loosen the pivot nut, locking nut, and adjusting screw.
2. Remove the belt and install replacement.
3. Adjust the belt to specification by tightening the adjusting screw.
4. Tighten the locking nut to 25 ft. lbs.
5. Tighten the pivot nut to 30 ft. lbs.

Power Steering Pump — 2.5L Engines

▶ See Figure 67

If replacement of the power steering belt is required, the A/C and alternator belts must first be remove.

1. Loosen the locking screw and pivot screw to replace, or adjust the belt.
2. Remove the belt and install replacement.
3. Using a ½ in. breaker bar positioned in adjusting bracket slot, adjust the belt to specification.
4. Tighten the locking screw followed by the pivot screw. Tighten to 40 ft. lbs.

Alternator/Air Conditioning Compressor — 2.6L Engine

▶ See Figure 68

1. Loosen the locking screw, jam nut, and pivot nut.
2. Loosen the adjusting screw.
3. Remove the belt and install replacement.
4. Adjust the belt to specification by tightening the adjusting screw.
5. Tighten the locking screw followed by the pivot nut. Tighten to 195 inch lbs.
6. Tighten the jam nut to 250 inch lbs.

Power Steering Pump Belt — 2.6L Engines

▶ See Figure 68

If replacement of the power steering belt is required, the alternator and A/C belt must first be remove.

1. Loosen the pivot screw, and the locking screw.
2. Remove the timing pickup.
3. Remove the belt and install replacement.
4. Install a ½ in. breaker bar in the adjusting bracket slot, torque to specification.
5. Tighten the locking screw, followed by the pivot screw. Tighten to 40 ft. lbs.
6. Install the timing pick-up, and tighten to 160 inch lbs.

Air Conditioning Compressor Belt — 3.0L Engine

▶ See Figures 69 and 70

1. Loosen the locknut on the idler pulley.
2. Loosen the adjusting screw on the idler pulley.
3. Remove the belt and install replacement.
4. Adjust to specification by tightening the adjusting screw.
5. Tighten the idler pulley locknut to 40 ft. lbs.

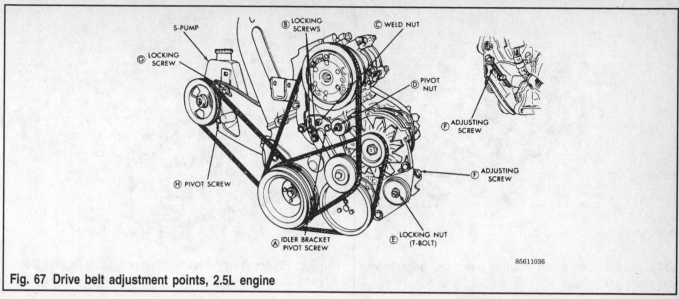

Fig. 67 Drive belt adjustment points, 2.5L engine

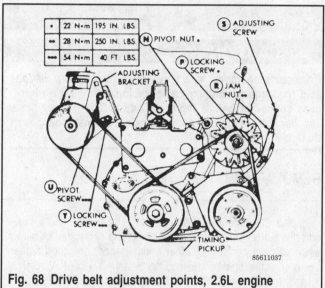

Fig. 68 Drive belt adjustment points, 2.6L engine

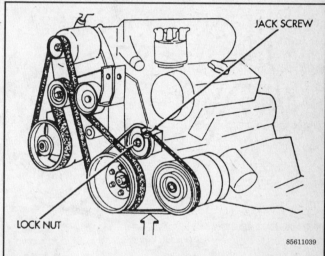

Fig. 70 Air conditioning compressor belt, 1991-94 3.0L engine

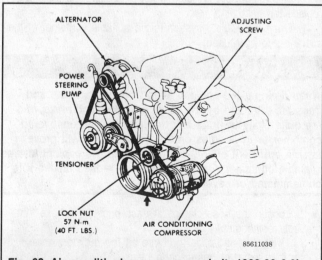

Fig. 69 Air conditioning compressor belt, 1988-90 3.0L engine

Alternator/Power Steering Pump Belt — 3.0L Engine

1988-90

▶ See Figure 71

If replacement of the alternator/power steering drive belt is required, the air conditioner drive belt must first be removed.

1. Install a ½ in. breaker bar into the tensioner slot, and rotate conterclockwise to release belt tension.
2. Remove the belt and install replacement.
3. Proper belt tension is maintain by the dynamic tensioner.

1991-94

▶ See Figure 72

The alternator/power steering pump belt is provided with a dynamic tensioner to maintain proper belt tension.

1. Raise the front of the vehicle and safely support it with jack stands.
2. Remove the right front splash shield.
3. Release tension by rotating the tensioner clockwise.
4. Remove the belt and install replacement.

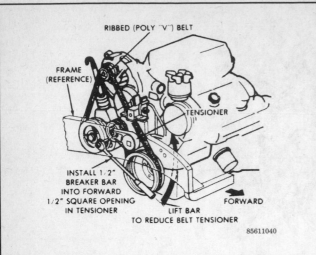

Fig. 71 Alternator/power steering pump belt adjustment, 1988-90 3.0L engine

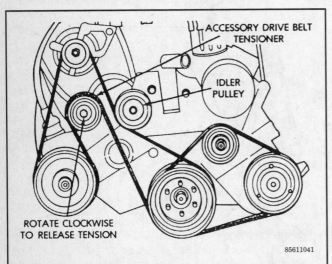

Fig. 72 Alternator/power steering pump belt adjustment, 1991-94 3.0L engine

5. Proper belt tension is maintain by the dynamic tension.
6. Install the right front splash shield. Lower the front of the vehicle.

Accessory Drive Belt — 3.3L and 3.8L Engines

▶ See Figure 73

All of the belt driven accessories on the 3.3L and 3.8L engines are driven by a single serpentine belt. The belt tension is maintained by am automatic tensioner.

1. Raise the front of the vehicle and safely support it with jack stands.
2. Remove the right front splash shield.
3. Release tension by rotating the tensioner clockwise.
4. Remove the belt and install replacement.
5. Proper belt tension is maintain by the dynamic tension.
6. Install the right front splash shield. Lower the front of the vehicle.

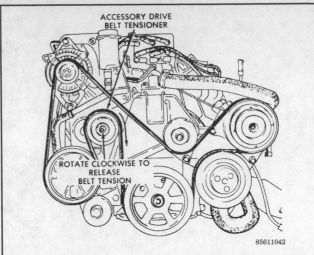

Fig. 73 Accessory drive belt adjustment, 3.3L and 3.8L engines

Hoses

❊❊CAUTION

On models equipped with an electric cooling fan, disconnect the negative battery cable, or fan motor wiring harness connector before replacing any radiator/heater hose. The fan may come on, under certain circumstances, even though the ignition is Off.

REMOVAL & INSTALLATION

Inspect the condition of the radiator and heater hoses periodically. Early spring and at the beginning of the fall or winter, when you are performing other maintenance, are good times. Make sure the engine and cooling system are cold. Visually inspect for cracking, rotting or collapsed hoses, replace as necessary. Run your hand along the length of the hose. If a weak or swollen spot is noted when squeezing the hose wall, replace the hose.

1. Drain the cooling system into a suitable container (if the coolant is to be reused).

❊❊CAUTION

When draining the coolant, keep in mind that cats and dogs are attracted by the ethylene glycol antifreeze, and are quite likely to drink any that is left in an uncovered container or in puddles on the ground. This will prove fatal in sufficient quantity. Always drain the coolant into a sealable container. Coolant should be reused unless it is contaminated or several years old.

2. Loosen the hose clamps at each end of the hose that requires replacement.
3. Twist, pull and slide the hose off the radiator, water pump, thermostat or heater connection.
4. Clean the hose mounting connections. Position the hose clamps on the new hose.

5. Coat the connection surfaces with a water resistant sealer and slide the hose into position. Make sure the hose clamps are located beyond the raised bead of the connector (if equipped) and centered in the clamping area of the connection.

6. Tighten the clamps to 20-30 inch lbs. Do not overtighten.

7. Fill the cooling system.

8. Start the engine and allow it to reach normal operating temperature. Check for leaks.

R-12 Air Conditioning System (1984-92)

SAFETY PRECAUTIONS

❋❋WARNING

R-12 refrigerant is a chlorofluorocarbon which, when released into the atmosphere, contributes to the depletion of the ozone layer in the upper atmosphere. Ozone filters out harmful radiation from the sun. Consult the laws in your area before servicing the air conditioning system. In some states it is illegal to perform repairs involving refrigerant unless the work is done by a certified technician equipped with a SAE standard refrigerant recovery/recycling station.

Because of the importance of the necessary safety precautions that must be exercised when working with air conditioning systems and R-12 refrigerant, a list of the safety precautions are outlined.

• Avoid contact with a charged refrigeration system, even when working on another part of the air conditioning system or vehicle. If a heavy tool comes into contact with a section of copper tubing or a heat exchanger, it can easily cause the relatively soft material to rupture.

• When it is necessary to apply force to a fitting which contains refrigerant, as when checking that all system couplings are securely tightened, use a wrench on both parts of the fitting involved, if possible. This will avoid putting torque on the refrigerant tubing. (It is advisable, when possible, to use tube or line wrenches when tightening these flare nut fittings.)

• Do not attempt to discharge the system by merely loosening a fitting, or removing the service valve caps and cracking these valves. Precise control is possibly only when using the service gauges. Place a rag under the open end of the center charging hose while discharging the system to catch any drops of liquid that might escape. Wear protective gloves when connecting or disconnecting service gauge hoses.

• Discharge the system only in a well ventilated area, as high concentrations of the gas can exclude oxygen and act as an anesthetic. When leak testing or soldering this is particularly important, as toxic gas is formed when R-12 contacts any flame. See WARNING above.

• Never start a system without first verifying that both service valves are back seated, if equipped, and that all fittings are throughout the system are snugly connected.

• Avoid applying heat to any refrigerant line or storage vessel. Charging may be aided by using water heated to less than 125°F (52°C) to warm the refrigerant container. Never allow a refrigerant storage container to sit out in the sun, or near any other source of heat, such as a radiator.

• Always wear goggles when working on a system to protect the eyes. If refrigerant contacts the eye, it is advisable in all cases to see a physician as soon as possible.

• Frostbite from liquid refrigerant should be treated by first gradually warming the area with cool water, and then gently applying petroleum jelly. A physician should be consulted.

• Always keep refrigerant can fittings capped when not in use. Avoid sudden shock to the can which might occur from dropping it, or from banging a heavy tool against it. Never carry a refrigerant can in the passenger compartment of a van.

• Always completely discharge the system before painting the vehicle (if the paint is to be baked on), or before welding anywhere near the refrigerant lines.

GENERAL SERVICING PROCEDURES

The most important aspect of air conditioning service is the maintenance of pure and adequate charge of refrigerant in the system. A refrigeration system cannot function properly if a significant percentage of the charge is lost. Leaks are common because the severe vibration encountered in an automobile can easily cause a sufficient cracking or loosening of the air conditioning fittings. As a result, the extreme operating pressures of the system force refrigerant out.

The problem can be understood by considering what happens to the system as it is operated with a continuous leak. Because the expansion valve regulates the flow of refrigerant to the evaporator, the level of refrigerant there is fairly constant. The receiver/drier stores any excess of refrigerant, and so a loss will first appear there as a reduction in the level of liquid. As this level nears the bottom of the vessel, some refrigerant vapor bubbles will begin to appear in the stream of liquid supplied to the expansion valve. This vapor decreases the capacity of the expansion valve very little as the valve opens to compensate for its presence. As the quantity of liquid in the condenser decreases, the operating pressure will drop there and throughout the high side of the system. As the R-12 continues to be expelled, the pressure available to force the liquid through the expansion valve will continue to decrease, and, eventually, the valve's orifice will prove to be too much of a restriction for adequate flow even with the needle fully withdrawn.

At this point, low side pressure will start to drop, and severe reduction in cooling capacity, marked by freeze-up of the evaporator coil, will result. Eventually, the operating pressure of the evaporator will be lower than the pressure of the atmosphere surrounding it, and air will be drawn into the system wherever there are leaks in the low side.

Because all atmospheric air contains at least some moisture, water will enter the system and mix with the R-12 and the oil. Trace amounts of moisture will cause sludging of the oil, and corrosion of the system. Saturation and clogging of the filter/drier, and freezing of the expansion valve orifice will eventually result. As air fills the system to a greater and greater extend, it will interfere more and more with the normal flows of refrigerant and heat.

A list of general precautions that should be observed while doing this follows:

1. Keep all tools as clean and dry as possible.

2. Thoroughly purge the service gauges and hoses of air and moisture before connecting them to the system. Keep them capped when not in use.

3. Thoroughly clean any refrigerant fitting before disconnecting it, in order to minimize the entrance of dirt into the system.

4. Plan any operation that requires opening the system beforehand in order to minimize the length of time it will be exposed to open air. Cap or seal the open ends to minimize the entrance of foreign material.

5. When adding oil, pour it through an extremely clean and dry tube or funnel. Keep the oil capped whenever possible. Do not use oil that has not been kept tightly sealed.

6. Use only refrigerant 12. Purchase refrigerant intended for use in only automotive air conditioning system. Avoid the use of refrigerant 12 that may be packaged for another use, such as cleaning, or powering a horn, as it is impure.

7. Completely evacuate any system that has been opened to replace a component, other than when isolating the compressor, or that has leaked sufficiently to draw in moisture and air. This requires evacuating air and moisture with a good vacuum pump for at least one hour.

If a system has been open for a considerable length of time it may be advisable to evacuate the system for up to 12 hours (overnight).

8. Use a wrench on both halves of a fitting that is to be disconnected, so as to avoid placing torque on any of the refrigerant lines.

ADDITIONAL PREVENTIVE MAINTENANCE CHECKS

Antifreeze

In order to prevent heater core freeze-up during A/C operation, it is necessary to maintain permanent type antifreeze protection of +15°F (-9°C) or lower. A reading of -15°F (-26°C) is ideal since this protection also supplies sufficient corrosion inhibitors for the protection of the engine cooling system.

❊❊WARNING

Do not use antifreeze longer than specified by the manufacturer.

Radiator Cap

For efficient operation of an cooling system, the radiator cap should have a holding pressure which meets manufacturer's specifications. A cap which fails to hold these pressure should be replaced.

Condenser

Any obstruction of or damage to the condenser configuration will restrict the air flow which is essential to its efficient opera-

tion. It is therefore, a good rule to keep this unit clean and in proper physical shape.

➡**Bug screens are regarded as obstructions.**

Condensation Drain Tube

This single molded drain tube expels the condensation, which accumulates on the bottom of the evaporator housing, into the engine compartment.

If this tube is obstructed, the air conditioning performance can be restricted and condensation buildup can spill over onto the vehicle's floor.

TEST GAUGES

▶ **See Figure 74**

Most of the service work performed in air conditioning requires the use of a set of two gauges, one for the high (head) pressure side of the system, the other for the low (suction) side.

The low side gauge records both pressure and vacuum. Vacuum readings are calibrated from 0 to 30 inches Hg and the pressure graduations read from 0 to no less than 150 psi.

The high side gauge measures pressure from 0 to at least 300 psi.

With the gauge set you can perform the following procedures:

1. Test high and low side pressures.
2. Remove air, moisture, and contaminated refrigerant.
3. Purge the system of refrigerant.
4. Charge the system with refrigerant.

All gauge sets must have 3 hoses, with 1 being for center manifold outlet.

❊❊WARNING

When connecting the hoses to the compressor service ports, the manifold gauge valves must be closed!

The suction gauge valve is opened to provide a passage between the suction gauge and the center manifold outlet. The discharge gauge valve is opened to provide a passage between the discharge pressure gauge and the center manifold outlet.

SYSTEM INSPECTION

❊❊CAUTION

The compressed refrigerant used in the air conditioning system expands into the atmosphere at a temperature of -21.7°F (-30°C) or lower. This will freeze any surface, including your eyes, that it contacts. In addition, the refrigerant decomposes into a poisonous gas in the presence of a flame. Do not open or disconnect any part of the air conditioning system.

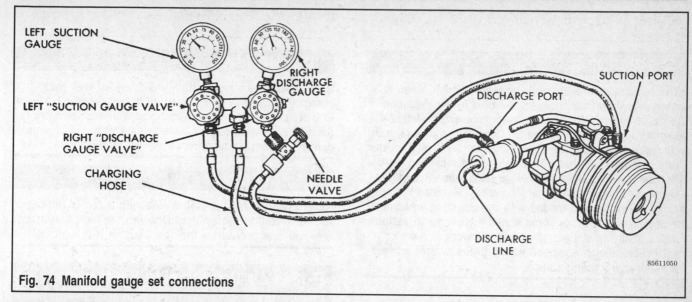

Fig. 74 Manifold gauge set connections

Sight Glass Check

You can safely make a few simple checks to determine if your air conditioning system needs service. The tests work best if the temperature is warm (about 70°F).

➡**If your vehicle is equipped with an after market air conditioner, the following system check may not apply. You should contact the manufacturer of the unit for instructions on systems checks.**

1. Place the automatic transmission in Park or the manual transmission in Neutral. Set the parking brake.

2. Run the engine at a fast idle (about 1,500 Rpm) either with the help of a friend or by temporarily readjusting the idle speed screw.

3. Set the controls for maximum cold with the blower on High.

4. Locate the sight glass in one of the system lines. Usually it is on the left alongside the top of the radiator.

5. If you see bubbles, the system must be recharged. Very likely there is a leak at some point.

6. If there are no bubbles, there is either no refrigerant at all or the system is fully charged. Feel the two hoses going to the belt driven compressor. If they are both at the same temperature, the system is empty and must be recharged.

7. If one hose (high pressure) is warm and the other (low pressure) is cold, the system may be all right. However, you are probably making these tests because you think there is something wrong, so proceed to the next step.

8. Have an assistant in the van turn the fan control on and off to operate the compressor clutch. Watch the sight glass.

9. If bubbles appear when the clutch is disengaged and disappear when it is engaged, the system is properly charged.

10. If the refrigerant takes more than 45 seconds to bubble when the clutch is disengaged, the system is overcharged. This usually causes poor cooling at low speeds.

✳✳WARNING

If it is determined that the system has a leak, it should be corrected as soon as possible. Leaks may allow moisture to enter and cause a very expensive rust problem. Exercise the air conditioner for a few minutes, every two weeks or so, during the cold months. This avoids the possibility of the compressor seals drying out from lack of lubrication.

TESTING THE SYSTEM

1. Connect a gauge set.

2. Close (clockwise) both gauge set valves.

3. Park the van in the shade, at least 5 feet from any walls. Start the engine, set the parking brake, place the transmission in **N** and establish an idle of 1100-1300 Rpm.

4. Run the air conditioning system for full cooling, in the **MAX** or **COLD** mode.

5. The low pressure gauge should read 5-20 psi; the high pressure gauge should indicate 120-180 psi.

✳✳WARNING

These pressures are the norm for an ambient temperature of 70-80°F (21-27°C). Higher air temperatures along with high humidity will cause higher system pressures. At idle speed and an ambient temperature of 110°F (43°C), the high pressure reading can exceed 300 psi. Under these extreme conditions, you can keep the pressures down by directing a large electric floor fan through the condenser.

DISCHARGING THE SYSTEM

✳✳WARNING

R-12 refrigerant is a chlorofluorocarbon which, when released into the atmosphere, contributes to the depletion of the ozone layer in the upper atmosphere. Ozone filters out harmful radiation from the sun.   Consult the laws in your area before servicing the air conditioning system. Chrysler Corp. recommends that a R-12 refrigerant recycling device that meets SAE standard J1991 be used when it is necessary to discharge the refrigerant system. Refer to the operating instructions provided with the recycling equipment for proper operation. In some states it is illegal to perform repairs involving refrigerant unless the work is done by a certified technician equipped with a SAE standard refrigerant recovery/recycling station.

EVACUATING THE SYSTEM

➡This procedure requires the use of a vacuum pump.

1. Connect the manifold gauge set.
2. Discharge the system.
3. Make sure that the low pressure gauge set hose is connected to the low pressure service gauge port on the top center of the accumulator/drier assembly and the high pressure hose connected to the high pressure service gauge port on the compressor discharge line.
4. Connect the center service hose to the inlet fitting of the vacuum pump.
5. Turn both gauge set valves to the wide open position.
6. Start the pump and note the low side gauge reading.
7. Operate the pump until the low pressure gauge reads 25-30 in.Hg. Continue running the vacuum pump for 10 minutes more. If you've replaced some component in the system, run the pump for an additional 20-30 minutes.
8. Leak test the system. Close both gauge set valves. Turn off the pump. The needle should remain stationary at the point at which the pump was turned off. If the needle drops to zero rapidly, there is a leak in the system which must be repaired.

LEAK TESTING

Some leak tests can be performed with a soapy water solution. There must be at least a $\frac{1}{2}$ lb. charge in the system for a leak to be detected. The most extensive leak tests are performed with either a Halide flame type leak tester or the more preferable electronic leak tester.

In either case, the equipment is expensive, and, the use of a Halide detector can be **extremely** hazardous!

CHARGING THE SYSTEM

✳✳WARNING

Refer to the operating instructions provided with the charging equipment being used. In some states it is illegal to perform repairs involving refrigerant unless the work is done by a certified technician equipped with a SAE standard refrigerant recovery/recycling/charging station.

✳✳CAUTION

Never open the high pressure side with a can of refrigerant connected to the system! Opening the high pressure side will over pressurize the can, causing it to explode!

R-134a Air Conditioning System (1993-94)

✳✳WARNING

These vehicles use a new type of refrigerent called R-134a. It is a non-toxic, non-flammable, clear colorless liquified gas and is NOT capatible with R-12 refrigerant. R-134a refrigerant also requires a special type of compressor oil. R-134a refrigerant is not available to the general public and when servicing the system, it is required that an air conditioning charging recovery/recycling machine be used and that the operating instructions provided with the equipment be followed. In some states it is illegal to perform repairs involving refrigerant unless the work is done by a certified technician.

SIGHT GLASS REFERIGERENT INSPECTION

You can safely make a few simple checks to determine if your air conditioning system needs service. The tests work best if the temperature is warm (about 70°F).

1. Place the automatic transmission in Park or the manual transmission in Neutral. Set the parking brake.
2. Run the engine at a fast idle (about 1,100 Rpm), with the help of a friend and allow the engine to reach normal operating temperature.
3. Remove the vehicle jack and clean the the sight glass.
4. Set the controls for A/C, RECIRC and high blower.
5. If the air conditioner compressor does not engage the refrigerent level is probably too low for the low pressure cut-off switch to detect and the systen should be tested for leaks.
6. Disconnect the low pressure cut-off switch. Place a jumper wire across the terminals in the connector boot. If the compressor still does not engage, a problem exists in the compressor clutch feed circuit.
7. If the compressor clutch engages, allow approximately one minute for the refrigerant to stabilize. View the refrigerant through the sight glass. The suction line should be cold to the touch and the sight glass should be clear.
8. If you see foam bubbles in the sight glass, the system must be recharged. Very likely there is a leak at some point.

9. If there are no bubbles, there is either no refrigerant at all or the system is fully charged. Occasional foam bubbles are normal when the work area temperature is above 110°F or below 70°F. If the suction line is cold and occasional bubbles are visible in the sight glass, block the condenser air flow. This will increase the compressor discharge pressure (do not allow the engine to over heat). Bubbles should dissipate. If not, the refrigerant level is low.

✳✳WARNING

If it is determined that the system has a leak, it should be corrected as soon as possible. Leaks may allow moisture to enter and cause a very expensive rust problem.   Exercise the air conditioner for a few minutes, every two weeks or so, during the cold months. This avoids the possibility of the compressor seals drying out from lack of lubrication.

Windshield Wipers

Wiper blades exposed to the weather over a period of time tend to lose their wiping effectiveness. Clean the wiping surface of the blade with a sponge and a mild solution of water and detergent. If the blades continue to smear, they should be replaced with either a new blade or refill.

BLADE REFILLS

1. Turn the wiper switch to the ON position. Turn the ignition switch ON. When the blades reach a convenient place on the windshield, turn the ignition switch to OFF, thus stopping the blades.
2. Lift the wiper arm to raise the blade from the windshield.
3. Insert a small blade type tool into the release slot of wiper blade and pry slightly upward.
4. Pinch lock on each end of blade and slide wiping element out of blade.
5. Install a new wiping element into blade. Make certain each release points are properly locked in position.
6. Install blade on wiper arm.

Most Anco® styles uses a release button that is pushed down to allow the refill to slide out of the yoke jaws. The new refill slides in and locks in place. Some Trico® refills are removed by locating where the metal backing strip of the refill is wider. Insert a small screwdriver blade between the frame and metal backing strip. Press down to release the refill from the retaining tab.

The Trico® style is unlocked at one end by squeezing 2 metal tabs, and the refill is slide out of the frame jaws. When the new refill is installed, the tabs will click into place, locking the refill.

The polycarbonate type is held in place by a locking lever that is pushed downward out of the groove in the arm to free the refill. When the new refill is installed, it will lock in place automatically.

The Tridon® refill has a plastic backing strip with a notch about 1 in. (25mm) from the end. Hold the blade (frame) on a hard surface so that the frame is tightly bowed. Grip the tip of the backing strip and pull up while twisting counter clockwise.

The backing strip will snap out of the retaining tab. Do this for the remaining tabs until the refill is free of the arm. The length of these refills is molded into the end and they should be replaced with identical types.

No matter which type of refill you use, be sure that all of the frame claws engage the refill. Before operating the wiper, be sure that no part of the metal frame is contacting the windshield.

Tires and Wheels

TIRE INFLATION

▶ **See Figure 75**

Check the air pressure in your vehicle's tires every few weeks. Make sure that the tires are cool. Air pressure increases with higher temperature, and will indicate false reading. A decal located on the glove box door or side door frame will tell you the proper tire pressure for the standard equipment tires.

➡**Never exceed the maximum inflation pressure on the side of the tire. Also never mixed tires of different size or construction (Belted vs Bias-ply, or Radial vs Belted etc.).**

It pays to buy a tire pressure gauge to keep in your vehicle, since those of service stations are often inaccurate or broken. While you are checking the tire pressure, take a look at the tread. The tread should be wearing evenly across the tire. Excessive wear in the center of the tread indicates over inflation. Excessive wear on the outer edges indicates under inflation. An irregular wear pattern is usually a sign of incorrect front wheel alignment or wheel balance.

A front end that is out of alignment will usually pull to one side when the steering wheel is released. Conditions which relate to front end alignment are associated by tire wear patterns. Tire treads being worn on one side more than the other, or wear on the tread edges may be noticeable. Front wheels which are incorrectly balance, is usually accompanied by high speed vibration.

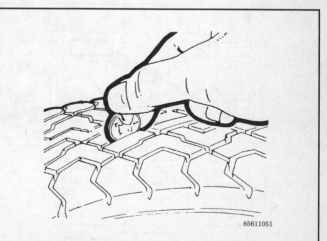

85611051

Fig. 75 Tread depth can be roughly checked with a Lincoln penney. If the top of Lincoln's head is visible, replace the tire

TIRE ROTATION

▶ **See Figure 76**

Tires installed on the front or rear of any vehicle are subjected to different loads, breaking, or steering functions. Because of these conditions, tires develop uneven wear patterns. Rotating the tires every 6000 miles or so will result in increased thread life. Use the correct pattern for tire rotation. Refer to Tire Rotation Patterns chart.

Most automotive experts are in agreement that radial tires are better all around performers, giving prolonged wear and better handling. An added benefit which you should consider when purchasing tires is that radials have less rolling resistance and can give up to a 10% increase in fuel economy over a bias-ply tire.

It is recommended that you have the tires rotated and the balance checked every 6,000 miles. There is no way to give a tire rotation diagram for every combination of tires and vehicles, but the accompanying diagrams are a general rule to follow. Radial tires should not be cross-switched; they last longer if their direction of rotation is not changed. Truck tires and some high-performance tires sometimes have directional tread, indicated by arrows on the sidewalls; the arrow shows the direction of rotation. They will wear very rapidly if reversed. Studded snow tires will lose their studs if their direction of rotation is reversed.

➡ **Mark the wheel position or direction of rotation on radial tires or studded snow tires before removing them.**

If your van is equipped with tires having different load ratings on the front and the rear, the tires should not be rotated front to rear. Rotating these tires could affect tire life (the tires with the lower rating will wear faster, and could become overloaded), and upset the handling of the van.

When installing the wheels on the vehicle, tighten the lug nuts in a criss-cross pattern. Lug nuts should be torqued to 85 ft. lbs.

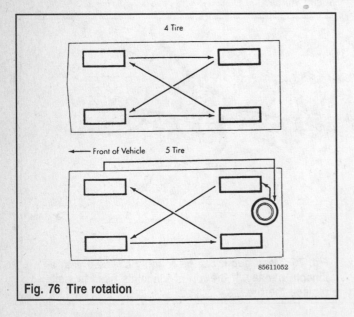

85611052

Fig. 76 Tire rotation

TIRE USAGE

The tires on your van were selected to provide the best all around performance for normal operation when inflated as specified. Oversize tires will not increase the maximum carrying capacity of the vehicle, although they will provide an extra margin of tread life. Be sure to check overall height before using larger size tires which may cause interference with suspension components or wheel wells. When replacing conventional tire sizes with other tire size designations, be sure to check the manufacturer's recommendations. Interchangeability is not always possible because of differences in load ratings, tire dimensions, wheel well clearances, and rim size. Also due to differences in handling characteristics, 70 Series and 60 Series tires should be used only in pairs on the same axle; radial tires should be used only in sets of four.

➡ **Many states have vehicle height restrictions; some states prohibit the lifting of vehicles beyond their design limits.**

The wheels must be the correct width for the tire. Tire dealers have charts of tire and rim compatibility. A mismatch can cause sloppy handling and rapid tread wear. The old rule of thumb is that the tread width should match the rim width (inside bead to inside bead) within 1 in. (25mm). For radial tires, the rim width should be 80% or less of the tire (not tread) width.

The height (mounted diameter) of the new tires can greatly change speedometer accuracy, engine speed at a given road speed, fuel mileage, acceleration, and ground clearance. Tire manufacturers furnish full measurement specifications. Speedometer drive gears are available for correction.

➡ **Dimensions of tires marked the same size may vary significantly, even among tires from the same manufacturer.**

The spare tire should be of the same size, construction and design as the tires on the vehicle. It's not a good idea to carry a spare of a different construction.

TIRE DESIGN

For maximum satisfaction, tires should be used in sets of five. Mixing or different types (radial, bias-belted, fiberglass belted) should be avoided. Conventional bias tires are constructed so that the cords run bead-to-bead at an angle. Alternate plies run at an opposite angle. This type of construction gives rigidity to both tread and sidewall. Bias-belted tires are similar in construction to conventional bias ply tires. Belts run at an angle and also at a 90° angle to the bead, as in the radial tire. Tread life is improved considerably over the conventional bias tire. The radial tire differs in construction, but instead of the carcass plies running at an angle of 90° to each other, they run at an angle of 90° to the bead. This gives the tread a great deal of rigidity and the sidewall a great deal of flexibility and accounts for the characteristic bulge associated with radial tires.

When radial tires are used, tire sizes and wheel diameters should be selected to maintain ground clearance and tire load capacity equivalent to the minimum specified tire. Radial tires should always be used in sets of five, but in an emergency,

radial tires can be used with caution on the rear axle only. If this is done, both tires on the rear should be of radial design.

✳✳WARNING

Radial tires should never be used on only the front axle!

FLUIDS AND LUBRICANTS

Fluid Disposal

Used fluids, such as engine oil, antifreeze, transmission oils and brake fluid are hazardous as waste material and must be disposed of properly.

Before draining any fluids, consult with your local municipal government. In may areas, waste oils are being accepted as part of the recycling program. A number of service stations, repair facilities and auto parts stores are accepting these waste fluids for recycling.

Be sure of the recycling center's policies before draining any fluids, as many will not accept different fluids that have been mixed together, such as oil and antifreeze.

Fuel Recommendations

Chrysler recommends that unleaded fuel only with a minimum octane rating of at least 87 be used in your vehicle, if equipped with a catalytic converter. The use of unleaded gasoline is required in order to meet all emission regulations, and provide excellent fuel economy.

Fuels of the same octane rating have varying anti-knock qualities. Thus, if your engine knocks or pings, try switching brands of gasoline before trying a more expansive higher octane fuel.

Your engine's fuel requirements can change with time, due to carbon buildup which changes the compression ratio. If switching brands or grades of gas doesn't work, check the ignition timing. If it is necessary to retard timing from specifications, don't change it more than about 4°. Retarded timing will reduce power output and fuel mileage and increase engine temperature.

Engine

OIL RECOMMENDATIONS

▶ **See Figures 77 and 78**

A high quality heavy-duty detergent oil having the proper viscosity for prevailing temperatures and an SG/CC service rating should be used in your vehicle. A high quality SG/CC rated oil should be used for heavy duty service or turbocharged equipped engines. The SG/CC and SG/CD rated oil contain sufficient chemical additives to provide maximum engine protection.

Pick an oil with the viscosity that matches the anticipated temperature of the region your vehicle will be operated in before the next oil change. A chart is provided to help you

with your selection. Choose the oil viscosity for the lowest expected temperature and you will be assured of easy cold weather starting and sufficient engine protection.

OIL LEVEL CHECK

▶ **See Figures 79, 80, 81, 82 and 83**

The engine oil level is checked with the dipstick which is located on the radiator side of the engine.

➡**The oil should be checked before the engine is started or five minutes after the engine has shut off. This gives the oil time to drain back to the oil pan and prevents an inaccurate oil level reading.**

Remove the dipstick from the tube, wipe it clean, and insert it back into the tube. Remove it again and observe the oil level. It should be maintained within the full range on the dipstick.

➡**Do not overfill the crankcase. This will cause oil aeration and loss of oil pressure.**

OIL AND FILTER CHANGE

▶ **See Figures 84, 85, 86 and 87**

The recommended mileage figures for oil and filter changes are 7,500 miles or 12 months whichever comes first, assuming normal driving conditions. If your vehicle is being used under dusty conditions, frequent trailer pulling, excessive idling, or

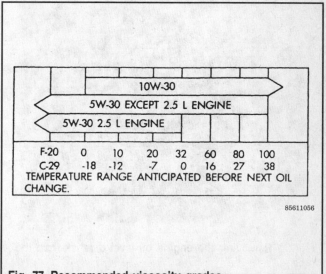

Fig. 77 Recommended viscosity grades

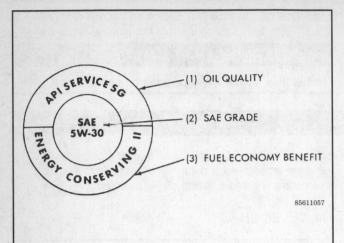

(1) OIL QUALITY

(2) SAE GRADE

(3) FUEL ECONOMY BENEFIT

85611057

Fig. 78 The top of the can will tell you what yo need to know about the oil

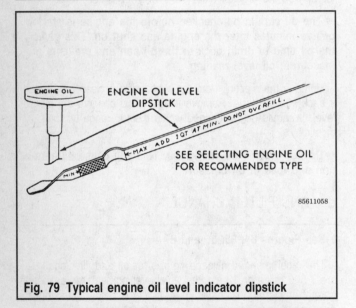

ENGINE OIL LEVEL DIPSTICK

MAX ADD 1QT AT MIN. DO NOT OVERFILL.

SEE SELECTING ENGINE OIL FOR RECOMMENDED TYPE

85611058

Fig. 79 Typical engine oil level indicator dipstick

85611112

Fig. 80 Removing the engine oil level dipstick from the tube

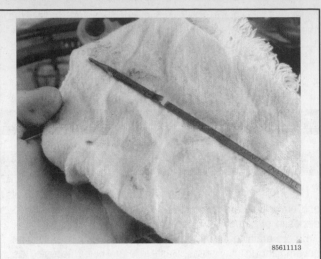

85611113

Fig. 81 Wipe the dipstick clean then insert it back into the tube

85611114

Fig. 82 Remove the oil fill cap from the top of the cover to add oil. This is a good time to check the condition of the cap sealing gasket

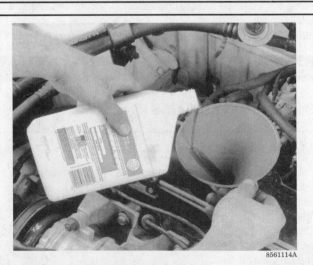

8561114A

Fig. 83 For easier filling and to avoid spilling, use a funnel when adding engine oil

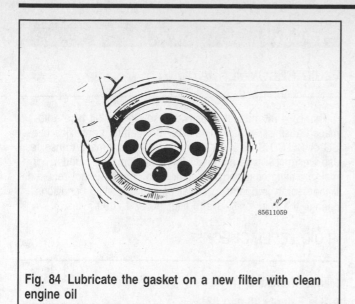

Fig. 84 Lubricate the gasket on a new filter with clean engine oil

85611059

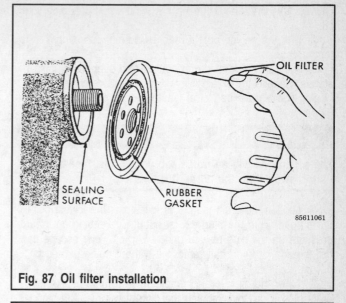

OIL FILTER

SEALING SURFACE

RUBBER GASKET

85611061

Fig. 87 Oil filter installation

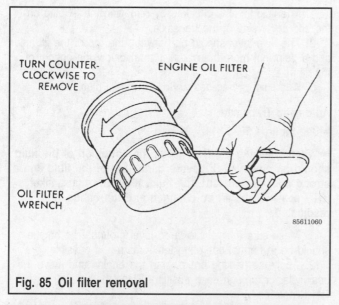

TURN COUNTER-CLOCKWISE TO REMOVE

ENGINE OIL FILTER

OIL FILTER WRENCH

85611060

Fig. 85 Oil filter removal

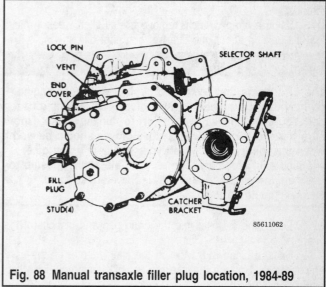

LOCK PIN

VENT

SELECTOR SHAFT

END COVER

FILL PLUG

STUD (4)

CATCHER BRACKET

85611062

Fig. 88 Manual transaxle filler plug location, 1984-89

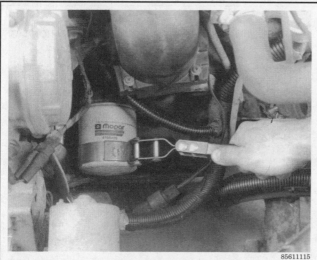

85611115

Fig. 86 Using an oil filter removal tool

stop and go driving, it is recommended to change the oil and filter at 3,000 miles.

➡Improper disposing of all lubricants (engine, trans., and differential), can result in environmental problems. Contact your local dealerships of service stations for advice on proper disposal.

Always drain the oil after the engine has been running long enough to bring it to operating temperature. Hot oil will flow easier and more contaminants will be removed along with the oil than if it were drained cold.

Chrysler recommends changing both the oil and filter during the first oil change and the filter every other oil change thereafter. For the small price of an oil filter, it's cheap insurance to replace the filter at every oil change. One of the larger filter manufacturers points out in its advertisements that not changing the filter leaves one quart of dirty oil in the engine. This claim is true and should be kept in mind when changing your oil.

1. Run the engine until it reaches normal operating temperature.

2. Jack up the front of the vehicle and support on jack stands, remove the shield if it will cause interference.

3. Slide a drain pan of at least 6 quarts capacity under the oil pan.

✳✳CAUTION

The engine oil will be hot! Keep your arms, face and hands away from the oil as it drains out!

4. Loosen the drain plug. It is located in the lowest point of the oil pan. Turn the plug out by hand. By keeping an inward pressure on the plug as you unscrew it, oil won't escape past the threads and you can remove it without being burned by hot oil.

5. Allow the oil to drain completely and then install the drain plug. Don't over tighten the plug, it will result in stripped threads.

6. Using a strap wrench, remove the oil filter. Keep in mind that it's holding about one quart of dirty, hot oil.

✳✳CAUTION

The EPA warns that prolonged contact with used engine oil may cause a number of skin disorders, including cancer! You should make every effort to minimize your exposure to used engine oil. Protective gloves should be worn when changing the oil. Wash your hands and any other exposed skin areas as soon as possible after exposure to used engine oil. Soap and water, or waterless hand cleaner should be used.

7. Empty the old filter into the drain pan and dispose of the filter.

8. Using a clean rag, wipe off the filter adapter on the engine block. Be sure that the rag doesn't leave any lint which could clog an oil passage.

9. Coat the rubber gasket on the filter with fresh oil. Spin it onto the engine by hand; when the gasket touches the adapter surface give it another 1/2-3/4 turn. No more, or you'll squash the gasket and it will leak.

10. Refill the engine with the correct amount of fresh oil. See the Capacities Chart.

11. Run the engine at idle for approximately one minute. Shut the engine off. Wait a few minutes and recheck oil level. Add oil, as necessary to bring the level up to **Fill**.

12. Shut the engine off and lower the vehicle.

✳✳CAUTION

You now have 4 quarts of used engine oil. Please store this oil in a secure container, such as a 1 gallon windshield washer fluid bottle. Locate a service station or garage which accepts used oil for recycling and dispose of it there.

Transaxle

FLUID RECOMMENDATION

The 1984-86 manual transaxles use Dexron®II type automatic transmission fluid. The 1987-94 manual transaxles use SG or SG/CD SAE 5W-30 engine oil. All automatic transaxles use Dexron®II type automatic transmission fluid. Under normal operating conditions, periodic fluid change is not required. If the vehicle is operating under severe operating conditions change the fluid, or fluid and filter every 15,000 miles.

FLUID LEVEL CHECK

Manual Transaxle

▶ **See Figures 88 and 89**

1. The fluid level is checked by removing the fill plug on the end cover side of the transaxle.

2. The fluid level should be between the top of the fill hole and a point not more than 1/8 in. (3mm) below the bottom of the fill hole.

3. Add fluid as necessary. Secure the fill plug.

Automatic Transaxle

▶ **See Figures 90, 91, 92, 93 and 94**

➡**When checking the fluid level, the condition of the fluid should be observed. If severe darkening of the fluid and a strong odor are present, the fluid, filter and pan gasket (RTV sealant) should be changed and the bands readjusted.**

1. Make sure the vehicle is on level ground. The engine should be at normal operating temperatures, if possible.

2. Apply the parking brake, start the engine and move the gear selector through each position. Place the selector in the PARK position.

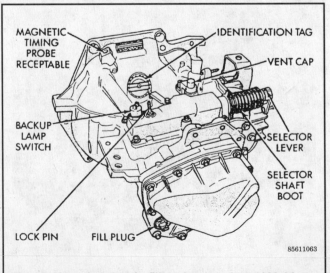

Fig. 89 Manual transaxle filler plug location, 1990-94

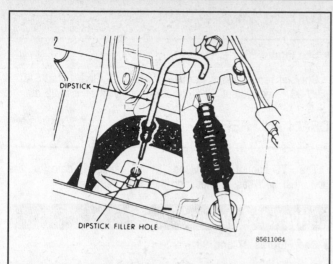

Fig. 90 Automatic transaxle dipdtick and filler hole location, Model A413 transaxle shown

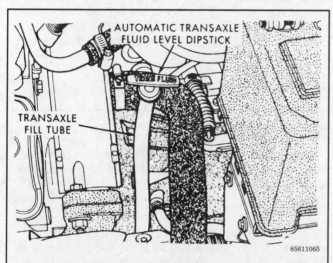

Fig. 91 Automatic transaxle dipdtick and filler hole location, Model A604 transaxle shown

Fig. 92 Removing the automatic transaxle fluid level dipstick

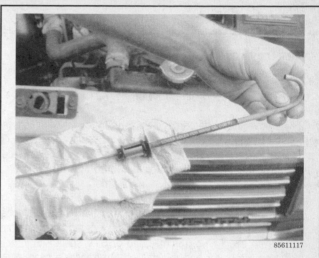

Fig. 93 Wipe the dipstick clean and reinsert it in the tube

Fig. 94 Using a funnel with a long neck is necessary for adding fluid to the automatic transmission

3. Remove the dipstick and determine if the fluid is warm or hot.

4. Wipe the dipstick clean and reinsert until fully seated. Remove and take note of the fluid level.

5. If the fluid is hot, the reading should be in the crosshatched area marked **HOT**.

6. If the fluid is warm, the fluid level should be in the area marked **WARM**.

7. If the fluid level checks low, add enough fluid (Dexron®II®) through the fill tube, to bring the level within the marks appropriate for average temperature of the fluid.

8. Insert the dipstick and recheck the level. Make sure the dipstick is fully seated to prevent dirt from entering. Do not overfill the transaxle.

DRAIN AND REFILL

Manual Transaxle

▶ **See Figure 95**

1. Raise and support the front of the vehicle on jack stands.
2. Remove the undercarriage splash shield if it will interfere with fluid change.
3. Position a drain pan underneath the end of the transaxle and remove the differential end cover where the fill plug is located. Loosen the bolt slightly and pry the lower edge away so that the fluid will drain.
4. Remove the cover completely. Clean the gasket surfaces of the case and cover. Clean the magnet located on the cover.
5. Use an even ⅛ in. (3mm) bead of RTV sealant to form a gasket on the cover and reinstall on the transaxle case.
6. Refill the transaxle with the correct fluid. (Refer to Transaxle Fluid Recommendations above)

Automatic Transaxle

Band readjustment and filter replacement are recommended when the fluid is changed. Refer to 'Drive Train' for required procedures.

Differential

The transmission and differential share a common housing. Fluid check and change procedures are covered in the 'Drive' Train Section.

Power Transfer Unit (PTU)

On models with All Wheel Drive (AWD), a power transfer unit is used that is connected to the transaxle. This unit is separate from the other drive train components.

FLUID RECOMMENDATION

▶ **See Figure 96**

Chrysler recommends the use of Mopar® Gear Lube, SAE 85W-90 or equivalent. The correct quantity of oil is 1.22 qts.

DRAIN AND REFILL

The PTU cannot be serviced. If fluid leakage is detected, the unit must be disassembled and the seals replaced.

Drive Line Module

▶ **See Figures 97 and 98**

On models with All Wheel Dive (AWD), the rear wheels are driven by shafts from the Drive Line Module. This module serves as the rear drive axle.

As well as containing the rear differential, this module contains a set of overrunning clutches in their own case. This clutch assembly serves to control differences in drive line speed and traction.

FLUID RECOMMENDATION

Drive Line Module

Chrysler recommends the use of Mopar® Gear Lube, SAE 85W-90 or equivalent. The module is full when the fluid level is ⅛ in. (3mm) below the fill plug.

Overrunning Clutch

Chrysler recommends the use of Mopar® ATF type 7176 or equivalent. The oil level should be at the bottom of the oil fill opening.

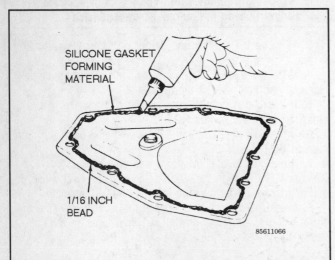

SILICONE GASKET
FORMING
MATERIAL

1/16 INCH
BEAD

85611066

Fig. 95 Form a silcone gasket as shown for the manual transaxle cover

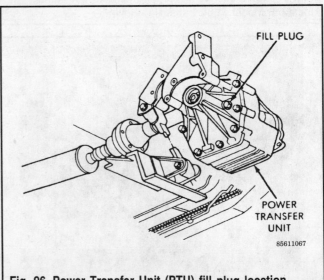

FILL PLUG

POWER
TRANSFER
UNIT

85611067

Fig. 96 Power Transfer Unit (PTU) fill plug location

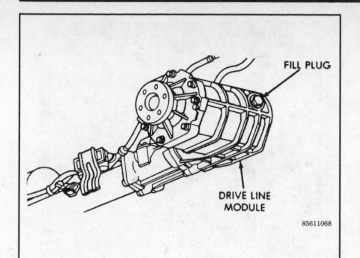

Fig. 97 Drive line module fill plug, All Wheel Drive equipped vehicles

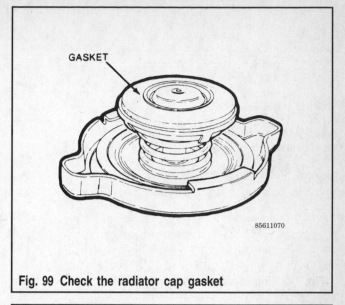

Fig. 99 Check the radiator cap gasket

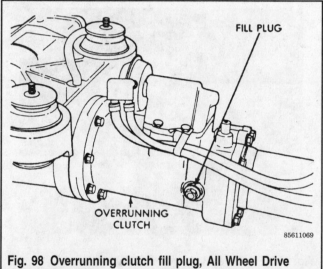

Fig. 98 Overrunning clutch fill plug, All Wheel Drive equipped vehicles

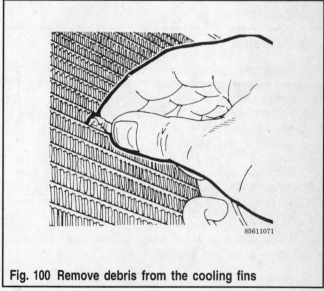

Fig. 100 Remove debris from the cooling fins

Cooling System

▶ See Figures 99, 100, 101 and 102

FLUID RECOMMENDATION

A 50/50 mixture of water and ethylene glycol type antifreeze (containing Alguard or silicate type inhibiter) that is safe for use in aluminum components is recommended. The 50/50 mixture offers protection to -34°F (-37°C). If addition cold weather protection is necessary a concentrate of 65% antifreeze may be used.

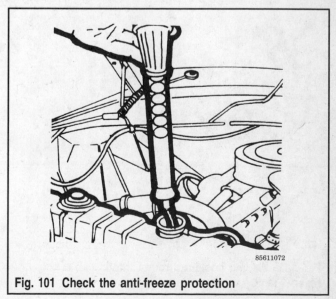

Fig. 101 Check the anti-freeze protection

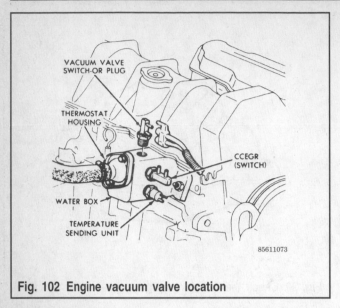

Fig. 102 Engine vacuum valve location

LEVEL CHECK

▶ **See Figure 103**

All vehicles are equipped with a transparent coolant reserve container. A minimum and maximum level mark are provided for a quick visual check of the coolant level.

1. Run the engine until normal operating temperature is reached.

2. Open the hood and observe the level of the coolant in the reserve.

3. Fluid level should be between the two lines. Add coolant, if necessary, through the fill cap of the reserve tank.

DRAIN AND REFILL

▶ **See Figures 104 and 105**

1. If the lower splash shield is in the way, remove it.

Fig. 103 Adding coolant through the fill cap of the reserve tank

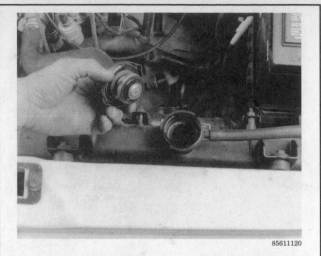

Fig. 104 Remove the radiator cap when the system is cool. Check the cap sealing gasket for deterioration

Fig. 105 Fill the system with a 50/50 mixture of ethylene glycol type antifreeze

2. Place the heater control lever on the dash control to full on.

3. Place a drain pan under the radiator and open the drain cock. When the coolant reserve tank is drained completely, remove the radiator cap.

✳✳CAUTION

When draining the coolant, keep in mind that cats and dogs are attracted by the ethylene glycol antifreeze, and are quite likely to drink any that is left in an uncovered container or in puddles on the ground. This will prove fatal in sufficient quantity. Always drain the coolant into a sealable container. Coolant should be reused unless it is contaminated or several years old.

4. If your vehicle is equipped with the 2.2L engine, removal of the vacuum valve (located above the thermostat housing), is necessary to provide air displacement. If your vehicle is equipped with the 2.5L engine, removal of the drain/fill plug

(located above the thermostat housing), is necessary to provide air displacement.

5. To remove the vacuum valve, disconnect the hose connector plug, and carefully unscrew the valve using the proper size wrench.

6. After draining the system, refill with water and run the engine until normal operating temperature is reached. (See the following refill procedures). Drain the system again, repeat procedure until the drained water runs clear.

7. Close the radiator drain cock.

8. Fill the system with a 50/50 mixture of ethylene glycol type antifreeze.

9. When the coolant reaches the hole in the water box at thermostat housing (2.2L and 2.5L engines), install the vacuum valve or drain/fill plug to 20 N.m (15 ft. lbs.)

10. Continue filling system until full.

11. Install the radiator cap, start the engine, and run until normal operating temperature is reached. Fill the coolant reserve tank to **Max** mark. Stop engine and allowed to cool.

➡️**It may be necessary to warm up and cool down engine several times to remove trapped air. Recheck level in reserve tank, and adjust level if necessary.**

CHECK THE RADIATOR CAP

While you are checking the coolant level, check the radiator cap for a worn or cracked gasket. If the cap doesn't seal properly, fluid will be lost in the form of steam and the engine will overheat. Replace the cap with a new one, if necessary.

CLEAN RADIATOR OF DEBRIS

Periodically clean any debris — leaves, paper, insects, etc. — from the radiator fins. Pick the large pieces off by hand. The smaller pieces can be washed away with water pressure from a hose.

Carefully straighten any bent radiator fins with a pair of needle nose pliers. Be careful — the fins are very soft! Don't wiggle the fins back and forth too much. Straighten them once and try not to move them again.

Master Cylinder

♦ **See Figures 106 and 107**

FLUID RECOMMENDATION

Use only a DOT 3 approved brake fluid in your vehicle. Always use fresh fluid when servicing or refilling the brake system.

LEVEL CHECK

The fluid level in both reservoirs of the master cylinder should be maintained at the bottom of the fill split rings visible

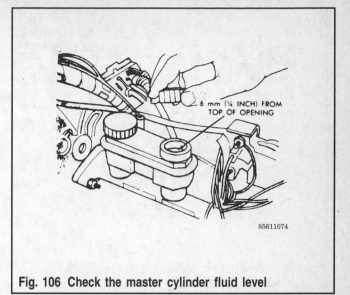

6 mm (¼ INCH) FROM TOP OF OPENING

85611074

Fig. 106 Check the master cylinder fluid level

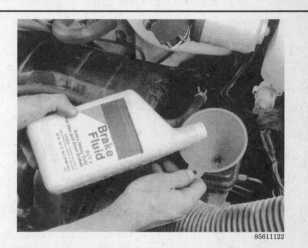

85611122

Fig. 107 Adding brake fluid to the reservoir. Use caution as brake fluid will remove paint from any surface

after removing the covers. Add the necessary fluid to maintain proper level. A drop in the fluid level should be expected as the brake pads and shoes wear. However, if an unusual amount of fluid is required, check for system leaks.

Power Steering Pump

♦ **See Figures 108, 109 and 110**

FLUID RECOMMENDATIONS

Power steering fluid such as Mopar Power Steering Fluid (Part Number 4318055) or equivalent should be used. Only petroleum fluids formulated for minimum effect on the rubber

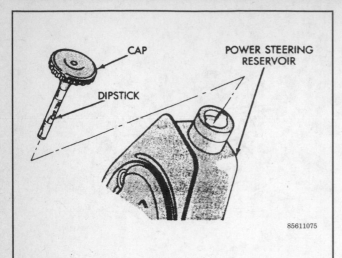

Fig. 108 Typical power steering reservoir dipstick, 2.2L, 2.5L, and 2.6L engine

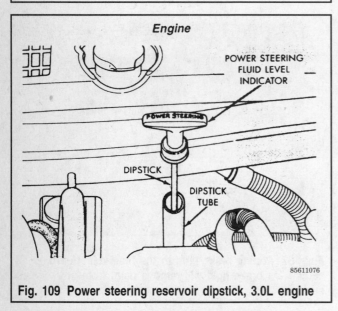

Fig. 109 Power steering reservoir dipstick, 3.0L engine

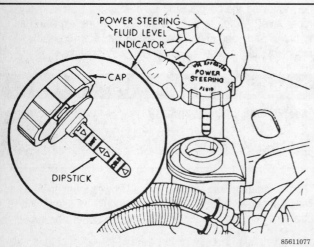

Fig. 110 Power steering reservoir dipstick, 3.3L and 3.8L engine

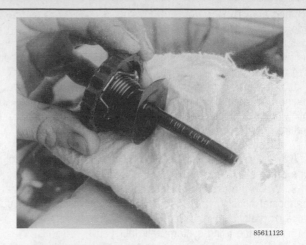

Fig. 111 When reading the power steering cap dipstick note that one side shows the correct hot level and the other shows a cold level reading

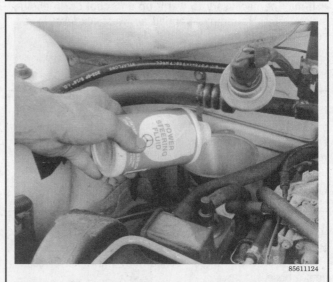

Fig. 112 Adding fluid to the power steering reservoir

hoses should be added. Do not use automatic transmission fluid.

✳✳CAUTION

Check the power steering fluid level with engine off, to avoid injury from moving parts.

LEVEL CHECK

▶ See Figures 111 and 112

1. Wipe off the power steering pump reservoir cap with a cloth before removal.
2. A dipstick is built into the cover. Remove the reservoir cover cap and wipe the dipstick with a cloth.
3. Reinstall the dipstick and check the level indicated.
4. Add fluid as necessary, but do not overfill.

Steering Gear

➡ The steering gear is lubricated and sealed at the factory, periodic lubrication is not necessary.

Chassis Lubrication

▶ **See Figures 113, 114 and 115**

All vehicles have two lower ball joints in the front suspension that are equipped with grease fittings as are the tie rod ends. Periodic lubrication (every 24,000 miles) using a hand grease gun and NLGI Grade 2, Multipurpose grease is required. Connect the grease gun to the fitting and pump until the boot seal on the tie rod ends or ball joints start to swell. Do not overfill until grease flows from under the boot edges.

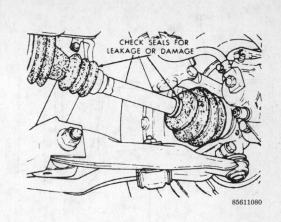

Fig. 115 Inspect CV-joint seals (boots) for cuts or damage

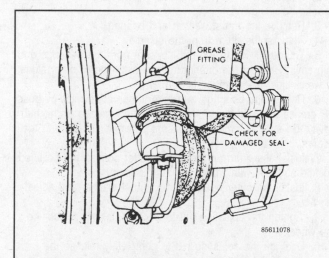

Fig. 113 Check the tie-rod end ball joint seals and lubricate at the grease fitting

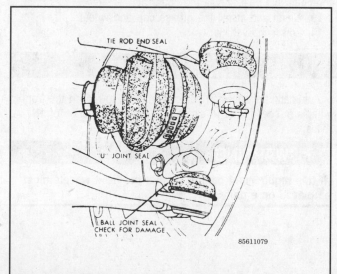

Fig. 114 Chck the ball joints for damaged seals

Body Lubrication

The following body parts and mechanisms should be lubricated periodically at all pivot and sliding points. Use the lubricant specified;

Engine Oil:
- Door Hinges at pin and pivot contact area.
- Hinges
- Liftgate Hinges
- Sliding Door at center hinge pivot.

White Spray Lube:
- Hood Hinge cam and slide
- Lock cylinders
- Parking Brake Mechanisms
- Window Regulator: remove trim panel
- Liftgate Latches
- Liftgate Prop Pivots
- Ash Tray Slide

Multi-purpose Lubricant (Water Resistant):
- Door Latch, Lock control Linkage and Remote Control Mechanism (trim panel must be removed)
- Latch Plate and Bolt

Multi-purpose Grease, NLGI Grade 2:
- Sliding Door: lower, center and upper tracks. Open position striker spring.
- Fuel Tank Door

Rear Wheel Bearings Front Wheel Drive Only

▶ **See Figure 116**

SERVICING

➡ Sodium-based grease is not compatible with lithium-based grease. Read the package labels and be careful not to mix the two types. If there is any doubt as to the type of grease used, completely clean the old grease from the bearing and hub before replacing.

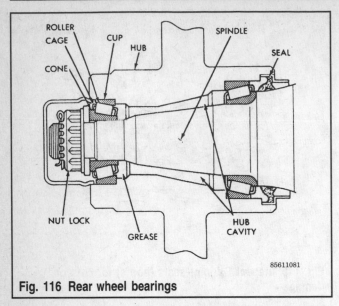

Fig. 116 Rear wheel bearings

Before handling the bearings, there are a few things that you should remember to do and not to do. **Remember to DO the following:**

• Remove all outside dirt from the housing before exposing the bearing.

• Treat a used bearing as gently as you would a new one.

• Work with clean tools in clean surroundings.

• Use clean, dry canvas gloves, or at least clean, dry hands.

• Clean solvents and flushing fluids are a must.

• Use clean paper when laying out the bearings to dry.

• Protect disassembled bearings from rust and dirt. Cover them up.

• Use clean rags to wipe bearings.

• Keep the bearings in oil-proof paper when they are to be stored or are not in use.

• Clean the inside of the housing before replacing the bearing. **Do NOT do the following:**

• Don't work in dirty surroundings.

• Don't use dirty, chipped or damaged tools.

• Try not to work on wooden work benches or use wooden mallets.

• Don't handle bearings with dirty or moist hands.

• Do not use gasoline for cleaning; use a safe solvent.

• Do not spin-dry bearings with compressed air. They will be damaged.

• Do not spin dirty bearings.

• Avoid using cotton waste or dirty cloths to wipe bearings.

• Try not to scratch or nick bearing surfaces.

• Do not allow the bearing to come in contact with dirt or rust at any time.

The rear wheel bearings should be inspected and relubricated whenever the rear brakes are serviced or at least every 30,000 miles. Repack the bearings with high temperature multi-purpose grease.

Check the lubricant to see if it is contaminated. If it contains dirt or has a milky appearance indicating the presence of water, the bearings should be cleaned and repacked.

Clean the bearings in kerosene, mineral spirits or other suitable cleaning fluid. Do not dry them by spinning the bearings. Allow them to air dry.

1. Raise and support the vehicle with the rear wheels off the floor.

2. Remove the wheel grease cap, cotter pin, nut-lock and bearing adjusting nut.

3. Remove the thrust washer and bearing.

4. Remove the drum from the spindle.

5. Thoroughly clean the old lubricant from the bearings and hub cavity. Inspect the bearing rollers for pitting or other signs of wear. Light discoloration is normal.

6. Repack the bearings with high temperature multi-purpose EP grease and add a small amount of new grease to the hub cavity. Be sure to force the lubricant between all rollers in the bearing.

7. Install the drum on the spindle after coating the polished spindle surfaces with wheel bearing lubricant.

8. Install the outer bearing cone, thrust washer and adjusting nut.

9. Tighten the adjusting nut to 20-25 ft. lbs. while rotating the wheel.

10. Back off the adjusting nut to completely release the preload from the bearing.

11. Tighten the adjusting nut finger-tight.

12. Position the nut-lock with one pair of slots in line with the cotter pin hole. Install the cotter pin.

13. Clean and install the grease cap and wheel.

14. Lower the vehicle.

TOWING

The vehicle can be towed from either the front or rear. If the vehicle is towed from the front for an extended distance make sure the parking brake is completely released.

Manual transmission vehicles may be towed on the front wheels at speeds up to 30 Mph, for a distance not to exceed 15 miles, provided the transmission is in neutral and the drive line has not been damaged. The steering wheel must be clamped in a straight ahead position.

✳✳WARNING

Do not use the steering column lock to secure front wheel position for towing.

Automatic transmission vehicles may be towed on the front wheels at speeds not to exceed 25 Mph for a period of 15 miles.

✳✳WARNING

If this requirement cannot be met the front wheels must be placed on a dolly.

JACKING

▶ **See Figure 117**

The standard jack utilizes special receptacles located at the body sills. They accept the scissors jack supplied with the vehicle, for emergency road service only. The jack supplied with the vehicle should never be used for any service operation other then tire changing. Never get under the vehicle while it is supported by only a jack. Always block the wheels when changing tires.

The service operations in this book often require that one end or the other, or both, of the vehicle be raised and safely supported. The ideal method, of course, would be a hydraulic hoist. Since this is beyond both the resource and requirement of the do-it-yourselfer, a small hydraulic floor jack is recommended for certain procedures in this guide. Two sturdy jack stands should be acquired if you intend to work under the vehicle at any time. An alternate method of raising the vehicle would be drive-on ramps, Which are available commercially. Be sure to block the wheels when using ramps.

❊❊CAUTION

Concrete blocks are not recommended for supporting the vehicle. They are likely to crumble if the load is not evenly distributed. Boxes and milk crates of any description must not be used to support the vehicle!

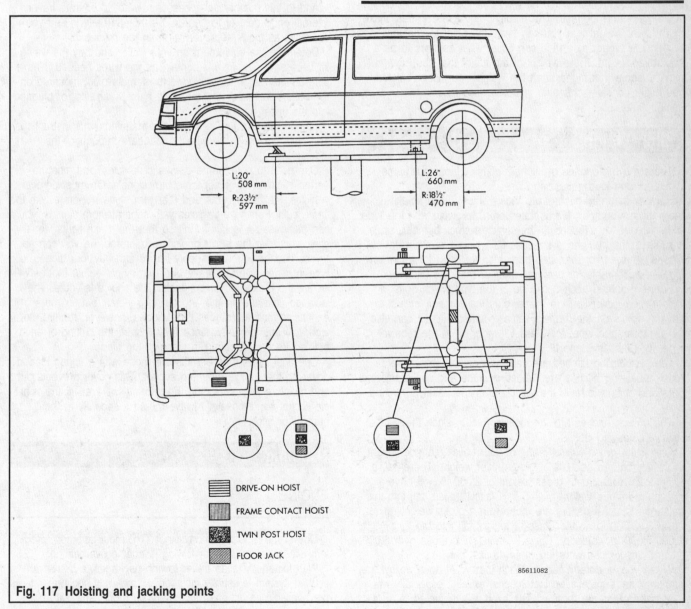

L:20″ 508 mm
R:23½″ 597 mm

L:26″ 660 mm
R:18½″ 470 mm

▦ DRIVE-ON HOIST

▥ FRAME CONTACT HOIST

▨ TWIN POST HOIST

▧ FLOOR JACK

85611082

Fig. 117 Hoisting and jacking points

TRAILER TOWING

Factory trailer towing packages are available on most vans. However, if you are installing a trailer hitch and wiring on your van, there are a few thing that you ought to know.

Trailer Weight

Trailer weight is the first, and most important, factor in determining whether or not your vehicle is suitable for towing the trailer you have in mind. The horsepower-to-weight ratio should be calculated. The basic standard is a ratio of 35:1. That is, 35 pounds of GVW for every horsepower.

To calculate this ratio, multiply you engine's rated horsepower by 35, then subtract the weight of the vehicle, including passengers and luggage. The resulting figure is the ideal maximum trailer weight that you can tow. One point to consider: a numerically higher axle ratio can offset what appears to be a low trailer weight. If the weight of the trailer that you have in mind is somewhat higher than the weight you just calculated, you might consider changing your rear axle ratio to compensate.

Hitch Weight

There are three kinds of hitches: bumper mounted, frame mounted, and load equalizing.

Bumper mounted hitches are those which attach solely to the vehicle's bumper. Many states prohibit towing with this type of hitch, when it attaches to the vehicle's stock bumper, since it subjects the bumper to stresses for which it was not designed. Aftermarket rear step bumpers, designed for trailer towing, are acceptable for use with bumper mounted hitches.

Frame mounted hitches can be of the type which bolts to two or more points on the frame, plus the bumper, or just to several points on the frame. Frame mounted hitches can also be of the tongue type, for Class I towing, or, of the receiver type, for Classes II and III.

Load equalizing hitches are usually used for large trailers. Most equalizing hitches are welded in place and use equalizing bars and chains to level the vehicle after the trailer is hooked up.

The bolt-on hitches are the most common, since they are relatively easy to install.

Check the gross weight rating of your trailer. Tongue weight is usually figured as 10% of gross trailer weight. Therefore, a trailer with a maximum gross weight of 2,000 lb. will have a maximum tongue weight of 200 lb. Class I trailers fall into this category. Class II trailers are those with a gross weight rating of 2,000-3,500 lb., while Class III trailers fall into the 3,500-6,000 lb. category. Class IV trailers are those over 6,000 lb. and are for use with fifth wheel trucks, only.

When you've determined the hitch that you'll need, follow the manufacturer's installation instructions, exactly, especially when it comes to fastener torques. The hitch will subjected to a lot of stress and good hitches come with hardened bolts. Never substitute an inferior bolt for a hardened bolt.

Wiring

Wiring the van for towing is fairly easy. There are a number of good wiring kits available and these should be used, rather than trying to design your own. All trailers will need brake lights and turn signals as well as tail lights and side marker lights. Most states require extra marker lights for overly wide trailers. Also, most states have recently required back-up lights for trailers, and most trailer manufacturers have been building trailers with back-up lights for several years.

Additionally, some Class I, most Class II and just about all Class III trailers will have electric brakes.

Add to this number an accessories wire, to operate trailer internal equipment or to charge the trailer's battery, and you can have as many as seven wires in the harness.

Determine the equipment on your trailer and buy the wiring kit necessary. The kit will contain all the wires needed, plus a plug adapter set which included the female plug, mounted on the bumper or hitch, and the male plug, wired into, or plugged into the trailer harness.

When installing the kit, follow the manufacturer's instructions. The color coding of the wires is standard throughout the industry.

One point to note, some domestic vehicles, and most imported vehicles, have separate turn signals. On most domestic vehicles, the brake lights and rear turn signals operate with the same bulb. For those vehicles with separate turn signals, you can purchase an isolation unit so that the brake lights won't blink whenever the turn signals are operated, or, you can go to your local electronics supply house and buy four diodes to wire in series with the brake and turn signal bulbs. Diodes will isolate the brake and turn signals. The choice is yours. The isolation units are simple and quick to install, but far more expensive than the diodes. The diodes, however, require more work to install properly, since they require the cutting of each bulb's wire and soldering in place of the diode.

One final point, the best kits are those with a spring loaded cover on the vehicle mounted socket. This cover prevents dirt and moisture from corroding the terminals. Never let the vehicle socket hang loosely. Always mount it securely to the bumper or hitch.

Cooling

ENGINE

One of the most common, if not THE most common, problem associated with trailer towing is engine overheating.

With factory installed trailer towing packages, a heavy duty cooling system is usually included. Heavy duty cooling systems are available as optional equipment on most vans, with or without a trailer package. If you have one of these extra-capacity systems, you shouldn't have any overheating problems.

If you have a standard cooling system, without an expansion tank, you'll definitely need to get an aftermarket expansion tank kit, preferably one with at least a 2 quart capacity. These kits are easily installed on the radiator's overflow hose, and come with a pressure cap designed for expansion tanks.

Another helpful accessory is a Flex Fan. These fan are large diameter units are designed to provide more airflow at low speeds, with blades that have deeply cupped surfaces. The blades then flex, or flatten out, at high speed, when less cooling air is needed. These fans are far lighter in weight than stock fans, requiring less horsepower to drive them. Also, they are far quieter than stock fans.

If you do decide to replace your stock fan with a flex fan, note that if your van has a fan clutch, a spacer between the flex fan and water pump hub will be needed.

Aftermarket engine oil coolers are helpful for prolonging engine oil life and reducing overall engine temperatures. Both of these factors increase engine life.

While not absolutely necessary in towing Class I and some Class II trailers, they are recommended for heavier Class II and all Class III towing.

Engine oil cooler systems consist of an adapter, screwed on in place of the oil filter, a remote filter mounting and a multi-tube, finned heat exchanger, which is mounted in front of the radiator or air conditioning condenser.

TRANSMISSION

An automatic transmission is usually recommended for trailer towing. Modern automatics have proven reliable and, of course, easy to operate, in trailer towing.

The increased load of a trailer, however, causes an increase in the temperature of the automatic transmission fluid. Heat is the worst enemy of an automatic transmission. As the temperature of the fluid increases, the life of the fluid decreases.

It is essential, therefore, that you install an automatic transmission cooler.

The cooler, which consists of a multi-tube, finned heat exchanger, is usually installed in front of the radiator or air conditioning compressor, and hooked in line with the transmission cooler tank inlet line. Follow the cooler manufacturer's installation instructions.

Select a cooler of at least adequate capacity, based upon the combined gross weights of the van and trailer.

Cooler manufacturers recommend that you use an aftermarket cooler in addition to, and not instead of, the present cooling tank in your van's radiator. If you do want to use it in place of the radiator cooling tank, get a cooler at least two sizes larger than normally necessary.

➡**A transmission cooler can, sometimes, cause slow or harsh shifting in the transmission during cold weather, until the fluid has a chance to come up to normal operating temperature. Some coolers can be purchased with or retrofitted with a temperature bypass valve which will allow fluid flow through the cooler only when the fluid has reached operating temperature, or above.**

ENGINE APPLICATION CHART

Year	Engine Code	No. Cyl.	Actual Displacement			Type	Fuel System	Built By
			Cu. In.	cc	Liters			
1984	C	4	135	2,212	2.2	OHC	2 bbl	Chrysler
	G	4	156	2,556	2.6	OHC	2 bbl	Mitsubishi
1985	C	4	135	2,212	2.2	OHC	2 bbl	Chrysler
	G	4	156	2,556	2.6	OHC	2 bbl	Mitsubishi
1986	C	4	135	2,212	2.2	OHC	2 bbl	Chrysler
	G	4	156	2,556	2.6	OHC	2 bbl	Mitsubishi
1987	C	4	135	2,212	2.2	OHC	2 bbl	Chrysler
	K	4	153	2,507	2.5	OHC	EFI	Chrysler
	G	4	156	2,556	2.6	OHC	2 bbl	Mitsubishi
	3	6	181	2,966	3.0	OHC	EFI	Mitsubishi
1988	K	4	153	2,507	2.5	OHC	EFI	Chrysler
	3	6	181	2,966	3.0	OHC	EFI	Mitsubishi
1989	K	4	153	2,507	2.5	OHC	EFI	Chrysler
	J	4	153	2,507	2.5	OHC	EFI ①	Chrysler
	3	6	181	2,966	3.0	OHC	EFI	Mitsubishi
1990	K	4	153	2,507	2.5	OHC	EFI	Chrysler
	J	4	153	2,507	2.5	OHC	EFI ①	Chrysler
	3	6	181	2,966	3.0	OHC	EFI	Mitsubishi
	R	6	201	3,294	3.3	OHV	EFI	Chrysler
1991	K	4	153	2,507	2.5	OHC	EFI	Chrysler
	3	6	181	2,966	3.0	OHC	EFI	Mitsubishi
	R	6	201	3,294	3.3	OHV	EFI	Chrysler
1992	K	4	153	2,507	2.5	OHC	EFI	Chrysler
	3	6	181	2,966	3.0	OHC	EFI	Mitsubishi
	R	6	201	3,294	3.3	OHV	EFI	Chrysler
1993	K	4	153	2,507	2.5	OHC	EFI	Chrysler
	3	6	181	2,966	3.0	OHC	EFI	Mitsubishi
	R	6	201	3,294	3.3	OHV	EFI	Chrysler
1994	K	4	153	2,507	2.5	OHC	EFI	Chrysler
	3	6	181	2,966	3.0	OHC	EFI	Mitsubishi
	R	6	201	3,294	3.3	OHV	EFI	Chrysler
	L	6	231	3,786	3.8	OHV	EFI	Chrysler

① Turbocharged Engine

85611C01

AUTOMATIC TRANSMISSION APPLICATION CHART

Year	Transmission	Models
1984	A-413 3 speed	Caravan, Voyager
	A-470 4 speed	Caravan, Voyager
1985	A-413 3 speed	Caravan, Voyager
	A-470 4 speed	Caravan, Voyager
1986	A-413 3 speed	Caravan, Voyager
	A-470 4 speed	Caravan, Voyager
1987	A-413 3 speed	Caravan, Voyager
	A-470 4 speed	Caravan, Voyager
1988	A-413 3 speed	Caravan, Voyager
	A-670 3 speed	Caravan, Voyager
1989	A-413 3 speed	Caravan, Voyager
	A-604 4 speed	Caravan, Voyager
	A-670 3 speed	Caravan, Voyager
1990	A-413 3 speed	Caravan, Voyager
	A-604 4 speed	Caravan, Voyager
	A-670 3 speed	Caravan, Voyager
1991	A-413 3 speed	Caravan, Voyager
	A-670 3 speed	Caravan, Voyager
	A-604 4 speed	Town & Country, Caravan, Voyager
1992	A-413 3 speed	Caravan, Voyager
	A-670 3 speed	Caravan, Voyager
	A-604 4 speed	Caravan, Voyager, Town & Country
1993	A-413 3 speed	Caravan, Voyager
	A-670 3 speed	Caravan, Voyager
	41TE 4 speed	Caravan, Voyager, Town & Country
1994	A-413 3 speed	Caravan, Voyager
	A-413 4 speed	Caravan, Voyager, Town & Country

85611C03

MANUAL TRANSMISSION APPLICATION CHART

Year	Transmission	Models
1984	A-460 4 speed	Caravan, Voyager
	A-465 4 speed	Caravan, Voyager
	A-525 5 speed	Caravan, Voyager
1985	A-460 4 speed	Caravan, Voyager
	A-465 4 speed	Caravan, Voyager
	A-525 5 speed	Caravan, Voyager
1986	A-460 4 speed	Caravan, Voyager
	A-525 5 speed	Caravan, Voyager
1987	A-460 4 speed	Caravan, Voyager
	A-520 5 speed	Caravan, Voyager
1988	A-520 5 speed	Caravan, Voyager
1989	A-520 5 speed	Caravan, Voyager
	A-555 5 speed	Caravan, Voyager
1990	A-523 5 speed	Caravan, Voyager
	A-568 5 speed	Caravan, Voyager
1991	NA	NA
1992	A-523 5 speed	Caravan, Voyager
1993	A-523 5 speed	Caravan, Voyager
1994	A-523 5 speed	Caravan, Voyager

85611C02

CAPACITIES

Year	VIN	Engine No. Cyl. Liters	Crankcase Includes Filter (qts.)	Transmission (pts.)			Power Transfer Unit (qts.) [8]	Fuel Tank (gal.)	Cooling System (qts.) [3]
				4-sp	5-sp	Auto. [4]			
1984	C	4-2.2L	4	4.8	—	[1]	—	15 [2]	8.5
	G	4-2.6L	5	—	4.8	[1]	—	15 [2]	9.5
1985	C	4-2.2L	4	4.8	—	[1]	—	15 [2]	8.5
	G	4-2.6L	5	—	4.8	[1]	—	15 [2]	9.5
1986	C	4-2.2L	4	4.8	—	[1]	—	15 [2]	8.5
	G	4-2.6L	5	—	4.8	[1]	—	15 [2]	9.5
1987	C	4-2.2L	4	4.8	—	[1]	—	15 [2]	8.5
	K	4-2.5L	4	—	4.8	[1]	—	15 [2]	8.5
	G	4-2.6L	5	—	4.8	[1]	—	15 [2]	9.5
	3	6-3.0L	4	—	—	[1]	—	15 [2]	10.5
1988	K	4-2.5L	4	—	5.0	[1]	—	15 [2]	8.5
	3	6-3.0L	4	—	—	[1]	—	15 [2]	10.5
1989	K	4-2.5L	4	—	5.0	[1]	—	15 [2]	8.5
	J	4-2.5L	4	—	5.0	[1]	—	15 [2]	8.5
	3	6-3.0L	4	—	—	[1]	—	15 [2]	10.5
1990	K	4-2.5L	4	—	4.6	[1]	—	15 [2]	8.5
	J	4-2.5L	4	—	4.6	[1]	—	15 [2]	8.5
	3	6-3.0L	4	—	—	[1]	—	15 [2]	10.5
	R	6-3.3L	4	—	—	[1]	—	15 [2]	10.5
1991	K	4-2.5L	4.5	—	—	[1]	1.22	15 [2]	8.5
	3	6-3.0L	4.5	—	—	[1]	1.22	15 [2]	10.5
	R	6-3.3L	4.5	—	—	[1]	1.22	15 [2]	10.5
1992	K	4-2.5L	4.5	—	4.8	[5]	1.22	[6]	9.5
	3	6-3.0L	4.5	—	4.8	[5]	1.22	[6]	10.0
	R	6-3.3L	4.5	—	—	[5]	1.22	[6]	10.0
1993	K	4-2.5L	4.5	—	4.8	[5]	1.22	[6]	9.5
	3	6-3.0L	4.5	—	4.8	[5]	1.22	[6]	10.0
	R	6-3.3L	4.5	—	—	[5]	1.22	[6]	10.0
1994	K	4-2.5L	4.5	—	4.6	[5]	1.22	[6]	9.5 [7]
	3	6-3.0L	4.5	—	4.6	[5]	1.22	[6]	10.5 [7]
	R	6-3.3L	4.5	—	—	[5]	1.22	[6]	10.5 [7]
	L	6-3.8L	4.5	—	—	[5]	1.22	[6]	10.5 [7]

[1] A413/A470 Transaxles (except Fleet): 17.8 pts.
A413/A470 Transaxles (Fleet): 18.4 pts.
A413/A460 Transaxles with Lockup Converter: 17.0 pts.
A604 Transaxles: 18.2 pts.
[2] Standard: 15 Gal.
Optional: 20 Gal.
[3] Add 1 qt. when equipped with rear heater
[4] Overhaul fill capacity with converter empty
[5] Three speed except fleet: 17 pts.
Three speed fleet: 18.4 pts.
4 speed: 18.2 pts.
[6] All wheel drive: 18 gal.
Front wheel drive: 20 gal.
[7] Includes heater and coolant recovery bottle
[8] All wheel drive vehicles

85611C04

TORQUE SPECIFICATIONS

Component	English	Metric
Air cleaner wing nut	14 inch lbs.	1.5 Nm
A/C Compressor		
Exc. 2.6L engine		
Locking and pivot screws	40 ft. lbs.	54 Nm
2.6L engine		
Locking screw and pivot nut	16 ft. lbs.	22 Nm
Jam nut	21 ft. lbs.	29 Nm
A/C Compressor idler pulley locknut		
3.0L engine	40 ft. lbs.	54 Nm
Air Pump locking and pivot bolts	25 ft. lbs.	34 Nm
Alternator		
Exc. 2.6L engine		
1984–89		
Locking screw	25 ft. lbs.	34 Nm
Pivot nut	30 ft. lbs.	41 Nm
1990–94 Locking & Pivot Nut	40 ft. lbs.	54 Nm
2.6L engine		
Locking screw and pivot nut	16 ft. lbs.	22 Nm
Jam nut	21 ft. lbs.	29 Nm
Carburetor stud nuts	14 inch lbs.	1.5 Nm
Cooling system hose clamps	20–30 inch lbs.	2–3 Nm
Cooling system vacuum valve or drain/fill plug	15 ft. lbs.	20 Nm
Fuel filter line clamps	10 inch lbs.	1 Nm
Fuel filter mounting screw	75 inch lbs.	8 Nm
Power Steering Pump locking and pivot screws	40 ft. lbs.	54 Nm
Wheel lug nuts	95 ft. lbs.	129 Nm

85611C05

2

ENGINE PERFORMANCE AND TUNE-UP

TUNE-UP PROCEDURES

Neither tune-up nor troubleshooting can be considered independently since each has a direct relationship with the other.

It is advisable to follow a definite and thorough tune-up procedure. Tune-up consists of three separate steps: Analysis, (the process of determining whether normal wear is responsible for performance loss, and whether parts require replacement or service); Parts Replacement or Service; and Adjustment, (where engine adjustments are performed).

The manufacturer's recommended interval for tune-ups on non-catalyst vehicles is 15,000 miles. Models with a converter, every 30,000 miles. Models equipped with a 2.6L engine require a valve lash adjustment every 15,000 miles. this interval should be shortened if the vehicle is subjected to severe operating conditions such as trailer pulling or stop and start driving, or if starting and running problems are noticed. It is assumed that the routine maintenance has been kept up, as this will have an effect on the result of the tune-up. All the applicable tune-up steps should be followed, as each adjustment complements the effects of the other. If the tune-up (emission control) sticker in the engine compartment disagrees with the information presented in the Tune-up Specifications chart in this section, the sticker figures must be followed. The sticker information reflects running changes made by the manufacturer during production.

Troubleshooting is a logical sequence of procedures designed to locate a particular cause of trouble. While the apparent cause of trouble, in many cases, is worn or damaged parts, performance problems are less obvious. The first job is to locate the problem and cause. Once the problem has been isolated, repairs, removal or adjustment procedures can be performed.

It is advisable to read the entire section before beginning a tune-up, although those who are more familiar with tune-up procedures may wish to go directly to the instructions.

Spark Plugs

A typical spark plug consists of a metal shell surrounding a ceramic insulator. A metal electrode extends downward through the center of the insulator and protrudes a small distance. Located at the end of the plug and attached to the side of the outer metal shell is the side electrode. The side electrode bends in at a 90° angle so that its tip is even with, and parallel to, the tip of the center electrode. The distance between these two electrodes (measured in thousandths of an inch) is called the spark plug gap. The spark plug in no way produces a spark but merely provides a gap across which the current can arc. The coil produces anywhere from 20,000 to 40,000 volts which travels to the distributor where it is distributed through the spark plug wires to the spark plugs. The current passes along the center electrode and jumps the gap to the side electrode, and, in do doing, ignites the air/fuel mixture in the combustion chamber.

SPARK PLUG HEAT RANGE

Spark plug heat range is the ability of the plug to dissipate heat. The longer the insulator (or the farther it extends into the engine), the hotter the plug will operate; the shorter the insulator the cooler it will operate. A plug that absorbs little heat and remains too cool will quickly accumulate deposits of oil and carbon since it is not hot enough to burn them off. This leads to plug fouling and consequently to misfiring. A plug that absorbs too much heat will have no deposits, but, due to the excessive heat, the electrodes will burn away quickly and in some instances, preignition may result. Preignition takes place when plug tips get so hot that they glow sufficiently to ignite the fuel/air mixture before the actual spark occurs. This early ignition will usually cause a pinging during low speeds and heavy loads.

The general rule of thumb for choosing the correct heat range when picking a spark plug is: if most of your driving is long distance, high speed travel, use a colder plug; if most of your driving is stop and go, use a hotter plug. Original equipment plugs are compromise plugs, but most people never have occasion to change their plugs from the factory-recommended heat range.

REMOVAL & INSTALLATION

▶ **See Figures 1, 2 and 3**

1. Before removing the spark plugs, number the plug wires so that the correct wire goes on the plug when replaced. This can be done with pieces of adhesive tape.

2. Next, clean the area around the plugs by blowing with compressed air. You can also loosen the plugs a few turns and crank the engine to blow the dirt away.

❋❋CAUTION

Wear safety glasses to avoid possible eye injury due to flying dust particles.

3. Disconnect the plugs wires by twisting and pulling on the rubber cap, not on the wire.

4. Remove each plug with a rubber insert spark plug socket. make sure that the socket is all the way down on the plug to prevent it from slipping and cracking the porcelain insulator.

5. After removing each plug, evaluate its condition. A spark plug's useful life is approximately 30,000 miles. Thus, it would make sense to replace a plug if it has been in service that long.

6. If the plugs are to be reused, file the center and side electrodes flat with a fine, flat point file. Heavy or baked on deposits can be carefully scraped off with a small knife blade, or the scraper tool of a combination spark plug tool. However, it is suggested that plugs be test and cleaned on a service station sandblasting machine. Check the gap between the electrodes with a round wire spark plug gapping gauge. Do not use a flat feeler gauge; it will give an inaccurate reading. If the

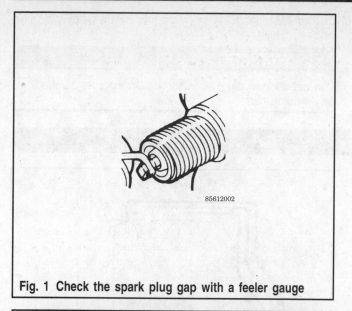

Fig. 1 Check the spark plug gap with a feeler gauge

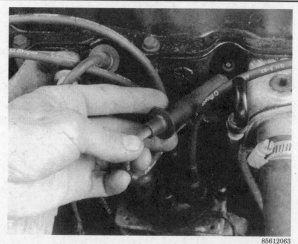

Fig. 2 Disconnect the spark plug wire by pulling on the boot and not the wire

Fig. 3 Removing the spark plug using a rachet and extension

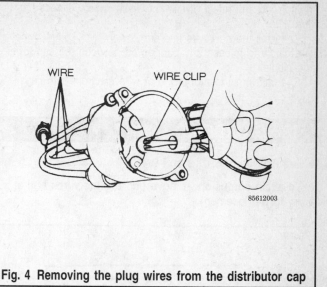

Fig. 4 Removing the plug wires from the distributor cap

gap is not as specified, use the bending tool on the spark plug gap gauge to bend the outside electrode. Be careful not to bend the electrode tool far or too often, because excessive bending may cause the electrode to break off and fall into the combustion chamber. This would require removing the cylinder head to reach the broken piece, and could also result in cylinder wall, piston ring, or valve damage.

7. Clean the threads of old plugs with a wire brush. Lubricate the threads with a drop of oil.

8. Screw the plugs in finger tight, and then tighten them with the spark plug socket to 20 ft. lbs. (27 Nm). Be very careful not to over tighten them.

9. Reinstall the wires. If, by chance, you have forgotten to number the plug wires, refer to the Firing Order illustrations.

Spark Plug Wires

▶ See Figure 4

Check the spark plug wire connections at the coil, distributor cap towers, and at the spark plugs. Be sure they are fully seated, and the boot covers are not cracked or split. Clean the cables with a cloth and a non-flammable solvent. Check for brittle or cracked insulation, replace wires as necessary. If a wire is suspected of failure, test it with an ohmmeter. Test as follows:

1. Remove the plug wire from the spark plug. Twist the boot and pull. Never apply pressure to the wire itself.

➡The 3.3L and 3.8L engines are equipped with a distributorless electronic ignition system. The plug wires run directly from the coil pack to the spark plugs.

2. Remove the distributor cap from the distributor with all wires attached.

➡Do not pull plugs wires from distributor cap, they must first be released from inside of cap.

3. Connect the ohmmeter between the spark plug terminal, and the corresponding electrode inside the distributor cap. Resistance should be within limits of the cable resistance chart. If resistance is not within specs, remove the wire from the dis-

tributor cap and retest. If still not within specs, replace the wire.

4. Install the new wire into cap tower, then squeeze the wire nipple to release any trapped air between the cap tower and nipple.

5. Push firmly to properly seat wire electrode into cap.

6. Install plug end of wire onto plug until it snaps into place.

✳✳WARNING

Do not allowed plug wires to contact exhaust manifold or any moving parts.

FIRING ORDERS

▶ See Figures 5, 6, 7, 8 and 9

➡To avoid confusion, remove and tag the wires one at a time, for replacement.

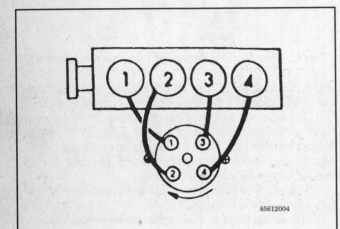

Fig. 5 2.2L and 2.5L engine
 Firing order: 1-3-4-2
Distributor rotation: Clockwise

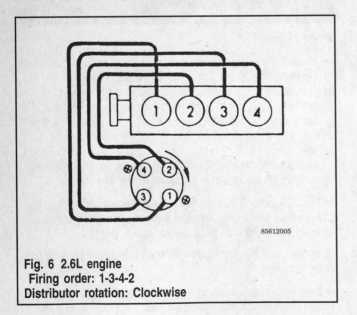

Fig. 6 2.6L engine
 Firing order: 1-3-4-2
Distributor rotation: Clockwise

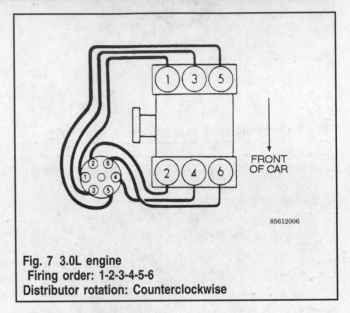

Fig. 7 3.0L engine
 Firing order: 1-2-3-4-5-6
Distributor rotation: Counterclockwise

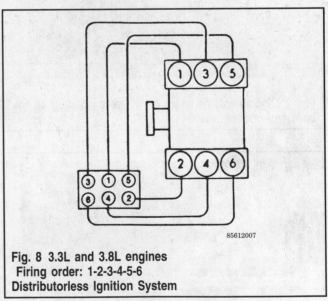

Fig. 8 3.3L and 3.8L engines
 Firing order: 1-2-3-4-5-6
Distributorless Ignition System

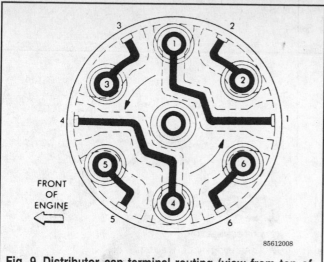

Fig. 9 Distributor cap terminal routing (view from top of cap), 3.0L engine

CHRYSLER HALL EFFECT ELECTRONIC IGNITION

Spark Control Computer (SCC) System

1984-87

The Hall Effect electronic ignition is used in conjunction with the Chrysler Spark Control Computer (SCC) controlling the entire ignition. It consists of a sealed Spark Control Computer, specially calibrated carburetor and various engine sensors, such as the vacuum transducer, coolant switch, Hall Effect pick-up assembly, oxygen sensor and carburetor switch.

SCC SYSTEM COMPONENTS

Spark Control Computer

During cranking, an electrical signal is sent from the distributor to the computer. This signal will cause the computer to fire the spark plugs at a fixed amount of advance. Once the engine starts, the timing will then be controlled by the computer based on the information received from the various sensors.

There are essentially 2 modes of operation of the Spark Control computer: the start mode and the run mode. The start mode is only used during engine cranking. During cranking, only the Hall Effect pick-up signals the computer. These signals are interpreted to provide a fixed number of degrees of spark advance.

After the engine starts and during normal engine operation, the computer functions in the run mode. In this mode, the Hall Effect pick-up serves as only one of the signals to the computer. It is a reference signal of maximum possible spark advance. The computer then determines, from information provided by the other engine sensors, how much of this advance is necessary and delays the coil saturation accordingly, firing the spark plug at the exact moment this advance (crankshaft position) is reached.

There is a third mode of operation which only becomes functional when the computer fails. This is the limp-in mode. This mode functions on signals from the pick-up only and results in very poor engine performance. However, it does allow the car to be driven to a repair shop. If a failure occurs in the pick-up assembly or the start mode of the computer, the engine will neither start nor run.

Hall Effect Pick-Up

The Hall Effect pick-up is located in the distributor assembly and supplies the engine Rpm and ignition timing data to the SCC to advance or retard the ignition spark as required by current operating conditions.

Coolant Sensor
▶ **See Figures 10, 11 and 12**

The coolant temperature sensor is located on the thermostat housing and provides the SCC with engine temperature data. The SCC uses this data to control various engine functions such as spark advance, fuel mixture, emission controls operation and radiator fan.

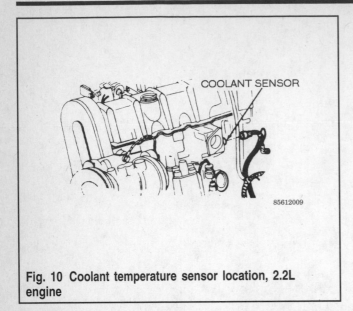

Fig. 10 Coolant temperature sensor location, 2.2L engine

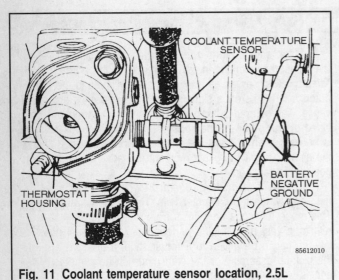

Fig. 11 Coolant temperature sensor location, 2.5L engine

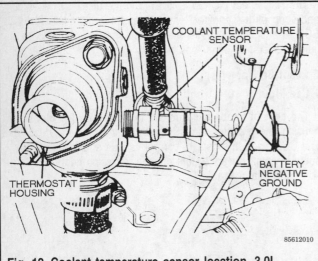

Fig. 12 Coolant temperature sensor location, 3.0L engine

Vacuum Sensor
◗ **See Figure 13**

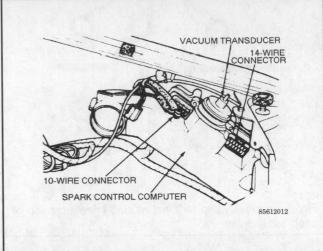

Fig. 13 Spark control vacuum transducer location, 2.2L engine

The vacuum transducer is located on the Spark Control Computer and informs the SCC as to the manifold vacuum during operation. The engine vacuum is one of the factors that will determine how the computer will advance/retard ignition timing and with the feedback carburetor, how the air/fuel ration will be changed.

Carburetor Switch
◗ **See Figure 14**

The carburetor switch is located on the left side of the carburetor; it provides the SCC with throttle open or throttle closed signal.

Oxygen Sensor
◗ **See Figure 15**

The oxygen sensor (used with feedback carburetors) is located in the exhaust manifold and signals the computer how

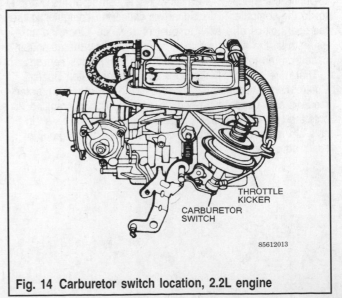

Fig. 14 Carburetor switch location, 2.2L engine

much oxygen is present in the exhaust gases. Since this amount is proportional to rich and lean mixtures, the computer will adjust the air/fuel ration to a level which will maintain operating efficiency of the 3-way catalyst system and engine.

DIAGNOSIS AND TESTING THE SCC SYSTEM

▶ **See Figures 16, 17 and 18**

➡**Apply parking brake and block wheels before performing any engine running tests, including idle or timing checks and adjustments.**

Testing for Spark at Coil

Remove coil secondary cable from distributor cap. Using a suitable tool, hold end of cable about ¼ in. from good engine ground. Crank engine and look for good, constant spark at coil secondary wire. If spark is constant, have a helper continue to crank engine while moving coil secondary cable away from ground. Look for arcing at the coil tower. If arcing occurs,

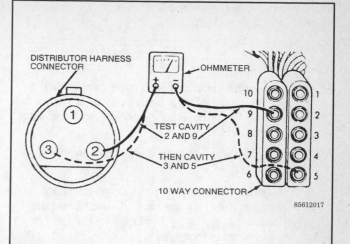

Fig. 17 Testing cavities 2 and 9, then cavities 3 and 5 for continuity

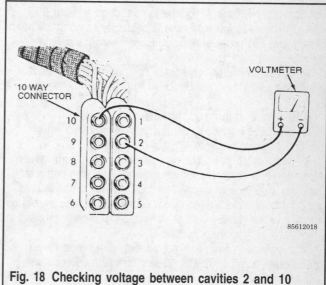

Fig. 18 Checking voltage between cavities 2 and 10

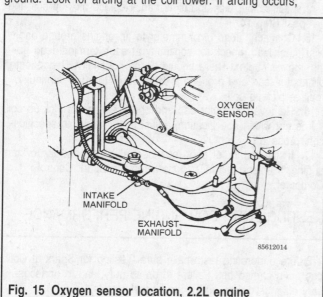

Fig. 15 Oxygen sensor location, 2.2L engine

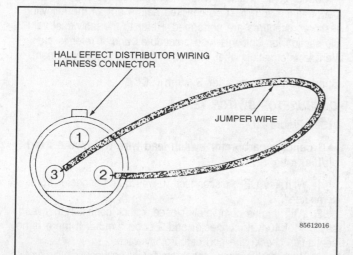

Fig. 16 Jumping cavities 2 and 3 of the distributor harness

replace the coil. If no arcing occurs, ignition system is producing the necessary high secondary voltage. Make certain this voltage is getting to spark plugs by checking distributor rotor, cap, spark plug wires and spark plugs. If all check in good condition, ignition system is NOT cause of problem.

If spark is weak, not constant or not present, continue with Failure To Start test.

Ignition System Starting Test

1. With a voltmeter measure voltage at battery and record it. Battery specific gravity must be 12.20. If if is not, charge batter to specification.
2. Turn ignition switch ON.
3. Remove coil wire from the distributor cap. Using a suitable tool, hold wire about a ¼ in. away from a good ground.
4. Intermittently jump coil negative to ground while looking for a good spark at coil wire.
5. If there is spark at coil wire it must be constant and bright blue in color. If spark is good, slowly move coil wire away from ground while looking for arcing at coil tower. If

arcing occurs replace coil. If spark is weak or not constant, proceed to 'Failure to Start Test'.

Failure to Start Test
▶ See Figure 19

➡Before proceeding with this test, make certain that 'Testing for Spark at Coil' has been performed. Failure to do so may lead to unnecessary diagnostic time and incorrect test results.

➡If a good spark was obtained during Ignition Starting Test, go to Step 8.

1. Turn ignition switch to OFF position and disconnect SCC 10-way connector. Turn ignition switch ON and remove coil wire from distributor cap. Using a suitable tool, hold end of wire 1/4 in. away from a good ground.

2. Intermittently short coil negative wire to ground. If spark is obtained replace spark control computer.

3. If no spark is obtained, check for battery voltage at coil positive terminal with ignition switch ON. It should be within 1 volt of battery voltage. If voltage is correct go to Step 5.

4. If voltage is incorrect, check continuity of wiring between battery and coil positive terminal. Repair wiring and repeat Step 3.

5. Check for battery voltage at coil negative terminal, it should be within 1 volt of battery voltage. If it is correct go to Step 7.

6. If voltage is incorrect, replace coil.

7. If voltage is correct, but no spark is obtained when shorting negative terminal, replace coil.

8. Spark is obtained but engine will not start, turn ignition switch to RUN position and with positive lead of a voltmeter, measure voltage from cavity 1 of SCC 10-way connector, to ground of disconnected lead from computer. Voltage should be within 1 volt of battery voltage. If voltage is correct, proceed to Step 10. If not, continue to Step 9.

9. If voltage in Step 8 is not correct, check wire for an open between coil and SCC 10-way connector. Repair wire and repeat Step 8.

10. Place a thin insulator (piece of paper or cardboard) between curb idle adjusting screw and carburator switch.

11. Connect negative lead of a voltmeter to a good engine ground.

12. Turn ignition switch to RUN position and measure voltage at carburator switch.

    a. If voltage is approximately 5 volts, proceed to Step 14.

    b. If voltage is not at least 5 volts, turn ignition switch to OFF position. Turn ignition switch back to RUN position and measure voltage at terminal 2 of SCC 10-way connector. Voltage should be within 1 volt of battery voltage.

    c. If voltage is correct, repeat Step 10.

    d. If voltage is incorrect, check wiring between terminal 2 and ignition switch for open, shorts or poor connections.

13. Turn ignition switch OFF, check for continuity between terminal 7 of SCC 10-way connector and carburator switch terminal. There should be continuity between these 2 points.

    a. If there is no continuity, check wire for opens, shorts or poor connections.

    b. If there is continuity, check for continuity between terminal 10 and engine ground.

    c. If there is continuity between terminal 10 and engine ground, replace Spark Control Computer (SCC).

    d. If there is no continuity, repeat Step 13; only proceed to Step 14 if engine still does not start.

14. Turn ignition switch to OFF position and, with an ohmmeter, measure resistance between terminals 5 and 9 of SCC 10-way connector for run pick-up coil and between terminals 3 and 9 for start pick-up coil. The resistance should be between 150-900 ohms.

    a. If resistance is correct, proceed to Step 15.

    b. If resistance is not correct, disconnect pick-up coil leads from distributor. Measure resistance at lead going into distributor.

    c. If resistance is now between 150-900 ohms, this means there is an open, shorted, or poor connection between the distributor connector and terminals 5 and 9 or 3 and 9 of the SCC 10-way connector.

    d. Repair wire and repeat Step 14. If resistance is still out of specification, pick-up coil is bad. Replace pick-up coil and repeat Step 14.

15. Connect 1 lead of ohmmeter to an engine ground and, with other lead, check for continuity at each terminal lead going into distributor. There should be no continuity. Reconnect distributor lead and proceed to Step 16. If there is continuity, replace pick-up coil.

16. Remove distributor cap and check air gap of pick-up coil. If it is not within specification, adjust it. If it is within specification, proceed to Step 17.

17. Install distributor cap, reconnect all wiring and try to start engine. If engine still fails to start, replace Spark Control Computer.

TESTING FOR POOR ENGINE PERFORMANCE

Before performing test, make sure 'Testing for Spark at Coil' has been carried out. Failure to do so may lead to unnecessary diagnostic time and incorrect test results.

Correct basic engine timing is essential for optimum vehicle performance and must be checked before any of the following testing procedures are performed. Refer to the individual vehicle section for ignition timing procedures and/or refer to the Vehicle Information label, located in the engine compartment.

Spark Control Computer System (SCC)

CARBURETOR SWITCH TEST

▶ See Figure 20

➡Grounding carburetor switch lead wire will give a fixed air/fuel ratio.

1. With key OFF, disconnect 10-way dual connector from computer.

2. With throttle completely closed, check continuity between cavity 7 of 10-way connector and a good ground. If there is no continuity, check wire and carburetor switch.

3. With throttle open, check continuity between cavity 7 of connector and a good ground. There should be no continuity.

HALL EFFECT ELECTRONIC SPARK ADVANCE SYSTEM DIAGNOSIS

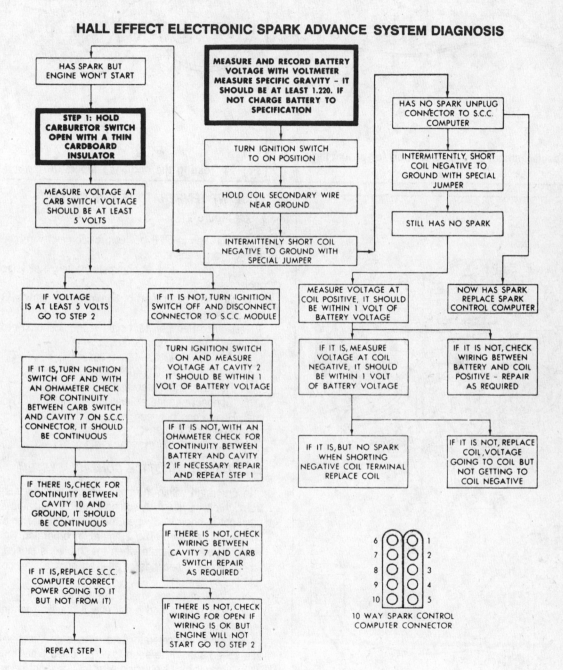

85612015

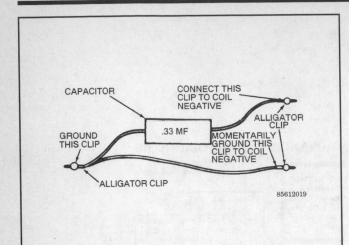

Fig. 19 Special jumper wire construction for grounding the coil

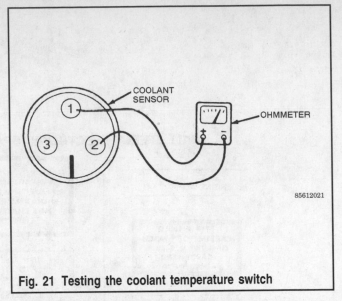

Fig. 21 Testing the coolant temperature switch

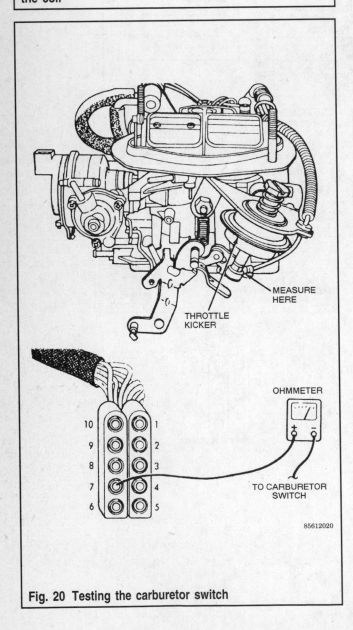

Fig. 20 Testing the carburetor switch

COOLANT TEMPERATURE SENSOR TEST

▶ See Figure 21

1. With key in OFF position, disconnect wire connector from coolant sensor.
2. Connect 1 lead of ohmmeter to terminal 1 (common) of coolant sensor.
3. Connect other lead of ohmmeter to terminal 3 (fan control circuit).
   Resistance between terminals 1 and 3 should be:
   Below 150°F (66°C): 20-200Ω
   150-200°F (66-93°C): 100-1500Ω
   Above 200°F (93°C): 400-6000Ω
4. Remove ohmmeter lead from terminal 3.
5. Connect ohmmeter lead to terminal 2 (SCC control circuit). Resistance between terminals 1 and 2 should be:
   50-100°F (10-38°C): 3,300-36,000Ω
   140-245°F (60-118°C): 176-3,900Ω

ELECTRONIC THROTTLE CONTROL SYSTEM

Incorporated within the spark control computer is the electronic throttle system. A solenoid, which regulates a vacuum dash-pot is energized when the air conditioner or electronic timers are activated. The 2 timers, incorporated within the ignition electronics, operate when the throttle is closed, plus a time delay of 2 seconds or after an engine start condition. To test the system:

1. Connect a tachometer to engine.
2. Start engine and run it until it reaches normal operating temperature.
3. Depress accelerator and release it. A higher than curb idle speed should be seen for a specified time.
4. On vehicles equipped with A/C, a slight decrease in idle speed will be noted when A/C is turned ON; turning OFF A/C will produce normal idle speed.

➡ **The A/C clutch will cycle on and off as system is in operation. This should not be mistaken as part of electronic control system.**

5. As A/C compressor clutch cycles on and off, sole kicker plunger should extend and retract.

6. If plunger does not move with A/C clutch cycling or after a start-up, check kicker system for vacuum leaks.

7. If speed increases do not occur, disconnect 6-way connector at carburetor.

8. Check solenoid with an ohmmeter by measuring resistance between terminal that contains black wire and ground. Resistance should be between 20-100 ohms. If not within specifications, replace solenoid.

9. Start vehicle and before time delay has timed out, measure voltage across vacuum solenoid terminals. The voltage should be within 2 volts of charging system voltage. If not within specifications, replace computer.

10. Turning A/C ON should also produce charging system voltage after time delay has timed out. If not, check wiring back to instrument panel for an open circuit.

SPARK ADVANCE OF SPARK CONTROL COMPUTER

Incorporated in the digital microprocessor electronics are some unique spark advance schedules, which will occur during cold and warm engine operation. These commands have been added to reduce engine emissions and improve driveability. Because they will be changing at different engine operating temperatures during the engine warm-up, all spark advance testing should be done with the engine at normal operating temperature.

1. Adjust the basic timing to specifications.

2. Have engine at normal operating temperature. The coolant temperature sensor must be connected and operating correctly.

3. Remove and plug vacuum hose at vacuum transducer.

4. Connect an auxiliary vacuum supply to vacuum transducer; draw and hold vacuum to 16 in Hg.

5. Start and raise engine speed to 2000 Rpm. Wait 1 minute and check specifications.

➡**The use of a metal exhaust tube is recommended for this test. Using rubber hose may result in a fire due to high temperatures and a long test period.**

6. The advance specifications are in addition to basic advance. If correct advance is not obtained, replace spark plug control computer.

Spark Control Computer (SCC) System — Component Replacement

REMOVAL & INSTALLATION

Spark Control Computer (SCC)
▶ See Figures 22, 23, 24, 25, 26, 27, 28 and 29

1. Disconnect the negative battery cable.

2. Disconnect the 10-way and 14-way connectors and outside air duct from SCC. Remove vacuum line from transducer.

3. Remove 4 mounting screws that hold computer in place.

4. Install new computer and secure mounting screws.

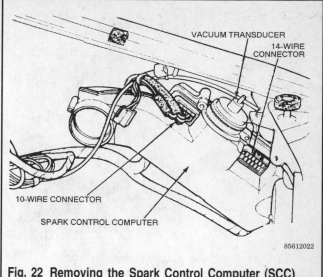

Fig. 22 Removing the Spark Control Computer (SCC)

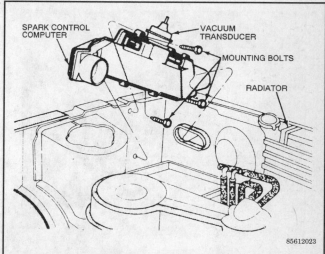

Fig. 23 Removing the Spark Control Computer (SCC) mounting bolts

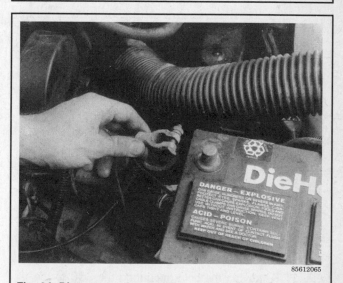

Fig. 24 Disconnect the negative battery cable

Fig. 25 Disconnect the 10-way connector from the controller assembly

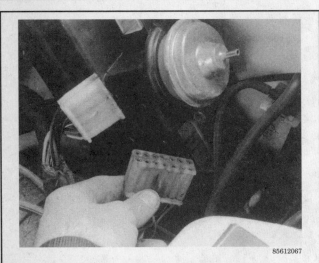

Fig. 26 Disconnect the 14-way connector from the controller assembly

Fig. 27 Removing the bolts mounting the SCC to the inside of the fender

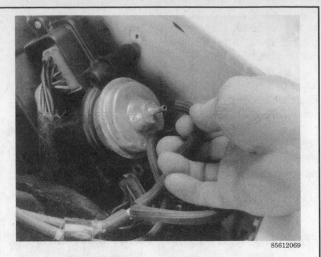

Fig. 28 Disconnect the vacuum lines from the transducer

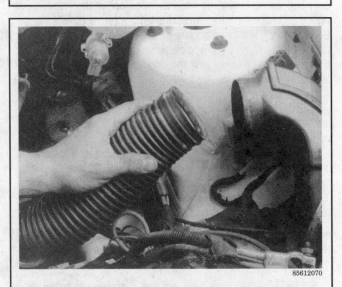

Fig. 29 Disconnect the outside air duct from the SCC

5. Reconnect vacuum line to transducer, making sure vacuum line is not pinched. Reconnect dual connectors and outside air duct to SCC unit.

➡Do not remove grease from 10-way or 14-way dual connector or connector cavities in spark control computer. The grease is used to prevent moisture from corroding terminals. If there isn't at least 1/8 in. grease on bottom of computer connector cavities, apply multi-purpose grease over entire end of connector plug before reinstalling.

Vacuum Transducer

If vacuum transducer fails, complete computer unit (SCC) must be replaced.

Coolant Temperature Sensor

1. Disconnect electrical connector from sensor. Remove sensor from engine. Some coolant may be lost from system.
2. Install new sensor and tighten to 20 ft lbs. Reconnect electrical connector.

3. Replace lost coolant.

Hall Effect Pick-Up

▶ **See Figures 30, 31, 32, 33, 34 and 35**

1. Remove splash shield from distributor and remove distributor cap.
2. Pull straight up on rotor and remove it from shaft.
3. Remove Hall Effect pick-up assembly.
4. Install new pick-up assembly onto distributor.

➡ **Hall Effect assembly wiring leads may be damaged if not properly reinstalled.**

5. Install distributor rotor.
6. Install distributor cap and splash shield.

Distributor

▶ **See Figures 36, 37, 38, 39, 40, 41 and 42**

1. Disconnect the negative battery cable.

Fig. 32 Removing the distributor splash shield

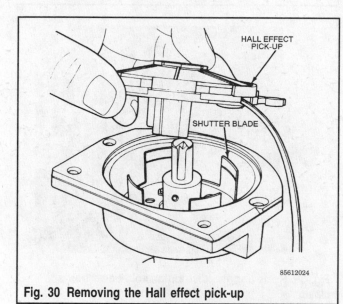

Fig. 30 Removing the Hall effect pick-up

Fig. 33 Removing the distributor cap with plug wires attached

Fig. 31 Remove the distributor splash shield retaining bolts

Fig. 34 After removing the distributor cap pull the rotor straight up and off the shaft

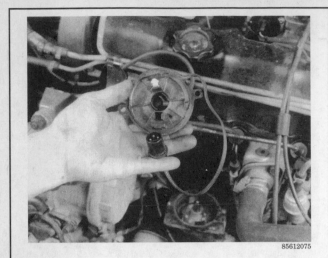

Fig. 35 Removing the Hall Effect pick-up assembly from the distributor

Fig. 38 Removing the distributor hold-down bolt

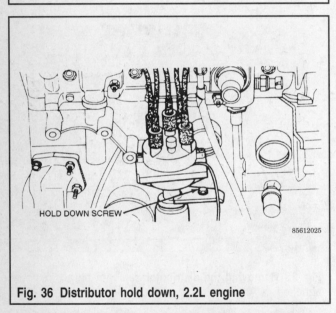

HOLD DOWN SCREW

Fig. 36 Distributor hold down, 2.2L engine

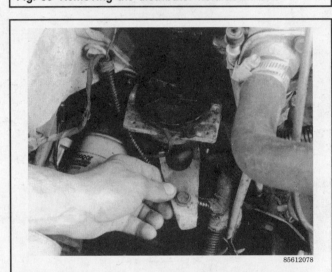

Fig. 39 Removing the distributor hold-down bolt and clamp

Fig. 37 Matchmark the rotor to the distributor housing

Fig. 40 Removing the distributor from the engine

Fig. 41 Removing the distributor O-ring from the distributor housing

Fig. 42 Install a new O-ring on the distributor housing

2. Disconnect the distributor pickup lead wires and vacuum hose(s), if equipped. Remove the splash shield, if equipped.

3. Unfasten the distributor cap retaining clips or screws and lift off the distributor cap with all ignition wires still connected. Remove the coil wire if necessary.

4. Matchmark the rotor to the distributor housing.

➡**Do not crank the engine during this procedure. If the engine is cranked, the matchmark must be disregarded.**

5. Remove the hold-down bolt and clamp.

6. Remove the distributor from the engine.

To install:

7. Install a new distributor housing O-ring.

8. Install the distributor in the engine so the rotor is lined up with the matchmark on the housing. Make sure the distributor is fully seated and that the distributor shaft is fully engaged.

9. If the engine has been cranked, position the engine so that the No. 1 piston is at TDC of the compression stroke and the mark on the vibration damper is lined up with **0** on the timing indicator. Then install the distributor so the rotor is aligned with the position of the No. 1 ignition wire on the distributor cap.

➡**There are distributor cap runners inside the cap on 3.0L engines. Make sure the rotor is pointing to where the No. 1 runner originates inside the cap and not where the No. 1 ignition wire plugs into the cap.**

10. Install the hold-down clamp and snug the hold-down bolt. Connect the vacuum hose(s), if equipped.

11. Connect the distributor pickup lead wires. Install the splash shield, if equipped.

12. Install the distributor cap and snap the retaining clips into place or tighten the screws.

13. Connect the negative battery cable.

14. Adjust the ignition timing and tighten the hold-down bolt.

Ignition Coil

▶ **See Figure 43**

The ignition coil is designed to operate without an external ignition resistor. Inspect coil for external leaks and arcing. Test primary and secondary circuit resistances, replacing any coil that dose not meet the manufacturers specifications.

Every time an ignition coil is replaced because of a burned tower or carbon tracking, always replace coil secondary wire.

Distributor Cap and Rotor

▶ **See Figure 44**

The distributor cap and rotor must be inspected for flash over, cracking, burning and/or worn terminals. Check carbon button in cap for cracking. Light scale may be removed with a sharp knife. Heavy deposits on the cap terminal or the rotor, require replacement of the component.

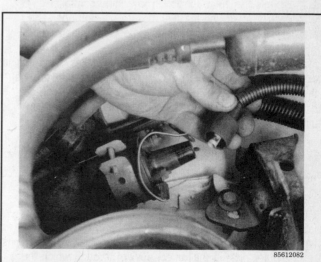

Fig. 43 Ignition coil with the secondary wire disconnected

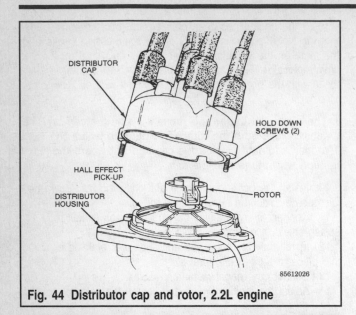

Fig. 44 Distributor cap and rotor, 2.2L engine

Single Module Engine Controller (SMEC) and Single Board Engine Controller (SBEC) Systems

1988-92

General Information

The Hall Effect Pick-Up ignition system is used in conjunction with an engine controller, also referred to the Single Module Engine Controller (SMEC) for 1988-89, a Single Board Engine Controller (SBEC) for 1990-91 or a Single Board Engine Controller II (SBEC II) for 1992 and a Powertrain Control Module (PCM) for 1993-94. The SMEC, SBEC, SBEC II or PCM controls the entire ignition. The engine controller gives the capability of igniting the fuel mixture over all operating conditions, by delivering an infinite amount of variable electronic spark advance curves.

The Hall Effect Pick-Up ignition system consists of an engine controller (SMEC, SBEC, SBEC II and PCM)), a conventional but pointless distributor, a hall effect pick-up, an ignition coil, an Auto Shutdown (ASD) relay and primary and secondary ignition wiring.

SYSTEM OPERATION

A shutter, sometimes referred to as an interrupter, is attached to the distributor shaft. The shutter contains a set of blades, 1 for each cylinder. A switch plate is mounted to the distributor housing above the shutter. The switch plate contains the distributor pick-up (hall effect device) through which the shutter blades rotate. As the shutter blades pass through the pick-up, they interrupt the magnetic field. The hall effect device in the pick-up senses the change in the magnetic field and switches ON and OFF, generating input signal (pulses) to the engine controller.

The engine controller energizes the ignition coil through the ASD relay. When the relay is energized by the controller, battery voltage is supplied to the ignition coil positive terminal. The engine controller will not energize the ASD relay until it receives input from the distributor pick-up. The engine controller calculates engine speed through the number of pulses generated.

On 2.5L turbocharged engines, 1 of the shutter blades has a window cut into it. The controller determines injector synchronization from that window.

During the crank-start period, the engine controller will provide a set amount of advanced timing to assure a quick efficient start. The amount of electronic spark advance provided by the engine controller is determined by 3 input factors:
- Coolant temperature
- Engine rpm
- Manifold Absolute Pressure (MAP)

The engine controller also receives information from the oxygen sensor and electronically adjusts the air fuel mixture to assure the most efficient fuel burn possible.

SYSTEM COMPONENTS

Engine Controller

The engine controller has a built in microprocessor which continuously monitor various engine sensors. The computer will then electronically advance or retard the ignition timing to provide even driveability during operation.

Hall Effect Pick-Up

The hall effect pick-up, located in the distributor, supplies the engine controller with engine rpm, fuel injection synchronization (turbocharged engines) and ignition timing information.

Manifold Absolute Pressure (MAP) Sensor

The MAP sensor, mounted under the hood, is a device which transmits information on manifold vacuum conditions and barometric pressure to the electronic controller. The MAP sensor data, along with data from other sensors, is used to determine proper air/fuel mixture.

Coolant Sensor

The coolant temperature sensor is located on the thermostat housing and provides the controller with engine temperature data. The controller uses this data to control various engine functions such as spark advance, fuel mixture, emission controls operation and radiator fan.

Auto Shutdown (ASD) Relay

The ASD relay is used basically as a fuel delivery safety factor. The ASD relay interrupts the power to the electrical fuel pump, fuel injectors and ignition coil if the ignition key is in **RUN** and there is no need for fuel delivery.

Detonation (Knock) Sensor

The detonation (knock) sensor, used on 2.5L turbocharged engines, is a device that generates a signal when spark knock occurs in the combustion chamber. The engine controller use this information to modify spark advance in order to eliminate detonation.

DIAGNOSIS AND TESTING THE SMEC SYSTEM

➡**Apply parking brake and block wheels before performing any engine running tests, including idle or timing checks and adjustments.**

Testing for Spark at Coil

Remove coil secondary cable from distributor cap. Using a suitable tool, hold end of cable about ¼ in. from good engine ground. Crank engine and look for good, constant spark at coil secondary wire. If spark is constant, have a helper continue to crank engine while moving coil secondary cable away from ground. Look for arcing at the coil tower. If arcing occurs, replace the coil. If no arcing occurs, ignition system is producing the necessary high secondary voltage. Make certain this voltage is getting to spark plugs by checking distributor rotor, cap, spark plug wires and spark plugs. If all check in good condition, ignition system is NOT cause of problem.

If spark is weak, not constant or not present, continue with Failure To Start test.

Ignition System Starting Test

1. With a voltmeter measure voltage at battery and record it. Battery specific gravity must be 12.20. If if is not, charge batter to specification.
2. Turn ignition switch ON.
3. Remove coil wire from the distributor cap. Using a suitable tool, hold wire about a ¼ in. away from a good ground.
4. Intermittently jump coil negative to ground while looking for a good spark at coil wire.
5. If there is spark at coil wire it must be constant and bright blue in color. If spark is good, slowly move coil wire away from ground while looking for arcing at coil tower. If arcing occurs replace coil. If spark is weak or not constant, proceed to 'Failure to Start Test'.

Failure To Start Test

▶ **See Figures 45 and 46**

➡**Apply parking brake and block wheels before performing any engine running tests, including idle or timing checks and adjustments.**

1. Check battery voltage and determine that a minimum of 12.4 volts is available for operation of cranking and ignition systems.
2. Crank engine for 5 seconds while monitoring voltage at coil positive terminal. If voltage remains near 0 during entire period of cranking, pleas refer to Section 5 in this book for on-board diagnostic checks of SMEC and ASD relay.
3. If measured voltage is near battery voltage but drops to 0 after 1-2 seconds of cranking, please refer to Section 5 in this book for on-board diagnostic checks of distributor reference pick-up circuit to SMEC.
4. If measured voltage remains near battery voltage for entire 5 second cranking period, turn key OFF and remove SMEC 14-way connector.Check 14-way connector for any spread terminals.
5. Remove wire to coil positive terminal and connect regular jumper wire between coil positive terminal and battery positive terminal.

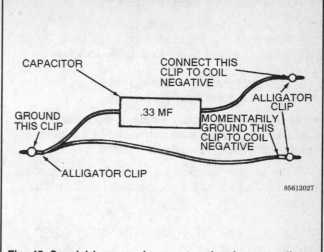

Fig. 45 Special jumper wire construction for grounding the coil

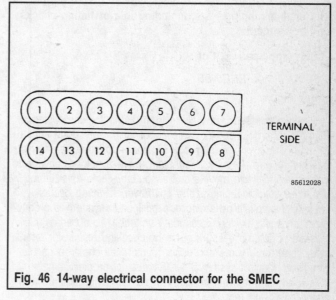

Fig. 46 14-way electrical connector for the SMEC

6. Using special jumper cable, momentarily ground terminal No. 12 of 14-way connector. A spark should be generated when ground is removed.
7. If spark is generated, replace SMEC.
8. If no spark is seen, use special jumper to ground coil negative terminal directly.
9. If spark is produced, trace and repair open condition within wiring harness.
10. If no spark is produced, replace ignition coil.

COOLANT TEMPERATURE SENSOR TEST

1. With key OFF, disconnect wire connector from coolant temperature sensor.
2. Connect one lead of an ohmmeter to one terminal of sensor.
3. Connect other ohmmeter lead to other sensor terminal; ohmmeter should read: Coolant at operating temperature (200°F)): Approximately 700-1000 ohms. Coolant at room temperature (70°F): Approximately 7,000-13,000 ohms.

SPARK ADVANCE OF SMEC SYSTEM

1. Adjust basic timing to specifications.
2. Have engine at normal operating temperature. The coolant temperature sensor must be connected and operating correctly.
3. Start and raise engine speed to 2000 Rpm. Wait 1 minute and check specifications.

➡The use of a metal exhaust tube is recommended for this test. Using rubber hose may result in a fire due to high temperatures and a long test period.

4. The advance specifications are in addition to basic advance. If correct advance is not obtained, SMEC must be replaced.

DIAGNOSIS AND TESTING THE SBEC, SBEC II AND PCM SYSTEM

➡Apply parking brake and block wheels before performing any engine running tests, including idle or timing checks and adjustments.

Testing for Spark at Coil

2.5L AND 3.0L ENGINES

▶ See Figure 47

Remove coil secondary cable from distributor cap. Using a suitable tool, hold end of cable about ¼ in. from good engine ground. Crank engine and look for good, constant spark at coil secondary wire. If spark is constant, have a helper continue to crank engine while moving coil secondary cable away from ground. Look for arcing at the coil tower. If arcing occurs, replace the coil. If no arcing occurs, ignition system is producing the necessary high secondary voltage. Make certain this voltage is getting to spark plugs by checking distributor rotor, cap, spark plug wires and spark plugs. If all check in good condition, ignition system is NOT cause of problem.

If spark is weak, not constant or not present, continue with Failure To Start test.

Failure To Start Test

2.5L AND 3.0L ENGINES

▶ See Figures 48, 49, 50 and 51

➡Apply parking brake and block wheels before performing any engine running tests, including idle or timing checks and adjustments.

1. Check battery voltage and determine that a minimum of 12.4 volts is available for operation of cranking and ignition systems.
2. Crank engine for 5 seconds while monitoring voltage at coil positive terminal. If voltage remains near 0 during entire period of cranking, please refer to Section 5 in this book for on-board diagnostic checks of SBEC, SBEC II or PCM and auto shutdown relay.
3. If measured voltage is near battery voltage but drops to 0 after 1-2 seconds of cranking, please refer to Section 5 in this book for on-board diagnostic checks of distributor reference pick-up circuit to SBEC, SBEC II or PCM.

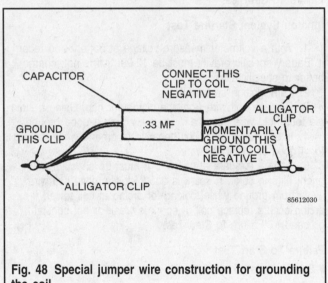

Fig. 48 Special jumper wire construction for grounding the coil

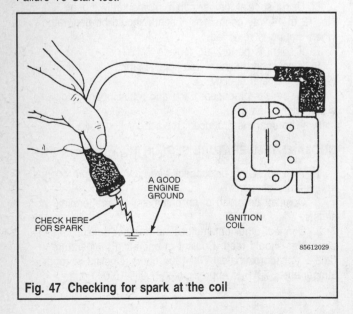

Fig. 47 Checking for spark at the coil

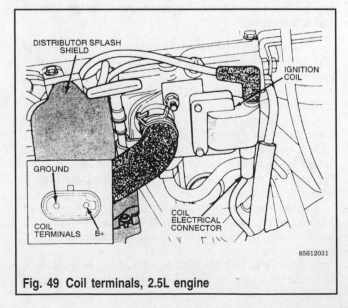

Fig. 49 Coil terminals, 2.5L engine

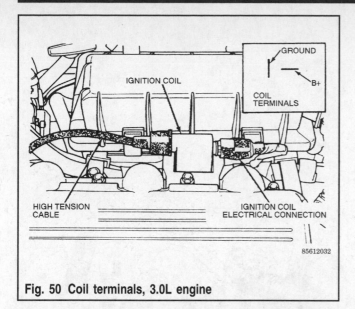

Fig. 50 Coil terminals, 3.0L engine

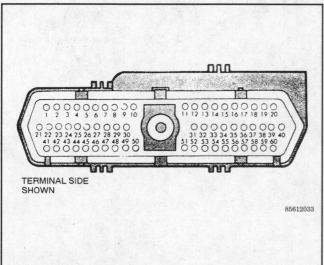

Fig. 51 60-way electrical connector engine controller

4. If measured voltage remains near battery voltage for entire 5 second cranking period, turn key OFF and remove SBEC 60-way connector. Check 60-way connector for any spread terminals.

5. Remove wire to coil positive terminal and connect regular jumper wire between coil positive terminal and battery positive terminal.

6. Using special jumper cable, momentarily ground terminal No. 19 of 60-way connector. A spark should be generated when ground is removed.

7. If spark is generated, replace the SBEC, SBEC II or PCM.

8. If no spark is seen, use special jumper to ground coil negative terminal directly.

9. If spark is produced, trace and repair open condition within wiring harness.

10. If no spark is produced, replace ignition coil.

Single Module Engine Controller (SMEC)System — Component Replacement

REMOVAL & INSTALLATION

Single Module Engine Control Unit
▶ See Figure 52

1. Disconnect the negative battery cable.
2. Disconnect the air cleaner duct from the SMEC unit.
3. Carefully disconnect the connectors from the unit.

➡**Make sure there is at least an ⅛ in. of grease in the connectors.**

4. Install the connectors on the replacement unit.
5. Mount the unit in position and make sure the connectors are secure.
6. Install the air cleaner duct and connect the battery cable.

Hall Effect Pick-Up
▶ See Figure 53

1. Disconnect the negative battery cable.
2. Remove the distributor cap and remove the rotor.
3. Remove the screws that retain the pick-up assembly. Disconnect the electrical lead from the pick-up.
4. Carefully remove the assembly from the distributor.
5. Install the new pick-up assembly and connect the electrical lead.
6. Install the retaining screws. Install the cap and rotor.
7. Connect the negative battery cable.

Coolant Temperature Sensor
▶ See Figures 54 and 55

1. Disconnect electrical connector from sensor. Remove sensor from engine. Some coolant may be lost from system.

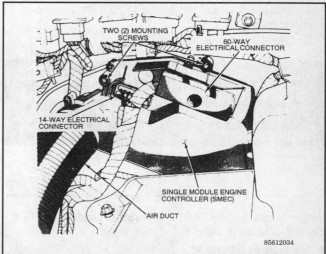

Fig. 52 The Single Module Engine Controller (SMEC) is retained with two mounting screws

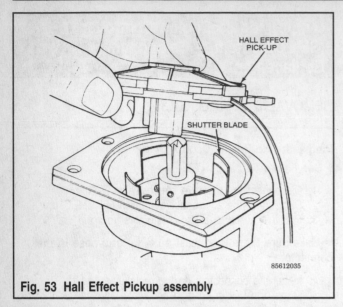

Fig. 53 Hall Effect Pickup assembly

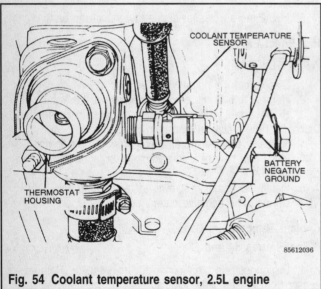

Fig. 54 Coolant temperature sensor, 2.5L engine

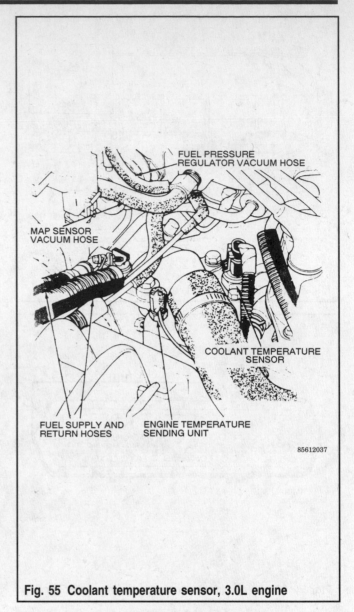

Fig. 55 Coolant temperature sensor, 3.0L engine

2. Install new sensor and tighten to 20 ft lbs. Reconnect electrical connector.
3. Replace lost coolant.

Single Board Engine Controller (SBEC, SBEC II) and Powertrain Control Module (PCM) Systems — Component Replacement

REMOVAL & INSTALLATION

Single Board Engine Control Unit (SBEC) and Powertrain Control Module (PCM)

▶ See Figures 56 and 57

➡The SBEC or PCM is located next to the battery.

1. Remove the battery.

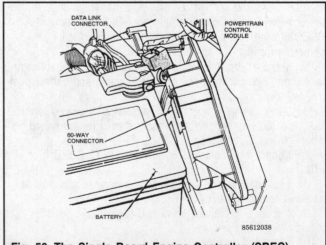

Fig. 56 The Single Board Engine Controller (SBEC), also referred to the Powertrain Control Module is located behind the battery

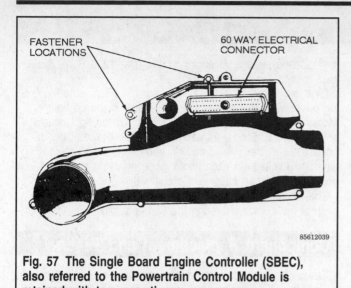

Fig. 57 The Single Board Engine Controller (SBEC), also referred to the Powertrain Control Module is retained with two mounting screws

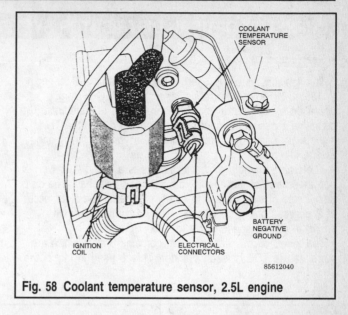

Fig. 58 Coolant temperature sensor, 2.5L engine

2. Remove the air cleaner duct or air cleaner assembly.
3. Remove the battery.
4. Carefully disconnect the 60-way wiring connector from the PCM.
5. Remove the PCM.

Hall Effect Pick-Up

▶ **See Figure 53**

1. Disconnect the negative battery cable.
2. Remove the distributor cap and remove the rotor.
3. Remove the screws that retain the pick-up assembly. Disconnect the electrical lead from the pick-up.
4. Carefully remove the assembly from the distributor.
5. Install the new pick-up assembly and connect the electrical lead.
6. Install the retaining screws. Install the cap and rotor.
7. Connect the negative battery cable.

Coolant Temperature Sensor

▶ **See Figures 58 and 59**

1. Disconnect electrical connector from sensor. Remove sensor from engine. Some coolant may be lost from system.
2. Install new sensor and tighten to 20 ft lbs. for the 2.5L engine and 60 inch lbs. for the 3.0L engine.
3. Replace lost coolant.

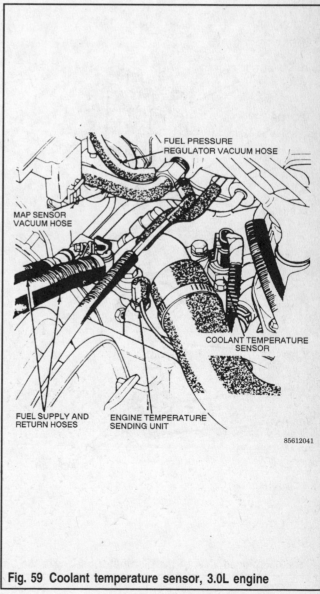

Fig. 59 Coolant temperature sensor, 3.0L engine

CHRYSLER OPTICAL DISTRIBUTOR SYSTEM

▶ **See Figure 60**

This ignition system is used in vehicles with the 3.0L engine in 1988-89. The system is similar to the SMEC system in operation except that it uses a different type of distributor. The computer receives its input from an optical distributor. The signals are used to control fuel injection, ignition timing and engine idle speed.

The timing member in the distributor is a thin disk, driven at half the speed of the engine, from the left camshaft. The disk has 2 sets of slots in it. The outer, high data rate slots, occur at 2 degrees of engine rotation. They are used for ignition timing at engine speed of up to 1200 Rpm.

The inner, or low data rate set, contains 6 slots which are correlated to TDC of each cylinder. This is used to trigger the fuel injection system. At engine speed over 1200 Rpm, this set also controls the ignition timing.

Light emitting diodes and photo sensors are mounted in facing positions on opposite sides of the disk in the distributor. Masks over the LED's and the diodes focus the light beams onto the photo diodes. As each slot passes between the diodes, the light beam is turned on and off. This creates an alternating voltage in each photo diode, which is converted into on/off pulses by an integrated circuit within the distributor.

The distributor also delivers firing pulses from the coil to each of the cylinders through the cap and rotor.

Component Replacement and Testing

The replacement of components and their testing in the optical distributor system are the same as the SMEC system.

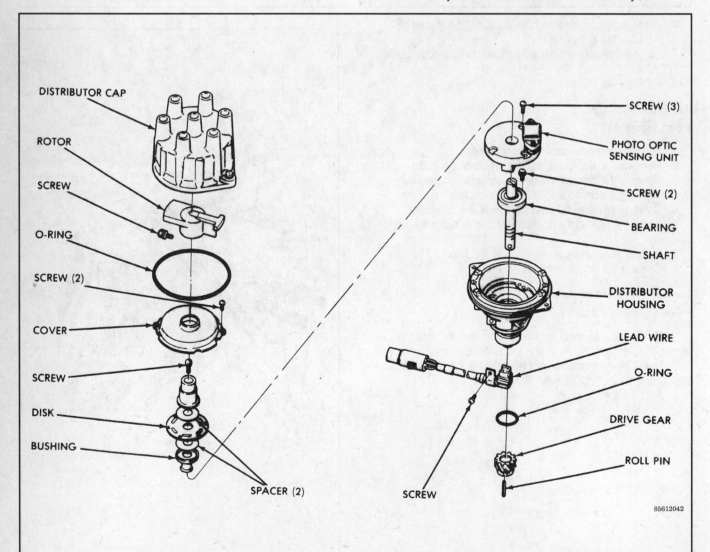

Fig. 60 Exploded view of the distributor used with the Chrysler Optical Distributor system, 1988-89 3.0L engine

85612042

DIRECT IGNITION SYSTEM (DIS)

General Information

Vehicle equipped with the 3.3L and 3.8L engines use a distributorless ignition system. The system has 3 main components, the coil, the camshaft reference sensor and the crankshaft timing sensor.

The Single Board Engine Controller (SBEC) receives its engine speed and crankshaft position signal from a sensor located in the transaxle housing. This crankshaft position sensor senses slots located around an extension on the torque converter drive plate. A camshaft sensor located in the timing case cover, supplies cylinder identification to the SBEC, by sensing slots located on the camshaft sprocket.

Diagnosis and Testing the DIS System

FAILURE TO START TEST

▶ See Figures 61, 62 and 63

➡Apply parking brake and block wheels before performing any engine running tests, including idle or timing checks and adjustments.

1990-91

➡Apply parking brake and block wheels before performing any engine running tests, including idle or timing checks and adjustments.

1. Check battery voltage and determine that a minimum of 12.4 volts is available for operation of cranking and ignition systems.

2. Connect a voltmeter to the wiring harness coil connector at the B+ pin.

3. Crank engine for 5 seconds while monitoring voltage at the B+ terminal. If voltage remains near 0 during entire period

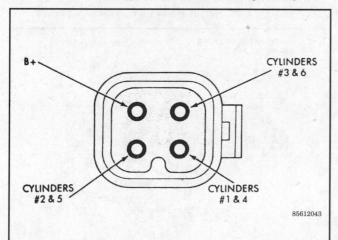

Fig. 61 Wiring harness coil connector, 3.3L and 3.8L engines with DIS

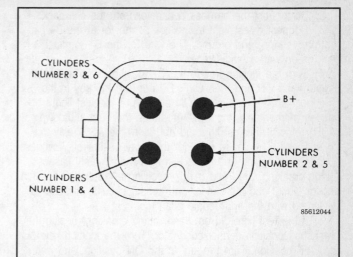

Fig. 62 Ignition coil terminal identification, 3.3L and 3.8L engines with DIS

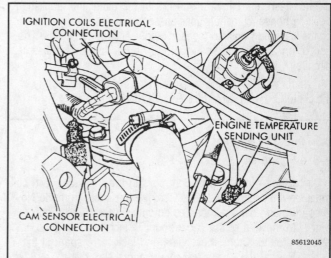

Fig. 63 Ignition coil electrical connection, 3.3L and 3.8L engines with DIS

of cranking, please refer to Section 5 in this book for on-board diagnostic checks of SBEC and auto shutdown relay.

4. If measured voltage is near battery voltage but drops to 0 after 1-2 seconds of cranking, please refer to Section 5 in this book for on-board diagnostic checks of distributor reference pick-up circuit to SBEC.

5. If measured voltage remains near battery voltage for entire 5 second cranking period, turn key OFF and remove SBEC 60-way connector. Check 60-way connector for any spread terminals.

1992-94

➡Apply parking brake and block wheels before performing any engine running tests, including idle or timing checks and adjustments.

1. Check battery voltage and determine that a minimum of 12.66 volts is available for operation of cranking and ignition systems.

2. Disconnect the harness connector from the coil pack.

3. Connect a test light to the coil connector at the B+ pin (battery voltage) and ground. The wire for the B+ terminal is dark green with a black tracer.

4. Turn the ignition key to the ON position. The test light should flash ON and then OFF. Do not turn the key to the OFF position, leave it in the ON position. If the test light flashes momentarily, the PCM grounded the auto shutdown (ASD) relay. If the test light did not flash, the ASD relay did no energize. The cause is either the relay or the relay circuits.

5. Crank engine and if the test light momentarily flashes during cranking, the PCM is not receiving a crankshaft position sensor signal and the sensor and sensor circuits will have to be tested with the appropriate scan tool.

6. If the test light did not flash during cranking, unplug the crankshaft position sensor connector. Turn the ignition key to the OFF position. Turn the key to the ON position, and wait for the test light to momentarily flash once, then crank the engine. If the test light momentarily flashes, the crankshaft position sensor is shorted and must be replaced. If the light did not flash, the cause of the no-start is either the crankshaft position sensor/camshaft position sensor 8-volt supply circuit, or the camshaft position sensor output or ground circuits. The use of an appropriate scan tool will be needed to test these circuits.

TESTING FOR SPARK AT COIL

3.3L and 3.8L Engines
▶ **See Figure 64**

Since their are 3 independent coils in the package, each coil must be checked individually. Remove the cable from the No. 2 spark plug. Insert a metal object into the spark plug boot and hold the end of the cable about ¼ inch from a good engine ground. Crank the engine and look for a spark at the cable. Repeat the above test for cylinders No. 4 and No. 6. If

there is no spark during all 3 cylinder tests, proceed to the Failure To Start Test.

Component Replacement-DIS System

REMOVAL & INSTALLATION

Ignition Coil
▶ **See Figure 65**

1. Disconnect the negative battery cable.
2. Remove the spark plug wires from the coil.
3. Disconnect the electrical connector.
4. Remove the coil fasteners.
5. Remove the coil from the ignition module.
6. The installation is the reverse of the removal procedure.

Crank Position Sensor
▶ **See Figures 66, 67 and 68**

1. Disconnect the negative battery cable.
2. Disconnect the sensor lead at the harness connector.
3. Remove the sensor retainer bolt.
4. Pull the sensor straight up and out of the transaxle housing.
5. If the removed sensor is being reinstalled, clean off the old spacer completely and attach a new spacer to the sensor. If a new spacer is not used, the sensor will not function properly. New sensors are equipped with a new spacer.

To install:

6. Install the sensor in the transaxle housing and push the sensor down until contact is made with the drive plate.
7. Hold in this position and install the retaining bolt. Torque to 105 inch lbs. (11.9 Nm).
8. Connect the sensor lead wire.

Cam Position Sensor
▶ **See Figure 69**

1. Disconnect the negative battery cable.
2. Disconnect the sensor lead at the harness connector.

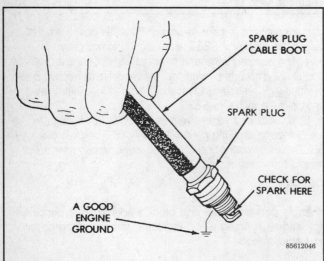

Fig. 64 Testing for spark at the coil, 3.3L and 3.8L engines with DIS

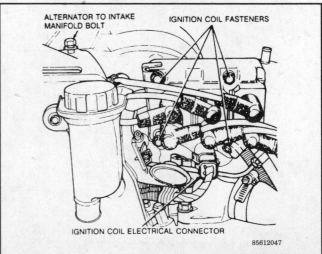

Fig. 65 Ignition coil removal, 3.3L and 3.8L engines with DIS

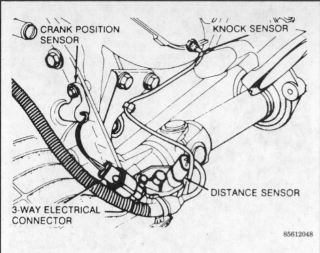

Fig. 66 Crankshaft position sensor location, 1990-91 3.3L engine with DIS

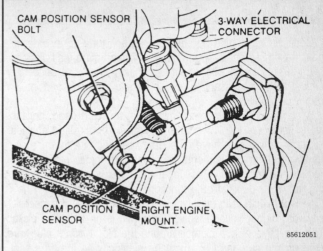

Fig. 69 Camshaft sensor location, 3.3L and 3.8L engine with DIS

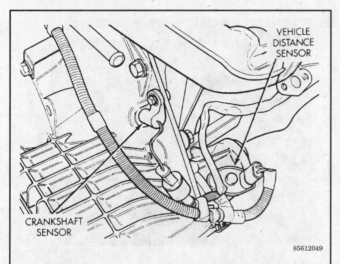

Fig. 67 Crankshaft position sensor location, 1992 3.3L engine with DIS

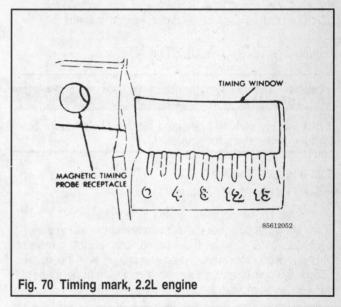

Fig. 70 Timing mark, 2.2L engine

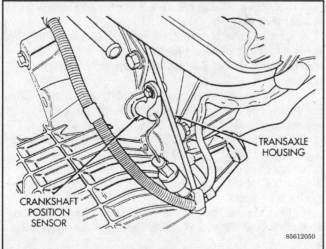

Fig. 68 Crankshaft position sensor location, 1993-94 3.3L and 3.8L engine with DIS

3. Loosen the sensor retaining bolt enough to allow the slot to slide past the bolt.

4. Pull the sensor (not by the wire) straight up and out of the chain case cover. Resistance may be high due to the presence of the rubber O-ring.

5. If the removed sensor is being reinstalled, clean off the old spacer completely and attach a new spacer to the sensor. If a new spacer is not used, the sensor will not function properly. New sensors are equipped with a new spacer.

To install:

6. Inspect the O-ring for damage and replace if necessary.

7. Lubricate the O-ring lightly with oil. Install the sensor to the chain case cover and push the sensor into its bore in the chain case cover until contact is made with the cam timing gear.

8. Hold in this position and tighten the bolt to 125 inch lbs. (14 Nm).

9. Connect the connector and rout it away from the belt.

Ignition Timing

Basic timing should be checked at each tune-up in order to gain maximum engine performance. While timing isn't likely to change very much with electronic ignition system, it become a critical factor necessary to reduce engine emission and improve driveability.

A stroboscopic (dynamic) timing light must be used, because static lights are too inaccurate for emission controlled engines.

Some timing light have other features built into them, such as dwell meters or tachometers. These are nice, in that they reduce the tangle of wires under the hood when you're working, but may duplicate the functions of tools your already have. One worthwhile feature, which is becoming more of a necessity with higher voltage ignition systems, is an inductive pickup. The inductive pickup clamps around the No. 1 spark plug wire, sensing the surges of high voltage electricity as they are sent to the plug. The advantage is that no mechanical connection is inserted between the wire and the plug, which eliminates false signals to the timing light. A timing light with an inductive pickup should be used on electronic ignition systems

IGNITION TIMING ADJUSTMENT

❋❋CAUTION

Always apply parking brake and block wheels before performing any engine running tests.

2.2L and 2.6L Engines
▶ **See Figures 70, 71, 72 and 73**

1. With engine off, clean off the timing marks.
2. Mark the pulley or damper notch and the timing scale with white chalk or paint. If the timing notch on the damper or pulley is not visible, bump the engine around with the starter or turn the crankshaft with a wrench on the front pulley bolt to get it to an accessible position.

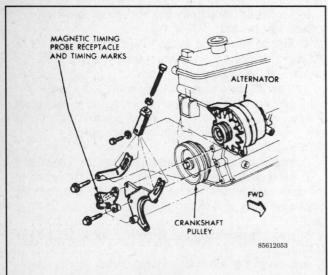

MAGNETIC TIMING PROBE RECEPTACLE AND TIMING MARKS

ALTERNATOR

FWD

CRANKSHAFT PULLEY

85612053

Fig. 71 Timing mark, 2.6L engine

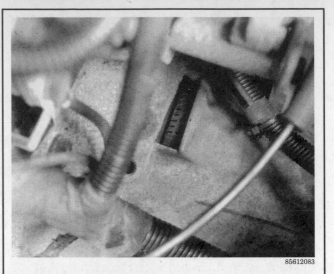
85612083

Fig. 72 Timing mark window

85612084

Fig. 73 Checking the timing with a timing light and adjusting by turning the distributor

3. Connect a suitable inductive timing light to number one cylinder plug wire.
4. Connect a tachometer unit, Positive Lead to the negative terminal of the coil and the Negative Lead to a known good engine ground. Select the tachometer appropriate cylinder position.
5. Warm the engine to normal operating temperature. Open the throttle and release to make sure idle speed screw is against its stop, and not on fast idle.
6. On vehicles equipped with a carburetor switch, connect a jumper wire between the carburetor switch and ground to obtain specified Rpm. Disconnect and plug vacuum hose at the Spark Control Computer. (See specifications decal under the hood for specific instructions).
7. Read engine Rpm on the tachometer 1,000 Rpm scale, and adjust curb idle to specification noted on the under hood label.
8. Aim the timing light toward timing indicator, and read degree marks. If flash occurs when timing mark is before

specification, timing is advanced. If flash occurs when timing mark is after specification, timing is retarded.

➡ **Models equipped with the 2.2L engine have a notch on the torque converter or flywheel, with the numerical timing marks on the bell housing. Models equipped with the 2.6L engine have the timing marks on the front crankshaft pulley.**

9. If adjustment is necessary, loosen the distributor hold down screw. Turn the distributor slowly to specified value, and tighten hold down screw. Recheck timing and curb idle. If curb idle have change, readjust to specified value and reset ignition timing. Repeat curb idle setting, and ignition timing until both are within specification.

10. Disconnect timing light, and reconnect all vacuum hoses necessary.

11. Turn engine off and remove jumper wire, and tachometer.

2.5L and 3.0L Engines

▶ **See Figures 74 and 75**

1. With the engine off, clean off the timing marks.

2. Mark the pulley or damper notch and the timing scale with white chalk or paint. If the timing notch on the damper or pulley is not visible, bump the engine around with the starter or turn the crankshaft with a wrench on the front pulley bolt to get it to an accessible position.

3. Connect a suitable inductive timing light to number one cylinder plug wire.

4. Connect a tachometer unit, positive lead to the negative terminal of the coil and the negative lead to a known good engine ground. Select the tachometer appropriate cylinder position.

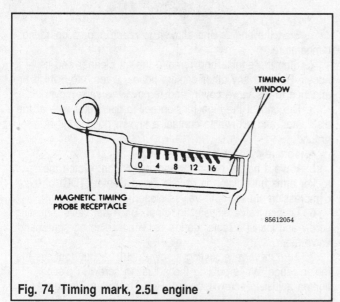

Fig. 74 Timing mark, 2.5L engine

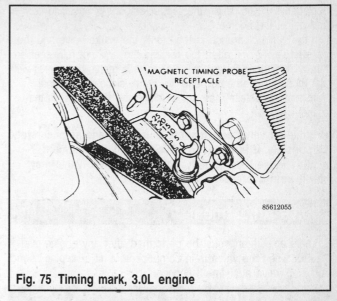

Fig. 75 Timing mark, 3.0L engine

5. Warm the engine to normal operating temperature.

6. With engine at normal operating temperature, disconnect coolant temperature sensor. Radiator fan and instrument panel check engine lamp should come on. (See specifications decal under the hood for specific instructions).

7. Read engine Rpm on the tachometer 1,000 Rpm scale, and adjust curb idle to specification noted on the under hood label.

8. Aim the timing light toward timing indicator, and read degree marks. If flash occurs when timing mark is before specification, timing is advanced. If flash occurs when timing mark is after specification, timing is retarded.

➡ **Models equipped with the 2.5L engine have the timing marks visible through a window on the transaxle housing. Models equipped with the 3.0L engine have the timing marks on the front crankshaft pulley.**

9. If adjustment is necessary, loosen the distributor hold down screw. Turn the distributor slowly to specified value, and tighten hold down screw. Recheck ignition timing.

10. Turn the engine off and removed the tachometer and timing light.

11. Connect the coolant temperature sensor.

➡ **Reconnecting the coolant temperature sensor will turn the check engine lamp off; however, a fault code will be stored in the SMEC. After 50 to 100 key on/off cycles the SMEC will cancel the fault code. The code can also be canceled by disconnecting the battery.**

3.3L and 3.8L Engines

The 3.3L and 3.8L engine use an electronic distributorless ignition system. The ignition timing cannot be changed or set in any way.

VALVE LASH

Valve adjustment determines how far the valves enter the cylinder and how long they stay open and closed.

If the valve clearance is too large, part of the lift of the camshaft will be used in removing the excess clearance. Con-

sequently, the valve will not be opening as far as it should. This condition has two effects: the valve train components will emit a tapping sound as they take up the excessive clearance and the engine will perform poorly because the valves does not open fully and allow the proper amount of gases to flow in and out of the engine.

If the valve clearance is too small, the intake valve and the exhaust valves will open too far and they will not fully seat on the cylinder head when they close. As a result, the valves will also become overheated and will warp, since they cannot transfer heat unless they are touching the valve seat in the cylinder head.

➡️While all valve adjustments must be made as accurately as possible, it is better to have the valve adjustment slightly loose then slightly tight as a burned valve may result from overly tight adjustments.

Valve Adjustment

Valve adjustment must be performed after any engine overhaul or when the valve train components emit a tapping sound requiring valve adjustment service.

✳️CAUTION

Always apply parking brake and block wheels before performing any engine running tests.

2.2L, 2.5L, 3.0L, 3.3L AND 3.8L ENGINES

The 2.2L, 2.5L, 3.0L, 3.3 and 3.8L engines use hydraulic lash adjusters. No periodic adjustment or checking is necessary.

2.6L ENGINE (WITH JET VALVES)

▶ **See Figure 76**

A jet valve is added on some models. The jet valve adjuster is located on the intake valve rocker arm and must be adjusted before the intake valve.

1. Start the engine and allow it to reach normal operating temperature.
2. Stop the engine and remove the air cleaner and its hoses. Remove any other cables, hoses, wires, etc., which are attached to the valve cover, and remove the valve cover.
3. Disconnect the high tension coil-to-distributor wire at the distributor, and allow it to contact a known good engine ground.
4. Torque the cylinder head bolts.
5. Have a helper bump the ignition switch. Watch the rocker arms until piston No. 4 cylinder is at Top Dead Center (TDC) and adjust jet valves as follow.
6. Back out the intake valve adjusting screw two or three turns.

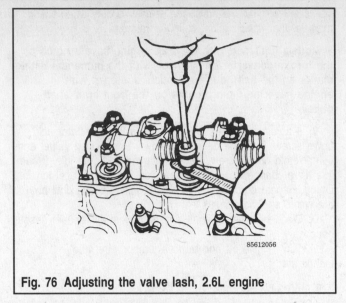

Fig. 76 Adjusting the valve lash, 2.6L engine

7. Loosen the locknut on the jet valve and back out jet valve adjusting screw.
8. Install a 0.15mm feeler gauge between the jet valve stem and the jet valve adjusting screw.
9. Turn in jet valve adjusting screw until it slightly makes contact with the jet valve stem. While holding jet valve adjusting screw in place tighten jet valve lock nut. Recheck clearance.
10. Complete the adjustment by adjusting intake and exhaust valve clearance on the same cylinder as jet valve you've finished. Refer to Valve Clearance Specification Chart.

2.6L ENGINE (WITHOUT JET VALVES)

1. Start the engine and allow it to reach normal operating temperature.
2. Stop the engine and remove the air cleaner and its hoses. Remove any other cables, hoses, wires, etc., which are attached to the valve cover, and remove the valve cover.
3. Disconnect the high tension coil-to-distributor wire at the distributor, and allow it to contact a known good engine ground.
4. Torque cylinder head bolts.
5. Have a helper bump the ignition switch. Watch the rocker arms until piston is at Top Dead Center (TDC) of the compression stroke (both valves closed).
6. Loosen valve adjuster lock nut. Back out valve adjusting screw and install a feeler gauge between adjusting screw and valve stem.
7. Turn in valve adjusting screw until it slightly touches the feeler gauge. While holding the adjusting screw in place tighten adjusting screw lock nut. Refer to Valve Clearance Specification Chart.
8. Perform Step 5 thru 7 on the remaining three cylinders.

IDLE SPEED AND MIXTURE ADJUSTMENTS

IDLE SPEED ADJUSTMENT

◆ **See Figures 77, 78, 79, 80, 81 and 82**

✳✳CAUTION

Always apply the parking brake and block wheels before performing idle adjustment, or any engine running tests.

HOLLEY 5220/6520 — 2.2L ENGINE

1. Check and adjust the ignition timing.
2. Disconnect and plug the vacuum connector at the Coolant Vacuum Switch Cold Closed (CVSCC) located on the top of the thermostat housing.
3. Unplug the connector at the radiator fan and connect a jumper wire so that the cooling fan will run constantly. Remove the PCV valve from the engine and allow it to draw under hood air.
4. Connect a tachometer to the engine.
5. Ground the carburetor switch with a jumper wire.
6. On models equipped with a 6250 carburetor (6250 models are equipped with an oxygen sensor) disconnect the oxygen system test connector on the left fender shield.
7. Start the engine and run until normal operating temperature is reached.
8. Turn the idle adjustment screw until required Rpm is reached. (Refer to the Under hood Specification Label or Tune-Up Chart). Shut off engine.
9. Reconnect the PCV valve, oxygen connector, vacuum connector (CVSCC) and remove the carburator switch jumper. Remove the radiator fan jumper and reconnect harness.

➡**After Step 9 is completed, the idle speed might change, this is normal and the engine speed should not be readjusted.**

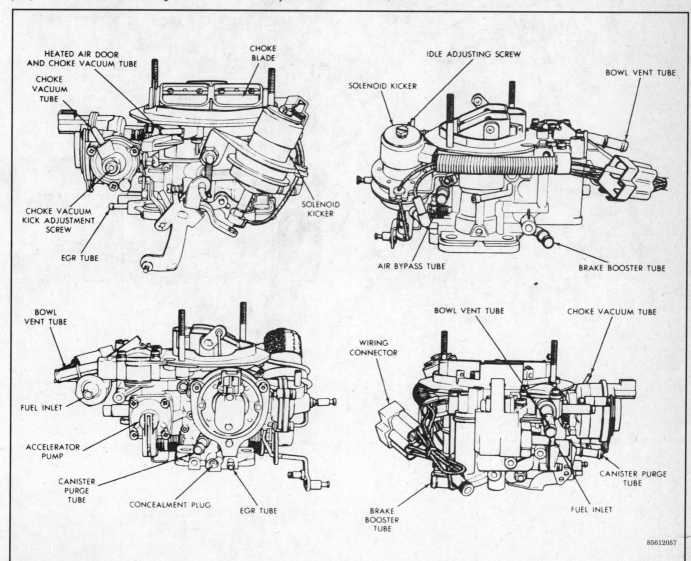

Fig. 77 Model 5220 carburetor

85612057

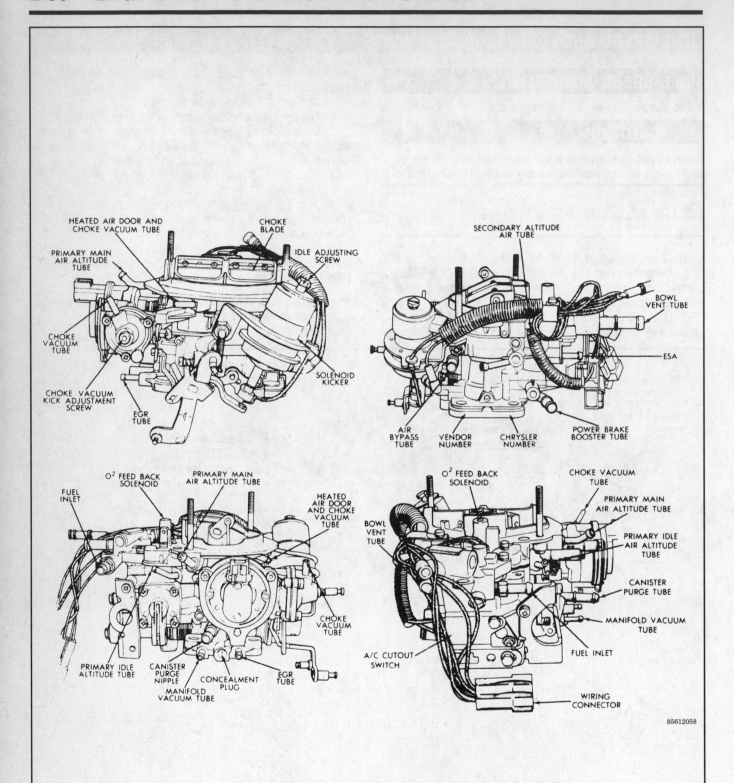

Fig. 78 Model 6520 carburetor

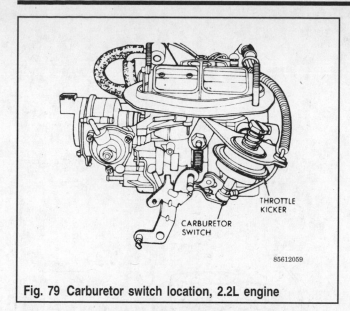

Fig. 79 Carburetor switch location, 2.2L engine

10. Refer to Fuel System Section for fast idle, air conditioning idle speed check and choke kick adjustment procedures.

MIKUNI CARBURETOR — 2.6L ENGINE

1. Connect a tachometer to the engine.
2. Check and adjust the ignition timing.
3. Start and run the engine until normal operating temperature is reached.
4. Disconnect the cooling fan harness connector.
5. Run at 2500 Rpm for 10 seconds. Return the engine to idle.
6. Wait two minutes and check engine Rpm indicated on the tachometer. If the idle speed is not within specs indicated on the under hood sticker or Tune-Up Chart, adjust the idle speed screw as necessary.
7. Models equipped with air condition, set temperature control lever to coldest position and turn on air conditioning. With compressor running, set idle speed to 900 Rpm with idle up screw.
8. After adjustment is complete, shut off the engine, disconnect the tachometer and reconnect the cooling fan harness.

ELECTRONIC FUEL INJECTED ENGINES

The idle speed is controlled by the Automatic Idle Speed motor (AIS) which is controlled by the logic module. The logic module receives data from various sensors in the system and adjusts the engine idle to a predetermined speed. Idle speed

specifications can be found on the Vehicle Emission Control Information (VECI) label, located in the engine compartment. If the idle speed is not within specification and there are no problems with the system, the vehicle should be taken to an authorized dealer for service.

IDLE MIXTURE ADJUSTMENT

The following procedure uses a propane enrichment method of adjusting the idle. Use extreme care when using the propane tank. Make sure that it is in a secure location and that the fittings are not leaking.

Holley and Mikuni Carburetors

1. Disconnect and plug the EGR hose. Disconnect the oxygen sensor, if equipped.
2. Disconnect and plug the hose at the canister.
3. Remove the PCV hose from the valve cover and allow it to draw under hood air.
4. Ground the carburetor switch with a jumper wire, if equipped.
5. Disconnect the vacuum hose from the computer, if equipped and connect an auxiliary vacuum supply of 16 Hg in.
6. Remove the concealment plug. Disconnect the vacuum supply hose to the tee and install a propane supply hose in its place.
7. Make sure all accessories are off. Install a tachometer and start the engine. Allow the engine to run for 2 minutes to stabilize.
8. Open the main propane valve. Slowly open the propane metering valve until the maximum engine Rpm is reached. When too much propane is added, the engine will begin to stumble; at this point back off until the engine stabilizes.
9. Adjust the idle Rpm to obtain the specified propane Rpm. Fine tune the metering valve to obtain the highest Rpm again. If there has been a change to the maximum Rpm, readjust the idle screw to the specified propane Rpm.
10. Turn the main propane valve off and allow the engine to run for 1 minute to stabilize.
11. Adjust the mixture screw to obtain the smoothest idle at the specified idle Rpm.
12. Open the main propane valve. Fine tune the metering valve to obtain the highest Rpm. If the maximum engine speed is more that 25 Rpm different than the specified propane Rpm, repeat the procedure.
13. Turn the propane valves off and remove the propane canister. Reinstall the vacuum supply hose to the tee.
14. Perform the idle speed adjustment procedure.
15. Connect all wires and hoses that were previously disconnected.

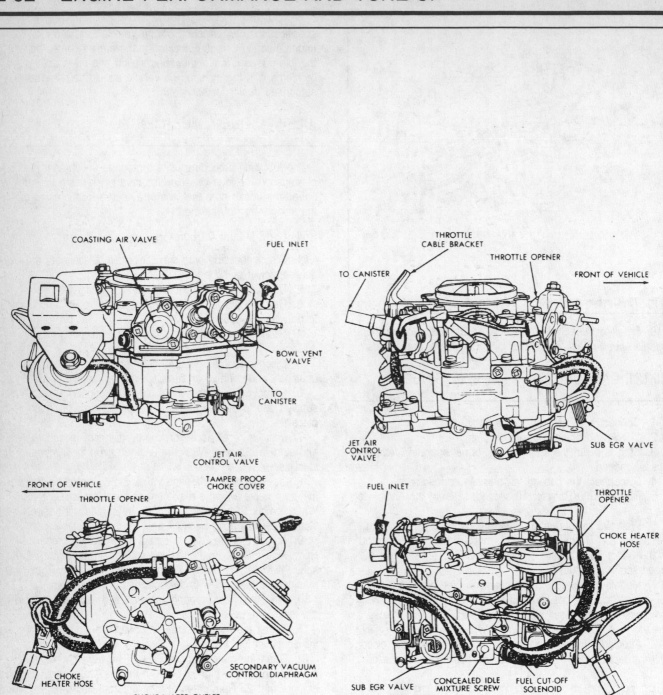

Fig. 80 Mikuni carburetor

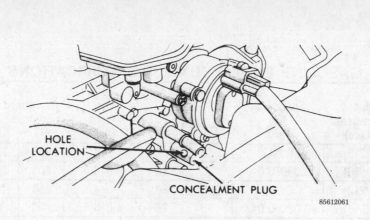

Fig. 81 Correct location for drilling the hole at the idle mixture screw

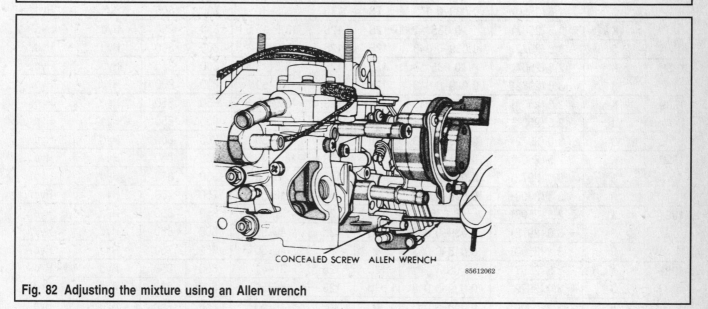

Fig. 82 Adjusting the mixture using an Allen wrench

GASOLINE ENGINE TUNE-UP SPECIFICATIONS

Year	Engine ID/VIN	Engine Displacement Liters (cc)	Spark Plug Gap (in.)	Ignition Timing (deg.) MT	AT	Fuel Pump (psi)	Idle Speed (rpm) MT	AT	Valve Clearance In.	Ex.
1984	C	2.2 (2212)	0.035	6B	6B	3–4	850	900	Hyd.	Hyd.
	G	2.6 (2556)	0.039–0.043	7B	7B	4.6–6.0	800	800	Hyd. ①	Hyd. ①
1985	C	2.2 (2212)	0.035	6B	6B	3–4	850	900	Hyd.	Hyd.
	G	2.6 (2556)	0.039–0.043	7B	7B	4.6–6.0	800	800	Hyd. ①	Hyd. ①
1986	C	2.2 (2212)	0.035	6B	6B	3–4	850	900	Hyd.	Hyd.
	G	2.6 (2556)	0.039–0.043	7B	7B	4.6–6.0	800	800	Hyd. ①	Hyd. ①
1987	C	2.2 (2212)	0.035	6B	6B	4.5–6.0	850	900	Hyd.	Hyd.
	G	2.6 (2556)	0.039–0.043	7B	7B	3–4	800	800	Hyd. ①	Hyd. ①
	K	2.5 (2507)	0.035	12B	12B	13.5–15.5	850	850	Hyd.	Hyd.
	3	3.0 (2972)	0.039–0.043	12B	12B	12–16	800	800	Hyd.	Hyd.
1988	K	2.5 (2507)	0.035	12B	12B	13.5–15.5	850	850	Hyd.	Hyd.
	3	3.0 (2972)	0.039–0.043	12B	12B	46–50	800	800	Hyd.	Hyd.
1989	K	2.5 (2507)	0.035–0.043	12B	12B	13.5–15.5	850	850	Hyd.	Hyd.
	J	2.5 (2507)	0.035–0.043	12B	12B	13.5–15.5	850	850	Hyd.	Hyd.
	3	3.0 (2972)	0.039–0.043	12B	12B	46–50	800	800	Hyd.	Hyd.
1990	K	2.5 (2507)	0.035–0.043	12B	12B	13.5–15.5	850	850	Hyd.	Hyd.
	3	3.0 (2972)	0.039–0.043	12B	12B	46–50	800	800	Hyd.	Hyd.
	R	3.3 (3300)	0.048–0.053	②	②	46–50	750	750	Hyd.	Hyd.
1991	K	2.5 (2507)	0.035	12B	12B	37–41	850	850	Hyd.	Hyd.
	3	3.0 (2972)	0.039–0.043	12B	12B	46–50	800	800	Hyd.	Hyd.
	R	3.3 (3300)	0.048–0.053	②	②	46–50	750	750	Hyd.	Hyd.
1992	K	2.5 (2507)	0.035	12B	12B	37–41	850	850	Hyd.	Hyd.
	3	3.0 (2972)	0.039–0.043	12B	12B	46–50	800	800	Hyd.	Hyd.
	R	3.3 (3300)	0.048–0.053	②	②	46–50	750	750	Hyd.	Hyd.
1993	K	2.5 (2507)	0.035	12B	12B	37–41	850	850	Hyd.	Hyd.
	3	3.0 (2972)	0.039–0.043	12B	12B	46–50	800	800	Hyd.	Hyd.
	R	3.3 (3300)	0.048–0.053	②	②	46–50	750	750	Hyd.	Hyd.
1994	K	2.5 (2507)	0.035	12B	12B	37–41	850	850	Hyd.	Hyd.
	3	3.0 (2972)	0.039–0.043	12B	12B	46–50	800	800	Hyd.	Hyd.
	R	3.3 (3300)	0.048–0.053	②	②	46–50	750	750	Hyd.	Hyd.
	L	3.8 (3785)	0.048–0.053	②	②	46–50	③	③	Hyd.	Hyd.

NOTE: The Vehicle Emission Control Information label often reflects specification changes made during production. The label figures must be used if they differ from those in this chart.

B—Before Top Dead Center
① Jet valve clearance: 0.010 in. (hot)
② Ignition timing cannot be adjusted; base engine timing is set at TDC during assembly
③ Refer to the Vehicle Emission Control Information (VECI) label for correct specification

85612C01

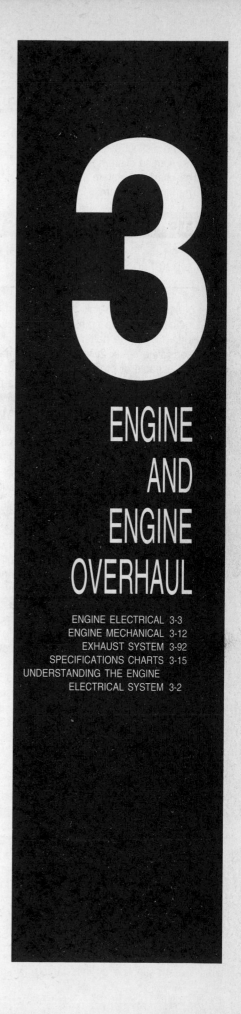

3

ENGINE AND ENGINE OVERHAUL

UNDERSTANDING THE ENGINE ELECTRICAL SYSTEM

The engine electrical system can be broken down into 3 separate and distinct systems:

1. The starting system.
2. The charging system.
3. The ignition system.

BATTERY AND STARTING SYSTEM

Basic Operating Principles

The battery is the first link in the chain of mechanisms which work together to provide cranking of the automobile engine. In most modern cars, the battery is a lead/acid electro-chemical device consisting of six 2v subsections connected in series so the unit is capable of producing approximately 12v of electrical pressure. Each subsection, or cell, consists of a series of positive and negative plates held a short distance apart in a solution of sulfuric acid and water. The 2 types of plates are of dissimilar metals. This causes a chemical reaction to be set up, and it is this reaction which produces current flow from the battery when its positive and negative terminals are connected to an electrical appliance such as a lamp or motor. The continued transfer of electrons would eventually convert the sulfuric acid in the electrolyte to water, and make the 2 plates identical in chemical composition. As electrical energy is removed from the battery, its voltage output tends to drop. Thus, measuring battery voltage and battery electrolyte composition are 2 ways of checking the ability of the unit to supply power. During the starting of the engine, electrical energy is removed from the battery. However, if the charging circuit is in good condition and the operating conditions are normal, the power removed from the battery will be replaced by the generator (or alternator) which will force electrons back through the battery, reversing the normal flow, and restoring the battery to its original chemical state.

The battery and starting motor are linked by very heavy electrical cables designed to minimize resistance to the flow of current. Generally, the major power supply cable that leaves the battery goes directly to the starter, while other electrical system needs are supplied by a smaller cable. During starter operation, power flows from the battery to the starter and is grounded through the car's frame and the battery's negative ground strap.

The starting motor is a specially designed, direct current electric motor capable of producing a very great amount of power for its size. One thing that allows the motor to produce a great deal of power is its tremendous rotating speed. It drives the engine through a tiny pinion gear (attached to the starter's armature), which drives the very large flywheel ring gear at a greatly reduced speed. Another factor allowing it to produce so much power is that only intermittent operation is required of it. This, little allowance for air circulation is required, and the windings can be built into a very small space.

The starter solenoid is a magnetic device which employs the small current supplied by the starting switch circuit of the ignition switch. This magnetic action moves a plunger which mechanically engages the starter and electrically closes the heavy switch which connects it to the battery. The starting switch circuit consists of the starting switch contained within the ignition switch, a transmission neutral safety switch or clutch pedal switch, and the wiring necessary to connect these in series with the starter solenoid or relay.

A pinion, which is a small gear, is mounted to a one-way drive clutch. This clutch is splined to the starter armature shaft. When the ignition switch is moved to the **start** position, the solenoid plunger slides the pinion toward the flywheel ring gear via a collar and spring. If the teeth on the pinion and flywheel match properly, the pinion will engage the flywheel immediately. If the gear teeth butt one another, the spring will be compressed and will force the gears to mesh as soon as the starter turns far enough to allow them to do so. As the solenoid plunger reaches the end of its travel, it closes the contacts that connect the battery and starter and then the engine is cranked.

As soon as the engine starts, the flywheel ring gear begins turning fast enough to drive the pinion at an extremely high rate of speed. At this point, the one-way clutch begins allowing the pinion to spin faster than the starter shaft so that the starter will not operate at excessive speed. When the ignition switch is released from the starter position, the solenoid is de-energized, and a spring contained within the solenoid assembly pulls the gear out of mesh and interrupts the current flow to the starter.

Some starter employ a separate relay, mounted away from the starter, to switch the motor and solenoid current on and off. The relay thus replaces the solenoid electrical switch, buy does not eliminate the need for a solenoid mounted on the starter used to mechanically engage the starter drive gears. The relay is used to reduce the amount of current the starting switch must carry.

THE CHARGING SYSTEM

Basic Operating Principles

The automobile charging system provides electrical power for operation of the vehicle's ignition and starting systems and all the electrical accessories. The battery services as an electrical surge or storage tank, storing (in chemical form) the energy originally produced by the engine driven generator. The system also provides a means of regulating generator output to protect the battery from being overcharged and to avoid excessive voltage to the accessories.

The storage battery is a chemical device incorporating parallel lead plates in a tank containing a sulfuric acid/water solution. Adjacent plates are slightly dissimilar, and the chemical reaction of the 2 dissimilar plates produces electrical energy when the battery is connected to a load such as the starter motor. The chemical reaction is reversible, so that when the generator is producing a voltage (electrical pressure) greater than that produced by the battery, electricity is forced into the battery, and the battery is returned to its fully charged state.

The vehicle's generator is driven mechanically, through V-belts, by the engine crankshaft. It consists of 2 coils of fine wire, one stationary (the stator), and one movable (the rotor). The rotor may also be known as the armature, and consists of fine wire wrapped around an iron core which is mounted on a shaft. The electricity which flows through the 2 coils of wire (provided initially by the battery in some cases) creates an intense magnetic field around both rotor and stator, and the interaction between the 2 fields creates voltage, allowing the generator to power the accessories and charge the battery.

There are 2 types of generators: the earlier is the direct current (DC) type. The current produced by the DC generator is generated in the armature and carried off the spinning armature by stationary brushes contacting the commutator. The commutator is a series of smooth metal contact plates on the end of the armature. The commutator is a series of smooth metal contact plates on the end of the armature. The commutator plates, which are separated from one another by a very short gap, are connected to the armature circuits so that current will flow in one directions only in the wires carrying the generator output. The generator stator consists of 2 stationary coils of wire which draw some of the output current of the generator to form a powerful magnetic field and create the interaction of fields which generates the voltage. The generator field is wired in series with the regulator.

Newer automobiles use alternating current generators or alternators, because they are more efficient, can be rotated at higher speeds, and have fewer brush problems. In an alternator, the field rotates while all the current produced passes only through the stator winding. The brushes bear against continuous slip rings rather than a commutator. This causes the current produced to periodically reverse the direction of its flow. Diodes (electrical one-way switches) block the flow of current from traveling in the wrong direction. A series of diodes is wired together to permit the alternating flow of the stator to be converted to a pulsating, but unidirectional flow at the alternator output. The alternator's field is wired in series with the voltage regulator.

The regulator consists of several circuits. Each circuit has a core, or magnetic coil of wire, which operates a switch. Each switch is connected to ground through one or more resistors. The coil of wire responds directly to system voltage. When the voltage reaches the required level, the magnetic field created by the winding of wire closes the switch and inserts a resistance into the generator field circuit, thus reducing the output. The contacts of the switch cycle open and close many times each second to precisely control voltage.

While alternators are self-limiting as far as maximum current is concerned, DC generators employ a current regulating circuit which responds directly to the total amount of current flowing through the generator circuit rather than to the output voltage. The current regulator is similar to the voltage regulator except that all system current must flow through the energizing coil on its way to the various accessories.

ENGINE ELECTRICAL

➡ Refer to Section 2 for further ignition system diagnosis and component replacement.

Ignition Coil

TESTING

All Models

▶ See Figure 1

➡ **On models equipped with the 3.3L and 3.8L engines, the spark at the coil is tested in the same ways as models with a distributor. But each of the coils towers must be checked for spark.**

1. Remove the coil wire from the distributor cap. Hold the end of the wire about ¼ in. away from a good engine ground point.

2. Have a helper crank the engine. Check for a spark between the coil wire end and the ground point.

3. If there is a spark, it must be constant and bright blue in color.

4. Continue to crank the engine. Slowly move the wire away from the ground point. If arching at the coil tower occurs, replace the coil.

5. If the spark is good and no arching at the coil tower occurs, the ignition system is producing the necessary high secondary voltage.

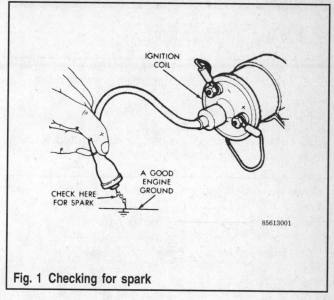

Fig. 1 Checking for spark

6. Check to make sure that the voltage is getting to the spark plugs. Inspect the distributor cap, rotor, spark plug wires and spark plugs.

7. If all of the components check okay, the ignition system is probably not the reason why the engine does not start.

8. Check the fuel system and engine mechanical items such as the timing belt.

Ignition Coil

REMOVAL & INSTALLATION

All Except 3.3L and 3.8L Engines

1. Disconnect the negative battery cable.
2. Remove the coil wire from the top of the coil.
3. Remove the wires from the top of the coil.
4. Remove the coil mounting bolt and remove the coil.
5. Mount the replacement coil in position and reconnect all of the wires.
6. Connect the battery cable.

3.3L and 3.8L Engines
▶ See Figure 2

1. Disconnect the negative battery cable.
2. Remove the electrical connector from the coil assembly. Tag and disconnect the spark plug wires from the coil assembly.
3. Remove the coil mounting bolts and remove the coil assembly from the engine.
4. Mount the coil in position and connect all of the wires. Tighten the coil assembly mounting bolts to 105 inch lbs. (12 Nm).
5. Connect the negative battery cable.

Distributor Cap

REMOVAL & INSTALLATION

1. Remove the splash shield retaining screws and the splash shield.
2. Loosen the distributor cap retaining screws.
3. Remove the distributor cap
4. Inspect the inside, of the cap, for spark flash over (burnt tracks on cap or terminals), center carbon button wear or

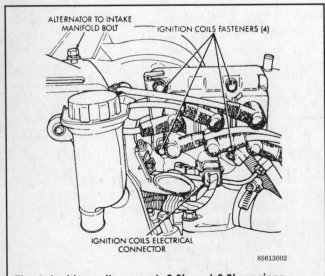

ALTERNATOR TO INTAKE MANIFOLD BOLT — IGNITION COILS FASTENERS (4)

IGNITION COILS ELECTRICAL CONNECTOR

85613002

Fig. 2 Ignition coil removal, 3.3L and 3.8L engines

cracking, and worn terminals. Replace the cap if any of these problems are present or suspected.

Light deposits on the terminals can be cleaned with a knife, heavy deposits or scaling will require cap replacement.

Wash the cap with a solution of warm water and mild detergent, scrub with a soft brush and dry with a clean soft cloth to remove dirt and grease.

5. If cap replacement is necessary, take notice of cap installed position in relationship to distributor assembly.
6. Number each plug wire so that the correct wire goes on the proper cap terminal when replaced. This can be done with pieces of adhesive tape.

➡**Do not pull plugs wires from distributor cap, they must first be released from inside of cap.**

7. Position the replacement cap on the distributor assembly, and tighten the distributor cap retaining screws.
8. Push the wire terminals firmly to properly seat the wires into the cap.
9. Reinstall the splash shield.

Distributor Rotor

With the distributor cap removed, remove the rotor. Inspect the rotor for cracks, excessive wear or burn marks and sufficient spring tension of the spring to cap carbon button terminal. Clean light deposits, replace the rotor if scaled or burnt heavily. Clean the ground strap on the inner side of the shaft mount. Take care not to bend any of the shutter blades, if blades are bent replace the rotor.

Distributor

REMOVAL & INSTALLATION

▶ See Figure 3

➡**Although not absolutely necessary, it is probably easier (for reference reinstallation, especially if the engine is rotated after distributor removal) to bring the engine to No. 1 cylinder at TDC (top dead center) before removing the distributor.**

1. Disconnect the distributor lead wires, and vacuum hose as necessary.
2. Remove the distributor cap.
3. Rotate the engine crankshaft (in the direction of normal rotation) until No. 1 cylinder is at TDC on compression stroke. make a mark on the block where the rotor points for installation reference.
4. Remove the distributor hold down bolt.
5. Carefully lift the distributor from the engine. The shaft will rotate slightly as the distributor is removed.
6. If the engine was not disturbed while the distributor was out, lower the distributor into the engine, engaging the gears and making sure that the gasket is properly seated in the block. The rotor should line up with the mark made before removal.
7. Install the distributor cap.
8. Tighten the hold down bolt. Connect the wires and vacuum hose as necessary.

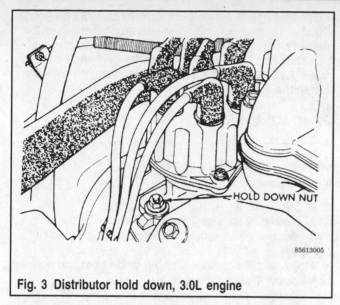

Fig. 3 Distributor hold down, 3.0L engine

9. Check and, if necessary, adjust the ignition timing.

➡**The following procedure is to be used if the engine was cranked with the distributor removed.**

10. If the engine has been cranked/turned while the distributor was removed, rotate the crankshaft until the number one piston is at TDC on the compression stroke. This will be indicated by the O mark on the flywheel (2.2L and 2.5L engines) aligned with the pointer on the clutch housing, or crank pulley (2.6L and 3.0L engines) aligned with the pointer on engine front cover.

11. Position the rotor just ahead of the No. 1 terminal of the cap and lower the distributor into the engine. With the distributor fully seated, the rotor should be directly under the No. 1 terminal.

12. Install the distributor cap.

13. Tighten the hold down bolt. Connect the wires and vacuum hose as necessary.

14. Check and, if necessary, adjust the ignition timing.

Alternator

The alternator charging system is a negative (-) ground system which consists of an alternator, a regulator, a charge indicator, a storage battery and wiring connecting the components, and fuse link wire.

The alternator is belt-driven from the engine. Energy is supplied from the alternator/regulator system to the rotating field through 2 brushes to 2 slip-rings. The slip-rings are mounted on the rotor shaft and are connected to the field coil. This energy supplied to the rotating field from the battery is called excitation current and is used to initially energize the field to begin the generation of electricity. Once the alternator starts to generate electricity, the excitation current comes from its own output rather than the battery.

The alternator produces power in the form of alternating current. The alternating current is rectified by 6 diodes into direct current. The direct current is used to charge the battery and power the rest of the electrical system.

When the ignition key is turned on, current flows from the battery, through the charging system indicator light on the instrument panel, to the voltage regulator, and to the alternator. Since the alternator is not producing any current, the alternator warning light comes on. When the engine is started, the alternator begins to produce current and turns the alternator light off. As the alternator turns and produces current, the current is divided in 2 ways: part to the battery to charge the battery and power the electrical components of the vehicle, and part is returned to the alternator to enable it to increase its output. In this situation, the alternator is receiving current from the battery and from itself. A voltage regulator is wired into the current supply to the alternator to prevent it from receiving too much current which would cause it to put out too much current. Conversely, if the voltage regulator does not allow the alternator to receive enough current, the battery will not be fully charged and will eventually go dead.

The battery is connected to the alternator at all times, whether the ignition key is turned on or not. If the battery were shorted to ground, the alternator would also be shorted. This would damage the alternator. To prevent this, a fuse link is installed in the wiring between the battery and the alternator. If the battery is shorted, the fuse link is melted, protecting the alternator.

ALTERNATOR PRECAUTIONS

Some precautions should be taken when working on this, or any other, AC charging system.

1. Never switch battery polarity.
2. When installing a battery, always connect the grounded terminal first.
3. Never disconnect the battery while the engine is running.
4. If the molded connector is disconnected from the alternator, never ground the hot wire.
5. Never run the alternator with the main output cable disconnected.
6. Never electric weld around the truck without disconnecting the alternator.
7. Never apply any voltage in excess of battery voltage while testing.
8. Never jump a battery for starting purposes with more than 12v.

CHARGING SYSTEM TROUBLESHOOTING

There are many possible ways in which the charging system can malfunction. Often the source of a problem is difficult to diagnose, requiring special equipment and a good deal of experience. This is usually not the case, however, where the charging system fails completely and causes the dash board warning light to come on or the battery to become dead. To troubleshoot a complete system failure only 2 pieces of equipment are needed: a test light, to determine that current is reaching a certain point; and a current indicator (ammeter), to determine the direction of the current flow and its measurement in amps.

This test works under 3 assumptions:

1. The battery is known to be good and fully charged.
2. The alternator belt is in good condition and adjusted to the proper tension.

3. All connections in the system are clean and tight.

➥**In order for the current indicator to give a valid reading, the car must be equipped with battery cables which are of the same gauge size and quality as original equipment battery cables.**

4. Turn off all electrical components on the car. Make sure the doors of the car are closed. If the car is equipped with a clock, disconnect the clock by removing the lead wire from the rear of the clock. Disconnect the positive battery cable from the battery and connect the ground wire on a test light to the disconnected positive battery cable. Touch the probe end of the test light to the positive battery post. The test light should not light. If the test light does light, there is a short or open circuit on the car.

5. Disconnect the voltage regulator wiring harness connector at the voltage regulator. Turn on the ignition key. Connect the wire on a test light to a good ground (engine bolt). Touch the probe end of a test light to the ignition wire connector into the voltage regulator wiring connector. This wire corresponds to the **I** terminal on the regulator. If the test light goes on, the charging system warning light circuit is complete. If the test light does not come on and the warning light on the instrument panel is on, either the resistor wire, which is parallel with the warning light, or the wiring to the voltage regulator, is defective. If the test light does not come on and the warning light is not on, either the bulb is defective or the power supply wire form the battery through the ignition switch to the bulb has an open circuit. Connect the wiring harness to the regulator.

6. Examine the fuse link wire in the wiring harness from the starter relay to the alternator. If the insulation on the wire is cracked or split, the fuse link may be melted. Connect a test light to the fuse link by attaching the ground wire on the test light to an engine bolt and touching the probe end of the light to the bottom of the fuse link wire where it splices into the alternator output wire. If the bulb in the test light does not light, the fuse link is melted.

7. Start the engine and place a current indicator on the positive battery cable. Turn off all electrical accessories and make sure the doors are closed. If the charging system is working properly, the gauge will show a draw of less than 5 amps. If the system is not working properly, the gauge will show a draw of more than 5 amps. A charge moves the needle toward the battery, a draw moves the needle away from the battery. Turn the engine off.

8. Disconnect the wiring harness from the voltage regulator at the regulator at the regulator connector. Connect a male spade terminal (solderless connector) to each end of a jumper wire. Insert one end of the wire into the wiring harness connector which corresponds to the **A** terminal on the regulator. Insert the other end of the wire into the wiring harness connector which corresponds to the **F** terminal on the regulator. Position the connector with the jumper wire installed so that it cannot contact any metal surface under the hood. Position a current indicator gauge on the positive battery cable. Have an assistant start the engine. Observe the reading on the current indicator. Have your assistant slowly raise the speed of the engine to about 2,000 Rpm or until the current indicator needle stops moving, whichever comes first. Do not run the engine for more than a short period of time in this condition. If the wiring harness connector or jumper wire becomes excessively hot during this test, turn off the engine and check for a grounded

wire in the regulator wiring harness. If the current indicator shows a charge of about 3 amps less than the output of the alternator, the alternator is working properly. If the previous tests showed a draw, the voltage regulator is defective. If the gauge does not show the proper charging rate, the alternator is defective.

REMOVAL & INSTALLATION

Chrysler Alternator- 2.2L Engine
▶ **See Figures 4, 5, 6, 7 and 8**

1. Disconnect the negative battery cable.
2. Disconnect the wiring and label for easy installation.
3. Remove the air conditioning compressor drive belt if equipped.
4. Loosen the alternator adjusting bracket bolt and adjusting bolt. Remove the alternator belt.
5. Remove the bracket bolt and the mounting bolt.

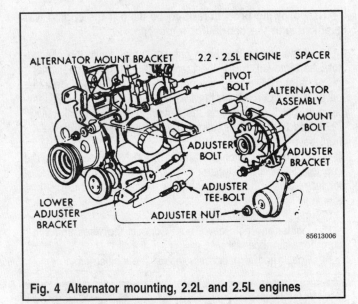

Fig. 4 Alternator mounting, 2.2L and 2.5L engines

Fig. 5 Disconnecting alternator wiring, 2.2L and 2.5L engines

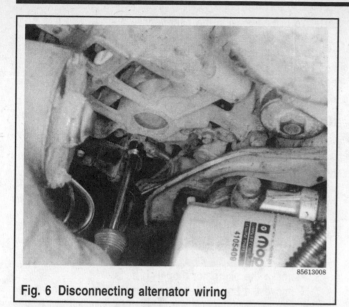

Fig. 6 Disconnecting alternator wiring

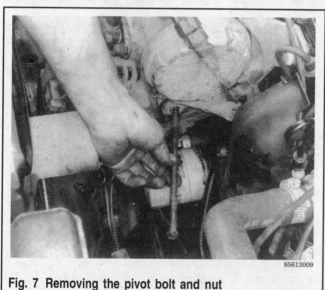

Fig. 7 Removing the pivot bolt and nut

Fig. 8 Removing the alternator from the vehicle

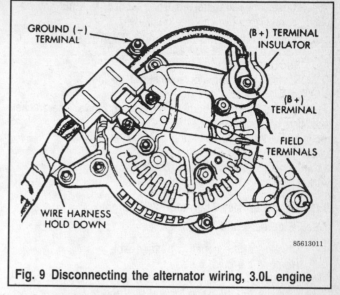

Fig. 9 Disconnecting the alternator wiring, 3.0L engine

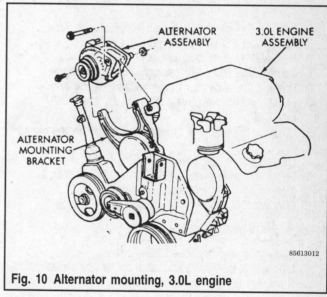

Fig. 10 Alternator mounting, 3.0L engine

6. Remove the pivot bolt and nut.
7. Lift the alternator from the vehicle.

➡When lifting the alternator out of the vehicle on some years with A/C, clearance may be restricted by the condensor cooling fan assembly or the A/C compressor and mounting bracket assembly, if so, removal of one of these items will be necessary.

8. Position the alternator against the engine.
9. Install the pivot bolt and nut.
10. Install the mounting bracket bolts, and adjusting bolt.
11. Install drive belts and adjust to specification.
12. Tighten all the mounting bolts and nuts.
13. Connect all alternator terminals.
14. Connect the negative battery cable.

Bosch Alternator 2.2L Engine

1. Disconnect the negative battery cable.
2. Disconnect the wiring and label for easy installation.
3. Remove the air conditioning compressor drive belt.

4. Loosen the alternator adjusting bracket lock nut and adjusting screw. Remove the alternator belt.

5. Remove the bracket locknut and mounting bolt.

6. Remove the pivot bolt and nut.

7. Remove the alternator.

8. Position the alternator against the engine.

9. Install pivot bolt and nut.

10. Set the mounting bracket in place and install the bracket mounting bolt and locknut.

11. Install the drive belts and adjust to specification.

12. Tighten all the mounting bolts and nuts.

13. Connect all alternator terminals.

14. Connect the negative battery cable.

Bosch and Chrysler Alternators 2.5L Engine

▶ See Figures 4 and 5

1. Disconnect the negative battery cable.

2. Remove the drive belts.

3. Remove the adjusting bracket to engine mounting bolt.

4. Remove the adjusting locking bolt and nut, and remove the mounting bracket.

5. Position the alternator to gain access to the wiring.

6. Disconnect the wiring and label for easy installation.

7. Remove the pivot bolt, nut, and washers.

8. Remove the alternator assembly from the engine.

9. Position the alternator assembly against the engine.

10. Loosely install the pivot bolt, washers, and nut.

11. Install all wiring.

12. Position the mounting bracket and install engine mounting bolt.

13. Loosely install the adjusting locking bolt and nut.

14. Install the drive belts, and adjust to specification.

15. Tighten all mounting bolts and nuts.

16. Connect the negative battery cable.

Mitsubishi Alternator 2.6L Engine

1. Disconnect the negative battery cable.

2. Disconnect the wiring and label for easy installation.

3. Remove the adjusting strap mounting bolt.

4. Remove the drive belts.

5. Remove the support mounting bolt and nut.

6. Remove the alternator assembly.

7. Position the alternator assembly against the engine and install the support bolt.

8. Install the adjusting strap mounting bolt.

9. Install the alternator belts and adjust to specification.

10. Tighten all the support bolts and nuts.

11. Connect all alternator terminals.

12. Connect the negative battery cable.

Bosch and Nippondenso Alternator 3.0L Engine

▶ See Figures 9 and 10

1. Disconnect the negative battery cable.

2. Install a 1/2 in. breaker bar in the tensioner slot. Rotate counterclockwise to release belt tension and remove poly-V belt.

3. Remove the alternator mounting bolts (2).

4. Remove the wiring and remove alternator.

5. To install, position the alternator and install wiring.

6. Set the alternator against the mounting bracket and install the mounting bolts.

7. Rotate the tensioner counterclockwise and install poly-V belt.

8. Connect the negative battery cable.

Nippondenso Alternator 3.3L and 3.8L Engines

1. Disconnect the negative battery cable.

2. Remove the alternator drive belt, by relieving the tension on the dynamic tensioner.

3. Loosen the nut on the support bracket at the exhaust manifold, do not remove it.

4. Remove the alternator tensioner/power steering bracket bolt.

5. Remove the tensioner stud nut and remove the tensioner.

6. Remove the alternator mounting bolts.

7. Remove the power steering reservoir from the mounting bracket, do not disconnect the hoses, and position it out of the way.

8. Remove the alternator support bracket bolts. Remove the intake plenum to alternator bracket bolt and remove the alternator support bracket from the engine.

9. Remove the alternator from the engine and disconnect the electrical leads.

To install:

10. Install the alternator in position on the engine and connect the electrical leads.

11. Install the alternator support bracket, tighten the retaining bolts to 40 ft. lbs. (54 Nm).

12. Install the power steering reservoir on the mounting bracket.

13. Install the alternator mounting bolts, tighten the bolts to 40 ft. lbs. (54 Nm).

14. Install the tensioner and tensioner mounting stud. Install the retaining nut on the exhaust manifold.

15. Install the alternator belt, insert a 1/2 in. extension into the square hole in the tensioner and turn the tensioner. Tighten the tensioner bolt.

16. Connect the negative battery cable.

Regulator

REMOVAL & INSTALLATION

Chrysler Alternator (Early Models)

1. Disconnect the negative battery cable.

2. Remove the electrical connection from voltage regulator assembly.

3. Remove the mounting bolts and remove the regulator.

4. This regulator is not adjustable and must be replaced as a unit if found to be defective.

5. Clean any dirt or corrosion from the regulator mounting surface, including mounting holes.

6. Install the replacement electronic voltage regulator.

7. Secured the mounting screws.

8. Connect the voltage regulator wiring connector. Connect the negative battery cable.

➡ **All Bosch, Nippondenso, Mitsubishi, and Chrysler (Late Models) alternators have an integral electronic voltage regulator. Voltage regulator replacement on these models requires removal and disassembly of the alternator.**

Starter

▶ See Figures 11, 12 and 13

TEST PROCEDURES (ON VEHICLE)

➡**The battery is the heart of the electrical system. If the battery is not up to specification it will not deliver the necessary amperage for proper starter operation.**

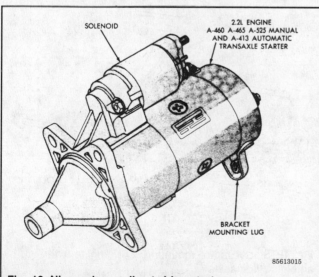

Fig. 11 Bosch direct drive starter

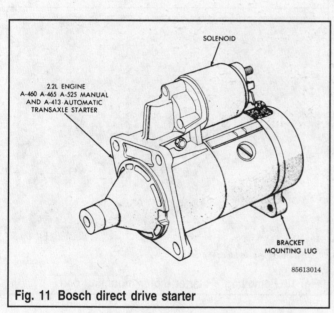

Fig. 12 Nippondenso direct drive starter

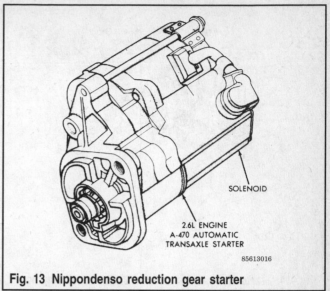

Fig. 13 Nippondenso reduction gear starter

Starter Does Not Operate

✳✳CAUTION

Before performing this test, disconnect the coil wire from the distributor cap center tower and secure to a good engine ground. This will prevent the engine from starting.

1. Connect a voltmeter across the battery terminals and confirm that battery voltage (12.4 volts) is available for the ignition and cranking system.
2. Turn the headlights on.
3. If the headlights do not operate. Check the battery cables for loose or corroded connection.
4. If the headlights glow normally, have a helper operate the ignition switch. Headlights should remained reasonably bright when ignition switch is operated. If the headlights dim considerably or go out when the ignition switch is operated, the problem is battery related.
5. If headlights remain bright when the ignition switch is operated. The problem is at the starter relay, wiring, or starter motor.
6. Connect a test light to the battery feed terminal of the starter relay. The test light should go on. If the test light is off, check the battery feed wire to starter relay.
7. Connect the test light to the ignition switch terminal of starter relay and a known good engine ground. Have a helper operate the ignition switch. If the test light does not come on when the ignition switch is operated, check the wiring from the ignition switch to the relay. Test light should have came on.
8. Test light on.
9. Connect a heavy jumper wire, between the battery relay feed and the relay solenoid terminal. If the starter motor operates replace the starter relay. If the motor does not operate, remove the starter for repairs.

REMOVAL & INSTALLATION

▶ See Figures 14, 15, 16, 17, 18 and 19

1. Disconnect the negative battery cable.

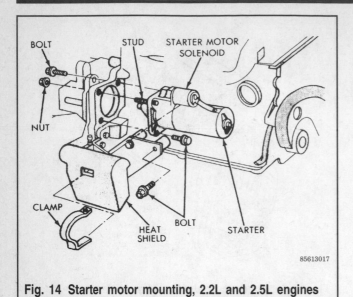

Fig. 14 Starter motor mounting, 2.2L and 2.5L engines

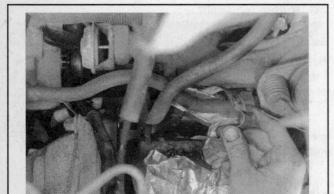

Fig. 15 Working from under the vehicle, disconnect the starter motor heat shield clamp

Fig. 16 View of the starter motor with the heat shield removed while looking over the crossmember

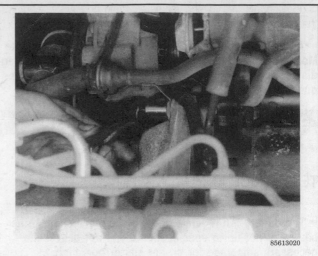

Fig. 17 Removing the starter motor mounting stud nut where the air pump tube bracket is also attached

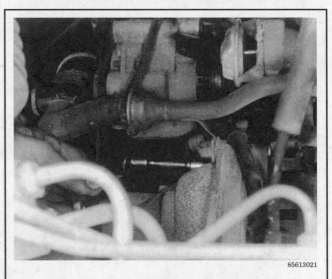

Fig. 18 Removing a starter motor mounting bolt

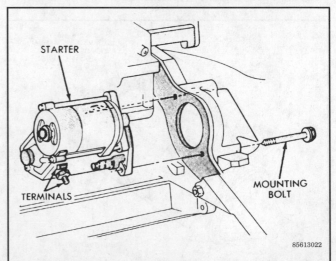

Fig. 19 Starter motor mounting, 2.6L engine with automatic transaxle

2. Raise and safely support the vehicle. The starter can be removed by reaching over the crossmember.

3. Remove the heat shield and its clamps, if so equipped.

4. On the 2.2L and 2.5L engine loosen the air pump tube at the exhaust manifold and move the tube bracket away from the starter.

5. Remove the electrical connections from the starter.

6. Remove the bolts attaching the starter to the flywheel housing and the rear bracket to the engine or transaxle.

7. Remove the starter.

8. Position the replacement starter against the mounting surface.

9. Install the mounting bolts.

10. Connect the starter wiring.

11. On 2.2L and 2.5L engines, position the air pump tube toward starter and connect tube bracket the to exhaust manifold.

12. Install the heat shield and clamp.

13. Connect the negative battery cable.

SOLENOID REPLACEMENT

▶ **See Figures 20, 21 and 22**

1. Remove the starter as previously outlined.

2. Disconnect the field coil wire from the solenoid.

3. Remove the solenoid mounting screws.

4. Work the solenoid off of shift fork lever and remove the solenoid.

5. Install plunger on replacement solenoid.

6. Install plunger on shift fork lever.

7. Secure solenoid with mounting screws.

STARTER GEAR AND CLUTCH REPLACEMENT

▶ **See Figure 23**

1. Disconnect the negative battery cable.

2. Remove the starter from the vehicle.

3. Remove the 2 gear housing attaching screws from the starter.

4. Separate the gear housing from the solenoid housing. The pinion, pinion gear bearing and drive gear will all be loose between the 2 housings. The starter gear and clutch can also be removed at this time.

5. To reinstall the pinion gear and bearing, wipe clean with a rag and coat with light weight wheel bearing grease.

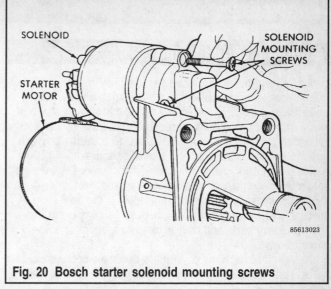

Fig. 20 Bosch starter solenoid mounting screws

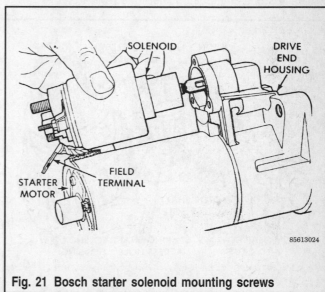

Fig. 21 Bosch starter solenoid mounting screws

6. Place the bearing and gear over the shaft in the housing. Reinstall the starter gear and clutch if removed.

7. Install the housings and reinstall the retaining screws.

8. Install the starter in the vehicle and connect the negative battery cable.

ENGINE MECHANICAL

Engine Overhaul Tips

Most engine overhaul procedures are fairly standard. In addition to specific parts replacement procedures and complete specifications for your individual engine, this section also is a guide to accept rebuilding procedures. Examples of standard rebuilding practice are shown and should be used along with specific details concerning your particular engine.

Competent and accurate machine shop services will ensure maximum performance, reliability and engine life.

In most instances it is more profitable for the do-it-yourself mechanic to remove, clean and inspect the component, buy the necessary parts and deliver these to a shop for actual machine work.

On the other hand, much of the rebuilding work (crankshaft, block, bearings, piston rods, and other components) is well within the scope of the do-it-yourself mechanic.

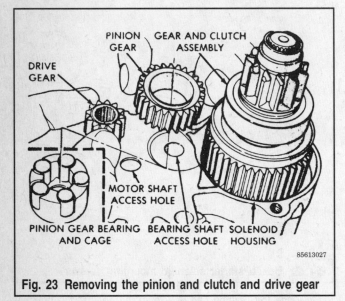

Fig. 23 Removing the pinion and clutch and drive gear

TOOLS

The tools required for an engine overhaul or parts replacement will depend on the depth of your involvement. With a few exceptions, they will be the tools found in a mechanic's tool kit (see "General Information and Maintenance"). More in-depth work will require any or all of the following:
- A dial indicator (reading in thousandths) mounted on a universal base
- Micrometers and telescope gauges
- Jaw and screw-type pullers
- Scraper
- Valve spring compressor
- Ring groove cleaner
- Piston ring expander and compressor
- Ridge reamer
- Cylinder hone or glaze breaker
- Plastigage®
- Engine stand

The use of most of these tools is illustrated in this section. Many can be rented for a one-time use from a local parts jobber or tool supply house specializing in automotive work.

Occasionally, the use of special tools is called for. See the information on Special Tools and Safety Notice in the front of this book before substituting another tool.

INSPECTION TECHNIQUES

Procedures and specifications are given in this section for inspecting, cleaning and assessing the wear limits of most major components. Other procedures such as Magnaflux® and Zyglo® can be used to locate material flaws and stress cracks. Magnaflux® is a magnetic process applicable only to ferrous materials. The Zyglo® process coats the material with a fluorescent dye penetrant and can be used on any material Check for suspected surface cracks can be more readily made

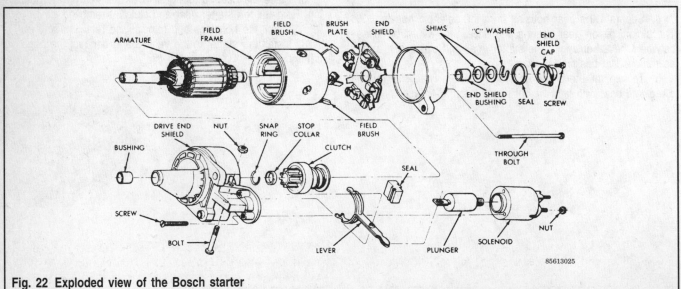

Fig. 22 Exploded view of the Bosch starter

using spot check dye. The dye is sprayed onto the suspected area, wiped off and the area sprayed with a developer. Cracks will show up brightly.

OVERHAUL TIPS

Aluminum has become extremely popular for use in engines, due to its low weight. Observe the following precautions when handling aluminum parts:

• Never hot tank aluminum parts (the caustic hot tank solution will eat the aluminum.

• Remove all aluminum parts (identification tag, etc.) from engine parts prior to the tanking.

• Always coat threads lightly with engine oil or anti-seize compounds before installation, to prevent seizure.

• Never over-torque bolts or spark plugs especially in aluminum threads.

Stripped threads in any component can be repaired using any of several commercial repair kits (Heli-Coil®, Microdot®, Keenserts®, etc.).

When assembling the engine, any parts that will be frictional contact must be prelubed to provide lubrication at initial start-up. Any product specifically formulated for this purpose can be used, but engine oil is not recommended as a prelube.

When semi-permanent (locked, but removable) installation of bolts or nuts is desired, threads should be cleaned and coated with Loctite® or other similar, commercial non-hardening sealant.

REPAIRING DAMAGED THREADS

▶ See Figures 24, 25, 26, 27 and 28

Several methods of repairing damaged threads are available. Heli-Coil® (shown here), Keenserts® and Microdot® are among the most widely used. All involve basically the same principle — drilling out stripped threads, tapping the hole and installing a prewound insert — making welding, plugging and oversize fasteners unnecessary.

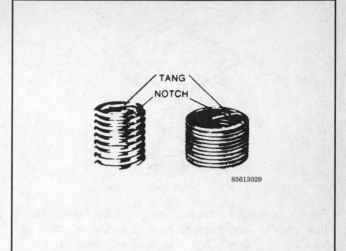

Fig. 25 Standard thread repair insert (left) and spark plug thread insert (right)

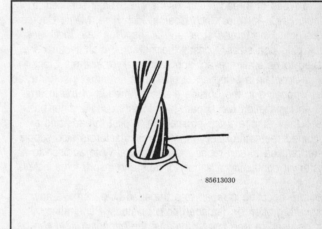

Fig. 26 Drill out the damaged threads with specified drill. Drill completely through the hole or to the bottom of a blind hole.

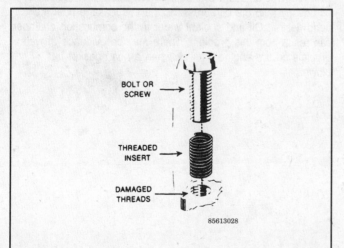

Fig. 24 Damaged bolt holes can be repaired with thread insert kits

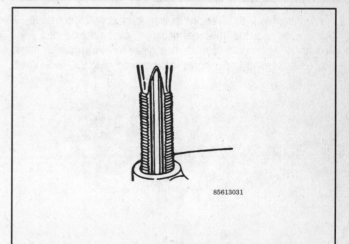

Fig. 27 With the tap supplied, tap the hole to receive the thread insert. Keep the tap well oiled and back it out frequently to avoid clogging the threads.

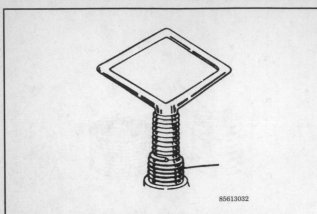

Fig. 28 Screw the threaded insert onto the installation tool until the tang engages the slot. Screw the insert into the tapped hole until it is ¼-½ turn below the top surface. After installation break off the tang with a hammer and punch.

Two types of thread repair inserts are usually supplied: a standard type for most Inch Coarse, Inch Fine, Metric Course and Metric Fine thread sizes and a spark lug type to fit most spark plug port sizes. Consult the individual manufacturer's catalog to determine exact applications. Typical thread repair kits will contain a selection of prewound threaded inserts, a tap (corresponding to the outside diameter threads of the insert) and an installation tool. Spark plug inserts usually differ because they require a tap equipped with pilot threads and a combined reamer/tap section. Most manufacturers also supply blister-packed thread repair inserts separately in addition to a master kit containing a variety of taps and inserts plus installation tools.

Before effecting a repair to a threaded hole, remove any snapped, broken or damaged bolts or studs. Penetrating oil can be used to free frozen threads; the offending item can be removed with locking pliers or with a screw or stud extractor. After the hole is clear, the thread can be repaired, as follows:

Checking Engine Compression

A noticeable lack of engine power, excessive oil consumption and/or poor fuel mileage measured over an extended period are all indicators of internal engine war. Worn piston rings, scored or worn cylinder bores, blown head gaskets, sticking or burnt valves and worn valve seats are all possible culprits here. A check of each cylinder's compression will help you locate the problems.

As mentioned in the Tools and Equipment section, a screw-in type compression gauge is more accurate that the type you simply hold against the spark plug hole, although it takes slightly longer to use. It's worth it to obtain a more accurate reading. Follow the procedures below.

1. Warm up the engine to normal operating temperature.
2. Remove all spark plugs.
3. Disconnect the high tension lead from the ignition coil.
4. On fully open the throttle either by operating the carburetor throttle linkage by hand or by having an assistant floor the accelerator pedal.
5. Screw the compression gauge into the no.1 spark plug hole until the fitting is snug.

➡**Be careful not to cross thread the plug hole. On aluminum cylinder heads use extra care, as the threads in these heads are easily ruined.**

6. Ask an assistant to depress the accelerator pedal fully on both carbureted and fuel injected trucks. Then, while you read the compression gauge, ask the assistant to crank the engine 2 or 3 times in short bursts using the ignition switch.
7. Read the compression gauge at the end of each series of cranks, and record the highest of these readings. Repeat this procedure for each of the engine's cylinders. Compare the highest reading of each cylinder to the compression pressure specification in the Tune-Up Specifications chart. The specs in this chart are maximum values.

A cylinder's compression pressure is usually acceptable if it is not less than 80% of maximum. The difference between each cylinder should be no more than 12-14 pounds.

8. If a cylinder is unusually low, pour a tablespoon of clean engine oil into the cylinder through the spark plug hole and repeat the compression test. If the compression comes up after adding the oil, it appears that the cylinder's piston rings or bore are damaged or worn. If the pressure remains low, the valves may not be seating properly (a valve job is needed), or the head gasket may be blown near that cylinder. If compression in any 2 adjacent cylinders is low, and if the addition of oil doesn't help the compression, there is leakage past the head gasket. Oil and coolant water in the combustion chamber can result from this problem. There may be evidence of water droplets on the engine dipstick when a head gasket has blown.

GENERAL ENGINE SPECIFICATIONS

Year	VIN	Engine No. Cyl. Liters	Fuel System Type	SAE Net Horsepower @ rpm	SAE Net Torque @ rpm (ft. lbs.)	Bore × Stroke (in.)	Compression Ratio	Oil Pressure @ rpm
1984	C	4-2.2L	2 bbl	84 @ 4800	111 @ 2400	3.44 × 3.62	8.5:1	60–90 @ 200
	G	4-2.6L	2 bbl	92 @ 4500	131 @ 2500	3.59 × 3.86	8.2:1	56 @ 2000
1985	C	4-2.2L	2 bbl	84 @ 4800	111 @ 2400	3.44 × 3.62	8.5:1	60–90 @ 200
	G	4-2.6L	2 bbl	92 @ 4500	131 @ 2500	3.59 × 3.86	8.2:1	56 @ 2000
1986	C	4-2.2L	2 bbl	96 @ 5200	119 @ 3200	3.44 × 3.62	9.5:1	50 @ 2000
	G	4-2.6L	2 bbl	101 @ 5600	140 @ 2800	3.59 × 3.86	8.7:1	85 @ 2500
1987	C	4-2.2L	2 bbl	96 @ 5200	119 @ 3200	3.44 × 3.62	9.5:1	50 @ 2000
	K	4-2.5L	EFI	100 @ 4800	135 @ 2800	3.44 × 4.09	8.9:1	30–80 @ 300
	G	4-2.6L	2 bbl	101 @ 5600	140 @ 2800	3.59 × 3.86	8.7:1	85 @ 2500
	3	6-3.0L	EFI	142 @ 5000	173 @ 2800	3.59 × 2.99	8.9:1	30–80 @ 300
1988	K	4-2.5L	EFI	100 @ 4800	135 @ 2800	3.44 × 4.09	8.9:1	30–80 @ 300
	3	6-3.0L	EFI	142 @ 5000	173 @ 2800	3.59 × 2.99	8.9:1	30–80 @ 300
1989	K	4-2.5L	EFI	100 @ 4800	135 @ 2800	3.44 × 4.09	8.9:1	30–80 @ 300
	J	4-2.5L	Turbo	150 @ 4800	180 @ 2000	3.44 × 4.09	7.8:1	30–80 @ 300
	3	6-3.0L	EFI	142 @ 5000	173 @ 2800	3.59 × 2.99	8.9:1	30–80 @ 300
1990	K	4-2.5L	EFI	100 @ 4800	135 @ 2800	3.44 × 4.09	8.9:1	30–80 @ 3000
	J	4-2.5L	Turbo	150 @ 4800	180 @ 2000	3.44 × 4.09	7.8:1	30–80 @ 3000
	3	6-3.0L	EFI	142 @ 5000	173 @ 2800	3.59 × 2.99	8.9:1	30–80 @ 3000
	R	6-3.3L	EFI	150 @ 4000	185 @ 3600	3.66 × 3.19	8.9:1	30–80 @ 3000
1991	K	4-2.5L	EFI	100 @ 4800	135 @ 2800	3.44 × 4.09	8.9:1	30–80 @ 3000
	3	6-3.0L	EFI	142 @ 5000	173 @ 2800	3.59 × 2.99	8.9:1	30–80 @ 3000
	R	6-3.3L	EFI	150 @ 4000	185 @ 3600	3.66 × 3.19	8.9:1	30–80 @ 3000
1992	K	4-2.5L	TFI	96 @ 4400	133 @ 2800	3.45 × 4.09	8.9:1	35–65 @ 2000
	3	6-3.0L	MFI	143 @ 5000	168 @ 2500	3.59 × 2.99	8.9:1	30–80 @ 3000
	R	6-3.3L	MFI	150 @ 4800	185 @ 3600	3.66 × 3.19	8.9:1	30–80 @ 3000
1993	K	4-2.5L	TFI	100 @ 4800	135 @ 2800	3.45 × 4.09	8.9:1	35–65 @ 2000
	3	6-3.0L	MFI	143 @ 5000	168 @ 2500	3.59 × 2.99	8.9:1	30–80 @ 3000
	R	6-3.3L	MFI	150 @ 4800	185 @ 3600	3.66 × 3.19	8.9:1	30–80 @ 3000
1994	K	4-2.5L	TFI	100 @ 4800	135 @ 2800	3.45 × 4.09	8.9:1	35–65 @ 2000
	3	6-3.0L	MFI	143 @ 5000	168 @ 2500	3.59 × 2.99	8.9:1	30–80 @ 3000
	R	6-3.3L	MFI	150 @ 4800	185 @ 3600	3.66 × 3.19	8.9:1	30–80 @ 3000
	L	6-3.8L	MFI	162 @ 4400	213 @ 3300	3.78 × 3.43	9.0:1	30–80 @ 3000

NOTE: Horsepower and torque are SAE net figures. They are measured at the rear of the transmission with all accessories installed and operating. Since the figures vary when a given engine is installed in different models, some are representative rather than exact.

85613C01

VALVE SPECIFICATIONS

Year	VIN	Engine No. Cyl. Liters	Seat Angle (deg.)	Face Angle (deg.)	Spring Test Pressure (lbs.)	Spring Installed Height (in.)	Stem-to-Guide Clearance (in.)		Stem Diameter (in.)	
							Intake	Exhaust	Intake	Exhaust
1984	C	4-2.2L	45	45	95	1.65	0.001–0.003	0.0030–0.0047	0.3124	0.3103
	G	4-2.6L	45	45	61	1.59	0.001–0.004	0.0020–0.0060	0.3150	0.3150
1985	C	4-2.2L	45	45	95	1.65	0.001–0.003	0.0030–0.0047	0.3124	0.3103
	G	4-2.6L	45	45	61	1.59	0.001–0.004	0.0020–0.0060	0.3150	0.3150
1986	C	4-2.2L	45	45	95	1.65	0.001–0.003	0.0030–0.0047	0.3124	0.3103
	G	4-2.6L	45	45	61	1.59	0.001–0.004	0.0020–0.0060	0.3150	0.3150
1987	C	4-2.2L	45	45	95	1.65	0.001–0.003	0.0030–0.0047	0.3124	0.3103
	K	4-2.5L	45	45	115	1.65	0.001–0.003	0.0030–0.0047	0.3124	0.3103
	G	4-2.6L	45	45	61	1.59	0.001–0.004	0.0020–0.0060	0.3150	0.3150
	3	6-3.0L	44.5	45.5	73	1.59	0.001–0.002	0.0020–0.0030	0.3130–0.3140	0.3120–0.3130
1988	K	4-2.5L	45	45	115	1.65	0.001–0.003	0.0030–0.0047	0.3124	0.3103
	3	6-3.0L	44.5	45.5	73	1.59	0.001–0.002	0.0020–0.0030	0.3130–0.3140	0.3120–0.3130
1989	K	4-2.5L	45	45	115	1.65	0.001–0.003	0.0030–0.0047	0.3124	0.3103
	J	4-2.5L	45	45	115	1.65	0.001–0.003	0.0030–0.0047	0.3124	0.3103
	3	6-3.0L	44.5	45.5	73	1.59	0.001–0.002	0.0020–0.0030	0.3130–0.3140	0.3120–0.3130
1990	K	4-2.5L	45	45	115	1.65	0.001–0.003	0.0030–0.0047	0.3124	0.3103
	J	4-2.5L	45	45	115	1.65	0.001–0.003	0.0030–0.0047	0.3124	0.3103
	3	6-3.0L	44.5	45.5	73	1.59	0.001–0.002	0.0020–0.0030	0.3130–0.3140	0.3120–0.3130
	R	6-3.3L	45	44.5	60	1.56				
1991	K	4-2.5L	45	45	115	1.65	0.001–0.003	0.0030–0.0047	0.3124	0.3103
	3	6-3.0L	44.5	45.5	73	1.59	0.001–0.002	0.0020–0.0030	0.3130–0.3140	0.3120–0.3130
	R	6-3.3L	45	44.5	60	1.56	0.002–0.016	0.0020–0.0160	0.3110–0.3120	0.3110–0.3120
1992	K	4-2.5L	45	45	115 @ 1.65	1.65	0.0009–0.0047	0.0030–0.0047	0.3124	0.3103
	3	6-3.0L	44.5	45.5	73 @ 1.59	1.59	0.001–0.002	0.0020–0.0030	0.3130–0.3140	0.3120–0.3130
	R	6-3.3L	45	44.5	95 @ 1.57	1.622–1.681	0.001–0.003	0.0020–0.0060	0.3120–0.3130	0.3110–0.3120
1993	K	4-2.5L	45	45	115 @ 1.65	1.65	0.0009–0.0047	0.0030–0.0047	0.3124	0.3103
	3	6-3.0L	44.5	45.5	73 @ 1.59	1.59	0.001–0.002	0.0020–0.0030	0.3130–0.3140	0.3120–0.3130
	R	6-3.3L	45	44.5	95 @ 1.57	1.622–1.681	0.001–0.003	0.0020–0.0060	0.3120–0.3130	0.3110–0.3120
1994	K	4-2.5L	45	45	115 @ 1.65	1.65	0.0009–0.0047	0.0030–0.0047	0.3124	0.3103
	3	6-3.0L	44.5	45.5	73 @ 1.59	1.59	0.001–0.002	0.0020–0.0030	0.3130–0.3140	0.3120–0.3130
	R	6-3.3L	45	44.5	95 @ 1.57	1.622–1.681	0.001–0.003	0.0020–0.0060	0.3120–0.3130	0.3110–0.3120
	L	6-3.8L	45	44.5	95 @ 1.57	1.622–1.681	0.001–0.003	0.0020–0.0060	0.3120–0.3130	0.3110–0.3120

85613C02

CAMSHAFT SPECIFICATIONS

Year	VIN	Engine No. Cyl. Liters	Journal Diameter (in.)					Bearing Clearance (in.)	Camshaft Endplay (in.)
			1	2	3	4	5		
1984	C	4-2.2L	1.375–1.376	1.375–1.376	1.375–1.376	1.375–1.376	1.375–1.376	0.002–0.004	0.005–0.013
	G	4-2.6L	—	—	—	—	—	0.002–0.008	0.004–0.008
1985	C	4-2.2L	1.375–1.376	1.375–1.376	1.375–1.376	1.375–1.376	1.375–1.376	0.002–0.004	0.005–0.013
	G	4-2.6L	—	—	—	—	—	0.002–0.008	0.004–0.008
1986	C	4-2.2L	1.375–1.376	1.375–1.376	1.375–1.376	1.375–1.376	1.375–1.376	0.002–0.004	0.005–0.013
	G	4-2.6L	—	—	—	—	—	0.002–0.008	0.004–0.008
1987	C	4-2.2L	1.375–1.376	1.375–1.376	1.375–1.376	1.375–1.376	1.375–1.376	0.002–0.004	0.005–0.013
	K	4-2.5L	1.375–1.376	1.375–1.376	1.375–1.376	1.375–1.376	1.375–1.376	0.002–0.004	0.005–0.020
	G	4-2.6L	—	—	—	—	—	0.002–0.008	0.004–0.008
	3	6-3.0L	—	—	—	—	—	—	—
1988	K	4-2.5L	1.375–1.376	1.375–1.376	1.375–1.376	1.375–1.376	1.375–1.376	0.002–0.004	0.005–0.020
	3	6-3.0L	—	—	—	—	—	—	—
1989	K	4-2.5L	1.375–1.376	1.375–1.376	1.375–1.376	1.375–1.376	1.375–1.376	0.002–0.004	0.005–0.020
	J	4-2.5L	1.375–1.376	1.375–1.376	1.375–1.376	1.375–1.376	1.375–1.376	0.002–0.004	0.005–0.020
	3	6-3.0L	—	—	—	—	—	—	—
1990	K	4-2.5L	1.375–1.376	1.375–1.376	1.375–1.376	1.375–1.376	1.375–1.376	0.002–0.004	0.005–0.020
	J	4-2.5L	1.375–1.376	1.375–1.376	1.375–1.376	1.375–1.376	1.375–1.376	0.002–0.004	0.005–0.020
	3	6-3.0L	—	—	—	—	—	—	—
	R	6-3.3L	1.997–1.999	1.980–1.982	1.965–1.96	1.949–1.952	—	0.001–0.005	0.005–0.012
1991	K	4-2.5L	1.375–1.376	1.375–1.376	1.375–1.376	1.375–1.376	1.375–1.376	0.002–0.004	0.005–0.020
	3	6-3.0L	—	—	—	—	—	—	—
	R	6-3.3L	1.997–1.999	1.980–1.982	1.965–1.96	1.949–1.952	—	0.001–0.005	0.005–0.012
1992	K	4-2.5L	1.375–1.376	1.375–1.376	1.375–1.376	1.375–1.376	1.375–1.376	0.002–0.004	0.005–0.013
	3	6-3.0L	NA	NA	NA	NA	NA	—	NA
	R	6-3.3L	1.997–1.999	1.980–1.982	1.965–1.96	1.949–1.952	—	0.001–0.005	0.005–0.012
1993	K	4-2.5L	1.375–1.376	1.375–1.376	1.375–1.376	1.375–1.376	1.375–1.376	0.002–0.004	0.005–0.013
	3	6-3.0L	NA	NA	NA	NA	NA	—	NA
	R	6-3.3L	1.997–1.999	1.980–1.982	1.965–1.96	1.949–1.952	—	0.001–0.005	0.005–0.012
1994	K	4-2.5L	1.375–1.376	1.375–1.376	1.375–1.376	1.375–1.376	1.375–1.376	0.002–0.004	0.005–0.013
	3	6-3.0L	NA	NA.	NA	NA	NA	—	NA
	R	6-3.3L	1.997–1.999	1.980–1.982	1.965–1.96	1.949–1.952	—	0.001–0.005	0.005–0.012
	L	6-3.8L	1.997–1.999	1.980–1.982	1.965–1.96	1.949–1.952	—	0.001–0.005	0.005–0.012

85613C03

CRANKSHAFT AND CONNECTING ROD SPECIFICATIONS

| Year | VIN | Engine No. Cyl. Liters | Crankshaft | | | | Connecting Rod | | |
			Main Brg. Journal Dia.	Main Brg. Oil Clearance	Shaft End-play	Thrust on No.	Journal Diameter	Oil Clearance	Side Clearance
1984	C	4-2.2L	2.3630–2.3630	0.0003–0.0031	0.002–0.007	3	1.9680–1.9690	0.0008–0.0034	0.005–0.013
	G	4-2.6L	2.3622	0.0008–0.0028	0.002–0.007	3	2.0866	0.0008–0.0028	0.004–0.010
1985	C	4-2.2L	2.3630–2.3630	0.0003–0.0031	0.002–0.007	3	1.9680–1.9690	0.0008–0.0034	0.005–0.013
	G	4-2.6L	2.3622	0.0008–0.0028	0.002–0.007	3	2.0866	0.0008–0.0028	0.004–0.010
1986	C	4-2.2L	2.3630–2.3630	0.0003–0.0031	0.002–0.007	3	1.9680–1.9690	0.0008–0.0034	0.005–0.013
	G	4-2.6L	2.3622	0.0008–0.0028	0.002–0.007	3	2.0866	0.0008–0.0028	0.004–0.010
1987	C	4-2.2L	2.3630–2.3630	0.0003–0.0031	0.002–0.007	3	1.9680–1.9690	0.0008–0.0034	0.005–0.013
	K	4-2.5L	2.3630–2.3630	0.0003–0.0031	0.002–0.007	3	1.9680–1.9690	0.0008–0.0034	0.005–0.013
	G	4-2.6L	2.3622	0.0008–0.0028	0.002–0.007	3	2.0866	0.0008–0.0028	0.004–0.010
	3	6-3.0L	2.3610–2.3630	0.0006–0.0020	0.002–0.010	3	1.9680–1.9690	0.0008–0.0028	0.004–0.010
1988	K	4-2.5L	2.3630–2.3630	0.0003–0.0031	0.002–0.007	3	1.9680–1.9690	0.0008–0.0034	0.005–0.013
	3	6-3.0L	2.3610–2.3630	0.0006–0.0020	0.002–0.010	3	1.9680–1.9690	0.0008–0.0028	0.004–0.010
1989	K	4-2.5L	2.3630–2.3630	0.0003–0.0031	0.002–0.007	3	1.9680–1.9690	0.0008–0.0034	0.005–0.013
	J	4-2.5L	2.3630–2.3630	0.0003–0.0031	0.002–0.007	3	1.9680–1.9690	0.0008–0.0034	0.005–0.013
	3	6-3.0L	2.3610–2.3630	0.0006–0.0020	0.002–0.010	3	1.9680–1.9690	0.0008–0.0028	0.004–0.010
1990	K	4-2.5L	2.3630–2.3630	0.0003–0.0031	0.002–0.007	3	1.9680–1.9690	0.0008–0.0034	0.005–0.013
	J	4-2.5L	2.3630–2.3630	0.0003–0.0031	0.002–0.007	3	1.9680–1.9690	0.0008–0.0034	0.005–0.013
	3	6-3.0L	2.3610–2.3630	0.0006–0.0020	0.002–0.010	3	1.9680–1.9690	0.0008–0.0028	0.004–0.010
	R	6-3.3L	2.5190	0.0007–0.0022	0.001–0.007	2	2.2830	0.0008–0.0030	0.005–0.015
1991	K	4-2.5L	2.3630–2.3630	0.0003–0.0031	0.002–0.007	3	1.9680–1.9690	0.0008–0.0034	0.005–0.013
	3	6-3.0L	2.3610–2.3630	0.0006–0.0020	0.002–0.010	3	1.9680–1.9690	0.0008–0.0028	0.004–0.010
	R	6-3.3L	2.5190	0.0007–0.0022	0.001–0.007	2	2.2830	0.0008–0.0030	0.005–0.015
1992	K	4-2.5L	2.3620–2.3630	0.0004–0.0028	0.002–0.007	3	1.9680–1.9690	0.0008–0.0034	0.005–0.013
	3	6-3.0L	2.3610–2.3630	0.0006–0.0020	0.002–0.010	3	1.9680–1.9690	0.0008–0.0028	0.004–0.010
	R	6-3.3L	2.5190	0.0004–0.0028	0.003–0.009	2	2.2830	0.0008–0.0030	0.005–0.015
1993	K	4-2.5L	2.3620–2.3630	0.0004–0.0028	0.002–0.007	3	1.9680–1.9690	0.0008–0.0034	0.005–0.013
	3	6-3.0L	2.3610–2.3630	0.0006–0.0020	0.002–0.010	3	1.9680–1.9690	0.0008–0.0028	0.004–0.010
	R	6-3.3L	2.5190	0.0004–0.0028	0.003–0.009	2	2.2830	0.0008–0.0030	0.005–0.015
1994	K	4-2.5L	2.3620–2.3630	0.0004–0.0028	0.002–0.007	3	1.9680–1.9690	0.0008–0.0034	0.005–0.013
	3	6-3.0L	2.3610–2.3630	0.0006–0.0020	0.002–0.010	3	1.9680–1.9690	0.0008–0.0028	0.004–0.010
	R	6-3.3L	2.5190	0.0004–0.0028	0.003–0.009	2	2.2830	0.0008–0.0030	0.005–0.015
	L	6-3.8L	2.5190	0.0007–0.0030	0.004–0.012	2	2.2830	0.0007–0.0030	0.005–0.015

85613C04

PISTON AND RING SPECIFICATIONS

Year	VIN	Engine No. Cyl. Liters	Piston Clearance	Ring Gap			Ring Side Clearance		
				Top Compression	Bottom Compression	Oil Control	Top Compression	Bottom Compression	Oil Control
1984	C	4-2.2L	0.0005–0.0015	0.0110–0.0120	0.0110–0.0120	0.0160–0.0550	0.0016–0.0028	0.0008–0.0020	0.0008–0.0020
	G	4-2.6L	0.0008–0.0016	0.0100–0.0180	0.0100–0.0180	0.0078–0.0350	0.0015–0.0031	0.0015–0.0037	—
1985	C	4-2.2L	0.0005–0.0015	0.0110–0.0120	0.0110–0.0120	0.0160–0.0550	0.0016–0.0028	0.0008–0.0020	0.0008–0.0020
	G	4-2.6L	0.0008–0.0016	0.0100–0.0180	0.0100–0.0180	0.0078–0.0350	0.0015–0.0031	0.0015–0.0037	—
1986	C	4-2.2L	0.0005–0.0015	0.0110–0.0120	0.0110–0.0120	0.0160–0.0550	0.0016–0.0028	0.0008–0.0020	0.0008–0.0020
	G	4-2.6L	0.0008–0.0016	0.0100–0.0180	0.0100–0.0180	0.0078–0.0350	0.0015–0.0031	0.0015–0.0037	—
1987	C	4-2.2L	0.0005–0.0015	0.0110–0.0120	0.0110–0.0120	0.0160–0.0550	0.0016–0.0028	0.0008–0.0020	0.0008–0.0020
	K	4-2.5L	0.0005–0.0015	0.0110–0.0120	0.0100–0.0120	0.0160–0.0550	0.0016–0.0028	0.0008–0.0020	0.0008–0.0020
	G	4-2.6L	0.0005–0.0015	0.0110–0.0120	0.0100–0.0120	0.0160–0.0550	0.0016–0.0028	0.0008–0.0020	0.0008–0.0020
	3	6-3.0L	0.0008–0.0015	0.0120–0.0180	0.0100–0.0160	0.0120–0.0350	0.0020–0.0035	0.0008–0.0020	—
1988	K	4-2.5L	0.0005–0.0015	0.0110–0.0120	0.0100–0.0120	0.0160–0.0550	0.0016–0.0028	0.0008–0.0020	0.0008–0.0020
	3	6-3.0L	0.0008–0.0015	0.0120–0.0180	0.0100–0.0160	0.0120–0.0350	0.0020–0.0035	0.0008–0.0020	—
1989	K	4-2.5L	0.0005–0.0015	0.0110–0.0120	0.0100–0.0120	0.0160–0.0550	0.0016–0.0028	0.0008–0.0020	0.0008–0.0020
	J	4-2.5L	0.0006–0.0018	0.0100–0.0200	0.0080–0.0190	0.0150–0.0550	0.0016–0.0030	0.0016–0.0030	0.0002–0.0080
	3	6-3.0L	0.0008–0.0015	0.0120–0.0180	0.0100–0.0160	0.0120–0.0350	0.0020–0.0035	0.0008–0.0020	—
1990	K	4-2.5L	0.0005–0.0015	0.0110–0.0120	0.0100–0.0120	0.0160–0.0550	0.0016–0.0028	0.0008–0.0020	0.0008–0.0020
	J	4-2.5L	0.0006–0.0018	0.0100–0.0200	0.0080–0.0190	0.0150–0.0550	0.0016–0.0030	0.0016–0.0030	0.0002–0.0080
	3	6-3.0L	0.0008–0.0015	0.0120–0.0180	0.0100–0.0160	0.0120–0.0350	0.0020–0.0035	0.0008–0.0020	—
	R	6-3.3L	0.0009–0.0022	0.0120–0.0220	0.0120–0.0220	0.0100–0.0400	0.0012–0.0037	0.0012–0.0037	0.0005–0.0089
1991	K	4-2.5L	0.0005–0.0015	0.0110–0.0120	0.0100–0.0120	0.0160–0.0550	0.0016–0.0028	0.0008–0.0020	0.0008–0.0020
	3	6-3.0L	0.0008–0.0015	0.0120–0.0180	0.0100–0.0160	0.0120–0.0350	0.0020–0.0035	0.0008–0.0020	—
	R	6-3.3L	0.0009–0.0022	0.0120–0.0220	0.0120–0.0220	0.0100–0.0400	0.0012–0.0037	0.0012–0.0037	0.0005–0.0089

85613C05

Standard Torque Specifications and Fastener Markings

In the absence of specific torques, the following chart can be used as a guide to the maximum safe torque of a particular size/grade of fastener.
• There is no torque difference for fine or coarse threads.
• Torque values are based on clean, dry threads. Reduce the value by 10% if threads are oiled prior to assembly.
• The torque required for aluminum components or fasteners is considerably less.

U.S. Bolts

Bolt Size (Inches)—(Thread)	1 or 2 Ft./Lbs.	Kgm	Nm	5 Ft./Lbs.	Kgm	Nm	6 or 7 Ft./Lbs.	Kgm	Nm
¼ — 20	5	0.7	6.8	8	1.1	10.8	10	1.4	13.5
— 28	6	0.8	8.1	10	1.4	13.6			
5/16 — 18	11	1.5	14.9	17	2.3	23.0	19	2.6	25.8
— 24	13	1.8	17.6	19	2.6	25.7			
3/8 — 16	18	2.5	24.4	31	4.3	42.0	34	4.7	46.0
— 24	20	2.75	27.1	35	4.8	47.5			
7/16 — 14	28	3.8	37.0	49	6.8	66.4	55	7.6	74.5
— 20	30	4.2	40.7	55	7.6	74.5			
½ — 13	39	5.4	52.8	75	10.4	101.7	85	11.75	115.2
— 20	41	5.7	55.6	85	11.7	115.2			
9/16 — 12	51	7.0	69.2	110	15.2	149.1	120	16.6	162.7
— 18	55	7.6	74.5	120	16.6	162.7			
5/8 — 11	83	11.5	112.5	150	20.7	203.3	167	23.0	226.5
— 18	95	13.1	128.8	170	23.5	230.5			
¾ — 10	105	14.5	142.3	270	37.3	366.0	280	38.7	379.6
— 16	115	15.9	155.9	295	40.8	400.0			
7/8 — 9	160	22.1	216.9	395	54.6	535.5	440	60.9	596.5
— 14	175	24.2	237.2	435	60.1	589.7			
1 — 8	236	32.5	318.6	590	81.6	799.9	660	91.3	894.8
— 14	250	34.6	338.9	660	91.3	849.8			

Metric Bolts

Bolt Size Thread Size x Pitch (mm)	4.6, 4.8 Ft./Lbs.	Kgm	Nm	8.8 Ft./Lbs.	Kgm	Nm
6 x 1.0	2–3	.2–.4	3–4	3–6	.4–.8	5–8
8 x 1.25	6–8	.8–1	8–12	9–14	1.2–1.9	13–19
10 x 1.25	12–17	1.5–2.3	16–23	20–29	2.7–4.0	27–39
12 x 1.25	21–32	2.9–4.4	29–43	35–53	4.8–7.3	47–72
14 x 1.5	35–52	4.8–7.1	48–70	57–85	7.8–11.7	77–110
16 x 1.5	51–77	7.0–10.6	67–100	90–120	12.4–16.5	130–160
18 x 1.5	74–110	10.2–15.1	100–150	130–170	17.9–23.4	180–230
20 x 1.5	110–140	15.1–19.3	150–190	190–240	26.2–46.9	160–320
22 x 1.5	150–190	22.0–26.2	200–260	250–320	34.5–44.1	340–430
24 x 1.5	190–240	26.2–46.9	260–320	310–410	42.7–56.5	420–550

85613034

Engine

▶ See Figures 29, 30, 31, 32, 33, 34, 35, 36, 37, 38, 39 and 40

REMOVAL & INSTALLATION

Engine Removal and Installation procedures are similar on all models.

1. Disconnect the negative battery cable.
2. Scribe the hood hinge outlines on the hood, and remove the hood.
3. Drain the cooling system. Remove the radiator hoses from the radiator and engine connections.

✳✳CAUTION

When draining the coolant, keep in mind that cats and dogs are attracted by the ethylene glycol antifreeze, and are quite likely to drink any that is left in an uncovered container or in puddles on the ground. This will prove fatal in sufficient quantity. Always drain the coolant into a sealable container. Coolant should be reused unless it is contaminated or several years old.

4. Remove the radiator and fan assembly.
5. Remove the air conditioner compressor from the engine and mounting brackets and hoses connected. Position the assembly to the side and secure out of the way.
6. Remove the power steering pump from the engine with mounting brackets and hoses connected. Position the assembly to the side and secure out of the way.
7. Disconnect all electrical connectors at the alternator, carburetor, injection unit and engine.
8. Disconnect the fuel line from the gas tank at the fuel pump. Disconnect the heat hoses from the engine. Disconnect the accelerator cable at the carburetor.
9. Remove the alternator. Disconnect the clutch cable from the clutch lever, if equipped with a manual transaxle.
10. Remove the transaxle case lower cover.

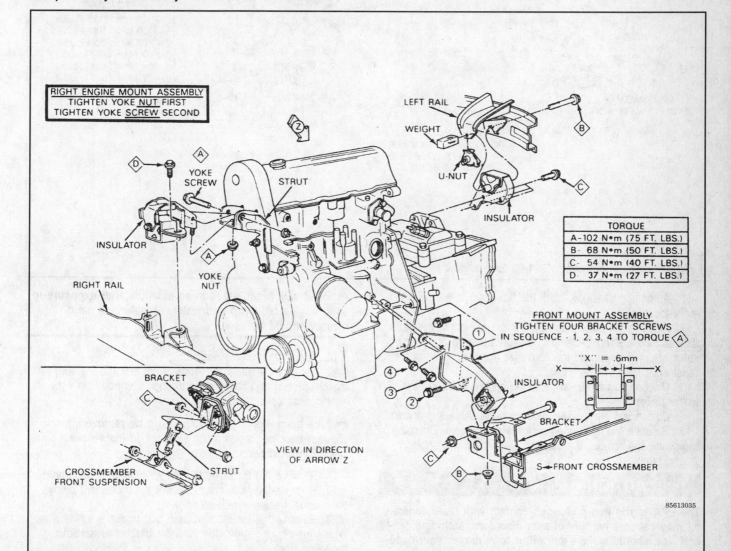

TORQUE	
A-	102 N•m (75 FT. LBS.)
B-	68 N•m (50 FT. LBS.)
C-	54 N•m (40 FT. LBS.)
D-	37 N•m (27 FT. LBS.)

85613035

Fig. 29 Engine mounting, 1989-90 2.5L engine

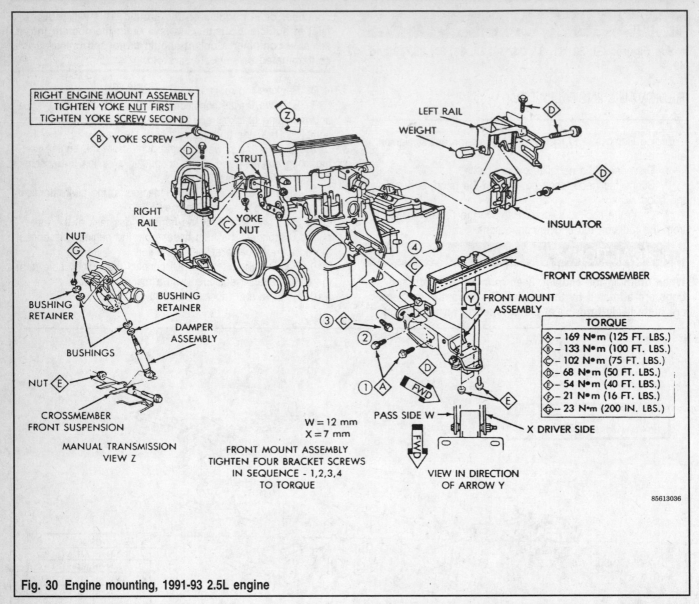

Fig. 30 Engine mounting, 1991-93 2.5L engine

11. Automatic transaxle, mark the flex plate to torque converter location.

12. Remove the bolts that mount the converter to the flex plate. Attach a small C-clamp to the front bottom of the converter housing to prevent the converter from falling off of the transaxle.

13. Disconnect the starter motor wiring and remove the starter motor.

14. Disconnect the exhaust pipe from the exhaust manifold.

15. Remove the right inner engine splash shield. Drain the engine oil and remove the oil filter. Disconnect the engine ground strap.

✷✷CAUTION

The EPA warns that prolonged contact with used engine oil may cause a number of skin disorders, including cancer! You should make every effort to minimize your exposure to used engine oil. Protective gloves should be worn when changing the oil. Wash your hands and any other exposed skin areas as soon as possible after exposure to used engine oil. Soap and water, or waterless hand cleaner should be used.

16. Attach hoist to the engine.

17. Support the transaxle. Apply slight upward pressure with the chain hoist and remove the through bolt from the right (timing case cover) engine mount.

➡**If the complete engine mount is to be removed, mark the insulator position on the side rail to insure exact reinstallation location.**

18. Remove the transaxle to cylinder block mounting bolts.

19. Remove the front engine mount through bolt. Remove the manual transaxle anti-roll strut.

20. Remove the insulator through bolt from the inside wheel house mount, or remove the insulator bracket to transaxle mounting bolt.

21. Raise the engine slowly with the hoist (transaxle supported). Separate the engine and transaxle and remove the engine.

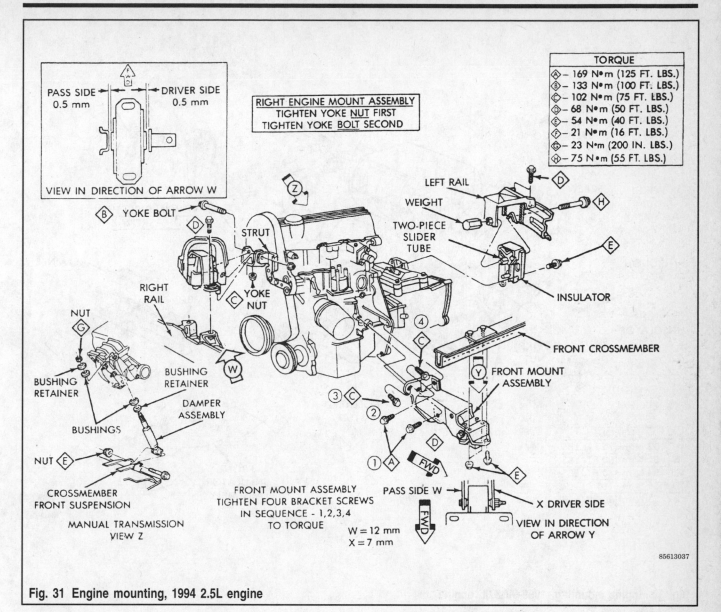

Fig. 31 Engine mounting, 1994 2.5L engine

To install:

22. With the hoist attached to the engine. Lower the engine into engine compartment.

23. Align the converter to flex plate and the engine mounts. Install all mounting bolts loosely until all are in position, then tighten to 40 ft. lbs.

24. Install the engine to transaxle mounting bolts. Tighten to 70 ft. lbs. for the 2.2L, 2.5L 3.0L engines and 75 ft. lbs. for the 3.3L and 3.8L engines.

25. Remove the engine hoist and transaxle support.

26. Secure the engine ground strap.

27. Install the inner splash shield.

28. Install the starter assembly.

29. Install the exhaust system.

30. Install the transaxle case lower cover. (Manual Transaxle)

31. Remove the C-clamp from the torque converter housing, (Automatic Transaxle).

32. Align flex plate and torque converter with mark previously made. (Automatic Transaxle).

33. Install the convertor to flex plate mounting screws. Tighten to (40 ft. lbs.).

34. Install the case lower cover. (Automatic Transaxle).

35. Connect the clutch cable. (Manual Transaxle)

36. Install the power steering pump.

37. Install the air conditioning compressor.

38. Install the alternator.

39. Connect all wiring.

40. Install the radiator, fan and shroud assembly.

41. Connect all cooling system hoses, accelerator cable and fuel lines.

42. Install the engine oil filter. Fill the crankcase to proper oil level.

43. Fill the cooling system.

44. Adjust linkages.

45. Install the air cleaner and hoses.

46. Install the hood.

47. Connect the battery cables, positive cable first.

48. Start the engine and run until normal operation temperature is indicated. Adjust the carburetor.

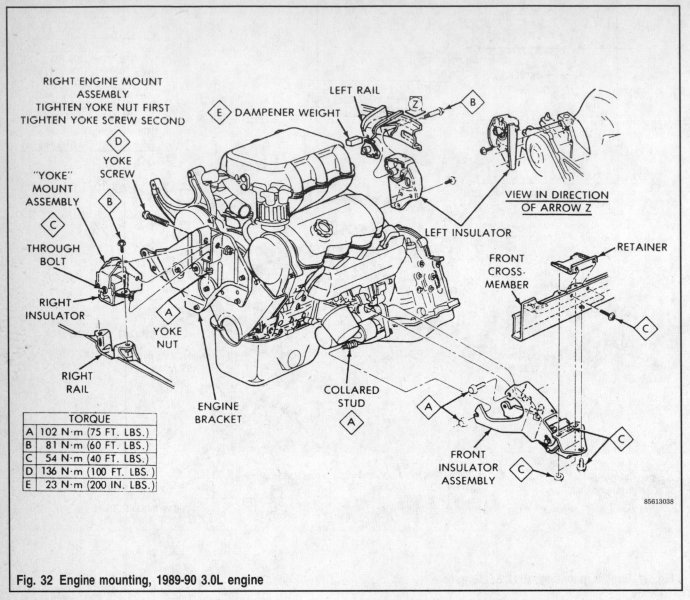

TORQUE		
A	102 N·m	(75 FT. LBS.)
B	81 N·m	(60 FT. LBS.)
C	54 N·m	(40 FT. LBS.)
D	136 N·m	(100 FT. LBS.)
E	23 N·m	(200 IN. LBS.)

85613038

Fig. 32 Engine mounting, 1989-90 3.0L engine

ENGINE/TRANSAXLE POSITIONING

The insulator on the frame rail (right side) and on the transmission bracket (left side) are adjustable to allow right/left drive train adjustment in relation to the driveshaft distress, front end damage or insulator replacement.

Adjustment

1. Remove the load on the engine mounts by carefully supporting the weight of the engine/transaxle assembly on a floor jack.
2. Loosen the right engine mount insulator vertical mounting bolts and the front engine mount bracket to cross member mounting nuts and bolts. The left insulator is sleeved to provide lateral movement.
3. Pry the engine/transaxle assembly to the left or right as required.
4. Tighten the right engine mount insulator vertical bolts to 20 ft. lbs. (29 Nm) for 1984-87 models, 27 ft. lbs. (37 Nm) for 1989-93 models and 50 ft. lbs. (68 Nm) for 1994. Tighten the center left engine mount insulator.

Solid Mount Compressor Bracket

REMOVAL & INSTALLATION

2.2L and 2.5 Engine
▶ See Figure 41

➡When service procedures require solid mount bracket removal and installation such as timing belt removal, it is important that the bracket fasteners numbered 1 through 7 be removed and installed in sequence.

1. Remove the drive belts.
2. Remove the air conditioner compressor with lines attached and set aside.
3. Remove the alternator pivot bolt and remove the alternator.

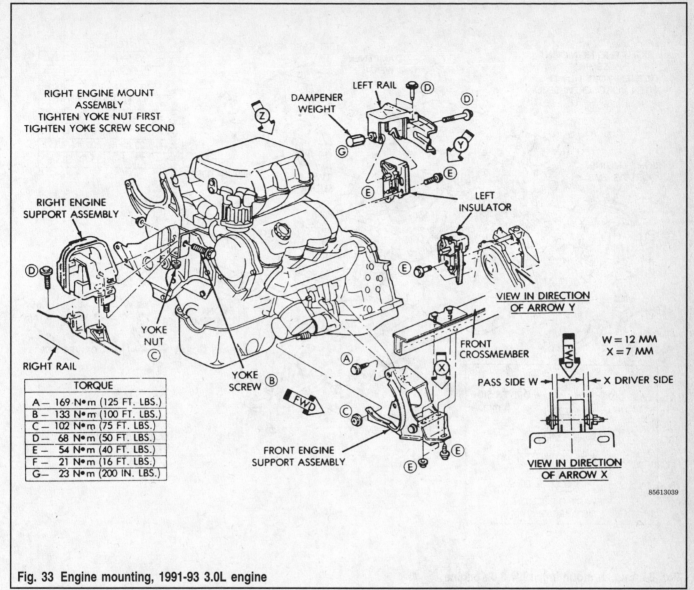

RIGHT ENGINE MOUNT
ASSEMBLY
TIGHTEN YOKE NUT FIRST
TIGHTEN YOKE SCREW SECOND

LEFT RAIL

DAMPENER
WEIGHT

LEFT
INSULATOR

RIGHT ENGINE
SUPPORT ASSEMBLY

RIGHT RAIL

YOKE
NUT
C

YOKE
SCREW   B

FRONT ENGINE
SUPPORT ASSEMBLY

VIEW IN DIRECTION
OF ARROW Y

FRONT
CROSSMEMBER

VIEW IN DIRECTION
OF ARROW X

W = 12 MM
X = 7 MM

PASS SIDE W   X DRIVER SIDE

TORQUE	
A —	169 N•m (125 FT. LBS.)
B —	133 N•m (100 FT. LBS.)
C —	102 N•m (75 FT. LBS.)
D —	68 N•m (50 FT. LBS.)
E —	54 N•m (40 FT. LBS.)
F —	21 N•m (16 FT. LBS.)
G —	23 N•m (200 IN. LBS.)

85613039

Fig. 33 Engine mounting, 1991-93 3.0L engine

4. Remove the air conditioner compressor belt idler.

5. Remove the right engine mount yoke screw securing the isolator support bracket to the engine mount bracket.

6. Remove the five side mounting bolts No. 1, 4, 5, 6 and 7.

7. Remove the front mounting nut No. 2 and remove or loosen front bolt No. 3.

8. Rotate the solid mount bracket away from the engine and slide on stud (No. 2 nut mounting stud) until free. The front mounting bolt and spacer will be removed with the bracket.

To install:

➡ The front mounting bolt and spacer need to be installed simultaneously.

9. Install the bracket on front No. 2 nut mounting stud) and slide the bracket over the timing belt cover into position.

10. Loosen the assembly bracket to engine fasteners No. 1 through 7.

11. The fasteners must be tighten to the specified torque and in the sequence as follows:

   a. First Bolt No. 1 to 30 inch lbs. (30 Nm).

   b. Second Nut No. 2 and Bolt No 3 to 40 ft. lbs. (54 Nm).

   c. Third Bolts No. 1 (second tightening) No. 4 and No. 5 to 40 ft. lbs. (54 Nm).

   d. Fourth Bolts No. 6 and No. 7 to 40 ft. lbs. (54 Nm). Install the alternator and compressor and tighten the compressor mounting bolts to 40 ft. lbs. (54 Nm).

Rocker (Valve) Cover

REMOVAL & INSTALLATION

2.2L Engine

▶ See Figures 42, 43, 44, 45, 46, 47, 48, 49, 50 and 51

1. Disconnect the negative battery cable.

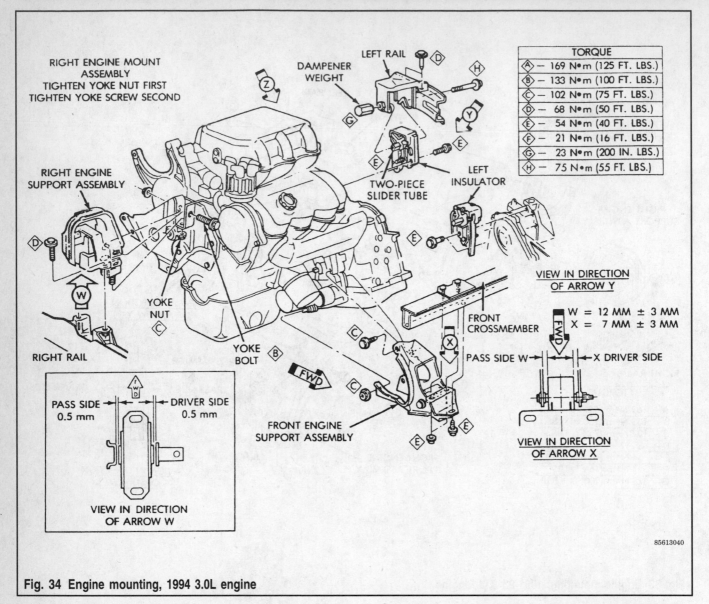

RIGHT ENGINE MOUNT ASSEMBLY
TIGHTEN YOKE NUT FIRST
TIGHTEN YOKE SCREW SECOND

DAMPENER WEIGHT

LEFT RAIL

RIGHT ENGINE SUPPORT ASSEMBLY

TWO-PIECE SLIDER TUBE

LEFT INSULATOR

	TORQUE
A	169 N•m (125 FT. LBS.)
B	133 N•m (100 FT. LBS.)
C	102 N•m (75 FT. LBS.)
D	68 N•m (50 FT. LBS.)
E	54 N•m (40 FT. LBS.)
F	21 N•m (16 FT. LBS.)
G	23 N•m (200 IN. LBS.)
H	75 N•m (55 FT. LBS.)

YOKE NUT

YOKE BOLT

RIGHT RAIL

FRONT CROSSMEMBER

FRONT ENGINE SUPPORT ASSEMBLY

VIEW IN DIRECTION OF ARROW Y

W = 12 MM ± 3 MM
X = 7 MM ± 3 MM

PASS SIDE W — X DRIVER SIDE

VIEW IN DIRECTION OF ARROW X

PASS SIDE 0.5 mm — DRIVER SIDE 0.5 mm

VIEW IN DIRECTION OF ARROW W

85613040

Fig. 34 Engine mounting, 1994 3.0L engine

2. Remove the air cleaner assembly. Remove or relocate any hoses or cables that will interfere with rocker cover removal.

3. Depress the retaining clip that holds the PCV module in the rocker cover and turn the module counterclockwise to remove the module.

4. Remove the upper timing belt cover upper and lower retaining bolts.

➡ **As the timing belt cover is lifted up a few inches the inside plastic ear of the cover will sometimes get caught on the pulley. Use a suitable tool to pry the ear away as the cover is being removed.**

5. Remove the upper cover from the engine.

6. At the other end of the valve cover, remove the air pump cover retaining bolts and remove the air pump pulley cover cover from the engine.

7. Carefully remove the rocker cover from the cylinder head.

8. Clean the cover and head mounting surfaces. Install the PCV module in rocker cover. Turn clockwise to install.

➡ **With PCV module installed, snorkel must point upward, toward top of valve cover. Snorkel should be free to rotate.**

9. Apply RTV sealant to the rocker cover mounting rail, or install a new cover gasket if provided.

10. Install the rocker cover and tighten to 105 inch lbs.

11. Install both front and rear belt covers.

12. Install the vacuum hoses and spark plug wires.

13. Install the air cleaner assembly.

14. Connect the battery cable.

2.5L Engine

▶ **See Figure 52**

A curtain aiding air/oil separation is located beneath the rocker cover on the cylinder head. The curtain is retained by rubber bumpers.

1. Disconnect the negative battery cable.

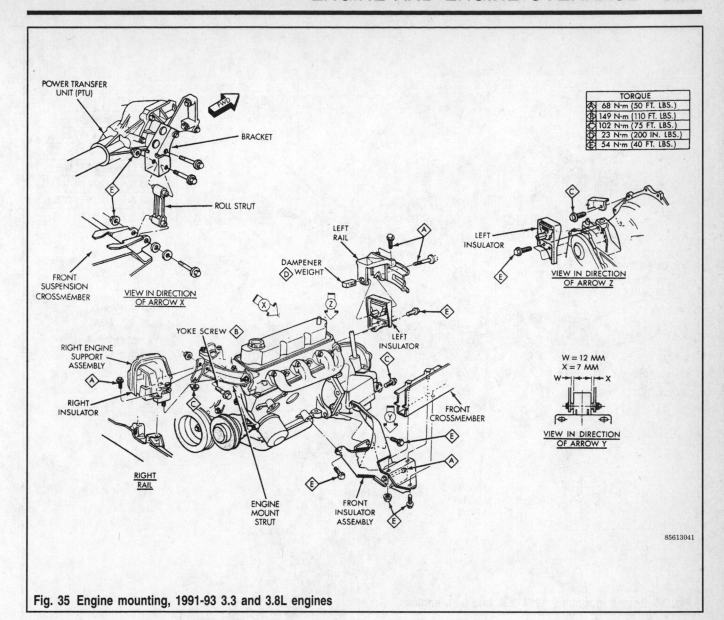

TORQUE	
Ⓐ	68 N·m (50 FT. LBS.)
Ⓑ	149 N·m (110 FT. LBS.)
Ⓒ	102 N·m (75 FT. LBS.)
Ⓓ	23 N·m (200 IN. LBS.)
Ⓔ	54 N·m (40 FT. LBS.)

Fig. 35 Engine mounting, 1991-93 3.3 and 3.8L engines

2. Remove the air cleaner assembly.

3. Remove any vacuum hoses necessary and relocate spark plug wires.

4. Remove the cover screws and remove the cover.

5. Remove the air/oil separation curtain.

6. Clean the cylinder head, curtain and cover mating surfaces before installation.

7. Install a gasket on the valve cover while pushing the tabs through slots in cover.

8. Install the curtain (manifold side first) with cutouts over cam towers and against cylinder head. Press opposite side into position below the cylinder head rail.

9. Install the cover and tighten to 105 inch lbs..

10. Install the vacuum hoses and spark plug wires.

11. Install the air cleaner assembly.

12. Connect the battery cable.

2.6L Engine

▶ See Figure 53

1. Disconnect the negative battery cable.

2. Remove the air cleaner assembly. Remove or relocate any hoses or cables that will interfere with rocker cover removal.

3. Disconnect the hoses to the PCV tube.

4. Remove the cover mounting bolts and remove the rocker cover from the cylinder head. The water pump pulley belt shield is attached at rear of rocker cover.

5. Clean the cover and head mounting surfaces.

6. Apply RTV sealant to the top of the rubber cam seal and install the rocker cover.

7. With rocker cover installed, apply RTV sealant to top of semi-circular packing.

8. Tighten screws to 55 inch lbs..

9. Install the vacuum hoses and spark plug wires.

10. Install the air cleaner assembly.

11. Connect the battery cable.

3.0L Engine

▶ See Figure 54

1. Disconnect the negative battery cable.

2. Remove the air cleaner assembly.

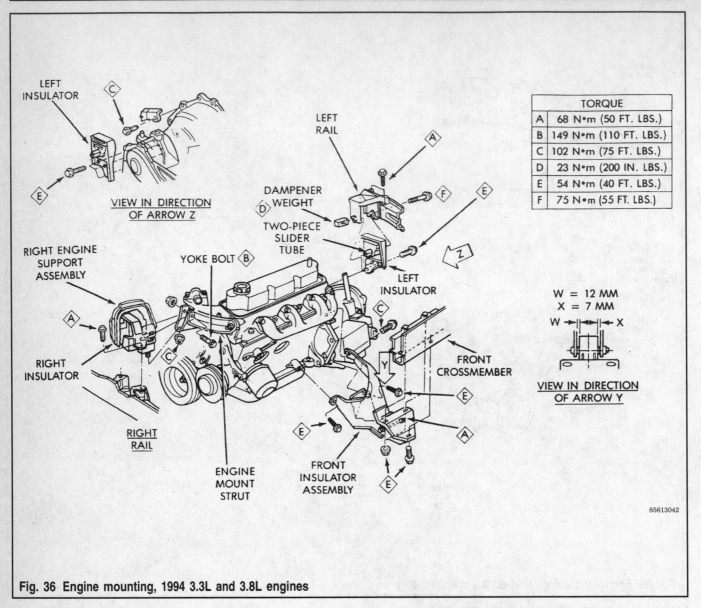

TORQUE	
A	68 N•m (50 FT. LBS.)
B	149 N•m (110 FT. LBS.)
C	102 N•m (75 FT. LBS.)
D	23 N•m (200 IN. LBS.)
E	54 N•m (40 FT. LBS.)
F	75 N•m (55 FT. LBS.)

W = 12 MM
X = 7 MM

VIEW IN DIRECTION OF ARROW Y

Fig. 36 Engine mounting, 1994 3.3L and 3.8L engines

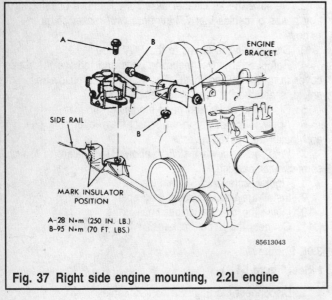

A-28 N•m (250 IN. LB.)
B-95 N•m (70 FT. LBS.)

Fig. 37 Right side engine mounting, 2.2L engine

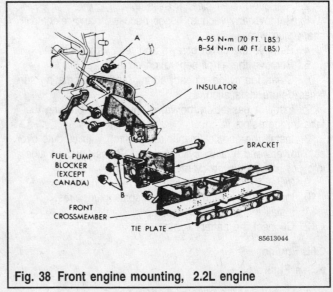

A-95 N•m (70 FT. LBS.)
B-54 N•m (40 FT. LBS.)

Fig. 38 Front engine mounting, 2.2L engine

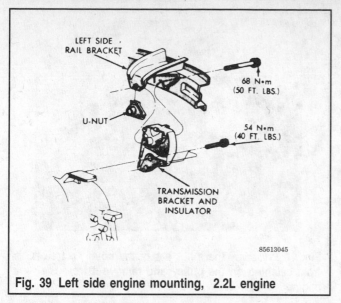

Fig. 39 Left side engine mounting, 2.2L engine

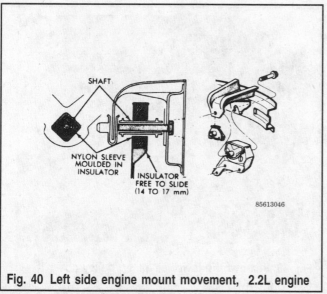

Fig. 40 Left side engine mount movement, 2.2L engine

Fig. 42 Depress the retaining clip to release the PCV module

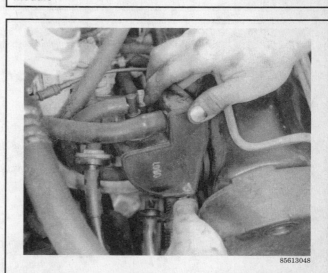

Fig. 43 Rotate the PCV module counterclockwise to remove from the valve cover

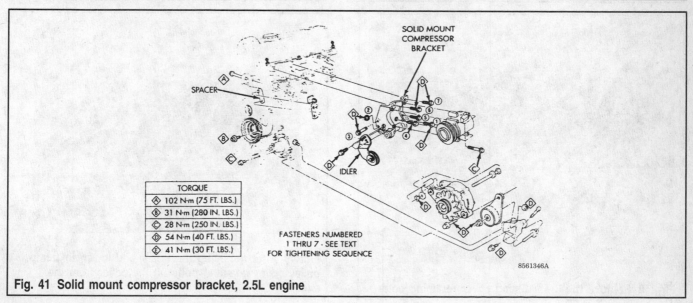

Fig. 41 Solid mount compressor bracket, 2.5L engine

Fig. 44 The PCV module shown disconnected from the valve cover

Fig. 47 Pry away the inner ear of the cover to free it from catching on the pulley and remove it from the engine

Fig. 45 Remove the upper timing cover/valve cover retaining bolts

Fig. 48 Remove the lower air pump pulley cover retaining bolts

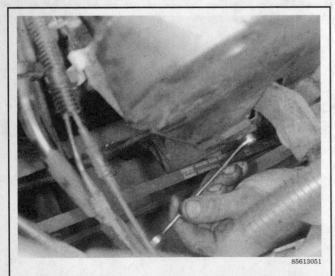

Fig. 46 Remove the lower timing cover retaining bolts

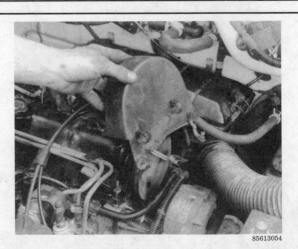

Fig. 49 After removing the upper and lower air pump pulley cover retaining bolts lift the cover from the engine

Fig. 50 Carefully lift the rocker cover from the cylinder head

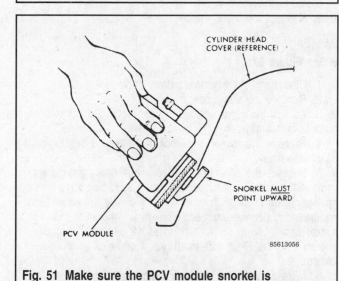

Fig. 51 Make sure the PCV module snorkel is positioned correctly during installation, 2.2L engine

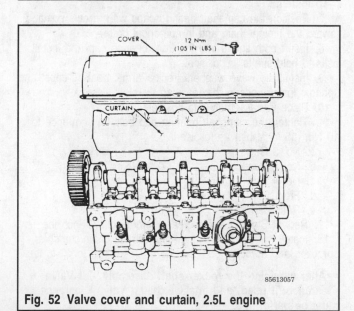

Fig. 52 Valve cover and curtain, 2.5L engine

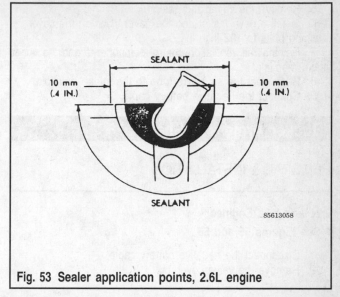

Fig. 53 Sealer application points, 2.6L engine

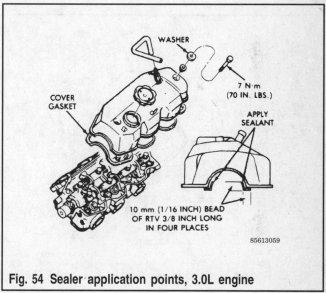

Fig. 54 Sealer application points, 3.0L engine

3. Remove any vacuum hoses necessary and relocate spark plug wires.

4. Remove the cover screws and remove cover.

5. Clean the cylinder head and cover mating surfaces before installation.

6. Install a new gasket. Apply RTV sealant to cover ends.

7. Install the cover and tighten to 68 inch lbs.

8. Install the vacuum hoses and spark plug wires.

9. Install the air cleaner assembly.

10. Connect the battery cable.

3.3L and 3.8L Engines

1. Disconnect the negative battery cable.

2. Remove the air intake tube and disconnect it from the intake manifold.

3. Remove the upper intake manifold, disconnecting any hoses or wires.

4. Remove the spark plug wires. Disconnect the closed ventilation system and evaporation control from the valve cover.

5. Remove the cover and gasket.

6. Install a new gasket and the cover. Tighten the cover retaining bolts to 102 inch lbs.

7. Reinstall all ventilation control components and the upper intake manifold.

8. Reconnect the air intake tube to the intake manifold.

9. Connect the negative battery cable.

Rocker Arms and Shafts

REMOVAL & INSTALLATION

2.2L and 2.5L Engines

▶ **See Figures 55 and 56**

1. Disconnect the negative battery cable.
2. Remove the valve cover.

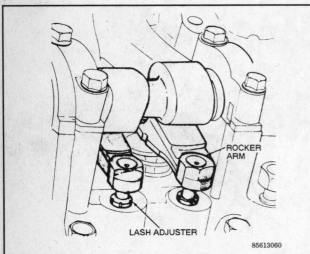

Fig. 55 Rocker arm and lash adjuster, 2.2L and 2.5L engines

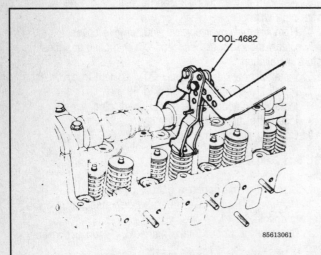

Fig. 56 Compressing a valve spring, 2.2L and 2.5L engines

3. Rotate the camshaft until the lobe base is on the rocker arm that is to be removed.

4. Slightly depress the valve spring using Chrysler tool-4682 or the equivalent. Slide the rocker off the lash adjuster and valve tip and remove. Label the rocker arms for position identification. Proceed to next rocker arm and repeat Steps 3 and 4.

5. Remove the lash adjuster if servicing is necessary.

To install:

6. If the lash adjuster was previously removed, partially fill with oil and install.

7. Rotate the camshaft until lobe base is in position with rocker arm. Slightly depress the valve spring using Chrysler tool 4682 or equivalent. Slide rocker arm in position.

➡**When depressing the valve spring with Chrysler tool 4682, or the equivalent, the valve locks can become dislocated. Check and make sure both locks are fully seated in the valve grooves and retainer.**

8. Install the valve cover.
9. Connect the battery cable.

2.6L Engine

▶ **See Figure 57**

1. Disconnect the negative battery cable.
2. Remove the valve cover.
3. Loosen the camshaft bearing cap bolts. Do not remove bolts from bearing cap.
4. Remove the rocker arm, rocker shafts and bearing caps as an assembly.
5. Remove the bolts from the camshaft bearing caps and remove the rocker shafts, waved washers, rocker arms and springs. Keep all parts in order. Note the way the rocker shaft, rocker arms, bearing caps and springs are mounted. The rocker arm shaft on the Left side has 12 oil holes at shaft bottom, and the Right side shaft has 4 oil holes at shaft bottom.
6. Inspect the rocker arms mounting area and rockers for damage. Replace if worn or heavily damaged.

To install:

7. Position the camshaft bearing caps with arrows pointing toward the timing chain and in numerical order.

8. Insert both shafts into the front bearing cap and install bolts to hold shafts in position.

9. Install the wave washers, rocker arms, bearing caps, and springs. Install bolts in the rear cap to retain assembly.

10. Place the assembly into position.

11. Tighten the camshaft bearing cap bolts in sequence to 10 Nm (85 inch lbs.) as followed:
    a. No. 3 Cap
    b. No. 2 Cap
    c. No. 4 Cap
    d. Front Cap
    e. Rear Cap

12. Repeat Step 12 and increase torque to 175 inch lbs.

13. Install the distributor drive gear, timing chain/camshaft sprocket, and sprocket bolt. Torque sprocket bolt to 40 ft. lbs.

➡**After servicing the rocker shaft assembly, Jet Valve Clearance (if used) and Intake/Exhaust Valve Clearance must be performed.**

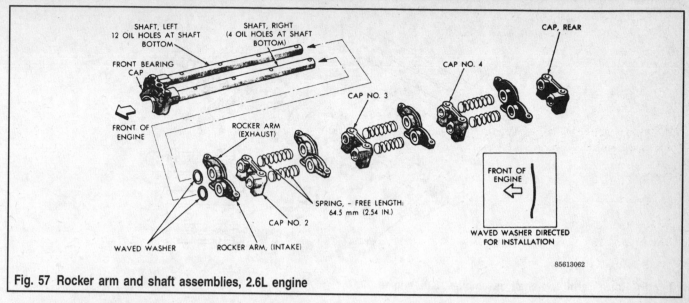

Fig. 57 Rocker arm and shaft assemblies, 2.6L engine

14. Install the water pump (upper shield) and valve cover.
15. Connect the battery cable.

3.0L Engine

▶ See Figures 58, 59, 60 and 61

1. Disconnect the negative battery cable.
2. Remove the valve cover.
3. Loosen the camshaft bearing cap bolts. Do not remove bolts from bearing cap.
4. Remove the rocker arm, rocker shafts and bearing caps as an assembly.
5. Remove the bolts from the camshaft bearing caps and remove the rocker shafts and arms. Keep all parts in order. Note the way the rocker shaft, rocker arms, bearing caps and springs are mounted. The rocker arm shaft on the Intake side has a 3mm diameter oil passage hole from the cylinder head. The exhaust side does not have this oil passage.
6. Inspect the rocker arm mounting area and rocker for damage. Replace if worn or heavily damaged.

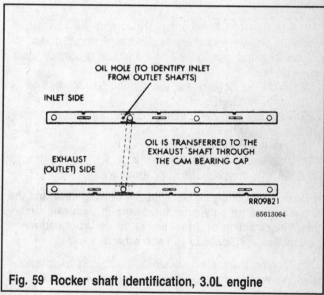

Fig. 59 Rocker shaft identification, 3.0L engine

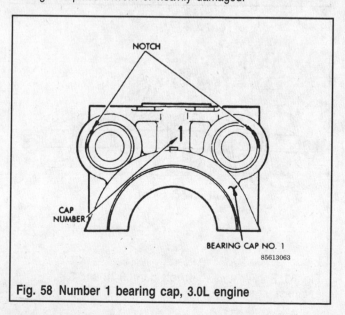

Fig. 58 Number 1 bearing cap, 3.0L engine

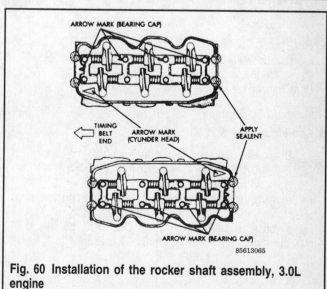

Fig. 60 Installation of the rocker shaft assembly, 3.0L engine

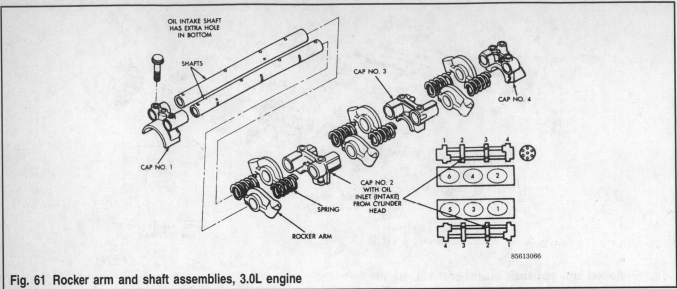

Fig. 61 Rocker arm and shaft assemblies, 3.0L engine

To install:

7. Identify No. 1 bearing cap, (No. 1 and No. 4 caps are similar). Install the rocker shafts into the bearing cap with notches in proper position. Insert the attaching bolts to retain assemble.

8. Install the rocker arms, springs and bearing caps on shafts in numerical sequence.

9. Align the camshaft bearing caps with arrows (depending on cylinder bank).

10. Install the bolts in number 4 cap to retain assembly.

11. Apply sealant at bearing cap ends.

12. Install the rocker arm shaft assembly.

➥Make sure the arrow mark on the bearing caps and the arrow mark on the cylinder heads are in the same direction. The direction of arrow marks on the front and rear assemblies are opposite to each other.

13. Tighten the bearing caps bolts to 85 inch lbs. in the following manner:
   a. No. 3 Cap
   b. No. 2 Cap
   c. No. 1 Cap
   d. No. 4 Cap

14. Repeat Step 13 increasing torque to 180 inch lbs.

15. Install the valve cover.

16. Connect the battery cable.

3.3L and 3.8L Engines

▶ See Figures 62 and 63

1. Disconnect the negative battery cable.

2. Remove the upper intake manifold assembly.

3. Remove the rocker arm cover.

4. remove the 4 rocker shaft retaining bolts and retainers.

5. remove the rocker arms and shaft assembly.

6. If you are disassembling the rocker shaft, be sure to install the rocker arms in their original locations.

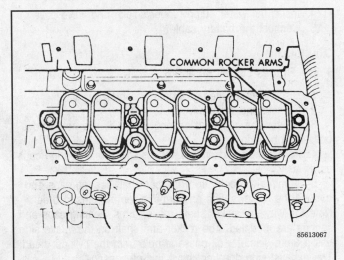

Fig. 62 Left bank rocker shaft assembly, 3.3L and 3.8L engines

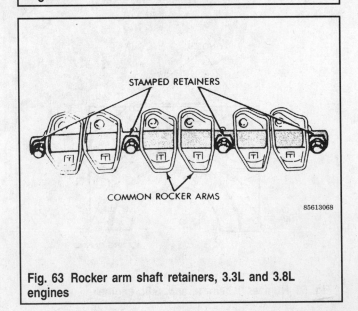

Fig. 63 Rocker arm shaft retainers, 3.3L and 3.8L engines

To install:

7. Install the rocker arm and shaft assembly, using the 4 retainers. Tighten the retaining bolts to 250 inch lbs. (28 Nm).

➡**The rocker arm shaft should be torqued down slowly, starting with the center bolts. Allow 20 minutes for tappet bleed down after installation, before engine operation.**

8. Install the rocker cover.
9. Install the crankcase ventilation components and connect the spark plug wires.
10. Install the upper intake manifold assembly. Connect the negative battery cable.

Thermostat

REMOVAL & INSTALLATION

◆ **See Figures 64, 65, 66, 67, 68, 69, 70 and 71**

The thermostat is located in a water box at the side of the engine (facing grille) 2.2L and 2.5L engines. The thermostat on 2.6L, 3.0L, 3.3L and 3.8L engines is located in a water box at the timing belt end of the intake manifold.

1. Drain the cooling system to a level below the thermostat.

❋❋CAUTION

When draining the coolant, keep in mind that cats and dogs are attracted by the ethylene glycol antifreeze, and are quite likely to drink any that is left in an uncovered container or in puddles on the ground. This will prove fatal in sufficient quantity. Always drain the coolant into a sealable container. Coolant should be reused unless it is contaminated or several years old.

2. Remove the hoses from the thermostat housing.
3. Remove the thermostat housing.
4. Remove the thermostat and discard the gasket. Clean the gasket surfaces thoroughly.

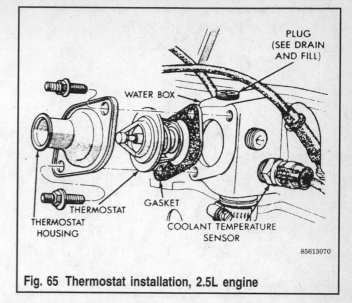

Fig. 65 Thermostat installation, 2.5L engine

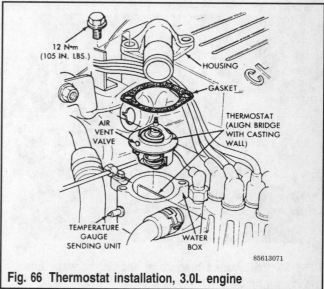

Fig. 66 Thermostat installation, 3.0L engine

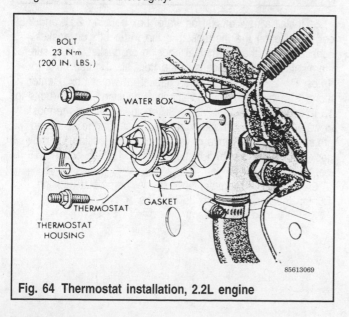

Fig. 64 Thermostat installation, 2.2L engine

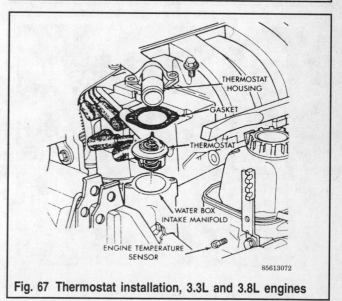

Fig. 67 Thermostat installation, 3.3L and 3.8L engines

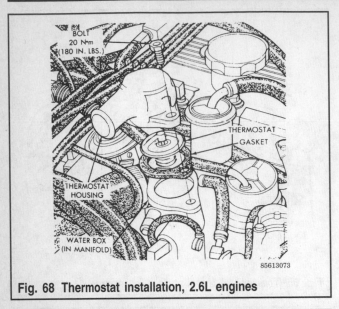

Fig. 68 Thermostat installation, 2.6L engines

Fig. 69 Removing a thermostat housing to water box retaining bolt

Fig. 70 Removing the thermostat housing

Fig. 71 Removing the thermostat from the water box

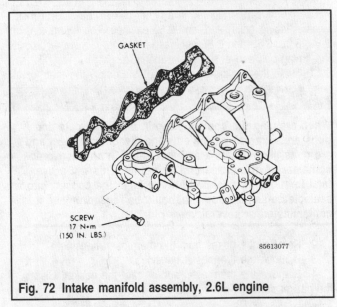

Fig. 72 Intake manifold assembly, 2.6L engine

5. Install a new gasket on water box housing 2.2L and 2.5L engines. Center the thermostat in the water box on gasket surface. Install the thermostat housing on gasket. Make sure thermostat sits in its recess of the housing. Tighten bolts to 15 ft. lbs. On 2.6L engine position gasket on water box. Center thermostat in water box and attached housing. Tighten bolts to 15 ft. lbs. On 3.0L, 3.3L and 3.8L engines position thermostat in water box pocket. Make sure thermostat flange in seated properly in flange groove of the water box. Position the new gasket on water box and install housing. Tighten bolts to 15 ft. lbs.

6. Connect the radiator hose to the thermostat housing. Tighten the hose clamp to 35 inch lbs.

7. Fill the cooling system.

Intake Manifold

REMOVAL & INSTALLATION

2.6L Engine

▶ See Figure 72

1. Disconnect the negative battery cable.
2. Drain the cooling system and disconnect the hoses from the water pump to the intake manifold.

✳✳CAUTION

When draining the coolant, keep in mind that cats and dogs are attracted by the ethylene glycol antifreeze, and are quite likely to drink any that is left in an uncovered container or in puddles on the ground. This will prove fatal in sufficient quantity. Always drain the coolant into a sealable container. Coolant should be reused unless it is contaminated or several years old.

3. Disconnect the carburetor air horn adapter and move to one side.
4. Disconnect the vacuum hoses and throttle link,age from the carburetor.
5. Disconnect the fuel inlet line at the fuel filter.
6. Remove the fuel filter and fuel pump and move to one side.
7. Remove the intake manifold retaining nuts and washers and remove the manifold.
8. Remove old gasket. Clean cylinder head and manifold gasket surface. Check for cracks or warpage. Install a new gasket on cylinder head.
9. Install manifold to cylinder head. Install washers and nuts. Refer to Torque Specification Chart.
10. Install the fuel pump and filter.
11. Install the carburetor air horn.
12. Install the throttle control cable.
13. Install the cooling system hose from water pump to manifold.
14. Install the vacuum hoses.
15. Connect the negative battery cable.

3.0L Engine

▶ See Figures 73, 74 and 80

1. Release fuel system pressure.
2. Disconnect the negative battery cable.
3. Drain the cooling system.

✳✳CAUTION

When draining the coolant, keep in mind that cats and dogs are attracted by the ethylene glycol antifreeze, and are quite likely to drink any that is left in an uncovered container or in puddles on the ground. This will prove fatal in sufficient quantity. Always drain the coolant into a sealable container. Coolant should be reused unless it is contaminated or several years old.

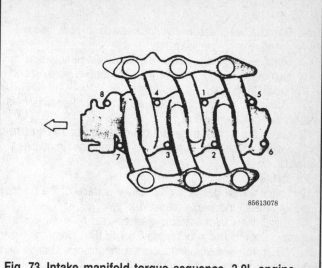

Fig. 73 Intake manifold torque sequence, 3.0L engine

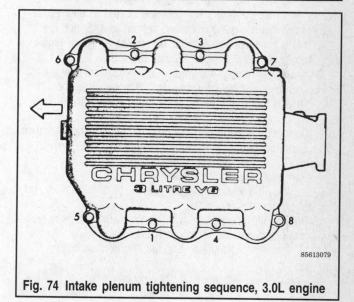

Fig. 74 Intake plenum tightening sequence, 3.0L engine

4. Remove the air cleaner.
5. Remove the throttle cable and transaxle kickdown cable.
6. Remove the electrical and vacuum connections from throttle body.
7. Remove the air intake hose from air cleaner to throttle body.
8. Remove the EGR tube to intake plenum.
9. Remove the electrical connection from charge temperature and coolant temperature sensor.
10. Remove the vacuum connection from the pressure regulator and remove the air intake connection from the manifold.
11. Remove fuel hoses to fuel rail connection.
12. Remove the air intake plenum to manifold bolts (8) and remove air intake plenum and gasket.

✳✳WARNING

Whenever the air intake plenum is removed, cover the intake manifold properly to avoid objects from entering cylinder head.

13. Disconnect the fuel injector wiring harness from the engine wiring harness.

14. Remove the pressure regulator attaching bolts and remove pressure regulator from rail.

15. Remove the fuel rail attaching bolts and remove fuel rail.

16. Remove the radiator hose from thermostat housing and heater hose from pipe.

17. Remove the intake manifold attaching nuts and washers and remove intake manifold.

18. Clean the gasket material from cylinder head and manifold gasket surface. Check for cracks or damaged mounting surfaces.

To install:

19. Install a new gasket on the intake surface of the cylinder head and install the intake manifold.

20. Install the intake manifold washers and nuts. Tighten in sequence shown. Refer to Torque Specification Chart.

21. Clean the injectors and lubricate the injector O-rings with a drop of clean engine oil.

22. Place the tip of each injector into their ports. Push assembly into place until the injectors are seated in their ports.

23. Install rail attaching bolts and tighten to 115 inch lbs.

24. Install pressure regulator to rail. Install pressure regulator mounting bolts and tighten to 95 inch lbs.

25. Install fuel supply and return tube holddown bolt and vacuum crossover tube holddown bolt. Torque to 95 inch lbs.

26. Torque fuel pressure regulator hose clamps to 10 inch lbs.

27. Connect injector wiring harness to engine wiring harness.

28. Connect vacuum harness to fuel rail and pressure regulator.

29. Remove covering from intake manifold.

30. Position the intake manifold gasket, beaded side up, on the intake manifold.

31. Put the air intake plenum in place. Install attaching bolts and tighten in sequence to 115 inch lbs.

32. Connect the fuel line to fuel rail. Tighten clamps to 10 inch lbs.

33. Connect the vacuum hoses to intake plenum.

34. Connect the electrical connection to coolant temperature sensor and charge temperature sensor.

35. Connect the EGR tube flange to intake plenum and torque to 15 ft. lbs.

36. Connect the throttle body vacuum hoses and electrical connections.

37. Install the throttle cable and transaxle kickdown linkage.

38. Install the radiator and heater hose. Fill the cooling system.

39. Connect the negative battery cable.

3.3L and 3.8L Engines

▶ **See Figures 75, 76, 77 and 78**

1. Disconnect the negative battery cable.

2. Relieve the fuel pressure as outlined in the beginning of Section One under Routine Maintenance.

3. Drain the cooling system.

4. Remove the air cleaner to throttle body hose assembly.

5. Disconnect the throttle cable and remove the wiring harness from the bracket.

6. Remove AIS motor and TPS wiring connectors from the throttle body.

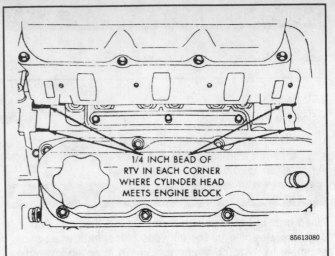

Fig. 75 Intake manifold gasket sealing, 3.3L and 3.8L engines

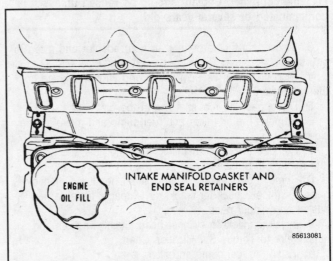

Fig. 76 Intake manifold gasket retainers, 3.3L and 3.8L engines

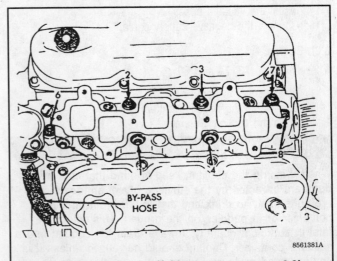

Fig. 77 Lower intake manifold torque sequence, 3.3L and 3.8L engines

Fig. 78 Upper intake manifold torque sequence, 3.3L and 3.8L engines

7. Remove the vacuum hose harness from the throttle body.

8. Remove the PCV and brake booster hoses from the air intake plenum.

9. Disconnect the charge temperature sensor electrical connector. Remove the vacuum harness connectors from the intake plenum.

10. Remove the cylinder head to the intake plenum strut.

11. Disconnect the MAP sensor and oxygen sensor connectors. Remove the engine mounted ground strap.

12. Remove the fuel hoses from the fuel rail and plug them.

13. Remove the DIS coils and the alternator bracket to intake manifold bolt.

14. Remove the upper intake manifold attaching bolts and remove the upper manifold.

15. Remove the vacuum harness connector from the fuel pressure regulator.

16. Remove the fuel tube retainer bracket screw and fuel rail attaching bolts. Spread the retainer bracket to allow for clearance when removing the fuel tube.

17. Remove the fuel rail injector wiring clip from the alternator bracket.

18. Disconnect the cam sensor, coolant temperature sensor and engine temperature sensor.

19. Remove the fuel rail.

20. Remove the upper radiator hose, bypass hose and rear intake manifold hose.

21. Remove the intake manifold bolts and remove the manifold from the engine.

22. Remove the intake manifold seal retaining screws and remove the manifold gasket.

23. Clean out clogged end water passages and fuel runners.

To install:

24. Clean and dry all gasket mating surfaces.

25. Place a drop of approximately ¼ inch diameter of silicone sealant onto each of the 4 manifold to cylinder head gasket corners.

✳✳CAUTION

The intake manifold gasket is made of very thin material and could cause personal injury.

26. Carefully install the intake manifold gasket and torque the end seal retainer screws to 105 inch lbs. (12 Nm).

27. Install the intake manifold and 8 retaining bolts and torque to 10 inch lbs. (1 Nm). Then torque the bolts to 200 inch lbs. (22 Nm) in the sequence shown.

28. When the bolts are torqued, inspect the seals to ensure that they have not become dislodged.

29. Lubricate the injector O-rings with clean oil to ease installation. Put the tip of each injector into their ports and position the fuel rail in place. Install the rail mounting bolts and tighten to 200 inch lbs. (22 Nm) .

30. Connect the cam sensor, coolant temperature sensor and engine temperature sensor.

31. Install the fuel injector harness wiring clip to the alternator bracket.

32. Install the vacuum harness to the pressure regulator.

33. Install the upper intake manifold with a new gasket. Install the bolts only finger tight. Install the alternator bracket to intake manifold bolt and the cylinder head to intake manifold strut and bolts. Torque the intake manifold mounting bolts to 250 inch lbs. (28 Nm) starting from the middle and working outward in the sequence shown. Torque the bracket and strut bolts to 40 ft. lbs. (54 Nm).

34. Install or connect all items that were removed or disconnected from the intake manifold and throttle body.

35. Connect the fuel hoses to the rail. Push the fittings in until they click in place.

36. Install the air cleaner assembly.

37. Connect the negative battery cable and check for leaks using the DRB I or II to activate the fuel pump.

Exhaust Manifold

REMOVAL & INSTALLATION

2.6L Engine

◗ **See Figure 79**

1. Disconnect the negative battery cable.

2. Remove the air cleaner assembly.

3. Remove the belt from the power steering pump.

4. Raise the vehicle and make sure it is supported safely.

5. Remove the exhaust pipe from the manifold.

6. Disconnect the air injection tube assembly from the exhaust manifold and lower the vehicle.

7. Remove the power steering pump assembly and move to one side.

8. Remove the heat cowl from the exhaust manifold.

9. Remove the exhaust manifold retaining nuts and remove the assembly from the vehicle.

10. Remove the carburetor air heater from the manifold.

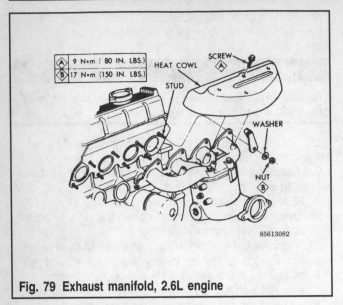

A 9 N•m (80 IN. LBS.)
B 17 N•m (150 IN. LBS.)

HEAT COWL   SCREW A
STUD
WASHER
NUT B

85613082

Fig. 79 Exhaust manifold, 2.6L engine

11. Separate the exhaust manifold from the catalytic converter by removing the retaining screws.

12. Clean gasket material from cylinder head and exhaust manifold gasket surfaces. Check mating surfaces for cracks or distortion.

13. Install a new gasket between the exhaust manifold an catalytic converter. Install mounting screws and tighten to 32 Nm (24 ft. lbs.).

14. Install the carburetor air heater on manifold and tighten to 80 inch lbs.

15. Lightly coat the new exhaust manifold gasket with sealant (P/N 3419115) or equivalent on cylinder head side.

16. Install the exhaust manifold and mounting nuts. Refer to Torque Specification Chart.

17. Install the heat cowl to manifold and tighten screws to 80 inch lbs.

18. Install the air cleaner support bracket.

19. Install the power steering pump assembly.

20. Install the air injection tube assembly to air pump.

21. Raise the vehicle and install air injection tube assembly to exhaust manifold.

22. Install the exhaust pipe to manifold.

23. Lower the vehicle and install power steering belt.

24. Fill the cooling system.

25. Install the air cleaner assembly.

26. Connect the negative battery cable.

3.0L Engine

▶ See Figure 80

1. Disconnect the negative battery cable.

2. Raise vehicle and support properly.

3. Disconnect the exhaust pipe from rear (cowl side) exhaust manifold at articulated joint.

4. Remove the EGR tube from the rear manifold and disconnect oxygen sensor lead.

5. Remove the attaching bolts from crossover pipe to manifold.

6. Remove the attaching nuts which retained manifold to cylinder head and remove manifold.

7. Lower the vehicle and remove bolt securing front heat shield to front exhaust manifold.

8. Remove the bolts retaining crossover pipe to front exhaust manifold and nuts retaining manifold to cylinder head. Remove manifold assembly.

9. Clean all gasket material from cylinder the head and exhaust manifold gasket surfaces. Check mating surfaces for cracks or distortion.

10. Install the new gasket with the numbers 1-3-5 stamped on the top on the rear bank. The gasket with the numbers 2-4-6 must be installed on the front bank (radiator side).

11. Install rear exhaust manifold and tighten attaching nuts to 15 ft. lbs.

12. Install exhaust pipe to manifold and tighten shoulder bolts to 20 ft. lbs.

13. Install crossover pipe to manifold and tighten bolts to 69 Nm (51 ft. lbs.).

14. Install oxygen sensor lead and EGR tube.

15. Install front exhaust manifold and attach exhaust crossover.

16. Install front manifold heat shield and tighten bolts to 10 ft. lbs.

17. Connect the negative battery cable.

3.3L and 3.8L Engines

1. Disconnect the negative battery cable.

2. If removing the rear manifold, raise the vehicle and support safely. Disconnect the exhaust pipe at the articulated joint from the rear exhaust manifold.

3. Separate the EGR tube from the rear manifold and disconnect the oxygen sensor wire.

4. Remove the alternator/power steering support strut.

5. Remove the bolts attaching the crossover pipe to the manifold.

6. Remove the bolts attaching the manifold to the head and remove the manifold.

7. If removing the front manifold, remove the heat shield, bolts attaching the crossover pipe to the manifold and the nuts attaching the manifold to the head.

8. Remove the manifold from the engine.

9. The installation is the reverse of the removal procedure. Torque all exhaust manifold attaching bolts to 17 ft. lbs. (23 Nm).

10. Start the engine and check for exhaust leaks.

Combination Manifold

REMOVAL & INSTALLATION

2.2L and 2.5L Engines

WITHOUT TURBOCHARGER

▶ See Figures 81, 82, 83, 84, 85, 86 and 87

➡When removing the combination manifold some bolts are easier accessed from under the vehicle by reaching over the crossmember, others are accessed from under the hood. You will need an assortment of extensions and universals to remove the various bolts and nuts.

1. Disconnect the battery negative cable.

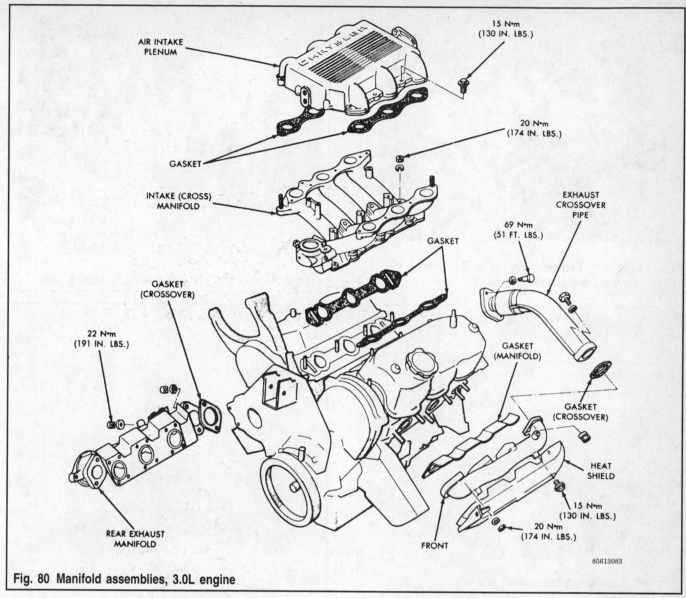

Fig. 80 Manifold assemblies, 3.0L engine

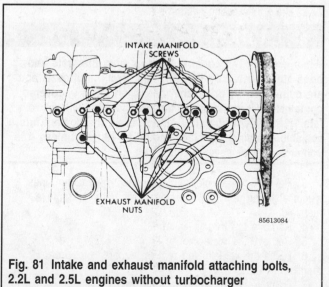

Fig. 81 Intake and exhaust manifold attaching bolts, 2.2L and 2.5L engines without turbocharger

Fig. 82 Disconnecting the throttle linkage bracket from the intake manifold (carburetor removed for viewing purposes)

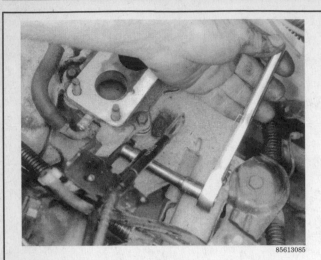

Fig. 83 Without disconnecting the hoses, remove the power steering pump and lay it aside

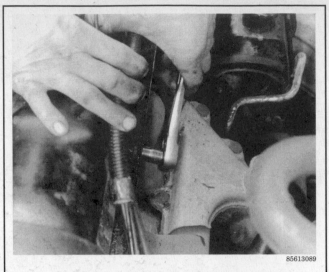

Fig. 86 Remove the exhaust manifold retaining bolts

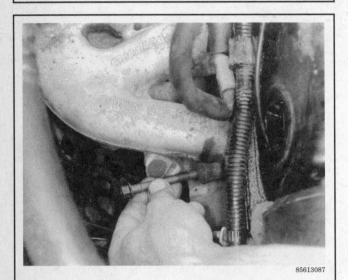

Fig. 84 Remove the intake manifold retaining bolts

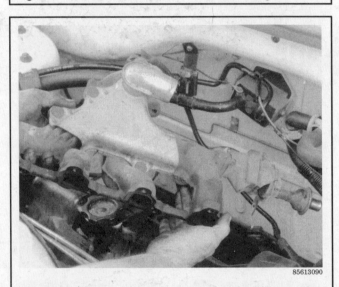

Fig. 87 Removing the exhaust manifold from the engine

2. Drain the cooling system.

✳✳CAUTION

When draining the coolant, keep in mind that cats and dogs are attracted by the ethylene glycol antifreeze, and are quite likely to drink any that is left in an uncovered container or in puddles on the ground. This will prove fatal in sufficient quantity. Always drain the coolant into a sealable container. Coolant should be reused unless it is contaminated or several years old.

3. Remove the air cleaner, disconnect all vacuum lines, electrical wiring and fuel lines from carburetor and intake manifold.
4. Remove the throttle linkage.
5. Remove the water hoses from water crossover.
6. Raise the vehicle and remove exhaust pipe from manifold.
7. Remove power steering pump and set aside.
8. Remove intake manifold support bracket and EGR tube.

Fig. 85 Removing the intake manifold from the engine

9. On Canadian cars remove (4) air injection tube bolts and injection tube assembly.

10. Remove the intake manifold retaining screws.

11. Lower vehicle and remove the intake manifold.

12. Remove exhaust manifold retaining nuts and remove exhaust manifold.

13. Clean gasket surface of both manifold and cylinder block surface.

14. Install a new gasket on exhaust and intake manifold. Coat manifold with Sealer (P/N 3419115) or equivalent on manifold side.

15. Position the exhaust manifold against cylinder block and install nuts. Tighten nuts from center while alternating outward in both direction. See Torque Specification Chart.

16. Position the intake manifold against cylinder head.

17. From beneath the vehicle tighten intake manifold screws. Start at the center while alternating outward in both direction. See Torque Specification Chart.

18. Install the exhaust pipe to exhaust manifold.

19. On Canadian cars install air injection tube assembly.

20. Install the intake manifold support bracket and EGR tube.

21. Install the power steering pump assembly and power steering belt.

22. Install the water hoses to water crossover.

23. Install the fuel lines, vacuum lines, and electrical wiring.

24. Fill the cooling system.

25. Connect the negative battery cable.

WITH TURBOCHARGER

▶ **See Figure 88**

➡**On some vehicles, some of the manifold attaching bolts are not accessible or too heavily sealed from the factory and cannot be removed on the vehicle. Head removal would be necessary in these situations.**

1. Disconnect the negative battery cable. Drain the cooling system. Raise and safely support the vehicle.

2. Disconnect the accelerator linkage, throttle body electrical connector and vacuum hoses.

3. Relocate the fuel rail assembly. Remove the bracket to intake manifold screws and the bracket to heat shield clips. Lift and secure the fuel rail (with injectors, wiring harness and fuel lines intact) up and out of the way.

4. Disconnect the turbocharger oil feed line at the oil sending unit Tee fitting.

5. Disconnect the upper radiator hose from the thermostat housing.

6. Remove the cylinder head, manifolds and turbocharger as an assembly.

7. With the assembly on a workbench, loosen the upper turbocharger discharge hose end clamp.

➡**Do not disturb the center deswirler retaining clamp.**

8. Remove the throttle body to intake manifold screws and throttle body assembly. Disconnect the turbocharger coolant return tube from the water box. Disconnect the retaining bracket on the cylinder head.

9. Remove the heat shield to intake manifold screws and the heat shield.

10. Remove the turbocharger to exhaust manifold nuts and the turbocharger assembly.

11. Remove the intake manifold bolts and the intake manifold.

12. Remove the exhaust manifold nuts and the exhaust manifold.

To install:

13. Place a new 2-sided Grafoil type intake/exhaust manifold gasket; do not use sealant.

14. Position the exhaust manifold on the cylinder head. Apply anti-seize compound to threads, install and torque the retaining nuts, starting at center and progressing outward in both directions, to 17 ft. lbs. (23 Nm). Repeat this procedure until all nuts are at 17 ft. lbs. (23 Nm).

15. Position the intake manifold on the cylinder head. Install and torque the retaining screws, starting at center and progressing outward in both directions, to 19 ft. lbs. (26 Nm). Repeat this procedure until all screws are at 19 ft. lbs. (26 Nm).

16. Connect the turbocharger outlet to the intake manifold inlet tube. Position the turbocharger on the exhaust manifold. Apply anti-seize compound to threads and torque the nuts to 30 ft. lbs. (41 Nm). Torque the connector tube clamps to 30 inch lbs. (41 Nm).

17. Install the tube support bracket to the cylinder head.

18. Install the heat shield on the intake manifold. Torque the screws to 105 inch lbs. (12 Nm).

19. Install the throttle body air horn into the turbocharger inlet tube. Install and torque the throttle body to intake manifold screws to 21 ft. lbs. (28 Nm). Torque the tube clamp to 30 inch lbs.

20. Install the cylinder head/manifolds/turbocharger assembly on the engine.

21. Reconnect the turbocharger oil feed line to the oil sending unit Tee fitting and bearing housing, if disconnected. Torque the tube nuts to 10 ft. lbs. (14 Nm).

22. Install the air cleaner assembly. Connect the vacuum lines and accelerator cables.

23. Reposition the fuel rail. Install and torque the bracket screws to 21 ft. lbs. (28 Nm). Install the air shield to bracket clips.

24. Connect the turbocharger inlet coolant tube to the engine block. Torque the tube nut to 30 ft. lbs. (41 Nm). Install the tube support bracket.

25. Install the turbocharger housing to engine block support bracket and the screws hand tight. Torque the block screw 1st to 40 ft. lbs. (54 Nm). Torque the screw to the turbocharger housing to 20 ft. lbs. (27 Nm).

26. Reposition the drain back hose connector and tighten the hose clamps. Reconnect the exhaust pi at the EGR valve.

Turbocharger

▶ **See Figure 88**

REMOVAL & INSTALLATION

2.5L Turbocharged Engine

1. Disconnect the negative battery cable. Drain the cooling system.

2. Disconnect the EGR valve tube at the EGR valve.

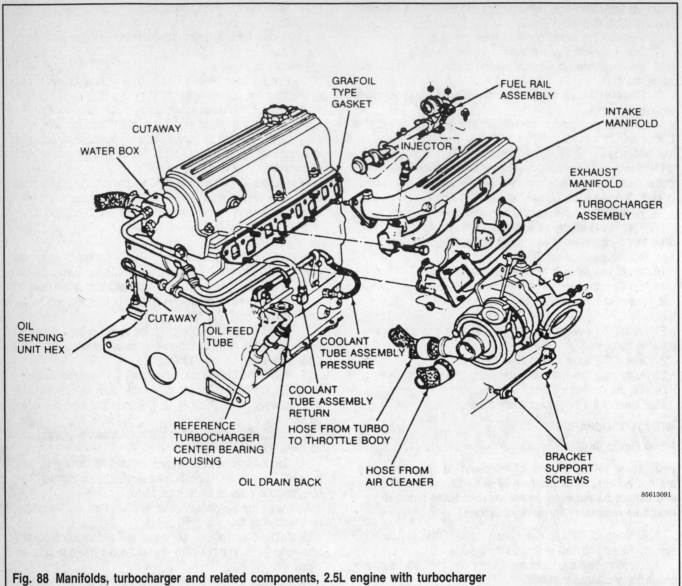

Fig. 88 Manifolds, turbocharger and related components, 2.5L engine with turbocharger

3. Disconnect the turbocharger oil feed at the oil sending unit hex and the coolant tube at the water box. Disconnect the oil/coolant support bracket from the cylinder head.

4. Remove the right intermediate shaft, bearing support bracket and outer drive shaft assemblies.

5. Remove the turbocharger to engine block support bracket.

6. Disconnect the exhaust pipe at the articulated joint. Disconnect the oxygen sensor at the electrical connection.

7. Loosen the oil drain-back tube connector clamps and move the tube hose down on the nipple.

8. Disconnect the coolant tube nut at the block outlet (below steering pump bracket) and tube support bracket.

9. Remove the turbocharger to exhaust manifold nuts. Carefully routing the oil and coolant lines, move the assembly down and out of the vehicle.

To Install:

➡Before installing the turbocharger assembly, be sure it is first charged with oil. Failure to do this may cause damage to the assembly.

10. Position the turbocharger on the exhaust manifold. Apply an anti-seize compound, Loctite® 771-64 or equivalent, to the threads and torque the retaining nuts to 40 ft. lbs. (54 Nm).

11. Connect the coolant tube to engine block fitting. Torque the tube nut to 30 ft. lbs. (41 Nm).

12. Position the oil drain-back hose and torque the clamps to 30 inch lbs.

13. Install and torque the:
   • Turbocharger to engine support bracket block screw to 40 ft. lbs. (54 Nm).
   • Turbocharger housing screw to 20 ft. lbs. (27 Nm).
   • Articulated joint shoulder bolts to 21 ft. lbs. (28 Nm).

14. Install the right drive shaft assembly, the starter and the oil feed line at the sending unit hex. Torque the oil feed tube nut to 10 ft. lbs. (14 Nm) and the EGR tube to EGR valve nut to 60 ft. lbs. (81 Nm).

15. Refill the cooling system. Connect the negative battery cable and check the turbocharger for proper operation.

Radiator

▶ See Figures 89, 90, 91, 92, 93, 94, 95, 96 and 97

REMOVAL & INSTALLATION

1. Disconnect the negative battery cable.
2. Drain the cooling system.

✳✳CAUTION

When draining the coolant, keep in mind that cats and dogs are attracted by the ethylene glycol antifreeze, and are quite likely to drink any that is left in an uncovered container or in puddles on the ground. This will prove fatal in sufficient quantity. Always drain the coolant into a sealable container. Coolant should be reused unless it is contaminated or several years old.

85613094

Fig. 90 Unscrew the upper radiator hose clamp at the radiator, 1987 2.2L shown

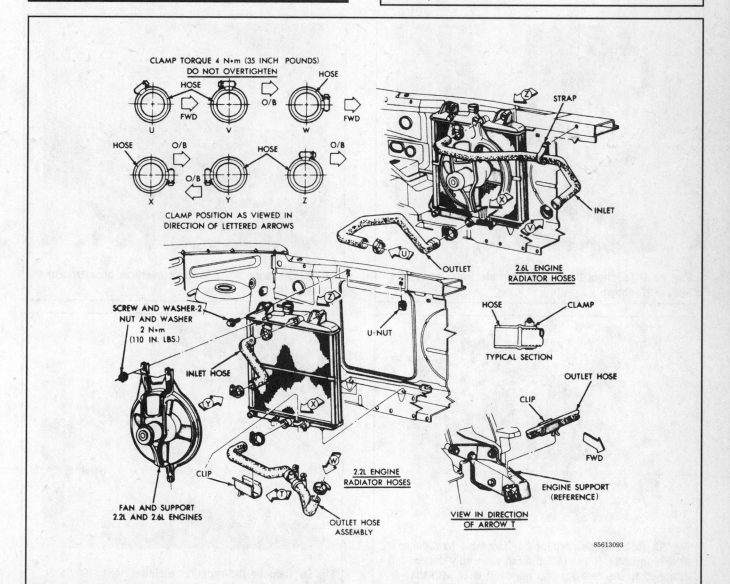

Fig. 89 Radiator mounting, 2.2L and 2.6L engines

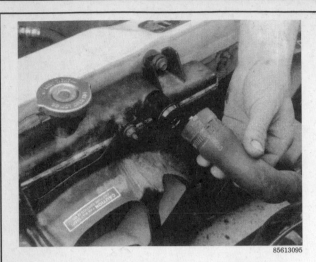

Fig. 91 Disconnect the upper radiator hose from the radiator, 1987 2.2L shown

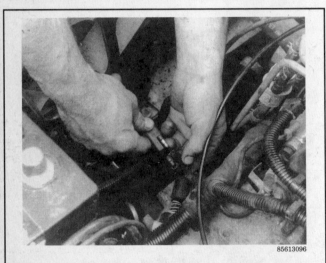

Fig. 92 Disconnect the radiator fan electrical connector, 1987 2.2L shown

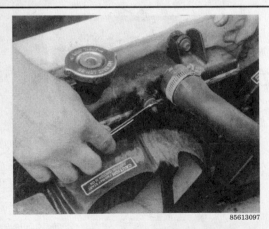

Fig. 93 Remove the radiator fan assembly to radiator attaching bolts. If desired, the fan assembly can be left attached to the radiator and removed later with the radiator out of the vehicle, 1987 2.2L shown

Fig. 94 Remove the radiator fan assembly from the vehicle, 1987 2.2L shown

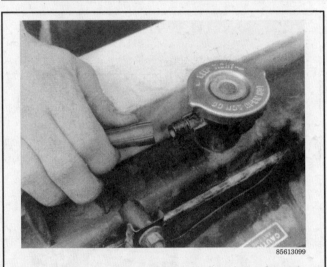

Fig. 95 Disconnect the radiator overflow hose from the radiator, 1987 2.2L shown

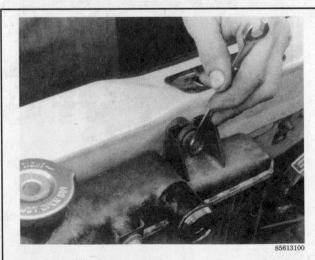

Fig. 96 Remove the radiator retaining bolts, 1987 2.2L shown

Fig. 97 Removing the radiator with the fan assembly attached from the vehicle, 1987 2.2L shown

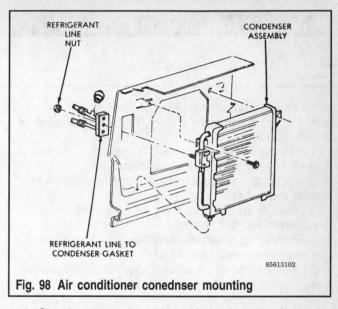

Fig. 98 Air conditioner conednser mounting

3. Remove the upper and lower hoses and coolant recovery tank tube to filler neck.
4. Disconnect the wiring harness from fan motor.
5. Remove the upper mounting bolts from fan assembly.
6. Lift fan assembly from bottom ring retaining clip.
7. Remove the radiator upper mounting bolts and carefully lift radiator from engine compartment.
8. Carefully slide the radiator into place while aligning radiator with holes in radiator support seat.
9. Install the upper radiator mounting bolts and tighten to 105 inch lbs.
10. Install the lower radiator hose and tighten to 35 inch lbs.
11. Carefully install the fan assembly while aligning lower fan support into retaining clip.
12. Attach washers and nuts to upper fan support.
13. Connect the fan electrical connector.
14. Install the upper radiator hose and tighten clamp to 35 inch lbs.
15. Fill the cooling system.

Air Conditioning Condenser

▶ **See Figure 98**

REMOVAL & INSTALLATION

1. Disconnect the negative battery cable.
2. Properly discharge the air conditioning system.
3. Remove the headlight bezels in order to gain access to the grille. Remove the grille assembly. A hidden screw fastens the grille to the center vertical support.
4. Remove the refrigerant lines attaching nut and separate the lines from the condenser sealing plate. Discard the gasket.
5. Cover the exposed ends of the lines to minimize contamination.
6. Remove the bolts that attach the condenser to the radiator support.
7. Remove the condenser from the vehicle.
To install:
8. Position the condenser and install the bolts.

9. Coat the new gasket with wax-free refrigerant oil and install. Connect the lines to the condenser sealing plate and tighten the nut.
10. Install the grille assembly.
11. Evacuate and recharge the air conditioning system. Add 1 oz. of refrigerant oil during the recharge.
12. Connect the negative battery cable and check the entire climate control system for proper operation and leaks.

Electric Cooling Fan

✳✳CAUTION

Make sure the key is in the OFF position when checking the electric cooling fan. If not, the fan could turn ON at any time, causing serious personal injury.

TESTING

1. Unplug the fan connector.
2. Using a jumper wire, connect the female terminal of the fan connector to the negative battery terminal.
3. The fan should turn on when the male terminal is connected to the positive battery terminal.
4. If not, the fan is defective and should be replaced.

REMOVAL & INSTALLATION

▶ **See Figures 92, 93 and 94**

1. Disconnect the negative battery cable.
2. Unplug the connector.
3. Remove the mounting screws.
4. Remove the fan assembly from the vehicle.
5. The installation is the reverse of the removal procedure.
6. Connect the negative battery cable and check the fan for proper operation.

Automatic Transmission Oil Cooler

REMOVAL & INSTALLATION

The transmission oil cooler used on these models are externally mounted ahead of the radiator. This is considered an oil-to-air type system.

1. Remove the electrical cooling fan assembly and remove radiator. Refer to Radiator Removal procedures.
2. Loosen the clamps retaining the hoses from the transmission cooler lines.
3. Place an oil drain pan under the hoses and remove hoses from the cooler assembly.
4. Remove (2) screws retaining the cooler assembly to support and remove cooler assembly.
5. If reusing the cooler assembly, reverse flush the cooler.
6. Position the cooler assembly against its support.
7. Install the cooler mounting bolts and tighten to 35 inch lbs.
8. Install hoses from the cooler lines to cooler assembly and tighten clamps to 16 inch lbs.
9. Install the radiator and cooling fan assembly. Refer to Radiator procedures previously outlined.

Water Pump

2.2L and 2.5L Engine

REMOVAL

▶ See Figure 99

1. Disconnect the negative battery cable.

2. Drain the cooling system.

✳✳CAUTION

When draining the coolant, keep in mind that cats and dogs are attracted by the ethylene glycol antifreeze, and are quite likely to drink any that is left in an uncovered container or in puddles on the ground. This will prove fatal in sufficient quantity. Always drain the coolant into a sealable container. Coolant should be reused unless it is contaminated or several years old.

➡Jack up the front of the vehicle, support on jack stands and remove the lower splash shield to access to the water pump and drive belts.

3. Remove the drive belts. (Refer to Section One).
4. Remove the upper radiator hose.
5. Without discharging the system, remove the air conditioning compressor from the engine mount and set to one side. If necessary remove the compressor mount (4 bolts) to gain access to the water pump retaining bolts.
6. Remove the alternator and move to one side.
7. Disconnect the lower radiator hose and heater hose.
8. Remove (3) upper screws and (1) lower screw retaining water pump to the engine and remove pump assembly.

DISASSEMBLY

▶ See Figure 100

1. Remove the 3 screws holding the pulley to the water pump.
2. Remove the 9 screws holding the water pump to the body. Because of the gasket seal a chisel is required to separate the pump from the body.
3. Clean the gasket surfaces on the pump and the body.
4. Remove and discard the O-ring gasket and clean the O-ring groove.

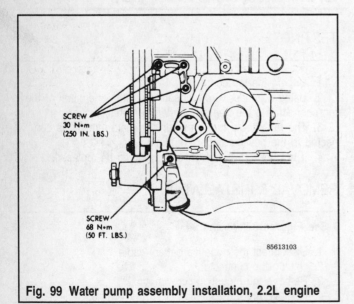

Fig. 99 Water pump assembly installation, 2.2L engine

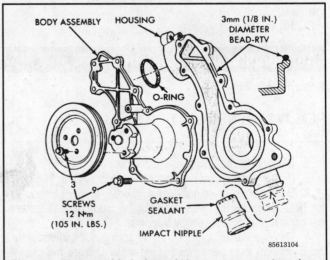

Fig. 100 Disassembled view of the water pump housing and body, 2.2L engine

ASSEMBLY

➡The body assembly, housing and impact nipple are serviced as separate components. On vehicles equipped with a carbureted engine, housing replacement is required. Install a new impact nipple.

1. Apply a sealer to the circumference of the new nipple and with a light mallet tap the nipple into the housing.
2. Apply RTV sealant to the body. Assemble the pump to the body and tighten the screws to 105 inch lbs. (12 Nm) and allow the sealant to set before filling and pressurizing the system.
3. Place a new O-ring in the groove.
4. Position the water pump pulley to the water pump and tighten the 3 retaining screws to 105 inch lbs. (12 Nm).

INSTALLATION

1. Position the replacement pump against the engine and install mounting screws. Tighten the (3) upper screws to 250 inch lbs. (30 Nm) and lower screw to 50 ft. lbs. (68 Nm).
2. Install heater hose and lower radiator hose. Tighten clamps to 16 inch lbs.
3. Install air conditioning compressor and alternator.
4. Install the drive belts and adjust to specification.
5. Fill the cooling system.
6. Connect the negative battery cable.

2.6L Engine

▶ See Figure 101

1. Drain the cooling system.

❄❄CAUTION

When draining the coolant, keep in mind that cats and dogs are attracted by the ethylene glycol antifreeze, and are quite likely to drink any that is left in an uncovered container or in puddles on the ground. This will prove fatal in sufficient quantity. Always drain the coolant into a sealable container. Coolant should be reused unless it is contaminated or several years old.

2. Remove the radiator hose, by-pass hose and heater hose from the water pump.
3. Remove the drive pulley shield.
4. Remove the locking screw and pivot screws.
5. Remove the drive belt and water pump from the engine.
6. Install a new O-ring gasket in O-ring groove of pump body assembly to cylinder block.
7. Position the water pump assembly against the engine and install pivot screws and locking screw finger tight.
8. Install the water pump drive belt and adjust to specification. New belt 8mm deflection, used belt 9mm deflection.
9. Install drive belt pulley cover.
10. Install the radiator hose, by-pass hose and heater hose.
11. Fill the cooling system.

3.0L Engine

▶ See Figure 102

1. Disconnect the negative battery cable.
2. Remove the drive belts.
3. Drain the cooling system.

❄❄CAUTION

When draining the coolant, keep in mind that cats and dogs are attracted by the ethylene glycol antifreeze, and are quite likely to drink any that is left in an uncovered container or in puddles on the ground. This will prove fatal in sufficient quantity. Always drain the coolant into a sealable container. Coolant should be reused unless it is contaminated or several years old.

4. Remove the timing case cover and timing belt. Refer to Timing Belt Covers and Timing Belt Removal procedures.
5. Remove the pump assembly mounting bolts.
6. Separate the pump assembly from water pipe and remove.
7. Clean gasket and O-ring mounting surfaces.
8. Install a new O-ring on water pipe and lubricate with water.
9. Install a new gasket on pump body.
10. Press the water pump assembly into water pipe.

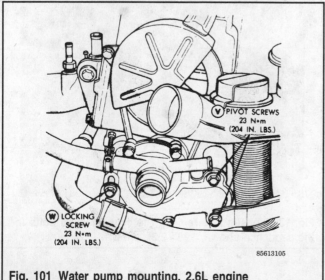

Fig. 101 Water pump mounting, 2.6L engine

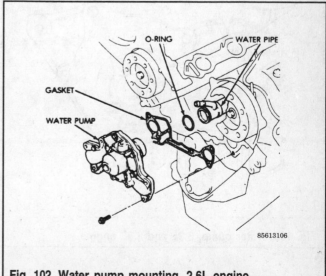

Fig. 102 Water pump mounting, 2.6L engine

11. Install pump mounting bolts and tighten to 27 Nm (20 ft. lbs.).

12. Install timing belt and cover. Refer to Timing Belt procedures.

13. Install drive belts.

14. Fill the cooling system.

3.3L and 3.8L Engines

▶ See Figure 103

1. Disconnect the negative battery cable.

2. Drain the cooling system.

3. Remove the serpentine belt.

4. Raise the vehicle and support safely. Remove the right front tire and wheel assembly and lower fender shield.

5. Remove the water pump pulley.

6. Remove the 5 mounting screws and remove the pump from the engine.

7. Discard the O-ring.

To install:

8. Using a new O-ring, install the pump to the engine. Torque the mounting bolts to 21 ft. lbs. (30 Nm).

9. Install the water pump pulley.

10. Install the fender shield and tire and wheel assembly. Lower the vehicle.

11. Install the serpentine belt.

12. Remove the engine temperature sending unit. Fill the radiator with coolant until the coolant comes out the sending unit hole. Install the sending unit and continue to fill the radiator.

13. Connect the negative battery cable, run the vehicle until the thermostat opens, fill the radiator completely and check for leaks.

14. Once the vehicle has cooled, recheck the coolant level.

Cylinder Head

REMOVAL & INSTALLATION

2.2L and 2.5L Engines

▶ See Figures 104, 105, 106, 107, 108, 109, 110 and 111

1. Relieve the fuel pressure if equipped with fuel injection. Disconnect the negative battery cable and unbolt it from the head. Drain the cooling system. Remove the dipstick bracket nut from the thermostat housing.

2. Remove the air cleaner assembly. Remove the upper radiator hose and disconnect the heater hoses.

3. Disconnect and label the vacuum lines, hoses and wiring connectors from the manifold(s), carburetor or throttle body and from the cylinder head. Remove the air pump, if equipped.

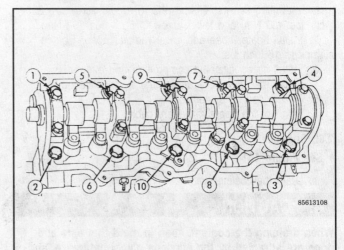

Fig. 104 Cylinder head bolt removal sequence, 2.2L and 2.5L engine

Fig. 105 Loosen and remove the cylinder head bolts in the sequence shown, 1987 2.2L shown

Fig. 103 Water pump, 3.3L and 3.8L engine

Fig. 106 Remove the cylinder head bolts in the sequence shown, 1987 2.2L shown

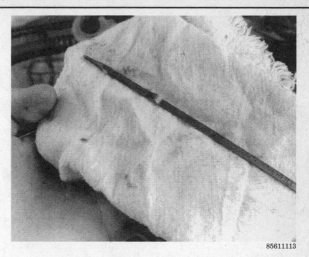

Fig. 109 Clean the gasket mating surfaces, 1987 2.2L shown

Fig. 107 Lifting the cylinder head from the engine compartment, 1987 2.2L shown

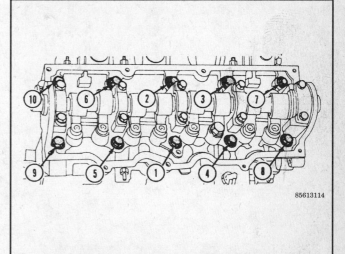

Fig. 110 Cylinder head bolt tightening sequence, 2.2L and 2.5L engine

4. Disconnect the all linkages and the fuel line from the carburetor or throttle body. Unbolt the cable bracket. Remove the ground strap attaching screw from the fire wall.

5. If equipped with air conditioning, remove the upper compressor mounting bolts. The cylinder head can be remove with the compressor and bracket still mounted. Remove the upper part of the timing belt cover.

6. Raise the vehicle and support safely. Disconnect the converter from the exhaust manifold. Disconnect the water hose and oil drain from the turbocharger, if equipped.

7. Rotate the engine by hand, until the timing marks align (No. 1 piston at TDC). Lower the vehicle.

8. With the timing marks aligned, remove the camshaft sprocket. The camshaft sprocket can be suspended to keep the timing intact. Remove the spark plug wires from the spark plugs.

9. Remove the valve cover and curtain, if equipped. Remove the cylinder head bolts and washers, starting from the middle and working outward.

Fig. 108 Remove the cylinder head gasket, 1987 2.2L shown

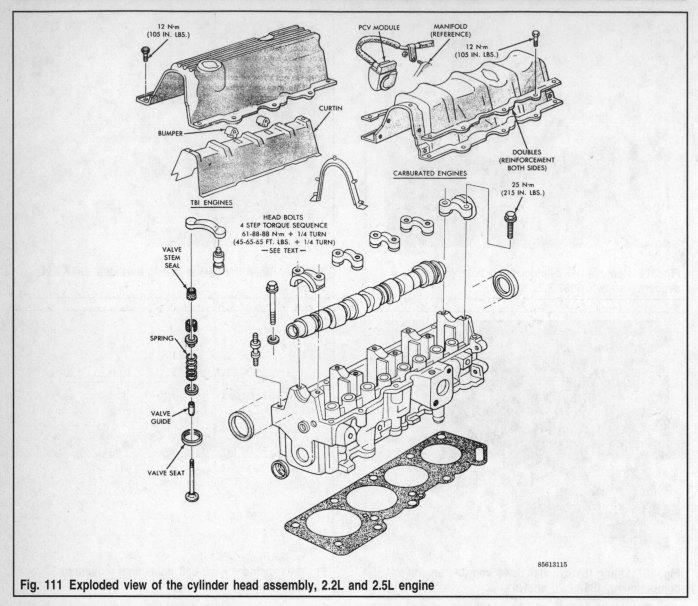

Fig. 111 Exploded view of the cylinder head assembly, 2.2L and 2.5L engine

10. Remove the cylinder head from the engine.

➡Before disassembling or repairing any part of the cylinder head assembly, identify factory installed oversized components. To do so, look for the tops of the bearing caps pained green and O/SJ stamped rearward of the oil gallery plug on the rear of the head. In addition, the barrel of the camshaft is painted green and O/SJ is stamped onto the rear end of the camshaft. Installing standard sized parts in an head equipped with oversized parts — or visa versa — will cause severe engine damage.

11. Clean the cylinder head gasket mating surfaces.
12. Using new gaskets and seals, install the head to the engine. Using new head bolts assembled with the old washers, torque the cylinder head bolts in sequence, to 45 ft. lbs. Repeating the sequence, torque the bolts to 65 ft. lbs. With the bolts at 65 ft. lbs., turn each bolt an additional ¼ turn.

➡Head bolt diameter for 1986-91 vehicles is 11mm. These bolts are identified with the number 11 on the head of the bolt. The 10mm bolts used on previous vehicles will

thread into an 11mm bolt hole, but will permanently damage the engine block. Make sure the correct bolts are being used.

13. Install the timing belt.
14. Install or connect all items that were removed or disconnected during the removal procedures.
15. Refill the cooling system. Connect the negative battery cable. Start the engine and check for leaks.

2.6L Engine

▶ See Figures 112 and 113

1. Disconnect the negative battery cable and unbolt if from the head.
2. Drain the cooling system. Remove the upper radiator hose and disconnect the heater hoses. Remove the air cleaner assembly.
3. Remove the dipstick bracket bolt from the thermostat housing.

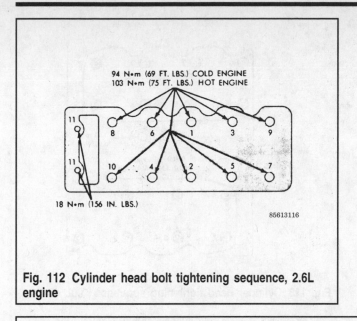

Fig. 112 Cylinder head bolt tightening sequence, 2.6L engine

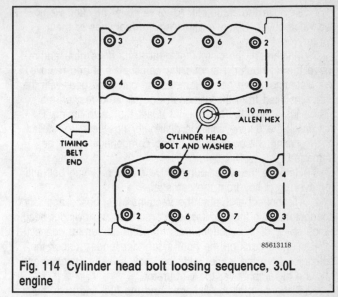

Fig. 114 Cylinder head bolt loosing sequence, 3.0L engine

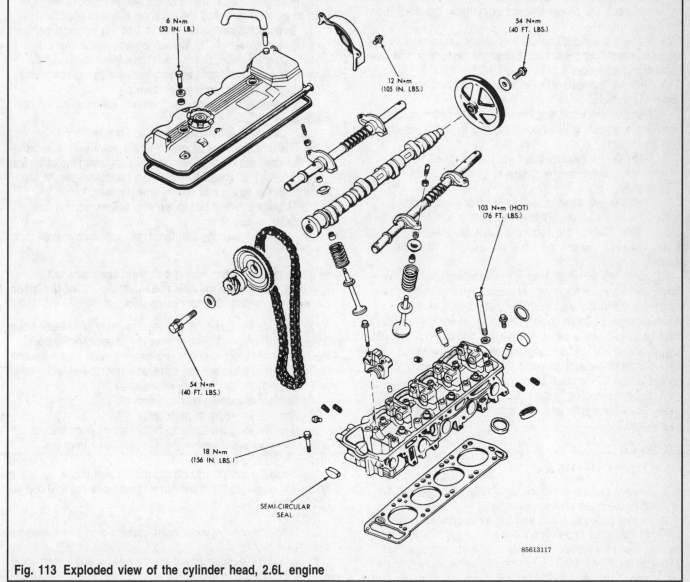

Fig. 113 Exploded view of the cylinder head, 2.6L engine

4. Remove the carburetor to valve cover bracket. Remove the valve cover. Remove and plug the fuel lines to the carburetor.

5. Matchmark the distributor gear to its drive gear and remove the distributor. Remove the camshaft bolt and remove the distributor drive gear. Remove the camshaft gear with the chain installed from the camshaft and allow to rest on the holder just below it. This will not upset the valve timing. Do not crank the engine until the distributor has been reinstalled or the timing will be lost and timing components could be damaged.

6. Remove the water pump drive pulley retaining bolt and remove the pulley from the camshaft.

7. Disconnect and label the vacuum lines, hoses and wiring connectors from the manifold(s), carburetor and cylinder head. Since some of the vacuum lines from the carburetor connect to a solenoid pack on the right side inner fender, unbolt the solenoids from the fender with the vacuum lines attached and fold the assembly over the carburetor.

8. Disconnect all the linkages and the fuel line from the carburetor. Remove the ground strap attaching screw from the fire wall. Unbolt the power steering pump from the bracket and position to the side.

9. Raise the vehicle and support safely. Disconnect the vacuum hoses from the source below the carburetor and disconnect the air feeder tubes.

10. Remove the exhaust pipe from the exhaust manifold. Lower the vehicle.

11. Remove the small end bolts from the head first, then remove the remaining head bolts, starting from the outside and working inward.

12. Remove the cylinder head from the engine.

13. Clean the cylinder head gasket mating surfaces.

To install:

14. Install a new head gasket to the block and install all head bolts and washers. Torque the bolts in sequence to 34 ft. lbs. (40 Nm). Repeat the sequence increasing the torque to 69 ft. lbs. (94 Nm). Tighten the small end bolts to 13 ft. lbs. (18 Nm).

15. Install the camshaft gear with the timing chain. If the timing will not allow for gear installation, reach into the case with a long, thin tool and push the rubber foot into the oil pump to allow for more chain movement. Install the distributor drive gear, bolt and washer. Torque the bolt to 40 ft. lbs. (54 Nm). Install the distributor, aligning the match marks.

16. Install or connect all items that were removed or disconnected during the removal procedure.

17. Refill the cooling system. Connect the negative battery cable. Start the engine and check for leaks. Adjust the timing as required.

3.0L Engine

▶ **See Figures 114, 115 and 116**

1. Relieve the fuel pressure. Disconnect the negative battery cable. Drain the cooling system.

2. Remove the drive belt and the air conditioning compressor from its mount and support it aside. Using a ½ in. drive breaker bar, insert it into the square hole of the serpentine drive belt tensioner, rotate it counterclockwise (to reduce the belt tension) and remove the belt. Remove the alternator and power steering pump from the brackets and move them aside.

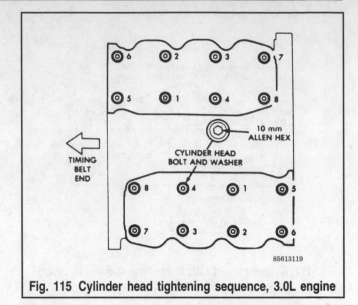

Fig. 115 Cylinder head tightening sequence, 3.0L engine

3. Raise the vehicle and support safely. Remove the right front wheel assembly and the right inner splash shield.

4. Remove the crankshaft pulleys and the torsional damper.

5. Lower the vehicle. Using a floor jack and a block of wood positioned under the oil pan, raise the engine slightly. Remove the engine mount bracket from the timing cover end of the engine and the timing belt covers.

6. To remove the timing belt, perform the following procedures:

   a. Rotate the crankshaft to position the No. 1 cylinder on the TDC of its compression stroke; the crankshaft sprocket timing mark should align with the oil pan timing indicator and the camshaft sprockets timing marks (triangles) should align with the rear timing belt covers timing marks.

   b. Mark the timing belt in the direction of rotation for reinstallation purposes.

   c. Loosen the timing belt tensioner and remove the timing belt.

➡**When removing the timing belt from the camshaft sprocket, make sure the belt does not slip off of the other camshaft sprocket. Support extension.**

7. Remove the camshaft bearing assembly to cylinder head bolts (do not remove the bolts from the assembly). Remove the rocker arms, rocker shafts and bearing caps as an assembly, as required. Remove the camshafts from the cylinder head and inspect them for damage, if necessary.

8. Remove the intake manifold assembly.

9. Remove the exhaust manifold.

10. Remove the cylinder head bolts starting from the outside and working inward. Remove the cylinder head from the engine.

11. Clean the gasket mounting surfaces and check the heads for warpage; the maximum warpage allowed is 0.008 in. (0.20mm).

To install:

12. Install the new cylinder head gaskets over the dowels on the engine block.

13. Install the cylinder heads on the engine and torque the cylinder head bolts in sequence using 3 even steps, to 70 ft. lbs. (95 Nm).

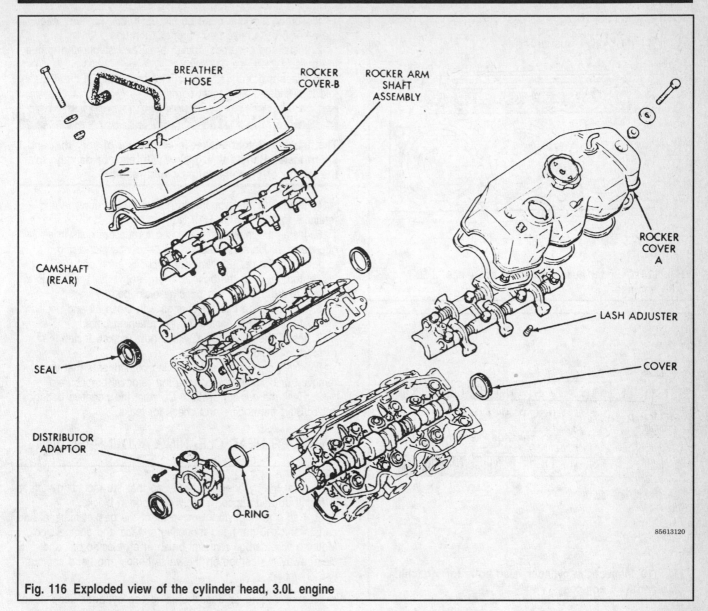

Fig. 116 Exploded view of the cylinder head, 3.0L engine

14. Install or connect all items that were removed or disconnected during the removal procedure.

15. When installing the timing belt over the camshaft sprocket, use care not to allow the belt to slip off the opposite camshaft sprocket.

16. Make sure the timing belt is installed on the camshaft sprocket in the same position as when removed.

17. Refill the cooling system. Connect the negative battery cable. Start the engine and check for leaks using the DRB I or II to active the fuel pump. Adjust the timing as required.

3.3L and 3.8L Engines

▶ See Figures 117, 118 and 119

1. Relieve the fuel pressure. Disconnect the negative battery cable. Drain the cooling system.
2. Remove the intake manifold with throttle body.
3. Disconnect the coil wires, sending unit wire, heater hoses and bypass hose.
4. Remove the closed ventilation system, evaporation control system and cylinder hear cover.
5. Remove the exhaust manifold.

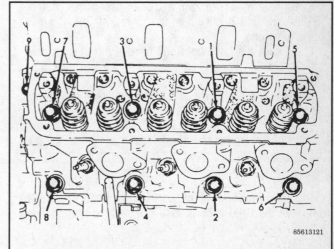

Fig. 117 Cylinder head gasket installation, 3.3L and 3.8L engines

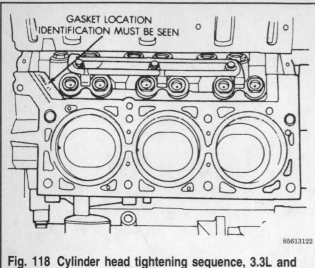

Fig. 118 Cylinder head tightening sequence, 3.3L and 3.8L engines

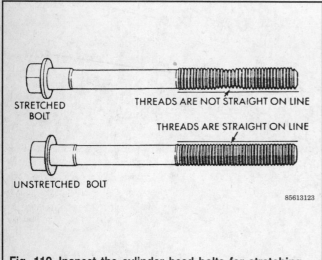

Fig. 119 Inspect the cylinder head bolts for stretching, 3.3L and 3.8L engines

6. Remove the rocker arm and shaft assemblies. Remove the pushrods and identify them in ensure installation in their original positions.

7. Remove the head bolts and remove the cylinder head from the block.

To install:

8. Clean the gasket mounting surfaces and install a new head gasket to the block.

9. Install the head to the block. Before installing the head bolts, inspect them for stretching. Hold a straight edge up to the threads. If the threads are not all on line, the bolt is stretched and should be replaced.

10. Torque the bolts in sequence to 45 ft. lbs. (61 Nm). Repeat the sequence and torque the bolts to 65 ft. lbs. (88 Nm). With the bolts at 65 ft. lbs., turn each bolt an additional ¼ turn.

11. Torque the lone head bolt to 25 ft. lbs. (33 Nm) after the other 8 bolts have been properly torqued.

12. Install the pushrods, rocker arms and shafts and torque the bolts to 21 ft. lbs. (12 Nm).

13. Place a drop of silicone sealer onto each of the 4 manifold to cylinder head gasket corners.

✳✳CAUTION

The intake manifold gasket is composed of very thin and sharp metal. Handle this gasket with care or damage to the gasket or personal injury could result.

14. Install the intake manifold gasket and torque the end retainers to 105 inch lbs. (12 Nm).

15. Install the intake manifold and torque the bolts in sequence to 10 inch lbs. Repeat the sequence increasing the torque to 17 ft. lbs. (23 Nm) and recheck each bolt for 17 ft. lbs. of torque. After the bolts are torqued, inspect the seals to ensure that they have not become dislodged.

16. Lubricate the injector O-rings with clean oil and position the fuel rail in place. Install the rail retaining bolts.

17. Install the valve cover with a new gasket. Install the exhaust manifold.

18. Install or connect all remaining components that were removed or disconnected during the removal procedures.

19. Refill the cooling system. Connect the negative battery cable. Start the engine and check for leaks.

CYLINDER HEAD CLEANING AND INSPECTION

1. Turn the cylinder head over so that the mounting surface is facing up and support evenly on wooden blocks.

2. Use a scraper and remove all of the gasket material and carbon stuck to the head mounting surface and engine block. Mount a wire carbon removal brush in an electric drill and clean away the carbon on the valve heads and head combustion chambers.

➡When scraping or decarbonizing the cylinder head, take care not to damage or nick the gasket mounting surface or combustion chamber.

3. Clean cylinder head oil passages.

4. After cleaning check cylinder head for cracks or damage.

5. Check cylinder head flatness. Flatness must be within 0.1mm.

CYLINDER HEAD RESURFACING

If the cylinder head is warped, resurfacing by a automotive machine shop will be required. After cleaning the gasket surface, place a straight-edge across the mounting surface of the head, diagonally from one end to the other. Using a feeler gauge, determine the clearance at the center and alone the length between the head and straight-edge.

Valves

▶ See Figure 120

REMOVAL

The following procedures to be performed with cylinder head removed from engine.

1. Compress valve springs using Tool C-3422A or equivalent. Do not mix removed parts. Place the parts from each valve in a separate container, numbered and identified for the valve and cylinder.
2. Remove valve retaining locks, valve spring retainers, valve stem seal, valve springs and valve spring seats.

➡**Before removing valve assembly remove any burrs from valve stem lock grooves to prevent damage to valve guides.**

3. Remove valve assembly.

INSPECTION

▶ See Figure 121

1. Clean valves thoroughly.
2. Check valve stem tip for pitting or depression.
3. Check for ridge wear on valve stem area.
4. Inspect valve (with Prussian blue) for even contact between valve face and cylinder head valve seat.
5. Gently remove valve stem seals with a pliers or screwdriver by prying side-to-side. Do not reused old seals.
6. Remove carbon and varnish deposits from inside of valve guides of cylinder head with a suitable guide cleaner.
7. Use an electric drill and soft rotary wire brush to clean the intake and exhaust valve ports, combustion chamber and valve seats. In some cases, the carbon build-up will have to

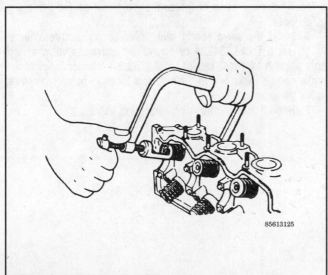

Fig. 120 Removing the valve springs

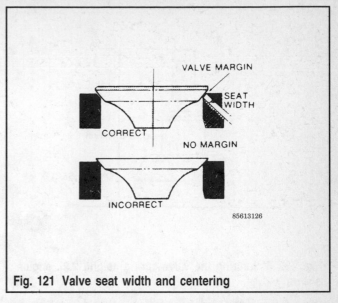

Fig. 121 Valve seat width and centering

be chipped away. Use a blunt pointed drift for carbon chipping, be careful around valve seat areas.

➡**When using a wire brush to clean carbon on the valve ports, valves, etc., be sure the deposits are actually removed, rather then burnished.**

8. Wash and clean all valve spring, locks, retainers etc., in safe solvent. Remember to keep parts from each valve separate.

➡**If valve guide replacement is necessary, or valve or seat refacing is necessary, the job must be handled by a qualified machine shop. If a valve seat is damaged, burnt or loose, the seat may be resurfaced or replaced as necessary. The automotive machine shop can handle the job for you.**

CHECKING VALVE SPRINGS

▶ See Figures 122 and 123

Place the valve spring on a flat surface next to a carpenters square. Measure the height of the spring, and rotate the spring against the edge of the square to measure distortion. If the spring height varies (by comparison) by more than $1/16$ in. or if the distortion exceeds $1/16$ in., replace the spring.

Have the valve springs tested for spring pressure at the installed and compressed (installed height minus valve lift) height using a valve spring tester. Springs should be within one pound, plug or minus each other. Replace springs as necessary.

INSTALLATION

▶ See Figure 124

1. Coat valve stems with lubrication oil and install in cylinder head.
2. Install a new valve stem seal on the valve. The valve stem seal should be install firmly and squarely over the valve

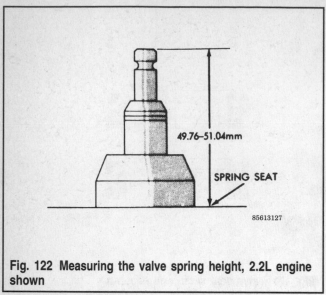

Fig. 122 Measuring the valve spring height, 2.2L engine shown

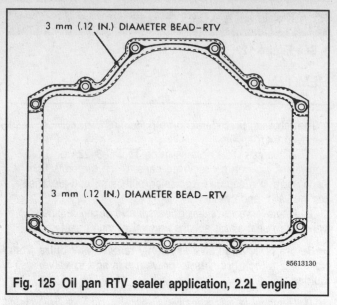

Fig. 125 Oil pan RTV sealer application, 2.2L engine

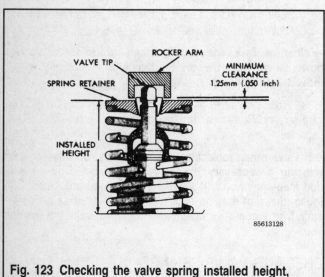

Fig. 123 Checking the valve spring installed height, 2.2L engine

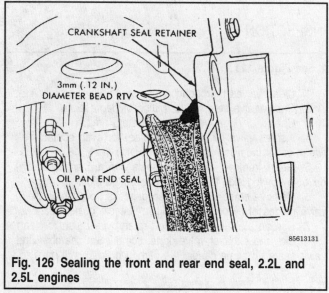

Fig. 126 Sealing the front and rear end seal, 2.2L and 2.5L engines

guide. The lower edge of the seal should rest on the valve guide boss.

3. Install the valve spring seat, valve spring, and retainer.

4. Using Tool C-3422A or equivalent compress valve spring only enough to install retainer locks. Install retainer locks and make certain locks are in their correct location before removing valve compressor.

5. Repeat step 1 thru 4 on remaining valves.

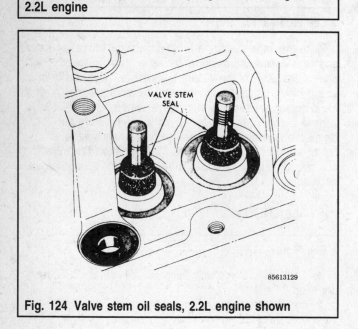

Fig. 124 Valve stem oil seals, 2.2L engine shown

Oil Pan

REMOVAL & INSTALLATION

2.2L Engine

▶ See Figures 125, 126, 127, 128 and 129

1. Raise and safely support the vehicle on jackstands. Drain the oil pan.

✳✳CAUTION

The EPA warns that prolonged contact with used engine oil may cause a number of skin disorders, including cancer! You should make every effort to minimize your exposure to used engine oil. Protective gloves should be worn when changing the oil. Wash your hands and any other

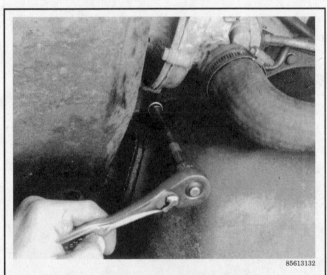

Fig. 127 Removing the oil pan retaining bolts

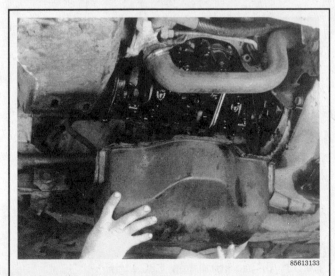

Fig. 128 Removing the oil pan

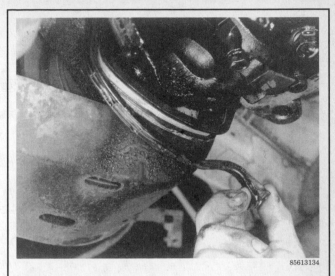

Fig. 129 Removing one of the end seals

exposed skin areas as soon as possible after exposure to used engine oil. Soap and water, or waterless hand cleaner should be used.

2. Remove the oil pan attaching bolts and remove oil pan.
3. Clean the oil pan and engine block gasket surfaces thoroughly.
4. Apply RTV sealant to oil pan side rails.
5. Install new oil pan seals and install oil pan. Torque the pan screws to 15 ft. lbs.
6. Refill the crankcase, start the engine and check for leaks.

2.5L Engine

▶ See Figures 126 and 130

1. Raise and safely support the vehicle on jackstands. Drain the oil pan.

✳✳CAUTION

The EPA warns that prolonged contact with used engine oil may cause a number of skin disorders, including cancer! You should make every effort to minimize your exposure to used engine oil. Protective gloves should be worn when changing the oil. Wash your hands and any other exposed skin areas as soon as possible after exposure to used engine oil. Soap and water, or waterless hand cleaner should be used.

2. Remove the oil pan attaching bolts and remove oil pan.
3. Clean oil pan and engine block gasket surfaces thoroughly.
4. Apply RTV sealant to oil pan rail at the front seal retainer parting line.
5. Attach the oil pan side gaskets using heavy grease or RTV to hold the gasket in place.
6. Install the new oil pan seals and apply RTV sealant to the ends of the seals at junction where seals and gasket meets.
7. Install oil pan and tighten M8 screws to 15 ft. lbs., and M6 screws to 105 inch lbs.

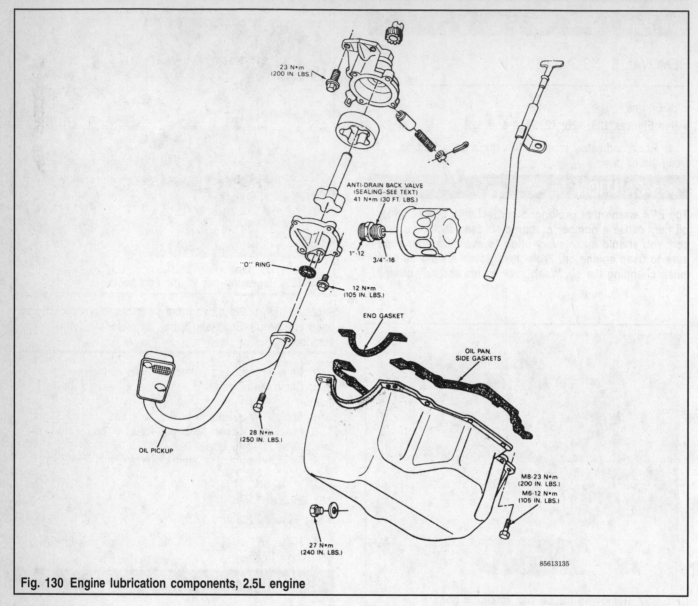

23 N•m
(200 IN. LBS.)

ANTI-DRAIN BACK VALVE
(SEALING--SEE TEXT)
41 N•m (30 FT. LBS.)

1"-12

3/4"-16

"O" RING

12 N•m
(105 IN. LBS.)

END GASKET

OIL PAN
SIDE GASKETS

OIL PICKUP

28 N•m
(250 IN. LBS.)

M8-23 N•m
(200 IN. LBS.)
M6-12 N•m
(105 IN. LBS.)

27 N•m
(240 IN. LBS.)

85613135

Fig. 130 Engine lubrication components, 2.5L engine

2.6L Engine

▶ See Figure 131

1. Raise and safely support the vehicle on jackstands. Drain the oil pan.

❋❋CAUTION

The EPA warns that prolonged contact with used engine oil may cause a number of skin disorders, including cancer! You should make every effort to minimize your exposure to used engine oil. Protective gloves should be worn when changing the oil. Wash your hands and any other exposed skin areas as soon as possible after exposure to used engine oil. Soap and water, or waterless hand cleaner should be used.

2. Remove the oil pan attaching bolts and remove oil pan.
3. Clean oil pan and engine block gasket surfaces thoroughly.
4. Install a new pan gasket.
5. Install oil pan and tighten screws to 60 inch lbs.

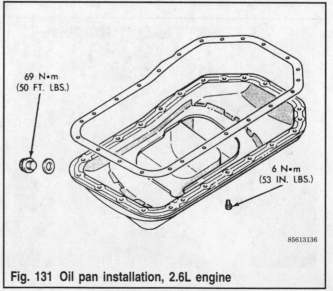

69 N•m
(50 FT. LBS.)

6 N•m
(53 IN. LBS.)

85613136

Fig. 131 Oil pan installation, 2.6L engine

3.0L Engine

▶ See Figure 132

1. Raise and safely support the vehicle on jackstands. Drain the oil pan.

※※CAUTION

The EPA warns that prolonged contact with used engine oil may cause a number of skin disorders, including cancer! You should make every effort to minimize your exposure to used engine oil. Protective gloves should be worn when changing the oil. Wash your hands and any other exposed skin areas as soon as possible after exposure to used engine oil. Soap and water, or waterless hand cleaner should be used.

2. Remove the oil pan attaching bolts and remove oil pan.
3. Clean oil pan and engine block gasket surfaces thoroughly.
4. Apply RTV sealant to oil pan.
5. Install oil pan to engine and tighten screws in sequence, working from the center toward the ends, to 50 inch lbs.

3.3L and 3.8L Engines

▶ See Figures 133 and 134

1. Disconnect the negative battery cable.
2. Raise the vehicle and support safely.
3. Remove the torque converter bolt access cover, if equipped.
4. Drain the engine oil.
5. Remove the oil pan retaining screws and remove the oil pan and gasket.
   To install:
6. Thoroughly clean and dry all sealing surfaces, bolts and bolt holes.
7. Apply silicone sealer to the chain cover to block mating seam and the rear main seal retainer to block seam, if equipped.

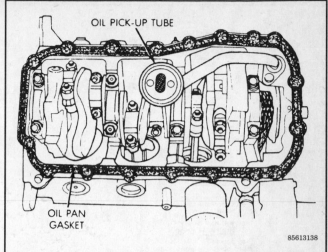

Fig. 133 Oil pan gasket installation, 3.3L and 3.8L engines

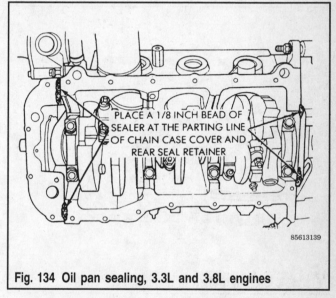

Fig. 134 Oil pan sealing, 3.3L and 3.8L engines

8. Install a new pan gasket or apply silicone sealer to the sealing surface of the pan and install to the engine.
9. Install the retaining screws and torque to 200 inch lbs. (23 Nm).
10. Install the torque converter bolt access cover, if equipped. Lower the vehicle.
11. Install the dipstick. Fill the engine with the proper amount of oil.
12. Connect the negative battery cable and check for leaks.

Oil Pump

REMOVAL & INSTALLATION

2.2L and 2.5L Engine

▶ See Figures 135, 136, 137 and 138

1. Raise and safely support the vehicle.

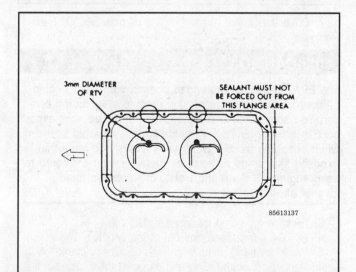

Fig. 132 Oil pan RTV sealer application, 3.0L engine

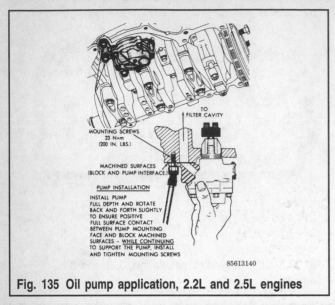

Fig. 135 Oil pump application, 2.2L and 2.5L engines

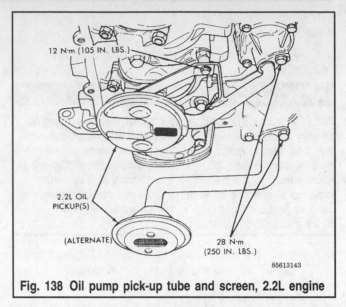

Fig. 138 Oil pump pick-up tube and screen, 2.2L engine

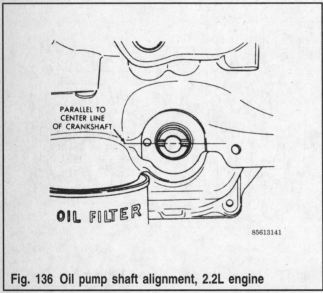

Fig. 136 Oil pump shaft alignment, 2.2L engine

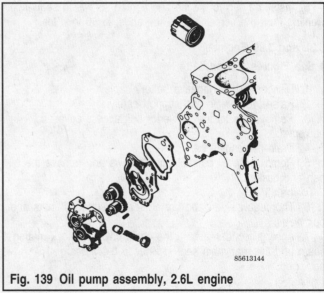

Fig. 139 Oil pump assembly, 2.6L engine

Fig. 137 Oil pump pick-up tube and screen

2. Drain the oil and remove engine oil pan. See Oil Pan Removal.

✳✳CAUTION

The EPA warns that prolonged contact with used engine oil may cause a number of skin disorders, including cancer! You should make every effort to minimize your exposure to used engine oil. Protective gloves should be worn when changing the oil. Wash your hands and any other exposed skin areas as soon as possible after exposure to used engine oil. Soap and water, or waterless hand cleaner should be used.

3. Remove the pump mounting bolts.
4. Pull the pump down and out of the engine.
5. Prime, by filling pump with fresh oil. Check crankshaft/intermediate shaft timing and oil pump drive alignment. Adjust if necessary.
6. Install pump and rotate back and forth slightly to ensure full surface contact of pump and block.

7. While holding pump in fully seated position, install pump mounting bolts. Torque to 15 ft. lbs.

8. Install engine oil pan. Refer to Oil Pan Installation procedures.

9. Refill crankcase, start engine.

10. Check engine oil pressure.

2.6L Engine

▶ See Figure 139

1. Remove accessory drive belts.

2. Remove the timing chain case cover. Refer to Timing Chain Case Cover Removal procedures.

3. Remove the silent shaft chain assembly and timing chain assembly. Refer to Timing Chain Removal procedures.

4. Remove the silent shaft bolt (bolt directly above the silent chain sprocket).

5. Remove the oil pump bolts and pull the pump housing straight forward. Remove the gaskets and the oil pump backing plate.

6. Clean gasket from mounting surfaces.

7. Install new gaskets/seals, align mating marks of the oil pump gears, refill the pump with oil, and install the pump assembly.

8. Install oil pump silent shaft sprocket and sprocket bolt. Tighten sprocket bolt to 34 Nm (25 ft. lbs.).

9. Install timing chain and silent shaft chain assembly. Refer to Timing Chain Installation procedures.

10. Install timing chain case cover. Refer to Timing Chain Case Cover Installation procedures.

11. Install accessory drive belts.

12. Reconnect battery negative cable.

13. Start engine and check engine oil pressure.

3.0L Engine

▶ See Figure 140

The oil pump assembly used on this engine is mounted at the front of the crankshaft. The oil pump also retains the crankshaft front oil seal.

1. Remove accessory drive belts.

2. Remove the timing belt cover and timing belt. Refer to Timing Belt Removal procedures.

3. Remove the crankshaft sprocket.

4. Remove the oil pump mounting bolts (5), and remove oil pump assembly. Mark mounting bolts for proper installation during reassembly.

5. Clean the oil pump and engine block gasket surfaces thoroughly.

6. Position a new gasket on pump assembly and install on cylinder block. Make sure correct length bolts are in proper locations and torque all bolts to 10 ft. lbs.

7. Install the crankshaft sprocket and timing belt. Recheck engine timing marks. Refer to Timing Belt Installation procedures.

8. Install the timing belt covers. Refer to Timing Belt Cover Installation procedures.

9. Install accessory drive belts.

10. Refill the crankcase and start the engine.

11. Check engine oil pressure.

3.3L and 3.8L Engines

▶ See Figures 141 and 142

1. Disconnect the negative battery cable. Remove the dipstick.

2. Raise the vehicle and support safely. Drain the oil and remove the oil pan.

3. Remove the oil pickup.

4. Remove the chain case cover.

5. Disassemble the oil pump as required.

To install:

6. Assemble the pump. Torque the cover screws to 10 ft. lbs. (12 Nm).

7. Prime the oil pump by filling the rotor cavity with fresh oil and turning the rotors until oil comes out the pressure port. Repeat a few times until no air bubbles are present.

8. Install the chain case cover.

9. Clean out the oil pickup or replace as required. Replace the oil pickup O-ring and install the pickup to the pump.

10. Install the oil pan.

11. Install the dipstick. Fill the engine with the proper amount of oil.

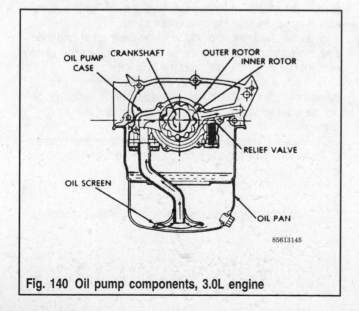

Fig. 140 Oil pump components, 3.0L engine

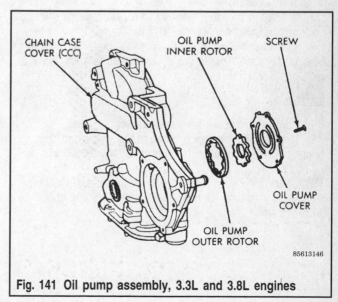

Fig. 141 Oil pump assembly, 3.3L and 3.8L engines

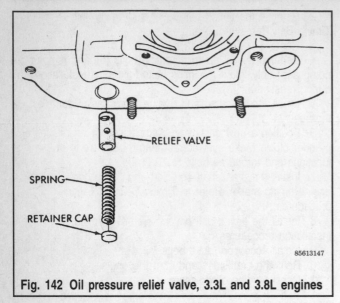

RELIEF VALVE

SPRING

RETAINER CAP

85613147

Fig. 142 Oil pressure relief valve, 3.3L and 3.8L engines

12. Connect the negative battery cable and check the oil pressure.

CHECKING

2.2L and 2.5L Engines

1. Remove the cover from the oil pump.
2. Check endplay of the inner rotor using a feeler gauge and a straight edge placed across the pump body. The specification is 0.001-0.004 in. (0.03-0.09mm).
3. Measure the clearance between the inner and outer rotors. The maximum clearance is 0.008 in. (0.20mm).
4. Measure the clearance between the outer rotor and the pump body. The maximum clearance is 0.014 in. (0.35mm).
5. The minimum thickness of the outer rotor is 0.944 in. (23.96mm). The minimum diameter of the outer rotor is 2.77 in. (62.70mm). The minimum thickness of the inner rotor is 0.943 in. (23.95mm).
6. Check the cover for warpage. The maximum allowable is 0.003 in. (0.076mm).
7. Check the pressure relief valve for damage. The spring's free length specification is 1.95 in. (49.50mm).
8. Assemble the outer rotor with the larger chamfered edge in the pump body. Torque the cover screws to 10 ft. lbs. (12 Nm).

2.6L Engine

1. Remove the cover from the oil pump.
2. Measure the clearance between the gears and their bearings. The specification for both is 0.0008-0.0020 in. (0.02-0.05mm).
3. Check the clearance between the gears and the housing. The specification for both gears is 0.004-0.006 in. (0.11-0.15mm).

4. Check endplay of the gears using a feeler gauge and a straight edge placed across the pump body. The specification for both is 0.002-0.004 in. (0.04-0.11mm).
5. Check the pressure relief valve for damage. The spring's free length specification is 1.85 in. (47.00mm).
6. If the gears were removed from the body, install them with the mating aligned. If they are not aligned properly, the silent shaft will be out of time.
7. Torque the cover screws to 13 ft. lbs. (18 Nm).

3.0L Engine

1. Remove the rear cover.
2. Remove the pump rotors and inspect the case for excessive wear.
3. Measure the diameter of the inner rotor hub that sits in the case. Measure the inside diameter of the inner rotor hub bore. Subtract the first measurement from the second; if the result is over 0.006 in. (0.15mm), replace the oil pump assembly.
4. Measure the clearance between the outer rotor and the case. The specification is 0.004-0.007 in. (0.10-0.18mm).
5. Check the side clearance of the rotors using a feeler gauge and a straight edge placed across the case. The specification is 0.0015-0.0035 in. (0.04-0.09mm).
6. Check the relief plunger and spring for damage and breakage.
7. Install the rear cover to the case.

3.3L and 3.8L Engines

1. Thoroughly clean and dry all parts. The mating surface of the chain case cover should be smooth. Replace the pump cover if it is scratched or grooved.
2. Lay a straight edge across the pump cover surface. If a 0.076mm feeler gauge can be inserted between the cover and the straight edge, the cover should be replaced.
3. The maximum thickness of the outer rotor is 0.301 in. (7.63mm). The minimum diameter of the outer rotor is 3.14 in. (79.78mm). The minimum thickness of the inner rotor is 0.301 in. (7.64m).
4. Install the outer rotor onto the chain case cover, press to one side and measure the clearance between the rotor and case. If the measurement exceeds 0.022 in. (56mm) and the rotor is good, replace the chain case cover.
5. Install the inner rotor to the chain case cover and measure the clearance between the rotors. If the clearance exceeds 0.008 in. (0.203mm), replace both rotors.
6. Place a straight edge over the chain case cover between bolt holes. If a 0.004 in. (0.102mm) thick feeler gauge can be inserted under the straight edge, replace the pump assembly.
7. Inspect the relief valve plunger for scoring and freedom of movement. Small marks may be removed with 400-grit wet or dry sandpaper.
8. The relief valve spring should have a free length of 1.95 in.
9. Assemble the pump using new parts where necessary.

Front Timing Cover and Seal

REMOVAL & INSTALLATION

2.2L and 2.5L Engine

▶ **See Figures 143, 144, 145, 146, 147, 148, 149 and 150**

1. Remove the accessory drive belts.
2. Support the vehicle on jackstands and remove the right inner splash shield.
3. Loosen and remove the 3 water pump pulley mounting screws and remove the pulley.
4. Remove the 4 crankshaft pulley retaining screws.
5. Remove the nuts at upper portion of timing cover and screws from lower portion and remove both halves of cover.
6. Install the cover. Secure the upper section to cylinder head with nuts and lower section to cylinder block with screws.
7. Install the crankshaft pulley and tighten the bolt to 20 ft. lbs., lower vehicle.

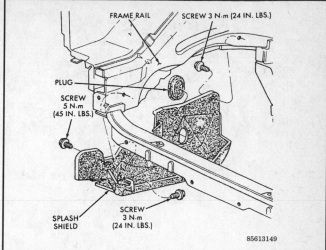

Fig. 144 Right inner splash shield, 2.2L and 2.5L engines

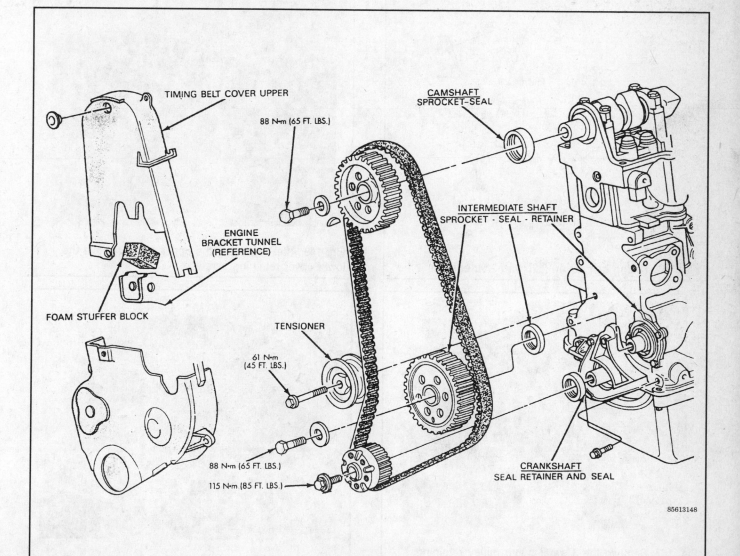

Fig. 143 Timing system and seals, 2.2L and 2.5L engines

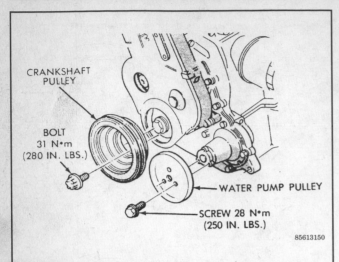

CRANKSHAFT PULLEY

BOLT
31 N·m
(280 IN. LBS.)

WATER PUMP PULLEY

SCREW 28 N·m
(250 IN. LBS.)

85613150

Fig. 145 Crankshaft and water pump pulley, 2.2L and 2.5L engines

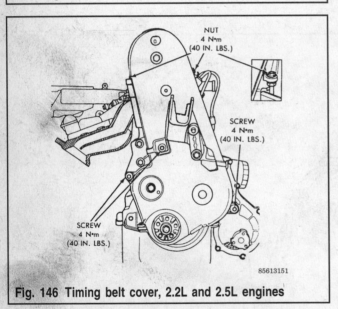

NUT
4 N·m
(40 IN. LBS.)

SCREW
4 N·m
(40 IN. LBS.)

SCREW
4 N·m
(40 IN. LBS.)

85613151

Fig. 146 Timing belt cover, 2.2L and 2.5L engines

85613152

Fig. 147 Remove the 3 water pump pulley retaining screws and remove the pulley

85613153

Fig. 148 Remove the 4 crankshaft pulley retaining screws and remove the pulley

85613154

Fig. 149 After removing the upper cover remove the lower cover retaining screws

85613155

Fig. 150 Removing the lower cover

8. Install the water pump pulley and tighten screws to 105 inch lbs.

9. Install the accessory drive belts.

2.6L Engine

▶ See Figure 151

1. Disconnect the negative battery cable.
2. Remove the air cleaner assembly.
3. Remove the accessory drive belts.
4. Remove the alternator mounting bolts and remove alternator.
5. Remove the power steering mounting bolts and set power steering pump aside.
6. Remove the air conditioner compressor mounting bolts and set compressor aside.
7. Support the vehicle on jackstands and remove right inner splash shield.
8. Drain the engine oil.

✷✷CAUTION

The EPA warns that prolonged contact with used engine oil may cause a number of skin disorders, including cancer! You should make every effort to minimize your exposure to used engine oil. Protective gloves should be worn when changing the oil. Wash your hands and any other exposed skin areas as soon as possible after exposure to used engine oil. Soap and water, or waterless hand cleaner should be used.

9. Remove the crankshaft pulley.
10. Lower the vehicle and place a jack under the engine with a piece of wood between jack and lifting point.
11. Raise the jack until contact is made with the engine. Relieve pressure by jacking slightly and remove the center bolt from the right engine mount. Remove right engine mount.
12. Remove the engine oil dipstick.
13. Remove the engine valve cover. Refer to Rocker Cover Removal procedures.

14. Remove the front (2) cylinder head to timing chain cover bolts. DO NOT LOOSEN ANY OTHER CYLINDER HEAD BOLTS.
15. Remove the oil pan retaining bolts and lower the oil pan.
16. Remove the screws holding the timing indicator and engine mounting plate.
17. Remove the bolts holding the timing chain case cover and remove cover.
18. Clean and inspect chain case cover for crack or other damage.
19. Position a new timing chain case cover gasket on case cover. Trim as required to assure fit at top and bottom.
20. Coat the cover gasket with sealant (P/N 3419115) or equivalent. Install chain case cover and tighten mounting bolts to 13 ft. lbs.
21. Install the (2) front cylinder head to timing chain case cover mounting bolts and tighten to 13 ft. lbs.
22. Install the engine oil pan tighten screws to 53 inch lbs.
23. Install the engine mounting plate and timing indicator.
24. Install the crankshaft pulley.
25. Install the right engine mount, lower engine and install right engine mount center bolt.
26. Install the engine valve cover. Refer to Rocker Cover Installation procedures.
27. Install the engine oil dipstick.
28. Install the air conditioner compressor.
29. Install the power steering pump.
30. Install the alternator.
31. Install the accessory drive belts.
32. Fill the engine crankcase with recommended engine oil.
33. Install the air cleaner assembly.
34. Connect the negative battery cable.

3.0L Engine

▶ See Figure 152

1. Disconnect the negative battery cable.
2. Remove the accessory drive belts.
3. Remove the air conditioner compressor mounting bracket bolts and lay compressor aside.
4. Remove the air conditioner mounting bracket and adjustable drive belt tensioner from engine.

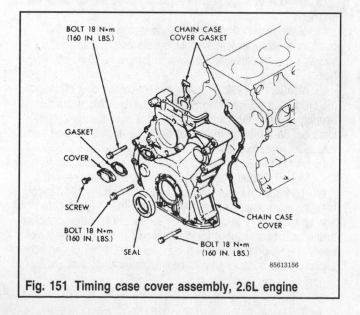

Fig. 151 Timing case cover assembly, 2.6L engine

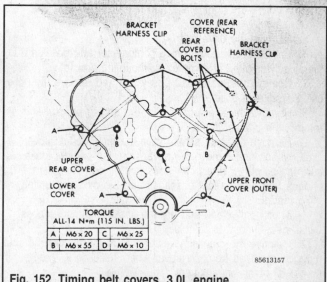

Fig. 152 Timing belt covers, 3.0L engine

5. Remove the steering pump/alternator belt tensioner mounting bolt and remove belt tensioner.

6. Remove the power steering pump mounting bracket bolts, rear support lock nut and set power steering pump aside.

7. Raise the vehicle and support on jackstands.

8. Remove the right inner splash shield.

9. Remove the crankshaft drive pulley bolt, drive pulley and torsional damper.

10. Lower the vehicle and place a floor jack under the engine. Separate engine mount insulator from engine mount bracket.

11. Raise the engine slightly and remove engine mount bracket.

12. Remove the timing belt covers.

13. Install the timing belt covers and tighten all screws to 10 ft. lbs.

14. Raise the engine slightly and install engine mount bracket.

15. Install the engine mount insulator into engine mount bracket.

16. Install the torsional damper, drive pulley and drive pulley bolt. Torque bolt to 110 Nm (150 ft. lbs.). Install the right inner splash shield.

17. Install the power steering mounting bracket and install the power steering pump.

18. Install the steering pump/alternator belt tensioner.

19. Install the air conditioner adjustable drive belt tensioner and mounting bracket.

20. Install the air conditioner compressor.

21. Install the accessory drive belts.

22. Connect the negative battery cable.

3.3L and 3.8L Engines

▶ See Figures 153 and 154

1. Disconnect the negative battery cable. Drain the cooling system.

2. Support the engine with a suitable engine support device and remove the right side motor mount.

3. Raise the vehicle and support safely. Drain the engine oil and remove the oil pan.

4. Remove the right wheel and tire assembly and the splash shield.

5. Remove the drive belt.

6. Unbolt the air conditioning compressor and position it to the side. Remove the compressor mounting bracket.

7. Remove the crankshaft pulley bolt and remove the pulley using a suitable puller.

8. Remove the idler pulley from the engine bracket and remove the bracket.

9. Remove the cam sensor from the timing chain cover.

10. Unbolt and remove the cover from the engine. Make sure the oil pump inner rotor does not fall out. Remove the 3 O-rings from the coolant passages and the oil pump outlet.

To install:

11. Thoroughly clean and dry the gasket mating surfaces. Install new O-rings to the block.

12. Remove the crankshaft oil seal from the cover. The seal must be removed from the cover when installing to ensure proper oil pump engagement.

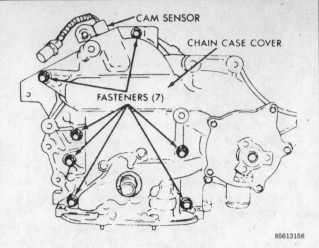

Fig. 153 Timing chain case cover retaining bolts, 3.3L and 3.8L engines

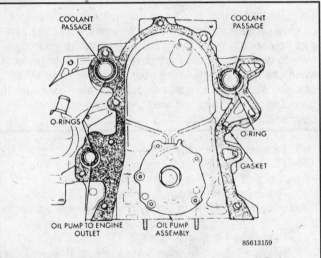

Fig. 154 Timing chain case cover gaskets and O-rings, 3.3L and 3.8L engines

13. Using a new gasket, install the chain case cover to the engine.

14. Make certain that the oil pump is engaged onto the crankshaft before proceeding, or severe engine damage will result. Install the attaching bolts and torque to 20 ft. lbs. (27 Nm).

15. Use tool C-4992 to install the crankshaft oil seal. Install the crankshaft pulley using a 5.9 in. suitable bolt and thrust bearing and washer plate L-4524. Make sure the pulley bottoms out on the crankshaft seal diameter. Install the bolt and torque to 40 ft. lbs. (54 Nm).

16. Install the engine bracket and torque the bolts to 40 ft. lbs. (54 Nm). Install the idler pulley to the engine bracket.

17. To install the cam sensor, first clean off the old spacer from the sensor face completely. Inspect the O-ring for damage and replace if necessary. A new spacer must be attached to the cam sensor, prior to installation; if a new spacer is not used, engine performance will be affected. Oil the O-ring lightly and push the sensor in to its bore in the timing case cover

until contact is made with the cam timing gear. Hold in this position and tighten it to 9 ft. lbs. (12 Nm).

18. Install the air conditioning compressor and bracket.
19. Install the drive belt.
20. Install the inner splash shield and the wheel and tire assembly.
21. Install the oil pan with a new gasket.
22. Install the motor mount.
23. Remove the engine temperature sensor and fill the cooling system until the level reaches the vacant sensor hole. Install the sensor and continue to fill the radiator. Fill the engine with the proper amount of oil.
24. Connect the negative battery cable and check for leaks.

Timing Belt and/or Chain

REMOVAL & INSTALLATION

2.2L and 2.5L Engine

▶ See Figures 155, 156, 157, 158 and 159

1. Remove the solid mount compressor bracket. Refer to Solid Mount Compressor Bracket Removal procedure outlined earlier in this Section.
2. Remove the accessory drive belts.
3. Remove the timing belt cover. Refer to Timing Belt Cover Removal procedures.
4. Place a jack under the engine.
5. Separate the right engine mount and raise the engine slightly.
6. Loosen the timing belt tensioner screw, rotate the hex nut, and remove timing belt.
7. Turn the crankshaft and intermediate shaft until markings on both sprockets are aligned.
8. Rotate the camshaft so that the arrows on the hub are in line with No. 1 camshaft cap to cylinder head line. Small hole must be in vertical center line.
9. Install the timing belt over the drive sprockets and adjust.

Fig. 156 After loosening the timing belt tensioner screw, rotate the hex nut to release the tension on the belt. When installing the belt rotate this hex nut to increase tension on the belt, then tighten the tensioner screw

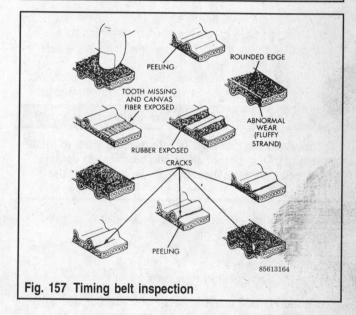

Fig. 157 Timing belt inspection

Fig. 155 Loosening the timing belt tensioner screw

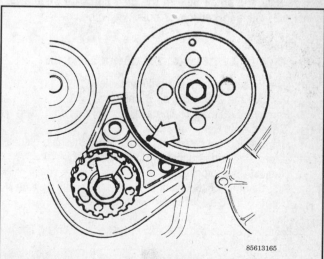

Fig. 158 Crankshaft and intermediate shaft timing mark alignment, 2.2L and 2.5L engine

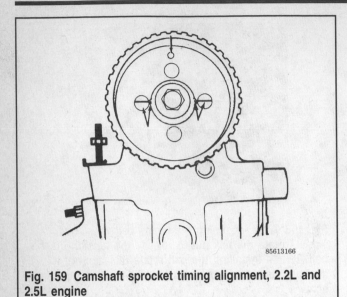

Fig. 159 Camshaft sprocket timing alignment, 2.2L and 2.5L engine

10. Tighten the tensioner by turning the tensioner hex to the right. Tension should be correct when the belt can be twisted 90 degrees with the thumb and forefinger, midway between the camshaft and intermediate sprocket.

11. Turn the engine clockwise from TDC 2 revolutions with crankshaft bolt. Check the timing marks for correct alignment.

✳✳WARNING

Do not used the camshaft or intermediate shaft to rotate the engine. Also, do not allow oil or solvent to contact timing belt as they will deteriorate the belt and cause slipping.

12. Tighten lock nut on tensioner while holding weighted wrench in position to 61 Nm (45 ft. lbs.).

13. Install the timing belt cover. Refer to Timing Belt Cover Installation procedures.

14. Install the accessory drive belts.

➡With timing belt cover installed and number one cylinder at TDC, the small hole in the cam sprocket should be centered in timing belt cover hole.

2.6L Engine

▶ **See Figures 160, 161, 162, 163, 164, 165 and 166**

1. Disconnect the negative battery cable.
2. Remove the accessory drive belts.
3. Remove the timing chain case cover. Refer to Timing Chain Case Cover Removal Procedures.
4. Remove the bolts securing the silent shaft chain guides. Mark all parts for proper location during assembly.
5. Remove the sprocket bolts, silent shaft drive chain, crankshaft/silent sprocket, silent shaft sprockets and spacer.
6. Remove the camshaft sprocket bolt and washer.
7. Remove the distributor drive gear.
8. Remove the camshaft sprocket holder and timing chain guides.
9. Depress the tensioner and remove the timing chain and camshaft sprocket.
10. Remove the crankshaft sprocket.
11. Remove the tensioner shoe, washer and spring.

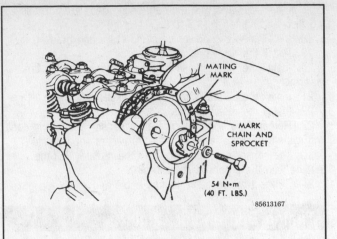

Fig. 160 Mark the chain and sprockets and remove the bolt, washer distributor drive gear and sprocket, 2.6L engine

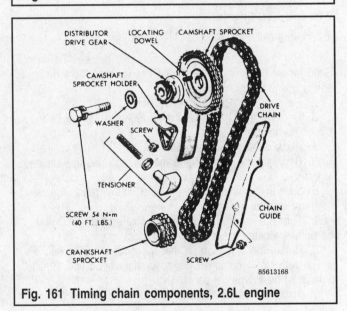

Fig. 161 Timing chain components, 2.6L engine

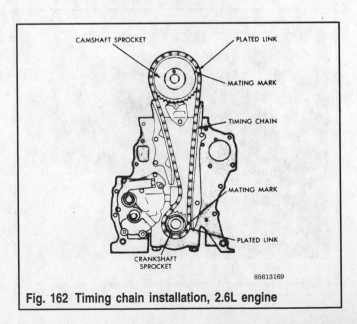

Fig. 162 Timing chain installation, 2.6L engine

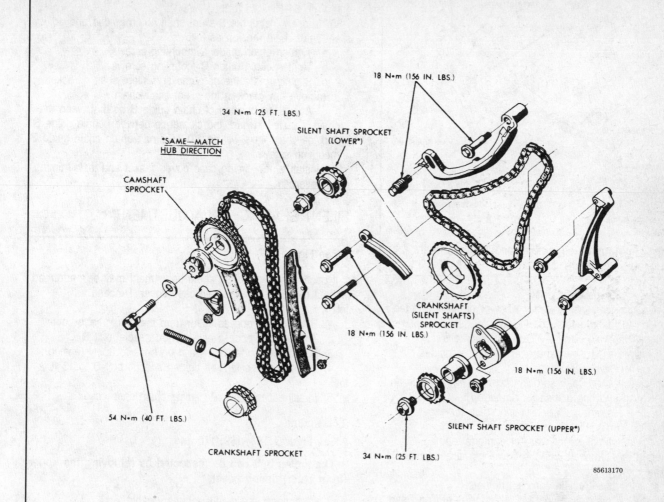

Fig. 163 Timing/silent shaft chain and drive components, 2.6L engine

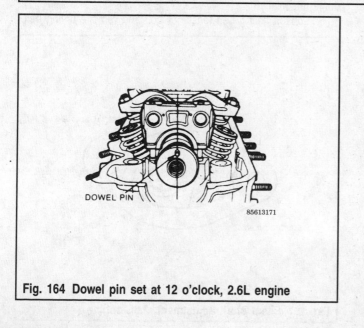

Fig. 164 Dowel pin set at 12 o'clock, 2.6L engine

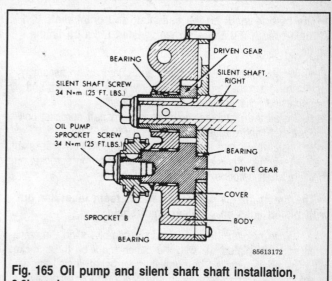

Fig. 165 Oil pump and silent shaft shaft installation, 2.6L engine

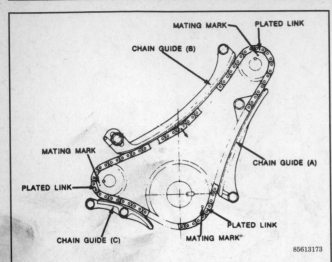

Fig. 166 Timing mark alignment for the silent shaft timing chain installation, 2.6L engine

12. Clean and inspect all parts.

13. Check the tensioner shoe for wear or damage and tensioner spring for deterioration. Spring free length 65.7mm.

14. Check the chain cover for damage or cracks.

15. Check the silent shaft and camshaft chain guides for damage or excessive wear.

16. Check the silent shaft sprocket cushion ring for free and smooth rotation and ring guides for damage.

17. Check the silent chain and timing chain for excessive play, wear or damage links.

18. Check all sprockets for wear or damage teeth.

19. Rotate the camshaft until the dowel pin is at vertical center line with cylinder.

20. Install the timing chain sprocket holders.

21. Rotate the crankshaft until No. 1 piston is at Top Dead Center (TDC) of its compression stroke.

22. Install the timing chain tensioner spring, washer and shoe on oil pump body.

23. Assemble the timing chain on the camshaft and crankshaft sprockets.

➡**The mating mark on the camshaft and crankshaft sprocket teeth must line up with plated links on timing chain.**

24. While holding the sprockets and chain as an assembly, install the crankshaft sprocket to key way of crankshaft and camshaft sprocket to dowel pin of camshaft.

25. Install the distributor drive gear, camshaft sprocket bolt and washer, and torque bolt to 54 Nm (40 ft. lbs.).

26. Install the silent shaft chain drive sprocket on crankshaft.

27. Assemble the silent shaft chain to oil pump sprocket and to silent shaft sprocket.

➡**The timing marks on the sprockets teeth must line up with plated links on of silent shaft chain.**

28. While holding the parts as an assembly, align the crankshaft sprocket plated link with the punch mark on the sprocket. With the chain installed on crankshaft sprocket, install the oil pump sprocket and silent chain sprocket on their respective shafts.

29. Install the oil pump and silent shaft sprocket bolts and tighten to 34 Nm (25 ft. lbs.).

30. Loosely install the 3 silent shaft chain guides and adjust silent shaft chain tension as follows.

   a. Tighten chain guide **A** mounting screws.

   b. Tighten chain guide **C** mounting screws.

   c. Slightly rotate the oil pump and silent shaft sprockets to remove any slack in the silent shaft chain.

   d. Adjust the position of chain guide **B** so that when the chain is pulled inward, the clearance between chain guide **B** and the chain links will be 1.0-3.5mm. Tighten chain guide **B** mounting screws.

31. Install a new timing case cover gasket and install timing case cover.

SILENT SHAFT CHAIN ADJUSTMENT

▸ **See Figure 167**

If necessary silent shaft chain adjustment may be performed without removing timing chain case cover. Proceed as followed:

1. Remove the access cover from the timing case cover.

2. Through the access hole loosen special bolt **B**

3. Using your finger only push on boss to apply tension.

4. While applying tension tighten special bolt **B** to 13 ft. lbs.

5. Install access cover to timing chain case cover.

3.0L Engine

▸ **See Figures 168, 169, 170 and 171**

➡**The timing belt can be inspected by removing the upper (front outer) timing cover.**

1. Disconnect the negative battery cable.

2. Remove the accessory drive belts.

3. Remove the timing belt covers. Refer to Timing Belt Cover Removal Procedures.

4. Identify the timing belt running direction to avoid reversal during installation.

5. Loosen timing belt tensioner bolt and remove timing belt.

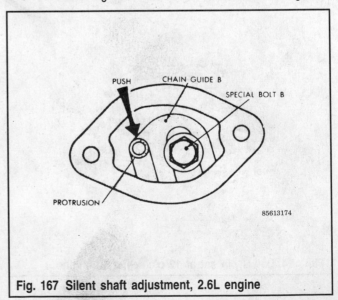

Fig. 167 Silent shaft adjustment, 2.6L engine

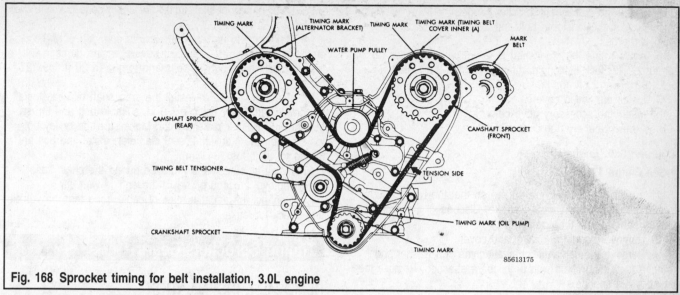

Fig. 168 Sprocket timing for belt installation, 3.0L engine

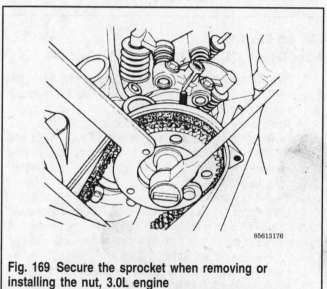

Fig. 169 Secure the sprocket when removing or installing the nut, 3.0L engine

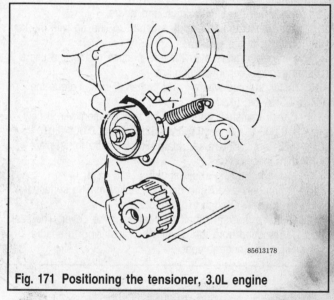

Fig. 171 Positioning the tensioner, 3.0L engine

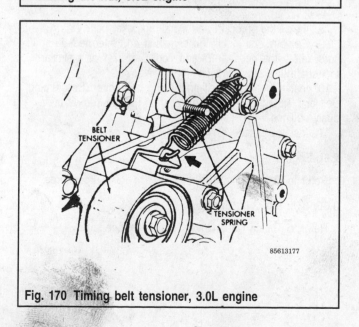

Fig. 170 Timing belt tensioner, 3.0L engine

6. Remove the crankshaft sprocket flange.

7. Rotate the crankshaft sprocket until timing mark on crankshaft sprocket is lined up with the oil pump timing mark at 1 o'clock position.

8. Rotate the (inner) camshaft sprocket until mark on (inner) camshaft sprocket is lined up with the timing mark on alternator bracket.

9. Rotate the (outer) camshaft sprocket (radiator side) until mark on the sprocket is lined up with the timing mark on the timing belt inner cover. Refer to timing belt illustration.

10. Install the timing belt on the crankshaft sprocket while maintaining pressure on the tensioner side.

11. Position the timing belt over the camshaft sprocket (radiator side). Next, position the belt under the water pump pulley, then over the (inner) sprocket and finally over the tensioner.

12. Apply rotating force in the opposite direction to the camshaft sprocket (radiator side) to create tension on the timing belt tension side.

13. Rotate the crankshaft in a clockwise direction and recheck engine timing marks.

14. Install the crankshaft sprocket flange.

15. Loosen the tensioner bolt and allow tensioner spring to tension the belt.

16. Again rotate the crankshaft in a clockwise direction (2) full turns. Recheck the engine timing. Tighten the tensioner bolt to 31 Nm (23 ft. lbs.).

17. Install the timing covers.

18. Install the accessory drive belts.

19. Connect battery negative cable.

3.3L and 3.8L Engines

▶ See Figure 172

1. If possible, position the engine so that the No. 1 piston is at TDC on the compression stroke. Disconnect the negative battery cable. Drain the coolant.

2. Remove the timing chain case cover.

3. Remove the camshaft gear attaching cup washer and remove the timing chain with both gears attached. Remove the timing chain snubber.

To install:

4. Assemble the timing chain and gears.

5. Turn the crankshaft and camshaft to line up with the key way locations of the gears.

6. Slide both gears over their respective shafts and use a straight edge to confirm alignment.

7. Install the cup washer and camshaft bolt. Torque the bolt to 35 ft. lbs. (47 Nm).

8. Check camshaft endplay. The specification with a new plate is 0.002-0.006 in. (0.051-0.052mm) and 0.002-0.010 in. (0.51-0.254mm) with a used plate. Replace the thrust plate if not within specifications.

9. Install the timing chain snubber.

10. Thoroughly clean and dry the gasket mating surfaces.

11. Install new O-rings to the block.

12. Remove the crankshaft oil seal from the cover. The seal must be removed from the cover when installing to ensure proper oil pump engagement.

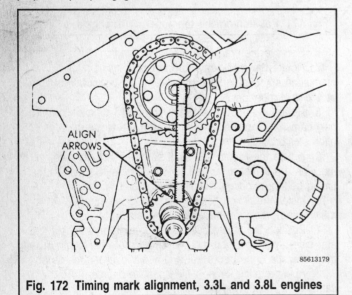

ALIGN
ARROWS

85613179

Fig. 172 Timing mark alignment, 3.3L and 3.8L engines

13. Using a new gasket, install the chain case cover to the engine.

14. Make certain that the oil pump is engaged onto the crankshaft before proceeding, or severe engine damage will result. Install the attaching bolts and torque to 20 ft. lbs. (27 Nm).

15. Use tool C-4992 to install the crankshaft oil seal. Install the crankshaft pulley using a 5.9 in. suitable bolt and thrust bearing and washer plate L-4524. Make sure the pulley bottoms out on the crankshaft seal diameter. Install the bolt and torque to 40 ft. lbs. (54 Nm).

16. Install all other parts removed during the chain case cover removal procedure and fill the engine with oil.

17. Connect the negative battery cable, road test the vehicle and check for leaks.

Timing Sprockets/Gears

REMOVAL & INSTALLATION

2.2L and 2.5L Engines

▶ See Figures 173, 174, 175, 176, 177, 178 and 179

1. Remove the drive belts, timing belt cover and timing belt. See Timing Belt Cover and Timing Belt Removal Procedures as previously outlined.

2. Remove the crankshaft sprocket bolt.

3. Remove the crankshaft sprocket using Tool C-4685 and Tool L-4524 or an equivalent puller. If crankshaft seal removal is necessary, remove with Tool C-4679 (2.2L) or Tool C-4991 (2.5L), or an equivalent tool.

4. Clean the crankshaft seal surface with 400 grit paper.

5. Lightly coat the seal (Steel case seal) outer surface with Loctite Stud N' Bearing Mount (P/N 4057987) or equivalent. A soap and water solution is recommended to lubricate (Rubber Coated Case Seal) outer surface.

6. Lightly lubricate the seal lip with engine oil.

7. Install seal with Tool No. C-4680 (2.2L) or Tool No. C-4992 (2.5L).

8. Install the sprocket and install sprocket bolt.

9. Remove and install the camshaft and intermediate shaft sprockets with Tool C-4687 and Tool C-4687-1 or a similar tool such as a strap wrench.

10. Install the timing belt and timing belt cover. See Timing Belt and Timing Belt Cover Installation Procedures as previously outlined.

11. Install the accessory drive belts.

2.6L Engine

Refer to Timing Chain Case Cover Removal procedures.

3.0L, 3.3L and 3.8L Engines

Refer to Timing Case Cover Removal procedures.

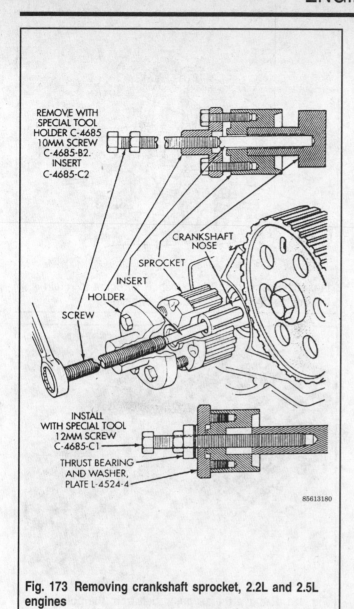

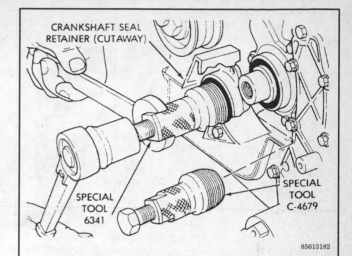

Fig. 175 Removing of the crankshaft, intermediate shaft and camshaft oil seal, 2.2L and 2.5L engines

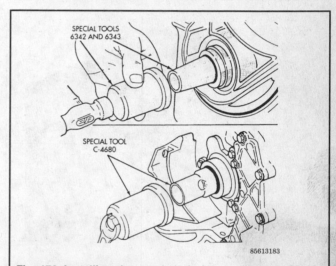

Fig. 176 Installing the crankshaft, intermediate shaft and camshaft oil seal, 2.2L and 2.5L engines

Fig. 173 Removing crankshaft sprocket, 2.2L and 2.5L engines

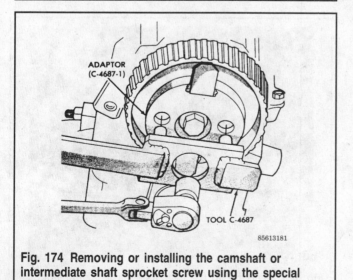

Fig. 174 Removing or installing the camshaft or intermediate shaft sprocket screw using the special tools, 2.2L and 2.5L engines

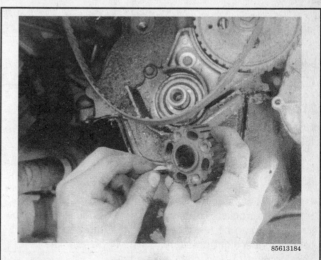

Fig. 177 The crankshaft sprocket and key removed from the shaft

Fig. 178 Using a strap wrench to the remove the intermediate shaft sprocket

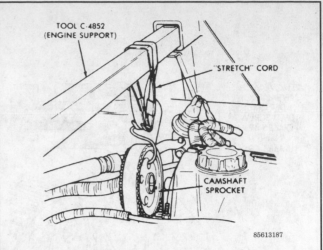

Fig. 180 Suspending the camshaft sprocket to retain the engine timing, 2.2L and 2.5L engines

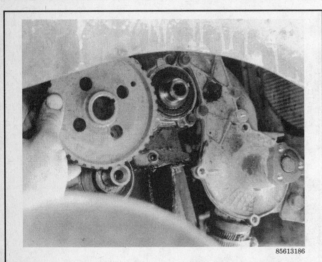

Fig. 179 The intermediate shaft sprocket shown removed from the shaft

Fig. 181 Remove the air pump belt from the pulley

Camshaft and Bearings

REMOVAL & INSTALLATION

2.2L and 2.5L Engines

▶ **See Figures 180, 181, 182, 183, 184, 185, 186, 187, 188, 189 and 190**

The following procedure is preformed with the engine in the vehicle.

➡Removal of the camshaft requires removal of the camshaft sprocket. To maintain proper engine timing, the timing belt can be left indexed on the sprockets and suspended under light pressure. This will prevent the belt from coming off and maintain timing.

1. Disconnect the negative battery cable. Relieve the fuel pressure, if equipped with fuel injection.

Fig. 182 Suspending the camshaft sprocket to retain timing before removing it from the camshaft

Fig. 183 Place a wrench on both ends of the camshaft and remove the camshaft sprocket leaving it suspended

Fig. 186 Removing the camshaft from the engine

Fig. 184 Removing the oil shield

Fig. 187 Removing the seal from the end of the camshaft

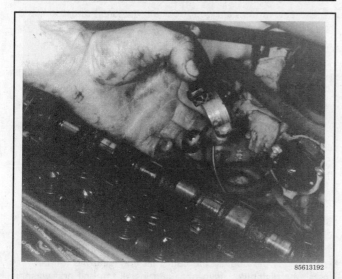

Fig. 185 Removing the bearing caps

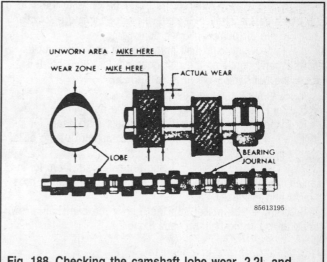

Fig. 188 Checking the camshaft lobe wear, 2.2L and 2.5L engine

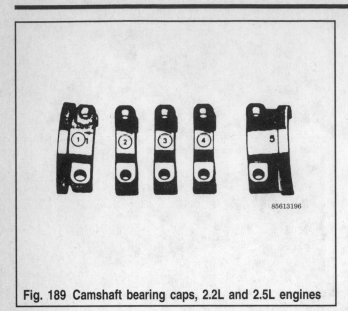

Fig. 189 Camshaft bearing caps, 2.2L and 2.5L engines

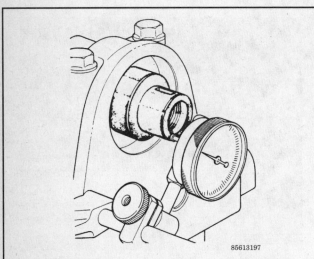

Fig. 190 Measuring the camshaft end play, 2.2L and 2.5L engines

2. Turn the crankshaft so the No. 1 piston is at the TDC of the compression stroke. Remove the upper timing belt cover. Remove the air pump pulley, if equipped.

3. Remove the camshaft sprocket bolt and the sprocket and suspend tightly so the belt does not lose tension. If it does, the belt timing will have to be reset.

4. Remove the valve cover.

5. Remove the air pump belt from the pulley.

6. If the rocker arms are being reused, mark them for installation identification and loosen the camshaft bearing bolts, evenly and gradually.

7. If the rocker arms are being reused, mark them for installation identification and loosen the camshaft bearing bolts, evenly and gradually.

8. Using a soft mallet, rap the rear of the camshaft a few times to break the bearing caps loose.

9. Remove the bolts, bearing caps and the camshaft with seals.

➡Before replacing the camshaft, identify factory installed oversized components. To do so, look for the tops of the bearing caps pained green and O/SJ stamped rearward of the oil gallery plug on the rear of the head. In addition, the barrel of the camshaft is painted green and O/SJ is stamped onto the rear end of the camshaft. Installing standard sized parts in an head equipped with oversized parts-or vice versa-will cause severe engine damage.

10. Check the oil passages for blockage and the parts for damage. Clean all mating surfaces.

To Install:

11. Transfer the sprocket key to the new camshaft. New rocker arms and a new camshaft sprocket bolt are normally included with the camshaft package. Install the rocker arms, lubricate the camshaft and install with end seals installed.

12. Place the bearing caps with No. 1 at the timing belt end and No. 5 at the transaxle end. The camshaft bearing caps are numbered and have arrows facing forward. Torque the camshaft bearing bolts evenly and gradually to 18 ft. lbs. (24 Nm).

➡Apply RTV silicone gasket material to the No. 1 and 5 bearing caps. Install the bearing caps before the seals are installed.

13. Mount a dial indicator to the front of the engine and check the camshaft endplay. Play should not exceed 0.006 in.

14. Install the camshaft sprocket and the new bolt. Install the air pump pulley, if equipped.

15. Install the valve cover with a new gasket.

16. Connect the negative battery cable and check for leaks.

2.6L Engine

1. Disconnect the negative battery cable.

2. Remove the valve cover.

3. Remove the camshaft gear retaining bolt and match mark the distributor gear to its drive gear. Remove the distributor. Pry the distributor drive gear off of the cam gear.

4. Remove the cam gear from the camshaft and allow it to rest on the holder below it.

5. Remove the water pump pulley.

6. Remove the camshaft cap bolts evenly and gradually.

7. Remove the caps, shafts, rocker arms and bolts together as an assembly.

8. Remove the camshaft with the rear seal from the engine.

To install:

9. Install a new roll pin to the camshaft. Lubricate the camshaft and install with the rear seal in place. Install the camshaft in position so the hole in the gear will line up with the roll pin.

10. Install the rocker caps, shafts and arms assembly. Tighten the camshaft bearing cap bolts in the following order to 85 inch lbs. (10 Nm): No. 3, No. 2, No. 4, front cap, rear cap. Repeat the sequence increasing the torque to 175 inch lbs. (19 Nm).

11. Install the gear to the camshaft engaging the roll pin. Install the distributor drive gear and install the bolt and washer. Torque the bolt to 40 ft. lbs. (54 Nm). Install the distributor.

12. Install the valve cover and all related parts.

3.0L Engine

1. Disconnect the negative battery cable. Remove the air cleaner assembly and valve covers.

2. Install auto lash adjuster retainers MD998443 or equivalent on the rocker arms.

3. If removing the right side (front) camshaft, remove the distributor extension.

4. Remove the camshaft bearing caps but do not remove the bolts from the caps.

5. Remove the rocker arms, rocker shafts and bearing caps, as an assembly.

6. Remove the camshaft from the cylinder head.

7. Inspect the bearing journals on the camshaft, cylinder head and bearing caps.

To Install:

8. Lubricate the camshaft journals and camshaft with clean engine oil and install the camshaft in the cylinder head.

9. Align the camshaft bearing caps with the arrow mark (depending on cylinder numbers) and in numerical order.

10. Apply sealer at the ends of the bearing caps and install the assembly.

11. Torque the bearing cap bolts, in the following sequence: No. 3, No. 2, No. 1 and No. 4 to 85 inch lbs. (10 Nm).

12. Repeat the sequence, increasing torque to 175 inch lbs. (18 Nm).

13. Install the distributor extension, if it was removed.

14. Install the valve cover and all related components.

3.3L and 3.8L Engines

▶ **See Figures 191 and 192**

1. Relieve the fuel system pressure. Disconnect the negative battery cable.

2. Remove the engine from the vehicle. Remove the intake manifold, cylinder heads, timing chain cover and timing chain from the engine.

3. Remove the rocker arm and shaft assemblies.

4. Label and remove the pushrod and lifters.

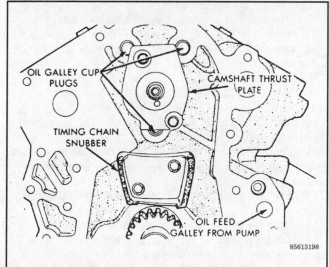

Fig. 191 Camshaft thrust plate, 3.3L and 3.8L engines

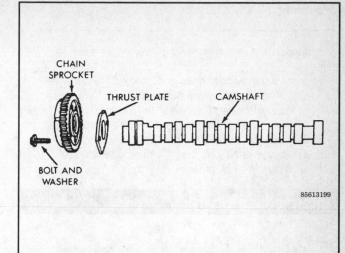

Fig. 192 Camshaft and sprocket assembly, 3.3L and 3.8L engines

5. Remove the camshaft thrust plate.

6. Install a long bolt into the front of the camshaft to facilitate its removal. Remove the camshaft being careful not to damage the cam bearings with the cam lobes.

To install:

7. Install the camshaft to within 2 in. of its final installation position.

8. Install the camshaft thrust plate and 2 bolts and torque to 10 ft. lbs. (12 Nm).

9. Place both camshaft and crankshaft gears on the bench with the timing marks on the exact imaginary center line through both gear bores as they are installed on the engine. Place the timing chain around both sprockets.

10. Turn the crankshaft and camshaft so the keys line up with the key ways in the gears when the timing marks are in proper position.

11. Slide both gears over their respective shafts and use a straight edge to check timing mark alignment.

12. Measure camshaft endplay. If not within specifications, replace the thrust plate.

13. If the camshaft was not replaced, lubricate and install the lifters in their original locations. If the camshaft was replaced, new lifters must be used.

14. Install the pushrods and rocker shaft assemblies.

15. Install the timing chain cover, cylinder heads and intake manifold.

16. Install the engine in the vehicle.

17. When everything is bolted in place, change the engine oil and replace the oil filter.

➡**If the camshaft or lifters have been replaced, add 1 pint of Mopar crankcase conditioner, or equivalent when replenishing the oil to aid in break in. This mixture should be left in the engine for a minimum of 500 miles and drained at the next normal oil change.**

18. Fill the radiator with coolant.

19. Connect the negative battery cable, set all adjustments to specifications and check for leaks.

CAMSHAFT INSPECTION

1. Inspect the camshaft bearing journals for wear or damage.
2. Inspect the cylinder head and check oil return holes.
3. Check the tooth surface of the distributor drive gear teeth of the right camshaft for wear or damage.
4. Check both camshaft surfaces for wear or damage.
5. Remove the distributor drive adaptor seal.
6. Check camshaft lobe height and replace if out of limit. Standard value is 41.00mm.

Intermediate Shaft

REMOVAL & INSTALLATION

2.2L and 2.5L Engines

▶ **See Figures 178 and 194**

The following procedures to be performed with engine removed from vehicle.
1. Remove the distributor assembly.
2. Remove the fuel pump.
3. Remove timing case cover, and timing belt.
4. Remove the intermediate shaft sprocket. See Sprocket Removal Procedures.
5. Remove the intermediate shaft retainer screws and remove retainer.
6. Remove the intermediate shaft and inspect journals and bushing.
7. When installing the shaft, lubricate the fuel pump eccentric and distributor drive gear. Install the intermediate shaft.
8. Inspect the shaft seal in retainer. Replace if necessary.
9. Lightly lubricate the seal lip with engine oil.
10. Install the intermediate shaft retainer assembly and retainer screws. Tighten screws to 105 inch lbs. On 2.5L engine apply anaerobic (Form-in-Place) gasket material to retainer sealing surface before installing.
11. Install the intermediate shaft sprocket.
12. Check engine timing. See Engine Timing Check Procedures.
13. Install the timing belt and adjust.
14. Install the timing belt cover.
15. Install the fuel pump.
16. Install the distributor. See Distributor Installation Procedures.

Balance Shafts

▶ **See Figures 193, 194, 195, 196, 197 and 198**

The 2.5L engine is equipped with 2 balance shafts located in a housing attached to the lower crankcase. These shafts are driven by a chain and 2 gears from the crankshaft at 2 times crankshaft speed. This counterbalance certain engine reciprocating masses.

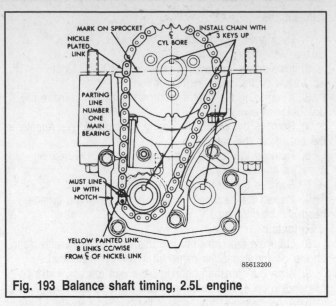

Fig. 193 Balance shaft timing, 2.5L engine

REMOVAL & INSTALLATION

1. Remove the engine from vehicle.
2. Remove the timing case cover, timing belt and sprockets.
3. Remove the engine oil pan.
4. Remove the front crankshaft seal retainer.
5. Remove the balance shafts chain cover.
6. Remove the chain guide and tensioner.
7. Remove the balance shafts sprocket retaining screws and crankshaft chain sprocket torx screws. Remove the chain and sprocket assembly.
8. Remove the balance shafts carrier front gear cover retaining double ended stud. Remove the cover and balance shafts gears.
9. Remove the carrier rear cover and balance shafts.
10. To separate the carrier, remove (6) crankcase to carrier attaching bolts and remove carrier.
11. Take notice of all parts to avoid interchanging.
   To install:
12. Install both shafts into carrier the assembly from rear of carrier.
13. Install the rear cover.
14. Install the balance shafts drive and driven gears to shafts.
15. Position the carrier assembly on crankcase and tighten (6) bolts to 54 Nm (40 ft. lbs.).
16. Crankshaft to Balance Shaft Timing must be established. Rotate both balance shafts until the key ways are in the Up position.
17. Install the short hub drive gear on balance shaft driving shaft.
18. Install the long hub gear on the driven shaft.
19. With both gears on the balance shafts and key ways Up, the timing marks should be meshed.
20. Align the balance shaft carrier cover with the carrier housing dowel pin and install double ended stud. Tighten to 105 inch lbs.
21. Install the crankshaft sprocket and tighten sprocket torx screw to 11 ft. lbs.

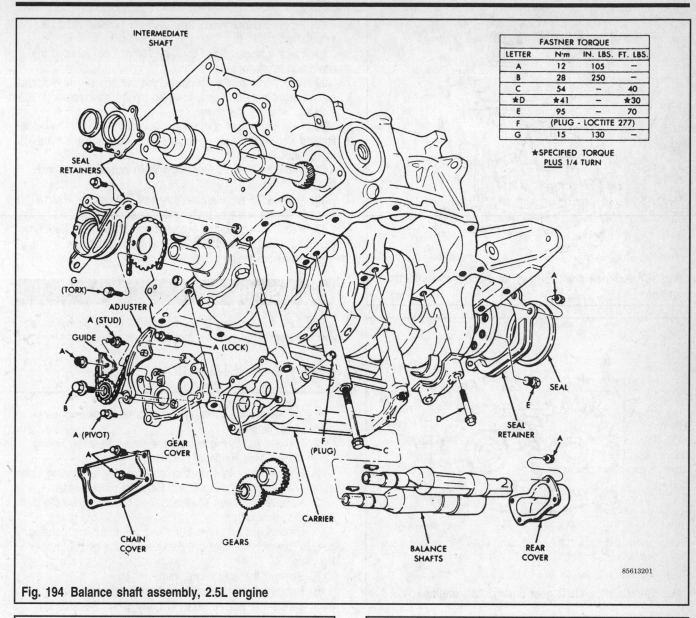

FASTNER TORQUE			
LETTER	N·m	IN. LBS.	FT. LBS.
A	12	105	—
B	28	250	—
C	54	—	40
★D	★41	—	★30
E	95	—	70
F	(PLUG - LOCTITE 277)		
G	15	130	—

★SPECIFIED TORQUE
PLUS 1/4 TURN

Fig. 194 Balance shaft assembly, 2.5L engine

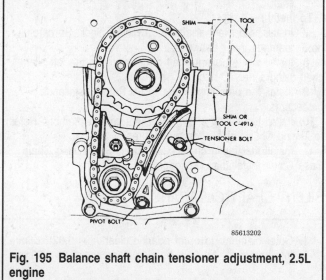

Fig. 195 Balance shaft chain tensioner adjustment, 2.5L engine

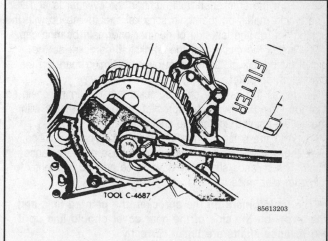

Fig. 196 Removing the intermediate shaft sprocket using the special tools, 2.5L engine

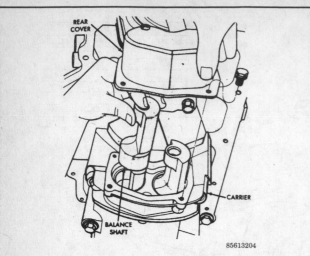

Fig. 197 Balance shaft removal and installation, 2.5L engine

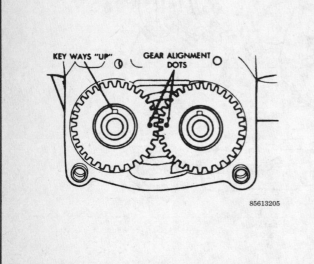

Fig. 198 Balance shaft gear timing, 2.5L engine

22. Turn the crankshaft until number one cylinder is at TDC. The timing marks on the chain sprocket should line up with the parting line on the left side of number one main bearing cap.

23. Install the chain over the crankshaft sprocket so the nickel plated link of the chain is over the timing mark on the crankshaft sprocket.

24. Install the balance shaft sprocket into the timing chain so that the timing mark on the sprocket (yellow dot) mates with the yellow painted link on the chain.

25. With the balance shaft key way in 12 o'clock position slide the balance shaft sprocket on the nose of the balance shaft. The balance shaft may have to be pushed in slightly to allow for clearance.

➡The timing mark on the sprocket, the painted link, and the arrow on the side of the gear cover should line up if the balance shafts are timed correctly.

26. Install the balance shaft bolt and tighten to 21 ft. lbs. Placed a wooden block between the crankcase and crankshaft counterbalance to prevent crankshaft from turning.

27. Proper balance shaft Timing Chain Tension must be established.

28. Place a shim 1.0mm thick by 70mm long between the chain and tensioner.

29. Apply firm hand pressure behind the adjustment slot and tighten adjustment bolt first, followed by the pivot screw to 105 inch lbs. Remove the shim.

30. Install the chain guide making sure the tab on the guide fits into slot on the gear cover. Install nut/washer and tighten to 105 inch lbs.

31. Install the chain cover and tighten screws to 105 inch lbs.

32. Apply a 1.5mm diameter bead of RTV gasket material to retainer sealing surface. Install retainer assembly.

33. Install the crankshaft sprocket and timing belt. See Timing Belt Adjustment and Engine Timing Procedures.

34. Install the timing cover.

Silent Shafts

The 2.6L engine uses 2 counter shafts (silent shafts) in the cylinder block to reduce engine noise and vibration.

REMOVAL & INSTALLATION

The following procedures to be performed with engine removed from vehicle.

1. Remove the timing chain case cover. Refer to Timing Chain Case Cover Removal procedures.

2. Remove the silent shaft chain assembly and timing chain assembly. Refer to Timing Chain Removal procedures.

3. Remove the silent shaft bolt (bolt directly above the silent chain sprocket).

4. Remove the oil pump bolts and pull the pump housing straight forward. Remove the gaskets and the oil pump backing plate.

5. Remove the right silent shaft.

6. Remove the left silent shaft thrust plate by screwing 2 8mm screws into tapped holes in thrust plate. Remove left silent shaft.

To install:

7. Install both silent shafts into cylinder block. Be careful not to damage inner bearings.

8. Install the left silent shaft thrust plate on the left silent shaft using a new O-ring.

9. Install the oil pump. Refer to Oil Pump Installation procedures.

10. Install the timing chain and silent chain assembly. Refer to Timing Chain Installation procedures.

11. Install the timing chain case cover. See Timing Chain Case Cover Installation procedures.

SILENT SHAFT CLEARANCE

1. Outer diameter to outer bearing clearance: 0.02-0.06mm.

2. Inner diameter to inner bearing clearance: 0.05-0.09mm.

Pistons and Connecting Rods

▶ **See Figures 199, 200, 201, 202, 203, 204, 205, 206, 207 and 208**

REMOVAL

The following procedures are performed with the engine removed from vehicle.

1. Remove the engine from the vehicle.
2. Remove the timing case cover, timing belt or chain and sprockets.
3. Remove the intake manifold.
4. Remove the cylinder head from engine.
5. Remove the engine oil pan.
6. Remove the oil pump.

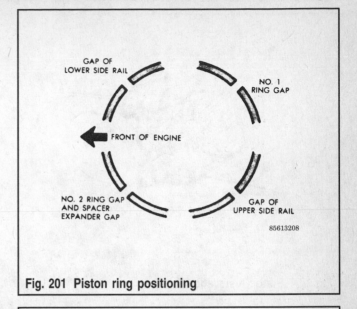

Fig. 201 Piston ring positioning

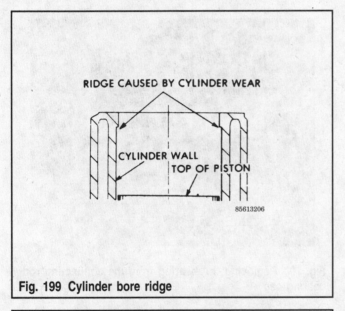

Fig. 199 Cylinder bore ridge

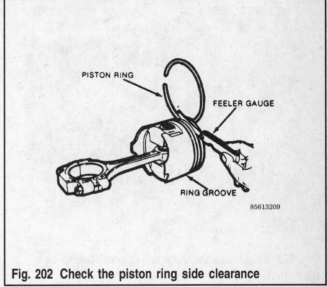

Fig. 202 Check the piston ring side clearance

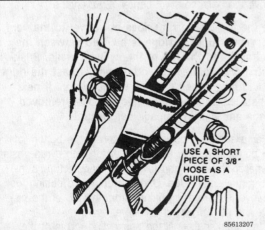

Fig. 200 Use lengths of rubber tubing to protect the crankshaft journal and cylinder linings during piston and rod removal and installation

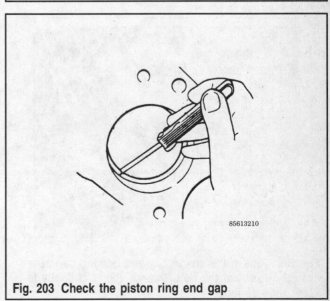

Fig. 203 Check the piston ring end gap

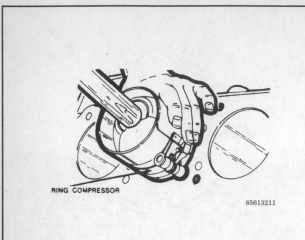

Fig. 204 Piston installation

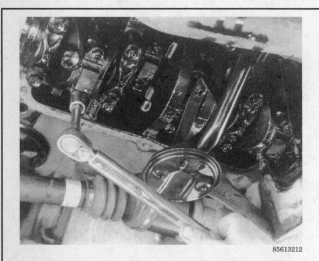

Fig. 205 Loosening the connecting rod bearing cap nuts

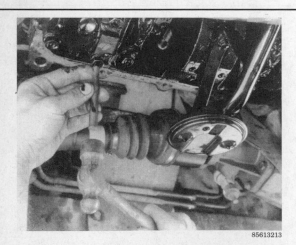

Fig. 206 Loosen the connecting rod bearing cap nuts enough to protect the bolt threads then tap lightly to break the cap loose

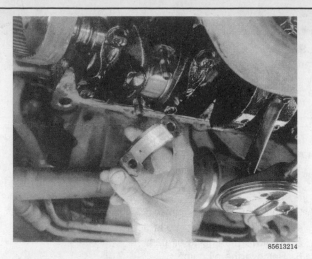

Fig. 207 The connecting rod bearing cap and bearing removed from the connecting rod

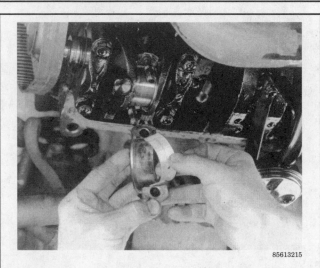

Fig. 208 Removing the bearing from the connecting rod bearing cap

7. Remove the balance shaft carrier (2.5L engine).

➡Because the top piston ring does not travel to the very top of the cylinder bore, a ridge is built up between the end of the travel and the top of the cylinder walls. Pushing the piston and connecting rod assembly past the ridge is difficult and may cause damage to the piston. If new rings are installed and the ridge has not been removed, ring breakage and piston damage can occur.

Turn the crankshaft to position the piston at the bottom of the cylinder bore. Cover the top of the piston with a rag. Install a ridge reamer in the bore and follow the manufacturer's instructions to remove the ridge. Use caution, avoid cutting too deeply. Remove the rag and cuttings from the top of the piston. Remove the ridge from all cylinders.

8. Turn the crankshaft until the connecting rod is at the bottom of travel.

9. Number all connecting rod caps if not already labeled to aid during assembly. Remove connecting rod bearing cap nuts and remove caps. Keep all parts separated.

10. Take 2 pieces of rubber tubing and cover the rod bolts to prevent cylinder wall scoring.

11. Before removing the piston assembly from cylinder bore scribe a mark indicating front position, or take notice of manufacturer identification mark. Using a wooden hammer handle, carefully tap piston assembly away from crankshaft and remove from cylinder block. Care should be taken not to damage crankshaft connecting rod journals or threads on connecting rod cap bolts.

12. Remove all the pistons from cylinder block in similar fashion.

➡It is not necessary to remove the crankshaft from cylinder block for piston service. If crankshaft service is necessary refer to Crankshaft Removal procedures.

CLEANING AND INSPECTION

▶ See Figures 209, 210, 211, 212 and 213

1. Use a piston ring expander and remove the rings from the piston.

2. Clean the ring grooves using an appropriate cleaning tool, exercise care to avoid cutting too deeply.

3. Clean all varnish and carbon from the piston with a safe solvent. Do not use a wire brush or caustic solution on the pistons.

4. Inspect the pistons for scuffing, scoring, cracks, pitting or excessive ring groove wear. If wear is evident, the piston must be replaced.

5. Have the piston and connecting rod assembly checked by a machine shop for correct alignment, piston pin wear and piston diameter. If the piston has collapsed it will have to be replaced or knurled to restore original diameter. Connecting rod bushing replacement, piston pin fitting and piston changing can be handled by the machine shop.

6. Check the cylinder bore diameter and cylinder bore for wear using a telescope gauge at 3 different levels. Cylinder bore out of round: 0.05mm maximum. Cylinder bore taper: 0.13mm maximum. Refer to General Engine Specification Chart for cylinder bore specification.

Fig. 210 Clean the piston grooves using a ring groove cleaner

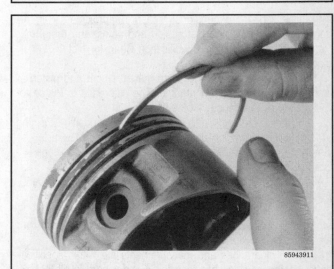

Fig. 211 You can use a piece of an old ring to clean the ring grooves, be careful the ring is sharp

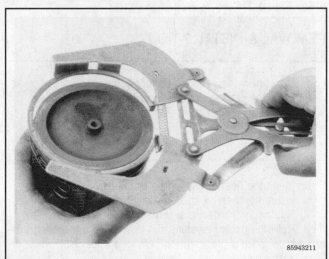

Fig. 209 Use a ring expander tool to remove the piston rings

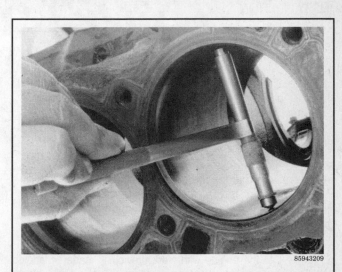

Fig. 212 An telescoping gauge may be used to measure the cylinder bore diameter

Fig. 213 Measure the piston's outer diameter using a micrometer

7. Check piston dimensions. Measure approximately 2mm above the bottom of the piston skirt and across the thrust face. Refer to Piston and Ring Specification Chart for piston diameter.

8. After recording cylinder bore measurement and piston diameter, subtract the low reading. The difference is Piston to Cylinder Wall Clearance: 0.02-0.04mm.

9. Check piston ring gap using a piston to position the ring at least 16mm from the bottom of cylinder bore. Measure clearance using a feeler gauge. Refer to Piston and Rings Specification Chart.

10. Check the piston ring to piston ring groove clearance using a feeler gauge.

11. Check the ring groove by rolling the new piston ring around the groove to check for burrs or carbon deposits. If any are found, remove with a fine file.

12. If all clearances and measurements are within specifications, honing or glaze breaking the cylinder bore is all that is required.

INSTALLATION

1. Start with the oil ring expander in the lower oil ring groove.

2. Install one oil rail at bottom of the oil ring expander and the other at top. The oil rails must be spaced 180 degrees apart from each other.

3. Using the ring expander install the intermediate piston ring.

4. Install the upper piston ring using the ring expander.

➡**Generally marks on the upper and intermediate piston rings must point toward the crown of piston. Consult the illustration with piston ring set instruction sheet for ring positioning.**

5. Install a ring compressor and insert the piston and rod assembly into the engine with mark previously made or labeled mark on piston head toward timing chain end of cylinder block.

6. Rotate the crankshaft so that the connecting rod journal is on center of cylinder bore. Install a new connecting rod bearing in connecting rod and cap. Check the connecting rod bearing oil clearance using Plastigage. Follow the manufacturer procedures. Refer to Crankshaft and Connecting Rod Specification Chart.

7. Tighten the connecting rod cap nuts to specification. Refer to Torque Specification Chart,

8. Install the remaining piston and rod assemblies.

9. Using a feeler gauge, check connecting rod side clearance.

10. On 2.5L engine install the balance shaft carrier.

11. Install the oil pump and pick-up.

12. Install the cylinder head.

13. Install the intake manifold.

14. Install the timing chain or belt and sprockets.

15. Install the timing case cover.

16. Install the engine oil pan. Refer to Oil Pan Installation procedures.

Freeze Plugs

REMOVAL & INSTALLATION

Freeze plugs can be removed with the engine in or out of the vehicle.

Using a blunt tool, such as a drift and hammer, strike the bottom edge of the plug. With the plug rotated, grasp it firmly with pliers and remove it. Do not drive the plug into the block as coolant flow restriction would occur.

When installing the replacement plug, thoroughly clean the plug bore, removing any old sealant. Coat the new plug with Loctite® Stud Mount, or equivalent. Position the plug on the block and drive it into the block so that the sharp edge is at least 0.020 in. (0.5mm) inside the chamfer. Check the plug for leaks after cooling system refilling.

Engine Block Heater

▶ **See Figure 214**

REMOVAL & INSTALLATION

1. Disconnect the negative battery cable.
2. Drain the cooling system, including the engine block.
3. Detach the power cord plug from the block heater assembly.
4. Loosen the screw in the center of the heater and pull the heater from the block.
To install:
5. Clean the heater hole in the block and the heater seat.
6. Insert the heater with the element loop facing upward.
7. Tighten the heater retaining screw securely.
8. Refill the cooling system and pressurize the cooling system with a radiator pressure tool. Check for leaks before operating block heater.
9. Connect the negative battery cable.

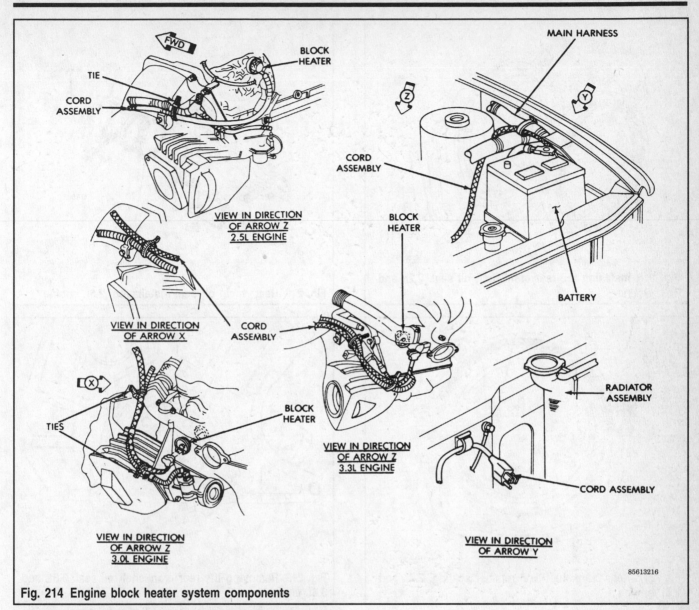

Fig. 214 Engine block heater system components

Rear Main Seal

REMOVAL & INSTALLATION

2.2L and 2.5L Engines

▶ See Figures 215, 216 and 217

1. With the engine or transaxle removed from vehicle, remove the flywheel or flexplate.

2. Pry out rear crankshaft oil seal from seal retainer. Be careful not to nick of damage crankshaft sealing surface or seal retainer.

3. Place Tool C-4681 or equivalent on the crankshaft.

4. Lubricate outer diameter with Loctite Stud N' Bearing Mount (PN. 4057987) or equivalent.

5. Lightly lubricate the seal lip with engine oil and tap in place with a plastic hammer.

6. Install the flywheel/flex plate and tighten bolts to 95 Nm (70 ft. lbs.).

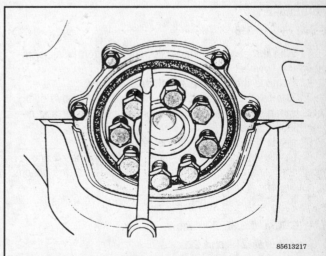

Fig. 215 Removing the rear crankshaft oil seal, 2.2L and 2.5L engine

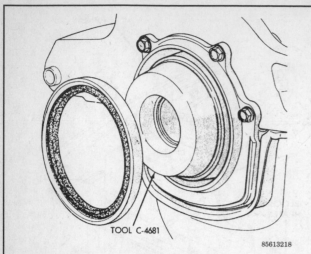

Fig. 216 Installing the rear crankshaft oil seal, 2.2L and 2.5L engine

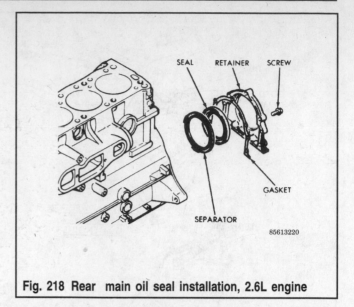

Fig. 218 Rear main oil seal installation, 2.6L engine

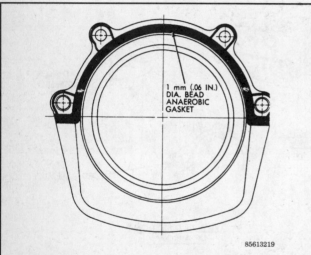

Fig. 217 Rear crankshaft seal retainer sealing, 2.2L and 2.5L engine

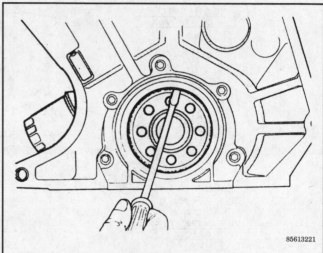

Fig. 219 Removing the rear crankshaft oil seal, 3.3L and 3.8L engine

2.6L Engine

◗ See Figure 218

1. With the engine or transaxle removed from vehicle, remove the flywheel or flex plate.

2. Remove the rear crankshaft seal retainer.

3. Remove the separator from retainer and remove seal.

4. Clean all old gasket material from the retainer and engine block surface.

5. Install a new gasket on the retainer.

6. Lightly lubricate the new seal lip with engine oil and install the separator making sure the oil hole is at the bottom of separator.

7. Install flywheel tighten bolts to 95 Nm (70 ft. lbs.).

3.0L, 3.3L and 3.8L Engines

◗ See Figures 219 and 220

1. With the engine or transaxle removed from vehicle, remove the flywheel or flex plate.

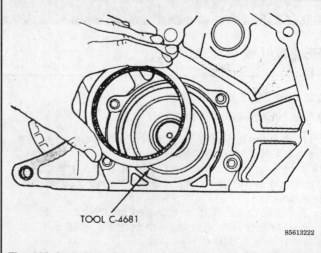

Fig. 220 Installing the rear crankshaft oil seal, 3.3L and 3.8L engine

2. Pry out the rear crankshaft oil seal from the seal retainer. Be careful not to nick or damage the crankshaft sealing surface or seal retainer.

3. Lightly lubricate the new seal lip with engine oil and install seal in retainer housing using Tool MD998718 or equivalent.

4. Install flywheel and tighten the bolts to 95 Nm (70 ft. lbs.).

Front Crankshaft Seal Retainer

REMOVAL & INSTALLATION

2.2L and 2.5L Engines

▶ **See Figures 221, 222, 223, 224, 225, 226 and 227**

➡**When the rear crankshaft seal retainer is required, provide retainer to block sealing during re-installation. Use form-in-place, anaerobic (cures in the absence of air) type gasket material applied as shown.**

1. Remove the timing belt covers, belt, crankshaft sprocket and seal as outlined earlier in this Section.

2. Remove the shield and retainer screws.

3. Apply a form-in-place, anaerobic (cures in the absence of air) type gasket material to the retainer.

4. Assemble the shield and retainer and tighten the screws to 105 inch lbs. (12 Nm).

Crankshaft and Main Bearings

▶ **See Figures 228, 229 and 230**

Although, crankshaft service can be performed without removing the engine from the vehicle, it is far easier to work on the engine after it has been removed from the vehicle.

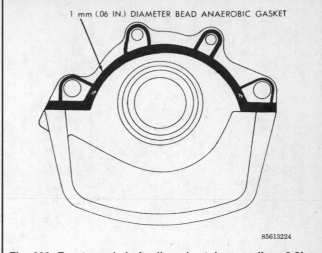

85613224

Fig. 222 Front crankshaft oil seal retainer sealing, 2.2L engine

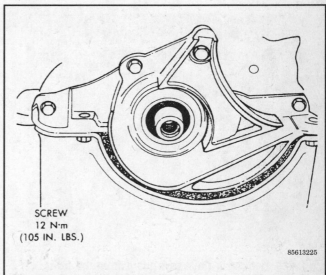

85613225

Fig. 223 Front crankshaft oil seal retainer, 2.5L engine

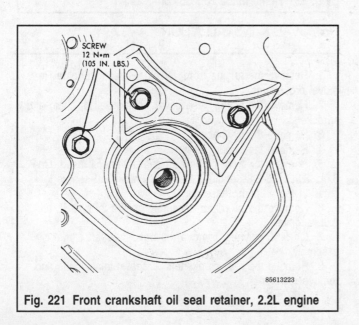

85613223

Fig. 221 Front crankshaft oil seal retainer, 2.2L engine

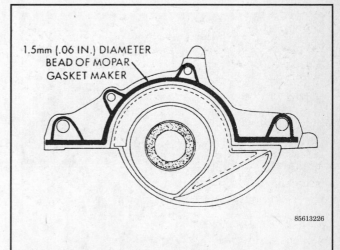

85613226

Fig. 224 Front crankshaft oil seal retainer sealing, 2.5L engine

Fig. 225 Removing the snow guard retaining bolts from the front crankshaft oil seal retainer

Fig. 226 Removing the snow guard from the front crankshaft oil seal retainer

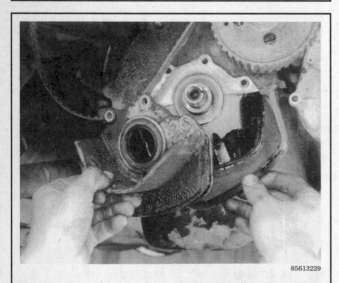

Fig. 227 Removing the front crankshaft oil seal retainer

Fig. 228 Remove the upper main bearing insert, using a roll out pin

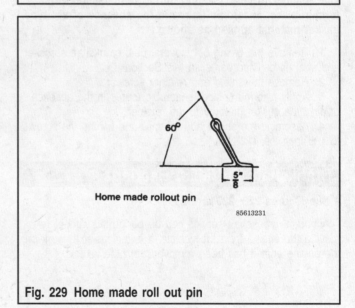

Fig. 229 Home made roll out pin

REMOVAL & INSTALLATION

1. Remove the engine from vehicle. Refer to Engine Removal procedures.

2. Remove the timing case cover, timing belt or chain and sprockets.

3. Remove the flywheel.

4. Remove the engine oil pan.

5. Remove the front crankshaft seal retainer if used. On 3.0L, 3.3L and 3.8L engines the front crankshaft seal is located in the oil pump assembly.

6. Remove the oil pump assembly on the 3.0L, 3.3L and 3.8L engines.

7. On 2.5L engines, remove the balance shaft carrier assembly.

8. Remove the rear crankshaft oil seal retainer bolts and remove retainer.

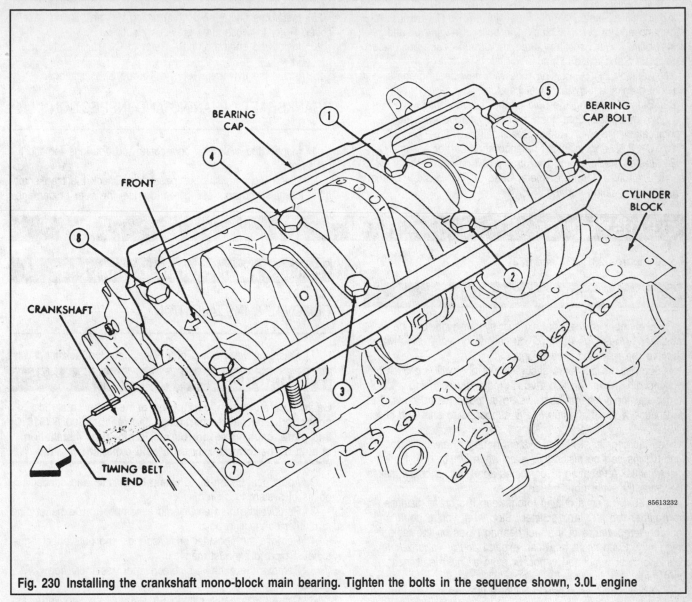

Fig. 230 Installing the crankshaft mono-block main bearing. Tighten the bolts in the sequence shown, 3.0L engine

9. Before removing the crankshaft check Crankshaft End Play. as follows:

   a. Position a screwdriver between a main bearing cap and crankshaft. Move the crankshaft all the way to the rear of its travel.

   b. Position a feeler gauge between the thrust bearing and crankshaft machined surface to determine end play. Refer to Crankshaft and Connecting Rod Specification Chart.

10. Use the following procedure if only crankshaft removal is necessary. If other engine repairs are being perform complete engine disassembly will be required.

11. Number all connecting rod caps if not already labeled to aid during assembly. Remove the connecting rod bearing caps nuts and remove caps.

12. Take 2 pieces of rubber tubing and cover the rod bolts to prevent crankshaft scoring.

13. Tap the piston assembly lightly away from crankshaft. Care should be taken not to damage crankshaft connecting rod journals or threads on connecting rod cap bolts.

14. Remove the main bearing cap bolts and remove caps. Remove crankshaft.

To install:

15. Install the main bearing shells with the lubrication groove in the cylinder block. Make certain the oil holes are in alignment, and bearing tabs seat in block.

16. Install the thrust bearing in journal No.

17. Oil the bearings and journals and install crankshaft.

18. Install the lower main bearing shells (without oil grooves) in lower bearing cap.

19. Check the main or connecting bearing oil clearance as followed:

   a. Wipe oil from bearing shells.

   b. Cut a piece of Plastigage to the same length as width of the bearing and place it in parallel with the journal.

   c. Install the bearing cap and torque to specification.

➡**Do not rotate crankshaft or the Plastigage will be smeared.**

   d. Carefully remove the bearing cap and measure the width of the Plastigage at the widest part using the scale printed on the Plastigage package. Refer to Crankshaft and Connecting Rod Specification Chart.

20. Install all main bearing caps with arrows toward the timing chain end of cylinder block. Dip bolts in engine oil and install bolts finger tight then alternately torque each bolt. Refer to Torque Specification Chart.

21. Position the connecting rods with new bearing shells against crankshaft. Install lower caps.

22. Before installing the nuts oil the threads. Install the nut on each bolt finger tight, then alternately torque each nut to specification. Refer to Torque Specification Chart.

23. On 2.5L engine install balance shaft carrier assembly.

24. Install the front and rear crankshaft oil seal retainer assembly. Apply a 1.5mm diameter bead of RTV gasket material to retainers sealing surface.

25. Install the timing sprockets, timing belt and timing case cover. Refer to procedures previously outlined.

26. Install the engine oil pan. Refer to Oil Pan Installation procedures.

27. Install the flywheel. Refer to Torque Specifications.

CRANKSHAFT CLEANING AND INSPECTION

1. Inspect the main and connecting rod bearings replace if necessary.

2. Clean the crankshaft oil passages. Check the crankshaft main journals and connecting rod journals for wear or damage.

EXHAUST SYSTEM

▶ See Figures 231, 232 and 233

Safety Precautions

For a number of reasons, exhaust system work can be the most dangerous type of work you can do on your car. Always observe the following precautions:

• Support the car extra securely. Not only will you often be working directly under it, but you'll frequently be using a lot of force, say, heavy hammer blows, to dislodge rusted parts. This can cause a car that's improperly supported to shift and possibly fall.

• Wear goggles. Exhaust system parts are always rusty. Metal chips can be dislodged, even when you're only turning rusted bolts. Attempting to pry pipes apart with a chisel makes the chips fly even more frequently.

• If you're using a cutting torch, keep it a great distance from either the fuel tank or lines. Stop what you're doing and feel the temperature of the fuel bearing pipes on the tank frequently. Even slight heat can expand and/or vaporize fuel, resulting in accumulated vapor, or even a liquid leak, near your torch.

• Watch where your hammer blows fall and make sure you hit squarely. You could easily tap a brake or fuel line when you hit an exhaust system part with a glancing blow. Inspect all lines and hoses in the area where you've been working.

❋❋CAUTION

Be very careful when working on or near the catalytic converter. External temperatures can reach 1,500°F (816°C) and more, causing severe burns. Removal or installation should be performed only on a cold exhaust system.

A number of special exhaust system tools can be rented from auto supply houses or local stores that rent special equipment. A common one is a tail pipe expander, designed to enable you to join pipes of identical diameter.

It may also be quite helpful to use solvents designed to loosen rusted bolts or flanges. Soaking rusted parts the night before you do the job can speed the work of freeing rusted parts considerably. Remember that these solvents are often flammable. Apply only to parts after they are cool!

Exhaust (Converter/Resonator) Pipe

REMOVAL & INSTALLATION

1. Raise the vehicle and properly support on jackstands.

❋❋CAUTION

Be very careful when working on or near the catalytic converter! External temperatures can reach 1,500°F (816°C) and more, causing severe burns! Removal or installation should be performed only on a cold exhaust system.

2. Apply penetrating oil to clamp bolts, nuts and connecting points of system to be remove.

3. Remove the nuts and clamp assembly from exhaust pipe to muffler connecting point.

4. Remove the shoulder bolts, springs and nuts attaching exhaust pipe to exhaust manifold.

5. Remove the exhaust pipe/converter assembly from muffler.

6. Clean the exhaust manifold to exhaust pipe/converter assembly gasket mating surfaces and the end of muffler with a wire brush.

7. Install the exhaust pipe/converter assembly or resonator into muffler. Make certain the key on the converter or resonator pipe bottomed in slot of muffler.

8. Install a new gasket on the exhaust pipe and position exhaust pipe into exhaust manifold. Install springs, shoulder bolts and nuts. Tighten nuts to 21 ft. lbs.

9. Align parts and install a new clamp assembly at exhaust pipe and muffler connecting point tighten clamps nuts to 23 ft. lbs.

Tailpipe

REMOVAL & INSTALLATION

1. Raise the vehicle and properly support on jackstands.

2. Apply penetrating oil to clamp bolts, nuts and connecting points of system to be remove.

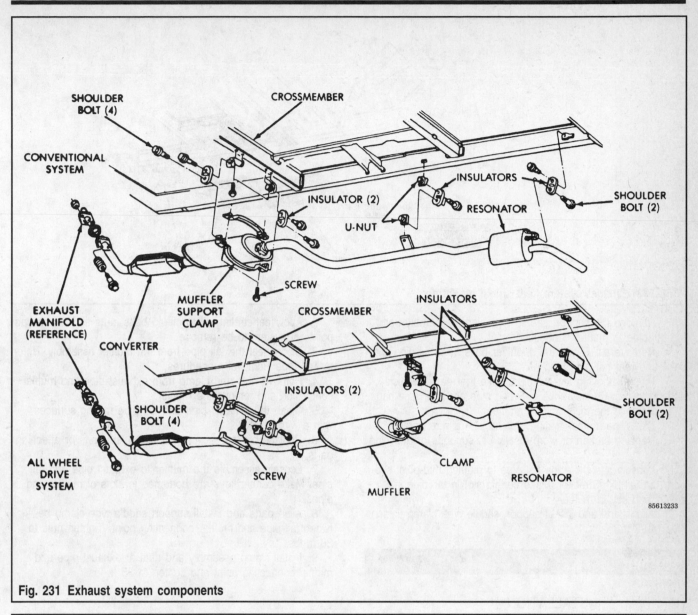

Fig. 231 Exhaust system components

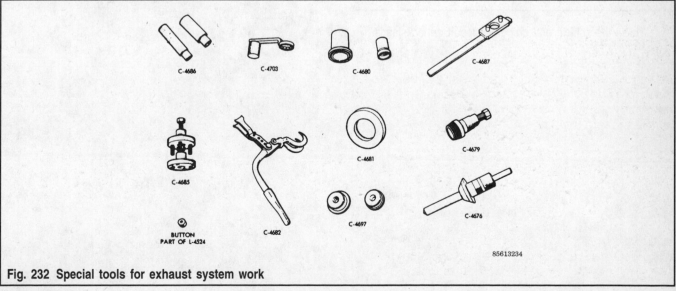

Fig. 232 Special tools for exhaust system work

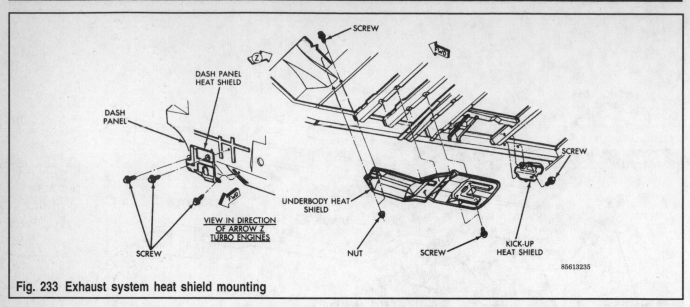

Fig. 233 Exhaust system heat shield mounting

3. Remove the support saddle type clamp assembly from the tail pipe to muffler connecting point.

4. Remove the U-nut and shoulder bolts from tail pipe mid-point and rear tail pipe bracket.

5. When removing the tail pipe, raise the rear of vehicle enough to provide clearance between pipe and rear axle parts.

6. Remove the tailpipe from muffler.

7. Clean the muffler mating surface with a wire brush.

8. Replace broken or worn insulators, supports or attaching parts.

9. Loosely assemble the tail pipe to muffler, mid-point support and tail pipe bracket. Make certain slot in tail pipe is keyed with key in muffler.

10. Align parts and install support saddle type clamp tighten nuts to 28 ft. lbs.

Muffler

REMOVAL & INSTALLATION

1. Raise the vehicle and properly support on jackstands.

2. Apply penetrating oil to clamp bolts, nuts and connecting points of system to be remove.

3. Disconnect the tail pipe from the muffler assembly. Refer to Tail Pipe Removal procedures.

4. Remove nuts and clamp from exhaust pipe and muffler connection and remove the muffler.

5. Clean the exhaust pipe and tail pipe mating surfaces with a wire brush.

6. Replace broken or worn insulators, supports or attaching parts.

7. Loosely assemble the muffler to exhaust pipe and tail pipe. Make certain keys are bottomed in slots of muffler and pipes.

8. Align parts and install support saddle type clamp between tail pipe and muffler connecting point. Tighten nuts to 28 ft. lbs.

9. Install clamp assembly and nuts at exhaust pipe and muffler connecting point and tighten to 25 ft. lbs.

TORQUE SPECIFICATIONS

Component	English	Metric
Air intake plenum attaching bolts		
3.0L engine	115 inch lbs.	13 Nm
Alternator support bracket	40 ft. lbs.	54 Nm
Alternator mounting bolts	40 ft. lbs.	54 Nm
Automatic transmission oil cooler mounting bolts	35 inch lbs.	4 Nm
Automatic transmission oil cooler lines-to-cooler clamps	16 inch lbs.	2 Nm
Balance shaft bolt		
2.5L engine	21 ft. lbs.	29 Nm
Balance shafts carrier assembly-to-crankcase bolts		
2.5L engine	40 ft. lbs.	54 Nm
Cam sensor bolt		
3.3L and 3.8L engines	105 inch lbs.	12 Nm
Camshaft bearing cap bolts		
2.2L and 2.5L engines	18 ft. lbs.	24 Nm
2.6L and 3.0L engines		
Step 1	85 inch lbs.	10 Nm
Step 2	15 ft. lbs.	19 Nm
Camshaft sprocket bolt		
Except 3.3L engine	40 ft. lbs.	54 Nm
3.3L and 3.8L engines	40 ft. lbs.	54 Nm
Camshaft thrust plate bolts		
3.3L engine	105 inch lbs.	12 Nm
Carburetor air heater-to-manifold		
2.6L engine	80 inch lbs.	9 Nm
Catalytic converter-to-manifold		
3.0L engine	24 ft. lbs.	32 Nm
Combination Manifold		
2.2L and 2.5L engines		
Exhaust manifold-to-cylinder head	17 ft. lbs.	23 Nm
Intake manifold-to-cylinder head	19 ft. lbs.	26 Nm
Connecting rod bearing cap bolts		
2.2L, 2.5L, 3.3L and 3.8L engines		
Step 1	40 ft. lbs.	54 Nm
Step 2	an additional 90° (1/4) turn	
2.6L engine	34 ft. lbs.	46 Nm
3.0L engine	38 ft. lbs.	52 Nm
Crankshaft damper bolt		
2.2L and 2.5L engines	50 ft. lbs.	68 Nm
2.6L engine	87 ft. lbs.	118 Nm
3.0L engine	110 ft. lbs.	150 Nm
Crankshaft pulley bolt		
2.2L and 2.5L engines	20 ft. lbs.	27 Nm
3.3L and 3.8L engines	40 ft. lbs.	54 Nm
Crankshaft sprocket Torx® screws		
2.5L engine	11 ft. lbs.	15 Nm

85613C07

TORQUE SPECIFICATIONS

Component	English	Metric
Cylinder Head		
2.2L and 2.5L engines		
Step 1	45 ft. lbs.	61 Nm
Step 2	65 ft. lbs.	88 Nm
Step 3	additional 90° (¼) turn	
2.6L engine		
Step 1	34 ft. lbs.	40 Nm
Step 2	69 ft. lbs.	94 Nm
3.0L engine		
Step 1	30 ft. lbs.	41 Nm
Step 2	50 ft. lbs.	68 Nm
Step 3	70 ft. lbs.	95 Nm
3.3L and 3.8L engines		
8 shorter bolts first		
Step 1	45 ft. lbs.	61 Nm
Step 2	65 ft. lbs.	88 Nm
Step 3	65 ft. lbs.	88 Nm
Step 4	an additional 90° (¼) turn	
2 longer bolts next	25 ft. lbs.	33 Nm
Distributor drive gear bolt		
2.6L engine	40 ft. lbs.	54 Nm
EGR tube flange-to-intake plenum		
3.0L engine	15 ft. lbs.	20 Nm
Engine-to-transaxle mounting bolts	70 ft. lbs.	95 Nm
Exhaust crossover pipe-to-manifold		
3.0L engine	51 ft. lbs.	69 Nm
Exhaust Manifold		
All exc. 2.6L engine	17 ft. lbs.	23 Nm
2.6L engine	13 ft. lbs.	18 Nm
Exhaust pipe-to-manifold		
3.0L engine	20 ft. lbs.	27 Nm
Exhaust pipe-to-exhaust manifold nuts	21 ft. lbs.	29 Nm
Exhaust pipe-to-muffler clamp nuts	23 ft. lbs.	31 Nm
Exhaust system saddle type clamp nuts	28 ft. lbs.	38 Nm
Flywheel/flex plate bolts		
All engines	70 ft. lbs.	95 Nm
Front engine mount	40 ft. lbs.	54 Nm
Fuel line-to-fuel rail clamps		
3.0L engine	10 inch lbs.	1 Nm
Fuel pressure regulator hose clamps		
3.0L engine	10 inch lbs.	1 Nm
Fuel pressure regulator mounting bolts		
3.0L engine	95 inch lbs.	11 Nm
Fuel rail bracket screws		
2.2L and 2.5L engines	21 ft. lbs.	28 Nm
Fuel supply and return tube holddown bolt		
3.0L engine	95 inch lbs.	11 Nm
Heat shield-to-manifold		
2.6L engine	80 inch lbs.	9 Nm
3.0L engine	10 ft. lbs.	14 Nm
Idler pulley-to-engine bracket bolts		
3.3L engine	40 ft. lbs.	54 Nm
Ignition coil mounting bolts	105 inch lbs.	12 Nm
Injector rail attaching bolts		
3.0L engine	115 inch lbs.	13 Nm

85613C08

TORQUE SPECIFICATIONS

Component	English	Metric
Intake Manifold		
2.2L and 2.5L engines	17 ft. lbs.	23 Nm
2.6L engine	13 ft. lbs.	18 Nm
3.0L engine	17 ft. lbs.	23 Nm
3.3L and 3.8L engines		
Step 1	10 inch lbs.	1 Nm
Step 2	17 ft. lbs.	23 Nm
Step 3	17 ft. lbs.	23 Nm
Intake manifold and retainers		
3.3L and 3.8L engines	105 inch lbs.	12 Nm
Intermediate shaft retainer screws		
2.2L and 2.5L engines	105 inch lbs.	12 Nm
Main bearing cap bolts		
2.2L, 2.5L, 3.3L and 3.8L engines		
Step 1	30 ft. lbs.	41 Nm
Step 2	an additional 90° (¼) turn	
2.6L engine	58 ft. lbs.	79 Nm
3.0L engine	60 ft. lbs.	82 Nm
Oil Pan		
2.2L engine	15 ft. lbs.	21 Nm
2.5L engine		
M8 screws	15 ft. lbs.	21 Nm
M6 screws	105 inch lbs.	12 Nm
2.6L engine		
Oil pan-to-block	60 inch lbs.	7 Nm
Oil pan-to-timing case	53 inch lbs.	6 Nm
3.0L engine	50 inch lbs.	6 Nm
3.3L and 3.8L engines	105 inch lbs.	12 Nm
Oil Pump attaching bolts		
2.2L and 2.5L engines	15 ft. lbs.	21 Nm
3.0L engine	10 ft. lbs.	14 Nm
Oil pump cover screws		
3.3L and 3.8L engines	105 inch lbs.	12 Nm
Oil pump sprocket bolt		
2.6L engine	25 ft. lbs.	34 Nm
Radiator mounting bolts	105 inch lbs.	12 Nm
Radiator hose-to-thermostat housing	35 inch lbs.	4 Nm
Radiator hose-to-radiator clamps	to 35 inch lbs.	4 Nm
Right engine mount	20 ft. lbs.	27 Nm
Rocker arm and shaft assembly bolts		
3.3L and 3.8L engines	21 ft. lbs.	28 Nm
Rocker (Valve) Cover		
2.2L engine	105 inch lbs.	12 Nm
2.5L engine	105 inch lbs.	12 Nm
2.6L engine	55 inch lbs.	6 Nm
3.0L engine	68 inch lbs.	7 Nm
3.3L and 3.8L engines	105 inch lbs.	12 Nm
Silent shaft chain tensioner bolt		
2.6L engine	13 ft. lbs.	18 Nm
Thermostat housing		
All engines	15 ft. lbs.	20 Nm
Throttle body-to-intake manifold screws		
2.2L and 2.5L engines	21 ft. lbs.	28 Nm
Timing belt cover screws		
3.0L engine	10 ft. lbs.	14 Nm

85613C09

TORQUE SPECIFICATIONS

Component	English	Metric
Timing belt tensioner lock nut		
2.2L and 2.5L engines	45 ft. lbs.	61 Nm
3.0L engine	23 ft. lbs.	31 Nm
Timing chain case cover		
2.6L engine	13 ft. lbs.	18 Nm
Timing chain cover screws		
2.5L engine	105 inch lbs.	12 Nm
3.3L and 3.8L engines		
M8x1.25 bolt	20 ft. lbs.	27 Nm
M10x1.50 bolt	40 ft. lbs.	54 Nm
Timing chain guide nut		
2.5L engine	105 inch lbs.	12 Nm
Timing chain tensioner adjustment and pivot bolts		
2.5L engine	105 inch lbs.	12 Nm
Torque converter-to-flex plate bolts	40 ft. lbs.	54 Nm
Turbocharger-to-exhaust manifold	40 ft. lbs.	54 Nm
Turbocharger articulated joint shoulder bolts	21 ft. lbs.	28 Nm
Turbocharger connector tube clamps	30 inch lbs.	41 Nm
Turbocharger inlet tube-to-throttle body tube clamp	30 inch lbs.	3 Nm
Turbocharger inlet coolant tube-to-engine block	30 ft. lbs.	41 Nm
Turbocharger mounting screws		
Block screw	40 ft. lbs.	54 Nm
Housing screw	20 ft. lbs.	27 Nm
Turbocharger oil feed line nuts	10 ft. lbs.	14 Nm
Turbocharger oil drain-back hose clamps	30 inch lbs.	3 Nm
Turbocharger outlet-to-exhaust manifold nuts	30 ft. lbs.	41 Nm
Upper intake manifold bolts		
3.3L and 3.8L engines	21 ft. lbs.	28 Nm
Upper intake manifold bracket and strut bolts		
3.3L and 3.8L engines	40 ft. lbs.	54 Nm
Water Pump		
2.2L and 2.5L engines		
3 upper bolts	20 ft. lbs.	27 Nm
1 lower bolt	50 ft. lbs.	68 Nm
2.6L and 3.0L engines	20 ft. lbs.	27 Nm
3.3L and 3.8L engines	105 inch lbs.	12 Nm
Water pump pulley screws		
2.2L and 2.5L engine	105 inch lbs.	12 Nm

85613C10

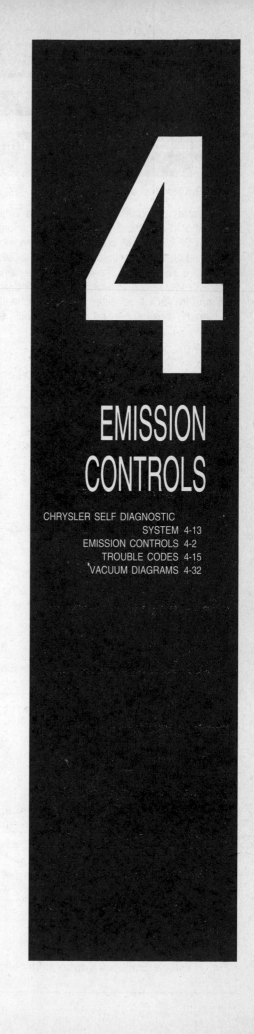

4

EMISSION CONTROLS

EMISSION CONTROLS

Vehicle Emission Control Information Label

▶ **See Figures 1 and 2**

All vehicles described in this Repair and Tune-Up Guide are equipped with a Vehicle Emission Control Information Label (VECI). The VECI label is located in the engine compartment and is permanently attached. No attempt should be made to remove the VECI label. The VECI label contains specific information for the vehicle to which it is attached. If the specifications on the VECI label differ from the information contain in this manual, those shown on the label should be followed.

Crankcase Ventilation System

The Positive Crankcase Ventilation System is described, and servicing procedures are detailed in the 'General Information and Maintenance' section of this book.

Evaporative Emission Controls

The Evaporative Emission Control System prevents gasoline vapor emissions from the fuel system, from entering the atmosphere.

Evaporating fuel from the gas tank or carburetor, passes through vent hoses and tubes to a charcoal canister where they are temporarily stored until they can be drawn into the intake manifold and burned when the engine is running.

CHARCOAL CANISTER

▶ **See Figures 3, 4 and 5**

The charcoal canister is a sealed, maintenance free unit which stores fuel vapors from the fuel tank and carburetor bowl. Although all carburetor bowls are vented internally, some models do not required venting to the canister. In cases where the carburetor is not vented to the canister, the bowl vent port on the canister will be capped. If the canister becomes damaged, replacement with a new unit is required. The hoses connecting the canister are of fuel resistant construction. Use only fuel resistant hoses if replacement is necessary.

DAMPING CANISTER

Some models are equipped with a damping canister that is connected in series with the charcoal canister. The damping canister cushions the effect of a sudden release of fuel rich vapors when the purge valve is signaled to open. The rich

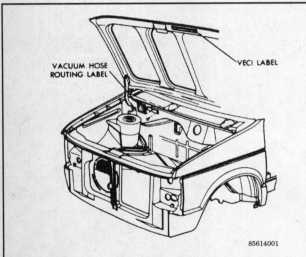

Fig. 1 Vehicle Emission Control Information Label, 1984-86

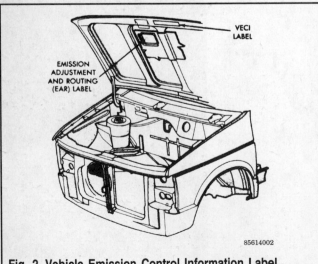

Fig. 2 Vehicle Emission Control Information Label, 1987-94

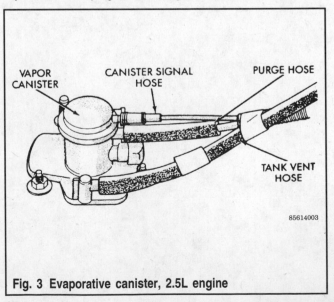

Fig. 3 Evaporative canister, 2.5L engine

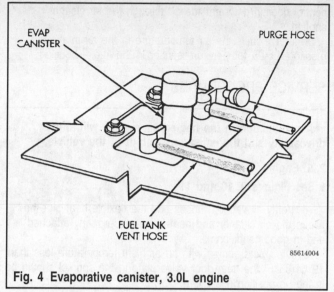

Fig. 4 Evaporative canister, 3.0L engine

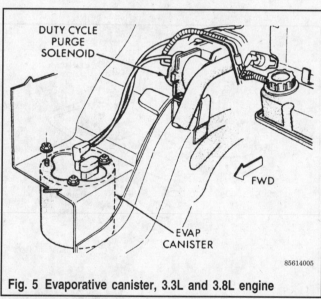

Fig. 5 Evaporative canister, 3.3L and 3.8L engine

vapors are held momentarily and then gradually fed into the intake manifold to be burned.

CANISTER PURGE SOLENOID

▶ See Figure 6

All engines except 1994 vehicles equipped with 3.0L, 3.3L and 3.8L engines are equipped with a canister purge solenoid which is connected in series with the charcoal canister. The canister purge solenoid is electrically operated by the SMEC, SBEC, SBEC II or PCM which grounds the solenoid if engine temperature is below 66°C. This prevents vacuum from reaching the charcoal canister. When the engine reaches operating temperature the SMEC de-energizes the solenoid and allows purge vapors from the canister to pass through the throttle body.

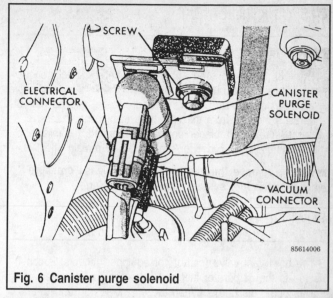

Fig. 6 Canister purge solenoid

DUTY CYCLE CANISTER PURGE SOLENOID

▶ See Figure 7

All 1994 vehicles equipped with 3.0L, 3.3L and 3.8L engines are equipped with a duty cycle EVAP canister purge solenoid. The duty cycle EVAP canister purge solenoid regulates the rate of vapor flow from the EVAP canister to the throttle body and is controlled by the PCM (Powertrain Control Module).

ROLLOVER VALVE

All vehicles pass a full 360° rollover without allowing fuel leakage. To accomplish this, fuel and vapor flow controls are needed for all fuel tank connections. A rollover valve is mounted in the top of the fuel tank to prevent leakage if the vehicle is involved in a rollover.

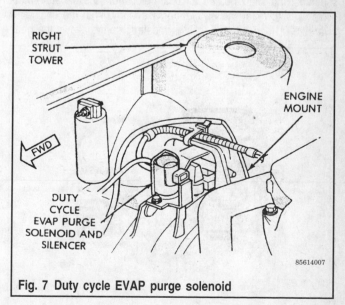

Fig. 7 Duty cycle EVAP purge solenoid

GAS TANK FILLER CAP

▶ **See Figure 8**

The fuel tank is covered and sealed with a specially engineered pressure/vacuum relief gas cap. The built-in relief valve is a safety feature, and allows pressure to be relieved without separating the cap from the filler tube eliminating excessive tank pressure. If a replacement cap is required, a similar cap must be installed in order for the system to remain effective.

➡ **Always remove the gas tank cap to release pressure whenever the fuel system requires servicing.**

BOWL VENT VALVE

The bowl vent valve (carburetor equipped models) is connected to the carburetor fuel bowl, the charcoal canister, and the air pump discharge. When the engine is not running and no air pump pressure is applied, a direct connection between the carburetor and canister exists. When the engine is running, air pump pressure closes the connection between the canister and the fuel bowl. When the engine is shut off, air pressure in the valve bleeds down and the   fuel bowl is allow to vent vapors into the canister.

Exhaust Emission Controls

HEATED INLET AIR SYSTEM

All 2.2L and 2.5L engines are equipped with a vacuum device located in the air cleaner air intake. A small door is operated by a vacuum diaphragm and a thermostatic spring. When the outside air temperature is below a specified level, the door will block off air entering from outside the air cleaner snorkel, and allow heated air channeled from the exhaust manifold area to enter the air cleaner assembly. With the engine warmed up and running the thermostatic spring allows the heat control door to draw outside air through the air cleaner snorkel.

On later models the air temperature in the air intake is monitored by a temperature sensor in the intake housing.

SERVICE PROCEDURES

➡ **A malfunction in the heated air system will affect driveability and the emissions output of the vehicle.**

2.2L Engine

▶ **See Figures 9, 10 and 11**

1. Verify all vacuum hoses and the flexible heat pipe between the air cleaner and heat stove are properly attached and in good condition.
2. On a cold engine with an ambient temperature less than 19°C (65°F) the heat door valve plate in the snorkel should be in the up position (Heat On).

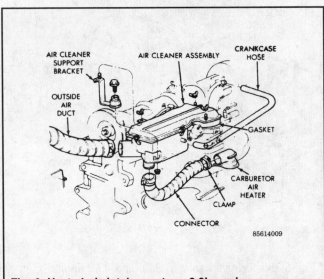

Fig. 9 Heated air intake system, 2.2L engine

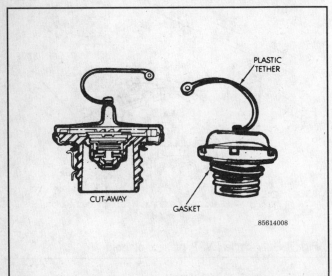

Fig. 8 Pressure vacuum gas filler cap

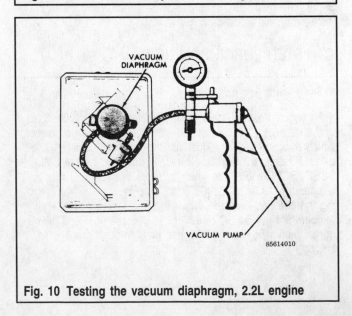

Fig. 10 Testing the vacuum diaphragm, 2.2L engine

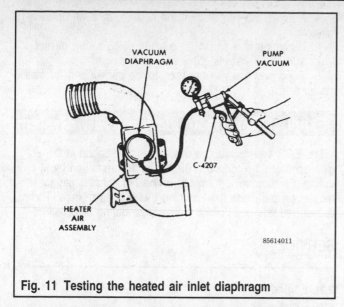

Fig. 11 Testing the heated air inlet diaphragm

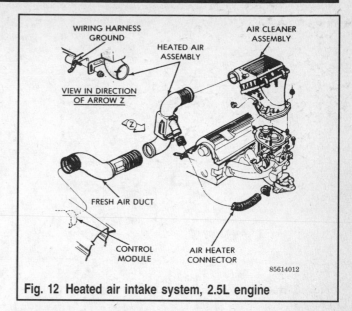

Fig. 12 Heated air intake system, 2.5L engine

3. With the engine running at normal operating temperature, the heat door should be in the down position (Heat Off).

4. If the heat door valve plate does not respond to hot and cold temperatures, the door diaphragm or the sensor may need replacing.

5. To test the diaphragm, remove the air cleaner from the engine and allow it to cool down to 19°C (65°F).

6. Connect a hand operated vacuum pump to the vacuum diaphragm and apply 20 inches of vacuum. The diaphragm should not leak down more than 10 inches in 5 minutes. The control door should not lift from the bottom of the snorkel at less than 2 inches of vacuum and be in the full up position with no more than 4 inches of vacuum. If the vacuum test proves the diaphragm defective, replace the air cleaner.

7. If the vacuum test shows the diaphragm in proper working condition, replace the sensor.

8. Label the vacuum hoses at the sensor to aid during reassemble. Disconnect the vacuum hoses, remove the retaining clips with a screwdriver and discard. Remove the sensor and mounting gasket.

9. Position the new gasket on the sensor and install sensor. Support the sensor on the outer diameter, and install the retaining clips.

10. Reconnect vacuum hoses.

2.5L Engine

▶ See Figure 12

1. Verify all vacuum hoses and the flexible heat pipe between the air cleaner and heat stove are properly attached and in good condition.

2. On a cold engine with an ambient temperature less than 46°C (115°F) the heat door valve plate in the snorkel should be in the up position (Heat On).

3. With the engine running at normal operating temperature, the heat door should be in the down position (Heat Off).

4. If the heat door valve plate does not respond to hot and cold temperatures, the door diaphragm or the sensor may need replacing.

5. To test the diaphragm, remove the air cleaner from the engine and allow it to cool down to 46°C (115°F).

6. Connect a hand operated vacuum pump to the sensor and apply 20 inches of vacuum. The door valve should be in the up position (Heat On).

7. If the door does not raise to 'Heat On' position, test the vacuum diaphragm for proper operation.

8. Apply 20 inches of vacuum with a hand operated vacuum pump to the vacuum diaphragm. The diaphragm should not leak down more than 10 inches in 5 minutes. The control door should not lift from the bottom of the snorkel at less than 2 inches of vacuum and be in the full up position with no more than 4 inches of vacuum. If the vacuum test proves the diaphragm defective, replace the air cleaner.

9. If the vacuum test shows the diaphragm in proper working condition, replace the sensor.

10. Label the vacuum hoses at the sensor to aid during assembly. Disconnect the vacuum hoses, remove the retaining clips with a screwdriver and discard. Remove the sensor and mounting gasket.

11. Position the new gasket on the sensor and install sensor. Support the sensor on the outer diameter, and install the retaining clips.

12. Connect the vacuum hoses.

2.6L Engine

▶ See Figure 13

1. Verify all vacuum hoses and the flexible heat pipe between the air cleaner and heat stove are properly attached and in good condition.

2. On a cold engine with an ambient temperature less than 30°C (84°F) the heat door valve plate in the snorkel should be in the up position (Heat On).

3. With the engine running at normal operating temperature, the heat door should be in the down position (Heat Off).

4. If the heat door valve plate does not respond to hot and cold temperatures, the door diaphragm or the sensor may need replacing.

5. To test the diaphragm, remove the air cleaner from the engine and allow it to cool down to 30°C (84°F).

6. Connect a hand operated vacuum pump to the sensor and apply 15 inches of vacuum. The valve should be in the up position (Heat On).

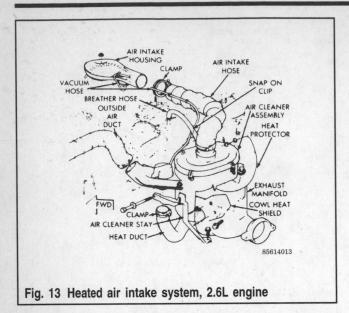

Fig. 13 Heated air intake system, 2.6L engine

7. If the door does not raise to Heat On position, test the vacuum motor for proper operation.

8. Apply 10 inches of vacuum to the vacuum motor with a hand operated vacuum pump, if the valve does not remain in the full up position replace the air cleaner body assembly.

9. If the door perform adequately with vacuum applied to the motor, replace the sensor.

HEATED AIR TEMPERATURE SENSOR REPLACEMENT

▶ **See Figure 14**

The heated air temperature sensor is located in the air cleaner housing and can be removed with the air filter removed from the housing.

1. Remove the top of the air cleaner housing, this can be done by releasing the clips.
2. Remove the air filter.
3. Disconnect the vacuum lines from the sensor.

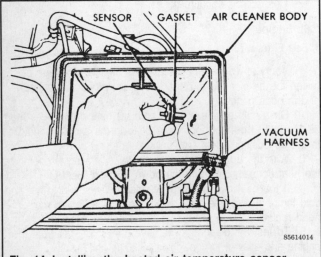

Fig. 14 Installing the heated air temperature sensor, 2.5L engine

4. Remove the sensor from the housing by prying it carefully out.

5. Install the new sensor in position using a new gasket. Make sure the sensor is firmly seated.

6. Reconnect the vacuum lines to the sensor and reinstall the air filter.

Exhaust Gas Recirculation (EGR) System

The EGR system reduces the oxides of nitrogen in the engine exhaust. The reduction of NOx is accomplished by allowing a predetermined amount of the hot exhaust gas to recirculate and dilute the incoming fuel and air mixture. This dilution reduces peak flame temperature during combustion.

SERVICE

2.2L Engine

▶ **See Figure 15**

The components of the EGR system on the 2.2L engine are; a Coolant Controlled Exhaust Gas Recirculation/Coolant Vacuum Switch Cold Closed (CVSCC) unit mounted in the thermostat housing, an EGR valve, and a EGR tube.

The CVSCC prevents vacuum from being supplied to the EGR system or other systems until the coolant temperature reaches a certain level. When a certain temperature is reached the CVSCC opens and vacuum is supplied as necessary. To assure proper operation test the system as follows:

1. Inspect all passages and moving parts for free movement.

2. Inspect all hoses. If any are hardened, cracked or have faulty connection, replacement is necessary.

3. Allow the engine to reach normal operating temperature. Locate the EGR valve at the end of the intake manifold. Allow the engine to idle for about a minute, then abruptly accelerate to about 2000 rpm, but not over 3000 rpm. Visible movement of the EGR valve stem should be noticed. Movement of the stem indicates the valve is operating normally. If no movement

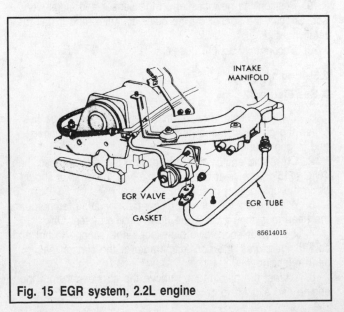

Fig. 15 EGR system, 2.2L engine

is noticed. Remove the EGR valve and inspect it for deposits and wear.

4. If deposits around the poppet and seat are more than a film, apply some heat control solvent to the area to help soften the deposits. Apply vacuum to the valve with a hand operated vacuum pump. When the valve opens, scrap away the deposits from the poppet and seat. If the valve poppet does not open when vacuum is applied, replace the valve. If the stem or seat is worn replace the valve.

5. If the EGR valve is functioning properly, check the CVSCC.

6. Check condition of vacuum hoses at the CVSCC and properly routed (see vacuum hose under hood sticker).

7. Check engine coolant level.

8. Disconnect the vacuum hoses and remove the valve from the thermostat housing. Place the valve in an ice bath below 4.4°C (40°F) so that the threaded portion is covered. Attach a vacuum pump to the lower connection on the valve (the one connected to the vacuum hose showing a yellow stripe). Apply 10 inches of vacuum. Pressure should drop no more than one inch in one minute. If the vacuum drops more, replace the CVSCC.

2.6L Engine
▶ See Figure 16

With this system exhaust gases are partially recirculated from an exhaust port in the cylinder head into a port at the intake manifold below the carburetor. EGR flow is controlled by thermo valves, and a combination of a Dual EGR valve and Sub EGR valve.

The dual EGR valve consists of a primary and secondary valve which are controlled by a different carburetor vacuums in response to the throttle opening. EGR flow is halted at idle and wide open throttle operation. The primary valve controls the EGR flow at narrow throttle openings, while the secondary valve allows flow into the intake mixture at wider throttle openings. Vacuum to the dual EGR valve is controlled by thermo valves.

A carburetor mounted Sub EGR valve is directly opened and closed by the throttle linkage in order to closely modulate the

EGR flow controlled by the EGR control valve, in response to the throttle opening.

Two thermo valves connected to the EGR system, sense coolant temperature changes and open and close accordingly to control the vacuum flow to the EGR system.**Test the system as follows:**

1. Check the vacuum hose for good condition and proper routing (see vacuum hose under hood sticker).

2. Engine must be cold. Cold start the engine and allow to idle.

3. Check to make sure that the fast idle does not cause the secondary EGR valve to operate. If the secondary EGR valve operates at cold start fast idle, replace the secondary EGR valve thermo valve.

4. Run the engine until the operating temperature exceeds 65°C (149°F). The secondary EGR valve should now be in operation. If if it does not operate, inspect the EGR valve or thermo valve.

5. Disconnect the green stripped vacuum hose from the carburetor. Connect a hand vacuum pump to the hose and apply 6 inches of vacuum while opening the sub EGR valve by hand. If the idle speed becomes unstable, the secondary valve is operating properly. If the idle speed remains the same, replace the secondary EGR valve and thermo valve.

6. Connect the green stripped hose to the carburetor. Disconnect the yellow stripped hose from the carburetor and connect it to the hand vacuum pump. Hold the sub EGR valve opened and apply 6 inches of vacuum.

7. If the idle speed becomes unstable, the primary EGR valve is operating properly. If the idle speed remains unchanged, replace the primary EGR valve and thermo valve.

2.5L, 3.0L, 3.3L and 3.8L Engines
▶ See Figures 17, 18, 19, 20 and 21

The EGR system on these engines, is a back pressure type. A back pressure transducer measures the amount of exhaust gas back pressure on the exhaust side of the EGR valve and varies the strength of the vacuum signal applied to the EGR valve. The transducer uses this back pressure signal to provide the correct amount of exhaust gas recirculation under all conditions.

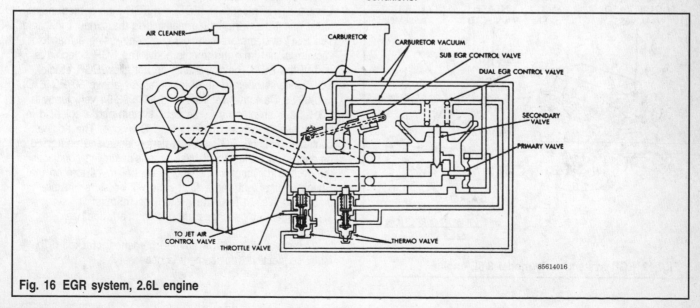

Fig. 16 EGR system, 2.6L engine

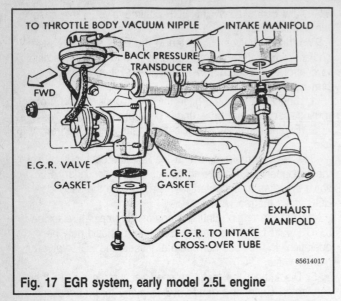

Fig. 17 EGR system, early model 2.5L engine

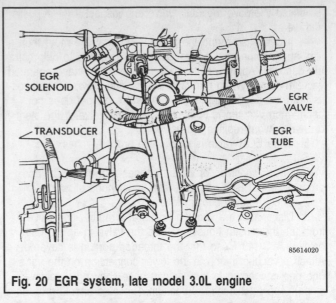

Fig. 20 EGR system, late model 3.0L engine

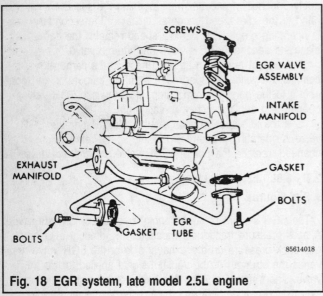

Fig. 18 EGR system, late model 2.5L engine

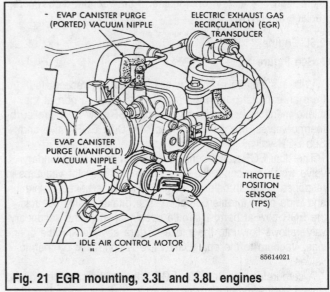

Fig. 21 EGR mounting, 3.3L and 3.8L engines

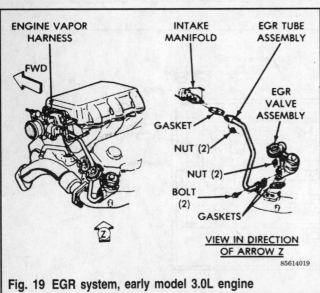

Fig. 19 EGR system, early model 3.0L engine

This utilizes an intake manifold mounted EGR valve and Electric EGR Transducer (EET). An EGR tube carries the exhaust gases from the intake manifold to the exhaust manifold. The EGR systems are solenoid controlled, using a manifold vacuum signal from the throttle body. The EGR solenoid is part of the EET. These systems do not allow EGR at idle. EGR systems operate at all temperatures above 60°F (16°C).

1989-92 California vehicles, and all 1993-94 vehicles with EGR, have an on-board diagnostic system and a solenoid in series with the vacuum line to the EGR valve. The engine controller monitors EGR system performance and energized or de-energized the solenoid base on engine/driving conditions. If the system malfunction the engine controller will turn on the Check Engine light and a fault code will be stored in the diagnostic system.**Test the system as follows:**

1. Inspect all passages and moving parts for free movement.

2. Inspect all hoses. If any are hardened, cracked or have faulty connection, replacement is necessary.

3. Warm the engine to normal operating temperature. Allow the engine to idle for about a minute, then abruptly accelerate to about 2000 rpm, but not over 3000 rpm. Visible movement of the groove on EGR valve stem should be noticed. Movement of the stem indicates the valve is operating normally. If no movement is noticed.

4. Disconnect the vacuum hoses from the EGR vacuum transducer, and attach a hand operated vacuum pump. Raise the engine to 2000 rpm and apply 10 inches of vacuum, while checking valve movement. If no valve movement occurs, replace the valve/transducer assembly.

➡**If the back-pressure EGR valve does not function satisfactory. Replace the entire Valve/Transducer assembly. No attempt should be made to clean the valve.**

5. If movement occurs, check the diaphragm for leaks. Valve should remain open at least 30 seconds.

6. If the valve is functioning satisfactory, remove the throttle body and inspect port in throttle bore and associated passages. Apply some heat control solvent to the area to help soften any deposit.

7. Install the throttle body and recheck EGR operation.

Air Injection System

▶ **See Figure 22**

2.2L engines are equipped with an air injection system. This system is designed to supply a controlled amount of air to the exhaust gases, through exhaust ports, aiding in the oxidation of the gases and reduction of carbon monoxide and hydrocarbons to an appreciable level.

During engine warm-up air is injected into the base of the exhaust manifold. After the engine warms up, the air flow is switched (by a Coolant Vacuum Switch Cold Open or by a vacuum solenoid) to the 3-way catalyst where it further aids in the reduction of carbon monoxide and hydrocarbons in the exhaust system.

The system consists of a belt driven air pump, hoses, a switch/relief valve and a check valve to prevent the components within the system from high temperature exhaust gases.

➡**No repairs are possible on any of the air injection system components. All replacement parts must be serviced as a unit.**

Coolant Vacuum Switch Cold Open

1. Locate the switch on the thermostat housing.
2. Label the hoses before removing. Remove hoses.
3. Remove the vacuum switch from housing.
4. Install a new vacuum switch and connect the vacuum hoses. (See under hood vacuum hose routing label).

AIR PUMP

▶ **See Figures 23, 24 and 25**

➡**The air injection system is not completely noiseless. Do not assume the air pump is defective because it squeals. If the system creates excessive noise, remove the drive belt and operate the engine. If the noise ceases, check all hoses connection for proper tightening. Replace pump if necessary.**

1. Remove all hoses and vacuum lines from the air pump and diverter valve or switch/relief valve (depending on how equipped).
2. Remove the air pump drive pulley shield.
3. Remove the air pump pivot bolt and remove air pump belt.
4. Remove the remaining mounting bolts and remove pump.
5. Remove the diverter valve or switch/relief valve from pump.
6. Clean all gasket material from valve and pump mounting surface.
7. Install the diverter valve or switch/relief valve using a new gasket, to the new pump.

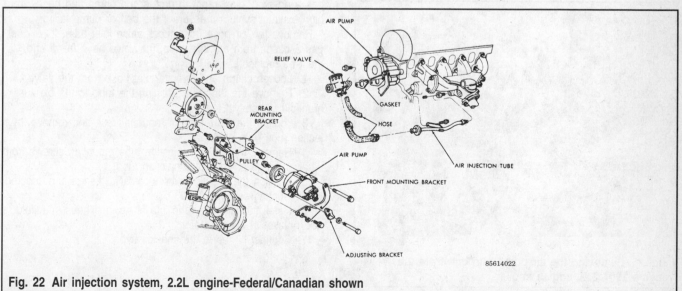

85614022

Fig. 22 Air injection system, 2.2L engine-Federal/Canadian shown

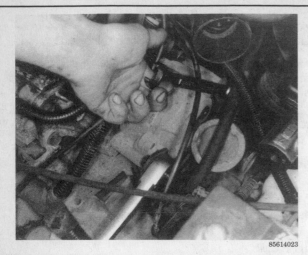

85614023

Fig. 23 Loosening the air pump mounting and pivot bolts

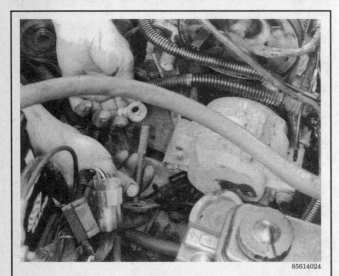

85614024

Fig. 24 Removing a mounting bolt from the air pump

85614025

Fig. 25 Removing the air pump and belt from the engine 1987 2.2L engine shown

8. Install the pump on the engine and loosely install pivot bolt.
9. Install drive belt and tighten pivot bolt.
10. Install air pump drive pulley shield.
11. Install all hoses and vacuum lines.

SWITCH/RELIEF VALVE

If vacuum is apply to the valve and air injection is not upstream, or if air injection is in both upstream and downstream, the valve is faulty and must be replaced.
1. Remove all air hoses and vacuum hoses.
2. Remove the valve to pump mounting bolts, and remove valve.
3. Clean all gasket material from mounting surfaces.
4. Install the new valve to the pump with a new gasket.
5. Secure the valve with mounting bolts, tighten bolts to 14Nm (125 inch lbs.).
6. Reinstall all air hoses and vacuum hoses.

RELIEF VALVE

The purpose of this valve is to control air pump pressure during high engine speeds. If the pump discharge pressure exceeds 9 PSI the valve will open and vent the excess pressure to the atmosphere.
1. Remove the air hoses from the valve.
2. Remove the valve mounting screws and remove valve.
3. Clean all gasket material from mounting surfaces.
4. Install a new gasket on valve and secure with mounting screws.
5. Reconnect air hoses.

CHECK VALVE

The check valve is located in the injection tube which lead to the exhaust manifold and converter assembly. The valve has a one-way diaphragm to protect the pump and hoses from high exhaust system pressure if the belt or pump failed.
Remove the air hose from check valve inlet tube. If exhaust gas escapes from the inlet tube, the valve have failed and must be replaced.
1. Loosen clamp and remove inlet hose from the valve.
2. Remove the tube nut retaining the tube to the exhaust manifold or catalyst.
3. Loosen the starter motor mounting bolt and remove injection tube from engine.
4. Remove the catalyst injection tube mounting screws from catalyst flange and remove injection tube.
5. Position the injection tube to catalyst flange and secured with mounting screws.
6. Install the injection tube into fitting in exhaust manifold and bracket at starter motor.
7. Connect hoses to the check valve.

Pulse Air Feeder System

▶ **See Figure 26**

2.6L engines use a pulse air feeder system to promote oxidation of exhaust emissions in the rear catalytic converter. The system consists of a main reed valve and sub-reed valve. The main reed valve is controlled by a diaphragm which is activated by pressure pulses from the crankcase. The sub-reed valve is activated by pulsation in the exhaust system between the front and rear converters.

1. Remove the air duct from the right side of the radiator.
2. Remove the carburetor protector shield.
3. Remove the engine oil dipstick and tube.
4. Remove the pulse air feeder mounting bolts.
5. Raise and support the front of the vehicle on jackstands. Disconnect the pulse air feeder hoses and remove the feeder.
6. Install hoses on pulse air feeder.
7. Lower the vehicle and tighten feeder mounting bolts.
8. Check O-ring on lower end of the dipstick tube. Replace if damaged.
9. Install carburetor protector shield.
10. Install the air deflector on radiator.

Dual Air Aspirator System

2.6L engines use an air aspirator system which aids in reducing carbon monoxide (CO) and hydrocarbon emissions. The system uses pulsating exhaust pressure to draw fresh air from the air cleaner assembly. Failure of the aspirator valve will result in excess noise.

SYSTEM TEST

1. Check the aspirator tube/exhaust manifold assembly joint and hoses. If aspirator tube/exhaust manifold joint is leaking, retighten to 68 Nm (50 ft. lbs.). If hoses are harden, replace as necessary.
2. Disconnect the inlet hose from aspirator valve.

3. With engine at idle, the negative (vacuum) exhaust pulses should be felt at the valve inlet.
4. If hot exhaust gases escaped from the aspirator inlet, replace the valve.

REMOVAL & INSTALLATION

1. Remove the air inlet hose from aspirator valve.
2. Remove screws from aspirator bracket, and remove tube assembly from engine.
3. Install tube and tighten nuts to 54 Nm (40 ft. lbs.).
4. Install tube bracket assembly and torque to 28 Nm (250 in.lbs.).
5. Connect the air hose to valve and air cleaner nipple, install clamps.

Electronic Feedback Carburetor (EFC) System

Some models are equipped with an Electronic Feedback Carburetor (EFC) System which is designed to convert Hydrocarbons(HC), Carbon Monoxide (CO) and Oxides of Nitrogen (NOx) into harmless substances. An exhaust gas oxygen sensor generates an electronic signal which is used by the Spark Control Computer to precisely control the air-fuel mixture ratio to the carburetor.

There are two operating modes in the EFC system:
1. OPEN LOOP-During cold engine operation the air-fuel ratio will be fixed to a richer mixture programmed into the computer by the manufacture.
2. CLOSED LOOP-The computer varies the air-fuel ratio based on information supplied by the oxygen sensor.

Oxygen Sensor

▶ **See Figure 27**

The oxygen sensor is a galvanic battery which produces electrical voltage after being heated by exhaust gases. The sensor monitors the oxygen content in the exhaust stream,

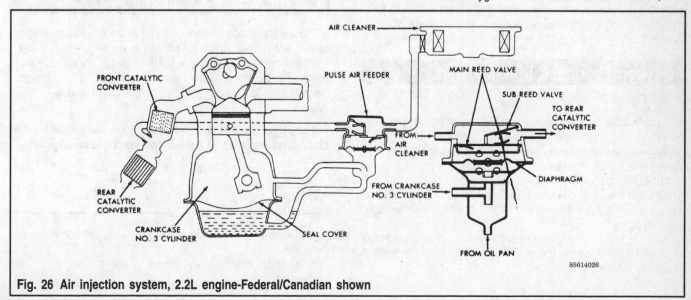

85614026

Fig. 26 Air injection system, 2.2L engine-Federal/Canadian shown

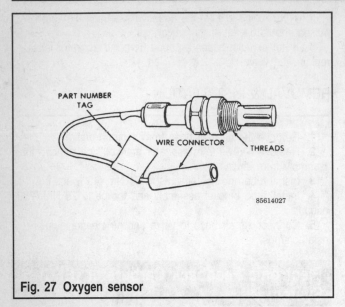

Fig. 27 Oxygen sensor

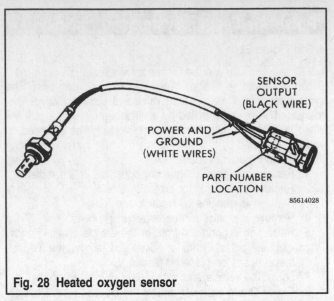

Fig. 28 Heated oxygen sensor

convert it to an electrical voltage and transmit this voltage to the Spark Control Computer.

❋❋WARNING

Use care when working around the oxygen sensor as the exhaust manifold may be extremely hot. The sensor must be remove using Tool C-4907.

When the sensor is removed, the exhaust manifold threads must be cleaned with an 18mm x 1.5 x 6E tap.

If the sensor is to be reinstalled, the sensor threads must be coated with an anti-seize compound such as Loctite 771-64 or equivalent. New sensors are coated with compound on the threads and no additional compound is required. The sensor should be torque to 27 Nm (20 ft. lbs.).

Heated Oxygen Sensor

▶ See Figure 28

The heated oxygen sensor is basically the same as the standard oxygen sensor, except that it is internally heated for faster switching during engine operation. Replacement of the heated oxygen sensor is the same as the standard sensor.

Oxygen Feedback Solenoid

▶ See Figure 29

In addition to the oxygen sensor, EFC uses an Oxygen Feedback Solenoid. It purpose is to regulate the fuel-air ratio of the feedback carburetor, along with a conventional fixed main metering jet, in response to the electrical signal generated by the Spark Control Computer.

With the feedback solenoid de-energized, the main metering orifice is fully uncovered and the richest condition exists within the carburetor.

With the feedback solenoid energized, the solenoid push rod seals the main metering orifice. This position offers the leanest condition within the carburetor.

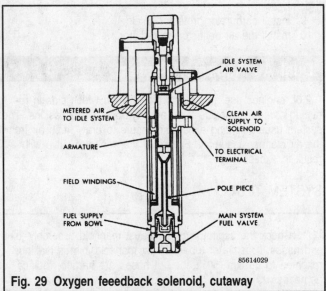

Fig. 29 Oxygen feeedback solenoid, cutaway

Electric Choke Assembly

The electric choke system is a heater and switch assembly sealed within the choke housing. When the engine is running and the engine oil pressure is 2.7 kPa (4 psi) or above, the contacts in the oil pressure switch closes and feed current to the automatic choke system to open the choke and keep it open.

➡ **The choke assembly must never be immersed in fluid as damage to the internal switch and heater assembly will result.**

TESTING

1. Disconnect the electrical lead from choke heater assembly.

2. Connect direct battery voltage to choke heater connection.

3. The choke valve should reach the open position within five minutes.

✳✳WARNING

Operation of any type should be avoided if there is a loss of choke power. This condition cause a very rich mixture to burn and result in abnormally high exhaust system temperatures, which may cause damage to the catalyst or other underbody parts of the vehicle.

Emission Maintenance Light

All models have an Emission Maintenance Reminder (EMR) lamp, this lamp is illuminated when the ignition key is turned

ON. The lamp is connected with the engine controller, which records the vehicle mileage and stores it into memory every 8 miles. At the time the mileage is stored, the controller checks for the 60,000, 82,500 and 120,000 mile trip points. When the current mileage matches one of these mileages, the EMR lamp is illuminated.

When the EMR lamp is illuminated some of the emission components are supposed to be changed. These components are: EGR valve, EGR tube and PCV valve at 60,000 miles and 120,000 miles. At 82,500 miles the oxygen sensor must also be replaced. The EMR lamp can then be reset using an appropriate DRB tester or equivalent.

CHRYSLER SELF DIAGNOSTIC SYSTEM

General Information

The Chrysler fuel injection systems combine electronic spark advance and fuel control. At the center of these systems is a digital, pre-programmed computer, known as a Single Module Engine Controller (SMEC) for 1987-89, a Single Board Engine Controller (SBEC) for 1990-91 or a Single Board Engine Controller II (SBEC II) for 1992 and a Powertrain Control Module (PCM) for 1993-94. The SMEC, SBEC, SBEC II or PCM regulates ignition timing, air-fuel ratio, emission control devices, cooling fan, charging system idle speed and speed control. It has the ability to update and revise its commands to meet changing operating conditions.

Various sensors provide the input necessary for controller to correctly regulate fuel flow at the injectors. These include the Manifold Absolute Pressure (MAP), Throttle Position Sensor (TPS), oxygen sensor, coolant temperature sensor, charge temperature sensor, and vehicle speed sensors.

In addition to the sensors, various switches are used to provide important information to the controller. These include the neutral safety switch, air conditioning clutch switch, brake switch and speed control switch. These signals cause the SMEC, SBEC, SBEC II or PCM to change either the fuel flow at the injectors or the ignition timing or both.

The SMEC, SBEC, SBEC II or PCM , are designed to test their own input and output circuits, If a fault is found in a major system, this information is stored in the SMEC, SBEC, SBEC II or PCM for eventual display to the technician. Information on this fault can be displayed to the technician by means of the instrument panel CHECK ENGINE light or by connecting a diagnostic read-out tester and reading a numbered display code, which directly relates to a general fault. Some inputs and outputs are checked continuously and others are checked under certain conditions. If the problem is repaired or no longer exists, the The SMEC, SBEC, SBEC II or PCM cancels the fault code after 50-100 key ON/OFF cycles.

When a fault code is detected, it appears as either a flash of the CHECK ENGINE light on the instrument panel or by watching the Diagnostic Readout Box II (DRB II). This indicates that an abnormal signal in the system has been recognized by the SMEC, SBEC, SBEC II or PCM . Fault codes do indicate the presence of a failure but they don't identify the failed component directly.

FAULT CODES

Fault codes are 2 digit numbers that tell the technician which circuit is bad. Fault codes do indicate the presence of a failure but they don't identify the failed component directly. Therefore a fault code and a result are not always the reason for the problem.

INDICATOR CODES

Indicator codes are 2 digit numbers that tell the technician if particular sequences or conditions have occurred. Such a condition where the indicator code will be displayed is at the beginning or the end of a diagnostic test. Indicator codes will not generate a CHECK ENGINE light or engine running test code.

ACTUATOR TEST MODE (ATM) CODES

ATM test codes are 2 digit numbers that identify the various circuits used by the technician during the diagnosis procedure.

ENGINE RUNNING TEST CODES

Engine running test codes are 2 digit numbers. The codes are used to access sensor readouts while the engine is running and place the engine in particular operating conditions for diagnosis.

CHECK ENGINE LIGHT

The CHECK ENGINE light has 2 modes of operation: diagnostic mode and switch test mode.

If a DRB II diagnostic tester is not available, the SMEC/SBEC can show the technician fault codes by flashing the CHECK ENGINE light on the instrument panel in the diagnostic mode. In the switch test mode, after all codes are displayed, switch function can be confirmed. The light will turn on and off when a switch is turned **ON** and **OFF**.

Even though the light can be used as a diagnostic tool, it cannot do the following:

1. Once the light starts to display fault codes, it cannot be stopped. If the technician loses count, he must start the test procedure again.

2. The light cannot display all of the codes or any blank displays.

3. The light cannot tell the technician if the oxygen feedback system is lean or rich and if the idle motor and detonation systems are operational.

4. The light cannot perform the actuation test mode, sensor test mode or engine running test mode.

➡ **Be advised that the CHECK ENGINE light can only perform a limited amount of functions and is not to be used as a substitute for a diagnostic tester. All diagnostic procedure described herein are intended for use with a Diagnostic Readout Box II (DRB II) or equivalent tool.**

ENTERING SELF-DIAGNOSTICS

➡ **The following diagnostic and test procedures are intended for use with the Diagnostic Readout Box II (DRB II). Since each available diagnostic readout box may differ in its interpretation and display of the sensor results, refer to the instructional procedure that accompanies each tester unit.**

Obtaining Fault Codes
▶ See Figures 30, 31 and 32

1. Connect the readout box to the diagnostic connector located in the engine compartment near SMEC/SBEC.

2. Start the engine, if possible, cycle the transmission selector and the A/C switch if applicable. Shut off the engine.

3. On 1988 models, turn the ignition switch **ON, OFF, ON, OFF, ON** within 5 seconds. On 1989-94 models, simply turn the ignition switch **ON** to access the read fault code data. Record all the fault code messages displayed on the readout box.

4. Observe the CHECK ENGINE light on the instrument panel. The light should illuminate for 3 seconds and then go out.

EXITING DIAGNOSTIC TEST

By turning the ignition switch to the **OFF** position, the test mode system is exited. With a Diagnostic Readout Box attached to the system and the ATM control button not pressed, the computer will continue to cycle the selected circuits for 5 minutes and then automatically shut the system down.

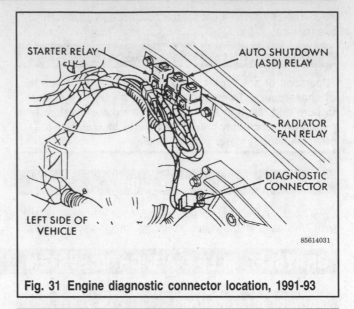

Fig. 31 Engine diagnostic connector location, 1991-93

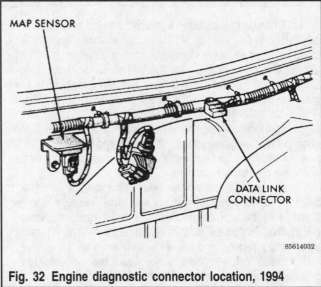

Fig. 32 Engine diagnostic connector location, 1994

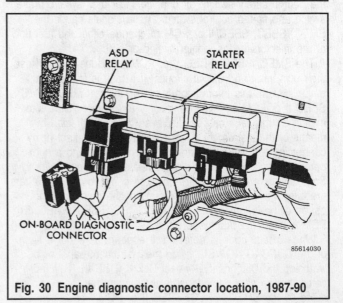

Fig. 30 Engine diagnostic connector location, 1987-90

TROUBLE CODES

▶ See Figures 33, 34, 35, 36, 37, 38, 39, 40, 41, 42, 43, 44, 45, 46, 47, 48 and 49

CHECK ENGINE LAMP FAULT CODE	DRB II DISPLAY	DESCRIPTION OF FAULT CONDITION
11	IGN REFERENCE SIGNAL	No distributor reference signal detected during engine cranking.
12	No. of Key-ons since last fault or since faults were erased.	Direct battery input to controller disconnected within the last 50-100 ignition key-ons.
13†**	MAP PNEUMATIC SIGNAL	No variation in MAP sensor signal is detected.
	or MAP PNEUMATIC CHANGE	No difference is recognized between the engine MAP reading and the stored barometric pressure reading.
14†**	MAP VOLTAGE TOO LOW	MAP sensor input below minimum acceptable voltage.
	or MAP VOLTAGE TOO HIGH	MAP sensor input above maximum acceptable voltage.
15**	VEHICLE SPEED SIGNAL	No distance sensor signal detected during road load conditions.
16†**	BATTERY INPUT SENSE	Battery voltage sense input not detected during engine running.
17	LOW ENGINE TEMP	Engine coolant temperature remains below normal operating temperatures during vehicle travel (Thermostat).
21**	OXYGEN SENSOR SIGNAL	Neither rich or lean condition is detected from the oxygen sensor input.
22†**	COOLANT VOLTAGE LOW	Coolant temperature sensor input below the minimum acceptable voltage.
	or COOLANT VOLTAGE HIGH	Coolant temperature sensor input above the maximum acceptable voltage.
23	T/B TEMP VOLTAGE LOW	Throttle body temperature sensor input below the minimum acceptable voltage.
	or T/B TEMP VOLTAGE HI	Throttle body temperature sensor input above the maximum acceptable voltage.
24†**	TPS VOLTAGE LOW	Throttle position sensor input below the minimum acceptable voltage.
	or TPS VOLTAGE HIGH	Throttle position sensor input above the maximum acceptable voltage.
25**	AIS MOTOR CIRCUITS	A shorted condition detected in one or more of the AIS control circuits.
26	INJ 1 PEAK CURRENT	High resistance condition detected in the injector output circuit.
27	INJ 1 CONTROL CKT	Injector output driver stage does not respond properly to the control signal.
31**	PURGE SOLENOID CKT	An open or shorted condition detected in the purge solenoid circuit.
32**	EGR SOLENOID CIRCUIT	An open or shorted condition detected in the EGR solenoid circuit. (California emissions only)
	or EGR SYSTEM FAILURE	Required change in Fuel/Air ratio not detected during diagnostic test. (California emissions only)
33	A/C CLUTCH RELAY CKT	An open or shorted condition detected in the A/C clutch relay circuit.
34	S/C SERVO SOLENOIDS	An open or shorted condition detected in the speed control vacuum or vent solenoid circuits.

85614C01

Fig. 33 Fault Code Identification, 1987-90 with TBI

CHECK ENGINE LAMP FAULT CODE	DRB II DISPLAY	DESCRIPTION OF FAULT CONDITION
35	RADIATOR FAN RELAY	An open or shorted condition detected in the radiator fan relay circuit.
41	CHARGING SYSTEM CKT	Output driver stage for alternator field does not respond properly to the voltage regulator control signal.
42	ASD RELAY CIRCUIT	An open or shorted condition detected in the auto shutdown relay circuit.
43	IGNITION CONTROL CKT	Output driver stage for ignition coil does not respond properly to the dwell control signal.
44	FJ2 VOLTAGE SENSE	No FJ2 voltage present at the logic board during controller operation.
46**	BATTERY VOLTAGE HIGH	Battery voltage sense input above target charging voltage during engine operation.
47	BATTERY VOLTAGE LOW	Battery voltage sense input below target charging voltage during engine operation.
51**	AIR FUEL AT LIMIT	Oxygen sensor signal input indicates lean fuel/air ratio condition during engine operation.
52**	AIR FUEL AT LIMIT	Oxygen sensor signal input indicates rich fuel/air ratio condition during engine operation.
	or EXCESSIVE LEANING	Adaptive fuel value leaned excessively due to a sustained rich condition.
53	INTERNAL SELF-TEST	Internal engine controller fault condition detected.
55		Completion of fault code display on the CHECK ENGINE lamp.
62	EMR MILEAGE ACCUM	Unsuccessful attempt to update EMR mileage in the controller EEPROM.
63	EEPROM WRITE DENIED	Unsuccessful attempt to write to an EEPROM location by the controller.
	FAULT CODE ERROR	An unrecognized fault ID received by DRB II.

†Check Engine Lamp On
**Check Engine Lamp On (California Only)

85614C02

Fig. 34 Fault Code Identification, 1987-90 with TBI

CHECK ENGINE LAMP FAULT CODE	DRB II DISPLAY	DESCRIPTION OF FAULT CONDITION
11	IGN REFERENCE SIGNAL	No distributor reference signal detected during engine cranking.
12	No. of Key-ons since last fault or since faults were erased.	Direct battery input to controller disconnected within the last 50-100 ignition key-ons.
13†**	MAP PNEUMATIC SIGNAL	No variation in MAP sensor signal is detected.
	or	
	MAP PNEUMATIC CHANGE	No difference is recognized between the engine MAP reading and the stored barometric pressure reading.
14†**	MAP VOLTAGE TOO LOW	MAP sensor input below minimum acceptable voltage.
	or	
	MAP VOLTAGE TOO HIGH	MAP sensor input above maximum acceptable voltage.
15**	VEHICLE SPEED SIGNAL	No distance sensor signal detected during road load conditions.
16†**	BATTERY INPUT SENSE engine running.	Battery voltage sense input not detected during
17	LOW ENGINE TEMP	Engine coolant temperature remains below normal operating temperatures during vehicle travel (Thermostat).
21**	OXYGEN SENSOR SIGNAL	Neither rich or lean condition is detected from the oxygen sensor input.
22†**	COOLANT VOLTAGE LOW	Coolant temperature sensor input below the minimum acceptable voltage.
	or	
	COOLANT VOLTAGE HIGH	Coolant temperature sensor input above the maximum acceptable voltage.
24	TPS VOLTAGE LOW	Throttle position sensor input below the minimum acceptable voltage.
	or	
	TPS VOLTAGE HIGH	Throttle position sensor input above the maximum acceptable voltage.
25	AIS MOTOR CIRCUITS	A shorted condition detected in one or more of the AIS control circuits.
26†**	INJ 1 PEAK CURRENT	High resistance condition detected in the INJ 1 injector bank circuit.
	or	
	INJ 2 PEAK CURRENT	High resistance condition detected in the INJ 2 injector bank circuit.
	or	
	INJ 3 PEAK CURRENT	High resistance condition detected in the INJ 3 injector bank circuit.
27†**	INJ 1 CONTROL CKT	INJ 1 injector bank output driver stage does not respond properly to the control signal.
	or	
	INJ 2 CONTROL CKT	INJ 2 injector bank output driver stage does not respond properly to the control signal.
	or	
	INJ 3 CONTROL CKT	INJ 3 injector bank output driver stage does not respond properly to the control signal.
31**	PURGE SOLENOID CKT	An open or shorted condition detected in the purge solenoid circuit.

85614C03

Fig. 35 Fault Code Identification, 1987-90 with MFI

CHECK ENGINE LAMP FAULT CODE	DRB II DISPLAY	DESCRIPTION OF FAULT CONDITION
33	A/C CLUTCH RELAY CKT	An open or shorted condition detected in the A/C clutch relay circuit.
34	S/C SERVO SOLENOIDS	An open or shorted condition detected in the speed control vacuum or vent solenoid circuits.
35	RADIATOR FAN RELAY	An open or shorted condition detected in the radiator fan relay circuit.
41	CHARGING SYSTEM CKT	Output driver stage for alternator field does not respond properly to the voltage regulator control signal.
42	ASD RELAY CIRCUIT	An open or shorted condition detected in the auto shutdown relay circuit.
	or Z1 VOLTAGE SENSE	No Z1 voltage sensed when the auto shutdown relay is energized.
43	IGNITION CONTROL CKT	Output driver stage for ignition coil does not respond properly to the dwell control signal.
44	FJ2 VOLTAGE SENSE	No FJ2 voltage present at the logic board during controller operation. (S-body only)
46†**	BATTERY VOLTAGE HIGH	Battery voltage sense input above target charging voltage during engine operation.
47	BATTERY VOLTAGE LOW	Battery voltage sense input below target charging voltage during engine operation.
51	AIR FUEL AT LIMIT	Oxygen sensor signal input indicates lean fuel/air ratio condition during engine operation.
52	AIR FUEL AT LIMIT	Oxygen sensor signal input indicates rich fuel/air ratio condition during engine operation.
53	INTERNAL SELF-TEST	Internal engine controller fault condition detected.
54†**	SYNC PICK-UP SIGNAL	No high data rate signal detected during engine rotation.
55		Completion of fault code display on the CHECK ENGINE lamp.
62	EMR MILEAGE ACCUM	Unsuccessful attempt to update EMR mileage in the controller EEPROM.
63	EEPROM WRITE DENIED	Unsuccessful attempt to write to an EEPROM location by the controller.
	FAULT CODE ERROR	An unrecognized fault ID received by DRB II.

†Check Engine Lamp On
**Check Engine Lamp On (California Only)

85614C04

Fig. 36 Fault Code Identification, 1987-90 with MFI

Fault Code	DRB II Display	Description of Fault Code
11	No Reference Signal During Cranking	No distributor reference signal detected during engine cranking.
13+**	Slow Change in Idle MAP Signal or No Change in MAP from Start to Run	No variation in MAP Sensor signal is detected. No difference is recognized between the engine MAP reading and the barometric pressure reading at start-up.
14+**	MAP Voltage Too Low or MAP Voltage Too High	MAP sensor input below minimum acceptable voltage. MAP sensor input above maximum acceptable voltage.
15**	No Vehicle Speed Signal	No distance sensor signal detected during road load conditions.
17	Engine Is Cold Too Long	Engine coolant temperature remains below normal operating temperatures during vehicle travel (Thermostat).
21**	O2 Signal Stays at Center or O2 Signal Shorted to Voltage	Neither rich or lean condition is detected from the oxygen sensor input. Oxygen sensor input voltage maintained above normal operating range.
22+**	Coolant Sensor Voltage Too High or Coolant Sensor Voltage Too Low	Coolant temperature sensor input above the maximum acceptable voltage. Coolant temperature sensor input below the minimum acceptable voltage.

85614C05

Fig. 37 Fault Code Identification, 1990-91 with TBI

Fault Code	DRB II Display	Description of Fault Code
24+**	Throttle Position Sensor Voltage High	Throttle position sensor input above the maximum acceptable voltage.
	or	
	Throttle Position Sensor Voltage Low	Throttle position sensor input below the minimum acceptable voltage.
25**	Automatic Idle Speed Motor Circuits	A shorted condition detected in one or more of the AIS control circuits.
27	Injector #1 Control Circuit	Injector #1 output driver does not respond properly to the control signal.
31**	Purge Solenoid Circuit	An open or shorted condition detected in the purge solenoid circuit.
32**	EGR Solenoid Circuit	An open or shorted condition detected in the EGR solenoid circuit. (All except Federal with Auto Trans.)
	or	
	EGR System Failure	Required change in Fuel/Air ratio not detected during diagnostic test. (California only)
33	A/C Clutch Relay Circuit	An open or shorted condition detected in the A/C clutch relay circuit.
34	Speed Control Solenoid Circuits	An open or shorted condition detected in the speed control vacuum or vent solenoid circuits.
35	Radiator Fan Relay Circuit	An open or shorted condition detected in the radiator fan relay circuit.
37	Torque Converter Unlock Solenoid CKT	An open or shorted condition detected in the torque converter part throttle unlock solenoid circuit. (automatic transmission only)

85614C06

Fig. 38 Fault Code Identification, 1990-91 with TBI

Fault Code	DRB II Display	Description of Fault Code
41+**	Alternator Field Not Switching Properly	An open or shorted condition detected in the alternator field control circuit.
42	Auto Shutdown Relay Control Circuit	An open or shorted condition detected in the auto shutdown relay circuit.
46+**	Charging System Voltage Too High	Battery voltage sense input above target charging voltage during engine operation.
47+**	Charging System Voltage Too Low	Battery voltage sense input below target charging voltage during engine operation and no significant change in voltage detected during active test of alternator output.
51**	O2 Signal Stays Below Center (Lean)	Oxygen sensor signal input indicates lean fuel/air ratio condition during engine operation.
52**	O2 Signal Stays Above Center (Rich)	Oxygen sensor signal input indicates rich fuel/air ratio condition during engine operation.
53	Internal Controller Failure	Internal engine controller fault condition detected.
62	Controller Failure EMR Miles Not Stored	Unsuccessful attempt to update EMR mileage in the controller EEPROM.
63	Controller Failure EEPROM Write Denied	Unsuccessful attempt to write to an EEPROM location by the controller.
55	N/A	Completion of fault code display on CHECK ENGINE lamp.

+ Check Engine Lamp On
** Check Engine Lamp On (California Only)

85614C07

Fig. 39 Fault Code Identification, 1990-91 with TBI

Fault Code	DRB II Display	Description of Fault Code
11	No Reference Signal During Cranking	No ignition reference signal detected during engine cranking.
13+**	Slow Change in Idle MAP Signal or No Change in MAP from Start to Run	No variation in MAP Sensor signal is detected. No difference is recognized between the engine MAP reading and the barometric pressure reading at start-up.
14+**	MAP Voltage Too Low or MAP Voltage Too High	MAP sensor input below minimum acceptable voltage. MAP sensor input above maximum acceptable voltage.
15**	No Vehicle Speed Signal	No distance sensor signal detected during road load conditions.
17	Engine Is Cold Too Long	Engine coolant temperature remains below normal operating temperatures during vehicle travel (Thermostat).
21**	O2 Signal Stays at Center or O2 Signal Shorted to Voltage	Neither rich or lean condition is detected from the oxygen sensor input. Oxygen sensor input voltage maintained above normal operating range.
22+**	Coolant Sensor Voltage Too High or Coolant Sensor Voltage Too Low	Coolant temperature sensor input above the maximum acceptable voltage. Coolant temperature sensor input below the minimum acceptable voltage.

85614C08

Fig. 40 Fault Code Identification, 1990-91 with MFI

Fault Code	DRB II Display	Description of Fault Code
24+**	Throttle Position Sensor Voltage High	Throttle position sensor input above the maximum acceptable voltage.
	or	
	Throttle Position Sensor Voltage Low	Throttle position sensor input below the minimum acceptable voltage.
25**	Automatic Idle Speed Motor Circuits	A shorted condition detected in one or more of the AIS control circuits.
26+**	Injector #1 Peak Current Not Reached	High resistance condition detected in the INJ 1 injector bank circuit.
	or	
	Injector #2 Peak Current Not Reached	High resistance condition detected in the INJ 2 injector bank circuit.
	or	
	Injector #3 Peak Current Not Reached	High resistance condition detected in the INJ 3 injector bank circuit.
27+**	Injector #1 Control Circuit	Injector #1 output driver does not respond properly to the control signal.
	or	
	Injector #2 Control Circuit	Injector #2 output driver does not respond properly to the control signal.
	or	
	Injector #3 Control Circuit	Injector #3 output driver does not respond properly to the control signal.
31**	Purge Solenoid Circuit	An open or shorted condition detected in the purge solenoid circuit.

85614C09

Fig. 41 Fault Code Identification, 1990-91 with MFI

Fault Code	DRB II Display	Description
11	No reference Signal During Cranking	No distributor reference signal detected during engine cranking.
13+**	No change in MAP from start to run	No difference recognized between the engine MAP reading and the barometric (atmospheric) pressure reading at start-up.
14+**	MAP voltage too low or MAP voltage too High	MAP sensor input below minimum acceptable voltage. MAP sensor input above maximum acceptable voltage.
15**	No vehicle speed signal	No vehicle distance (speed) sensor signal detected during road load conditions.
17	Engine is cold too long	Engine coolant temperature remains below normal operating temperatures during vehicle travel (thermostat).
21**	O₂ signal stays at center or O₂ signal shorted to voltage	Neither rich or lean condition detected from the oxygen sensor input. Oxygen sensor input voltage maintained above the normal operating range.
22+**	Coolant sensor voltage too high or Coolant sensor voltage too low	Coolant temperature sensor input above the maximum acceptable voltage. Coolant temperature sensor input below the minimum acceptable voltage.
24+**	Throttle position sensor voltage high or Throttle position sensor voltage low	Throttle position sensor input above the maximum acceptable voltage. Throttle position sensor input below the minimum acceptable voltage.
25**	Automatic idle speed motor circuits	A shorted condition detected in one or more of the AIS control circuits.
27	Injector control circuit (DRB II)	Injector output driver does not respond properly to the control signal (DRB II specifies the injector by cylinder number).
31**	Purge solenoid circuit	An open or shorted condition detected in the purge solenoid circuit.
33	A/C clutch relay circuit	An open or shorted condition detected in the A/C clutch relay circuit.
34	Speed control solenoid circuits	An open or shorted condition detected in the speed control vacuum or vent solenoid circuits.

+ Check Engine Lamp On
** Check Engine Lamp On (California Only)

85614C10

Fig. 42 Fault Code Identification, 1992-93 with TBI

Fault Code	DRB II Display	Description
35	Radiator fan relay circuits	An open or shorted condition detected in the radiator fan circuit
37	Torque convertor unlock solenoid CKT	An open or shorted condition detected in the torque convertor part throttle unlock solenoid circuit (automatic transmission).
41+**	Alternator field not switching properly	An open or shorted condition detected in the alternator field control circuit.
42	Auto shutdown relay control circuit	An open or shorted condition detected in the auto shutdown relay circuit.
44	Battery temp voltage	An open or shorted condition exists in the coolant temperature sensor circuit or a problem exists in the engine controller's battery temperature voltage circuit.
46+**	Charging system voltage too high	Battery voltage sense input above target charging voltage during engine operation.
47+**	Charging system voltage too low	Battery voltage sense input below target charging during engine operation. Also, no significant change detected in battery voltage during active test of alternator output.
51**	O$_2$ signal stays below center (lean)	Oxygen sensor signal input indicates lean air/fuel ratio condition during engine operation.
52**	O$_2$ signal stays above center (rich)	Oxygen sensor signal input indicates rich air/fuel ratio condition during engine operation.
53	Internal controller	Engine controller internal fault condition detected.
62	Controller Failure EMR miles not stored	Unsuccessful attempt to update EMR milage in the controller EEPROM.
63	Controller Failure EEPROM write denied	Unsuccessful attempt to write to an EEPROM location by the engine controller.
55	N/A	Completion of fault code display on Check Engine lamp.

+ Check Engine Lamp On
** Check Engine Lamp On (California Only)

85614C11

Fig. 43 Fault Code Identification, 1992-93 with TBI

Fault Code	DRB II Display	Description
11	No reference Signal During Cranking	No distributor reference signal detected during engine cranking.
13+**	No change in MAP from start to run	No difference recognized between the engine MAP reading and the barometric (atmospheric) pressure reading at start-up.
14+**	MAP voltage too low or MAP voltage too High	MAP sensor input below minimum acceptable voltage. MAP sensor input above maximum acceptable voltage.
15**	No vehicle speed signal	No vehicle distance (speed) sensor signal detected during road load conditions.
17	Engine is cold too long	Engine coolant temperature remains below normal operating temperatures during vehicle travel (thermostat).
21**	O2 signal stays at center or O2 signal shorted to voltage	Neither rich or lean condition detected from the oxygen sensor input. Oxygen sensor input voltage maintained above the normal operating range.
22+**	Coolant sensor voltage too high or Coolant sensor voltage too low	Coolant temperature sensor input above the maximum acceptable voltage. Coolant temperature sensor input below the minimum acceptable voltage.
24+**	Throttle position sensor voltage high or Throttle position sensor voltage low	Throttle position sensor input above the maximum acceptable voltage. Throttle position sensor input below the minimum acceptable voltage.
25**	Automatic idle speed motor circuits	A shorted condition detected in one or more of the AIS control circuits.
27	Injector control circuit (DRB II)	Injector output driver does not respond properly to the control signal (DRB II specifies the injector by cylinder number).
31**	Purge solenoid circuit	An open or shorted condition detected in the purge solenoid circuit.
33	A/C clutch relay circuit	An open or shorted condition detected in the A/C clutch relay circuit.
34	Speed control solenoid circuits	An open or shorted condition detected in the speed control vacuum or vent solenoid circuits.

+ Check Engine Lamp On
** Check Engine Lamp On (California Only)

85614C12

Fig. 44 Fault Code Identification, 1992-93 with MFI

Fault Code	DRB II Display	Description
35	Radiator fan relay circuits	An open or shorted condition detected in the radiator fan circuit
41+**	Alternator field not switching properly	An open or shorted condition detected in the alternator field control circuit.
42	Auto shutdown relay control circuit	An open or shorted condition detected in the auto shutdown relay circuit.
43+**	Ignition coil #1 primary circuit or	Peak primary circuit current not achieved with maximum dwell time.
	Ignition coil #2 primary circuit or	Peak primary circuit current not achieved with maximum dwell time.
	Ignition coil #3 primary circuit	Peak primary circuit current not achieved with maximum dwell time.
44	Battery temp voltage	An open or shorted condition exists in the coolant temperature sensor circuit or a problem exists in the engine controller's battery temperature voltage circuit.
46+**	Charging system voltage too high	Battery voltage sense input above target charging voltage during engine operation.
47+**	Charging system voltage too low	Battery voltage sense input below target charging during engine operation. Also, no significant change detected in battery voltage during active test of alternator output.
51**	O_2 signal stays below center (lean)	Oxygen sensor signal input indicates lean air/fuel ratio condition during engine operation.
52**	O_2 signal stays above center (rich)	Oxygen sensor signal input indicates rich air/fuel ratio condition during engine operation.
53	Internal controller	Engine controller internal fault condition detected.
54+**	No sync pick-up signal	No fuel sync signal detected during engine rotation.
62	Controller Failure EMR miles not stored	Unsuccessful attempt to update EMR milage in the controller EEPROM.
63	Controller Failure EEPROM write denied	Unsuccessful attempt to write to an EEPROM location by the engine controller.
55	N/A	Completion of fault code display on Check Engine lamp.

+ Check Engine Lamp On
** Check Engine Lamp On (California Only)

85614C13

Fig. 45 Fault Code Identification, 1992-93 with MFI

Diagnostic Trouble Code	DRB Scan Tool Display	Description of Diagnostic Trouble Code
11*	No Crank Reference Signal at PCM	No crank reference signal detected during engine cranking.
12*	Battery Disconnect	Direct battery input to PCM was disconnected within the last 50 Key-on cycles.
13**	No Change in MAP From Start to Run or Slow Change in Idle MAP Signal	No difference recognized between the engine MAP reading and the barometric (atmospheric) pressure reading at start-up. MAP output change is slower and/or smaller than expected.
14**	MAP Sensor Voltage Too Low or MAP Sensor Voltage Too High	MAP sensor input below minimum acceptable voltage. MAP sensor input above maximum acceptable voltage.
15**	No Vehicle Speed Sensor Signal	No vehicle distance (speed) sensor signal detected during road load conditions.
17*	Engine is Cold Too Long	Engine coolant temperature remains below normal operating temperatures during vehicle travel (thermostat).
21**	O2S Stays at Center or O2S Shorted to Voltage	Neither rich or lean condition detected from the oxygen sensor input. Oxygen sensor input voltage maintained above the normal operating range.
22**	ECT Sensor Voltage Too High or ECT Sensor Voltage Too Low	Engine coolant temperature sensor input above maximum acceptable voltage. Engine coolant temperature sensor input below minimum acceptable voltage.
24**	Throttle Position Sensor Voltage High or Throttle Position Sensor Voltage Low	Throttle position sensor input above the maximum acceptable voltage. Throttle position sensor input below the minimum acceptable voltage.
25**	Idle Air Control Motor Circuits	A shorted condition detected in one or more of the IAC motor control circuits.
27**	Injector Control Circuit	Injector output driver does not respond properly to the control signal.
31**	EVAP Solenoid Circuit	An open or shorted condition detected in the EVAP purge solenoid circuit.
33*	A/C Clutch Relay	An open or shorted condition detected in the A/C clutch relay circuit.

* Check Engine Lamp will not illuminate at all times if this Diagnostic Trouble Code was recorded. Cycle Ignition key as described in manual and observe code flashed by Check Engine lamp.

** Check Engine Lamp will illuminate during engine operation if this Diagnostic Trouble Code was recorded.

85614C14

Fig. 46 Fault Code Identification, 1994 with TBI

Diagnostic Trouble Code	DRB Scan Tool Display	Description of Diagnostic Trouble Code
34*	Speed Control Solenoid Circuits	An open or shorted condition detected in the speed control vacuum or vent solenoid circuits.
35*	Low Speed Fan CTRL Relay Circuits or	An open or shorted condition detected in the radiator fan low speed relay circuit.
	High Speed Fan CTRL Relay Circuits	An open or shorted condition detected in the radiator fan high speed relay circuit.
37*	Torque Convertor Clutch Solenoid CKT	An open or shorted condition detected in the torque convertor clutch solenoid circuit.
41*	Generator Field Not Switching Properly	An open or shorted condition detected in the generator field control circuit.
42*	Auto Shutdown Relay Control Circuit or	An open or shorted condition detected in the automatic shut down relay circuit.
	No ASD Relay Output Voltage at PCM	PCM did not detect ASD sense signal after grounding the ASD relay.
46**	Charging System Voltage Too High	Battery voltage sense input above target charging voltage during engine operation.
47**	Charging System Voltage Too Low	Battery voltage sense input below target charging during engine operation. Also, no significant change detected in battery voltage during active test of generator output.
51**	O2S Signal Stays Below Center (Lean)	Oxygen sensor signal input indicates lean air/fuel ratio condition during engine operation.
52**	O2S Signal Stays Above Center (Rich)	Oxygen sensor signal input indicates rich air/fuel ratio condition during engine operation.
53*	Internal Controller Failure	Powertrain Control Module internal fault condition detected.
62*	PCM Failure SRI Mile Not Stored	Unsuccessful attempt to update SRI Milage.
63*	PCM Failure EEPROM Write Denied	Unsuccessful attempt to write to an EEPROM location by the Powertrain Control Module.
55	N/A	Completion of fault code display on Malfunction Indicator Lamp (Check Engine lamp).

* Check Engine Lamp will not illuminate at all times if this Diagnostic Trouble Code was recorded. Cycle Ignition key as described in manual and observe code flashed by Check Engine lamp.

** Check Engine Lamp will illuminate during engine operation if this Diagnostic Trouble Code was recorded.

85614C15

Fig. 47 Fault Code Identification, 1994 with TBI

Diagnostic Trouble Code	DRB Scan Tool Display	Description of Diagnostic Trouble Code
34*	Speed Control Solenoid Circuits	An open or shorted condition detected in the speed control vacuum or vent solenoid circuits.
35*	Low Speed Fan CTRL Relay Circuits or High Speed Fan CTRL Relay Circuits	An open or shorted condition detected in the radiator fan low speed relay circuit. An open or shorted condition detected in the radiator fan high speed relay circuit.
37*	Torque Convertor Clutch Solenoid CKT	An open or shorted condition detected in the torque convertor clutch solenoid circuit.
41*	Generator Field Not Switching Properly	An open or shorted condition detected in the generator field control circuit.
42*	Auto Shutdown Relay Control Circuit or No ASD Relay Output Voltage at PCM	An open or shorted condition detected in the automatic shut down relay circuit. PCM did not detect ASD sense signal after grounding the ASD relay.
46**	Charging System Voltage Too High	Battery voltage sense input above target charging voltage during engine operation.
47**	Charging System Voltage Too Low	Battery voltage sense input below target charging during engine operation. Also, no significant change detected in battery voltage during active test of generator output.
51**	O2S Signal Stays Below Center (Lean)	Oxygen sensor signal input indicates lean air/fuel ratio condition during engine operation.
52**	O2S Signal Stays Above Center (Rich)	Oxygen sensor signal input indicates rich air/fuel ratio condition during engine operation.
53*	Internal Controller Failure	Powertrain Control Module internal fault condition detected.
54*	No Cam Sync Signal at PCM	No fuel sync signal detected during engine rotation.
62*	PCM Failure SRI Mile Not Stored	Unsuccessful attempt to update SRI Milage.
63*	PCM Failure EEPROM Write Denied	Unsuccessful attempt to write to an EEPROM location by the Powertrain Control Module.
55	N/A	Completion of fault code display on Malfunction Indicator Lamp (Check Engine lamp).

* Check Engine Lamp will not illuminate at all times if this Diagnostic Trouble Code was recorded. Cycle Ignition key as described in manual and observe code flashed by Check Engine lamp.

** Check Engine Lamp will illuminate during engine operation if this Diagnostic Trouble Code was recorded.

85614C16

Fig. 48 Fault Code Identification, 1994 with MFI

Diagnostic Trouble Code	DRB Scan Tool Display	Description of Diagnostic Trouble Code
11*	No Crank Reference Signal at PCM	No crank reference signal detected during engine cranking.
12*	Battery Disconnect	Direct battery input to PCM was disconnected within the last 50 Key-on cycles.
13**	No Change in MAP From Start to Run	No difference recognized between the engine MAP reading and the barometric (atmospheric) pressure reading at start-up.
14**	MAP Sensor Voltage Too Low	MAP sensor input below minimum acceptable voltage.
	or	
	MAP Sensor Voltage Too High	MAP sensor input above maximum acceptable voltage.
15**	No Vehicle Speed Sensor Signal	No vehicle distance (speed) sensor signal detected during road load conditions.
17*	Engine is Cold Too Long	Engine coolant temperature remains below normal operating temperatures during vehicle travel (thermostat).
21**	O2S Stays at Center	Neither rich or lean condition detected from the oxygen sensor input.
	or	
	O2S Shorted to Voltage	Oxygen sensor input voltage maintained above the normal operating range.
22**	ECT Sensor Voltage Too High	Engine coolant temperature sensor input above maximum acceptable voltage.
	or	
	ECT Sensor Voltage Too Low	Engine coolant temperature sensor input below minimum acceptable voltage.
24**	Throttle Position Sensor Voltage High	Throttle position sensor input above the maximum acceptable voltage.
	or	
	Throttle Position Sensor Voltage Low	Throttle position sensor input below the minimum acceptable voltage.
25**	Idle Air Control Motor Circuits	A shorted condition detected in one or more of the IAC motor control circuits.
27**	Injector Control Circuit	Injector output driver does not respond properly to the control signal. DRB scan tool specifies which injector.
31**	EVAP Solenoid Circuit	An open or shorted condition detected in the duty cycle EVAP purge solenoid circuit.
32**	EGR Solenoid Circuit	An open or shorted condition detected in the EGR transducer solenoid circuit.
	or	
	EGR System Failure	Required change in air/fuel ratio not detected during diagnostic test.
33*	A/C Clutch Relay	An open or shorted condition detected in the A/C clutch relay circuit.

* Check Engine Lamp will not illuminate at all times if this Diagnostic Trouble Code was recorded. Cycle Ignition key as described in manual and observe code flashed by Check Engine lamp.
** Check Engine Lamp will illuminate during engine operation if this Diagnostic Trouble Code was recorded.

85614C17

Fig. 49 Fault Code Identification, 1994 with MFI

VACUUM DIAGRAMS

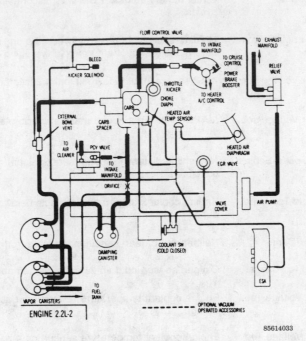

Fig. 50 Vacuum hose routing, 1984 with 2.2L engine (Federal)

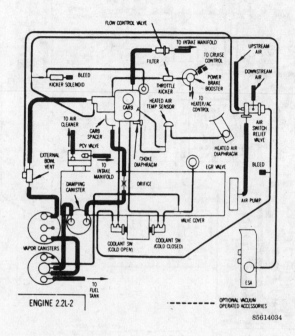

Fig. 51 Vacuum hose routing, 1984 with 2.2L engine (California)

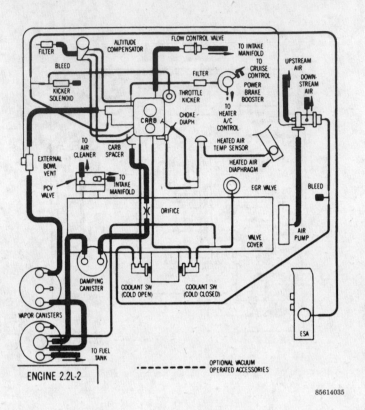

Fig. 52 Vacuum hose routing, 1984 with 2.2L engine (Altitude)

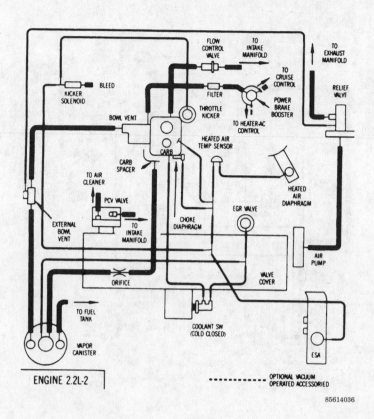

Fig. 53 Vacuum hose routing, 1984 with 2.2L engine (Canada)

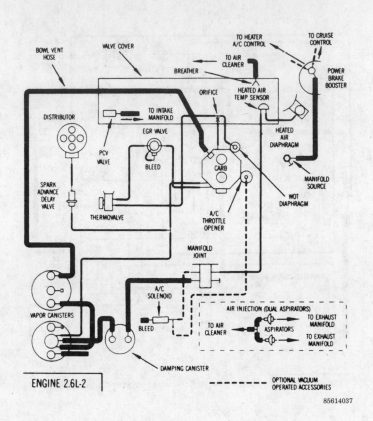

ENGINE 2.6L-2

85614037

Fig. 54 Vacuum hose routing, 1984 with 2.6L engine (Federal)

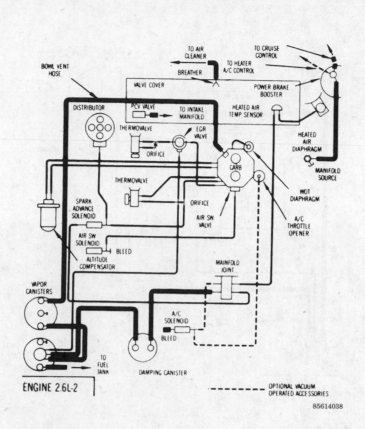

Fig. 55 Vacuum hose routing, 1984 with 2.6L engine (California)

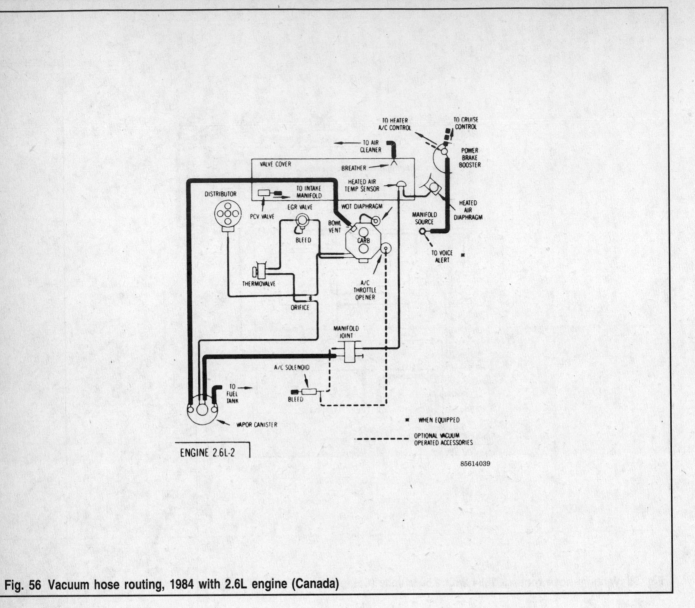

Fig. 56 Vacuum hose routing, 1984 with 2.6L engine (Canada)

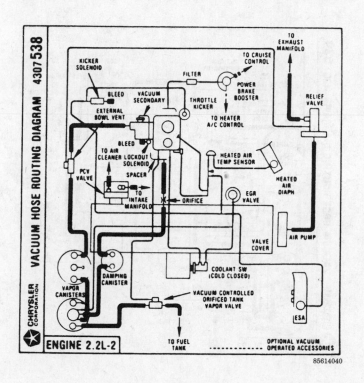

Fig. 57 Vacuum hose routing, 1985 with 2.2L engine (Federal)

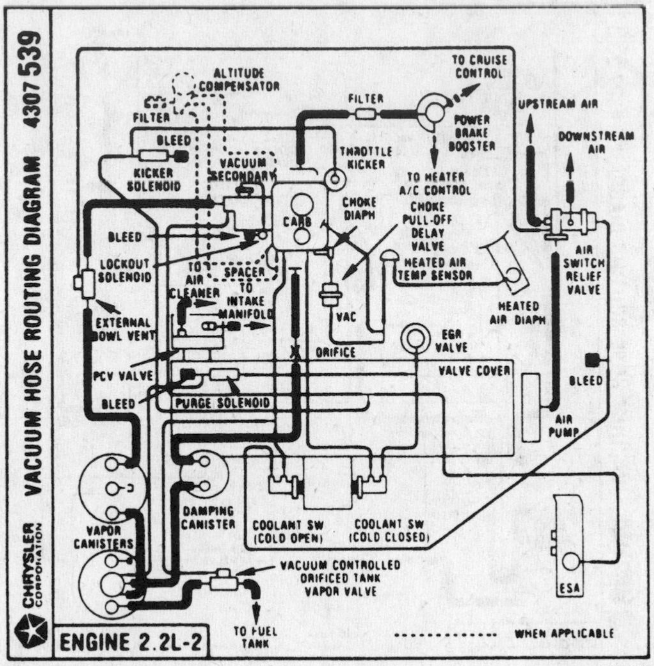

VACUUM HOSE ROUTING DIAGRAM 4307 539

ALTITUDE COMPENSATOR

FILTER

TO CRUISE CONTROL

FILTER

UPSTREAM AIR

DOWNSTREAM AIR

BLEED

KICKER SOLENOID

VACUUM SECONDARY

THROTTLE KICKER

POWER BRAKE BOOSTER

TO HEATER A/C CONTROL

BLEED

CARB

CHOKE DIAPH

CHOKE PULL-OFF DELAY VALVE

AIR SWITCH RELIEF VALVE

LOCKOUT SOLENOID

TO AIR CLEANER

SPACER

TO INTAKE MANIFOLD

HEATED AIR TEMP SENSOR

EXTERNAL BOWL VENT

VAC

HEATED AIR DIAPH

BLEED

PCV VALVE

ORIFICE

EGR VALVE

BLEED

PURGE SOLENOID

VALVE COVER

AIR PUMP

VAPOR CANISTERS

DAMPING CANISTER

COOLANT SW (COLD OPEN)

COOLANT SW (COLD CLOSED)

ESA

VACUUM CONTROLLED ORIFICED TANK VAPOR VALVE

CHRYSLER CORPORATION

ENGINE 2.2L-2

TO FUEL TANK

- - - - - - WHEN APPLICABLE

85614041

Fig. 58 Vacuum hose routing, 1985 with 2.2L engine (California)

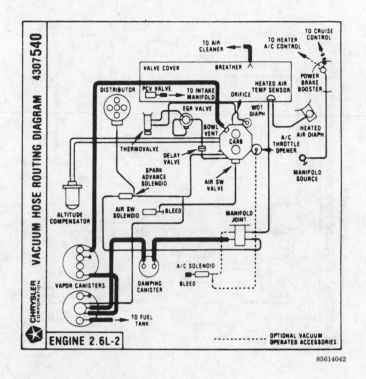

Fig. 59 Vacuum hose routing, 1985 with 2.6L engine (Altitude)

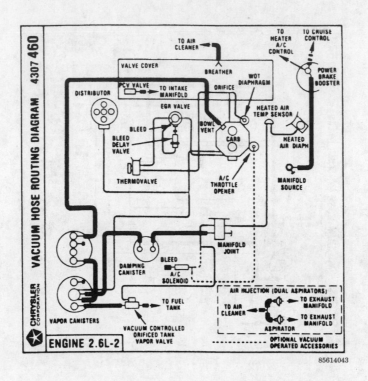

Fig. 60 Vacuum hose routing, 1985 with 2.6L engine (Federal)

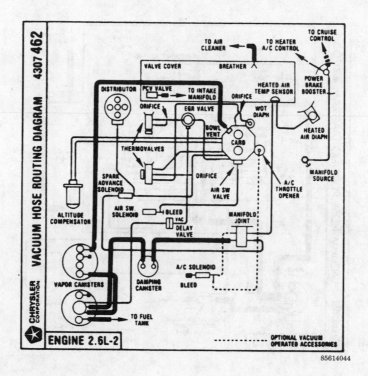

Fig. 61 Vacuum hose routing, 1985 with 2.6L engine (California)

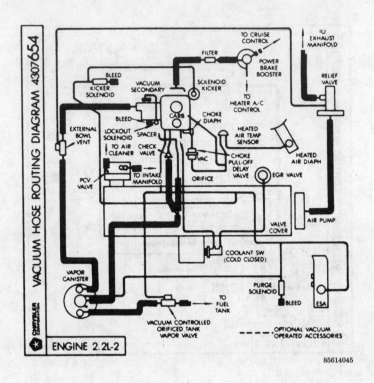

Fig. 62 Vacuum hose routing, 1986 with 2.2L engine (Federal)

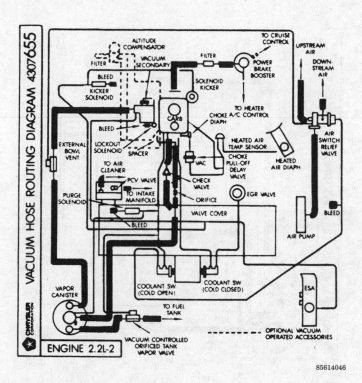

Fig. 63 Vacuum hose routing, 1986 with 2.2L engine (California)

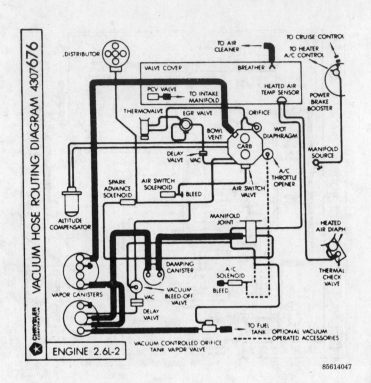

Fig. 64 Vacuum hose routing, 1986 with 2.6L engine (Altitude)

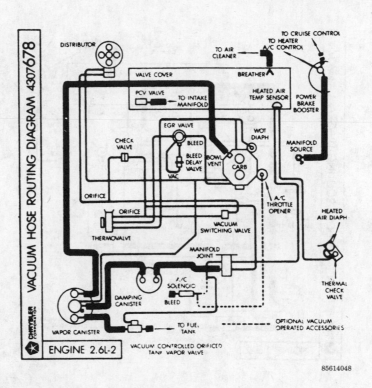

Fig. 65 Vacuum hose routing, 1986 with 2.6L engine (Federal)

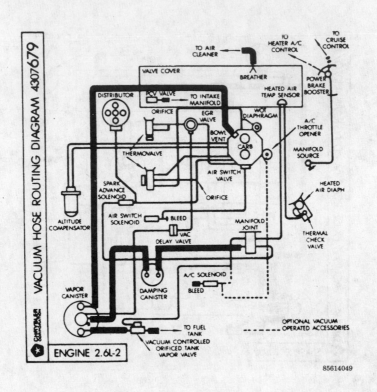

Fig. 66 Vacuum hose routing, 1986 with 2.6L engine (California)

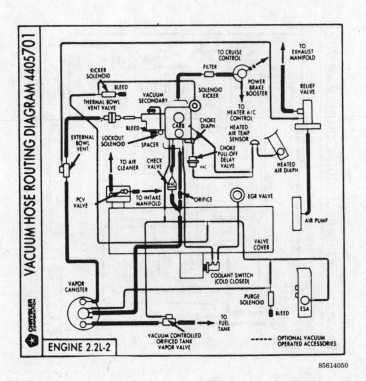

Fig. 67 Vacuum hose routing, 1987 with 2.2L engine (Federal)

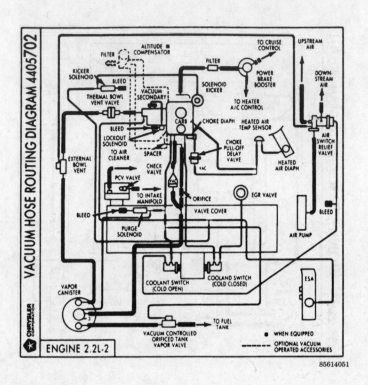

Fig. 68 Vacuum hose routing, 1987 with 2.2L engine (California)

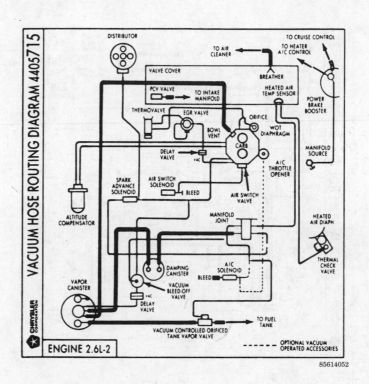

Fig. 69 Vacuum hose routing, 1987 with 2.6L engine (Federal)

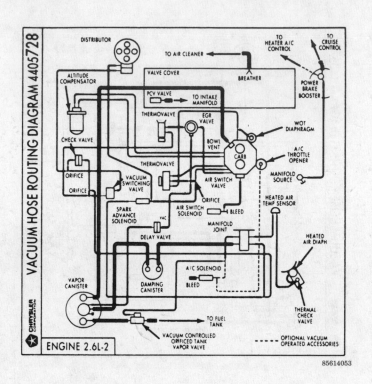

Fig. 70 Vacuum hose routing, 1987 with 2.6L engine (California)

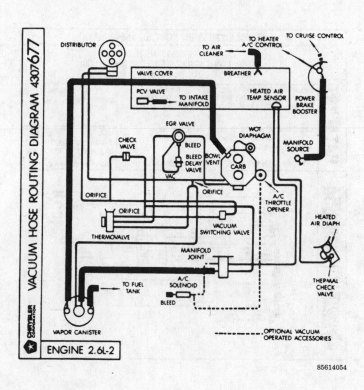

Fig. 71 Vacuum hose routing, 1987 with 2.6L engine (Canada)

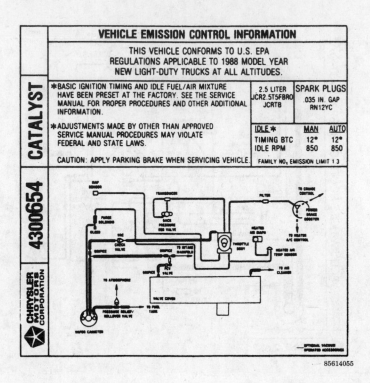

Fig. 72 Vacuum hose routing, 1988 with 2.5L engine (Federal)

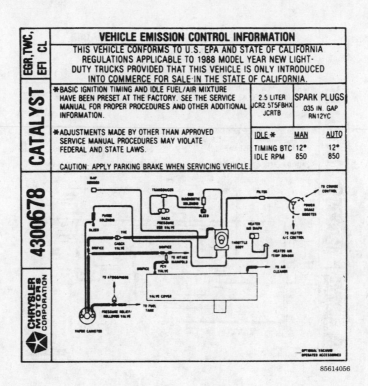

85614056

Fig. 73 Vacuum hose routing, 1988 with 2.5L engine (California)

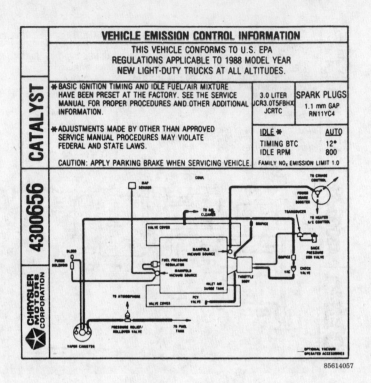

Fig. 74 Vacuum hose routing, 1988 with 3.0L engine (Federal)

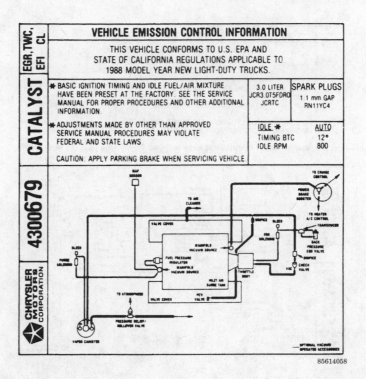

VEHICLE EMISSION CONTROL INFORMATION

THIS VEHICLE CONFORMS TO U.S. EPA AND
STATE OF CALIFORNIA REGULATIONS APPLICABLE TO
1988 MODEL YEAR NEW LIGHT-DUTY TRUCKS.

✱ BASIC IGNITION TIMING AND IDLE FUEL/AIR MIXTURE
HAVE BEEN PRESET AT THE FACTORY. SEE THE SERVICE
MANUAL FOR PROPER PROCEDURES AND OTHER ADDITIONAL
INFORMATION.

✱ ADJUSTMENTS MADE BY OTHER THAN APPROVED
SERVICE MANUAL PROCEDURES MAY VIOLATE
FEDERAL AND STATE LAWS.

CAUTION: APPLY PARKING BRAKE WHEN SERVICING VEHICLE

3.0 LITER
JCR3.0T5FDRO
JCRTC

SPARK PLUGS
1.1 mm GAP
RN11YC4

IDLE ✱	AUTO
TIMING BTC	12°
IDLE RPM	800

85614058

Fig. 75 Vacuum hose routing, 1988with 3.0L engine (California)

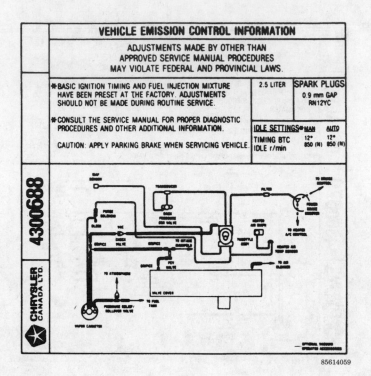

VEHICLE EMISSION CONTROL INFORMATION

ADJUSTMENTS MADE BY OTHER THAN
APPROVED SERVICE MANUAL PROCEDURES
MAY VIOLATE FEDERAL AND PROVINCIAL LAWS.

✳ BASIC IGNITION TIMING AND FUEL INJECTION MIXTURE
HAVE BEEN PRESET AT THE FACTORY. ADJUSTMENTS
SHOULD NOT BE MADE DURING ROUTINE SERVICE.

✳ CONSULT THE SERVICE MANUAL FOR PROPER DIAGNOSTIC
PROCEDURES AND OTHER ADDITIONAL INFORMATION.

CAUTION: APPLY PARKING BRAKE WHEN SERVICING VEHICLE.

2.5 LITER | **SPARK PLUGS**
0.9 mm GAP
RN12YC

IDLE SETTINGS | MAN | AUTO
TIMING BTC | 12° | 12°
IDLE r/min | 850 (N) | 850 (N)

4300688

CHRYSLER CANADA LTD.

85614059

Fig. 76 Vacuum hose routing, 1988 with 2.5L engine (Canada)

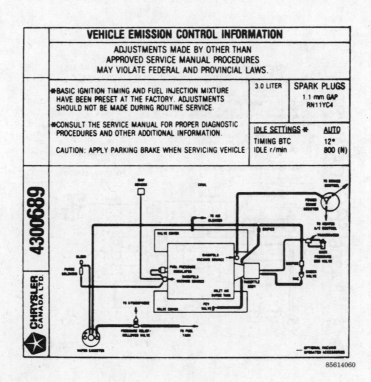

Fig. 77 Vacuum hose routing, 1988 with 3.0L engine (Canada)

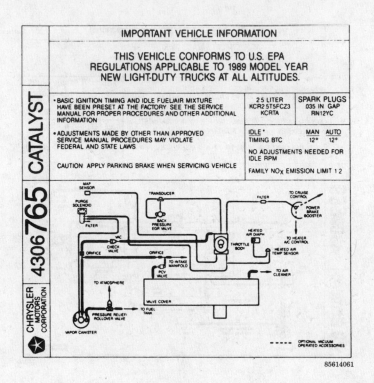

Fig. 78 Vacuum hose routing, 1989 with 2.5L engine (Federal, Altitude)

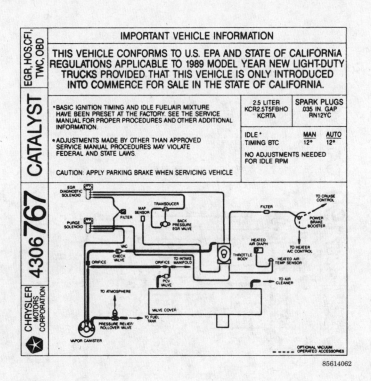

Fig. 79 Vacuum hose routing, 1989 with 2.5L engine (California)

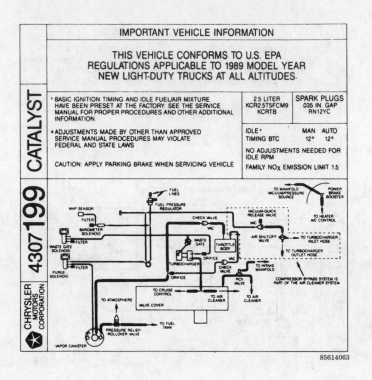

Fig. 80 Vacuum hose routing, 1989 with 2.5L turbo engine (Federal, California)

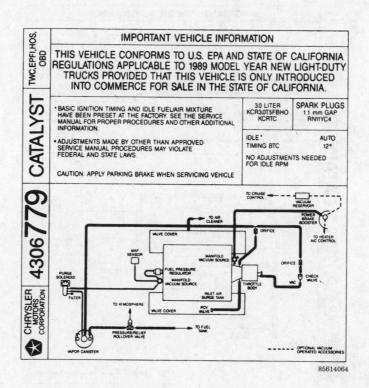

IMPORTANT VEHICLE INFORMATION

THIS VEHICLE CONFORMS TO U.S. EPA AND STATE OF CALIFORNIA REGULATIONS APPLICABLE TO 1989 MODEL YEAR NEW LIGHT-DUTY TRUCKS PROVIDED THAT THIS VEHICLE IS ONLY INTRODUCED INTO COMMERCE FOR SALE IN THE STATE OF CALIFORNIA.

• BASIC IGNITION TIMING AND IDLE FUEL/AIR MIXTURE HAVE BEEN PRESET AT THE FACTORY. SEE THE SERVICE MANUAL FOR PROPER PROCEDURES AND OTHER ADDITIONAL INFORMATION.

• ADJUSTMENTS MADE BY OTHER THAN APPROVED SERVICE MANUAL PROCEDURES MAY VIOLATE FEDERAL AND STATE LAWS.

CAUTION: APPLY PARKING BRAKE WHEN SERVICING VEHICLE

3.0 LITER
KCR3.0T5FBHO
KCRTC

SPARK PLUGS
1.1 mm GAP
RN11YC4

IDLE •
TIMING BTC

AUTO
12°

NO ADJUSTMENTS NEEDED
FOR IDLE RPM

TWC,EPFI,HOS, OBD
CATALYST
43067779
CHRYSLER MOTORS CORPORATION

85614064

Fig. 81 Vacuum hose routing, 1989 with 3.0L engine (Federal, California)

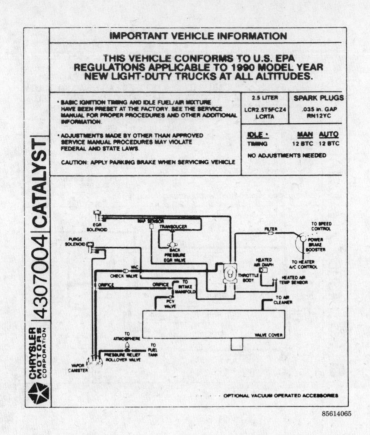

Fig. 82 Vacuum hose routing, 1990 with 2.5L engine (Federal, Altitude)

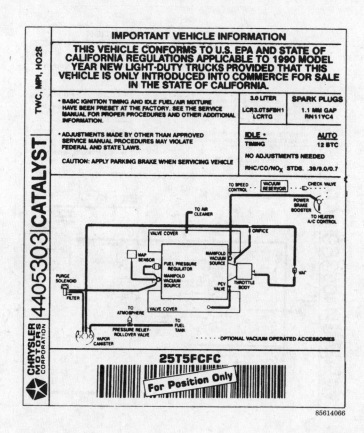

IMPORTANT VEHICLE INFORMATION

THIS VEHICLE CONFORMS TO U.S. EPA AND STATE OF CALIFORNIA REGULATIONS APPLICABLE TO 1990 MODEL YEAR NEW LIGHT-DUTY TRUCKS PROVIDED THAT THIS VEHICLE IS ONLY INTRODUCED INTO COMMERCE FOR SALE IN THE STATE OF CALIFORNIA.

TWC, MPI, HO2S

CHRYSLER MOTORS CORPORATION 4405303 CATALYST

- BASIC IGNITION TIMING AND IDLE FUEL/AIR MIXTURE HAVE BEEN PRESET AT THE FACTORY. SEE THE SERVICE MANUAL FOR PROPER PROCEDURES AND OTHER ADDITIONAL INFORMATION.

- ADJUSTMENTS MADE BY OTHER THAN APPROVED SERVICE MANUAL PROCEDURES MAY VIOLATE FEDERAL AND STATE LAWS.

CAUTION: APPLY PARKING BRAKE WHEN SERVICING VEHICLE

3.0 LITER	SPARK PLUGS
LCR3.0T5FBH1 LCRTG	1.1 MM GAP RN11YC4

| IDLE · TIMING | AUTO 12 BTC |

NO ADJUSTMENTS NEEDED

RHC/CO/NO$_X$ STDS. .39/9.0/0.7

TO SPEED CONTROL — VACUUM RESERVOIR — CHECK VALVE

POWER BRAKE BOOSTER

TO HEATER A/C CONTROL

TO AIR CLEANER

VALVE COVER

ORIFICE

MAP SENSOR

FUEL PRESSURE REGULATOR

MANIFOLD VACUUM SOURCE

MANIFOLD VACUUM SOURCE

PCV VALVE

THROTTLE BODY

VAC

PURGE SOLENOID

FILTER

TO ATMOSPHERE

VALVE COVER

TO FUEL TANK

PRESSURE RELIEF ROLLOVER VALVE

VAPOR CANISTER

· · · · · OPTIONAL VACUUM OPERATED ACCESSORIES

25T5FCFC

For Position Only

85614066

Fig. 83 Vacuum hose routing, 1990 with 3.0L engine (Federal, Altitude)

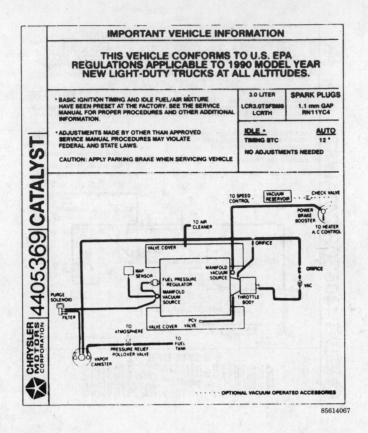

Fig. 84 Vacuum hose routing, 1990 with 3.0L engine (Federal, Altitude)

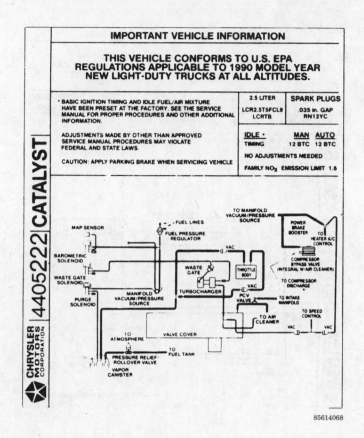

Fig. 85 Vacuum hose routing, 1990 with 2.5L turbo engine (Federal, Altitude)

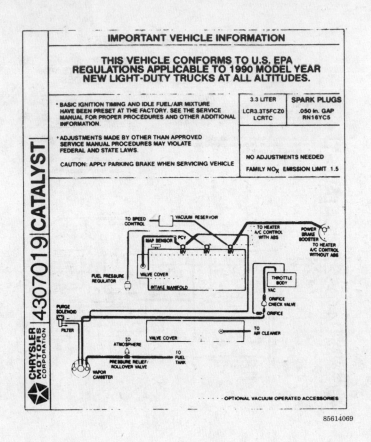

Fig. 86 Vacuum hose routing, 1990 with 3.3L engine (Federal, Altitude)

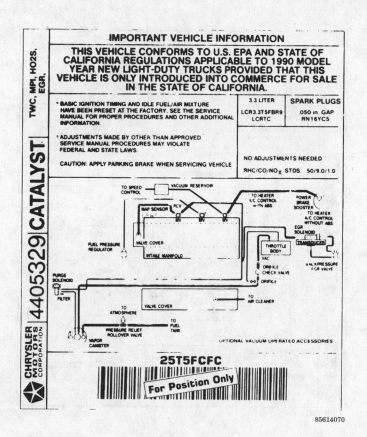

Fig. 87 Vacuum hose routing, 1990 with 3.3L engine (California)

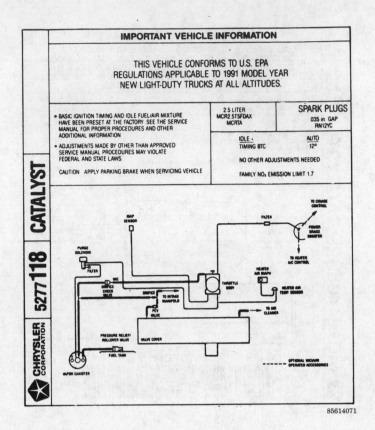

Fig. 88 Vacuum hose routing, 1991 with 2.5L engine (Federal)

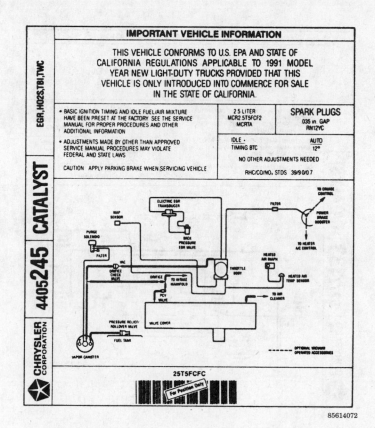

Fig. 89 Vacuum hose routing, 1991 with 2.5L engine (California)

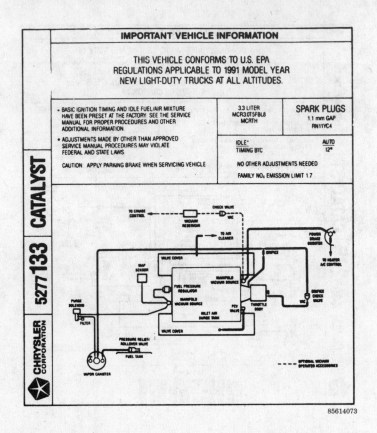

Fig. 90 Vacuum hose routing, 1991 with 3.0L engine (Federal, California)

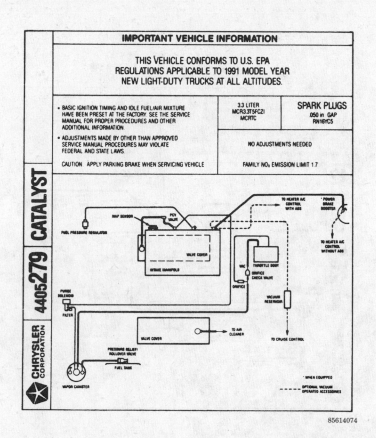

Fig. 91 Vacuum hose routing, 1991 with 3.3L engine with front wheel drive (Federal, California)

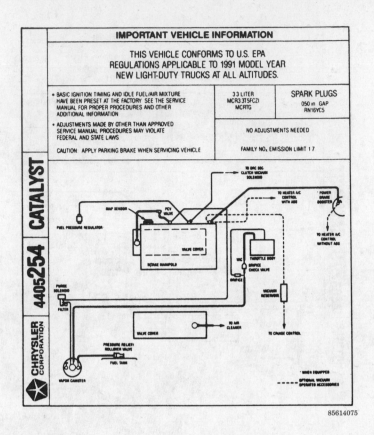

Fig. 92 Vacuum hose routing, 1991 with 3.3L engine with all wheel drive (Federal, California)

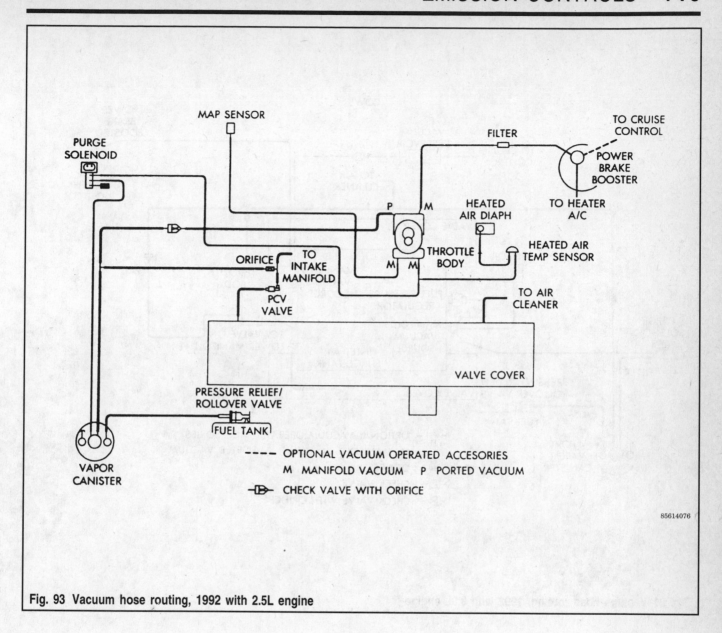

Fig. 93 Vacuum hose routing, 1992 with 2.5L engine

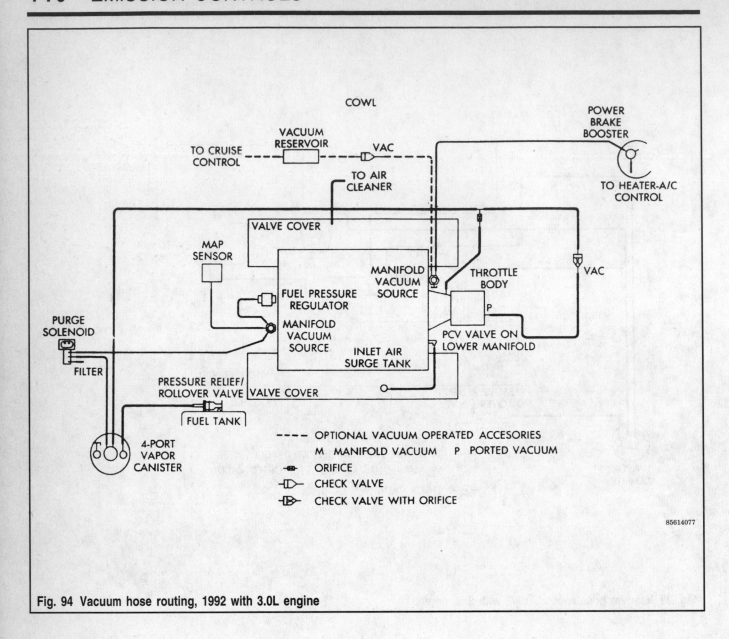

Fig. 94 Vacuum hose routing, 1992 with 3.0L engine

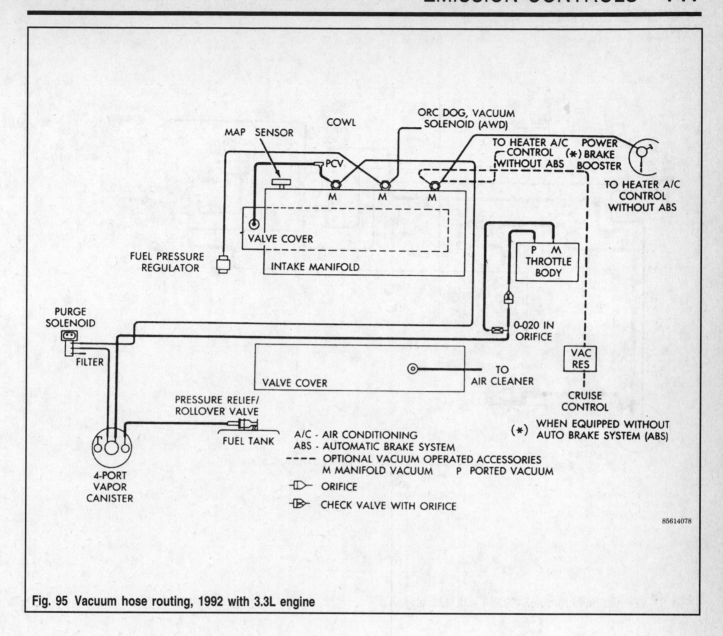

Fig. 95 Vacuum hose routing, 1992 with 3.3L engine

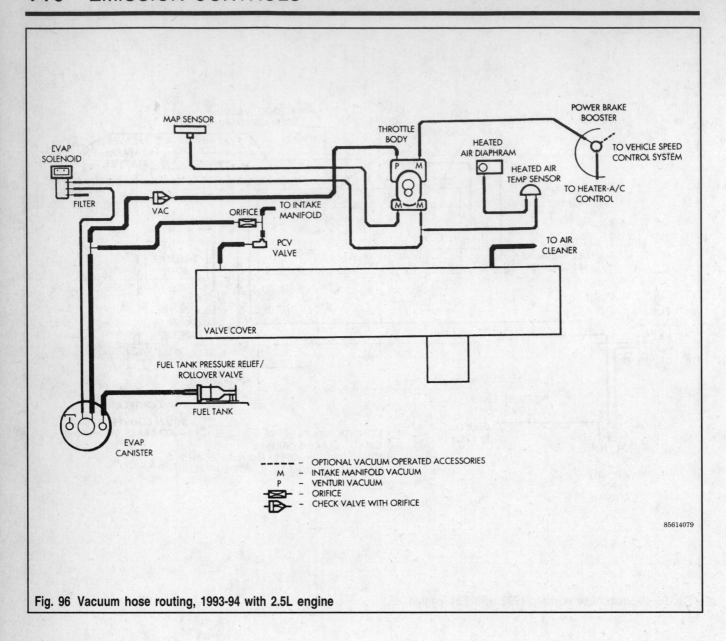

Fig. 96 Vacuum hose routing, 1993-94 with 2.5L engine

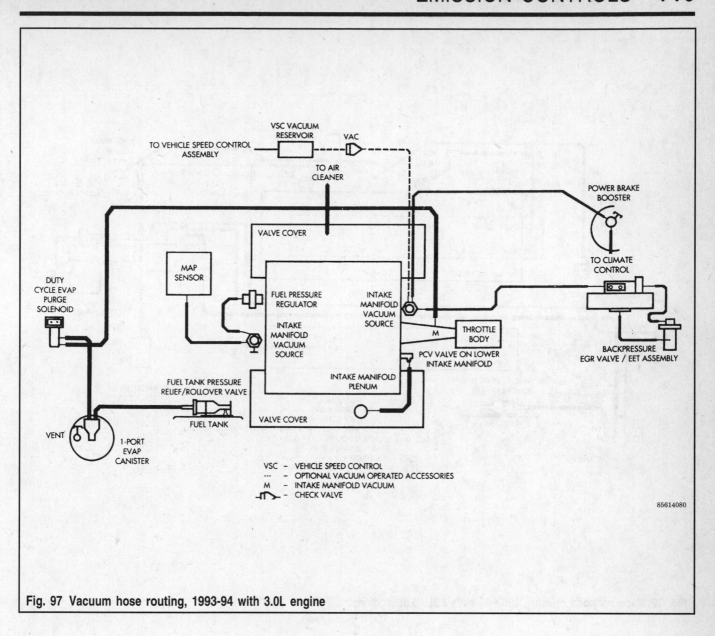

Fig. 97 Vacuum hose routing, 1993-94 with 3.0L engine

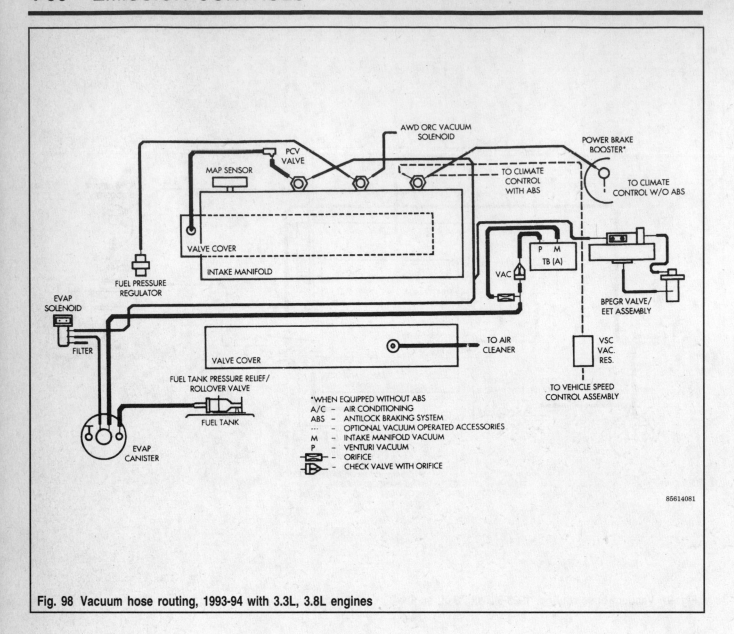

Fig. 98 Vacuum hose routing, 1993-94 with 3.3L, 3.8L engines

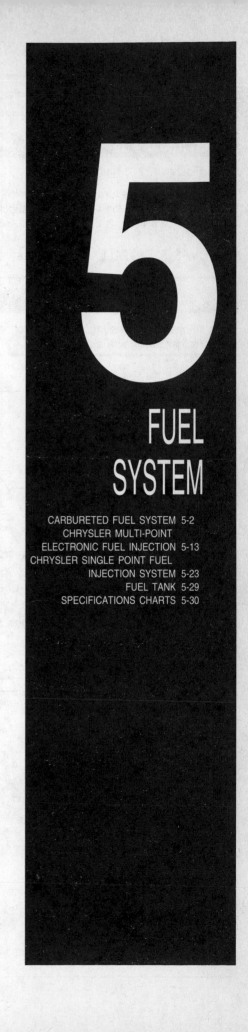

5

FUEL
SYSTEM

CARBURETED FUEL SYSTEM

Mechanical Fuel Pump

▶ **See Figures 1, 2, 3 and 4**

The 2.2L and 2.6L engine use a mechanical type fuel pump located on the side of the engine. The fuel pump is driven by an eccentric cam which is cast on the accessory drive shaft.

REMOVAL & INSTALLATION

✳✳CAUTION

Don't smoke when working around gasoline, cleaning solvent or other flammable substances.

1. Remove the oil filter.

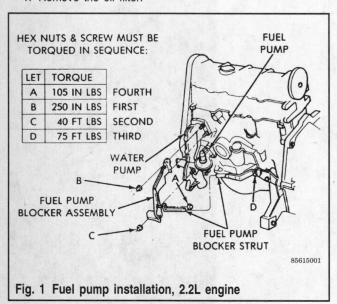

HEX NUTS & SCREW MUST BE TORQUED IN SEQUENCE:

LET	TORQUE	
A	105 IN LBS	FOURTH
B	250 IN LBS	FIRST
C	40 FT LBS	SECOND
D	75 FT LBS	THIRD

FUEL PUMP

WATER PUMP

FUEL PUMP BLOCKER ASSEMBLY

FUEL PUMP BLOCKER STRUT

85615001

Fig. 1 Fuel pump installation, 2.2L engine

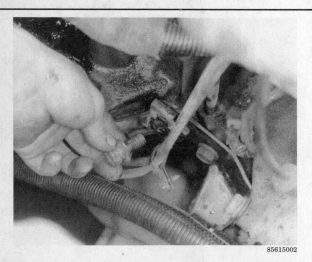

85615002

Fig. 2 Removing the fuel pump blocker strut retaining bolt

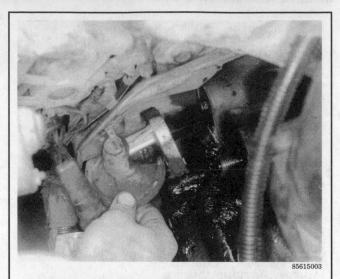

85615003

Fig. 3 Removing the fuel pump blocker strut

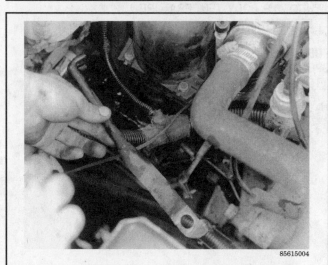

85615004

Fig. 4 The fuel pump removed from the engine. Oil filter removed for illustration purposes

2. Disconnect the fuel lines from the pump.
3. Plug the lines to prevent fuel leakage.
4. Remove the fuel pump blocker strut from front engine mount to blocker assembly.
5. Remove the fuel pump mounting bolts.
6. Clean all gasket material from engine block mounting surface and spacer block.
7. Assemble the new gaskets and spacer block to fuel pump.
8. Install the fuel pump mounting bolts in pump mounting flange.
9. Position the pump assembly on engine block and torque bolts alternately to 250 inch lbs.
10. Connect the fuel lines to the pump.
11. Position the fuel pump blocker strut on blocker assembly and front engine mount. Tighten assembly.
12. Install the oil filter. Check and adjust oil level.

13. Start the engine and check fuel fittings for leaks.

TESTING

Volume Test

The fuel pump should supply 1 qt. of fuel in 1 minute or less at idle.

Pressure Test

1. Insert a T-fitting in the fuel line at the carburetor.

✳✳CAUTION

Never smoke when working around gasoline! Avoid all sources of sparks or ignition. Gasoline vapors are EXTREMELY volatile!

2. Connect a six inch piece of hose between the T-fitting and a pressure gauge. A longer piece of hose will result in an inaccurate reading.
3. Disconnect the inlet line to the carburetor at the fuel pump and vent the pump. Failure to vent the pump will result in low pressure reading. Reconnect the fuel line.
4. Connect a tachometer to the engine. Start the engine and allow to idle. The pressure gauge should show a constant $4\frac{1}{2}$-6 psi reading. When the engine is turned off, the pressure should slowly drop to zero. An instant drop to zero indicates a leaky diaphragm or weak spring. If pressure is too high, the main spring is too strong or the air vent is plugged.
5. Proceed with vacuum test.

Vacuum Test

1. Remove the inlet and outlet fuel lines from the pump.

✳✳CAUTION

Never smoke when working around gasoline! Avoid all sources of sparks or ignition. Gasoline vapors are EXTREMELY volatile!

2. Plug the fuel line to the carburetor to prevent fuel leakage.
3. Connect a vacuum gauge to the fuel pump inlet fitting.
4. Using the starter motor, turn the engine over several times and observe the vacuum gauge. The fuel pump should develop a minimum of 11 inches of vacuum.
5. If the vacuum readings are below specification, replace the pump.

Carburetor

ADJUSTMENTS

Idle Speed/Solenoid Kicker Check — Holley
▶ See Figure 5

2.2L air conditioned vehicles are equipped with a solenoid kicker.
1. Start engine and run until operating temperature is reached.
2. Turn air conditioning switch on and set temperature control lever to the coldest position.
3. Notice the kicker solenoid for in and out movement as the compressor cycles on and off. If no movement occurred, check the kicker system for vacuum leaks. Check the operation of the vacuum solenoid. If no problems are found, replace the kicker.
4. If the kicker solenoid functions properly, turn off the air conditioning switch and shut engine off.

Solenoid Kicker Adjustment — Holley

1. Check ignition timing and adjust if necessary.
2. Disconnect and plug vacuum connector at the CVSCC.
3. Unplug connector at cooling fan and jumper harness so fan will run continuously.
4. Remove the PCV valve and allow it to draw underhood air.
5. Connect a tachometer to the engine.
6. Ground the carburetor switch with a jumper wire.
7. Disconnect the oxygen system test lead located on the left fender shield on vehicles equipped with 6520 carburetors.
8. Start the engine and run until normal operating temperature is reached.
9. Adjust idle speed screw to specification given in under hood label.
10. Reconnect PCV valve, oxygen connector and CVSCC vacuum connector.
11. Remove the jumper from carburetor switch.
12. Remove the jumper from radiator fan and reconnect harness.

➡**After Steps 10, 11 and 12 are completed, the idle speed may change slightly. This is normal and engine speed should not be readjusted.**

Fast Idle — Holley
▶ See Figure 6

Before adjusting fast idle, check and adjust ignition timing.
1. Disconnect the electrical harness at the radiator fan and install a jumper wire so the fan will run continuously.
2. Remove the PCV valve and allow it to draw under hood air.
3. Disconnect and plug the vacuum connector at the CVSCC.
4. Install a tachometer.
5. Jumper the carburetor switch.
6. Disconnect oxygen system test connector located on the left fender shield by shock tower.

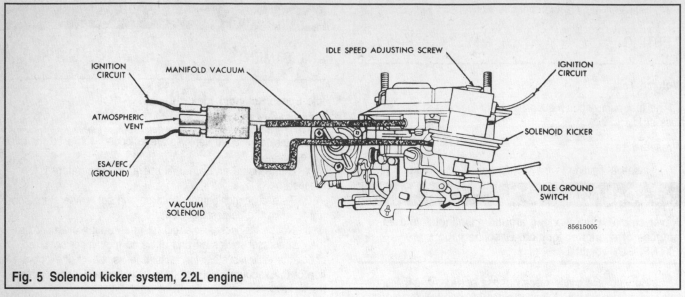

Fig. 5 Solenoid kicker system, 2.2L engine

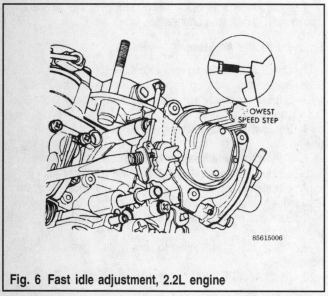

Fig. 6 Fast idle adjustment, 2.2L engine

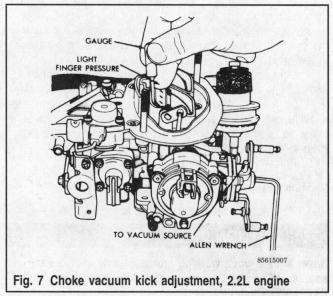

Fig. 7 Choke vacuum kick adjustment, 2.2L engine

7. Start engine and allow to reach normal operating temperature.

8. Open throttle slightly and place adjustment screw on the lowest step of fast idle cam.

9. Adjust the fast idle screw to specification shown on under hood VECI label. Return engine to idle and repeat Step 8, readjust if necessary.

10. Stop engine, remove jumper wire from radiator fan harness and reconnect connector.

11. Reinstall PCV valve.

12. Reconnect oxygen system test connector, and vacuum connector at CVSCC.

Choke Vacuum Kick — Holley

▶ **See Figures 7, 8 and 9**

1. Open the carburetor throttle and hold choke valve in closed position. While maintaining choke valve in closed position, release the throttle. Fast idle system should now be trapped at closed choke condition.

2. Disconnect carburetor vacuum source at carburetor.

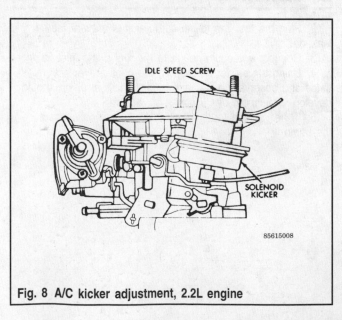

Fig. 8 A/C kicker adjustment, 2.2L engine

Vacuum Kick Specifications

Carb Number	Setting
4288460	.07 in.
4288461	.07 in.
4288262	.07 in.
4288263	.07 in.
4288456	.08 in.
4288458	.08 in.
4288459	.08 in.

85615009

Fig. 9 Vacuum kick adjustment specifications, 2.2L engine

3. Using light finger pressure, close choke valve to the smallest opening possible without disturbing linkage system.

4. Using the proper size drill or gauge, insert between choke valve and air horn wall at primary throttle end of carburetor. Refer to Choke Vacuum Kick Specification Chart.

5. Using an allen head screw in center of diaphragm housing, adjust by turning clockwise or counterclockwise to obtain correct setting.

6. Reconnect vacuum hose to carburetor vacuum source.

Mixture Adjustment (Propane Assisted)

➡**The following procedures require the use of a propane cylinder, vacuum hose and a special control valve to provide proper enrichment. Any adjustments made other than those in the following procedures, may violate Federal and State Laws.**

1. Remove the concealment plug. Refer to Steps 18 through 20 under carburetor disassembling procedure.

2. Set the parking brake and place the transaxle in neutral position. Turn off all accessories. Start engine and allow to idle on second highest step of fast idle cam until normal operating temperature is reached. Return engine to idle.

3. Disconnect vacuum connector at CVSCC and plug. Disconnect the vacuum hose to the heated air door sensor at the three way connector, and in its place, install the supply hose from the propane bottle.

4. Unplug the radiator fan connector and jumper harness so the fan will run continuously. Remove PCV valve and allow it to draw under hood air. Connect a jumper wire between the carburetor switch and ground. On vehicles equipped with 6520 carburetors, disconnect the oxygen test lead located on the left fender shield.

5. With the air cleaner installed. Open the propane main valve. Slowly open the propane metering valve until maximum engine RPM idle is reached. If too much propane is added engine RPM will decrease. Adjust metering valve for the highest engine RPM.

6. With the propane still flowing, adjust the idle speed screw on top of the solenoid to obtain specified RPM on under hood label. Again adjust the propane metering valve to get the

highest engine RPM. If the maximum RPM changes, readjust the idle speed screw to the specified propane RPM.

7. Shut off the propane main valve and allow the engine to stabilize. With the air cleaner still in place, slowly adjust the mixture screws to obtain the specified set RPM. Pause for a few seconds after each adjustment to allow engine speed to stabilized.

8. Again turn on the propane main valve and adjust the metering valve to obtain the highest engine RPM. If the maximum speed differs more than 25 RPM, repeat Steps 5 through 8.

9. Shut off both valves on propane cylinder. Disconnect the propane vacuum supply hose and connect the vacuum hose to the heated air door sensor at the three way connector.

10. Install concealment plug. Proceed with fast idle adjustment starting at Step 7.

Anti-Dieseling Adjustment — Holley

➡**Always check and adjust ignition timing before any idle speed adjustment is performed.**

1. Warm engine to normal operating temperature. Place transaxle in neutral position and set parking brake.

2. Turn off all accessories. Jumper wire between carburetor switch and ground.

3. Remove the RED wire from the 6-Way connector (carburetor side).

4. Adjust the throttle stop speed screw to obtain 700 rpm.

5. Reconnect RED wire and remove jumper from carburetor switch.

Idle RPM — Mikuni Carburetor

▶ **See Figure 10**

1. Check and adjust ignition timing.

2. Set the parking brake and place transaxle in neutral. Turn off all accessories.

3. Disconnect the radiator fan.

4. Connect a tachometer to the engine.

5. Start engine and run until operating temperature is reached.

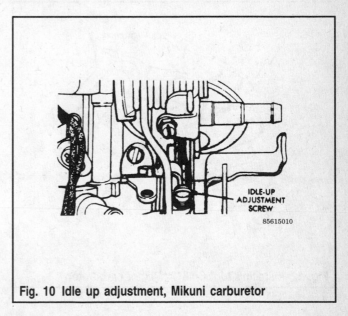

IDLE-UP
ADJUSTMENT
SCREW

85615010

Fig. 10 Idle up adjustment, Mikuni carburetor

6. Disconnect cooling fan. Run engine at 2500 RPM for 10 seconds and return to idle.

7. Wait 2 minutes and record RPM. If RPM differs from VECI under hood specification label, turn idle speed adjusting screw until specification is obtained.

8. On air condition models, set the temperature lever to the coldest position and turn air conditioning switch on. With the air condition running, set the engine speed to 900 RPM using the idle-up adjustment screw.

9. Shut engine off. Connect the cooling fan and remove tachometer.

Fast Idle — Mikuni Carburetor

♦ See Figures 11 and 12

1. Connect a tachometer to the engine. Check and adjust ignition timing.

2. Set the parking brake and place transaxle in neutral. Turn off all accessories.

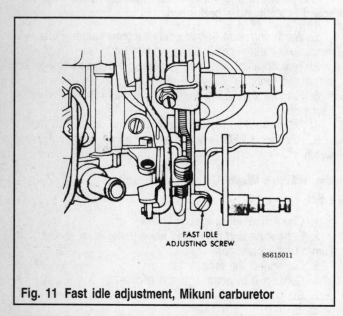

Fig. 11 Fast idle adjustment, Mikuni carburetor

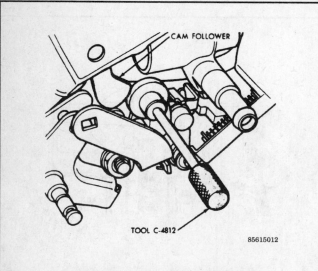

Fig. 12 Installing tool C-4812, Mikuni carburetor

3. Start engine and run until operating temperature is reached.

4. Disconnect radiator fan. Remove and plug vacuum advance hose at distributor.

5. Open the throttle slightly and install Tool C-4812 on cam follower pin.

6. Release throttle lever and adjust fast idle adjusting screw to specification shown on VECI under hood label.

7. Remove tool and shut engine off. Reconnect fan, unplug and reconnect vacuum hose, and remove tachometer.

Idle Mixture (Propane Assist)Mikuni Carburetor

➡**The following procedures require the use of a propane cylinder, vacuum hose and a special control valve to provide proper enrichment. Any adjustments made other than those in the following procedures, may violate Federal and State Laws.**

1. Remove concealment plug. Refer to Concealment Plug Removal procedure. Check and adjust ignition timing.

2. Set the parking brake and place transaxle in neutral. Turn off all accessories.

3. Disconnect the cooling fan.

4. Connect a tachometer to the engine.

5. Start engine and run until operating temperature is reached.

6. Disconnect cooling fan. Run engine at 2500 RPM for 10 seconds and return to idle. Allow engine to idle for 2 minutes.

7. Remove the air cleaner fresh air duct. Place the propane bottle in a safe location and in an upright position. Insert the propane supply hose approximately 4 inches into the air cleaner snorkel.

8. Open the propane bottle main valve. Slowly open the metering valve until the highest engine RPM is reached. If too much propane is added, the engine RPM will decrease. Fine Tune the propane metering valve to obtain the highest engine RPM.

9. With the propane still flowing, adjust the idle speed screw to the specified RPM shown on VECI under hood label. Again Fine Tune the propane metering valve to get the highest engine RPM. If the RPM increases, readjust the idle speed screw to specification.

10. Shut off the propane main valve and allow the engine speed to stabilize. Slowly adjust the carburetor mixture screws to obtain the specified idle RPM. Pause between each adjustment to allow engine speed to stabilize.

11. Again turn on the propane main valve, Fine Tune the metering valve to get the highest engine RPM. If the RPM changes, repeat Step 8 through 10.

12. Shut off the propane main valve and metering valve. Remove the propane supply hose. Install the air cleaner fresh air duct. Install the concealment plug and impact plate.

Concealment Plug Removal Mikuni Carburetor

1. Remove the impact plate, if used.

2. Remove the vacuum connector from high altitude compensator (HAC) fitting on carburetor, if used.

3. With an eight inch long ¼" diameter drill bit, drill out concealment plug at location show.

4. Remove concealment plug.

REMOVAL & INSTALLATION

2.2L Engine

▶ See Figures 13, 14, 15, 16, 17, 18, 19, 20, 21, 22, 23 and 24

> ✳✳CAUTION
>
> **Never remove a carburetor from an engine that has just been road tested. Allow the engine to cool down to prevent accidental fuel ignition or personal injury.**

1. Disconnect the negative battery cable.
2. Remove the air cleaner.
3. Remove the fuel tank filler cap to relieve fuel system pressure.

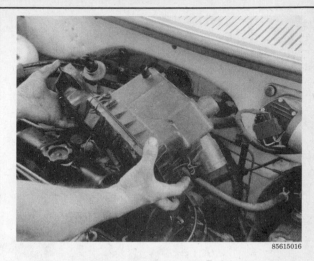

Fig. 15 Disconnecting the breather hose to the air cleaner, 1987 2.2L engine

Fig. 13 After disconnecting the air intake duct disconnect the air heat tube to the air cleaner

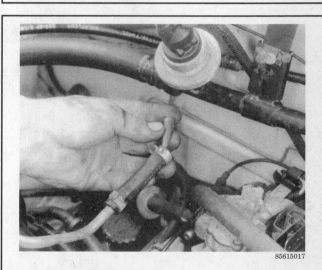

Fig. 16 Disconnect the carburetor inlet line, 1987 2.2L engine

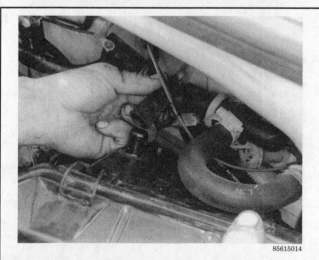

Fig. 14 Disconnecting the breather hose to the air cleaner, 1987 2.2L engine

Fig. 17 Disconnect the electrical connector to the electric choke, 1987 2.2L engine

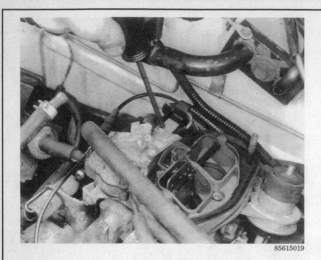

Fig. 18 Disconnect the wiring harness and vacuum tube retaining bracket, 1987 2.2L engine

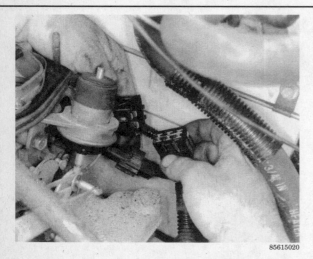

Fig. 19 Disconnect the main wiring harness connector, 1987 2.2L engine

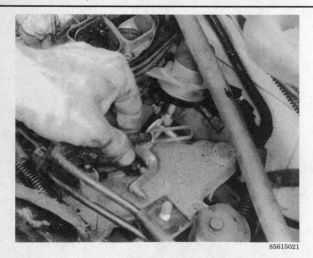

Fig. 20 Disconnect the throttle linkage from the carburetor, 1987 2.2L engine

Fig. 21 Disconnect the vacuum tube, 1987 2.2L engine

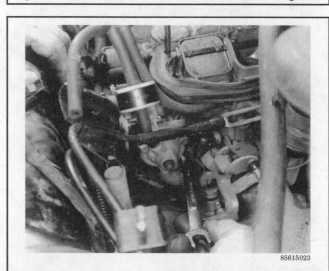

Fig. 22 Removing the carburetor mounting nuts, 1987 2.2L engine

Fig. 23 Removing the carburetor mounting nuts, 1987 2.2L engine

85615025

Fig. 24 Removing the carburetor assembly from the manifold, 1987 2.2L engine

4. Disconnect all carburetor electrical wiring.

✷✷**CAUTION**

Never smoke when working around gasoline! Avoid all sources of sparks or ignition. Gasoline vapors are EXTREMELY volatile!

5. Disconnect the carburetor inlet line and block off line to prevent fuel leakage.
6. Disconnect the throttle linkage. Label and remove all vacuum hoses.
7. Remove the carburetor mounting nuts and remove carburetor.
8. Inspect the mating surfaces of the carburetor and isolator for nicks, burrs, dirt or other damage. It is not necessary to disturb the isolator to intake manifold mounting screws, unless the isolator is damage.
9. Carefully install carburetor on engine. Install nuts evenly and torque to 200 inch lbs. Make certain throttle plates and choke plate opens and closes properly when operated.
10. Connect the throttle linkage and fuel inlet line.
11. Connect the vacuum hoses.
12. Connect the negative battery cable.
13. Install the air cleaner and adjust the carburetor.

2.6L Engine

✷✷**CAUTION**

Never remove a carburetor from an engine that has just been road tested. Allow the engine to cool down to prevent accidental fuel ignition or personal injury.

1. Disconnect the negative battery cable.
2. Remove the air cleaner.
3. Remove the fuel tank filler cap.to relieve fuel system pressure.
4. Disconnect the carburetor protector and all carburetor electrical wiring.

5. Drain the cooling system. Label and remove the vacuum hoses and coolant hoses at carburetor.

✷✷**CAUTION**

When draining the coolant, keep in mind that cats and dogs are attracted by the ethylene glycol antifreeze, and are quite likely to drink any that is left in an uncovered container or in puddles on the ground. This will prove fatal in sufficient quantity. Always drain the coolant into a sealable container. Coolant should be reused unless it is contaminated or several years old.

6. Disconnect the carburetor inlet line and block off line to prevent fuel leakage.

✷✷**CAUTION**

Never smoke when working around gasoline! Avoid all sources of sparks or ignition. Gasoline vapors are EXTREMELY volatile!

7. Disconnect the throttle linkage.
8. Remove the carburetor mounting bolts and nuts and remove carburetor.
9. Inspect the mating surfaces of the carburetor and intake manifold for nicks, burrs, dirt or other damage.
10. Install a new gasket on intake manifold.
11. Carefully install the carburetor on the engine. Install mounting bolts and nuts. Tighten evenly and torque to 150 inch lbs. Make certain throttle plates and choke plate opens and closes properly when operated.
12. Connect the throttle linkage, fuel line and electrical connectors.
13. Install and tighten carburetor protector.
14. Fill the cooling system.
15. Connect the negative battery cable.
16. Install the air cleaner and adjust the carburetor.

OVERHAUL

Holley Model 5220/6520

1. Remove the carburetor from the engine as described in carburetor removal procedure.
2. Using a small screwdriver disconnect and remove choke valve operating rod and seal.
3. Remove the idle stop solenoid mounting screws and remove solenoid.
4. Remove the oxygen solenoid retaining screws and carefully remove the sensor.
5. Remove the retaining clip securing the vacuum diaphragm control rod, remove the vacuum diaphragm mounting screws and remove vacuum diaphragm assembly.
6. Make a mark for proper alignment during assembly, on the air conditioning wide open throttle cut-out switch, and remove switch and wiring assembly.
7. Remove the (5) air horn screws and separate the air horn from carburetor body.
8. Invert the air horn and remove the float pin, float and inlet needle.
9. Remove the fuel inlet needle and seat.

10. Notice the size and position of the secondary main metering jets, and remove jets.

11. Notice the size and position of the primary main metering jets, and remove jets.

12. Using a small screwdriver remove the secondary high speed bleed and secondary main well tube. Note the size and position so it can be reinstalled in its proper location.

13. Remove the primary high speed bleed and primary main well tube. Note the size and position so it can be reinstalled in its proper location.

14. Remove the pump discharge nozzle retaining screw, nozzle and gasket. Invert the carburetor and remove the pump discharge weight ball and check ball. (Both are the same size).

15. Remove the accelerator pump cover retaining screws, cover, pump diaphragm and spring.

16. Remove the choke diaphragm retaining screws and remove cover and spring.

17. Rotate the choke shaft and lever assembly counterclockwise. Rotate choke diaphragm assembly clockwise and remove from housing. Remove end of lower screw from housing. If the choke diaphragm need replacement, the diaphragm cover must also be replaced.

18. To remove concealment plug, center punch at a point ¼″ from the end of the mixture screw housing.

19. Drill through the outer housing with a ⅛ in. drill bit.

20. Pry out the concealment plug and save for reinstallation.

21. Remove the idle mixture screws from carburetor body.

CLEANING AND INSPECTION

Efficient carburetion depends greatly on careful cleaning and inspection during overhaul, since dirt, gum, water, or varnish in or on the carburetor parts are often responsible for poor performance. There are many commercial carburetor cleaning solvent which can give satisfactory results.

➡Avoid placing any seals, O-rings, float, choke and vacuum diaphragm in cleaning solvent. Such components can be damage if immerse in cleaning solvent. Clean the external surfaces of these parts with a clean lint free cloth or brush.

Soak carburetor parts in cleaning solvent, but do not leave parts in solvent no longer than necessary to loosen deposits. Remove parts and rinse with clean hot water. Blow out all passages and jets with compressed air. Blow dry all parts.Inspect the following:

1. Check the float needle and seat for wear. If wear is found, needle/seat assembly.

2. Check the float pin for wear and the float for damage. Replace if necessary.

3. Check the throttle and choke shaft bores for wear or an out-of-round condition. Damage or wear to the throttle arm, shaft, or shaft bore will often require replacement of the throttle body. These parts require a close tolerance fit. Wear on these parts may allow air leakage, which could affect starting and idling.

4. Inspect the idle mixture adjusting needles for burrs or grooves, Any such condition requires replacement of the needle, since you will not be able to obtain a satisfactory idle.

5. Check the bowl cover for warped surfaces with a straight edge.

ASSEMBLY

1. Install the choke shaft, while rotating counterclockwise. Install the diaphragm with a clockwise motion. Position spring and cover over diaphragm, and install retaining screws. Be certain fast idle link has been properly installed.

2. Install the accelerator pump spring, diaphragm cover and screws.

✳✳CAUTION

Never smoke when working around gasoline! Avoid all sources of sparks or ignition. Gasoline vapors are EXTREMELY volatile!

3. Install the accelerator pump discharge check ball in discharge passage. Check the accelerator pump and seat operation before complete reassembling as follows:

a. Fill the fuel bowl with clean fuel.

b. Hold the discharge check ball down with a small brass rod and operate the pump plunger by hand. If the check ball and seat is leaking, no resistance will be felt when the plunger is operated. If the valve is leaking, use the old ball and carefully stake the ball using a suitable drift punch. Avoid damaging the bore containing the pump weight.

c. After staking the old ball, remove and replace with the new ball. Recheck for leaks.

4. Install a new gasket, discharge nozzle and nozzle retaining screw.

5. Install the primary main well tube and primary high speed bleed.

6. Install the secondary main well tube and secondary high speed bleed.

7. Install the primary main metering (smaller size number) jet.

8. Install the secondary main metering (larger size number) jet.

9. Install the needle and seat assembly with a new gasket.

10. Invert the air horn and install float, inlet needle and float lever pin. Reset "dry float setting" and "float drop." Refer to carburetor adjustment procedures.

11. Install a new gasket on air horn, and install choke rod seal and choke rod.

12. Carefully position the air horn on carburetor body.

13. Install a new retainer on choke shaft lever and fast idle cam pickup lever and connect choke rod.

14. Install air horn retaining screws and torque to 30 inch lbs.

15. Install idle stop solenoid, and reinstall anti-rattle spring.

16. Install the air conditioning wide open throttle cut-out switch and aligned with mark previously made. The switch must be position so that the air conditioning clutch circuit is open 10 before wide open throttle position.

17. Install the oxygen solenoid gasket on air horn. Install new O-ring seal on oxygen solenoid. Coat the new O-ring seal with petroleum jelly and install solenoid in carburetor body. Tighten solenoid mounting screws and secure wiring and clamps.

18. Install the vacuum solenoid.
19. Install the vacuum control valve.

Float Setting

1. Invert the air horn. With gasket remove, insert a 12.2mm gauge or drill between air horn and float.
2. To obtain proper dry float level bend adjusting tang with a small screwdriver.

Float Drop

▶ **See Figures 25 and 26**

1. With the air horn upright, check float drop with a depth gauge.
2. To obtain proper float drop adjustment, hold float assembly securely with one hand. Using a small screwdriver, carefully bend adjusting tang to obtain a float drop of 47.6mm.

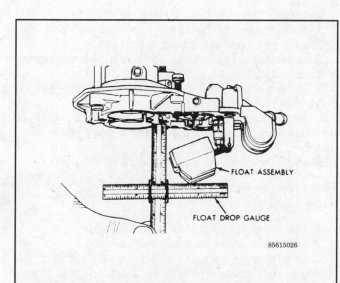

Fig. 25 Measuring the float drop, 2.2L engine shown

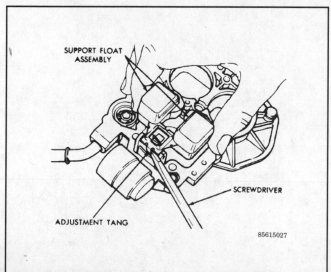

Fig. 26 Float drop adjustment, 2.2L engine shown

Mikuni Carburetor

2.6L engines are equipped with a downdraft type two barrel carburetor, which can be identified with its black resin compound main body. The automatic choke is a thermowax type which is controlled by engine coolant temperature.

This carburetor also features a diaphragm type accelerator pump, bowl vent, fuel cut-off solenoid, air switching valve (ASV), sub-EGR valve, coasting air valve (CAV), jet air control valve (JACV) and a high altitude compensation (HAC) system. (California Only).

OVERHAUL

1. Grind head from screws of choke cover. Gently tap the remaining screw portions using a hammer and a pointed punch in a counterclockwise direction until screws are removed.
2. Take notice of the painted punch mark and scribed lines on choke pinion plate. During reassembly, these marks must be aligned.
3. Remove the E-clip from the throttle opener link. Remove the throttle opener mounting screws and set aside.
4. Remove the ground wire from the fuel cut-off solenoid, remove solenoid mounting screws, and remove solenoid.
5. Remove the throttle return spring and damper spring.
6. Remove the choke unloader E-clip from its link and remove choke unloader.
7. Remove vacuum hose and link from vacuum chamber. Remove vacuum chamber mounting screws and remove vacuum chamber.
8. Remove accelerator rod link from throttle lever.
9. Remove the air horn mounting screws (6) and carefully separate air horn from carburetor body.
10. Slide out float pivot pin and remove float assembly. Remove air horn gasket.
11. Unscrew needle/seat retainer, remove needle/seat, O-ring and screen.
12. Remove the primary and secondary venturi and O-rings. Mark both venturi for proper location during reassembly.
13. Remove primary and secondary main jets. Mark both jets for proper location during reassembly.
14. Remove primary and secondary pedestals and gaskets.
15. Remove bowl vent solenoid mounting screws, solenoid, bowl vent assembly, seal and gasket.
16. Remove the coasting air valve (CAV) mounting screws and remove valve assembly from air horn. (California and Altitude Models).
17. Remove enrichment valve mounting screws and remove enrichment valve assembly.
18. Remove air switching valve (ASV) mounting screws and remove air switching valve assembly from air horn.
19. Remove the primary and secondary pilot jet set screw and lock. Remove pilot jet set assembly.
20. Remove primary and secondary air bleed jets from top of air horn. Mark both jets for proper location during reassembly.
21. Invert the air horn, carefully drop out and note pump weight, check ball and hex nut.
22. Remove accelerator pump mounting screws and remove pump cover, diaphragm, spring, pump body and gasket.

23. Remove jet air control valve mounting screws and remove J.A.C.V. cover, spring, retainer and diaphragm seal.

24. Remove E-clip from sub-EGR lever. The sub-EGR valve is under pressure by a steel ball and spring. Care should be used when removing lever to prevent accidental lost of spring or ball. Carefully slide the pin from lever and sub-EGR valve. Remove the steel ball, spring, sub-EGR valve and boot seal.

CLEANING AND INSPECTION

Efficient carburetion depends greatly on careful cleaning and inspection during overhaul, since dirt, gum, water, or varnish in or on the carburetor parts are often responsible for poor performance. There are many commercial carburetor cleaning solvents which can give satisfactory results.

➡ **Avoid placing any seals, O-rings, float, choke and vacuum diaphragm in cleaning solvent. Such components can be damage if immerse in cleaning solvent. Clean the external surfaces of these parts with a clean lint free cloth or brush.**

Soak carburetor parts in cleaning solvent, but do not leave parts in solvent longer than necessary to loosen deposits. Remove parts and rinse with clean hot water. Blow out all passages and jets with compressed air. Blow dry all parts. Inspect the following:

1. Check the float needle and seat for wear. If wear is found, needle/seat assembly.

2. Check the float pin for wear and the float for damage. Replace if necessary.

3. Check the throttle and choke shaft bores for wear or an out-of-round condition. Damage or wear to the throttle arm, shaft, or shaft bore will often require replacement of the throttle body. These parts require a close tolerance fit. Wear on these parts may allow air leakage, which could affect starting and idling.

4. Inspect the idle mixture adjusting needles for burrs or grooves, Any such condition requires replacement of the needle, since you will not be able to obtain a satisfactory idle.

5. Check the bowl cover for warped surfaces with a straight edge.

ASSEMBLY

1. Install the sub-EGR valve to throttle valve and check for proper operation.

2. Assemble the jet air control valve to throttle body and secure with mounting screws.

3. Assemble the accelerator pump to throttle body and secure with mounting screws.

4. Install the primary and secondary air bleed jets. The secondary air bleed jet has the largest number.

5. Position new O-ring seals on primary and secondary pilot jet side. Slide assembly into place and install lock and screw.

6. Assemble the air switching valve to air horn and secure with mounting screws.

7. Assemble the enrichment valve to air horn.

8. Assemble the coasting air valve to air horn.

9. Position a new O-ring and gasket on bowl vent assembly and install on air horn.

10. Position a new gasket on air horn and install primary and secondary pedestals.

11. Install primary and secondary main jets in their pedestals. The secondary main jet has the largest number.

12. Position new O-rings on both primary and secondary venturi. Install primary and secondary venturi and retainers.

13. Position a new O-ring on needle seat. Install a new screen on needle seat. Install shim and needle seat into air horn. Install retainer and screw.

14. Position the float on air horn and install float pivot pin. Refer to Float Level Adjustment procedure.

15. Position a new gasket on throttle body. Install main body to throttle and install nut, check ball and weight in main body.

16. Position a new gasket on main body and carefully assemble air horn to main body.

17. Install vacuum hoses to air horn.

18. Connect accelerator rod link to throttle lever.

19. Install vacuum chamber to air horn. Connect vacuum hose and secondary throttle lever link.

20. Connect choke unloader link and install E-clip.

21. Position a new O-ring on fuel cut-off solenoid. Install the solenoid to main body and connect ground wire.

22. Install throttle opener to air horn. Connect throttle opener link and install E-clip.

23. Replace tamper-proof choke cover screws. Align the punch mark with the painted mark on gear.

24. Install the choke cover and peen over screws. Tighten the remaining screw using a pointed punch and a small hammer.

25. Install the choke water hose and clamp.

Float Level
▶ **See Figure 27**

1. Remove air horn from carburetor main body.

2. Remove air horn gasket and invert air horn.

3. Using a gauge measure the distance from bottom of float to air horn surface. The distance should be 20mm ± 1mm. If distance is not within specification, the shim under the needle and seat must be changed. Shim pack MD606952 or

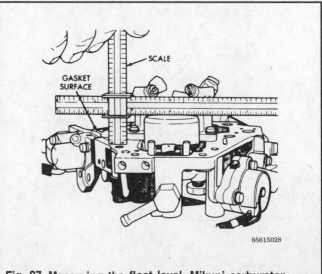

Fig. 27 Measuring the float level, Mikuni carburetor

equivalent has three shims: 0.3mm, 0.4mm, or 0.5mm. Adding or removing one shim will change the float level three its thickness.

CHRYSLER MULTI-POINT ELECTRONIC FUEL INJECTION

General Information

The turbocharged and non-turbocharged Multi-Point Electronic Fuel Injection (MPI) system combines an electronic fuel and spark advance control system with a turbocharged intake system or cross type intake system. At the center of this system is a digital computer containing a microprocessor known also known as an engine controller that regulates ignition timing, air/fuel ratio, emission control devices, idle speed, cooling fan, charging system, turbocharger waste gate (on turbo models) and speed control. This component has the ability to update and revise its programming to meet changing operating conditions.

Various sensors provide the input necessary for the engine controller to correctly regulate fuel flow at the fuel injectors. These include the manifold absolute pressure, throttle position, oxygen sensor, coolant temperature, charge temperature, vehicle speed (distance) sensors and detonation sensor. In addition to the sensors, various switches also provide important information. These include the neutral-safety, air conditioning clutch switch, brake switch and speed control switch.

Check Engine Light

The check engine light comes on each time the ignition key is turned **ON** and stays on for a few seconds as a bulb test. If the engine controller receives an incorrect signal or no signal from either the coolant temperature sensor, charge temperature sensor, manifold absolute pressure sensor, throttle position sensor, battery voltage sensor input or emission related system on California vehicles the check engine light on the instrument panel is illuminated.

This is a warning that the engine controller has gone into Limp In Mode in an attempt to keep the system operational. The light can also be used to display fault codes. Cycle the ignition switch **ON, OFF, ON, OFF, ON** within 5 seconds and any fault codes stored in the memory will be displayed.

Limp In Mode is the attempt by the engine controller to compensate for the failure of certain components by substituting information from other sources.

Diagnosis and Testing

➡**For Self-Diagnostic System and Accessing Trouble Code Memory, see the diagnostic procedures in Section 4. These procedures require an extensive knowledge of electronic fuel injection systems, use extreme care when performing any of these procedures.**

The SMEC has been programmed to monitor several different circuits of the fuel injection system. This monitoring is called On Board Diagnosis. If a problem is sensed with a monitored circuit, often enough to indicate an actual problem, its fault code is stored in the SMEC for eventual display to the service technician. If the problem is repaired or ceases to exist, the engine controller cancels the fault code after 50-100 ignition key **ON/OFF** cycles.

Fault codes are 2 digit numbers that identify which circuit is bad. In most cases, they DO NOT identify which component is bad in a circuit. When a fault code appears it indicates that the engine controller has recognized an abnormal signal in the system. Fault codes indicate the results of a failure but do not always identify the failed component directly.

Fuel System Pressure Release Procedure

1987-92

2.5L, 3.0L and 3.3L Engines

1. Loosen the gas cap to release tank pressure.
2. Disconnect injector wiring harness from the engine or main harness.
3. Connect a jumper to ground terminal No. 1 of the injector harness to engine ground.
4. Connect a jumper to the positive terminal No. 2 of the injector harness and momentarily touch the positive terminal of the battery for no longer than 5 seconds. This releases the system pressure. Remove the jumper wires.

1993-94

3.0L Engine

1. Loosen the gas cap to release tank pressure.
2. Disconnect the fuel rail electrical harness from the engine harness.
3. Connect one end of a jumper wire to the A142 circuit terminal of the fuel rail harness connector.
4. Connect the other end of the jumper wire to a good ground source.
5. Momentarily ground one of the injectors by connecting the other end of the jumper wire to an injector terminal in the harness connector. Repeat the procedure for 2 or 3 injectors.

3.3L and 3.8L Engine

1. Disconnect the negative battery cable.
2. Loosen the gas cap to release tank pressure.
3. Remove the protective cap from the fuel pressure test port on the fuel rail.
4. Place the open end of fuel pressure release hose, tool No. C-4799-1, into an approved gasoline container. Connect the other end of hose C-4799-1 to the fuel pressure test port. Fuel pressure will bleed off through the hose into the gasoline container.

➡**Fuel gauge C-4799-A contains hose C-4799-1**

FUEL PRESSURE

Testing

2.5L TURBO ENGINES

1. Release fuel system pressure.
2. Remove the protective cover from the service valve on the fuel rail.
3. Connect a suitable fuel pressure gauge to fuel rail service valve.
4. Using the DRBII tester, with the key in the **RUN** position, use "Actuate Outputs Test-Auto Shutdown Relay" this will activate the fuel pump for 1.5 seconds to pressurize the system.
5. If the gauge reads 53-57 psi fuel pressure is correct and no further testing is necessary. Remove all test equipment.
6. If pressure is not correct, record the pressure and continue with the test procedure.
7. If the fuel pressure is below specifications, install the fuel pressure gauge in the fuel supply line, between the fuel tank and fuel filter at the rear of the vehicle.
8. Repeat test. If pressure is 5 psi higher than recorded pressure replace the fuel filter. If no change in pressure is observed, gently squeeze the return hose. If the pressure increases replace the pressure regulator. If no change is observed check for a defective fuel pump or plugged filter sock.

➡**The test (Step 9) should be performed when fuel tank is a least ¹/₂-³/₄ full.**

9. If the fuel pressure is above specifications, remove the fuel return line hose from the chassis line at fuel tank and connect a 3 foot piece of fuel hose to the return line. Position the other end in suitable container (2 gallons or more). Repeat test and, if pressure is now correct, check in-tank return hose for kinking.
10. Replace the fuel tank assembly if the in-tank reservoir check valve or the aspirator jet is blocked.
11. If the pressure is still above specifications, remove fuel return hose from fuel pressure regulator. Connect a suitable hose to the fuel pressure regulator nipple and place the other in a suitable container. Repeat test. If pressure is now correct, check for restricted fuel line. If no change is observed, replace fuel pressure regulator.

3.0L, 3.3L AND 3.8L ENGINE

1. Release fuel system pressure.
2. Disconnect the fuel supply hose from the engine fuel line assembly. Connect a suitable fuel pressure gauge between fuel supply hose and engine fuel line assembly.
3. Using the DRBII tester, with the key in the **RUN** position, use "Actuate Outputs Test-Auto Shutdown Relay" this will activate the fuel pump for 1.5 seconds to pressurize the system.
4. If the gauge reads 46-50 psi fuel pressure is correct and no further testing is necessary. Remove all test equipment.
5. If pressure is not correct, record the pressure and continue with the test procedure.
6. If the fuel pressure is below specifications, install the fuel pressure gauge in the fuel supply line, between the fuel tank and fuel filter at the rear of the vehicle.
7. Repeat test. If pressure is 5 psi higher than recorded pressure replace the fuel filter. If no change in pressure is

observed, gently squeeze the return hose. If the pressure increases replace the pressure regulator. If no change is observed check for a defective fuel pump or plugged filter sock.

➡**The test (Step 8) should be performed when fuel tank is a least ¹/₂-³/₄ full.**

8. If the fuel pressure is above specifications, remove the fuel return line hose from the chassis line at fuel tank and connect a 3 foot piece of fuel hose to the return line. Position the other end in suitable container (2 gallons or more). Repeat test and, if pressure is now correct, check in-tank return hose for kinking.
9. Replace the fuel tank assembly if the in-tank reservoir check valve or the aspirator jet is blocked.
10. If the pressure is still above specifications, remove fuel return hose from fuel pressure regulator. Connect a suitable hose to the fuel return line and place the other end in a suitable container. Repeat the test. If the pressure is now correct, check for restricted fuel line. If no change has occurred, replace the fuel pressure regulator.

WASTEGATE CALIBRATION

Check

2.5L Turbo Engines

1. Disconnect the vacuum hose from the wategate diaphragm.
2. Connect a cooling system pressure tester or equivalent to the wastegate diaphragm.
3. Slowly apply pressure while watching the actuator rod.
4. If the wastegate actuator rod moves more than 0.015 inch before 2-4 psi (4 psi on Turbo II) or does not move after 5 psi is applied the wastegate is faulty.
5. Service faulty component as necessary.

Component Replacement

THROTTLE BODY

Removal and Installation
▶ **See Figures 28, 29 and 30**

When servicing the fuel portion of the throttle body, it will be necessary to bleed fuel pressure before opening any hoses refer to Fuel Pressure Release procedure. Always reassemble throttle body components with new O-rings and seals where applicable. Use care when removing fuel hoses to prevent damage to hose or hose nipple. Always use new hose clamps of the correct type when reassembling and torque hose clamps to 10 inch lbs. (1 Nm).

1. Drain engine coolant, if necessary, and release fuel pressure. Disconnect negative battery cable.
2. Remove air cleaner to throttle body screws (or nuts), loosen hose clamp and remove air cleaner adaptor.

➡**When removing accelerator cable, note position or adjustment for correct installation.**

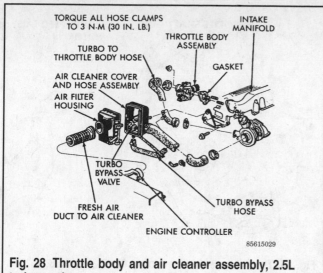

Fig. 28 Throttle body and air cleaner assembly, 2.5L turbo engine

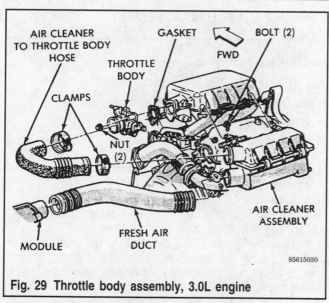

Fig. 29 Throttle body assembly, 3.0L engine

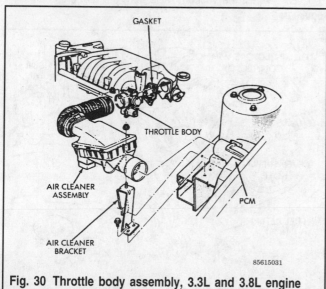

Fig. 30 Throttle body assembly, 3.3L and 3.8L engine

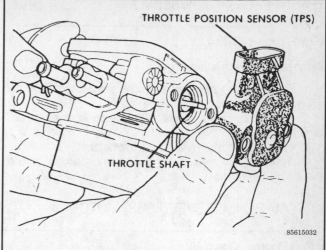

Fig. 31 Throttle position sensor, 2.5L turbo, 3.3L and 3.8L engines

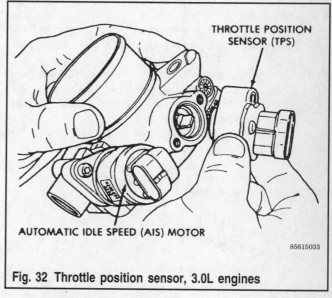

Fig. 32 Throttle position sensor, 3.0L engines

3. Remove accelerator, speed control and transaxle kick-down cables and return spring.

4. Remove throttle cable bracket from throttle body.

5. Disconnect all necessary electrical connector(s).

6. Disconnect vacuum hoses from throttle body.

7. Loosen throttle body-to-turbocharger hose clamp if so equipped.

8. Remove throttle body-to-intake manifold or adapter screws (or nuts). Always note position of retaining bolts as some may be different in length.

9. Remove throttle body and gasket.

10. Reverse the above procedure for installation.

➥If fuel system hoses are to be replaced, only hoses marked EFI/EFM may be used.

THROTTLE POSITION SENSOR

▶ See Figures 31 and 32

Removal and Installation

1. Disconnect negative battery cable and 3-way throttle position sensor wiring connector.
2. Remove 2 screws, mounting throttle position sensor to throttle body.
3. Lift throttle position sensor off throttle shaft.
4. To install, reverse removal procedure and torque screws to 17 inch lbs. (2 Nm).

AUTOMATIC IDLE SPEED (AIS) MOTOR

▶ See Figures 33 and 34

Removal and Installation

1. Disconnect negative battery cable and 4-way AIS motor wiring connector.
2. Remove 2 screws that mount AIS motor to throttle body.
3. Remove AIS motor from throttle body. Make certain that the O-ring is on the AIS motor.
4. To install, place new O-ring on AIS motor. If pintle measures more than 1 inch, it must be retracted by using the AIS Motor Test in the Actuate Outputs mode of the DRBII. (Battery must be reconnected for this operation.)
5. Carefully place AIS motor into throttle body.
6. Install 2 mounting screws and torque to 17 inch lbs. (2 Nm).
7. Connect 4 way wiring connector to AIS motor and reconnect negative battery cable.

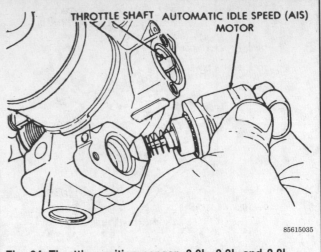

Fig. 34 Throttle position sensor, 3.0L, 3.3L and 3.8L engines

FUEL INJECTOR RAIL ASSEMBLY

Removal and Installation

2.5L TURBO ENGINES

▶ See Figures 28, 35, 36, 37, 38 and 39

1. Perform fuel system pressure release procedure.
2. Disconnect negative battery cable.
3. Remove air cleaner assembly.
4. Disconnect detonation (knock) sensor and fuel injector wiring connectors.
5. Loosen fuel supply hose clamp at fuel rail inlet and remove hose. Wrap a shop towel around hose to absorb any fuel spillage which may occur when removing.
6. Loosen fuel return hose clamp at the fuel pressure regulator and remove the hose. Wrap a shop towel around the hose to absorb any fuel spillage, which may occur when removing the hose.
7. Disconnect the vacuum hose from the fuel pressure regulator.

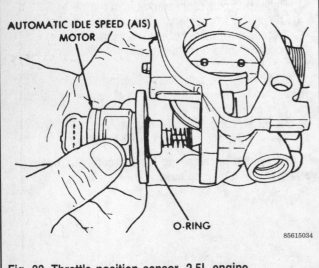

Fig. 33 Throttle position sensor, 2.5L engine

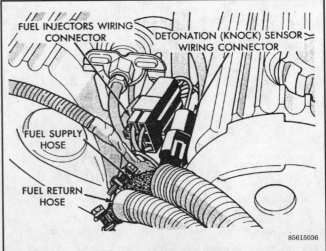

Fig. 35 Fuel hoses and electrical connections, 2.5L engine

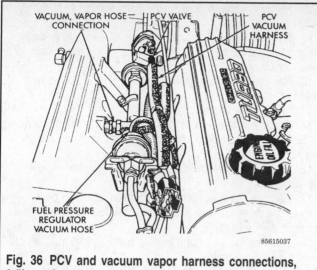

Fig. 36 PCV and vacuum vapor harness connections, 2.5L engine

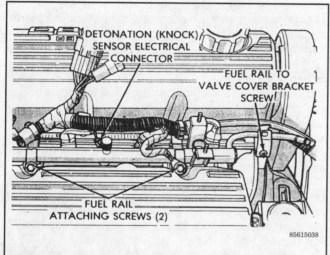

Fig. 37 Fuel hoses and electrical connections, 2.5L engine

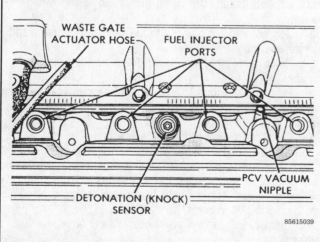

Fig. 38 Detonation (knock sensor) and PCV vacuum nipple, 2.5L engine

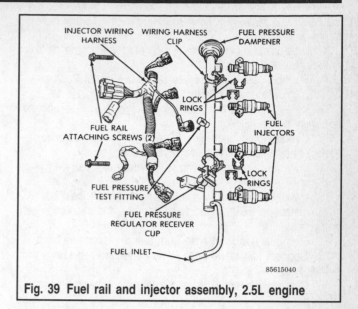

Fig. 39 Fuel rail and injector assembly, 2.5L engine

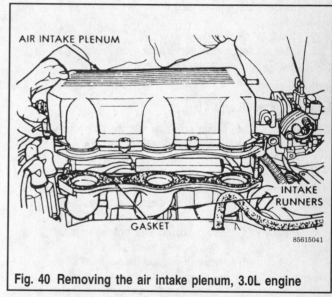

Fig. 40 Removing the air intake plenum, 3.0L engine

8. Remove the fuel pressure regulator mounting bolts from the fuel rail.

9. Remove the fuel pressure regulator from the fuel rail.

10. Remove the PCV vacuum harness and vacuum vapor harness from the intake manifold.

11. Remove the fuel rail to the valve cover bracket screw. Remove the knock sensor connector from the sensor.

12. Remove the fuel rail to intake manifold mounting bolts.

13. Remove fuel rail and injector assembly by pulling rail so that injectors come straight out of there ports.

14. Be careful not to damage rubber injector O-ring upon removal from ports.

15. Remove fuel rail assembly from vehicle.

16. Do not remove fuel injectors until fuel rail assembly has been completely removed from vehicle.

To install:

17. To install, be sure injectors are seated into receiver cup, with lock ring in place.

18. Install injector wiring harness to injectors and fasten into wiring clips.

19. Make sure injector holes are clean and all plugs have been removed.

20. Lube injector O-ring with a drop of clean engine oil to ease installation.

21. Put tip of each injector into respective ports. Push assembly into place until injectors are seated in ports.

22. Install attaching bolts and ground eyelet. Torque bolts to 250 inch lbs. (28 Nm).

23. Connect detonation (knock) sensor wire connector to sensor. Install fuel rail to valve cover bracket screw.

24. Lube fuel pressure O-ring with a drop of clean engine oil and install into receiver cup on fuel rail.

25. Install attaching nuts and torque to 65 inch lbs. (7 Nm).

26. Install the PCV system hose harness and vacuum hose harness.

27. Reconnect vacuum hose from fuel pressure regulator.

28. Connect fuel return hose to fuel pressure regulator tighten hose clamp.

29. Connect fuel supply hose to fuel rail inlet and tighten hose clamp.

30. Connect fuel injector and detonation (knock) sensor wiring connector.

31. Install air cleaner assembly.

32. Connect negative battery cable.

33. Use ATM tester to test for leaks.

3.0L ENGINE

▶ **See Figures 40 and 41**

1. Perform fuel system pressure release procedure.
2. Disconnect negative battery cable.
3. Remove air cleaner to throttle body hose.
4. Remove throttle cable and transaxle kickdown linkage.
5. Remove Automatic Idle Speed (AIS) motor and Throttle Position Sensor (TPS) wiring connectors from throttle body.
6. Remove vacuum hose harness from throttle body.
7. Remove PCV and brake booster hoses from air intake plenum.
8. If equipped, remove EGR tube flange from intake plenum.
9. Remove wiring connectors from charge temperature sensor and coolant temperature sensor.

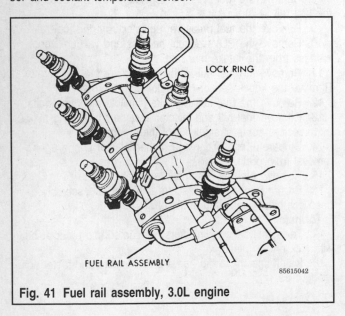

LOCK RING

FUEL RAIL ASSEMBLY

85615042

Fig. 41 Fuel rail assembly, 3.0L engine

10. Remove vacuum connections from air intake plenum vacuum connector.

11. Remove fuel hoses from fuel rail. Wrap a shop towel around hose to absorb any fuel spillage which may occur when removing.

12. Remove fasteners from air intake plenum to intake manifold.

13. Remove air intake plenum.

14. Cover intake manifold with suitable cover when servicing.

15. Remove vacuum hoses from fuel rail and fuel pressure regulator.

16. Disconnect fuel injector wiring harness from engine wiring harness.

17. Remove the fuel pressure regulator attaching bolts. Loosen the hose clamps and remove the fuel pressure regulator from the fuel rail.

18. Remove the fuel rail attaching bolts and lift the fuel rail from the intake manifold.

19. Be careful not to damage the injector ports when removing.

20. Remove the fuel rail assembly from the vehicle.

21. Do not remove the injectors until the fuel rail has been completely removed from the vehicle.

To install:

22. Make sure the injectors are completely seated with the lockring in place.

23. Make sure the injector holes are clean and that all plugs have been removed.

24. Lube injector O-ring with a drop of clean engine oil to ease installation.

25. Put tip of each injector into respective ports. Push assembly into place until injectors are seated in ports.

26. Install fuel rail attaching bolts. Torque bolts to 115 inch lbs. (13 Nm).

27. Install fuel pressure regulator and hose assembly onto fuel rail. Install attaching bolts to intake manifold. Torque to 77 inch lbs. (8.7 Nm).

28. Install fuel supply and return tube hold-down bolt and vacuum crossover tube hold-down bolt. Torque to 95 inch lbs. (10 Nm).

29. Tighten fuel pressure regulator hose clamps.

30. Connect fuel injector wiring harness to engine wiring harness.

31. Connect vacuum harness to fuel pressure regulator and fuel rail assembly.

32. Remove covering from lower intake manifold and clean surface.

33. Place intake manifold gaskets, with beaded sealer up, on lower manifold. Put air intake in place. Install attaching fasteners and torque to 115 inch lbs. (13 Nm).

34. Connect fuel line to fuel rail and tighten.

35. Connect vacuum harness to air intake plenum.

36. Connect charge temperature sensor and coolant temperature sensor electrical connectors to sensors.

37. If equipped, connect EGR tube flange to intake plenum and torque to 200 inch lbs. (22 Nm).

38. Connect PCV and brake booster supply hose to intake plenum.

39. Connect Automatic Idle Speed (AIS) motor and Throttle Position Sensor (TPS) electrical connectors.

40. Connect vacuum vapor harness to throttle body.

41. Install throttle cable and transaxle kickdown linkage.

42. Install air inlet hose assembly.
43. Connect negative battery cable.
44. Use ATM tester to test for leaks.

3.3L AND 3.8L ENGINES

▶ See Figures 42, 43, 44, 45, 46, 47, 48, 49, 50 and 51

1. Relieve the fuel pressure.
2. Disconnect the negative battery cable.
3. Remove the air cleaner and hose assembly.
4. Disconnect the throttle cable. Remove the wiring harness from the throttle cable bracket and intake manifold water tube.
5. Remove the vacuum hose harness from the throttle body.
6. Remove the PCV and brake booster hoses from the air intake plenum.
7. Remove the EGR tube flange from the intake plenum, if equipped.
8. Unplug the charge temperature sensor and unplug all vacuum hoses from the intake plenum.
9. Remove the cylinder head to intake plenum strut.
10. Disconnect the MAP sensor and oxygen sensor connector. Remove the engine mounted ground strap.
11. Release the fuel hose quick disconnect fittings and remove the hoses from the fuel rail. Plug the hoses.
12. Remove the Direct Ignition System (DIS) coils and the alternator bracket to intake manifold bolt.
13. Remove the intake manifold bolts and rotate the manifold back over the rear valve cover. Cover the intake manifold.
14. Remove the vacuum harness from the pressure regulator.
15. Remove the fuel tube retainer bracket screw and the fuel rail attaching bolts. Spread the retainer bracket to allow for clearance when removing the fuel tube.
16. Remove the fuel rail injector wiring clip from the alternator bracket.
17. Disconnect the camshaft sensor, coolant temperature sensor and engine temperature sensor.
18. Remove the fuel rail.
19. Position the fuel rail on a work bench, so that the injectors are easy to get at.

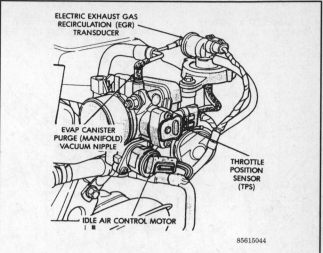
Fig. 43 Electrical and vacuum connection to the throttle body, 3.3L and 3.8L engines

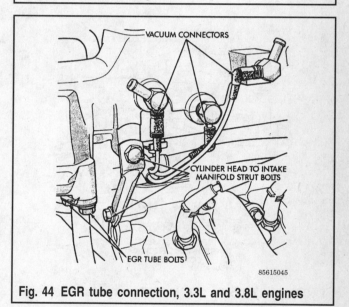
Fig. 44 EGR tube connection, 3.3L and 3.8L engines

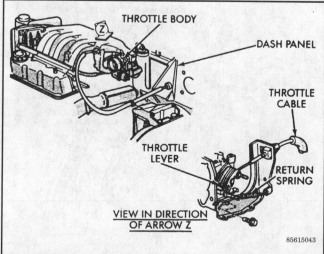
Fig. 42 Throttle cable attachment, 3.3L and 3.8L engines

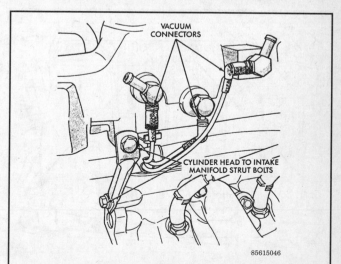
Fig. 45 Electrical and vacuum connections to the intake manifold, 3.3L and 3.8L engines

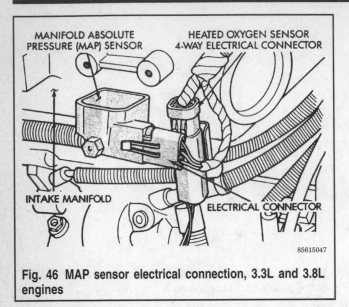

Fig. 46 MAP sensor electrical connection, 3.3L and 3.8L engines

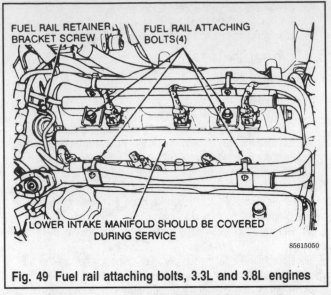

Fig. 49 Fuel rail attaching bolts, 3.3L and 3.8L engines

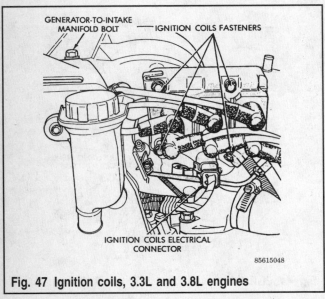

Fig. 47 Ignition coils, 3.3L and 3.8L engines

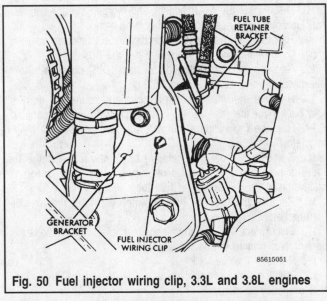

Fig. 50 Fuel injector wiring clip, 3.3L and 3.8L engines

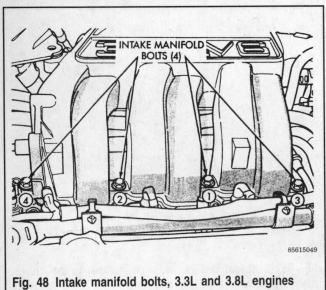

Fig. 48 Intake manifold bolts, 3.3L and 3.8L engines

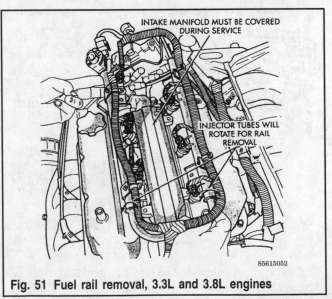

Fig. 51 Fuel rail removal, 3.3L and 3.8L engines

20. Remove the small connector retaining clip and unplug the injector. Remove the injector clip from the fuel rail and injector. Pull the injector straight off of the rail.

To install:

21. Lubricate the rubber O-ring with clean oil and install to the rail receiver cap. Install the injector clip to the slot in the injector, plug in the connector and install the connector clip.

22. Install the fuel rail.

23. Connect the cam sensor, coolant temperature sensor and engine temperature sensor.

24. Install the fuel rail injector wiring clip to the alternator bracket.

25. Install the fuel rail attaching bolts and fuel tube retainer bracket screw.

26. Install the vacuum harness to the pressure regulator.

27. Install the intake manifold with a new gasket. Install the bolts only fingertight. Install the alternator bracket to intake manifold bolt and the cylinder head to intake manifold strut and bolts. Torque the intake manifold mounting bolts to 21 ft. lbs. (28 Nm) starting from the middle and working outward. Torque the bracket and strut bolts to 40 ft. lbs. (54 Nm).

28. Install or connect all items that were removed or disconnected from the intake manifold and throttle body.

29. Connect the fuel hoses to the rail. Push the fittings in until they click in place.

30. Install the air cleaner assembly.

31. Connect the negative battery cable and check for leaks using the DRB I or II to activate the fuel pump.

FUEL INJECTOR

▶ **See Figures 39, 41, 52 and 53**

Removal and Installation

1. Remove fuel rail.
2. Disconnect injector wiring connector from injector.
3. Position fuel rail assembly so that fuel injectors are easily accessible.
4. Remove injector clip off fuel rail and injector. Pull injector straight out of fuel rail receiver cup.

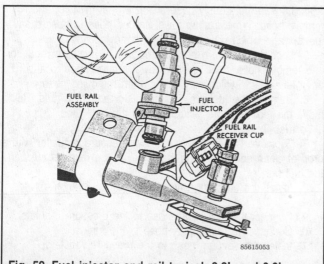

Fig. 52 Fuel injector and rail typical, 3.3L and 3.8L engines

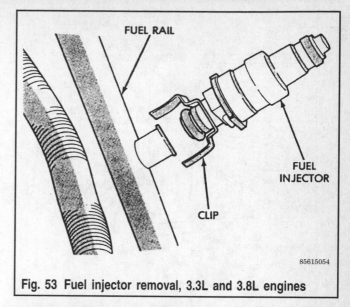

Fig. 53 Fuel injector removal, 3.3L and 3.8L engines

5. Check injector O-ring for damage. If O-ring is damaged, it must be replaced. If injector is to be reused, a protective cap must be installed on injector tip to prevent damage while injector is out for service.

6. Repeat for remaining injectors.

7. Before installing an injector, the rubber O-ring must be lubricated with a drop of clean engine oil to aid in installation.

8. Install injector top end into fuel rail receiver cup. Be careful not to damage O-ring during installation.

9. Install injector clip by sliding open end into top slot of injector and onto receiver cup ridge into side slots of clip.

10. Repeat steps for remaining injectors.

FUEL PRESSURE REGULATOR

Removal and Installation
▶ **See Figures 54, 55, 56, 57 and 58**

1. Perform fuel system pressure release procedure.
2. Disconnect negative battery cable.

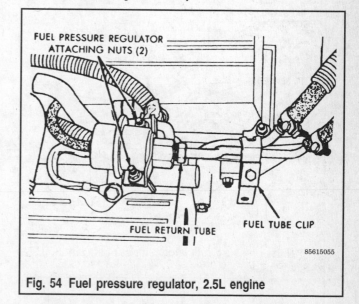

Fig. 54 Fuel pressure regulator, 2.5L engine

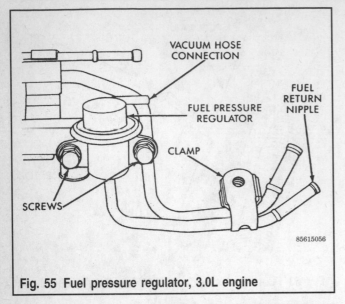

Fig. 55 Fuel pressure regulator, 3.0L engine

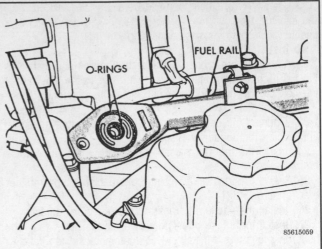

Fig. 58 Fuel pressure regulator O-rings, 3.3L and 3.8L engine

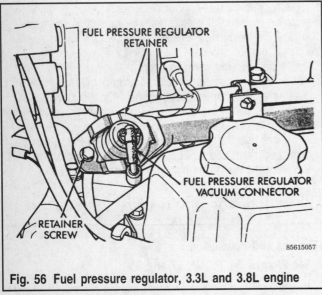

Fig. 56 Fuel pressure regulator, 3.3L and 3.8L engine

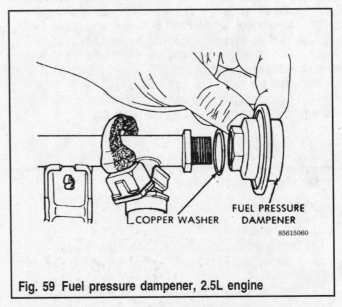

Fig. 59 Fuel pressure dampener, 2.5L engine

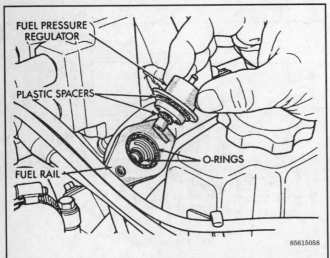

Fig. 57 Fuel pressure regulator removal/installation, 3.3L and 3.8L engine

3. Remove vacuum hose from fuel pressure regulator.

4. Loosen fuel supply hose clamp at fuel rail inlet and remove hose. Wrap a shop towel around hose to absorb any fuel spillage which may occur when removing hose.

5. Loosen fuel return hose clamp at fuel pressure regulator and remove hose. Wrap a shop towel around hose to absorb any fuel spillage which may occur when removing hose.

6. Remove the fuel pressure regulator attaching nuts. Remove the fuel pressure regulator from the fuel rail.

To install:

7. Lubricate the O-ring for the fuel pressure regulator with a drop of clean engine oil and install it into the receiver cup, on the fuel rail.

8. Install the attaching nuts and torque to 65 inch lbs. (7 Nm).

9. Connect the fuel return hose to the pressure regulator.

10. Connect the fuel supply hose to the fuel rail.

11. Install the vacuum hose to the pressure regulator.

12. Connect the negative battery cable. Using the DRBII tester or equivalent, use the Actuate Outputs Test-Auto Shutdown Relay to pressurize the system and check for leaks.

FUEL PRESSURE DAMPENER

▶ **See Figure 59**

Removal and Installation

1. Perform fuel system pressure release procedure.
2. Remove PCV system hose assembly from intake manifold and valve cover.
3. Place a shop towel under fuel pressure dampener to absorb any fuel spillage.
4. Using 2 open end wrenches, 1 on the flats of fuel rail and the other on fuel pressure dampener. Remove fuel pressure dampener and copper washer.
5. To install, place a new copper washer on fuel rail and install fuel pressure dampener torque to 30 ft. lbs. (41 Nm) using a wrench to hold fuel rail while tightening fuel pressure dampener.
6. Connect fuel injector wiring harness reinstall PCV system hose assembly.
7. Using the DRBII tester use the Actuate Outputs Test — Auto Shutdown Relay to pressurize system to check for leaks.

ENGINE CONTROLLER OR CONTROL MODULE

▶ **See Figure 60**

Removal And Installation

➡ **Refer to Section 4 for more information on the engine controller or control module.**

1. Remove the air cleaner duct from the engine controller.
2. Remove the battery.
3. Remove 2 module mounting screws. Remove the 14 and 60 way wiring connectors from the module and remove the module.
4. Reverse the above procedure for installation.

HEATED OXYGEN SENSOR

▶ **See Figure 61**

Removal and Installation

Removing the oxygen sensor from the exhaust manifold may be difficult if the sensor was overtorqued during installation.

Use tool C-4907 or equivalent, to remove the sensor. The threads in the exhaust manifold must be cleaned with an 18mm · 1.5 · 6E tap. If the same sensor is to be reinstalled, the threads must be coated with an anti-seize compound such as Loctite® 771-64 or equivalent. New sensors are packaged with anti-seize compound on the threads and no additional compound is required. Sensors must be torqued to 20 ft. lbs. (27 Nm).

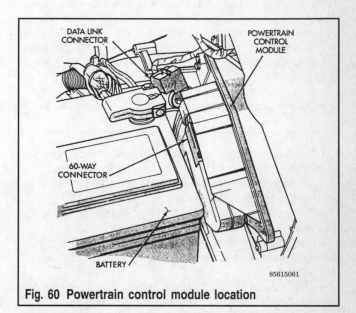

Fig. 60 Powertrain control module location

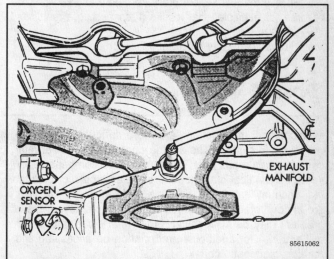

Fig. 61 Typical oxygen sensor location, 3.0L engine shown

CHRYSLER SINGLE POINT FUEL INJECTION SYSTEM

General Information

The electronic fuel injection system is a computer regulated single point fuel injection system that provides precise air/fuel ratio for all driving conditions. At the center of this system is a digital pre-programmed computer also known as an engine controller or powertrain control module, that regulates ignition timing, air/fuel ratio, emission control devices, idle speed and cooling fan and charging system. This component has the ability to update and revise its programming to meet changing operating conditions.

Various sensors provide the input necessary for the engine controller to correctly regulate the fuel flow at the fuel injector. These include the manifold absolute pressure, throttle position, oxygen sensor, coolant temperature, vehicle speed (distance) sensors and throttle body temperature. In addition to the sensors, various switches also provide important information. These include the neutral-safety switch, air conditioning clutch relay, and auto shut-down relay.

All inputs to the engine controller are converted into signals which are used by the computer. Based on these inputs, air-fuel ratio, ignition timing or other controlled outputs are adjusted accordingly.

The engine controller tests many of its own input and output circuits. If a fault is found in a major system this information is stored in the memory. Information on this fault can be displayed to a technician by means of the instrument panel check engine light or by connecting a diagnostic read out and reading a numbered display code which directly relates to a specific fault.

SERVICE PRECAUTIONS

When working around any part of the fuel system, take precautionary steps to prevent possible fire and/or explosion:
- Disconnect the negative battery terminal, except when testing with battery voltage is required.
- Whenever possible, use a flashlight instead of a drop light to inspect fuel system components or connections.
- Keep all open flames and smoking material out of the area and make sure there is adequate ventilation to remove fuel vapors.
- Use a clean shop cloth to catch fuel when opening a fuel system. Dispose of gasoline-soaked rags properly.
- Relieve the fuel system pressure before any service procedures are attempted that require disconnecting a fuel line.
- Use eye protection.
- Always keep a dry chemical (class B) fire extinguisher near the area.

DIAGNOSIS AND TESTING

➡**Mechanical malfunctions are more difficult to diagnose with the EFI system. The engine controller or powertrain control module has been programmed to compensate for some mechanical malfunctions such as incorrect cam timing, vacuum leaks, etc. If engine performance problems are encountered, and no fault codes are displayed, the problem may be mechanical rather than electronic. Refer to Section 4 for additioinal information on accessing and reading diagnostic codes**

VISUAL INSPECTION

A visual inspection for loose, disconnected or misrouted wires and hoses should be made before attempting to diagnose or service the fuel injection system. A visual check will help spot these faults and save unnecessary test and diagnostic time. A thorough visual inspection will include the following checks:
1. Check that vacuum connections on rear and/or front of throttle body are secure and not leaking.

2. Check that vacuum connection(s) at EGR and/or purge solenoid is secure and not leaking.
3. Check that hoses are securely attached to vapor canister.
4. Check that hose from PCV valve is securely attached to the intake manifold vacuum port.
5. Check that hoses are attached to back pressure transducer.
6. Check that alternator wiring and belt are correctly installed and tight.
7. Check that heated air door vacuum connection is connected and not leaking.
8. Check vacuum connections at MAP sensor.
9. Check that hose and wiring connections at the fuel pump are tight and wires are making contact with the terminals on pump.
10. Check power brake and speed control vacuum connections are tight.
11. Check that the following electrical connections are clean, tight and have good contact:
   a. Connectors to the engine controller or powertrain control module
   b. Connector at EGR solenoid and/or purge solenoid
   c. Connector at speed (distance) sensor
   d. Connector at cooling fan relay
   e. Connector to oxygen sensor
   f. Connector at fuel injector(s)
   g. Connector at automatic idle speed (AIS) and throttle position sensor (TPS)
   h. Connector at coolant temperature sensor
   i. Connector at throttle body temperature sensor
   j. Connector to distributor
   k. Connectors for engine-to-main harness
   l. Connectors for all relays
   m. Connector to neutral safety switch (automatic only)
   n. All ignition cables are in order and seated
   o. Ground straps to engine and dash panel
   p. Connection to battery

FUEL SYSTEM PRESSURE TEST

1987-91

✳✳CAUTION

Fuel system pressure must be released as previously described each time a fuel hose is to be disconnected. Take precautions to avoid the risk of fire.

1. Remove fuel intake hose from throttle body and connect fuel system pressure testers C-3292, and C-4749, or equivalent, between fuel filter hose and throttle body.
2. Start engine and read gauge. Pressure should be 14.5 psi (100 kPa).

➡**ATM tester C-4805 or equivalent can be used. With ignition in RUN, depress ATM button. This activate the fuel pump and pressure system**

3. If fuel pressure is below specifications:
   a. Install tester between fuel filter hose and fuel line.

b. Start engine. If pressure is now correct, replace fuel filter. If no change is observed, gently squeeze return hose. If pressure increases, replace pressure regulator. If no change is observed, problem is either a plugged pump filter sock or defective fuel pump.

4. If pressure is above specifications:

a. Remove fuel return hose from throttle body. Connect a substitute hose and place other end of hose in clean container.

b. Start engine. If pressure is now correct, check for restricted fuel return line. If no change is observed, replace fuel regulator.

1991-94

❋❋CAUTION

Fuel system pressure must be released as previously described each time a fuel hose is to be disconnected. Take precautions to avoid the risk of fire.

1. Release the fuel system pressure as outlined below.
2. Remove the fuel supply hose quick connector from the chassis lines (at the engine).
3. Connect fuel pressure Gauge C-4799 or equivalent to the Fuel Pressure Test Adapter 6539. Install the adapter between the fuel supply hose and the chassis fuel line assembly.

❋❋CAUTION

When using the ASD Fuel System Test, the ASD relay and fuel pump relay remain energized for 7 minutes or until the test is stoped, or until the ignition switch is turned to the OFF position.

4. Place the ignition key to the ON position. Using the DRB scan tool, access the ASD Fuel System Test. The ASD Fuel System Test will activate the fuel pump and pressurize the system. If the gauge reads 39 psi, further testing is not required. If the pressure is not correct , record the pressure and remove the gauge.
5. If the fuel pressure reading was below specifications, proceed to next step.
6. Perform the fuel pressure release procedure.
7. Remove the fuel supply hose quick connector from the chassis lines (at the engine).
8. Connect fuel pressure Gauge C-4799 and Fuel Pressure Adapter 6433 in the fuel supply fuel line between the fuel tank and the fuel filter.
9. Using the DRB scan tool, with the ignition key in the ON position, repeat the ASD Fuel System Test.
10. If the pressure is at least 5 psi higher than the reading recorded earlier, replace the fuel filter.
11. If no change is observed, gently squeeze the return hose. If the gauge reading does not change when the return hose is squeezed, the problem is either a plugged inlet strainer or defective fuel pump.
12. If the fuel pressure reading was above specifications in Step 4, proceed to next step.
13. Perform the fuel pressure release procedure.
14. Connect fuel pressure Gauge C-4799 and Fuel Pressure Adapter 6433 in the fuel supply fuel line between the fuel tank and the fuel filter.

15. Remove the fuel return hose from the fuel pump at the fuel tank. Connect the Fuel Pressure Test Adapter 6541 to the return line. Place the other end of adapter 6541 into an approved gasoline container (minimum 2 gallon size). All return fuel will flow into the container.
16. Using the DRB scan tool, with the ignition key in the ON position, repeat the ASD Fuel System Test.
17. If the pressure is now correct, replace the fuel pump assembly.
18. If the pressure is still above specifications, remove the fuel return hose from the chassis fuel tubes at engine.
19. Connect the Fuel Pressure Test Adapter 6541 to the return line. Place the other end of adapter 6541 into an approved gasoline container. Repeat the test. If pressure is now correct, check for a restricted fuel return line. If no change is observed, replace the fuel pressure regulator.

FUEL SYSTEM PRESSURE RELEASE

❋❋CAUTION

The fuel injection system is under a constant pressure of approximately 14.5 psi (100 kPa). Before servicing any part of the fuel injection system, the system pressure must be released. Use a clean shop towel to catch any fuel spray and take precautions to avoid the risk of fire.

1. Loosen gas cap to release tank pressure.
2. Remove wiring harness connector from injector.
3. Ground 1 terminal of the injector harness.
4. Connect jumper wire to positive second terminal of the harness and touch battery positive post for no longer than 10 seconds. This releases system pressure.
5. Remove jumper wire and continue fuel system service.

Throttle Body

▶ **See Figure 62**

REMOVAL & INSTALLATION

1. Remove air cleaner.
2. Perform fuel system pressure release.
3. Disconnect negative battery cable.
4. Disconnect vacuum hoses and electrical connectors.
5. Remove throttle cable and, if so equipped, speed control and transaxle (or transmission) kickdown cables.
6. Remove return spring.
7. Remove fuel intake and return hoses.
8. Remove throttle body mounting screws and lift throttle body from vehicle.
9. When installing throttle body, use a new gasket. Install throttle body and torque mounting screws to 175 inch lbs. (20 Nm).
10. Install fuel intake and return hoses using new original equipment type clamps.
11. Install return spring.
12. Install throttle cable and, if so equipped, install kickdown and speed control cables.

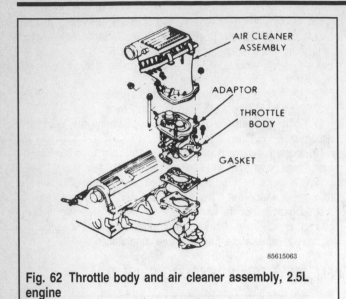

Fig. 62 Throttle body and air cleaner assembly, 2.5L engine

13. Install wiring connectors and vacuum hoses.
14. Install air cleaner.
15. Reconnect negative battery cable.

Fuel Fittings

▶ See Figures 63 and 64

REMOVAL & INSTALLATION

1. Remove air cleaner assembly.
2. Perform fuel system pressure release.
3. Disconnect negative battery cable.
4. On 1991-94 models, loosen the fuel tube clamp on the valve cover.
5. On 1987-90 models, loosen fuel intake and return hose clamps. On 1991-94 models remove the fuel tubes from the quick disconnect fittings. Wrap a shop towel around each hose, twist and pull off each hose.

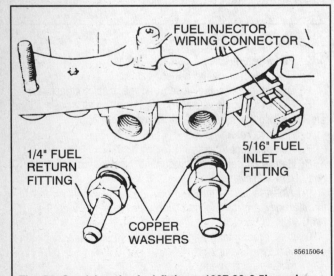

Fig. 63 Servicing the fuel fittings, 1987-90 2.5L engine

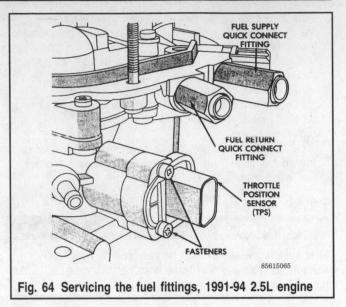

Fig. 64 Servicing the fuel fittings, 1991-94 2.5L engine

6. Remove each fitting and note inlet diameter. Remove copper washers.
7. To install, replace copper washers with new washers.
8. Install fuel fittings in proper ports and torque to 175 inch lbs. (20 Nm).
9. On 1987-90 models, using new original equipment type hose clamps, install fuel return and supply hoses.
10. On 1991-94 models, Lubricate the ends of the fuel tubes with 30 weight oil. Insert the tubes into the quick disconnect fittings and pull to make sure they are securely locked.
11. On 1991-94 models, tighten the fuel tube clamp on the valve cover.
12. Reconnect negative battery cable.
13. Test for leaks using ATM tester C-4805 or equivalent. With ignition in the **RUN** position depress ATM button. This will activate pump and pressurize the system. Check for leaks.
14. Reinstall air cleaner assembly.

Fuel Pressure Regulator

▶ See Figure 65

REMOVAL & INSTALLATION

1. Remove air cleaner assembly.
2. Perform fuel system pressure release.
3. Disconnect negative battery cable.
4. Remove 3 screws attaching pressure regulator to throttle body. Place a shop towel around inlet chamber to contain any fuel remaining in the system.
5. Pull pressure regulator from throttle body.
6. Carefully remove O-ring from pressure regulator and remove gasket.
7. To install, place new gasket on pressure regulator and carefully install new O-ring.
8. Position pressure regulator on throttle body press into place.
9. Install 3 screws and torque to 40 inch lbs. (5 Nm).
10. Connect negative battery cable.

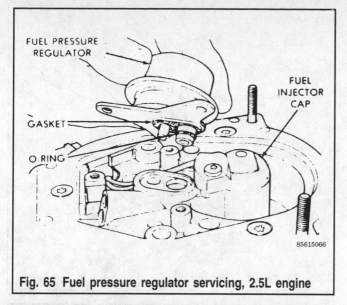

Fig. 65 Fuel pressure regulator servicing, 2.5L engine

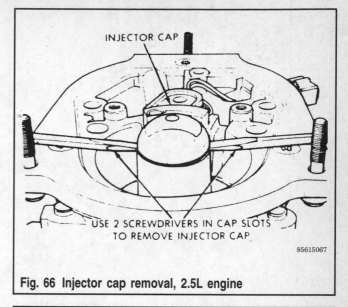

Fig. 66 Injector cap removal, 2.5L engine

11. Test for leaks using ATM tester C-4805 or equivalent. With ignition in the **RUN** position depress ATM button. This will activate pump and pressurize the system. Check for leaks.

12. Reinstall air cleaner assembly.

Fuel Injector

REMOVAL & INSTALLATION

▶ **See Figures 66, 67, 68, 69 and 70**

1. Remove air cleaner assembly.
2. Perform fuel system pressure release.
3. Disconnect negative battery cable.
4. Remove fuel pressure regulator.
5. Remove Torx® screw holding down injector cap.
6. With 2 small prying tools, lift cap off injector using slots provided.
7. Using a small prying tool placed in hole in front of electrical connector, gently pry injector from pod.
8. Make sure injector lower O-ring has been removed from pod.
9. To install, place a new lower O-ring on injector and a new O-ring on injector cap. The injector will have upper O-ring already installed.
10. Put injector cap on injector. (Injector and cap are keyed). Cap should sit on injector without interference. Apply a light coating of castor oil or petroleum jelly on O-rings. Place assembly in pod.
11. Rotate cap and injector to line up attachment hole.
12. Push down on cap until it contacts injector pod.
13. Install Torx® screw and torque to 35-45 inch lbs. (4-5 Nm).
14. Install fuel pressure regulator.
15. Connect negative battery cable.
16. Test for leaks using ATM tester C-4805 or equivalent. With ignition in the **RUN** position depress ATM button. This will activate pump and pressurize the system. Check for leaks.
17. Reinstall air cleaner assembly.

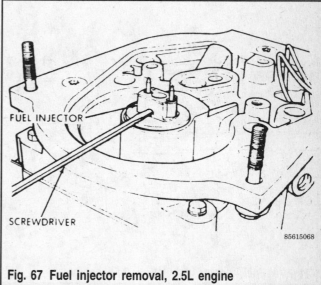

Fig. 67 Fuel injector removal, 2.5L engine

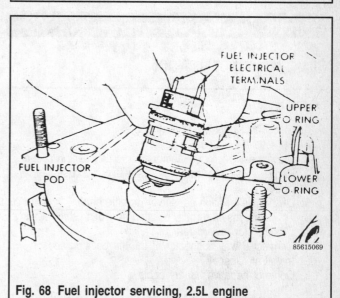

Fig. 68 Fuel injector servicing, 2.5L engine

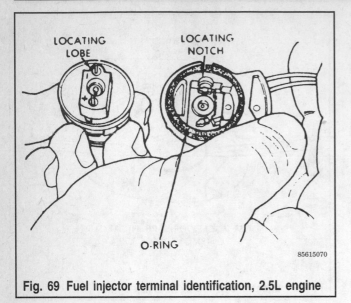

Fig. 69 Fuel injector terminal identification, 2.5L engine

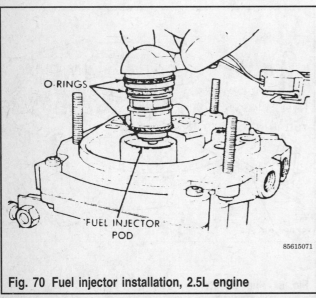

Fig. 70 Fuel injector installation, 2.5L engine

Throttle Position Sensor

REMOVAL & INSTALLATION

▶ See Figure 71

1. Disconnect negative battery cable.
2. Remove air cleaner.
3. Disconnect 3 way connector at throttle position sensor.
4. Remove 2 screws mounting throttle position sensor to throttle body.
5. Lift throttle position sensor off throttle shaft.
6. To install, install throttle position sensor to throttle body, position connector toward rear of vehicle.
7. Connect 3 way connector at throttle position sensor.
8. Install air cleaner.
9. Connect negative battery cable.

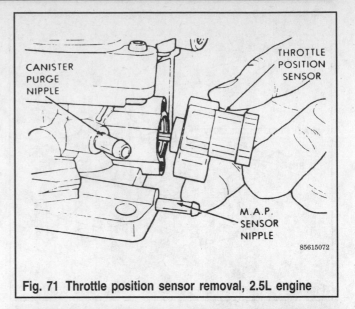

Fig. 71 Throttle position sensor removal, 2.5L engine

Throttle Body Temperature Sensor

▶ See Figure 72

REMOVAL & INSTALLATION

1. Remove air cleaner.
2. Disconnect throttle cables from throttle body linkage.
3. Remove 2 screws from throttle cable bracket and lay bracket aside.
4. Disconnect wiring connector.
5. Unscrew sensor.
6. To install, apply heat transfer compound to tip portion of new sensor.
7. Install and torque to 100 inch lbs. (11 Nm).
8. Connect wiring connector.
9. Install throttle cable bracket with 2 screws.
10. Connect throttle cables to throttle body linkage and install clips.
11. Install air cleaner.

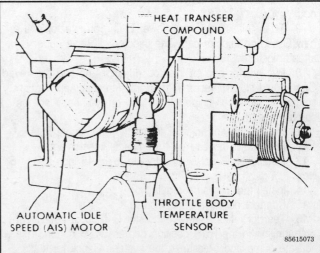

Fig. 72 Throttle body temperature sensor removal, 1988-90 2.5L engine shown

Automatic Idle Speed (AIS) Motor Assembly

➡ The Automatic Idle Speed (AIS) motor is sometimes referred to as the idle air control motor.

REMOVAL & INSTALLATION

▶ **See Figure 73**

1. Remove air cleaner.
2. Disconnect negative battery cable.
3. Disconnect 4 pin connector on AIS.
4. Remove temperature sensor from throttle body housing.
5. Remove 2 Torx® head screws.
6. Remove AIS from throttle body housing, making sure that O-ring is with AIS.
7. To install, be sure that pintle is in the retracted position. If pintle measures more than 1 in. (25mm), it must be retracted by using ATM test code No. 03. (Battery must be connected for this operation.)
8. Install new O-ring on AIS.
9. Install AIS into housing making sure O-ring is in place.

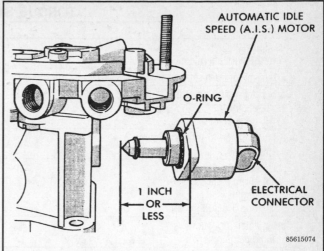

Fig. 73 Servicing the Automatic Idle Speed (AIS) motor, 2.5L engine

10. Install 2 Torx® head screws.
11. Connect 4 pin connector to AIS.
12. Install temperature sending unit into throttle body housing.
13. Connect negative battery cable.

FUEL TANK

REMOVAL & INSTALLATION

➡ — All Wheel Drive vehicles, have a fuel tank that is made of plastic. Care should be taken to avoid damaging this tank. The fuel tank in AWD vehicles is mounted at the side of the vehicle instead of the rear.

1. Release the fuel system pressure. Refer to fuel system pressure release procedure in this section.

✳✳CAUTION

Never smoke when working around gasoline! Avoid all sources of sparks or ignition. Gasoline vapors are EXTREMELY volatile!

2. Disconnect battery negative cable.
3. Raise the vehicle and support properly.
4. Remove drain tube rubber cap on left rail and connect a siphon hose to drain tube. Drain fuel into a safe gasoline container.
5. Remove screws supporting filler tube to inner and outer quarter panel.
6. Disconnect wiring and lines from the tank.
7. Position a transmission jack to support the fuel tank and remove the bolts from fuel tank straps.

8. Lower tank slightly, and carefully work filler tube from tank.
9. Lower tank, disconnect vapor separator rollover valve hose and remove the fuel tank and insulator pad from vehicle.
To install:
10. Support the fuel tank with a transmission jack. Connect the vapor separator rollover valve hose and position insulator pad on fuel tank.

➡ Be certain vapor vent hose is clipped to the tank and not pinch between tank and floor pan during installation.

11. Raise tank into position and carefully work filler tube into tank.
12. Install straps and tighten bolts to 54.2 Nm (40 ft. lbs.). Remove transmission jack.
13. Connect lines, drain tube cap and wiring connector, use new hose clamps.
14. Install and tighten filler tube to inner and outer quarter panel. On some models be sure to install the gasket between the filler tube and the inner quarter panel, before installing the mounting screws.
15. Replace cap on drain tube using a new hose clamp.
16. Fill the fuel tank, install the cap, connect battery cable and check operation.

TORQUE SPECIFICATIONS

Component	English	Metric
AIS Motor		
Multi-Point Fuel Injection	17 inch lbs.	2 Nm
Carburetor air horn retaining screws	30 inch lbs.	3 Nm
Carburetor mounting nuts		
2.2L engine	17 ft. lbs.	23 Nm
2.6L engine	13 ft. lbs.	17 Nm
EGR tube flange-to-intake plenum		
3.0L engine	200 inch lbs.	22 Nm
Fuel injector rail assembly		
2.5L turbo engines	21 ft. lbs.	28 Nm
3.0L engine	10 ft. lbs.	13 Nm
3.3L and 3.8L engines	200 inch lbs.	25 Nm
Fuel injector Torx® screws		
Single point injection	35–45 inch lbs.	4–5 Nm
Fuel pressure damper		
Multi-point injection systems	30 ft. lbs.	41 Nm
Fuel pressure regulator attaching screws		
Single point injection	40 inch lbs.	5 Nm
3.0L engine	77 inch lbs.	9 Nm
3.3L and 3.8L engines	65 inch lbs.	7 Nm
Fuel supply and return tube hold-down bolt		
3.0L engine	95 inch lbs.	10 Nm
Fuel tank strap bolts	40 ft. lbs.	54.2 Nm
Heated oxygen sensor	20 ft. lbs.	27 Nm
Mechanical fuel pump-to-engine block	21 ft. lbs.	28 Nm
Throttle body fuel fittings		
Single point injection	15 ft. lbs.	20 Nm
Throttle body mounting screws		
Single point injection	175 inch lbs.	20 Nm
Throttle position sensor		
Multi-Point Fuel Injection	17 inch lbs.	2 Nm
Throttle body temperature sensor		
Single point injection	100 inch lbs.	11 Nm
Vacuum crossover tube hold-down bolt		
3.0L engine	95 inch lbs.	10 Nm

85615C01

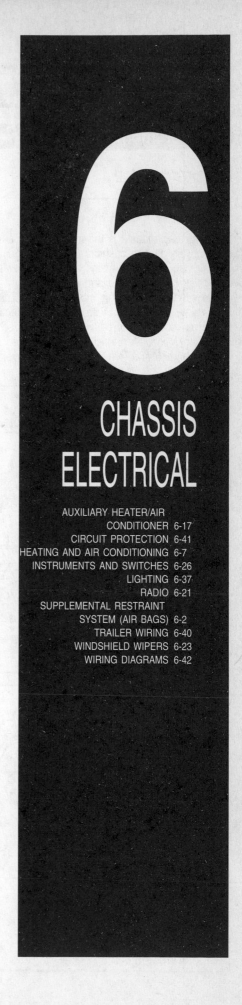

6

CHASSIS ELECTRICAL

SUPPLEMENTAL RESTRAINT SYSTEM (AIR BAGS)

General Information

AIR BAG MODULE

▶ **See Figures 1 and 2**

The air bag module is the most visible part of the system. It contains the air bag cushion and its supporting components. The air bag module contains a housing to which the cushion and inflator are attached and sealed.

The inflator assembly is mounted to the back of the module housing. When supplied with the proper electrical signal the inflator assembly will produce a gas and discharges it directly into the cushion. A protective cover is fitted to the front of the air bag module and forms a decorative cover in the center of the steering wheel. The air bag module is mounted directly to the steering wheel.

FRONT IMPACT SENSORS

▶ **See Figures 3 and 4**

The driver air bag system is a safety device designed to reduce the risk of fatality or serious injury, caused by a frontal impact of the vehicle.

The impact sensors provide verification of the direction and severity of the impact. Three impact sensors are used. One is called a safing sensor. It is located inside the diagnostic module which is mounted on the floor pan, just forward of the center console. The other two sensors are mounted on the upper crossmember of the radiator closure panel on the left and right side of the vehicle under the hood.

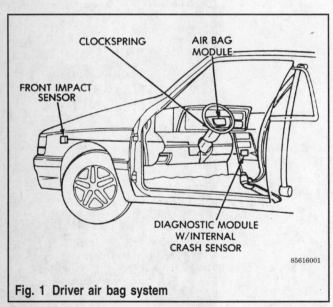

Fig. 1 Driver air bag system

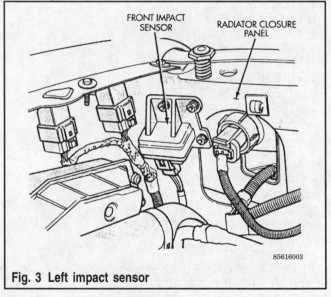

Fig. 3 Left impact sensor

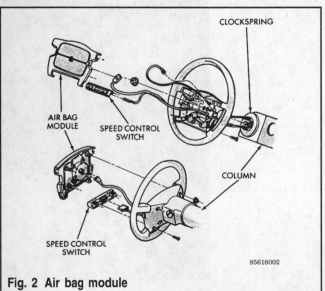

Fig. 2 Air bag module

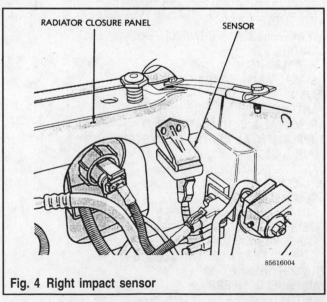

Fig. 4 Right impact sensor

The impact sensors are threshold sensitive switches that complete an electrical circuit when an impact provides a sufficient G force to close the switch. The sensors are calibrated for the specific vehicle and react to the severity and direction of the impact.

CLOCKSPRING

▶ See Figure 5

The clockspring is mounted on the steering column behind the steering wheel, and is used to maintain a continuous electrical circuit between the wiring harness and the driver's air bag module. This assembly consists of a flat ribbon-like electrically conductive tape which winds and unwinds with the steering wheel rotation.

DIAGNOSTIC MODULE

▶ See Figures 6 and 7

The Air Bag System Diagnostic Module (ASDM) contains the safing sensor and energy reserve capacitor. The ASDM monitors and system to determine the system readiness. The ASDM will store sufficient energy to deploy the air bag for only two minutes after the battery is disconnected. If both front impact sensors are open the air bag could be deployed up to 9.5 minutes after the battery is disconnected. The ASDM contains on-board diagnostics, and will illuminate the AIR BAG warning lamp in the cluster when a fault occurs.

STORAGE

The air bag module must be stored in its original special container until used for service. Also, it must be stored in a clean, dry environment, away from sources of extreme heat, sparks, and sources of high electrical energy. Always place or store the module on a surface with the trim cover facing up to minimize movement in case of accidental deployment.

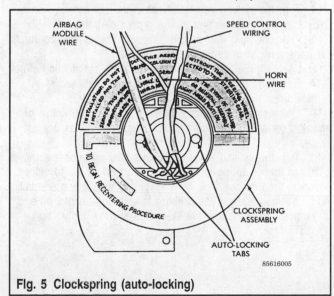

Fig. 5 Clockspring (auto-locking)

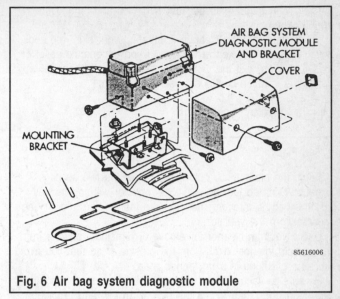

Fig. 6 Air bag system diagnostic module

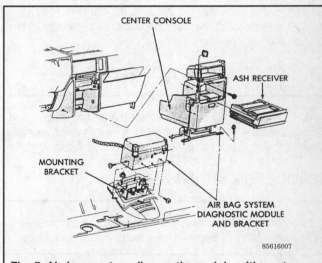

Fig. 7 Air bag system diagnostic module with center console

HANDLING LIVE MODULE

At no time should any source of electricity be permitted near the inflator on the back of the module. When carrying a live module, the trim cover should be pointed away from the body to minimize injury in the event of accidental deployment. In addition, if the module is placed on a bench or other surface, the plastic trim cover should be face up to minimize movement in case of accidental deployment.

When handling a steering column with an air bag module attached, never place the column of the floor or other surface with the steering wheel or module face down.

DEPLOYED MODULE

The vehicle interior may contain a very small amount of sodium hydroxide powder, a byproduct of air bag deployment. Since this powder can irritate the skin, eyes, nose or throat, be sure to wear safety glasses, rubber gloves and long sleeves during cleanup.

If you find that the cleanup is irritating your skin, run cool water over the affected area. Also, if you experience nasal or throat irritation, exit the vehicle for fresh air until the irritation ceases. If irritation continues, see a physician.

CLEAN UP PROCEDURE

▶ **See Figure 8**

Begin the cleanup by putting tape over the two air bag exhaust vents so that no additional powder will find its way into the vehicle interior. Then remove the air bag and air bag module from the vehicle.

Use a vacuum cleaner to remove any residual powder from the vehicle interior. Work from the outside in so that you avoid kneeling or sitting in a uncleaned area.

Be sure to vacuum the heater and A/C outlets as well. In fact it's a good idea to run the blower on low and to vacuum up any powder expelled from the plenum. You may need to vacuum the interior of the car a second time to recover all of the powder.

SERVICE OF A DEPLOYED AIR BAG

After an air bag has been deployed, the air bag module and clockspring must be replaced because they cannot be reused. Other air bag system components are replaced if damaged.

SERVICE PRECAUTIONS

This system is a sensitive, complex electro-mechanical unit. Before attempting to diagnose, remove or install the air bag

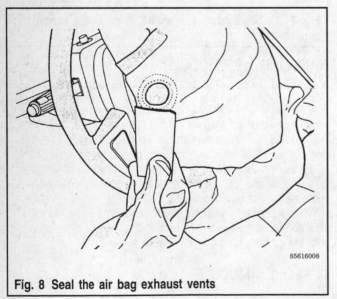

Fig. 8 Seal the air bag exhaust vents

85616008

system components, you must first disconnect and isolate the negative (ground) battery cable. Failure to do so could result in accidental deployment and possible personal injury.

When an undeployed air bag assembly is to be removed from the steering wheel, disconnect battery ground cable and isolate. Allow system capacitor to discharge for two minutes then begin air bag system component removal.

If the Air Bag Module Assembly is defective and non-deployed, refer to Chrysler Motors current return list for proper handling procedures.

✳✳WARNING

Replace air bag system components with Chrysler Mopar specified replacement parts. Substitute parts may visually appear interchangeable, but internal differences may result in inferior occupant protection. The fasteners, screws, and bolts, originally used for the air bag components, have special coatings and are specifically designed for the air bag system. They must never be replaced with any substitutes. Anytime a new fastener is needed, replace with the correct fasteners provided in the service package or fasteners listed in the Chrysler parts books.

Airbag System Check

✳✳WARNING

Disconnect and isolate the battery negative cable before beginning any airbag system component removal or installation procedure. This will disable the airbag system. Failure to disconnect the battery could result in accidental airbag deployment and possible personal injury. Allow system capacitor to discharge for 2 minutes before removing any airbag components.

1. Disconnect the battery negative cable and isolate.
2. Remove forward console or cover as necessary.
3. Connect DRB to ACM data link 6-way connector, located at right of steering column.
4. Turn the ignition key to ON position. Exit vehicle with DRB. Use the latest version of the proper cartridge.
5. After checking that no one is inside the vehicle, connect the battery negative cable.
6. Using the DRB, read and record active diagnostic data.
7. Read and record any stored diagnostic codes.
8. Correct any problems found in steps 6 and 7.
9. Erase stored diagnostic codes if there are no active diagnostic codes. If problems remain, diagnostic codes will not erase.
10. Turn the ignition key to OFF then ON and observe the message center airbag lamp. It should go on for six to eight seconds, then go out; indicating system is functioning normally.
11. If airbag warning lamp either fails to light, blinks on and off or goes on and stays on, there is a system malfunction.

Driver Airbag Module

❋❋WARNING

Disconnect and isolate the battery negative cable before beginning any airbag system component removal or installation procedure. This will disable the airbag system. Failure to disconnect the battery could result in accidental airbag deployment and possible personal injury. Allow system capacitor to discharge for 2 minutes before removing any airbag components.

REMOVAL

When removing a deployed module, rubber gloves, eye protection and long sleeve shirt should be worn, as there may be deposits on the surface which could irritate the skin and eyes.

1. Disconnect the battery negative cable and isolate.
2. Wait two minutes for the reserve capacitor to discharge before removing non deployed module.
3. Remove four nuts attaching airbag module to steering wheel.
4. Lift module and disconnect electrical connector from rear of module.
5. Remove module.
6. When replacing a deployed modue, the clockspring must also be replaced. Refer to Clockspring Removal and Installation for proper procedure.
   To install:
7. Connect clockspring squib connector to the module, by pressing straight in on the connector. Push connector past the secondary latching fingers until it is FULLY SEATED into the module squib.
8. Install four nuts and tighten to 80 to 100 in. lbs. (9 to 11 Nm) torque.
9. Do not connect battery negative cable. Refer to Airbag System Check for proper procedure.

Passenger Airbag Module

REMOVAL

❋❋WARNING

Disconnect and isolate the battery negative cable before beginning any airbag system component removal or installation procedure. This will disable the airbag system. Failure to disconnect the battery could result in accidental airbag deployment and possible personal injury. Allow system capacitor to discharge for 2 minutes before removing any airbag components.

Non Deployed

1. Disconnect and isolate the battery negative cable.
2. Disconnect glove box door check straps and allow door to open fully.

3. Remove the four screws attaching the module to the bracket.
4. Using a large flat tipped screwdriver by hand, pry module up to unsnap door from the trim pad and lift away from snaps. The access hole for the screwdriver is located at the center of the module mounting bracket.
5. Hold on to the door and raise module from opening. Rest module on trim pad and disconnect the two connectors and remove module. Use a shop towel to protect trim pad before placing module on it.
6. For installation, reverse above procedures. Tighten module attaching screws to 6 N.n (50 in. lbs.) torque.

Deployed Module

1. When removing a deployed module:
   a. Rubber gloves
   b. Eye protection
2. Long-sleeved shirt should be worn. There may be deposits on the surface which could irritate the skin and eyes.
3. Disconnect and isolate the battery negative cable.
4. Roll/fold airbag towards instrument panel.
5. Close door over folded airbag and tape door closed.
6. Refer to Cleanup Procedure above.
7. Disconnect glove box door check straps and allow door to open fully.
8. Remove the four screws attaching the module to the bracket.
9. Using a large flat tipped screwdriver or by hand, pry module up to unsnap door from the trim pad and lift away from snaps. The access hole for the screwdriver is located at the center of the module mounting bracket.
10. Hold on to the door and raise module from opening. Rest module on trim pad and disconnect the two connectors and remove module. Use a shop towel to protect trim pad before placing module on it.
11. Check trim pad for any cracking or surface marks and replace as necessary.
12. For installation, reverse above procedures. Check door for fit and finish while tightening modue screws. Tighten module attaching screws to 6 N.n (50 in. lbs.) torque.

Airbag Control Module (ACM)

❋❋WARNING

Disconnect and isolate the battery negative cable before beginning any airbag system component removal or installation procedure. This will disable the airbag system. Failure to disconnect the battery could result in accidental airbag deployment and possible personal injury. Allow system capacitor to discharge for 2 minutes before removing any airbag components.

REMOVAL

1. Disconnect the battery negative cable and isolate cable.
2. Remove the two screws attaching lower console to instrument panel support brackets.
3. Slide cupholder out.

4. Remove the two upper console attaching screws behind the cupholder.

5. Slide console rearward and up to remove.

6. Disconnect wiring at ACM and remove module.

7. Remove the four ACM mounting screws.

8. Slide the ACM off the mounting bracket toward the drive side and remove module.

❋❋WARNING

Use Correct Screws

9. For installation, reverse above procedures. Attach module and bracket with screws and tighten to 10.7 N.n (95 in. lbs.) torque.

10. Do not connect battery negative cable. Refer to Airbag System Check for proper procedure.

Clockspring

❋❋WARNING

Disconnect and isolate the battery negative cable before beginning any airbag system component removal or installation procedure. This will disable the airbag system. Failure to disconnect the battery could result in accidental airbag deployment and possible personal injury. Allow system capacitor to discharge for 2 minutes before removing any airbag components.

REMOVAL

1. Place the front wheels in the straight ahead position before starting the repair.

2. Disconnect the battery negative cable and isolate.

3. Wait two minutes for the reserve capacitor to discharge before removing non deployed module.

4. Remove the airbag module.

5. Remove Speed Control switch and connector if so equipped or cover.

6. Disconnect horn terminals.

7. Remove the steering wheel.

8. Remove upper and lower steering column shrouds to gain access to clockspring wiring.

9. Disconnect the 2-way connector between the clockspring and the instrument panel wiring harness on top of the fuse block.

10. To remove, pull clockspring assembly from the steering column by lifting locating fingers as necessary. The clockspring cannot be repaired and must be replaced if faulty.

To install:

11. Snap clockspring onto the steering column. If the clockspring is not properly positioned, follow the clockspring centering procedure before installing steering wheel.

12. Connect the clockspring to the instrument panel harness, ensure wiring locator clips are properly seated on wiring trough. Ensure harness locking tabs are properly engaged.

13. Install steering column shrouds. Be sure airbag wire is inside of shrouds.

14. Front wheels should still be in the straightahead position. Install steering wheel, ensure the flats on hub align with clockspring. Pull the horn lead through the smaller upper hole. Pull the airbag and speed control leads through the larger bottom hole. Ensure leads are not pinched under the steering wheel.

15. Connect the horn lead wire, then the airbag lead wire to the airbag module.

16. Install the airbag module and tighten nuts to 9 to 11 N.m (80 to 100 in. lb.) torque.

17. Install vehicle speed control switch and connector or cover.

18. Do not connect battery negative cable. Refer to Airbag Systems Check for proper procedure.

Clockspring Centering Procedure

❋❋WARNING

If the rotating tape within the clockspring is not positioned properly with the steering wheel and the front wheels, the clockspring may fail during use. The following procedure MUST BE USED to center the clockspring if it is not known to be properly positioned, or if the front wheels were moved from the straight ahead position.

❋❋WARNING

Disconnect and isolate the battery negative cable before beginning any airbag system component removal or installation procedure. This will disable the airbag system. Failure to disconnect the battery could result in accidental airbag deployment and possible personal injury. Allow system capacitor to discharge for 2 minutes before removing any airbag components.

1. Place front wheels in the straight ahead position.

2. Wait two minutes for the reserve capacitor to discharge before removing non deployed module.

3. Refer to Steering Wheel procedures for removal of airbag module and steering wheel.

4. Depress the two plastic locking pins to disengage locking mechanism.

5. Keeping locking mechanism disengaged, rotate the clockspring rotor in the CLOCKWISE DIRECTION to the end of travel. Do not apply excessive torque.

6. From the end of travel, rotate the rotor two full turns and a half in the counterclockwise direction. The horn wire should end up at the top and the squib wire at the bottom. Engage clockspring locking mechanism.

7. Refer to Steering Wheel procedures for installation of steering wheel and airbag module.

8. Do not connect battery negative cable. Refer to Airbag System Check for proper procedure.

Steering Column Switches

REMOVAL

This procedure covers the removal and installation of the steering wheel and clockspring. Once the steering wheel and clockspring have been removed, refer to the appropriate section of this service manual for switch replacement.

✳✳WARNING

Disconnect and isolate the battery negative cable before beginning any airbag system component removal or installation procedure. This will disable the airbag system. Failure to disconnect the battery could result in accidental airbag deployment and possible personal injury. Allow system capacitor to discharge for 2 minutes before removing any airbag components.

1. Disconnect the battery negative cable and isolate.

HEATING AND AIR CONDITIONING

Service such as blower motor and heater core replacement on 1984-87 models, requires the removal of the Heater/Evaporator unit from the vehicle. Two persons will be required for the operation.

➡**Properly discharge the refrigerant system before any work requiring the disconnecting of the refrigerant lines. Refer to Section 1 for the proper discharging, evacuating and recharging procedures.**

Air Conditioning Compressor

▸ **See Figures 9, 10, 11, 12, 13, 14, 15 and 16**

REMOVAL & INSTALLATION

1. Disconnect the negative battery cable.
2. Properly discharge the air conditioning system. Refer to Section 1 for discharge, evacuate and recharge procedures.
3. Remove the compressor drive belt(s). Disconnect the compressor lead.
4. Raise and safely support the vehicle, if necessary. Remove the refrigerant lines from the compressor and discard the gaskets. Cover the exposed ends of the lines to minimize contamination.
5. Remove the compressor mounting nuts and bolts.
6. Lift the compressor off of its mounting studs and remove from the engine compartment.

2. Wait two minutes for the reserve capacitor to discharge before removing non deployed module.
3. Remove four nuts attaching airbag module from the back side of steering wheel.
4. Lift module and disconnect connector from rear of module.
5. Remove vehicle speed control switch and connector if so equipped or cover.
6. Remove steering wheel.
7. Unsnap clockspring and remove it.
8. Refer to the appropriate section for switch replacement.
To install:
9. Snap clockspring on to steering column. Assure the 4-way connector is still seated.
10. Install steering wheel.
11. Install vehicle speed control switch and connector or cover.
12. Connect clockspring wiring connector to the module.
13. Install four nuts to module and tighten to 9 to 11 N.m 80 to 100 in. lbs. (9 to 11 Nm) torque.
14. Do not connect battery negative cable. Refer to Airbag System Check for proper procedure.

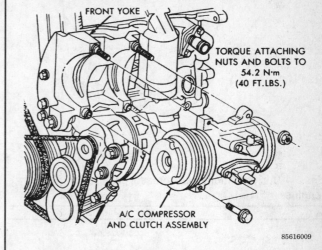

Fig. 9 Air conditioner compressor installation, 2.2L and 2.5L engines

To install:
7. Install the compressor and tighten all mounting nuts and bolts.
8. Coat the new gaskets with wax-free refrigerant oil and install. Connect the refrigerant lines to the compressor and tighten the bolts.
9. Install the drive belt(s) and adjust to specification. Connect the electrical lead.
10. Evacuate and recharge the air conditioning system.
11. Connect the negative battery cable and check the entire climate control system for proper operation and leaks.

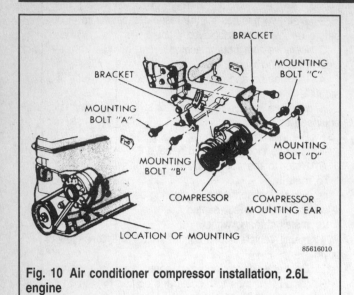

Fig. 10 Air conditioner compressor installation, 2.6L engine

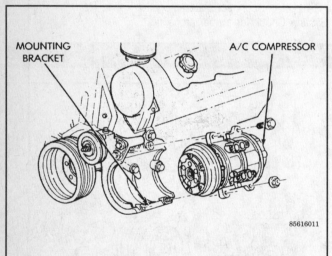

Fig. 11 Air conditioner compressor installation, 3.0L engine

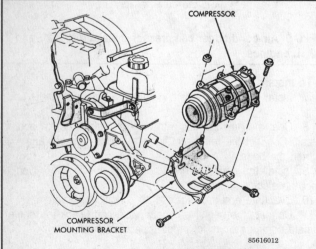

Fig. 12 Air conditioner compressor installation, 3.3L and 3.8L engines

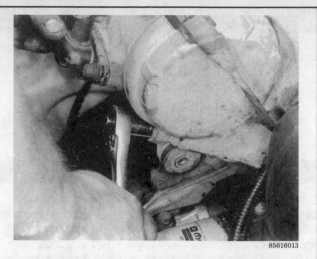

Fig. 13 Removing the air conditioner compressor lower mounting bolts

Fig. 14 Removing the upper air conditioner compressor mounting nuts

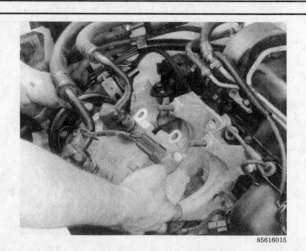

Fig. 15 After removing the air conditioner compressor mounting bolts and nuts the compressor may be lifted from the mounting bracket

Fig. 16 If necessary, remove the air conditioner compressor mounting bracket

Heater/Evaporator Unit

REMOVAL & INSTALLATION

1984-87
▶ See Figures 17, 18, 19, 20, 21, 22, 23 and 24

✳✳CAUTION

The air conditioning system contains refrigerant under high pressure. Severe personal injury may result from improper service procedures. If the knowledge and necessary equipment are not on hand, have the system serviced by qualified service the refrigerant system completely.

1. Discharge the air conditioning system. See the CAUTION notice above.
2. Block the vehicle wheels and apply the parking brake.

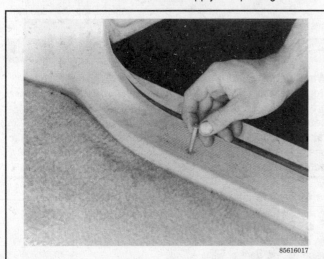

Fig. 17 Removing the passenger side cowl and sill trim panel lower retaining screws, 1987 Voyager shown

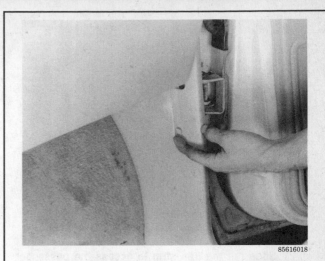

Fig. 18 Remove the screw hole cover plugs from the upper cowl and sill trim panel, 1987 Voyager shown

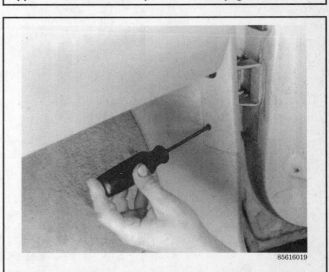

Fig. 19 Remove the screws from the upper cowl and sill trim panel, 1987 Voyager shown

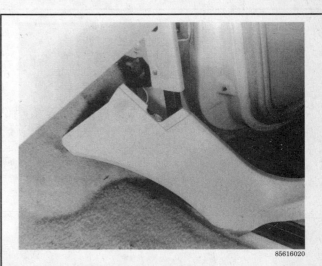

Fig. 20 Removing the passenger side cowl and sill trim panel, 1987 Voyager shown

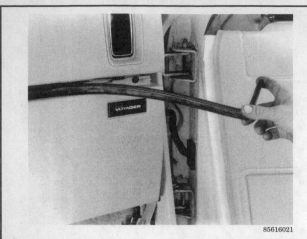

Fig. 21 Slide out the trim strip to access the passenger side lower dash panel retaining screws, 1987 Voyager shown

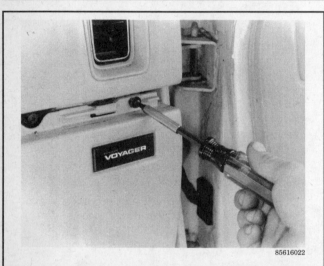

Fig. 22 Removing the passenger side lower dash panel retaining screws, 1987 Voyager shown

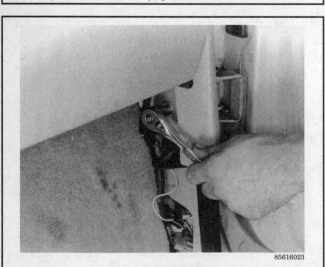

Fig. 23 Removing the passenger side lower dash panel mounting bolt, 1987 Voyager shown

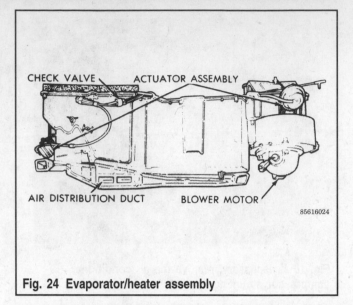

Fig. 24 Evaporator/heater assembly

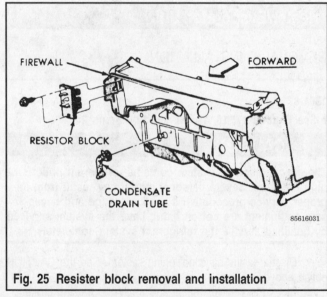

Fig. 25 Resister block removal and installation

3. Disconnect the negative battery cable. Drain the cooling system.

> **✳✳CAUTION**
>
> When draining the coolant, keep in mind that cats and dogs are attracted by the ethylene glycol antifreeze, and are quite likely to drink any that is left in an uncovered container or in puddles on the ground. This will prove fatal in sufficient quantity. Always drain the coolant into a sealable container. Coolant should be reused unless it is contaminated or several years old.

4. Remove the passenger side lower instrument panel.
5. Remove the steering column lower cover.
6. Remove the right side cowl and sill trim.
7. Remove the mounting bolt from the right side instrument panel to the right cowl.
8. Loosen the (2) brackets supporting the lower edge to air conditioning and heater unit housing.

9. Remove the mid-reinforcement instrument panel trim molding.

10. Remove the attaching screws from the right side to center of the steering column.

11. From the engine compartment; disconnect the vacuum line at brake booster and water valve.

12. Remove the hoses from the heater core. Plug the heater tubes.

13. Disconnect the air conditioning plumbing at the H-valve.

14. Remove the (4) nuts from engine compartment package mounting studs.

15. From the passenger compartment, pull the right side of lower instrument panel rearward until it reaches the passenger seat. Disconnect the electrical connectors and temperature control cable.

16. Remove the hangar strap from the unit assembly and bend rearward.

17. Carefully remove the unit assembly from the vehicle.

18. Place the heater/evaporator unit assembly on a work bench.

19. Remove the vacuum harness attaching screw and remove the harness through the access hole in the cover.

20. Remove the (13) attaching screws from the cover and remove the cover. The temperature control door will come out with the cover.

21. Remove the retaining bracket screws and the remove heater core assembly.

22. Remove the evaporator core assembly.

23. Disconnect the actuator linkage from the recirculation door and remove the vacuum line. Remove the actuator retaining screws and remove the actuator.

24. Remove the (4) attaching screws from the recirculation door cover to evaporator/heater assembly. Lift the cover from the unit and remove the recirculation door from its housing.

25. Remove the (5) attaching screws from the blower assembly sound helmet.

26. Remove the retaining clamp from the blower wheel hub and slide the blower wheel from the blower motor shaft.

27. Remove the blower motor (3) mounting screws from the helmet and remove the blower motor assembly.

To install:

28. Install the blower wheel to the blower motor shaft and secure it with the retaining clamp.

29. Feed the blower motor electrical wires through the access hole in the sound helmet and lower the blower motor into helmet.

30. Secure the blower motor with the (3) mounting screws.

31. Install the blower assembly and helmet into the fan scroll and secure it with (5) retaining screws.

32. Install the recirculation door into its housing. Place the recirculation door cover onto the unit and secure with the (4) retaining screws.

33. Install the actuator shaft onto the recirculation door and slide the actuator into its bracket. Secure the actuator assembly with (2) nuts.

34. Install the evaporator core into the unit.

35. Install the heater core into the unit and secure the core tube retaining bracket with attaching screws.

36. Install the unit cover and secure with (13) attaching screws.

37. Install the vacuum harness through the access hole in the cover and secure the vacuum harness.

38. Place the heater/evaporator assembly into the vehicle and position it against the dash panel.

39. Install the hangar strap.

40. Connect the temperature control cable, vacuum and electrical connectors.

41. Install the (4) retaining nuts to the unit mounting studs from the engine compartment.

42. Connect the air conditioning plumbing to the H-valve.

43. Connect the vacuum line at the brake booster and water valve.

44. Install the attaching screws from the right side to the center of the steering column.

45. Install the mid-reinforcement instrument panel trim molding.

46. Tighten the (2) brackets supporting the lower edge to the heater/evaporator unit housing.

47. Install the mounting bolt from the right side of the instrument panel to the right cowl.

48. Install the right side cowl and sill trim.

49. Install the steering column lower cover.

50. Install the passenger side lower instrument panel

51. Connect the heater hoses to heater core in the engine compartment.

52. Connect the negative battery cable.

53. Fill the cooling system.

54. Evacuate, charge and leak test the air conditioning system.

Blower Motor

REMOVAL & INSTALLATION

1984-87

1. Remove the heater/evaporator unit from the vehicle.

2. Remove the 4 screws retaining the recirculation cover to the unit and remove the cover and recirculating door.

3. Remove the blower assembly, sound helmet, motor and wheel.

4. To remove the blower wheel, remove the retaining clamp from the blower wheel hub and slide the blower wheel from the shaft.

5. Remove the 3 screws in the helmet and remove the blower motor and wires.

To install:

6. Install the blower wheel to the shaft and install the spring clip. Inspect the blower mounting plate seal and repair, as necessary. Apply rubber adhesive to the seal to aid in assembly.

7. Install the blower into the helmet and install the 3 mounting screws.

8. The entire blower assembly and helmet can be installed into the fan scroll with the 5 screws.

9. Install the recirculating door and cover.

1988-91

1. Disconnect the negative battery cable.

2. Locate and disconnect the 2-way connector at the blower motor lead under the instrument panel on the passen-

ger side of the vehicle. The wire connector insulator may be wrapped with a foam silencer material.

3. Remove the 5 blower motor screws attaching the the motor to the A/C-heater unit.

4. Allow the blower assembly to drop downward to clear the instrument panel.

5. Install in reverse of removal.

1992-94

1. Disconnect the negative battery cable.

2. Remove the lower right instrument panel assembly.

3. Remove the blower motor screws attaching the the motor to the A/C-heater unit.

4. Allow the blower assembly to drop downward to clear the instrument panel.

5. Install in reverse of removal.

Blower Motor Resistor

REMOVAL & INSTALLATION

▶ **See Figure 25**

The resistor block is located at the left rear corner of the engine compartment on Caravan, Voyager and Town & Country.

1. Disconnect the negative battery cable.

2. Remove the glovebox, if necessary. Locate the resistor block and disconnect the wire harness.

3. Remove the attaching screws and remove the resistor from the housing.

4. Make sure there is no contact between any of the coils before installing.

5. The installation is the reverse of the removal procedure. Make sure the foam seal is in good condition.

6. Connect the negative battery cable and check the blower system for proper operation.

Heater Core and Evaporator

▶ **See Figures 26, 27, 28, 29, 30 and 31**

REMOVAL & INSTALLATION

1984-90

1. Disconnect the negative battery cable. Properly discharge the air conditioning system, if equipped. Drain the cooling system.

2. Remove the lower steering column cover.

3. Remove the lower reinforcement under the steering column, right side cowl and sill trim. Remove the bolt holding the right side instrument panel to the right cowl.

4. Loosen the 2 brackets supporting the lower edge of the heater housing. Remove the instrument panel trim covering and reinforcement. Remove the retaining screws from the right side of the steering column.

5. Disconnect the vacuum lines at the brake booster and water valve.

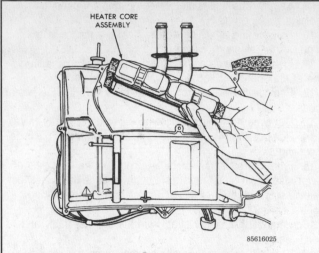

Fig. 26 Removing and installing the heater core assembly

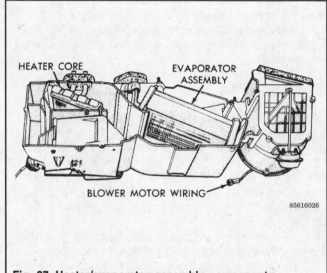

Fig. 27 Heater/evaporator assembly components

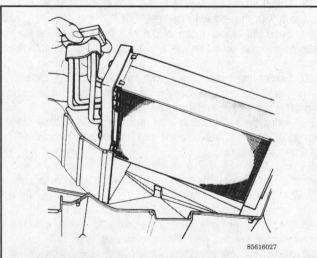

Fig. 28 Removing or installing the actuator and linkage on the blower housing

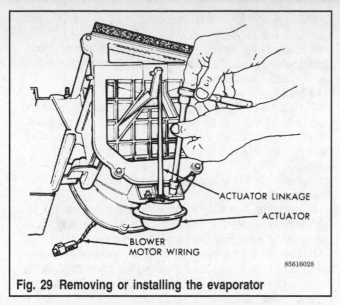

Fig. 29 Removing or installing the evaporator

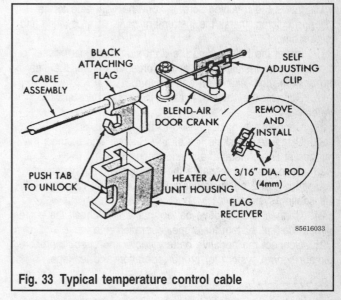

Fig. 32 Air conditioning and heater control head removal

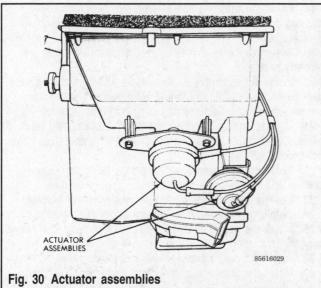

Fig. 30 Actuator assemblies

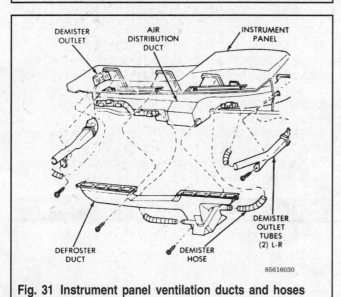

Fig. 31 Instrument panel ventilation ducts and hoses

Fig. 33 Typical temperature control cable

6. Clamp off the heater hoses at the heater core and remove them from the heater core tubes. Plug the ends to prevent leakage.

7. Disconnect the H-valve at the water valve and remove it. Remove the retaining nuts at the package tray mounting studs. Remove the drain tube.

8. Disconnect the blower motor wiring and temperature control cable. Disconnect the vacuum harness at the top of the heater unit.

9. Remove the retaining nuts from the package mounting studs at the firewall. Disconnect the hanger strap from the package and rotate it aside.

10. Pull the right side of the instrument panel out as far as possible. Fold the carpeting and insulation back to provide a little more working room and to prevent spillage from staining the carpeting.

11. Remove the entire housing assembly from the dash panel and remove it from the vehicle.

12. To disassemble the housing assembly, remove the vacuum diaphragm and retaining screws from the cover and remove the cover.

13. Remove the retaining screw from the heater core and/or evaporator and remove from the housing assembly.

To install:

14. Remove the temperature control door from the unit and clean the unit out with solvent. Lubricate the lower pivot rod and its well and install. Wrap the heater core and/or evaporator with foam tape and place in position. Secure with the screws.

15. Assemble the unit, making sure all vacuum tubes are properly routed.

16. Install the assembly to the vehicle and connect the vacuum harness. Install the nuts to the firewall and install the condensation tube. Fold the carpeting back into position.

17. Connect the hanger strap from the package and rotate it aside. Install the 2 brackets supporting the lower edge of the heater housing. Connect the blower motor wiring, resistor wiring and the temperature control cable.

18. Install the retaining screws from the right side to the steering column. Install the instrument panel trim covering and reinforcement.

19. Install the bolt holding the right side instrument panel to the right cowl. Install the lower reinforcement under the steering column, right side cowl and sill trim.

20. Connect the vacuum lines at the brake booster and water valve.

21. Connect the heater hoses to the core tubes.

22. Using new gaskets, install the H-valve and connect the refrigerant lines. Install the condensation tube.

23. Evacuate and recharge the air conditioning system, if equipped. Add 2 oz. of refrigerant oil during the recharge. Fill the cooling system.

24. Connect the negative battery cable and check the entire climate control system for proper operation and leaks.

25. Connect the negative battery cable and check the entire climate control system for proper operation and leakage.

1991-94

1. Disconnect the negative battery cable. Properly discharge the air conditioning system, if equipped. Drain the cooling system.

2. Remove the steering column cover and left and right side under panel silencers.

3. Remove the center bezel by unclipping it from the instrument panel.

4. Remove the accessory switch carrier and the heater/air conditioning control head.

5. Remove storage bin and lower right instrument panel.

6. Disconnect the blower motor lead under the right side of the instrument panel.

7. Remove the right side 40-way connector wiring bracket.

8. Remove the lower right reinforcement, body computer bracket and mid-to-lower reinforcement as an assembly.

9. Disconnect the vacuum lines at the brake booster and water valve.

10. Clamp off the heater hoses near the heater core and remove the hoses from the core tubes. Plug the hose ends and the core tubes to prevent spillage of coolant.

11. If equipped with air conditioning, remove the H-valve and condensation tube.

12. Disconnect the temperature control cable and vacuum harness at the connection at the top of the unit.

13. Remove the retaining nuts from the package mounting studs at the firewall. Disconnect the hanger strap from the package and rotate it aside.

To install:

14. Remove the temperature control door from the unit and clean the unit out with solvent. Lubricate the lower pivot rod and its well and install. Wrap the heater core and/or evaporator with foam tape and place in position. Secure with the screws.

15. Assemble the unit, making sure all vacuum tubes are properly routed.

16. Install the assembly to the vehicle and connect the vacuum harness. Install the nuts to the firewall and install the condensation tube. Fold the carpeting back into position.

17. Connect the hanger strap from the package and rotate it aside. Install the 2 brackets supporting the lower edge of the heater housing. Connect the blower motor wiring, resistor wiring and the temperature control cable.

18. Install the retaining screws from the right side to the steering column. Install the instrument panel trim covering and reinforcement.

19. Assemble the unit, making sure all vacuum tubes are properly routed.

20. Install the assembly to the vehicle and connect the vacuum harness. Install the nuts to the firewall and install the condensation tube. Fold the carpeting back into position.

21. Connect the hanger strap from the package and rotate it aside. Connect the blower motor wiring and temperature control cable.

22. Install the lower right reinforcement, body computer bracket and mid-to-lower reinforcement as an assembly.

23. Install the right side 40-way connector wiring bracket.

24. Install the lower right instrument panel and storage bin.

25. Install the heater/air conditioning control head and accessory switch carrier.

26. Install the center bezel to the instrument panel.

27. Install the under panel silencers and steering column cover.

28. Install the vacuum lines at the brake booster and water valve.

29. Connect the heater hoses to the core tubes.

30. Using new gaskets, install the H-valve and connect the refrigerant lines. Install the condensation tube.

31. Evacuate and recharge the air conditioning system, if equipped. Add 2 oz. of refrigerant oil during the recharge. Fill the cooling system.

32. Connect the negative battery cable and check the entire climate control system for proper operation and leaks.

33. Connect the negative battery cable and check the entire climate control system for proper operation and leakage.

Climate Control Head

▶ **See Figure 32**

REMOVAL & INSTALLATION

1. Disconnect the negative battery cable.

2. Remove the necessary bezel(s) in order to gain access to the control head.

3. Remove the screws that fasten the control head to the instrument panel.

4. Pull the unit out and unplug the electrical and vacuum connectors. Disconnect the temperature control cable by pushing the flag in and pulling the end from its seat.

5. Remove the control head from the instrument panel.

6. The installation is the reverse of the removal proceed that fasten the control head to the instrument panel.

Heater/Air Conditioning Control Cables

▶ See Figure 33

REMOVAL & INSTALLATION

1. Disconnect the negative battery cable.

2. Remove the necessary bezel(s) in order to gain access to the control head.

3. Remove the screws that fasten the control head to the instrument panel.

4. Pull the unit out and disconnect the temperature control cable by pushing the flag in and pulling the end from its seat.

5. The temperature control cable end is located at the bottom of the heater/air conditioning housing. Disconnect the cable end by pushing the flag in and pulling the end from its seat.

6. Disconnect the self-adjusting clip from the blend air or mode door crank.

7. Take note of the cable's routing and remove the from the vehicle.

To install:

8. Install the cable by routing it in exactly the same position as it was prior to removal.

9. Connect the self-adjusting clip to the door crank and click the flag into the seat.

10. Connect the upper end of the cable to the control head.

11. Place the temperature lever on the coolest side of its travel. Allowing the self-adjusting clip to slide on the cable, rotate the blend air door counterclockwise by hand until it stops.

12. Cycle the lever back and forth a few times to make sure the cable moves freely.

13. Connect the negative battery cable and check the entire climate control system for proper operation.

Filter/Drier

▶ See Figure 34

REMOVAL & INSTALLATION

1. Disconnect the negative battery cable.

2. Properly discharge the air conditioning system. Refer to Section 1.

3. On 1992-94 vehicles, remove the vehicle jack.

4. Remove the nuts that fasten the refrigerant lines to sides of the receiver/drier assembly.

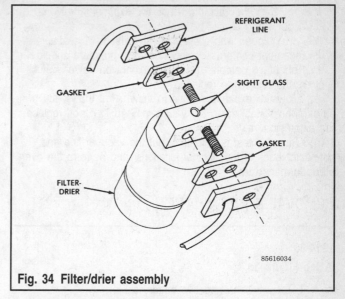

Fig. 34 Filter/drier assembly

5. Remove the refrigerant lines from the receiver/drier and discard the gaskets. Cover the exposed ends of the lines to minimize contamination.

6. Remove the mounting strap bolts and remove the receiver/drier from the engine compartment.

To install:

7. Transfer the mounting strap to the new receiver/drier.

8. Coat the new gaskets with wax-free refrigerant oil and install. Connect the refrigerant lines to the receiver/drier and tighten the nuts.

9. Evacuate and recharge the air conditioning system. Add 1 oz. of refrigerant oil during the recharge. Check for leaks.

Expansion Valve (H-Valve)

TESTING

1. Connect a manifold gauge set or charging station to the air conditioning system. Verify adequate refrigerant level.

2. Disconnect and plug the vacuum hose at the water control valve.

3. Disconnect the low pressure or differential pressure cut off switch connector and jump the wires inside the boot.

4. Close all doors, windows and vents to the passenger compartment.

5. Set controls to **MAX A/C**, full heat and high blower speed.

6. Start the engine and hold the idle speed at 1000 rpm. After the engine has reached normal operating temperature, allow the passenger compartment to heat up to create the need for maximum refrigerant flow into the evaporator.

7. The discharge (high pressure) gauge should read 140-240 psi and suction (low pressure) gauge should read 20-30 psi, providing the refrigerant charge is sufficient.

8. If the suction side is within specifications, freeze the expansion valve control head using a very cold substance (liquid CO_2 or dry ice) for 30 seconds:

  a. If equipped with a silver H-valve used with fixed displacement compressor, the suction side pressure should drop to 15 in. Hg vacuum. If not, the expansion valve is stuck open and should be replaced.

b. If equipped with a black H-valve used with variable displacement compressor, the discharge pressure should drop about 15 percent. If not, the expansion valve is stuck open and should be replaced.

9. Allow the expansion valve to thaw. As it thaws, the pressures should stabilize to the values in Step 7. If not, replace the expansion valve.

10. Once the test is complete, put the vacuum line and connector back in the original locations, and perform the overall performance test.

REMOVAL & INSTALLATION

1984-90

▶ See Figure 35

1. Disconnect the negative battery cable.
2. Properly discharge the air conditioning system.
3. Disconnect the low or differential pressure cut off switch.
4. Remove the attaching bolt at the center of the refrigerant plumbing sealing plate.
5. Pull the refrigerant lines assembly away from the expansion valve. Cover the exposed ends of the lines to minimize contamination.
6. Remove the 2 Torx® screws that mount the expansion valve to the evaporator sealing plate.
7. Remove the valve and discard the gaskets.

To install:

8. Transfer the low pressure cutoff switch to the new valve, if necessary.
9. Coat the new 'figure-8' gasket with wax-free refrigerant oil and install to the evaporator sealing plate.
10. Install the expansion valve and torque the Torx® screws to 100 inch lbs.

11. Lubricate the remaining gasket and install with the blower motor lead under the right side of the instrument panel.
12. Connect the refrigerant lines and sealing plate, tighten to 200 inch lbs. (23 Nm).
13. Connect the electrical leads and connect the negative battery cable.
14. Evacuate and properly recharge the air conditioning system.

1991-94

▶ See Figure 36

1. Disconnect the negative battery cable.
2. Properly discharge the air conditioning system.
3. Disconnect the boot-type wire connector from pressure cut off switch.
4. Disconnect the 3-pin connector from the ECCS.
5. Remove the attaching bolt at the center of the refrigerant plumbing sealing plate.
6. Pull the refrigerant lines assembly away from the expansion valve. Cover the exposed ends of the lines to minimize contamination.
7. Remove the 2 screws that mount the expansion valve to the evaporator sealing plate.
8. Remove the valve and discard the gaskets.

To install:

9. Remove and replace the aluminum gasket on the evaporator sealing plate.
10. Carefully hold the expansion valve sealing plate and torque the 2 screws to 100 inch lbs.
11. Remove and replace the aluminum gasket on the refrigerent line sealing plate.
12. Connect the refrigerant lines and sealing plate, tighten to 200 inch lbs. (23 Nm).
13. Connect the electrical leads and connect the negative battery cable.
14. Evacuate and properly recharge the air conditioning system.

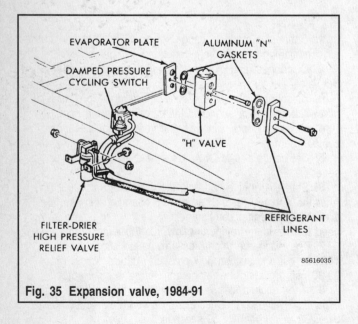

Fig. 35 Expansion valve, 1984-91

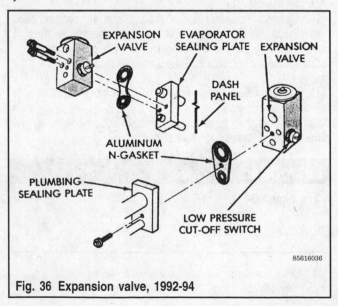

Fig. 36 Expansion valve, 1992-94

AUXILIARY HEATER/AIR CONDITIONER

▶ See Figure 37

Expansion Valve

REMOVAL & INSTALLATION

1. Disconnect the negative battery cable.
2. Properly discharge the air conditioning system.
3. Remove the middle bench, if equipped. Remove the interior left lower quarter trim panel.
4. Remove the 7 screws that attach the air distribution duct to the floor and unit. Pull the distribution duct straight up to remove.
5. Remove the 6 screws from the top surface of the unit and remove the unit cover.
6. Remove the bolt that secures the refrigerant lines to the evaporator sealing plate and separate the parts. Discard the gasket. Cover the exposed ends of the lines to minimize contamination.
7. Pull the evaporator and expansion valve straight up in order to clear the extension tube pilots and remove from the vehicle. Cover the exposed ends of the lines to minimize contamination.
8. Remove the Torx® screws and remove the expansion valve from the evaporator. Discard the gasket.

To install:

9. Remove and replace the aluminum gasket on the evaporator sealing plate.
10. Carefully hold the expansion valve sealing plate and torque the 2 screws to 100 inch lbs.
11. Remove and replace the aluminum gasket on the refrigerent line sealing plate.
12. Connect the refrigerant lines and sealing plate, tighten to 200 inch lbs. (23 Nm).
13. Install the unit cover and air distribution duct.
14. Install the interior trim cover and middle bench.

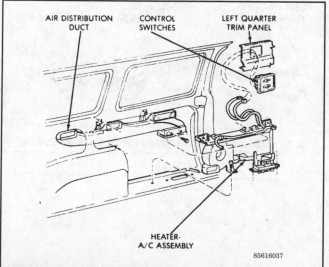

AIR DISTRIBUTION DUCT   CONTROL SWITCHES   LEFT QUARTER TRIM PANEL

HEATER-A/C ASSEMBLY

85616037

Fig. 37 Rear air conditioning/heater components

15. Evacuate and recharge the air conditioning system.
16. Connect the negative battery cable and check the entire climate control system for proper operation and leaks.

Blower Motor

REMOVAL & INSTALLATION

1. Disconnect the negative battery cable.
2. Remove the middle bench, if equipped. Remove the left lower quarter trim panel.
3. Remove 1 blower scroll cover to floor screw and 7 scroll to unit screws.
4. Remove the blower relay.
5. Rotate the blower scroll cover from under the unit.
6. Remove the fan from the blower motor, remove the 3 motor attaching screws and remove the motor from the unit.
7. The installation is the reverse of the removal procedure.
8. Connect the negative battery cable and check the blower motor for proper operation.

Blower Motor Resistor

REMOVAL & INSTALLATION

1. Disconnect the negative battery cable.
2. Remove the middle bench, if equipped. Remove the left lower quarter trim panel.
3. Disconnect the wiring harness from the resistor.
4. Remove the screws that attach the resistor to the rear unit and remove the resistor.
5. The installation is the reverse of the removal procedure.
6. Connect the negative battery cable and check for proper operation.

Heater Core

REMOVAL & INSTALLATION

1. Disconnect the negative battery cable. Pinch off the hoses to the rear heater core.
2. Raise the vehicle and support safely. Disconnect the underbody heater hoses from the rear heater core tubes.
3. Remove the middle bench, if equipped. Remove the interior left lower quarter trim panel.
4. Remove the 7 screws that attach the air distribution duct to the floor and unit. Pull the distribution duct straight up to remove.
5. Remove the 6 screws from the top surface of the unit and remove the unit cover.
6. Pull the heater core straight up and out of the unit.
7. The installation is the reverse of the removal procedure.
8. Connect the negative battery cable and check for leaks.

Evaporator

REMOVAL & INSTALLATION

1. Disconnect the negative battery cable.
2. Properly discharge the air conditioning system.
3. Remove the unit cover and duct.
4. Remove the middle bench, if equipped. Remove the interior left lower quarter trim panel.
5. Remove the 7 screws that attach the air distribution duct to the floor and unit. Pull the distribution duct straight up to remove.
6. Remove the 6 screws from the top surface of the unit and remove the unit cover.
7. Pull the evaporator and expansion valve straight up in order to clear the extension tube pilots and remove from the vehicle. Cover the exposed ends of the lines to minimize contamination.
8. Remove the Torx® screws and remove the expansion valve from the evaporator. Discard the gasket.
To install:
9. Lubricate the gasket with wax-free refrigerant oil and assemble the expansion valve and evaporator.
10. Lubricate the gasket with wax-free refrigerant oil and install the evaporator and expansion valve assembly to the refrigerant lines and install the bolt.
11. Install the unit cover and air distribution duct.
12. Install the interior trim cover and middle bench.
13. Evacuate and recharge the air conditioning system. If the evaporator was replaced, measure the amount of oil that was in the original evaporator and add that amount during the recharge.
14. Connect the negative battery cable and check the entire climate control system for proper operation and leaks.

Refrigerant Lines

▶ **See Figures 38 and 39**

REMOVAL & INSTALLATION

1. Disconnect the negative battery cable.
2. Properly discharge the air conditioning system.
3. Raise the vehicle and support safely.
4. Remove the nuts or bolts that attach the refrigerant line sealing plates to the adjoining components. If the lines are connected with flare nuts, use a back-up wrench when disassembling. Cover the exposed ends of the lines to minimize contamination.

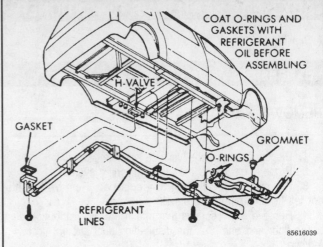

Fig. 39 Rear air conditioner assembly underbody line routing

5. Remove the support mount.
6. Remove the lines and discard the gaskets or O-rings.
To install:
7. Coat the new gaskets or O-rings with wax-free refrigerant oil and install. Connect the refrigerant lines to the adjoining components and tighten the nuts or bolts.
8. Install the support mount.
9. Evacuate and recharge the air conditioning system.
10. Connect the negative battery cable and check the entire climate control system for proper operation and leaks.

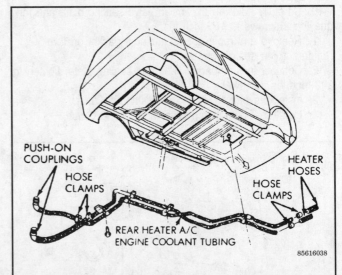

Fig. 38 Rear heater assembly, underbody hose routing

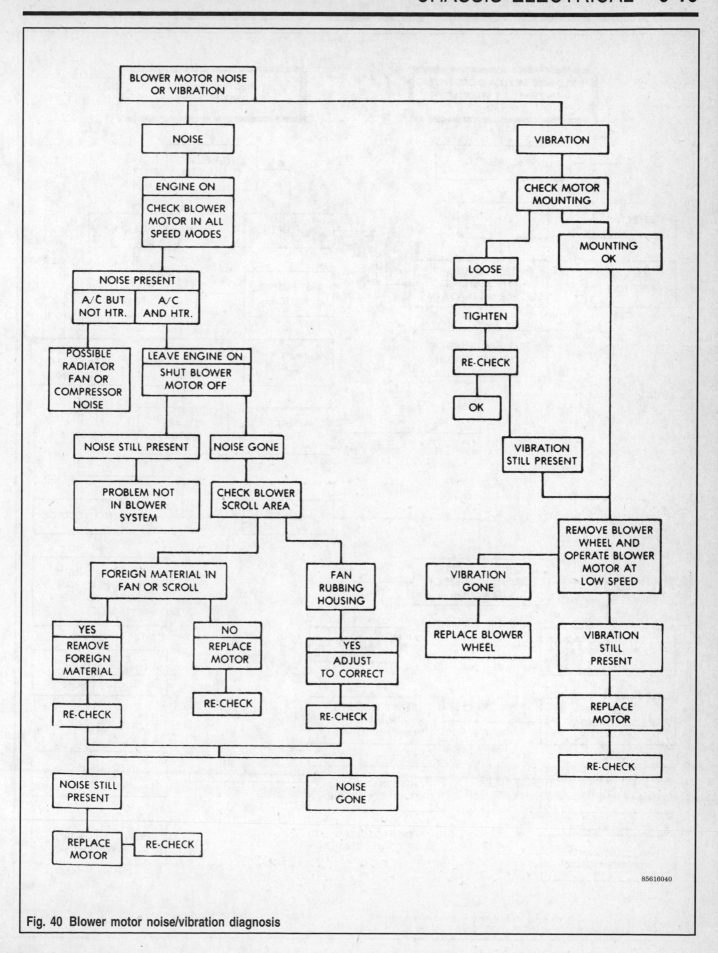

Fig. 40 Blower motor noise/vibration diagnosis

85616040

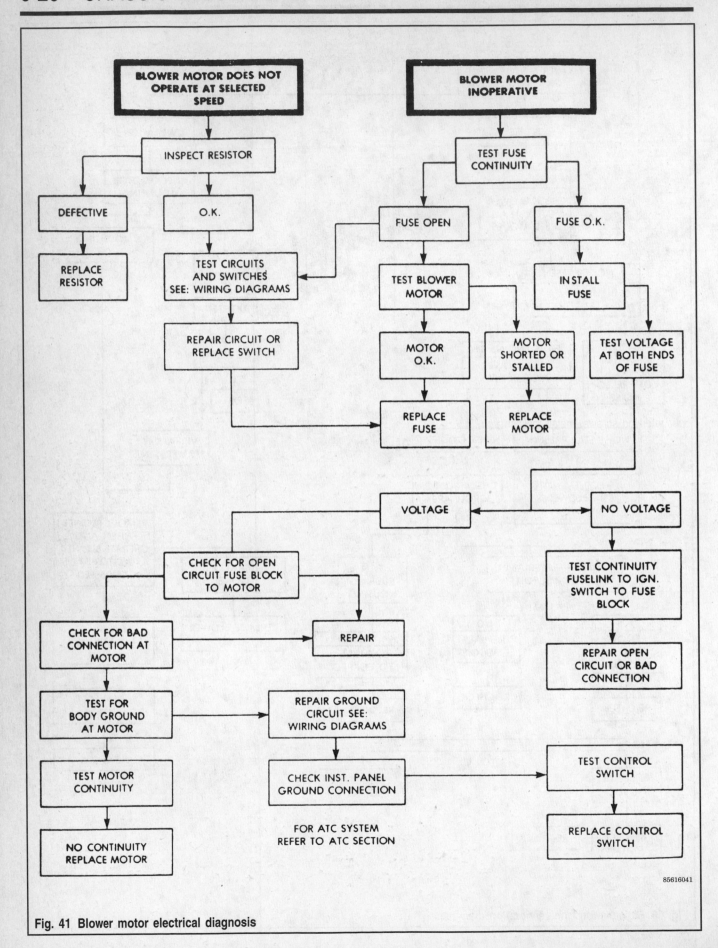

Fig. 41 Blower motor electrical diagnosis

85616041

RADIO

REMOVAL & INSTALLATION

▶ **See Figures 42, 43, 44, 45, 46, 47, 48, 49 and 50**

1. Disconnect the negative battery cable.
2. Remove the control knobs by pulling them from the mounting stalks.
3. Remove the three (3) screws from the top of the radio trim bezel.
4. Remove the ash tray to gain access to the trim bezel lower screws.
5. Remove the two (2) screws from the lower portion of the trim bezel.
6. Pull outward on the left side of bezel to unsnap the mounting clips. Remove the bezel.
7. Remove the radio to instrument panel retaining screws.
8. Pull the radio through the front of the instrument panel and unplug the wiring harness, ground strap and antenna plug.
9. Connect the radio wiring harness, ground strap and antenna lead.
10. Position the radio into the instrument panel and install the retaining screws.
11. Install the trim bezel and secure it with the lower and upper retaining screws. Install the ash tray.

Antenna

▶ **See Figure 51**

REMOVAL & INSTALLATION

1. Remove the radio.
2. Disconnect the antenna cable from the radio.

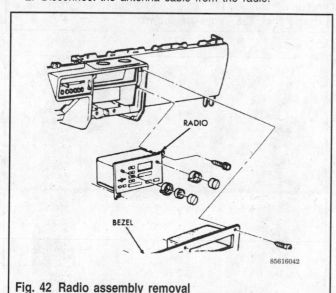

Fig. 42 Radio assembly removal

Fig. 43 Pull the radio control knobs off of the shafts, 1987 Voyager shown

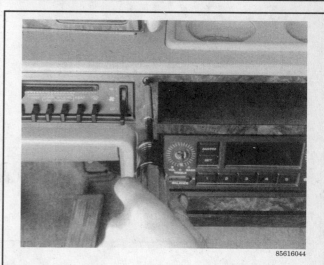

Fig. 44 Removing the trim bezel 3 upper retaining screws, 1987 Voyager shown

3. Remove the antenna cable from the harness retaining clips.
4. Unscrew the antenna mast from the upper adapter.
5. Remove the cap mounting nut.
6. Remove the adapter and mounting gasket.
7. From beneath the fender remove the antenna lead and body assembly.
8. Install the new antenna body and cable assembly from under fender.
9. Install the adapter gasket, adapter and cap nut.
10. Install the antenna cable through harness mounting clips and install the cable into radio receiver.
11. Install the radio into the instrument panel.

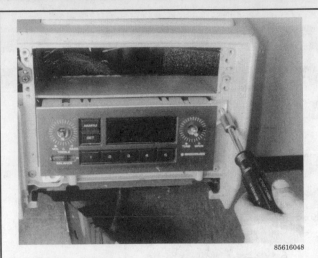

Fig. 45 Remove the ash tray to gain access to the lower trim bezel retaining screws, 1987 Voyager shown

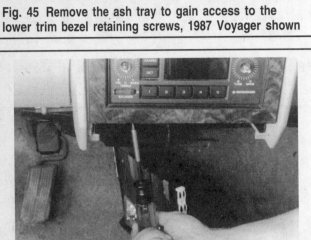

Fig. 46 Remove the 2 lower trim bezel retaining screws, 1987 Voyager shown

Fig. 47 Unsnap from the mounting clips and remove the trim bezel from the dash panel, 1987 Voyager shown

Fig. 48 Removing the radio to instrument panel retaining screws, 1987 Voyager shown

Fig. 49 After removing the radio to instrument panel retaining screws, the radio can be pulled out from the dash panel, 1987 Voyager shown

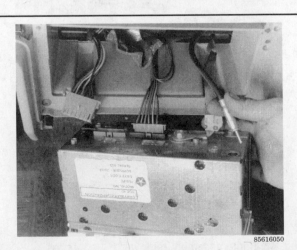

Fig. 50 Pull the radio through the front of the instrument panel and unplug the wiring harness, ground strap and antenna plug, 1987 Voyager shown

WINDSHIELD WIPERS

♦ See Figure 52

Wiper Blade

Refer to 'General Information and Maintenance' for removal and installation procedure.

Wiper Arm (Windshield)

REMOVAL & INSTALLATION

♦ **See Figures 53, 54, 55, 56 and 57**

1. Remove the head cover from the wiper arm base.
2. Remove the arm to pivot attaching nut.
3. Remove the wiper arm from pivot using a rocking motion.
4. With the wiper motor in Park position, position the arm on the pivot shaft. Choose a point where the tip of the left wiper arm is approximately 2 to 3 inches above the windshield cowl top, and the right arm 1 to 1.5 inches above the windshield cowl top.
5. Install the attaching nut and torque to 120 in. lbs.
6. Install the pivot head cover on the wiper arm.

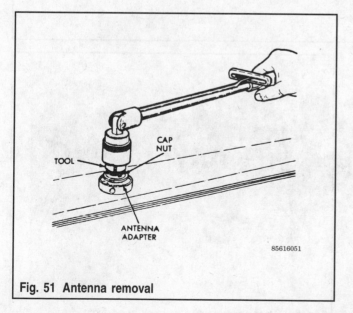

Fig. 51 Antenna removal

Wiper Arm (Liftgate)

♦ See Figure 58

REMOVAL & INSTALLATION

1. Insert Tool C-3982 or the equivalent between the wiper arm and wiper motor output shaft.

➡**The use of screwdrivers or other prying tool may damaged the spring clip in the base of the arm, while trying to release the arm. Damage of the spring clip will result in the arm coming off the shaft regardless of how carefully it is installed.**

2. Lift the arm and remove it from motor output shaft.
3. With motor in the Park position, position the arm on the motor output shaft. Choose a point where the tip of blade is about 38mm parallel with the bottom lower edge of liftgate glass. Push the wiper arm onto the motor shaft.

Windshield Wiper Motor

REMOVAL & INSTALLATION

♦ **See Figures 59, 60, 61 and 62**

1. The motor and wiper linkage are serviced as a unit. Disconnect the negative battery cable. Remove the wiper arm and blade assemblies. Refer to the windshield wiper arm removal and installation procedure in this section.
2. Open the hood and remove the cowl plenum grille and plastic screen.
3. Remove the hoses from the turret connector. Remove the pivot mounting screws.
4. Disconnect the motor wiring connector from the motor.
5. Remove the retaining nut from the wiper motor shaft to linkage drive crank, and remove the drive crank from the wiper motor shaft.
6. Remove the wiper motor assembly mounting screws and nuts, and remove the wiper motor.
   To install:
7. Position the wiper motor against it's mounting surface and secure in position with the mounting screws and nuts Connect the wiring harness.
8. Install the linkage drive crank onto the wiper motor shaft and secure it with the retaining nut. Torque the nut to 95 in. lbs.
9. Install cowl plenum grille plastic screen.
10. Connect hoses to turret connector.
11. Install the cowl plenum grille. Connect the negative battery cable. Close the hood.
12. Install the windshield wiper arm and blade assemblies.

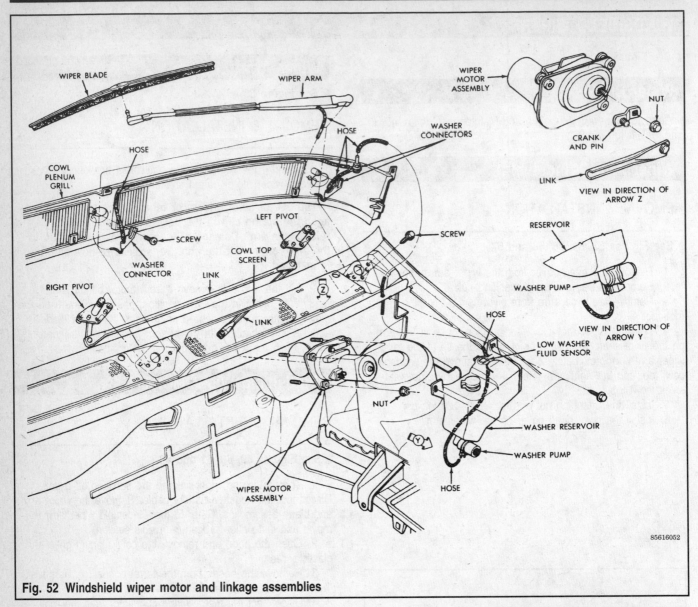

Fig. 52 Windshield wiper motor and linkage assemblies

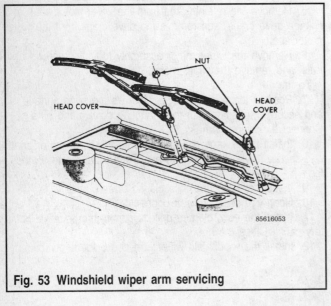

Fig. 53 Windshield wiper arm servicing

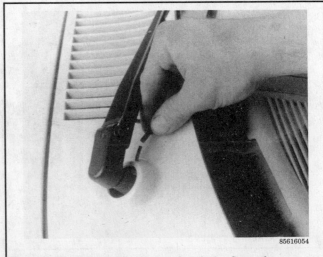

Fig. 54 Disconnecting the washer hose from the connector, 1987 Voyager shown

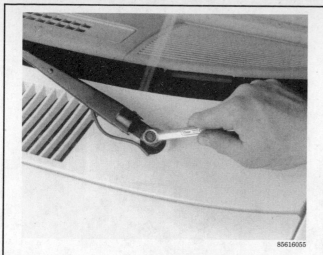

Fig. 55 Removing the wiper arm retaining nut, 1987 Voyager shown

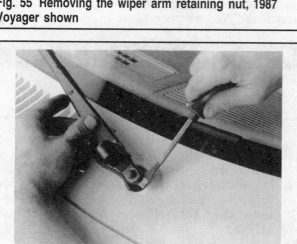

Fig. 56 After removing the wiper arm retaining nut, carefully pry off the base of the arm from the shaft, using a suitable prying tool, 1987 Voyager shown

Fig. 57 The wiper arm shown removed from the right pivot shaft, 1987 Voyager shown

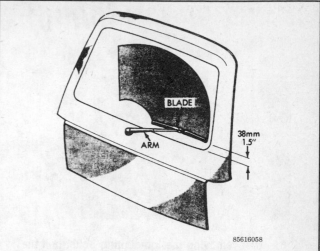

Fig. 58 1984-91 liftgate wiper arm installation, on 1992-94 models the measurement is 3.5 inches

Fig. 59 Remove the wiper motor harness connector, 1987 Voyager shown

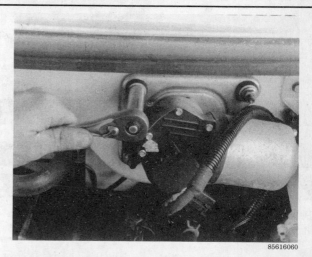

Fig. 60 Removing the wiper motor mounting screws, 1987 Voyager shown

Fig. 61 After removing the 3 mounting bolts, pull the wiper motor away enough to expose the linkage, 1987 Voyager shown

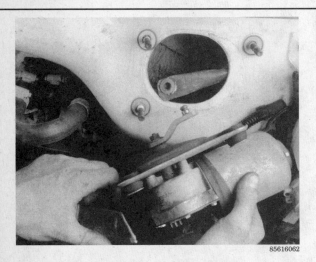

Fig. 62 Disconnect the arm from the linkage and remove the wiper motor, 1987 Voyager shown

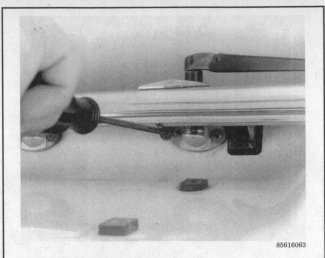

Fig. 63 Disconnecting the wiper linakge pivot retaining screws, 1987 Voyager shown

Liftgate Wiper Motor

REMOVAL & INSTALLATION

1. Disconnect the negative battery cable. Remove the wiper arm and blade assembly.
2. Open the liftgate and remove the trim panel.
3. Remove the four (4) mounting screws from liftgate wiper motor and bracket assembly.
4. Disconnect the electrical harness connector and remove the liftgate motor.
   To install:
5. Install the liftgate wiper motor and bracket assembly. Secure it with the mounting screws.
6. Connect the wiring harness to the wiper motor.
7. Install the liftgate trim panel and secure it with the mounting screws.
8. Install the liftgate wiper arm and blade assembly.

Windshield Wiper Linkage

▶ See Figures 59, 60, 61, 62 and 63

Refer to the Wiper Motor procedures in this section.

INSTRUMENTS AND SWITCHES

Instrument Cluster Assembly

❋❋WARNING

Before servicing the instrument cluster or components, disconnect the negative battery.

REMOVAL & INSTALLATION

1984-90
▶ See Figures 64 and 65

1. Disconnect the negative battery cable.
2. Remove the cluster assembly bezel mounting (7) screws and remove the cluster bezel.
3. On vehicles equipped with an automatic transaxle, remove the steering column lower cover.
4. Disconnect the shift indicator wire.

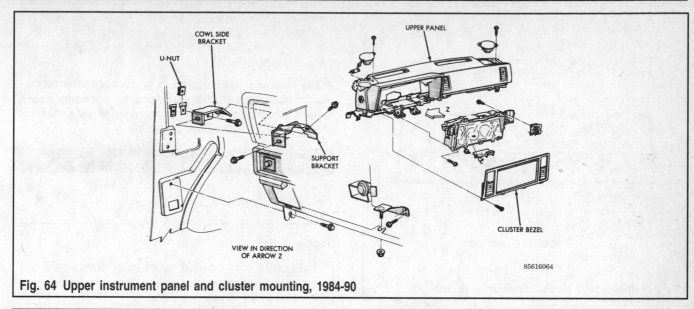

Fig. 64 Upper instrument panel and cluster mounting, 1984-90

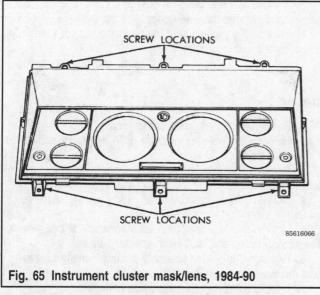

Fig. 65 Instrument cluster mask/lens, 1984-90

5. Remove the cluster assembly retaining screws.

6. Remove the cluster assembly retaining screws.

7. Carefully pull the cluster assembly from the panel and disconnect the speedometer cable.

8. Remove the cluster assembly wiring harness.

9. Remove the cluster assembly past the right side of the steering column.

To install:

10. Position the cluster assembly to the dash from the right side of the steering column.

11. Connect the cluster wiring.

12. Connect the speedometer cable.

13. Install the cluster assembly and retaining screws.

14. On models equipped with an automatic transaxle, place the selector lever in (D) Drive position.

15. Connect the shift indicator wire to the steering column shift housing. Route the wire on the outside of slotted flange.

16. Place the shift lever in (P) Park position to make the indicator self-adjust.

17. Connect the shift indicator wire.

18. Install the steering column lower cover.

19. Install the cluster assembly bezel. Secure the bezel with the retaining screws.

➡The following instruments can be serviced after removing the instrument cluster mask/lens. Do not completely remove the cluster assembly if only instrument service or cluster bulb replacement is necessary.

1991-94

◗ See Figures 66, 67 and 68

1. Disconnect the negative battery cable.

2. Remove the warning indicator grille by prying up with a flat bladed tool.

3. Remove the 3 mounting screws from the warning indicator module assembly and disconnect the wire connector.

4. On vehicles equipped with an automatic transaxle, remove the steering column lower cover.

5. On vehicles equipped with an automatic transaxle, set the parking brake and shift gear selector into low.

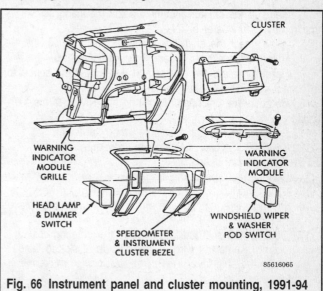

Fig. 66 Instrument panel and cluster mounting, 1991-94

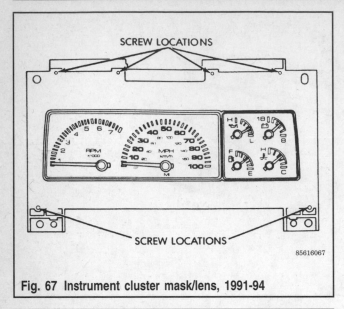

Fig. 67 Instrument cluster mask/lens, 1991-94

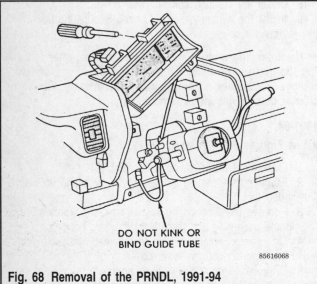

DO NOT KINK OR
BIND GUIDE TUBE

85616068

Fig. 68 Removal of the PRNDL, 1991-94

6. Remove the cluster assembly bezel mounting screws and remove the cluster bezel.

7. Disconnect the shift indicator wire.

8. Remove the cluster assembly retaining screws.

9. Carefully rotate the cluster and disconnect the connector, to access the PRNDL attaching screws.

10. Remove the 2 screws attaching the PRNDL to the cluster.

11. Remove the cluster assembly wiring harness.

12. To install, reverse the removal procedure.

13. Connect the cluster wiring.

14. Connect the speedometer cable.

15. Install the cluster assembly and retaining screws.

16. On models equipped with an automatic transaxle, place the selector lever in (D) Drive position.

17. Connect the shift indicator wire to the steering column shift housing. Route the wire on the outside of slotted flange.

18. Place the shift lever in (P) Park position to make the indicator self-adjust.

19. Connect the shift indicator wire.

20. Install the steering column lower cover.

21. Install the cluster assembly bezel. Secure the bezel with the retaining screws.

→ **The following instruments can be serviced after removing the instrument cluster mask/lens. Do not completely remove the cluster assembly if only instrument service or cluster bulb replacement is necessary.**

Fuel Gauge

REMOVAL & INSTALLATION

1984-90

1. Disconnect the negative battery cable. Remove the cluster bezel retaining screws and remove the cluster bezel.

2. Remove the cluster mask/lens.

3. Remove the fuel gauge attaching screws to cluster assembly and remove the fuel gauge.

4. Position the replacement gauge to the cluster assembly and secure it with attaching screws.

5. Install the cluster mask/lens, bezel and bezel retaining screws.

1991-94

1. Disconnect the negative battery cable.

2. Remove the warning indicator grille by prying up with a flat bladed tool.

3. Remove the 3 mounting screws from the warning indicator module assembly and disconnect the wire connector.

4. On vehicles equipped with an automatic transaxle, remove the steering column lower cover.

5. On vehicles equipped with an automatic transaxle, set the parking brake and shift gear selector into low.

6. Remove the cluster assembly bezel mounting screws and remove the cluster bezel.

7. Disconnect the POD switch wire connectors.

8. Remove the 4 screws attaching the gauge to the cluster and remove the fuel gauge.

9. Installation is the reverse of removal.

Voltmeter

REMOVAL & INSTALLATION

1984-90

1. Disconnect the negative battery cable. Remove the cluster bezel retaining screws and remove the cluster bezel.

2. Remove the cluster mask/lens.

3. Remove the voltmeter attaching screws to cluster assembly and remove the voltmeter.

4. Position the replacement voltmeter to cluster assembly and secure with the attaching screws.

5. Install the cluster mask/lens, bezel and bezel retaining screws.

1991-94

1. Disconnect the negative battery cable.
2. Remove the warning indicator grille by prying up with a flat bladed tool.
3. Remove the 3 mounting screws from the warning indicator module assembly and disconnect the wire connector.
4. On vehicles equipped with an automatic transaxle, remove the steering column lower cover.
5. On vehicles equipped with an automatic transaxle, set the parking brake and shift gear selector into low.
6. Remove the cluster assembly bezel mounting screws and remove the cluster bezel.
7. Disconnect the POD switch wire connectors.
8. Remove the 4 screws attaching the gauge to the cluster and remove the voltmeter.
9. Installation is the reverse of removal.

Temperature Gauge

REMOVAL & INSTALLATION

1984-90

1. Disconnect the negative battery cable. Remove the cluster bezel retaining screws and remove the cluster bezel.
2. Remove the cluster mask/lens.
3. Remove the temperature/oil pressure gauge attaching screws to cluster assembly and remove the temperature gauge.
4. Position the replacement temperature/oil pressure gauge to cluster assembly and secure with the attaching screws.
5. Install the cluster mask/lens, bezel and bezel retaining screws.

1991-94

1. Disconnect the negative battery cable.
2. Remove the warning indicator grille by prying up with a flat bladed tool.
3. Remove the 3 mounting screws from the warning indicator module assembly and disconnect the wire connector.
4. On vehicles equipped with an automatic transaxle, remove the steering column lower cover.
5. On vehicles equipped with an automatic transaxle, set the parking brake and shift gear selector into low.
6. Remove the cluster assembly bezel mounting screws and remove the cluster bezel.
7. Disconnect the POD switch wire connectors.
8. Remove the 4 screws attaching the gauge to the cluster and remove the temperature gauge.
9. Installation is the reverse of removal.

Oil Pressure Gauge

REMOVAL & INSTALLATION

1984-90

1. Disconnect the negative battery cable. Remove the cluster bezel retaining screws and remove the cluster bezel.
2. Remove the cluster mask/lens.
3. Remove the oil pressure/temperature gauge attaching screws to cluster assembly and remove the temperature gauge.
4. Position the replacement oil pressure/temperature gauge to cluster assembly and secure with the attaching screws.
5. Install the cluster mask/lens, bezel and bezel retaining screws.

1991-94

1. Disconnect the negative battery cable.
2. Remove the warning indicator grille by prying up with a flat bladed tool.
3. Remove the 3 mounting screws from the warning indicator module assembly and disconnect the wire connector.
4. On vehicles equipped with an automatic transaxle, remove the steering column lower cover.
5. On vehicles equipped with an automatic transaxle, set the parking brake and shift gear selector into low.
6. Remove the cluster assembly bezel mounting screws and remove the cluster bezel.
7. Disconnect the POD switch wire connectors.
8. Remove the 4 screws attaching the gauge to the cluster and remove the oil pressure gauge.
9. Installation is the reverse of removal.

Printed Circuit Board

▶ **See Figures 69 and 70**

REMOVAL & INSTALLATION

1. Disconnect the negative battery cable.
2. Remove the instrument cluster from the instrument panel.
3. Remove the circuit board retaining screws.
4. Remove the lamp sockets, by twisting them out.
5. Carefully remove the circuit board.
6. Install the new circuit board in position and install the lamp sockets.
7. Connect the negative battery cable.

Cluster Lamp Bulbs

REMOVAL & INSTALLATION

1. Disconnect the negative battery cable. Remove the cluster bezel retaining screws and remove the cluster bezel.

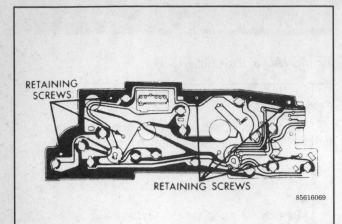

Fig. 69 Printed circuit board retaining screws, 1984-90

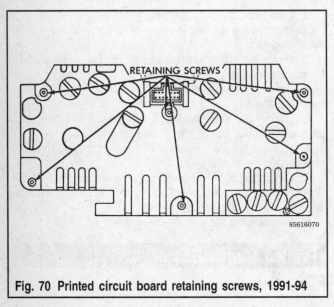

Fig. 70 Printed circuit board retaining screws, 1991-94

2. Remove the cluster mask/lens.
3. Remove the gauge assembly in front of blown bulbs and replace the bulbs.
4. Install the gauge to the cluster assembly.
5. Install the cluster mask/lens, bezel and bezel retaining screws.

Cluster Lamp Sockets

REMOVAL & INSTALLATION

All cluster lamp sockets are twist out sockets and are removed from the rear of the instrument cluster. Refer to Instrument Cluster Removal & Installation procedure in this section.

Instrument Panel (Lower)

REMOVAL & INSTALLATION

1984-90
▶ See Figure 71

✳✳CAUTION

Before servicing the lower instrument panel, chock the wheels. Servicing the steering column may cause an automatic transaxle to come out of the (P) Park position. Always release the parking brake before the release cable is disconnected. Disconnecting the parking brake cable without releasing the parking brake may cause personal injury.

1. Block the vehicle wheels and release the parking brake. Disconnect the negative battery cable.
2. Remove the steering column lower left cover.
3. Remove the side cowl and the sill molding.
4. Remove the instrument panel silencer and reinforcement.
5. Loosen the bolt in the side cowl, but do not remove the bolt.
6. Place the gear selector into the (N) Neutral position and disconnect the shift indicator cable.
7. Remove the steering wheel.
8. Remove the (5) nuts securing the steering column to the support bracket.
9. Lower the steering column. Use a cover to protect the steering column and the front seat.
10. Remove the right side instrument panel trim molding.
11. Remove the (9) screws securing the lower panel to the upper panel and mid-reinforcement.
12. Lower the instrument panel approximately six inches.
13. Disconnect the park brake release cable, heater attachment or air conditioning control cables, antenna and wiring connectors from the radio and fresh air ducts.
14. Disconnect the electrical connections and label them with tape for identification.
15. Pry the A-pillar garnish off the door opening weatherstrip at the panel bolt.
16. Pull the weatherstrip from the body and remove the lower panel from the vehicle.
To install:
17. Position the lower panel into the vehicle.
18. Install the weatherstrip and garnish molding.
19. Connect the park brake release cable, heater attachment or air conditioning control cables, antenna and wiring connectors to the radio and fresh air ducts.
20. Connect all electrical connections.
21. Secure the lower instrument panel to upper panel and mid-reinforcement with (9) retaining screws.
22. Install the right side instrument panel trim molding.
23. Raise the steering column and install the (5) nuts securing steering column to the support bracket.
24. Install the steering wheel.
25. Connect the shift indicator cable.
26. Install the lower reinforcement, silencer and the lower left steering column cover. Connect the negative battery cable.

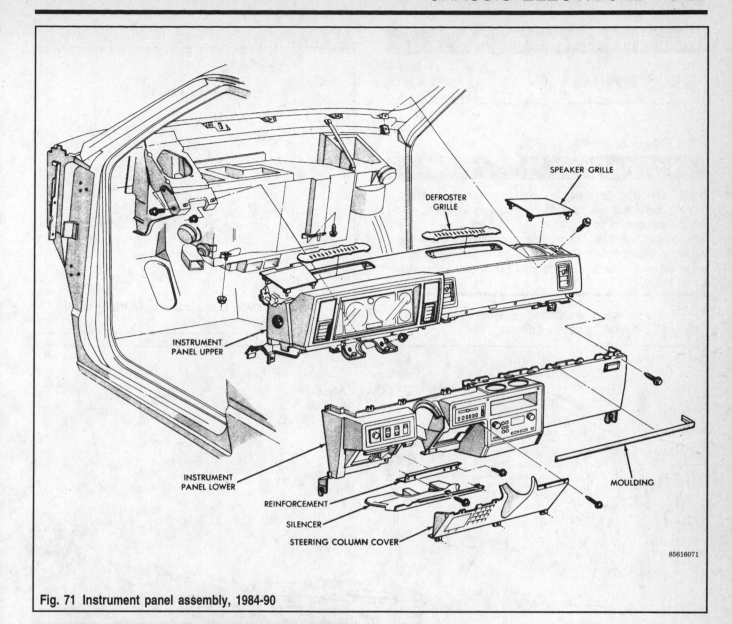

Fig. 71 Instrument panel assembly, 1984-90

Instrument Panel (Upper)

▶ See Figure 71

REMOVAL & INSTALLATION

1984-90

1. Disconnect the negative battery cable. Separate the lower instrument panel from the upper half (see Steps 1 through 12 of the Lower Instrument Panel procedure).
2. Disconnect the speedometer cable from the engine compartment.
3. Remove (2) nuts at the steering column floating bracket.
4. Disconnect the gear shift selector indicator wire.
5. Disconnect the electrical connector at the radio speakers.
6. Remove the radio speaker and defroster grilles.
7. Remove the (2) mounting screws from each side cowl brackct.

8. Remove the (4) upper panel attaching screws from the defroster duct slots and the (2) screws next to the radio speakers.
9. Pull the panel and disconnect the speedometer cable from the speedometer.
10. Remove upper instrument panel from vehicle.
To install:
11. Position the upper instrument panel into the vehicle.
12. Connect the speedometer cable.
13. Install the (6) upper panel attaching screws.
14. Install the cowl bracket retaining screws.
15. Install the radio speaker and defroster grilles.
16. Connect the radio speaker wiring.
17. Connect the gear shift selector indicator wire.
18. Install the retaining nuts at the steering column floating bracket.
19. Connect the speedometer cable in the engine compartment.
20. Install the lower panel to the upper.

Instrument Panel Assembly

REMOVAL & INSTALLATION

1991

▶ See Figures 72 and 73

❊❊CAUTION

Before servicing the lower instrument panel, chock the wheels. Servicing the steering column may cause an automatic transaxle to come out of the (P) Park position.   Always release the parking brake before the release cable is disconnected. Disconnecting the parking brake cable without releasing the parking brake may cause personal injury.

1. Block the vehicle wheels and release the parking brake. Disconnect the negative battery cable.

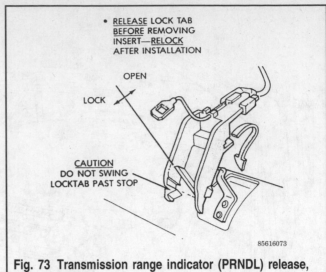

● RELEASE LOCK TAB <u>BEFORE</u> REMOVING INSERT—<u>RELOCK</u> AFTER INSTALLATION

OPEN

LOCK

CAUTION
DO NOT SWING
LOCKTAB PAST STOP

85616073

Fig. 73 Transmission range indicator (PRNDL) release, 1991-93

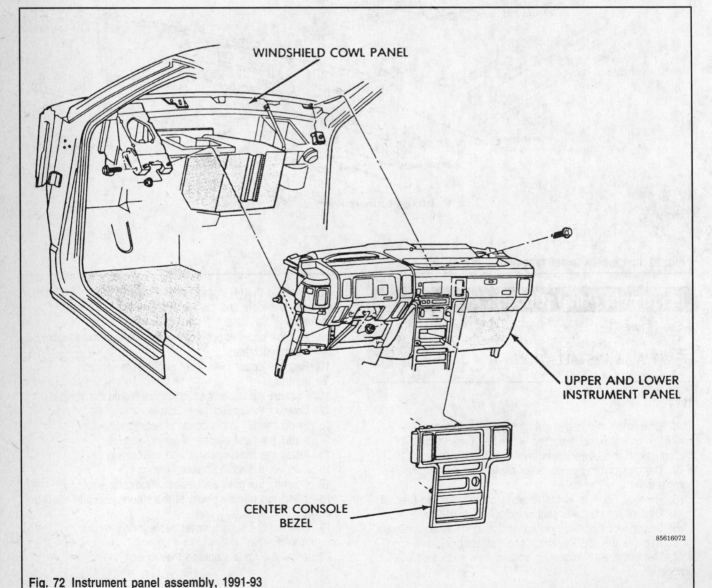

WINDSHIELD COWL PANEL

UPPER AND LOWER INSTRUMENT PANEL

CENTER CONSOLE BEZEL

85616072

Fig. 72 Instrument panel assembly, 1991-93

2. Remove the steering column lower left cover.

3. Disconnect the PRNDL at the column.

4. Remove the steering column.

5. Remove the lower right instrument panel silencer.

6. Remove the forward console if necessary.

7. Remove the instrument panel speaker grilles.

8. Remove the A-pillar intermediate and sill scuff garnish mouldings.

9. Unfasten the hood release mechanism from the side cowl.

10. Unfasten the parking brake handle bracket.

11. Disconnect the parking brake light switch, parking brake switch and bulk head wiring connectors.

12. Under the hood disconnect the ABS connector and resistor block. Unseat the grommet at the dash panel and feed the wiring back into the passenger compartment.

13. Remove the 2 nuts securing the instrument panel at the steering column support brace.

14. Loosen the instrument panel roll up bolts.

15. Remove the screws securing the instrument panel at the left cowl side ramp bracket.

16. Remove the 6 screws securing the instrument panel at the fence line.

17. Lift upward on the instrument panel to clear the roll up ramp. Roll the instrument panel back and hang it from the short position of the roll up hook.

18. With the instrument panel hanging in this position, disconnect the left and right side body wiring connections, vacuum lines and cables.

19. Remove the instrument panel from the vehicle.

20. To install, reverse the above removal steps.

1992-94
▶ See Figures 72, 73 and 74

✳✳CAUTION

Before servicing the lower instrument panel, chock the wheels. Servicing the steering column may cause an automatic transaxle to come out of the (P) Park position. Always release the parking brake before the release cable is disconnected. Disconnecting the parking brake cable without releasing the parking brake may cause personal injury.

1. Block the vehicle wheels and release the parking brake.

2. Disconnect the negative battery cable.

3. Remove the instrument panel cluster bezel.

4. Remove the lower right instrument panel.

5. Remove the lower left instrument panel silencer.

6. Remove the steering column lower left cover.

7. Remove the premium console or module cover.

8. Remove the lower left reinforcement.

9. Remove the floor braces.

10. Remove the steering column.

11. Remove the lower right instrument panel silencer.

12. Remove the premium console or module cover.

13. Remove the A-pillar intermediate and sill scuff garnish mouldings.

14. Unfasten the hood relaese mechanism from the side cowl.

15. Unfasten the parking brake handle bracket.

16. Disconnect the parking brake light switch, parking brake switch and bulk head wiring connectors.

17. Under the hood disconnect the ABS connector and resistor block. Unseat the grommet at the dash panel and feed the wiring back into the passenger compartment.

18. Remove the 2 nuts securing the instrument panel at the steering column support brace.

19. Loosen the instrument panel roll up bolts.

20. Remove the screws securing the instrument panel at the left cowl side ramp bracket.

21. Remove the 6 screws securing the instrument panel at the fence line.

22. Lift upward on the instrument panel to clear the roll up ramp. Roll the instrument panel back and hang it from the short position of the roll up hook.

23. With the instrument panel hanging in this position, disconnect the left and right side body wiring connections, vacuum lines and cables.

24. Remove the instrument panel from the vehicle.

25. To install, reverse the above removal steps.

Forward Console

▶ See Figure 75

REMOVAL & INSTALLATION

1. Remove the cigar lighter and ash receiver.

2. Remove the retaining screws securing the forward console to the upper mounting bracket.

3. Remove the retaining screws securing the forward console to the lower bracket.

4. Pull the console rearward and disconnect the cigar lighter and illumination electrical wiring connectors.

5. Remove the forward console from vehicle.

6. Position the forward console into the vehicle.

7. Connect the cigar lighter and illumination wiring connectors.

8. Install the console lower bracket retaining screws.

9. Install the console upper bracket retaining screws.

10. Install the cigar lighter and ash receiver.

Windshield Wiper Switch

The windshield wiper switch is a stalk mounted control on all except 1991 models. On 1991 models, the wiper switch is mounted on the instrument cluster pod along with the rear wiper switch.

REMOVAL & INSTALLATION

1984-90 Models With Standard Steering Column
▶ See Figures 76 and 77

1. Disconnect negative battery cable.

2. Remove the steering wheel horn pad assembly.

3. Remove the lower steering column cover, silencer and reinforcement.

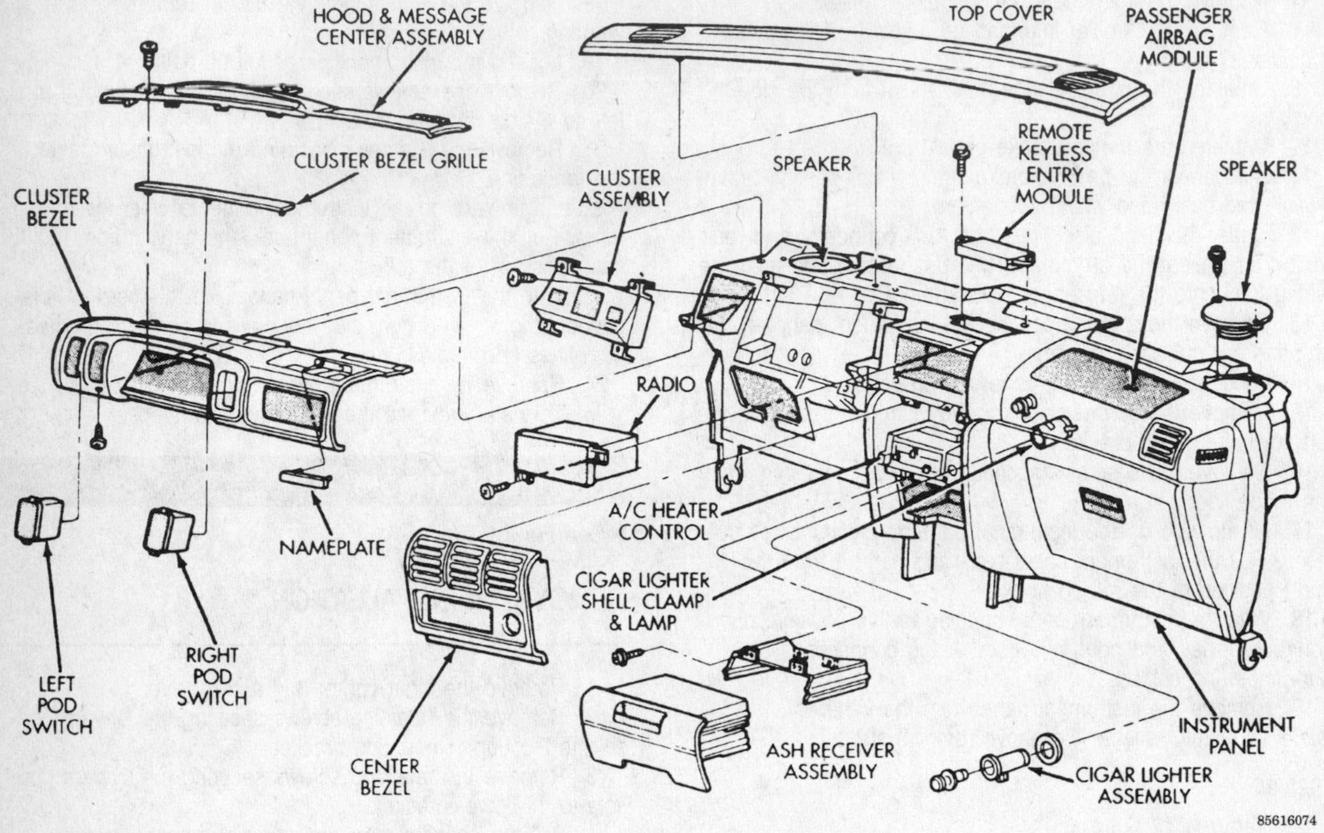

Fig. 74 Instrument panel assembly, 1994

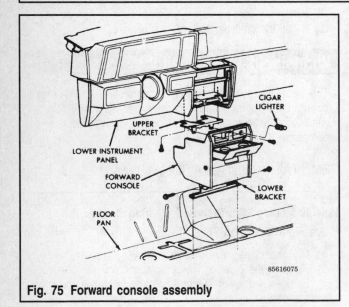

Fig. 75 Forward console assembly

4. Remove the wiper switch wiring harness from the steering column retainer.

5. Remove the wash/wipe switch cover. Rotate the cover upward.

6. Disconnect the wipe/wash seven terminal electrical connector. Disconnect intermittent the wipe switch electrical connector or speed control electrical connector, if equipped.

7. Unlock the steering column and turn the wheel so that the access hole provided in the wheel base is in the 9 o'clock position.

8. Reach through the access hole using a small screwdriver and loosen the turn signal lever mounting screw.

9. Remove the wipe/wash switch assembly the from steering column.

10. Slide the circular hider up the control stalk and remove the (2) screws that attach the control stalk sleeve to wipe/wash switch.

11. Remove the wipe/wash switch control knob from the multifunction control stalk. Rotate the control stalk to full clockwise position and pull the shaft from the switch.

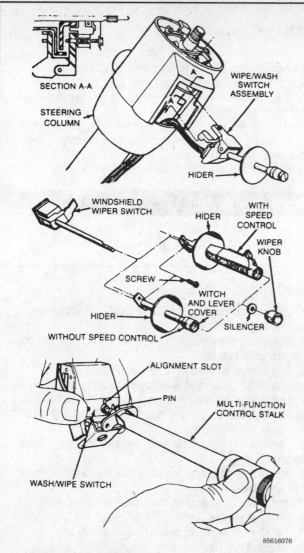

Fig. 76 Removing the wiper switch on the standard steering column, 1984-90

To install:

12. Install the stalk shaft into the wash/wipe switch and rotate full counterclockwise.

13. Install the wash/wipe switch control knob onto the end of the multifunction control stalk.

14. Install (2) retaining screws that secure the wipe/wash switch to the control stalk sleeve.

15. Install the wipe/wash switch assembly to the steering column.

16. Install and tighten the turn signal lever screw (through the access hole).

17. Connect the wipe/wash seven terminal electrical connector. Connect the intermittent wipe switch electrical connector or speed control electrical connector, if equipped.

18. Install the wash/wipe switch cover.

19. Secure the wiring harness into the steering column retainer.

20. Install the reinforcement, silencer and lower steering column cover.

21. Install the steering wheel horn pad assembly.

22. Connect the negative batter cable.

1984-90 Models With Tilt Steering Column
▶ **See Figure 77**

1. Disconnect the negative battery cable.

2. Remove the horn cover pad from the steering wheel. Remove steering column cover. Remove the steering wheel nut.

3. Remove the steering wheel using puller C-3428B or equivalent.

4. Carefully remove the plastic cover from the locking plate. Install locking plate depressing tool C-4156 or equivalent onto the steering shaft. Depress the locking plate and remove the retaining ring from the mounting groove using a small screwdriver. To avoid difficulty when removing the retaining ring, the full load of the upper bearing spring should not be relieved. Remove the locking plate, canceling cam, and upper bearing spring.

5. Remove the switch stalk actuator screw and arm.

6. Remove the hazard warning knob.

7. Disconnect the wipe/wash seven terminal electrical connector. Disconnect the intermittent wipe switch electrical connector or speed control electrical connector, if equipped.

8. Remove the turn signal switch (3) retaining screws.

9. Tape the connectors at end of the wiring to prevent snagging when removing. Place the shift bowl in low (1st) position. Remove the switch and wiring.

10. Remove the ignition key lamp located next to the hazard warning knob.

11. Insert a thin screwdriver into the lock release slot next to the lock cylinder mounting and depress the spring latch at the bottom of the slot. Remove the lock cylinder.

12. Insert a straightened paper clip or similar piece of wire with a hook bent on one end into the exposed loop of the wedge spring of key buzzer switch. Pull on the clip to remove both spring and switch.

➡ **If the wedge spring is dropped, it could fall into steering column, requiring complete disassembly of the column.**

13. Remove the column housing cover (3) screws and remove the housing cover.

14. Use a punch, and tap the wiper switch pivot pin from the lock housing. Use tape to hold the dimmer switch rod in place.

15. Remove the wipe/wash switch assembly.

16. Slide the circular hider up the control stalk and remove the (2) screws that attach the control stalk sleeve to the wipe/wash switch.

17. Remove the wipe/wash switch control knob from the multifunction control stalk. Rotate the control stalk to full clockwise position and pull the shaft from the switch.

To install:

18. Install the stalk shaft into the wash/wipe switch and rotate full counterclockwise.

19. Install the wash/wipe switch control knob on the end of the multifunction control stalk.

20. Install the (2) retaining screws that secure the wipe/wash switch to the control stalk sleeve.

21. Install the wipe/wash switch assembly to the steering column.

22. Install the wiper switch pivot pin.

23. Install the housing cover and secure with retaining screws.

24. Install the lock cylinder.
25. Assemble the wedge spring to key buzzer and install the key buzzer switch.
26. Install the ignition key lamp.
27. With the shift bowl in low (1st) position, install the turn signal switch and secure with retaining screws.
28. Connect the wipe/wash seven terminal electrical connector. Connect the intermittent wipe switch electrical connector or speed control electrical connector, if equipped.
29. Secure the wiring harness in retainer.
30. Install the hazard warning knob.
31. Install the switch stalk actuator screw and arm.
32. Install the locking plate, canceling cam, and upper bearing spring. Install the locking plate. Depress the locking plate with tool C-4156 or equivalent and install the retaining ring in groove of steering shaft. Install the plastic cover on locking plate.
33. Install the reinforcement, silencer and lower steering column cover.
34. Install the steering wheel and steering shaft nut.
35. Install the horn contact, horn pad and install the horn pad retaining screws.
36. Connect the negative battery cable.

1992-94

1. Disconnect the negative battery cable.
2. With tilt column, remove the tilt lever.
3. Remove both upper and lower steering column covers.
4. Remove the multi-function switch tamper proof mounting screws.
5. Pull the switch away from the column and loosen the connector screw. The screw will remain in the connector.
6. Remove the wiring connector from the multi-function switch.
   To install:
7. Install the wiring connector to the switch and tighten the connector retaining screw to 17 inch lbs.
8. Mount the multi-function switch to the column and tighten the retaining screws to 17 inch lbs.
9. With tilt column, install the tilt lever.

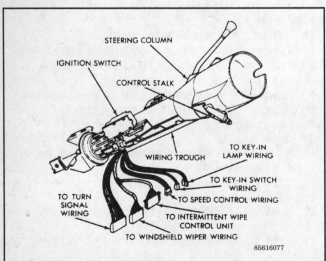

Fig. 77 Steering column wiring connector identification, 1984-90

10. Connect the negative battery cable.

1991 Models — Pod Mounted

1. Disconnect the negative battery cable.
2. Remove the cluster bezel retaining screws.
3. Tilt the steering column down, if equipped.
4. Pull the cluster bezel out enough to gain access to the switch retaining tabs.
5. Release the tabs and pull the switch from the cluster.
6. Install the switch in position and seat it firmly. Install the cluster bezel retaining screws.
7. Connect the negative battery cable.

Headlamp Switch

REMOVAL & INSTALLATION

1984-90

1. Disconnect the negative battery cable. Remove the headlamp switch plate bezel.
2. Remove the switch plate (4) retaining screws and pull the switch plate rearward.
3. Disconnect the electrical connectors. Remove the headlamp switch knob and shaft by depressing button on the switch body. Pull the knob and shaft out of the switch.
4. Remove the (2) screws retaining the headlamp switch to switch plate assembly.
5. Remove the headlamp switch retainer.
   To install:
6. Install the replacement switch into the headlamp switch plate with retainer.
7. Install the headlamp switch retaining screws to the switch plate assembly.
8. Install the headlamp switch knob and shaft.
9. Connect the electrical connectors.
10. Secure the headlamp switch plate with (4) attaching screws.
11. Install the headlamp switch plate bezel.

1991

On the 1991 models, the headlight switch is removed in the same manner as the windshield wiper switch. Refer to the windshield wiper switch removal procedure on these models.

1992-94

On these models, the left pod switch consists of the headlamp, parking lamp and hazard switches.
1. To remove the left POD switch, place a tool fabricated from a metal rod, shown in the illustration, in the hole right of the switch in the cluster bezel below the POD switch.
2. Move the tool to the lower tab and depress. Pull the switch out to free the lower tab.
3. Move the tool upward along the right side of the switch to place on the top tab. Pull down on the tab and pull the switch out of the bezel.
4. Disconnect the wire connector.
5. To install, connect the wire connector and push the switch into position until the tab locks in place.

Headlamp Dimmer Switch

REMOVAL & INSTALLATION

1984-90

➡ On 1991-94 models, the headlight dimmer switch is part of the turn signal, wiper (multi-function switch). Refer to the Wiper Switch removal and installation procedure outlined earlier in this Section

1. Remove the lower left steering column cover.
2. Tape the actuator control rod to prevent the rod from falling out.
3. Remove the dimmer switch retaining screws.
4. Disconnect the switch electrical connector and remove the switch.

5. Install a new switch and connect the electrical connector.
6. Position the actuator control rod into the dimmer switch and secure the switch onto the steering column.
7. Remove the tape from the actuator control rod.
8. Install the lower left steering column cover.

ADJUSTMENT

1984-90

1. Loosen the dimmer switch retaining screws.
2. Insert a 24mm drill bit or pin in the adjusting pin hole. Push the switch lightly against the control rod to remove free play. Tighten the switch retaining screws while maintaining light pressure on the dimmer switch.
3. Remove the drill bit or pin.

LIGHTING

Headlights

REMOVAL & INSTALLATION

Sealed Beam
▶ See Figure 78

1. Remove the headlight bezel retaining screws and remove the bezel.
2. Remove the headlamp retaining ring screws and remove the retaining ring. Do not disturb the headlamp adjusting crews.
3. Pull the sealed beam forward and disconnect the electrical connector.
4. Install the replacement beam and connect the electrical connector.

5. Install the retaining ring.
6. Install the headlight bezel.

Aerodynamic Headlamp
▶ See Figures 79, 80, 81, 82, 83, 84, 85, 86, 87 and 88

1. From the engine compartment, remove the three wire connector behind the headlamp assembly.
2. Rotate the bulb retaining ring counterclockwise and remove the retaining ring and lamp bulb.
3. Install the replacement bulb and retaining ring assembly. Rotate the ring clockwise.
4. Connect the three wire connector.

Signal and Marker Lights

REMOVAL & INSTALLATION

Front Park, Turn Signal and Side Marker
▶ See Figures 81, 82, 83 and 84

1. Remove the headlamp bezel retaining screws and remove the bezel.
2. Twist the bulb from the lamp socket.
3. Install the replacement bulb and twist into position.
4. Install the headlamp bezel and retaining screws.

Rear Tail, Stop, Turn Signal, Back Up, Side Marker and License Lamp
▶ See Figures 89, 90, 91, 92, 93 and 94

1. To replace the bulb, remove (4) attaching screws.
2. Pull out the lamp assembly. Twist the socket from the lamp and replace the bulb.
3. Install the replacement bulb and twist the socket into the lamp assembly.
4. Position the lamp assembly in place and secure with (4) attaching screws.

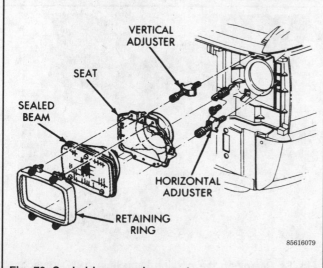

VERTICAL ADJUSTER

SEAT

SEALED BEAM

HORIZONTAL ADJUSTER

RETAINING RING

85616079

Fig. 78 Sealed beam replacement

Fig. 79 Removing the headlamp assembly bezel attaching screws, 1987 Voyager shown

Fig. 80 Removing the headlamp assembly bezel attaching screws, 1987 Voyager shown

Fig. 81 Removing the headlamp retaining bezel, 1987 Voyager shown

Fig. 82 Removing the headlamp retaining bezel, 1987 Voyager shown

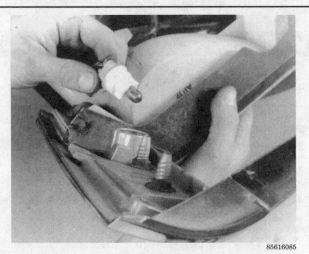

Fig. 83 Removing the side marker lamp bulb, 1987 Voyager shown

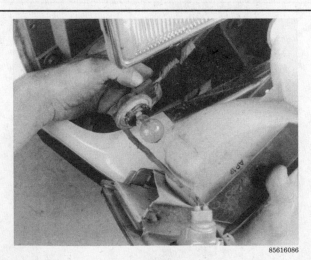

Fig. 84 Removing the parking lamp bulb, 1987 Voyager shown

Fig. 85 Disconnecting the wire connector from the back of the headlamp assembly, 1987 Voyager shown

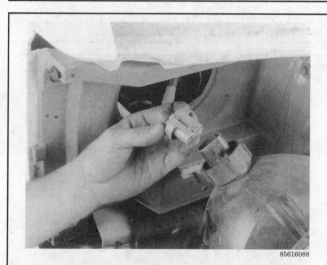

Fig. 86 Removing the wire connector from the back of the headlamp assembly, 1987 Voyager shown

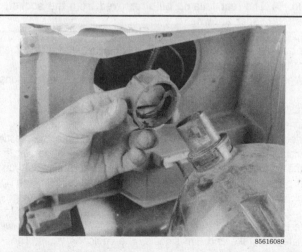

Fig. 87 Rotate counterclockwise and remove the ring from the back of the headlamp assembly, 1987 Voyager shown

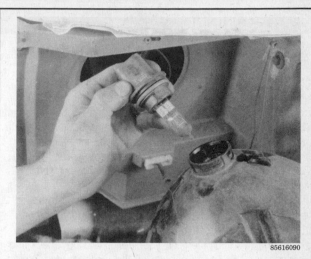

Fig. 88 Removing the bulb from the back of the headlamp assembly, 1987 Voyager shown

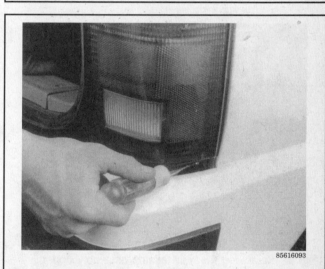

Fig. 89 Removing the rear tailamp assembly lower retaining screw, 1987 Voyager shown

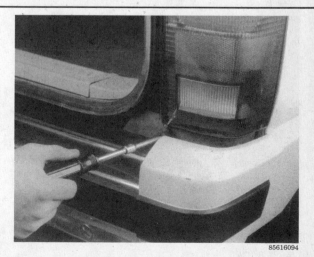

Fig. 90 Removing the rear tailamp assembly lower retaining screw, 1987 Voyager shown

TRAILER WIRING

Wiring the truck for towing is fairly easy. There are a number of good wiring kits available and these should be used, rather than trying to design your own. All trailers will need brake lights and turn signals as well as tail lights and side marker lights. Most states require extra marker lights for overly wide trailers. Also, most states have recently required back-up lights for trailers, and most trailer manufacturers have been building trailers with back-up lights for several years.

Additionally, some Class I, most Class II and just about all Class III trailers will have electric brakes.

Add to this number an accessories wire, to operate trailer internal equipment or to charge the trailer's battery, and you can have as many as seven wires in the harness.

Determine the equipment on your trailer and buy the wiring kit necessary. The kit will contain all the wires needed, plus a plug adapter set which included the female plug, mounted on

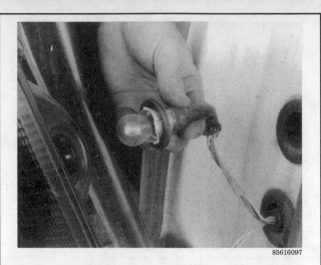

85616097

Fig. 93 Removing the rear tailamp bulb and socket assembly, 1987 Voyager shown

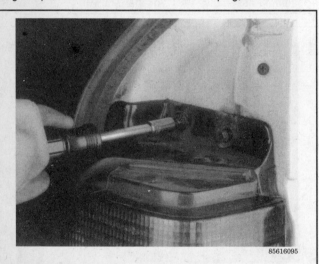

85616095

Fig. 91 Removing the rear tailamp assembly upper retaining screw, 1987 Voyager shown

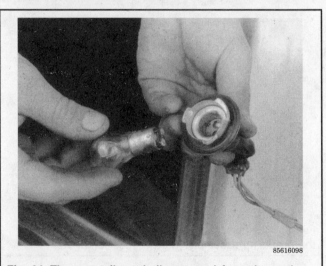

85616098

Fig. 94 The rear tailamp bulb removed from the socket, 1987 Voyager shown

85616096

Fig. 92 Removing the rear tailamp assembly, 1987 Voyager shown

the bumper or hitch, and the male plug, wired into, or plugged into the trailer harness.

When installing the kit, follow the manufacturer's instructions. The color coding of the wires is standard throughout the industry.

One point to note, some domestic vehicles, and most imported vehicles, have separate turn signals. On most domestic vehicles, the brake lights and rear turn signals operate with the same bulb. For those vehicles with separate turn signals, you can purchase an isolation unit so that the brake lights won't blink whenever the turn signals are operated, or, you can go to your local electronics supply house and buy four diodes to wire in series with the brake and turn signal bulbs. Diodes will isolate the brake and turn signals. The choice is yours. The isolation units are simple and quick to install, but far more expensive than the diodes. The diodes, however, require more work to install properly, since they require the cutting of each bulb's wire and soldering in place of the diode.

One final point, the best kits are those with a spring loaded cover on the vehicle mounted socket. This cover prevents dirt and moisture from corroding the terminals. Never let the vehicle socket hang loosely. Always mount it securely to the bumper or hitch.

CIRCUIT PROTECTION

Fuse Block

▶ **See Figure 95**

The fuse block and relay bank is located on the driver's side under the lower instrument panel. The fuse block contains fuses for various circuits as well as circuit breakers, horn relay, ignition lamp thermal time delay, and the turn signal flasher. The hazard warning flasher is mounted into a bracket below the fuse block. The individual fuse and relay locations can be found in the wiring diagrams at the end of this section.

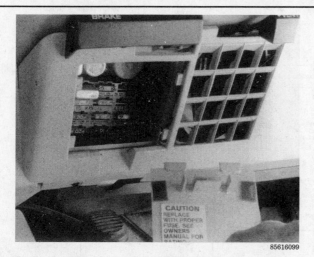

85616099

Fig. 95 The fuse box is located under a cover at the lower left instrument panel, 1987 Voyager shown

Fusible Links

The main wiring harnesses are equipped with fusible links to protect against harness damage should a short circuit develop.

Never replace a fusible link with standard wire. Only fusible link wire of the correct gauge with hypalon insulation should be used.

When a fusible link blows, it is very important to locate and repair the short. Do not just replace the link to correct the problem.

Always disconnect battery negative cable when servicing the electrical system.

REPLACEMENT

1. Disconnect the negative battery cable.
2. Cut off the remaining portion of the blown fusible link flush with the multiple connection insulator. Take care not to cut any of the other fusible links.
3. Carefully remove about one inch of insulation from the main harness wire at a point one inch away from the connection insulator.
4. Remove one inch of insulation from the replacement fusible link wire and wrap the exposed area around the main harness wire at the point where the insulation was removed.
5. Heat the splice with a high temperature soldering gun and apply resin type solder until it runs freely. Remove the soldering gun and confirm that a 'bright' solder joint has been made. Resolder if 'cold' (dull) joint.
6. Cut the other end of the fusible link off at a point just behind the small single wire insulator. Strip one inch of insulation from fusible link and connection wires. Wrap and solder.
7. After the connections have cooled, wrap the splices with at least three layers of electrical tape.

WIRING DIAGRAMS

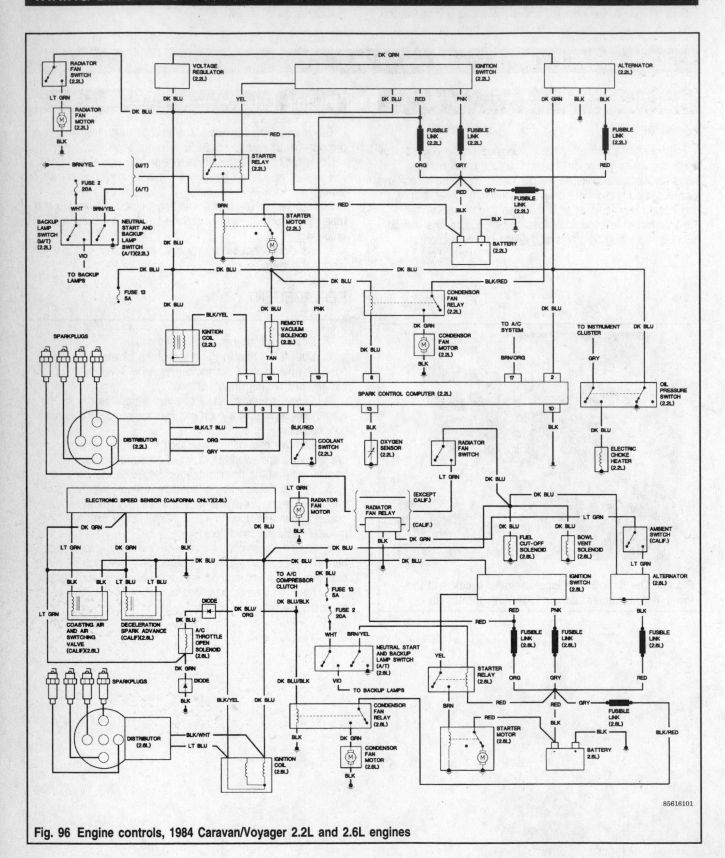

Fig. 96 Engine controls, 1984 Caravan/Voyager 2.2L and 2.6L engines

85616101

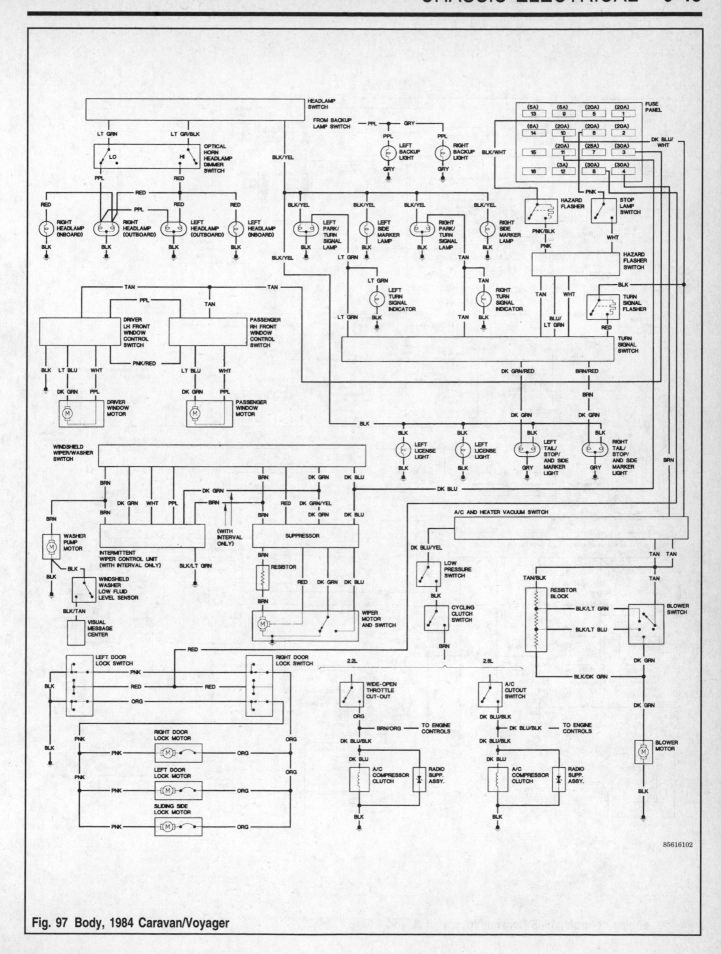

Fig. 97 Body, 1984 Caravan/Voyager

85616102

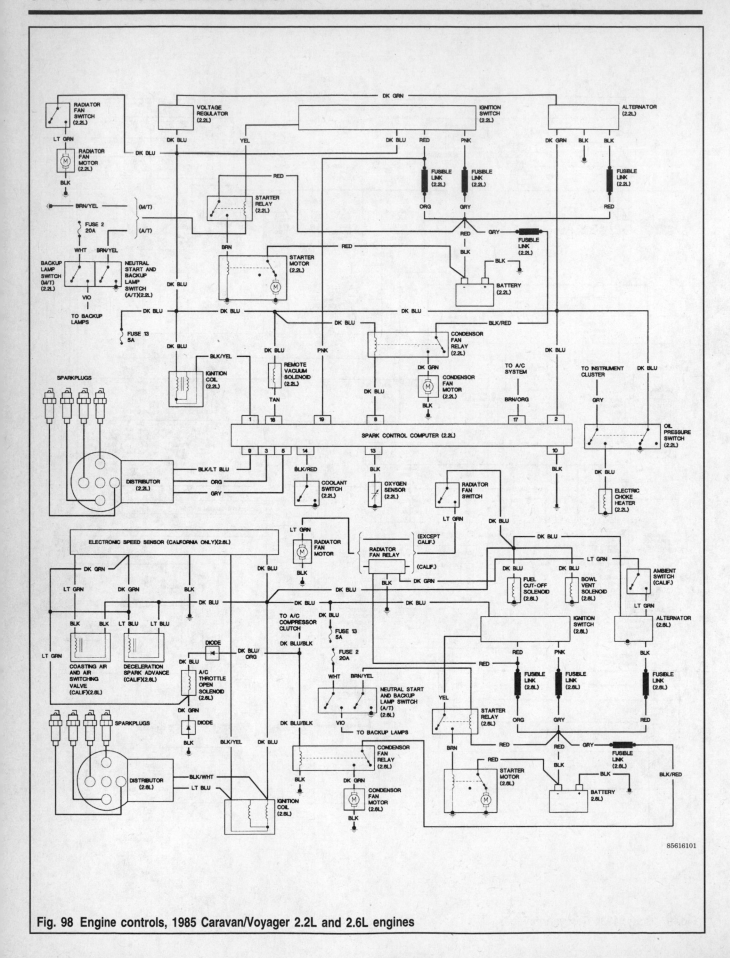

Fig. 98 Engine controls, 1985 Caravan/Voyager 2.2L and 2.6L engines

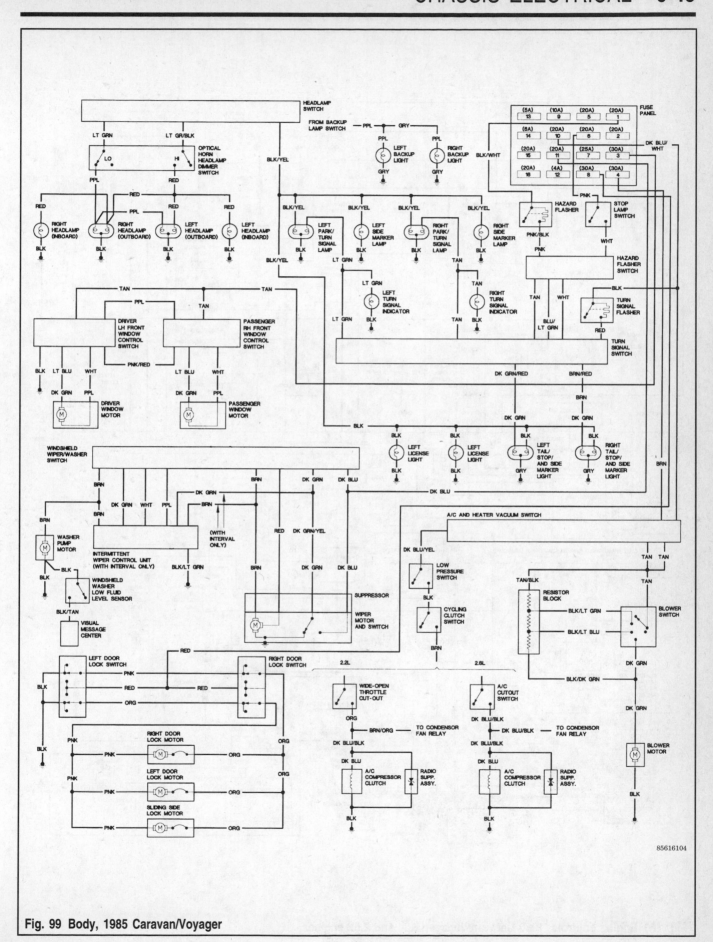

Fig. 99 Body, 1985 Caravan/Voyager

85616104

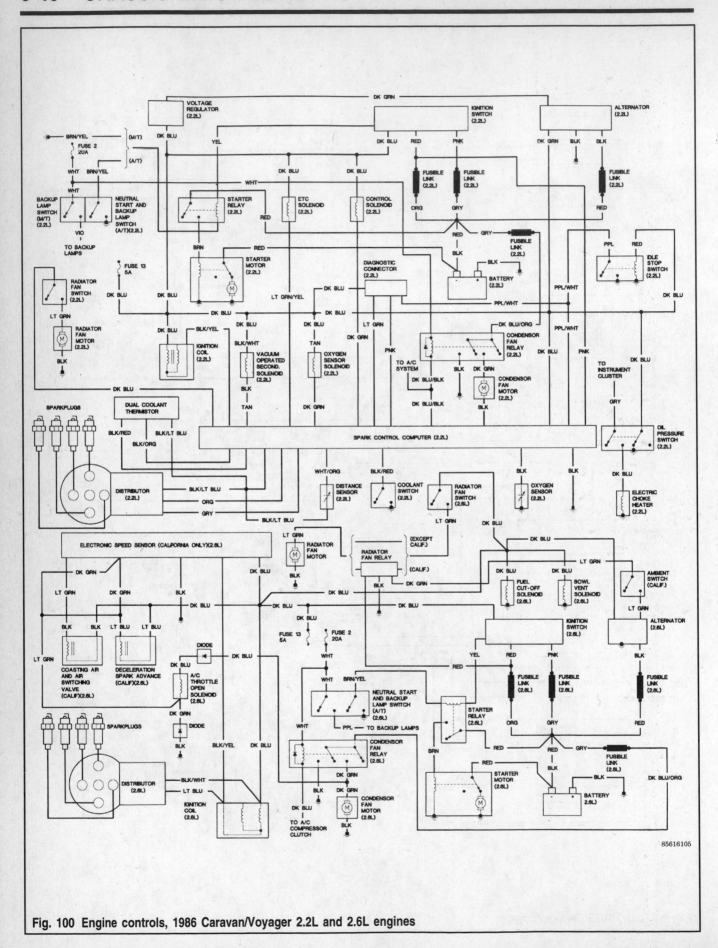

Fig. 100 Engine controls, 1986 Caravan/Voyager 2.2L and 2.6L engines

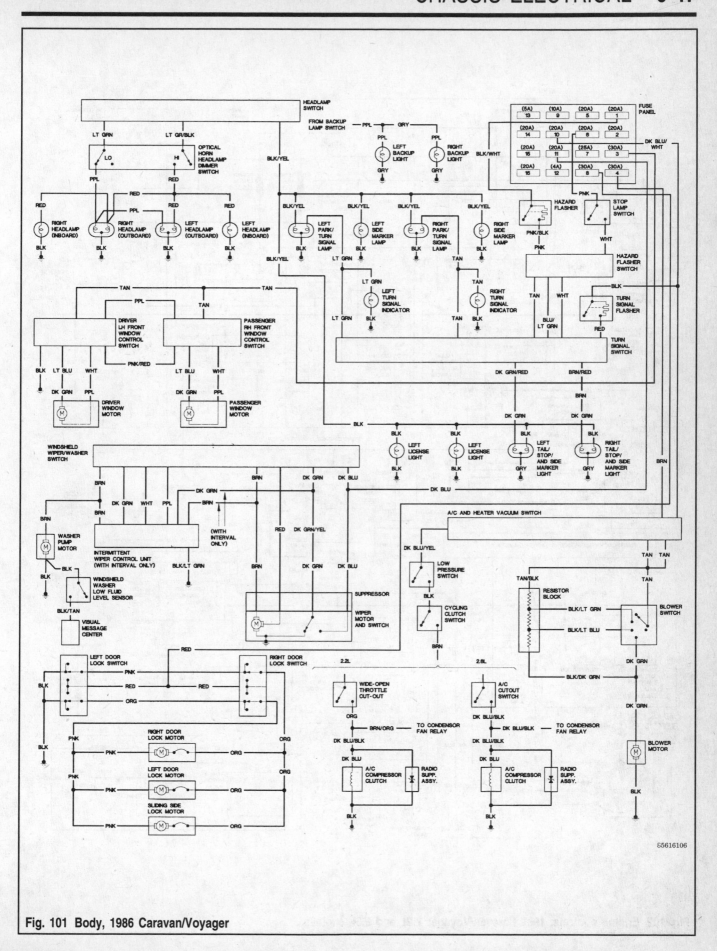

Fig. 101 Body, 1986 Caravan/Voyager

85616106

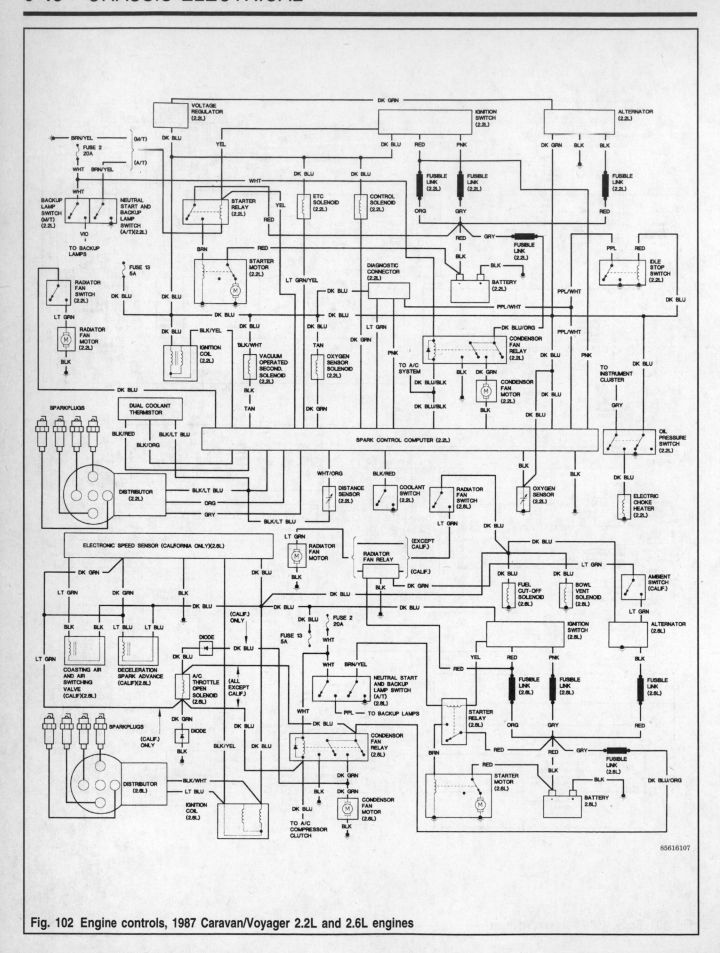

Fig. 102 Engine controls, 1987 Caravan/Voyager 2.2L and 2.6L engines

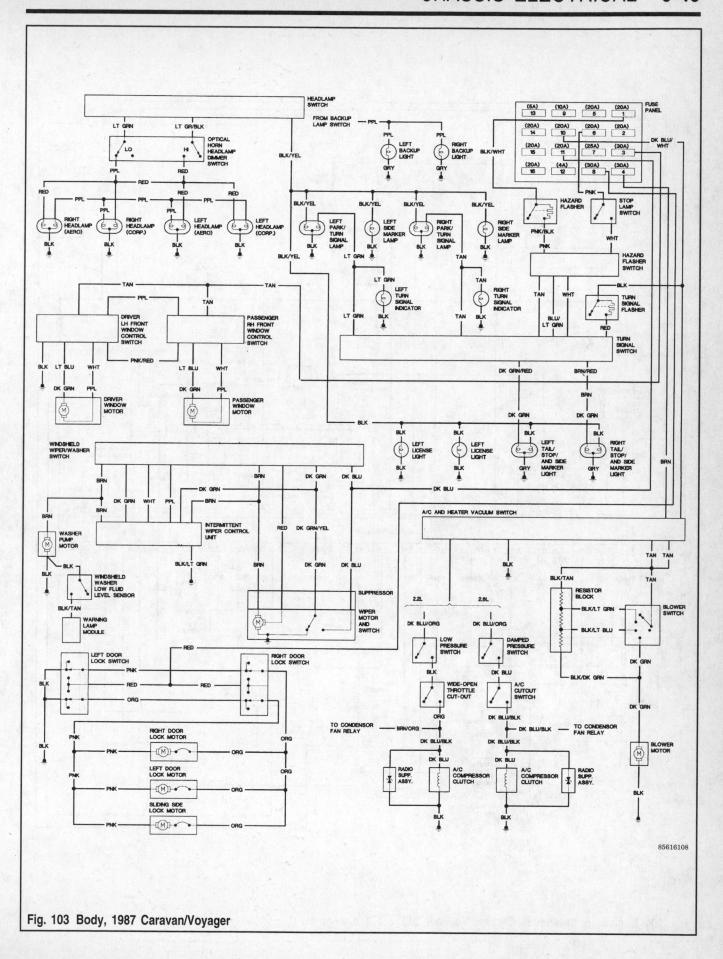

Fig. 103 Body, 1987 Caravan/Voyager

85616108

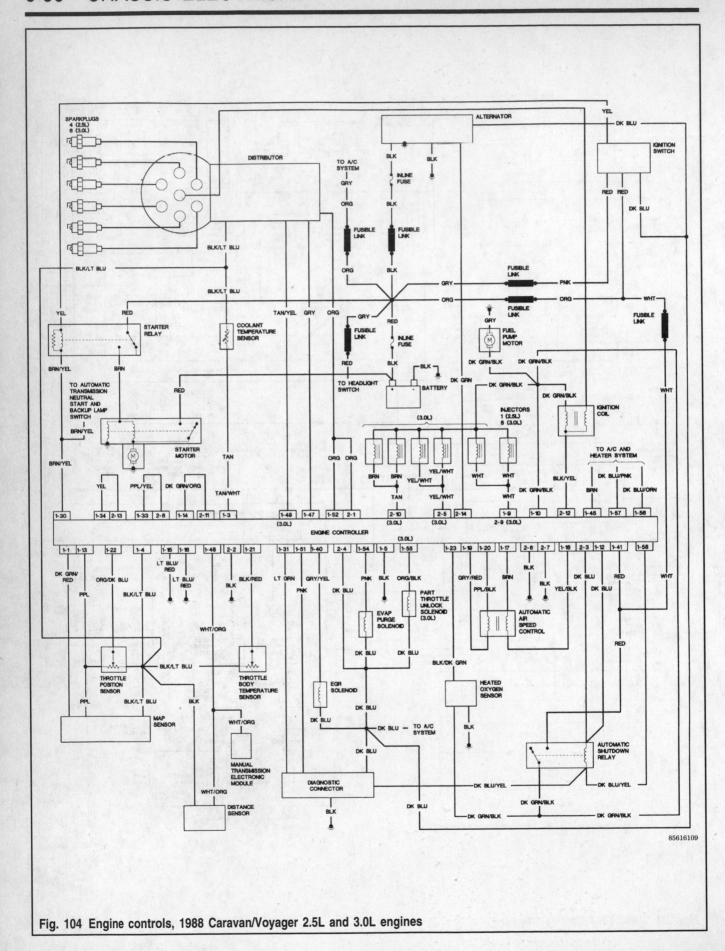

Fig. 104 Engine controls, 1988 Caravan/Voyager 2.5L and 3.0L engines

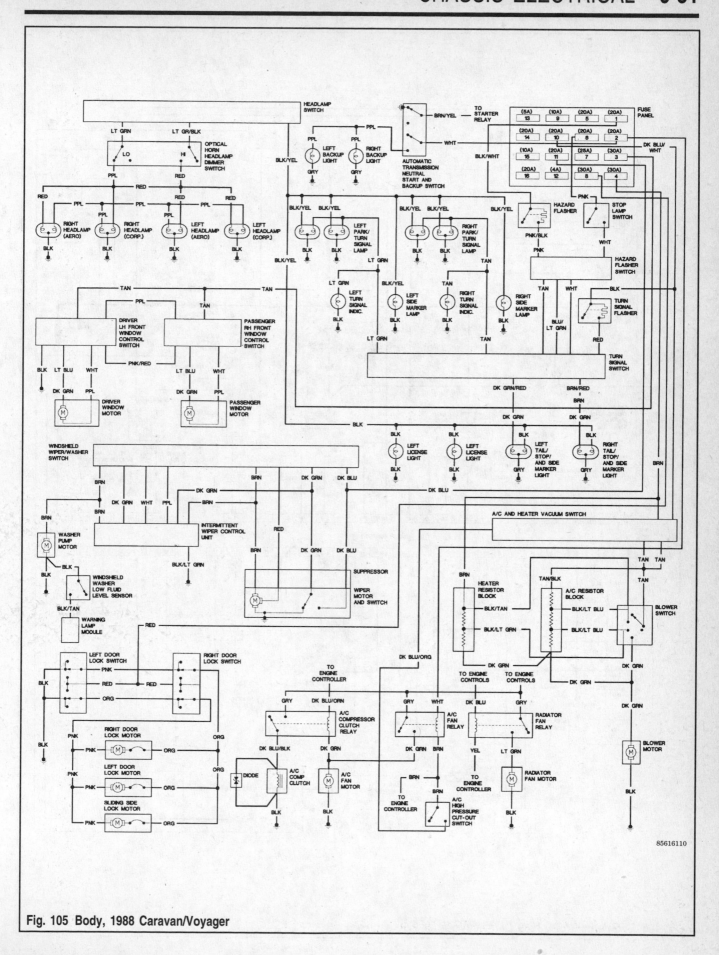

Fig. 105 Body, 1988 Caravan/Voyager

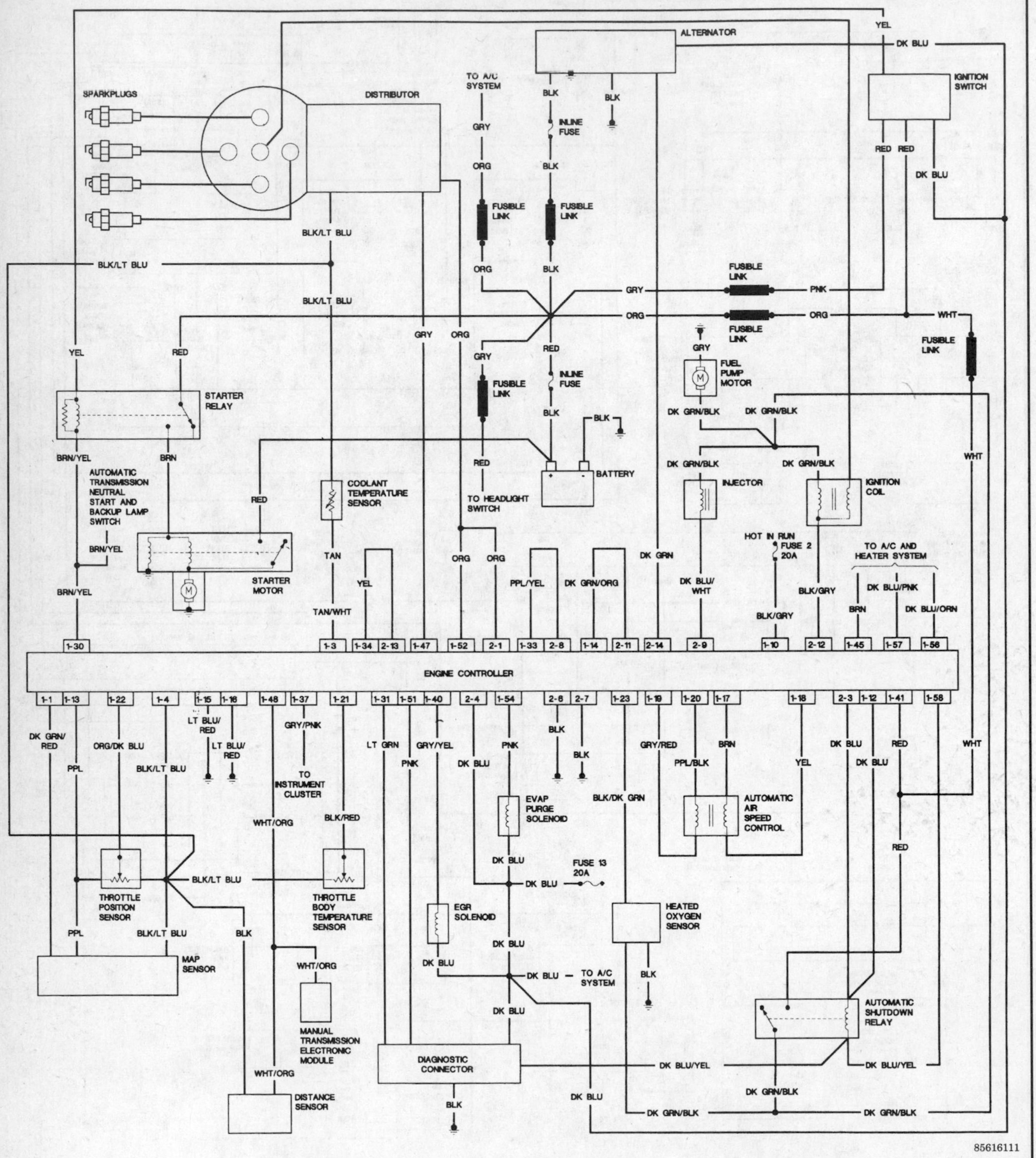

Fig. 106 Engine controls, 1989 Caravan/Voyager 2.5L engine

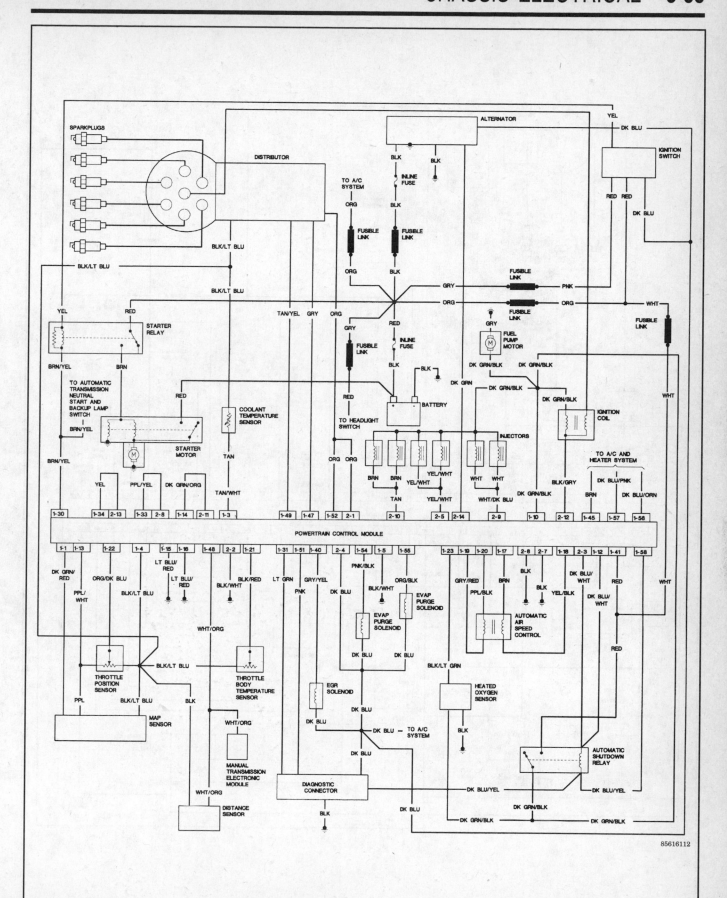

Fig. 107 Engine controls, 1989 Caravan/Voyager 3.0L engine

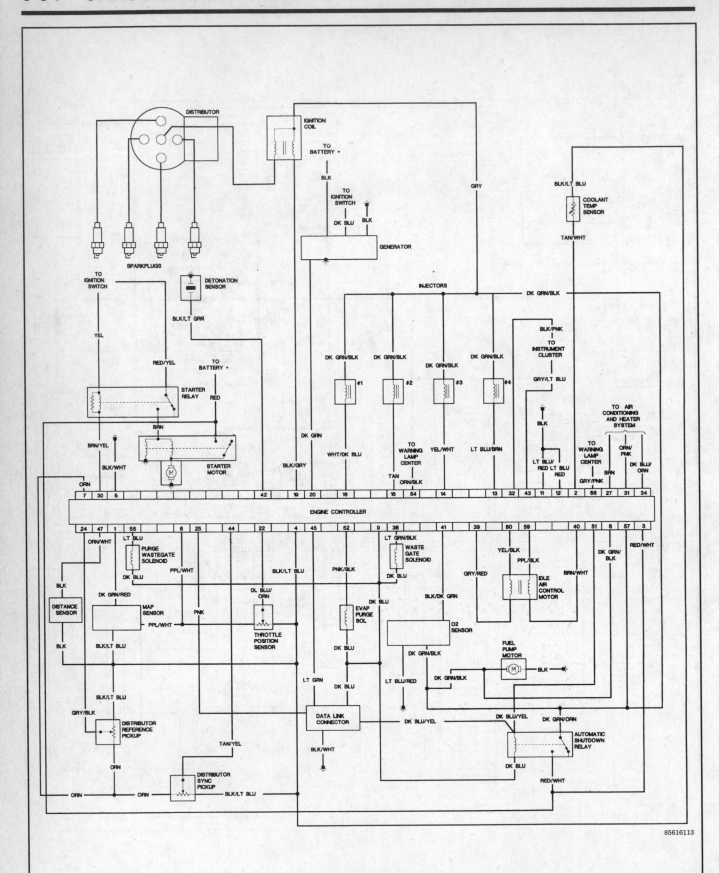

Fig. 108 Engine controls, 1989 Chrysler Town And Country, Caravan, Voyager, 2.5L turbo engine

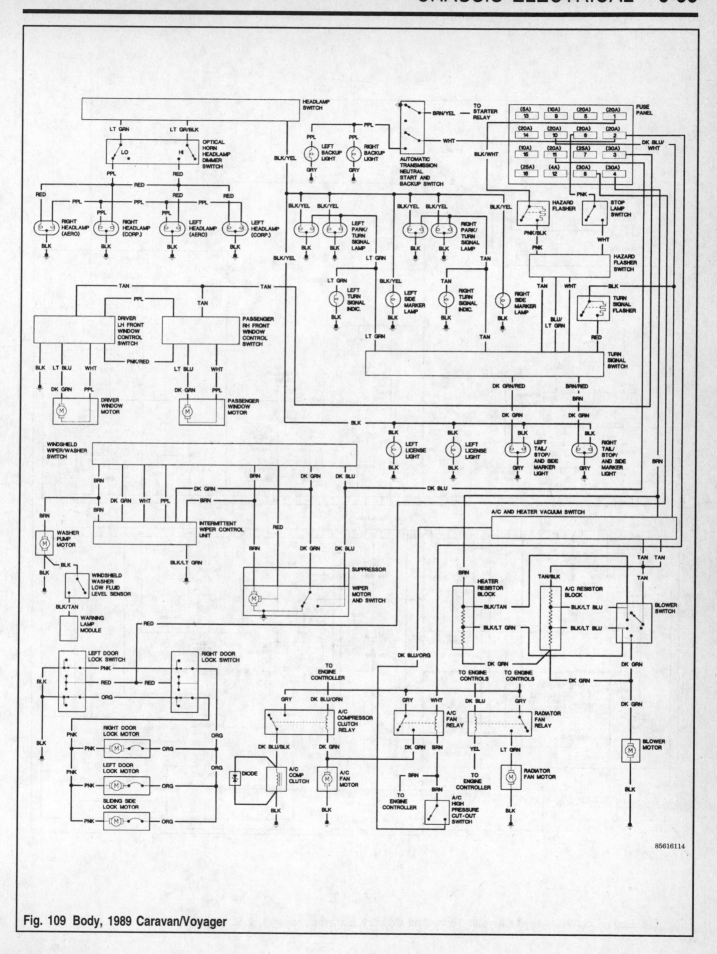

Fig. 109 Body, 1989 Caravan/Voyager

85616114

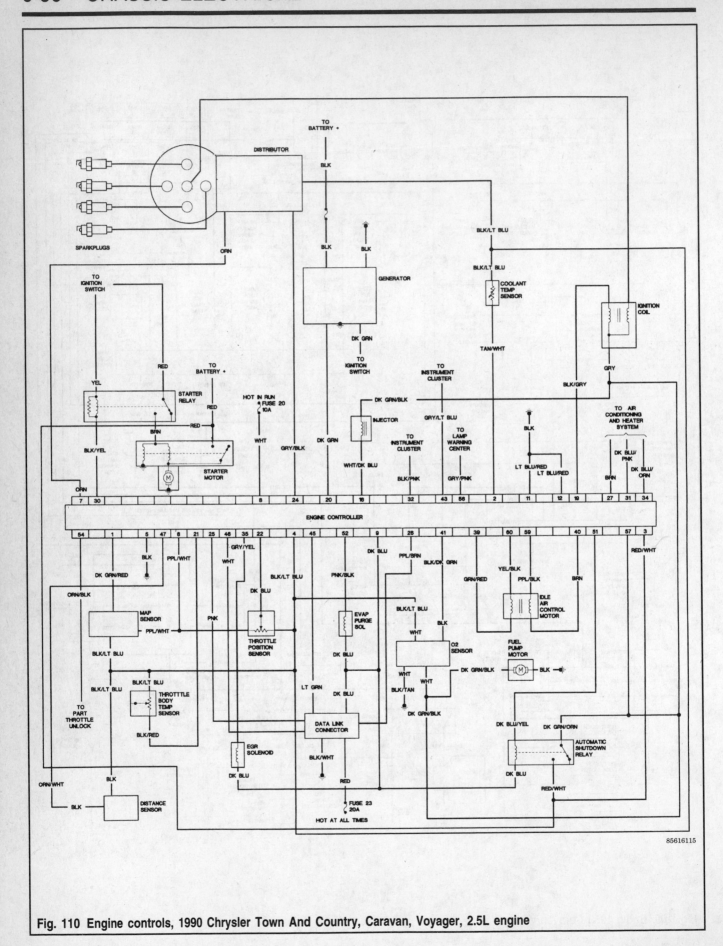

Fig. 110 Engine controls, 1990 Chrysler Town And Country, Caravan, Voyager, 2.5L engine

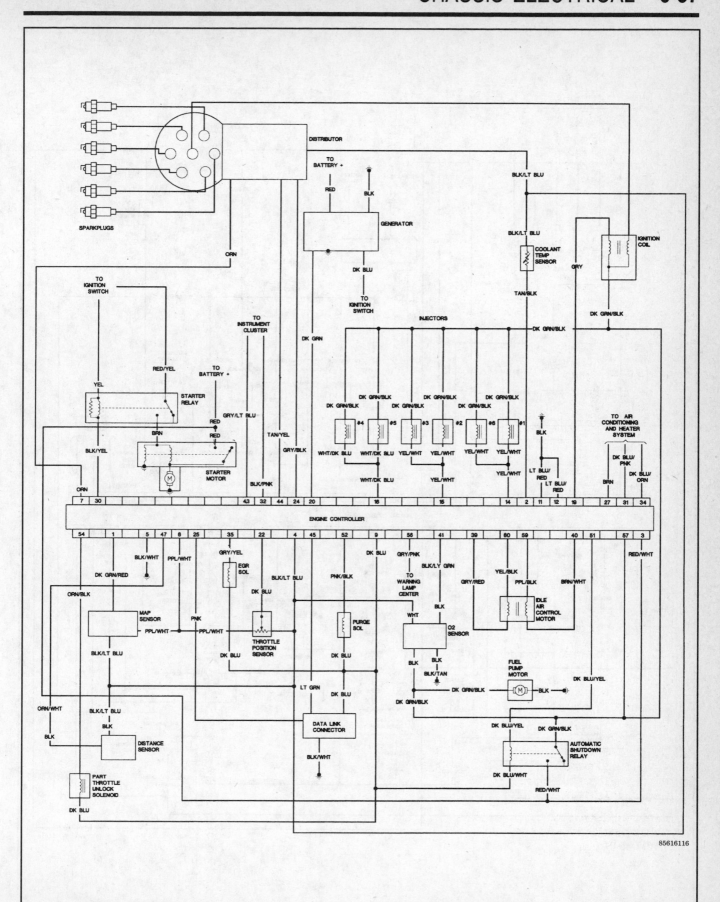

Fig. 111 Engine controls, 1990 Chrysler Town And Country, Caravan, Voyager, 3.0L engine

85616116

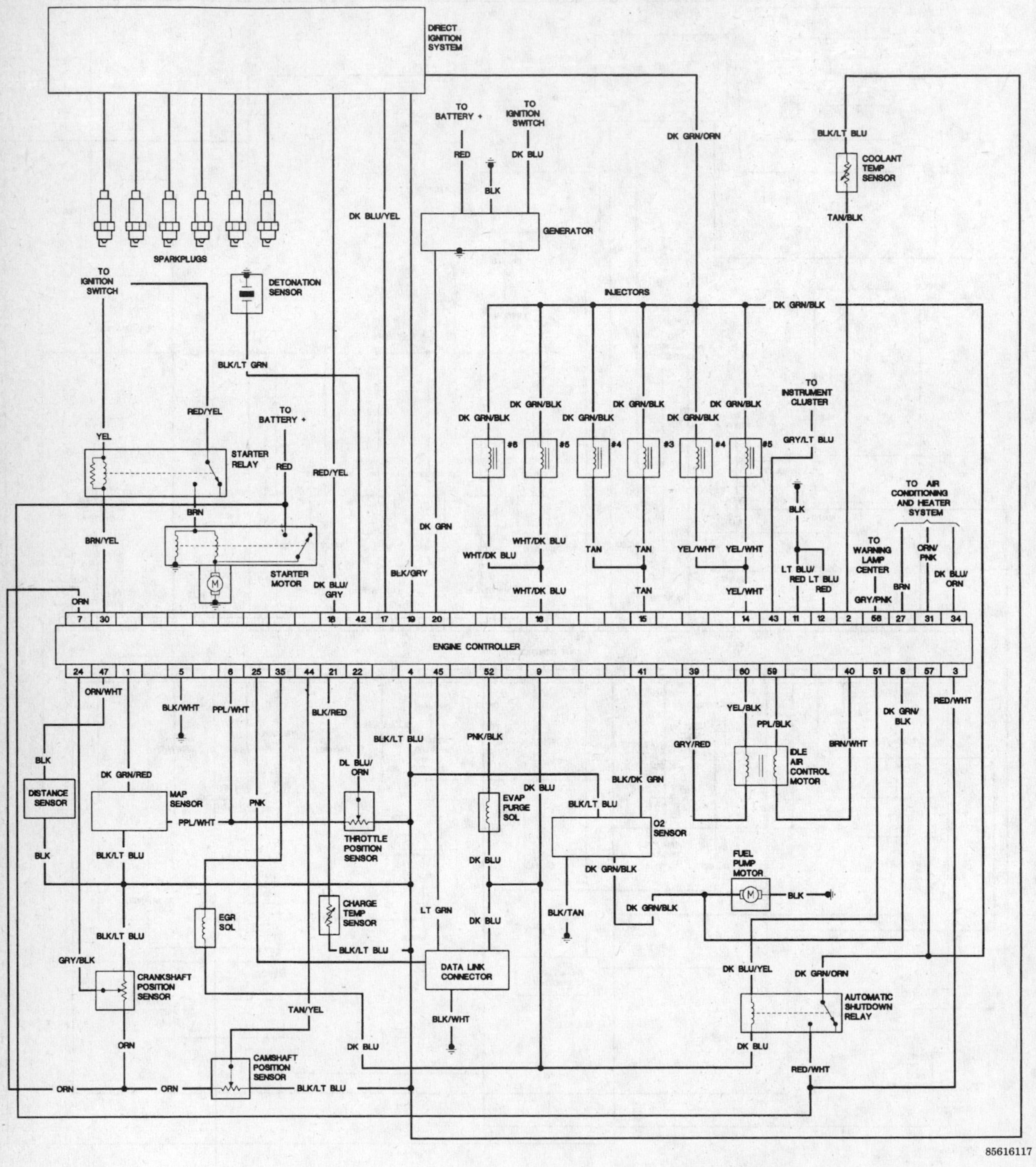

DIRECT IGNITION SYSTEM

TO BATTERY +
TO IGNITION SWITCH
RED
DK BLU
BLK
GENERATOR

DK GRN/ORN

BLK/LT BLU
COOLANT TEMP SENSOR
TAN/BLK

DK BLU/YEL

SPARKPLUGS

TO IGNITION SWITCH

DETONATION SENSOR

DK GRN/BLK

INJECTORS

TO INSTRUMENT CLUSTER

BLK/LT GRN

RED/YEL
TO BATTERY +
YEL
STARTER RELAY
RED
RED/YEL
BRN

DK GRN/BLK #8   DK GRN/BLK #5   DK GRN/BLK #4   DK GRN/BLK #3   DK GRN/BLK #4   DK GRN/BLK #5

GRY/LT BLU

TO AIR CONDITIONING AND HEATER SYSTEM

BRN/YEL
STARTER MOTOR
M

BLK

DK BLU/GRY

DK GRN
BLK/GRY

WHT/DK BLU   WHT/DK BLU
TAN   TAN
YEL/WHT   YEL/WHT

TO WARNING LAMP CENTER

ORN/PNK
DK BLU/ORN

ORN

WHT/DK BLU
TAN
YEL/WHT

LT BLU/RED LT BLU RED

GRY/PNK
BRN

7   30   18 42 17 19 20   16   15   14 43 11 12 2 58 27 31 34

ENGINE CONTROLLER

24 47 1   5   6   25 35 44 21 22   4   45   52   9   41   39   60 59   40 51 8 57 3

ORN/WHT
BLK/WHT   PPL/WHT   BLK/RED
YEL/BLK
PPL/BLK
DK GRN/BLK
RED/WHT

BLK
BLK/LT BLU
PNK/BLK
GRY/RED
IDLE AIR CONTROL MOTOR
BRN/WHT

DISTANCE SENSOR
DK GRN/RED
MAP SENSOR
PNK
PPL/WHT
DL BLU/ORN
BLK/LT BLU
EVAP PURGE SOL
DK BLU
BLK/DK GRN
BLK/LT BLU
O2 SENSOR

BLK
BLK/LT BLU
THROTTLE POSITION SENSOR
DK GRN/BLK

FUEL PUMP MOTOR
M   BLK

EGR SOL
CHARGE TEMP SENSOR
LT GRN
DK BLU
BLK/TAN
DK GRN/BLK

GRY/BLK
BLK/LT BLU
CRANKSHAFT POSITION SENSOR
BLK/LT BLU

DK BLU/YEL   DK GRN/ORN
AUTOMATIC SHUTDOWN RELAY

ORN
TAN/YEL
DK BLU
BLK/WHT
DATA LINK CONNECTOR
BLK/WHT
DK BLU

ORN
ORN
CAMSHAFT POSITION SENSOR
BLK/LT BLU
RED/WHT

85616117

Fig. 112 Engine controls, 1990 Chrysler Town And Country, Caravan, Voyager, 3.3L engine

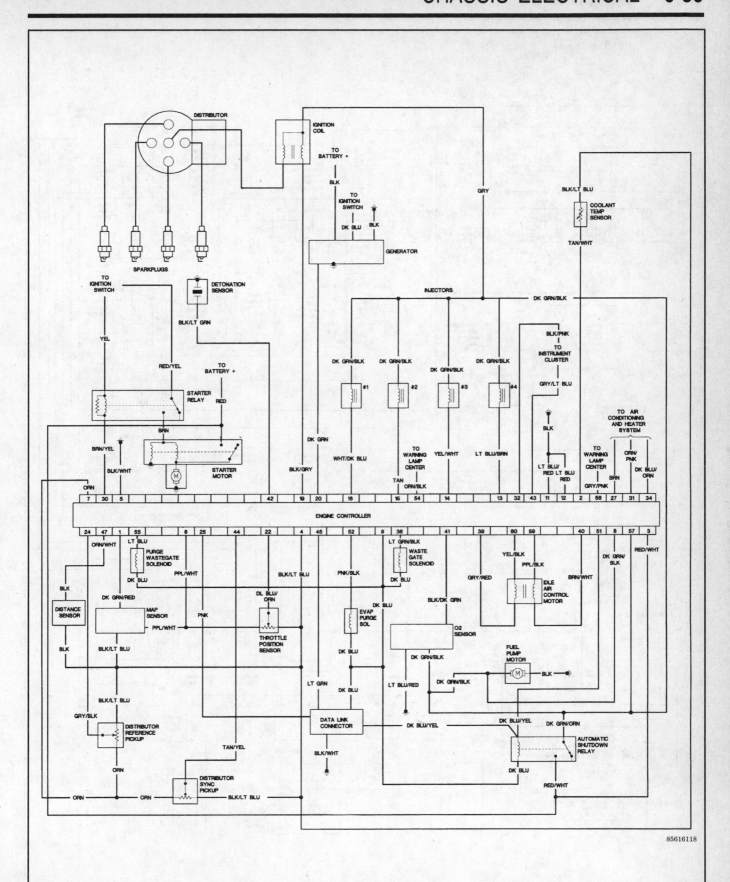

Fig. 113 Engine controls, 1990 Chrysler Town And Country, Caravan, Voyager, 2.5L Turbo engine

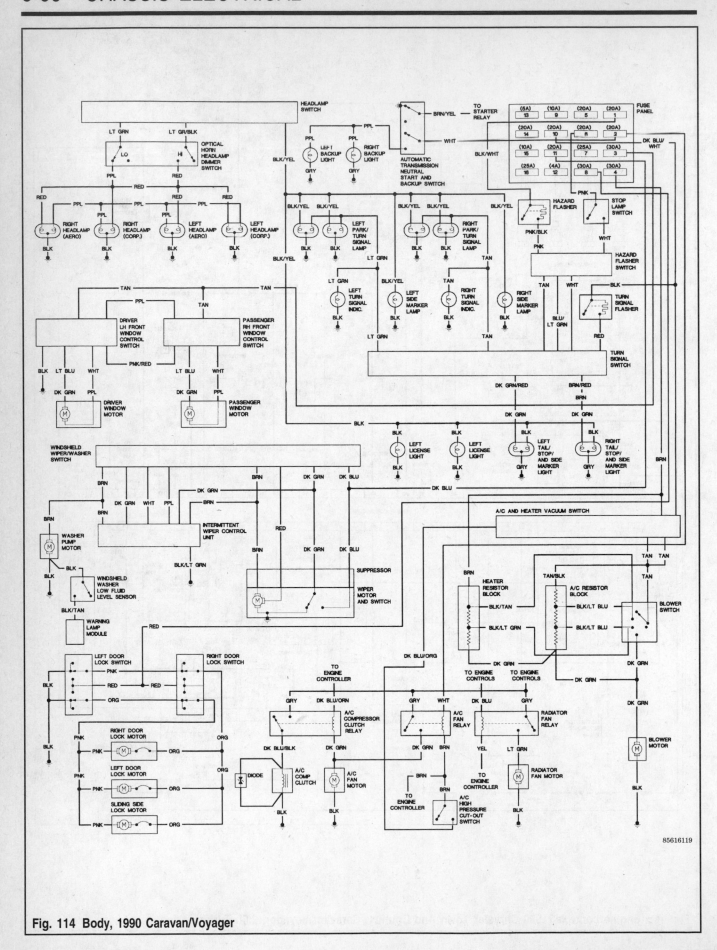

Fig. 114 Body, 1990 Caravan/Voyager

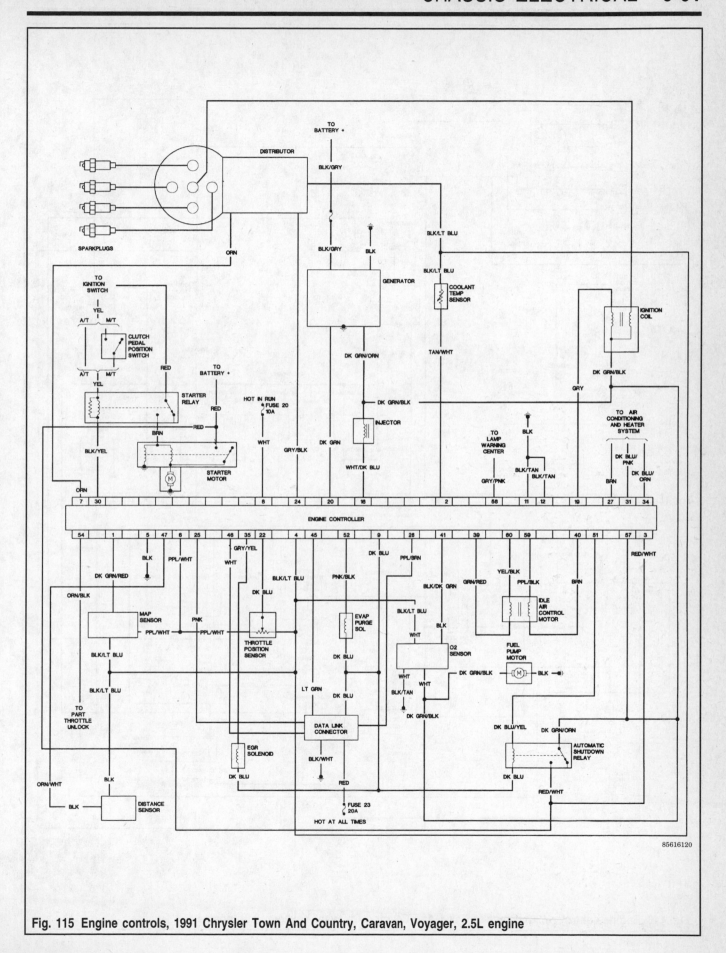

Fig. 115 Engine controls, 1991 Chrysler Town And Country, Caravan, Voyager, 2.5L engine

85616120

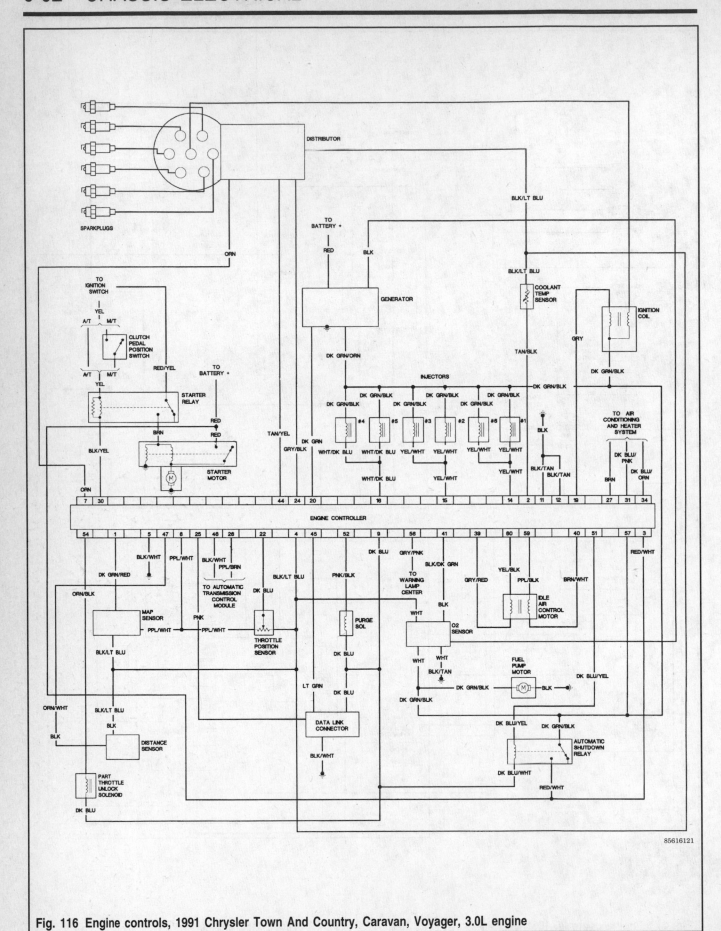

Fig. 116 Engine controls, 1991 Chrysler Town And Country, Caravan, Voyager, 3.0L engine

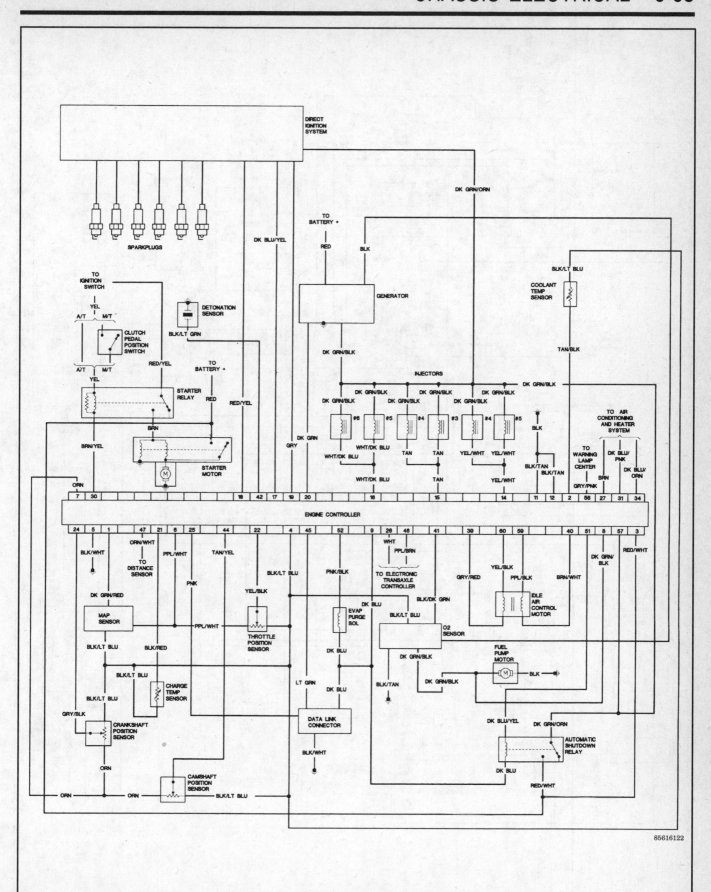

Fig. 117 Engine controls, 1991 Chrysler Town And Country, Caravan, Voyager, 3.3L engine

85616122

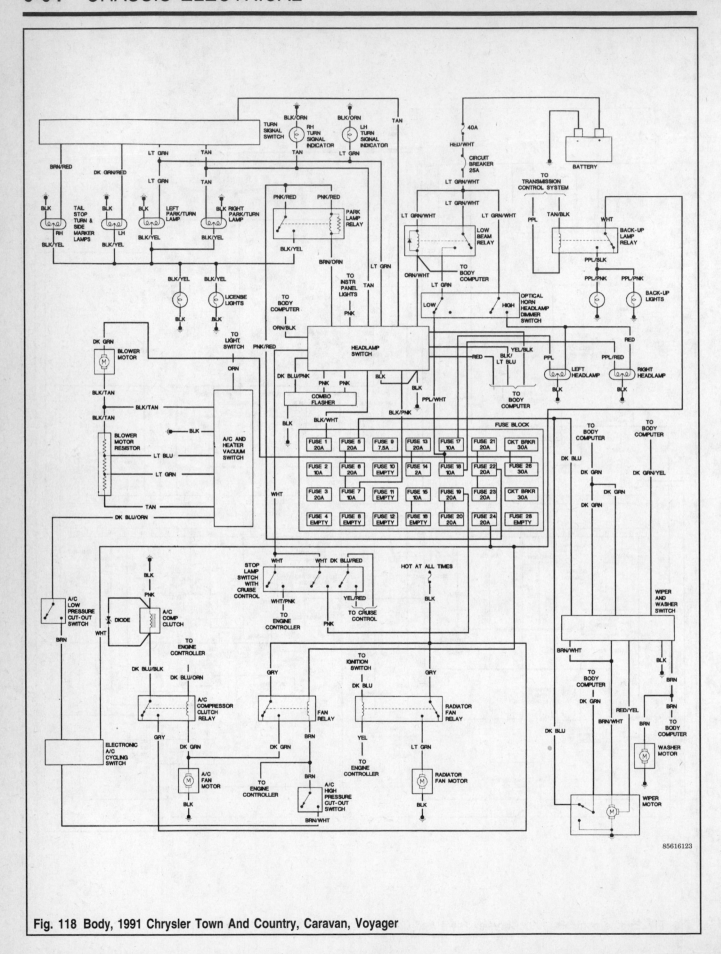

Fig. 118 Body, 1991 Chrysler Town And Country, Caravan, Voyager

85616123

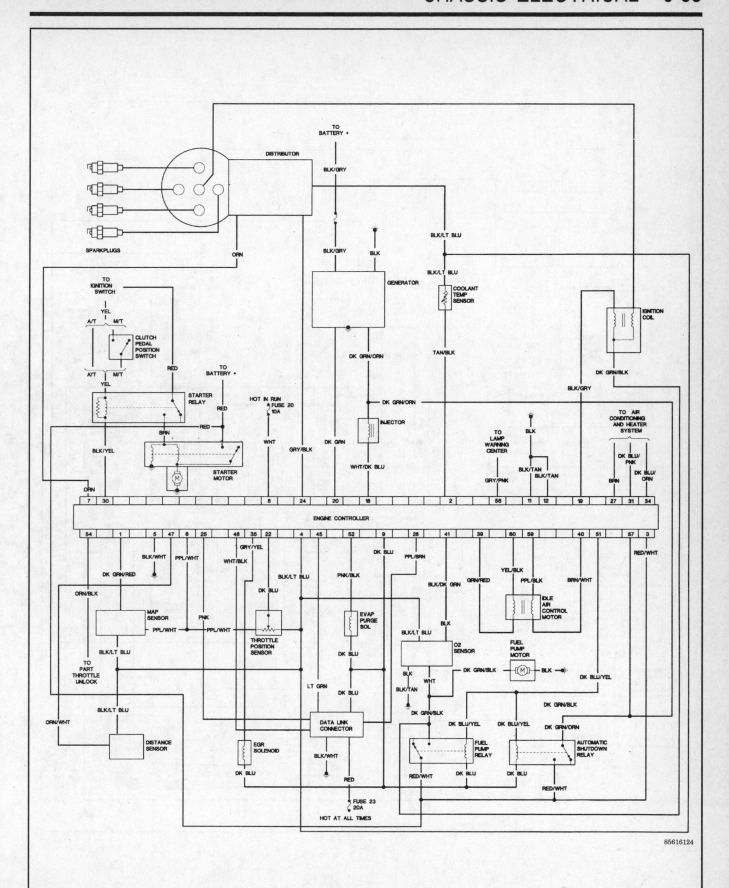

Fig. 119 Engine controls, 1992 Chrysler Town And Country, Caravan, Voyager, 2.5L engine

85616124

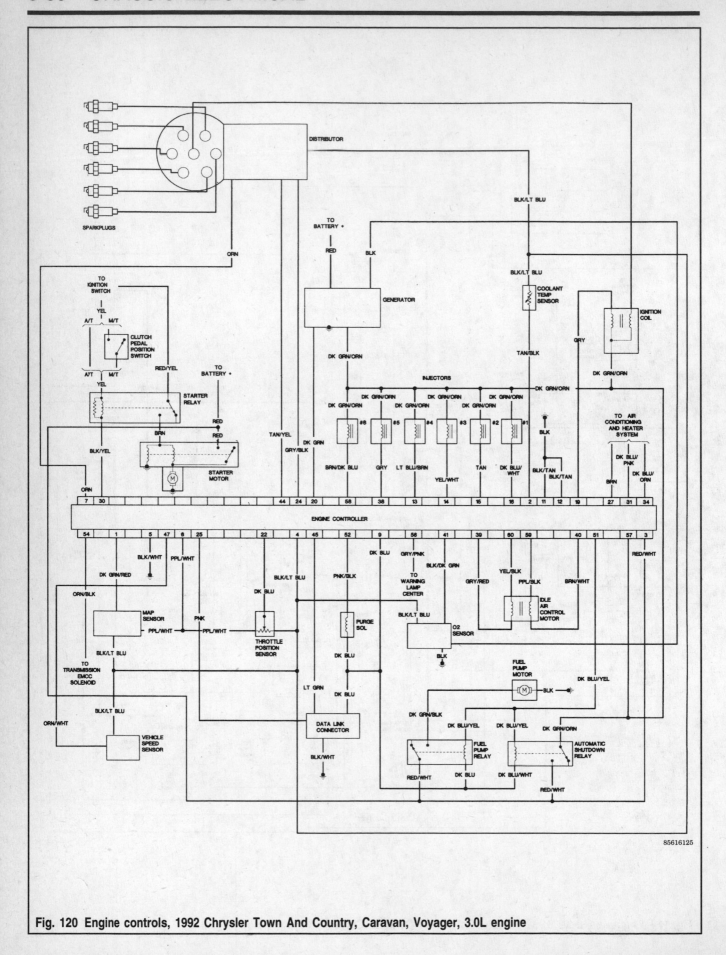

Fig. 120 Engine controls, 1992 Chrysler Town And Country, Caravan, Voyager, 3.0L engine

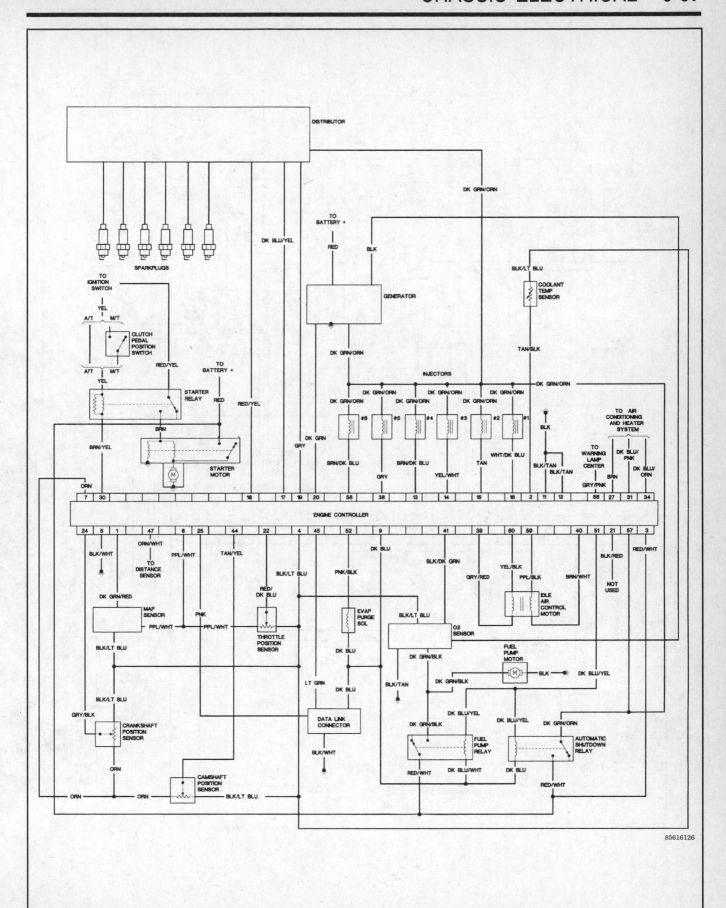

Fig. 121 Engine controls, 1992 Chrysler Town And Country, Caravan, Voyager, 3.3L engine

85616126

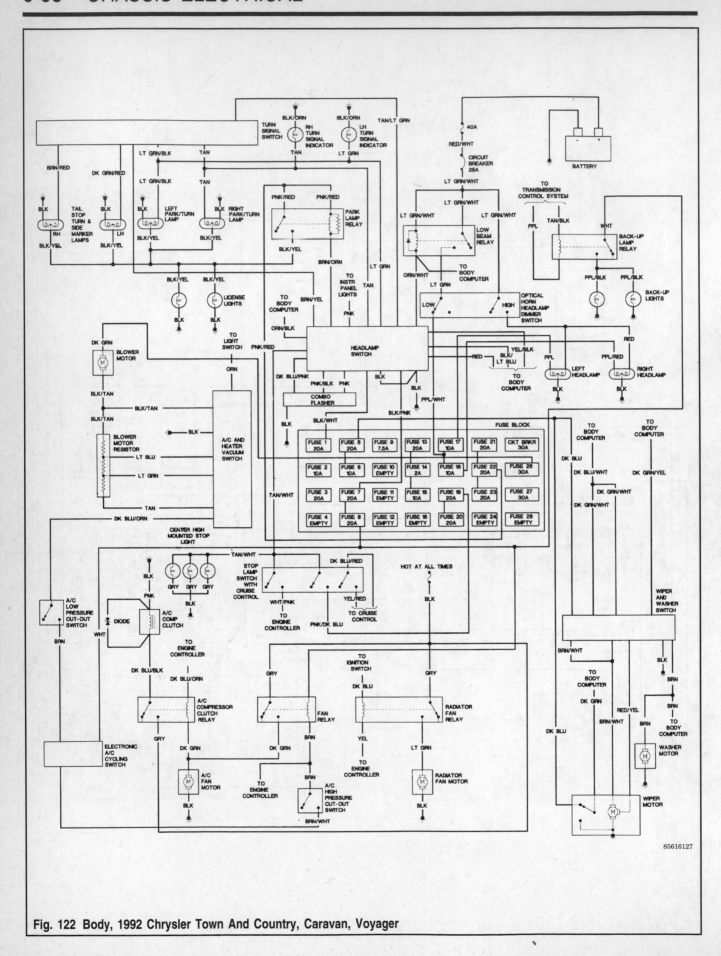

Fig. 122 Body, 1992 Chrysler Town And Country, Caravan, Voyager

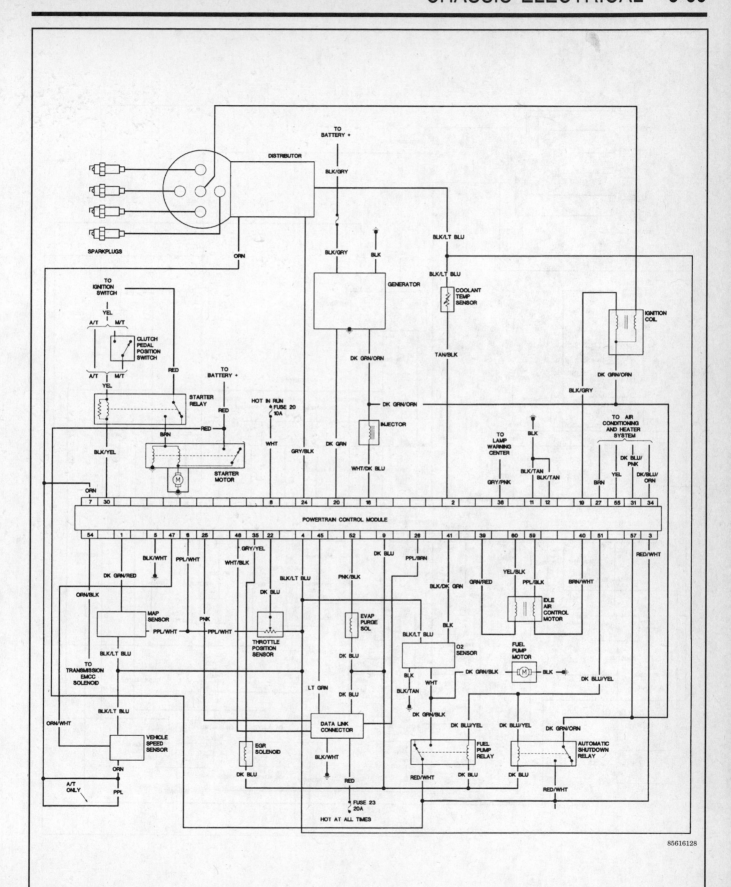

Fig. 123 Engine controls, 1993 Chrysler Town And Country, Caravan, Voyager, 2.5L engine

85616128

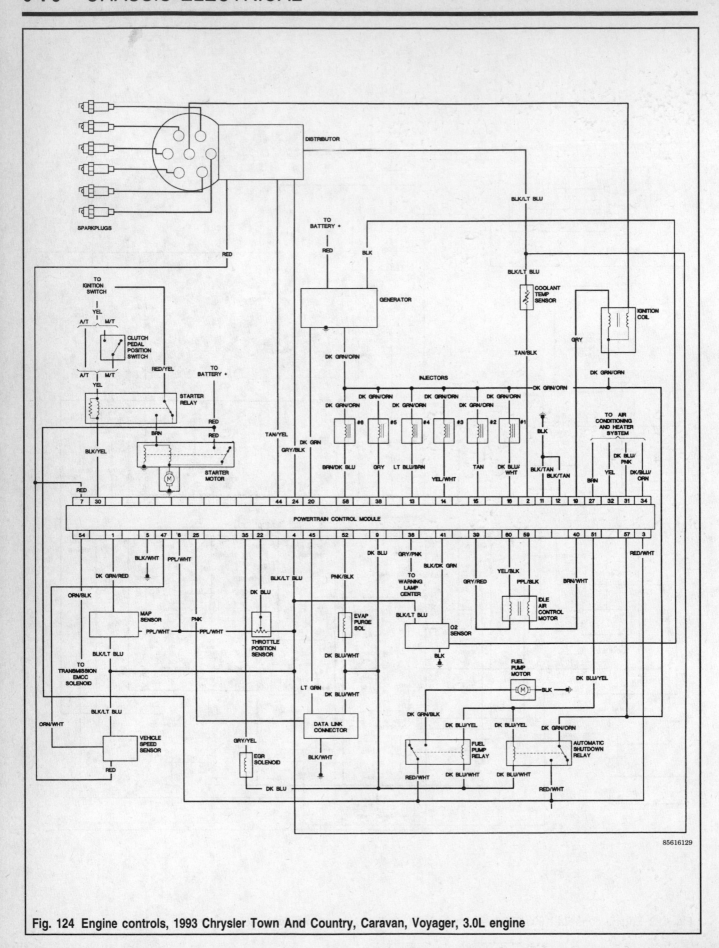

Fig. 124 Engine controls, 1993 Chrysler Town And Country, Caravan, Voyager, 3.0L engine

85616129

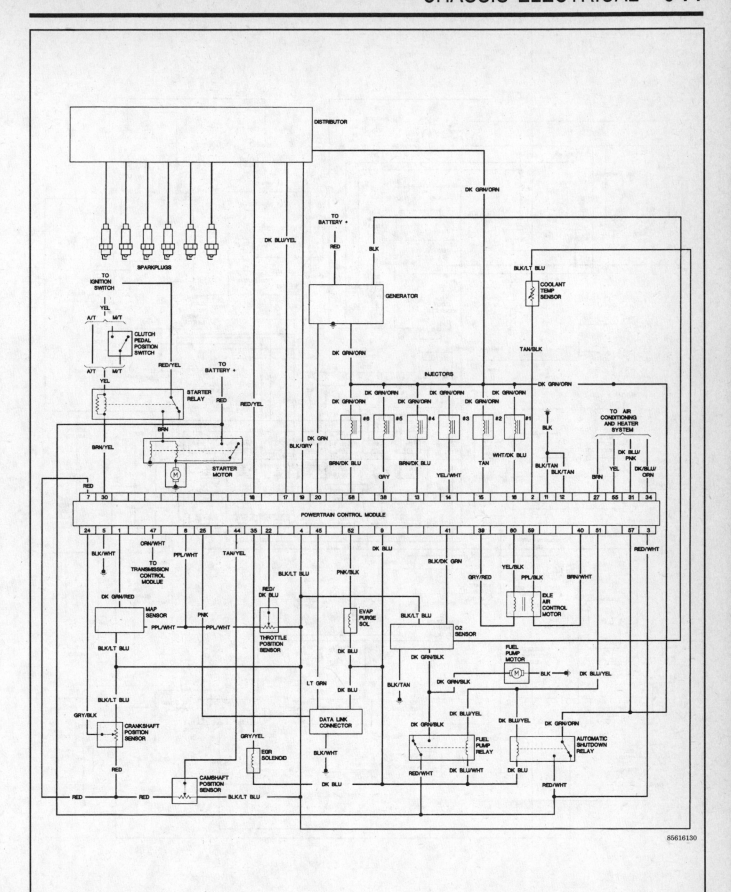

Fig. 125 Engine controls, 1993 Chrysler Town And Country, Caravan, Voyager, 3.3L engine

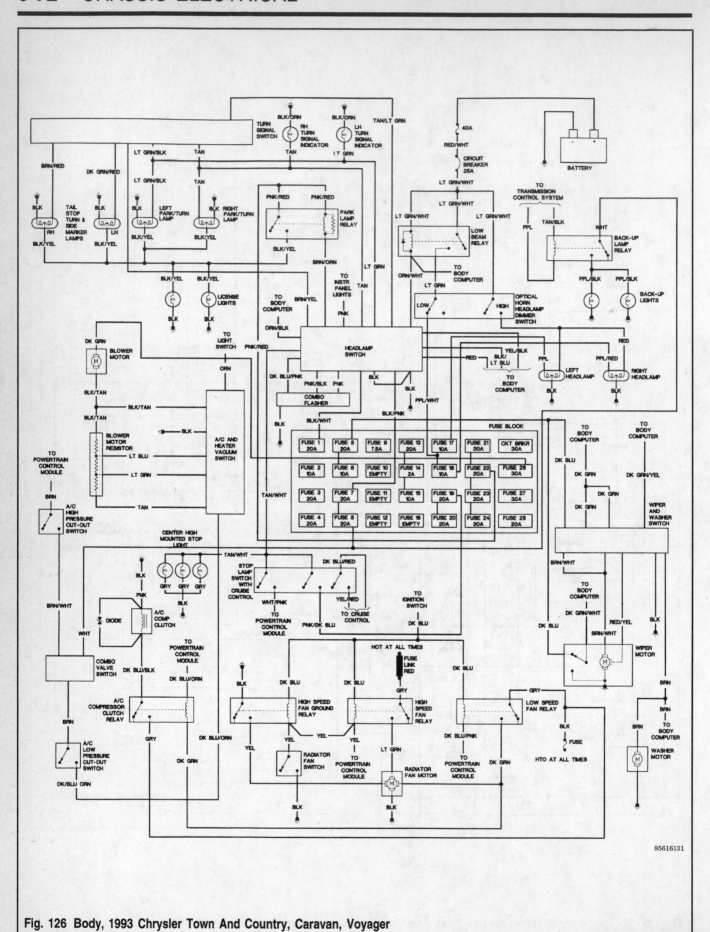

Fig. 126 Body, 1993 Chrysler Town And Country, Caravan, Voyager

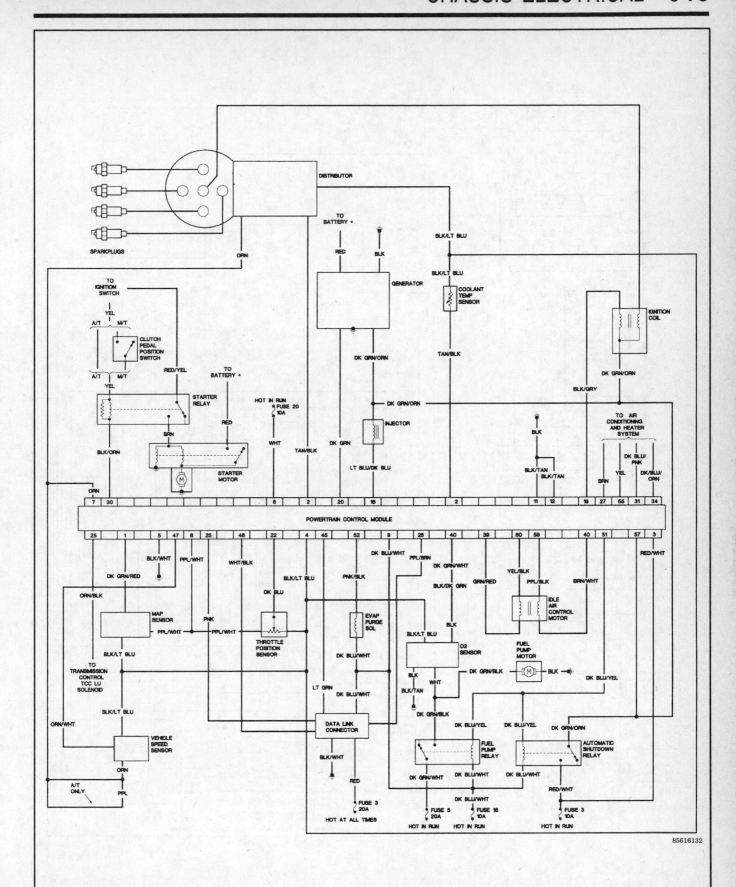

Fig. 127 Engine controls, 1994 Chrysler Town And Country, Caravan, Voyager, 2.5L engine

85616132

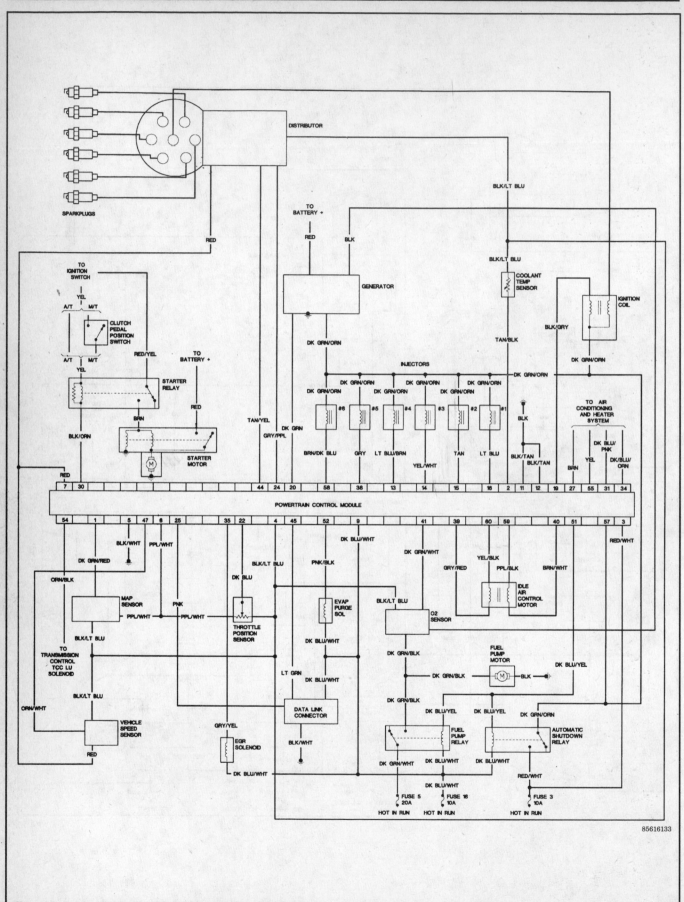

Fig. 128 Engine controls, 1994 Chrysler Town And Country, Caravan, Voyager, 3.0L engine

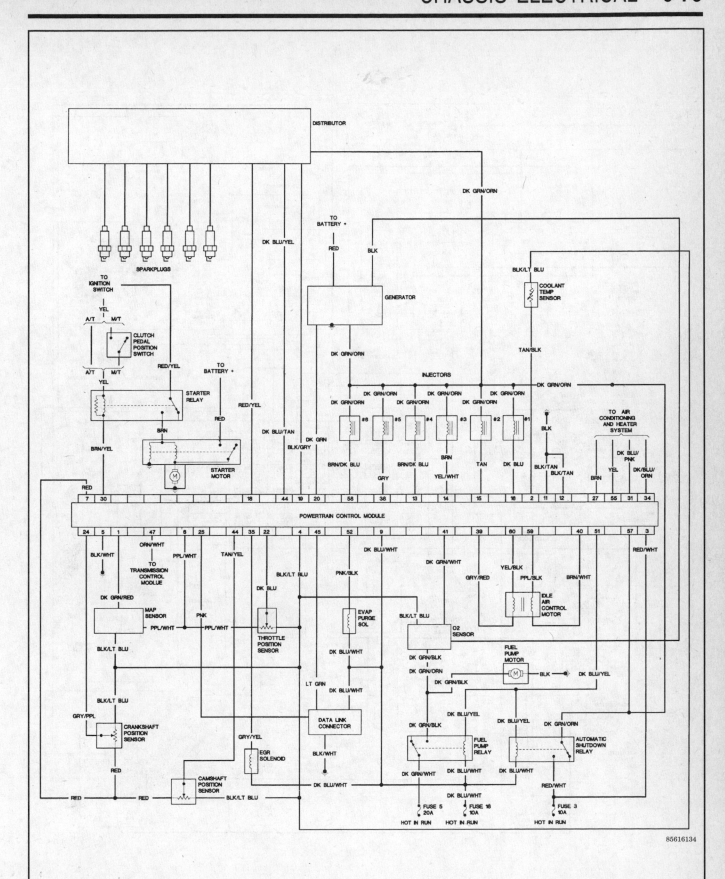

Fig. 129 Engine controls, 1994 Chrysler Town And Country, Caravan, Voyager, 3.3L and 3.8L engines

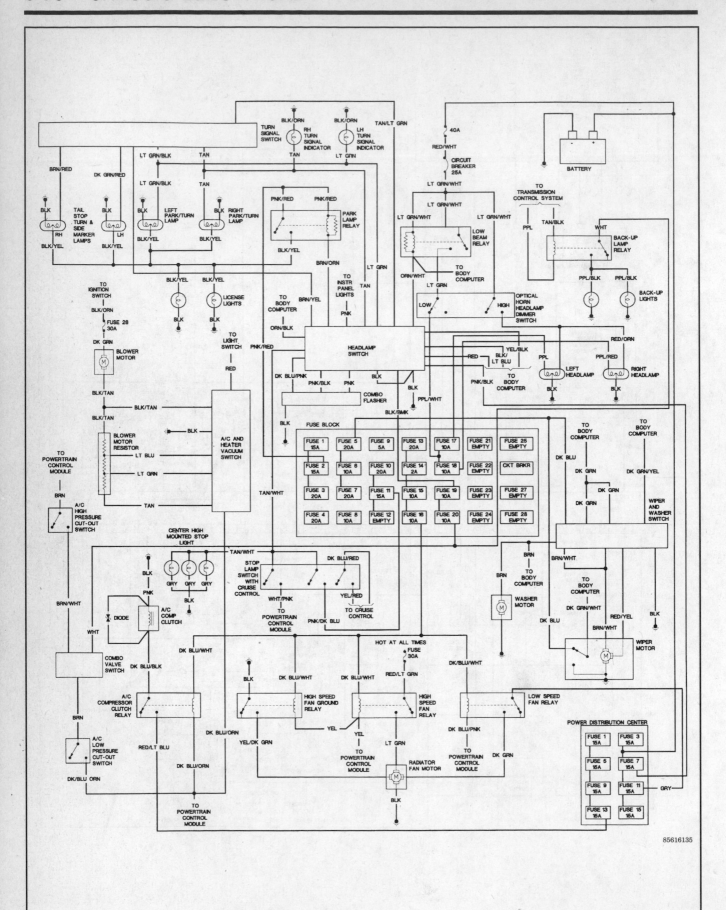

Fig. 130 Body, 1994 Chrysler Town And Country, Caravan, Voyager

85616135

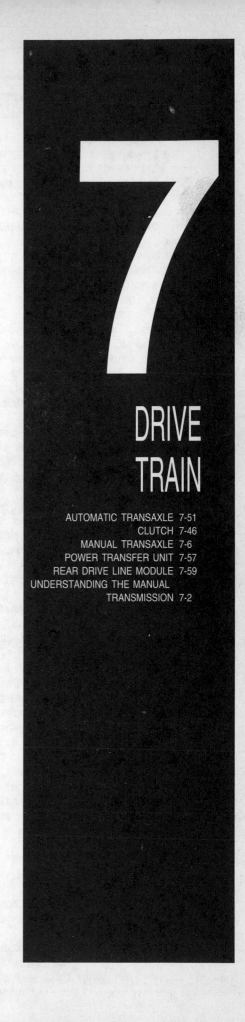

7

DRIVE
TRAIN

UNDERSTANDING THE MANUAL TRANSMISSION

Because of the way an internal combustion engine breathes, it can produce torque, or twisting force, only within a narrow speed range. Most modern, overhead valve engines must turn at about 2,500 rpm to produce their peak torque. By 4,500 rpm they are producing so little torque that continued increases in engine speed produce no power increases.

The torque peak on overhead camshaft engines is, generally, much higher, but much narrower.

The manual transmission and clutch are employed to vary the relationship between engine speed and the speed of the wheels so that adequate engine power can be produced under all circumstances. The clutch allows engine torque to be applied to the transmission input shaft gradually, due to mechanical slippage. The car can, consequently, be started smoothly from a full stop.

The transmission changes the ratio between the rotating speeds of the engine and the wheels by the use of gears. 4-speed or 5-speed transmissions are most common. The lower gears allow full engine power to be applied to the wheels during acceleration at low speeds.

The clutch drive plate is a thin disc, the center of which is splined to the transmission input shaft. Both sides of the disc are covered with a layer of material which is similar to brake lining and which is capable of allowing slippage without roughness or excessive noise.

The clutch cover is bolted to the engine flywheel and incorporates a diaphragm spring which provides the pressure to engage the clutch. The cover also houses the pressure plate. The driven disc is sandwiched between the pressure plate and the smooth surface of the flywheel when the clutch pedal is released, thus forcing it to turn at the same speed as the engine crankshaft.

The transmission contains a mainshaft which passes all the way through the transmission, from the clutch to the halfshafts. This shaft is separated at one point, so that front and rear portions can turn at different speeds.

Power is transmitted by a countershaft in the lower gears and reverse. The gears of the countershaft mesh with gears on the mainshaft, allowing power to be carried from one to the other. All the countershaft gears are integral with that shaft, while several of the mainshaft gears can either rotate independently of the shaft or be locked to it. Shifting from one gear to the next causes one of the gears to be freed from rotating with the shaft and locks another to it. Gears are locked and unlocked by internal dog clutches which slide between the center of the gear and the shaft. The forward gears usually employ synchronizers; friction members which smoothly bring gear and shaft to the same speed before the toothed dog clutches are engaged.

The clutch is operating properly if:

1. It will stall the engine when released with the vehicle held stationary.

2. The shift lever can be moved freely between 1st and reverse gears when the vehicle is stationary and the clutch disengaged.

A clutch pedal free-play adjustment is incorporated in the linkage. If there is about 1-2 in. (25-50mm) of motion before the pedal begins to release the clutch, it is adjusted properly. Inadequate free-play wears all parts of the clutch releasing

mechanisms and may cause slippage. Excessive free-play may cause inadequate release and hard shifting of gears.

Some clutches use a hydraulic system in place of mechanical linkage. If the clutch fails to release, fill the clutch master cylinder with fluid to the proper level and pump the clutch pedal to fill the system with fluid. Bleed the system in the same way as a brake system. If leaks are located, tighten loose connections or overhaul the master or slave cylinder as necessary.

Front wheel drive cars do not have conventional rear axles or drive shafts. Instead, power is transmitted from the engine to a transaxle, or a combination of transmission and drive axle, in one unit. Both the transmission and drive axle accomplish the same function as their counterparts in a front engine/rear drive axle design. The difference is in the location of the components.

In place of a conventional driveshaft, a front wheel drive design uses two driveshafts, sometimes called halfshafts, which couple the drive axle portion of the transaxle to the wheels. Universal joints or constant velocity joints are used just as they would in a rear wheel drive design.

Identification

Seven manual transaxles, built by Chrysler, are used; a 4-speed, A-460 and six 5-speeds; A-465, A-520, A-523, A-525, A-555 and A-568. All of these transaxles are based on the same design and components, therefore servicing each is almost identical. The transmission and differential are contained together in a single die-cast aluminum case. All of the transmissions are fully synchronized in all gears. Dexron®II automatic transmission type fluid (models through 1987) or 5W-30 motor oil (1988 and later models) is used for lubrication. Please refer to Section 1 for additional lubrication information. The transaxle model, build date and final drive ratio are stamped on a tag that is attached to the top of the transaxle. Always give the tag information when ordering parts for the unit.

Adjustments

SHIFT LINKAGE

▶ **See Figures 1, 2, 3, 4, 5, 6, 7, 8, 9, 10, 11, 12, 13, 14 and 15**

➡**If a hard shifting situation is experienced, determine if the cables are binding and need replacement, or if a linkage adjustment is necessary. Disconnect both cables at the transaxle and move the selector through the various positions. If the selector moves freely an adjustment may be all that is necessary; if not, cable replacement might be indicated.**

1. Working over the left front fender, unscrew the lock pin, from the transaxle selector shaft housing.

2. Reverse the lock pin so that the long end faces down and insert into the same threaded hole it was removed from.

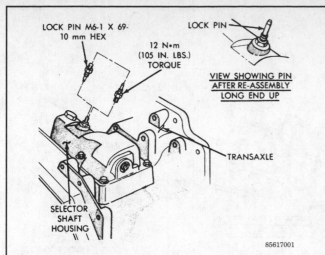

Fig. 1 Transaxle pinned in the neutral position to adjust gearshift linkage, 1984-90

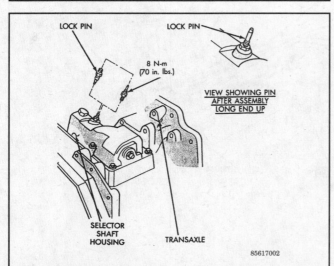

Fig. 2 Transaxle pinned in the neutral position to adjust gearshift linkage, 1992-94

Push the selector shaft into the selector housing while inserting the pin. A hole in the selector shaft will align with the lock pin, allowing the pin to be threaded into the housing. This will lock the selector shaft into the neutral position.

3. From inside the vehicle, remove the gearshift knob by pulling straight up. Remove the reverse pull up ring by first removing the retaining nut and then pull the ring up and off of the lever.

4. Remove the shift lever boot. Remove the console.

5. For models built through 1987: Fabricate two adjusting lock pins out of ¹⁄₁₆ in. rod. Total length of the pins should be 5 inches with a hook shaped on one end.

6. Loosen the selector and cross-over cable end adjusting/retainer bolts. Be sure the transaxle end of the cables are connected.

7. Install one adjusting lock pin on the side of the lever bracket in hole provided while moving lever slightly to help alignment. Install the other lock pin at the rear of the lever bracket (cross-over cable). Be sure that both cable end pieces are free to move.

8. After pins are inserted, the cable ends will be positioned to the correct adjustment point. Tighten the adjustment/retainer bolts to 55 inch lbs.

9. On model built in late 1986 and later: Loosen the selector and crossover cable adjusting screws. Remove the adjusting screw tool and attached spacer block from the shifter support.

10. Install the adjusting screw tool through the attached spacer, and screw the tool into the base of the shifter tower base.

11. Tighten the adjusting screw tool to 20 in. lbs.

12. Tighten the selector/crossover cable retaining screws to 70 in. lbs. Proper torque on the selector/crossover cable bracket is very important for proper operation.

13. Remove the adjusting screw tool and attach it to the bracket.

14. Check the gearshift cables for proper connection to the transaxle.

15. Install console and remainder of the removed parts.

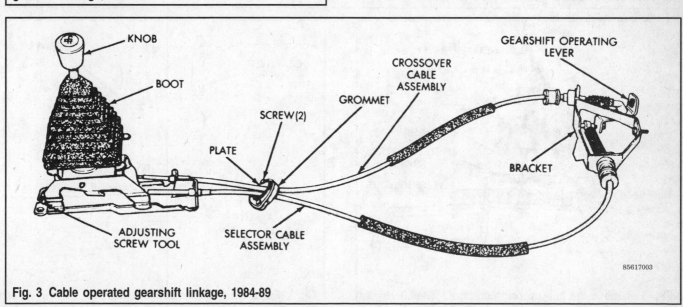

Fig. 3 Cable operated gearshift linkage, 1984-89

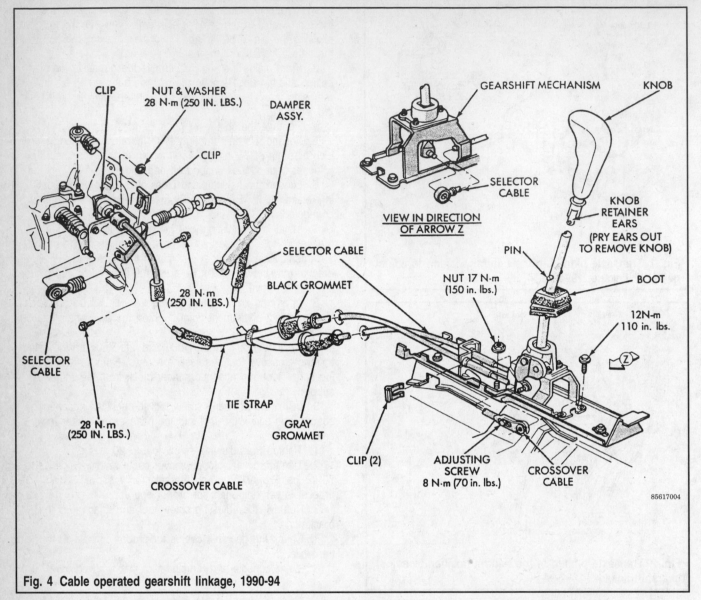

CLIP

NUT & WASHER
28 N·m (250 IN. LBS.)

CLIP

DAMPER
ASSY.

GEARSHIFT MECHANISM

KNOB

SELECTOR
CABLE

**VIEW IN DIRECTION
OF ARROW Z**

KNOB
RETAINER
EARS
(PRY EARS OUT
TO REMOVE KNOB)

SELECTOR CABLE

BLACK GROMMET

PIN

BOOT

NUT 17 N·m
(150 in. lbs.)

12N·m
110 in. lbs.

SELECTOR
CABLE

28 N·m
(250 IN. LBS.)

TIE STRAP

GRAY
GROMMET

CLIP (2)

ADJUSTING
SCREW
8 N·m (70 in. lbs.)

CROSSOVER
CABLE

28 N·m
(250 IN. LBS.)

CROSSOVER CABLE

85617004

Fig. 4 Cable operated gearshift linkage, 1990-94

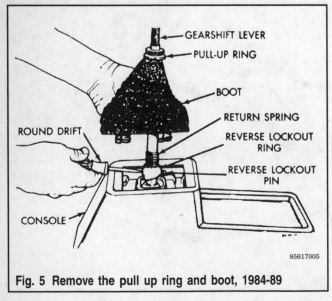

GEARSHIFT LEVER

PULL-UP RING

BOOT

RETURN SPRING

REVERSE LOCKOUT
RING

REVERSE LOCKOUT
PIN

ROUND DRIFT

CONSOLE

85617005

Fig. 5 Remove the pull up ring and boot, 1984-89

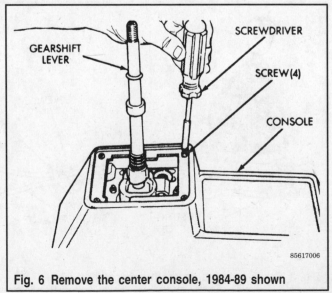

GEARSHIFT
LEVER

SCREWDRIVER

SCREW (4)

CONSOLE

85617006

Fig. 6 Remove the center console, 1984-89 shown

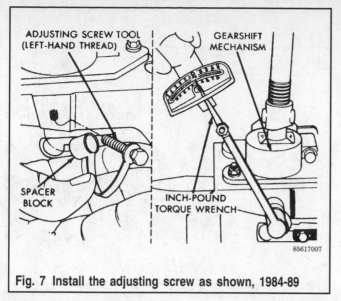

Fig. 7 Install the adjusting screw as shown, 1984-89

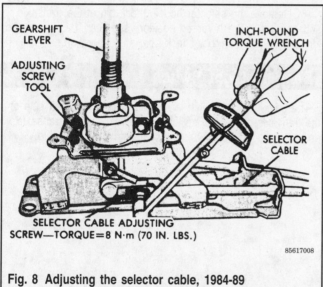

Fig. 8 Adjusting the selector cable, 1984-89

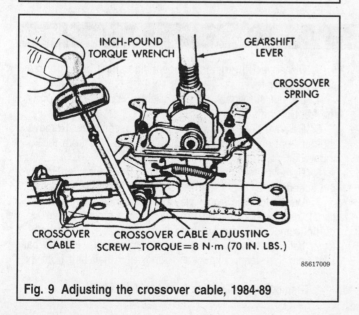

Fig. 9 Adjusting the crossover cable, 1984-89

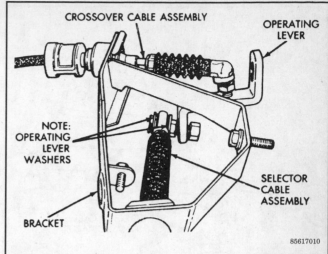

Fig. 10 Gearshift cable connections at the transaxle, 1984-89

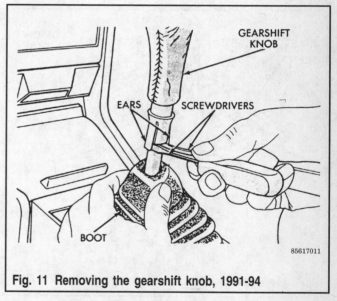

Fig. 11 Removing the gearshift knob, 1991-94

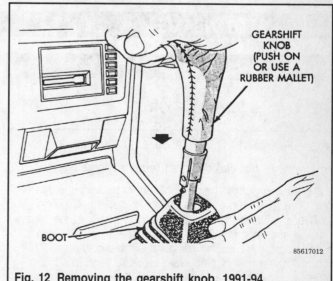

Fig. 12 Removing the gearshift knob, 1991-94

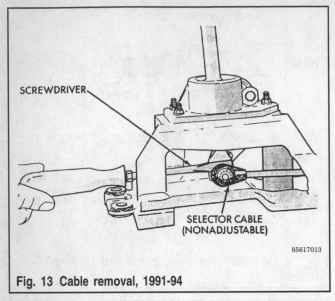

Fig. 13 Cable removal, 1991-94

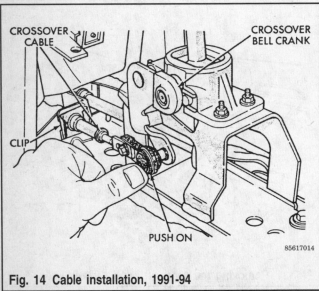

Fig. 14 Cable installation, 1991-94

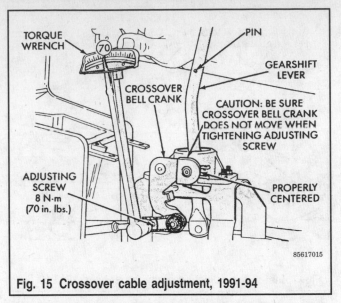

Fig. 15 Crossover cable adjustment, 1991-94

16. Remove the selector housing lock pin at the transaxle and install it in the reversed position (see Step 1). Tighten the lock pin to 105 inch lbs. check gear shift operation.

Back-up Light Switch

The back-up light switch is located at the upper left side of the transaxle case. The switch is screwed into the transaxle and serviced by replacement. No adjustment is possible.

MANUAL TRANSAXLE

Transaxle Assembly

REMOVAL & INSTALLATION

▶ **See Figures 16, 17, 18, 19, 20, 21, 22 and 23**

➡**Transaxle removal does not require engine removal.**

1. Disconnect the negative battery cable from the battery.
2. Install a sling or lifting bracket to the No. 4 cylinder exhaust manifold mounting bolt (through 1987), or the battery ground strap bolt (1988 and later). Place an engine support device across the engine compartment and connect to the sling. Tighten until slight upward pressure is applied to the engine.

3. Disconnect the gearshift operating control from the transaxle selector lever.
4. Loosen the wheel lug nuts slightly. Raise and support the front of the vehicle.
5. Remove both front wheel and tire assemblies. Remove the left front engine splash shield. Drain the fluid from the transaxle.
6. Remove the left front mount from the transaxle. Remove the speedometer cable adapter and pinion from the transaxle.
7. Disconnect the front sway bar. Disconnect the anti-rotational link (anti-hop damper) from the cross member bracket, do not remove the bracket from the transaxle. Remove both lower ball joint-to-steering knuckle mounting bolts. Pry the ball joint from the steering knuckle. Remove the halfshaft from the drive wheel hub.
8. Remove the halfshafts from the differential.

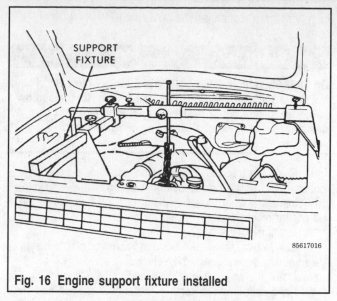
Fig. 16 Engine support fixture installed

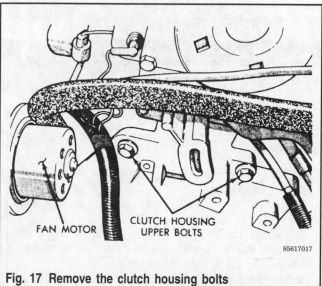
Fig. 17 Remove the clutch housing bolts

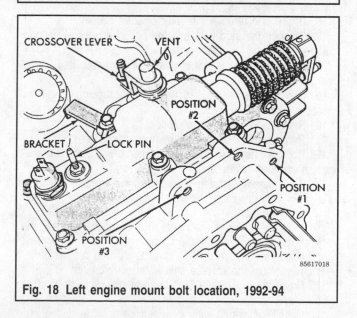
Fig. 18 Left engine mount bolt location, 1992-94

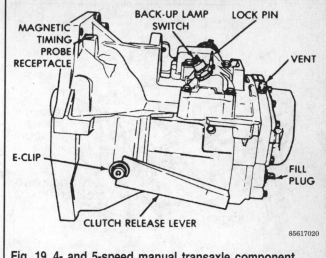
Fig. 19 4- and 5-speed manual transaxle component, left side

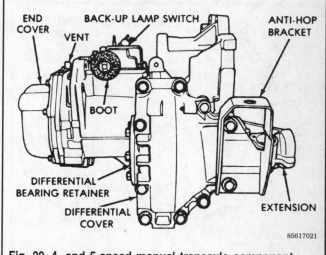
Fig. 20 4- and 5-speed manual transaxle component, right side

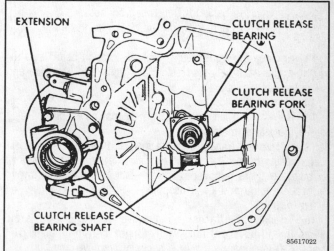
Fig. 21 4- and 5-speed manual transaxle component, front

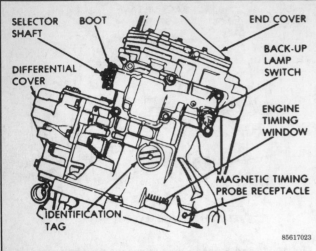

Fig. 22 4- and 5-speed manual transaxle component, top

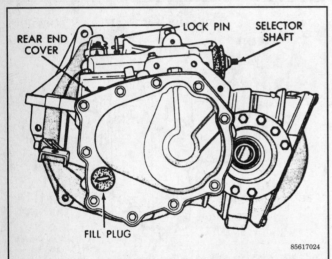

Fig. 23 4- and 5-speed manual transaxle component, rear

9. Remove the back-up light switch connector.

10. Remove the engine mount bracket from the front crossover.

11. Remove the front mount insulator through bolt. Place a suitable floor jack or transmission jack under the transaxle and raise to gently support.

12. Remove the top bell housing bolts.

13. Remove the left engine mount at rear cover plate. Remove the starter motor.

14. Secure the transaxle to the jack and remove the lower bell housing bolts. Check that all transaxle support mounts or through bolts are removed. Slide the jack and transaxle away from the engine and lower assembly.

To install:

15. To install the transaxle; make two locating pins for extra same thread bolts that are slightly longer than the mounting bolts. Cut the heads off with a hacksaw, remove any burrs or sharp edges with a file. Install the bolts into the rear of the engine and guide the transaxle over them. After the transaxle

is in position, remove the guide bolts and install mounting bolts.

✳✳WARNING

On 1992-93 vehicles, the bolts used for position No. 1 and No. 3 are the same length. The bolt in the No. 2 position is longer. If bolt No. 2 is used in position No. 3, it can damage the selector shaft housing when the bolt is seated.

16. Raise the transaxle into position and slide it over the locating pins. Install the top bell housing bolts.

17. Install the front mount insulator through bolt. Install the left engine mount and the starter motor.

18. Install the halfshafts.

19. Connect the sway bar and anti-hop/rotation link. Install the front wheels and lower the vehicle.

20. Install the speedometer drive and cable. Connect the throttle and shift linkage. Remove the engine support and connect the negative battery cable. Fill the transaxle with the correct lubrication fluid.

4-Speed Manual Transaxle Overhaul

▶ See Figure 24

TRANSAXLE CASE DISASSEMBLY

▶ See Figure 25

1. Remove the transaxle from the vehicle and position on suitable holding fixture.

2. Remove the differential cover bolts and the stud nuts, then remove the cover.

3. Remove the differential bearing retainer bolts.

4. Using tool No. L-4435 or equivalent spanner, rotate the differential bearing retainer to remove it.

5. Remove the extension housing bolts, differential assembly and extension housing.

6. Unbolt and remove the selector shaft housing.

7. Remove the stud nuts and the bolts from the rear end cover then pry off the rear end cover.

8. Remove the large snapring from the intermediate shaft rear ball bearing.

9. Remove the bearing retainer plate by tapping it with a plastic hammer.

10. Remove the 3rd/4th shift fork rail.

11. Remove the reverse idler gear shaft and gear.

12. Remove the input shaft gear assembly and the intermediate shaft gear assembly.

13. To remove the clutch release bearing, remove the E-clips from the clutch release shaft, then disassemble the clutch shaft components.

14. Remove the input shaft seal retainer bolts, the seal, the retainer assembly and the select shim.

15. Remove the reverse shift lever E-clip and flat washer and disassemble the reverse shift lever components.

16. Press the input shaft front bearing cup from the transaxle case.

17. Unbolt and remove the intermediate shaft front bearing retaining strap.

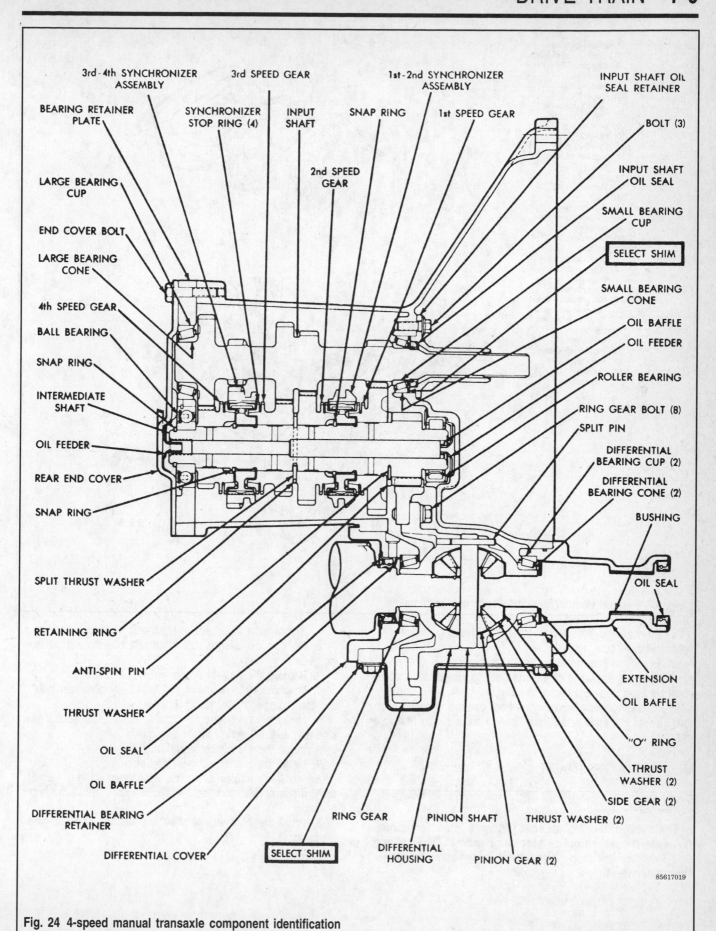

Fig. 24 4-speed manual transaxle component identification

3rd-4th SYNCHRONIZER ASSEMBLY

3rd SPEED GEAR

1st-2nd SYNCHRONIZER ASSEMBLY

INPUT SHAFT OIL SEAL RETAINER

BEARING RETAINER PLATE

SYNCHRONIZER STOP RING (4)

INPUT SHAFT

SNAP RING

1st SPEED GEAR

BOLT (3)

2nd SPEED GEAR

INPUT SHAFT OIL SEAL

LARGE BEARING CUP

SMALL BEARING CUP

SELECT SHIM

END COVER BOLT

LARGE BEARING CONE

SMALL BEARING CONE

4th SPEED GEAR

OIL BAFFLE

BALL BEARING

OIL FEEDER

SNAP RING

ROLLER BEARING

INTERMEDIATE SHAFT

RING GEAR BOLT (8)

OIL FEEDER

SPLIT PIN

REAR END COVER

DIFFERENTIAL BEARING CUP (2)

SNAP RING

DIFFERENTIAL BEARING CONE (2)

BUSHING

SPLIT THRUST WASHER

OIL SEAL

RETAINING RING

ANTI-SPIN PIN

THRUST WASHER

EXTENSION

OIL SEAL

OIL BAFFLE

OIL BAFFLE

"O" RING

DIFFERENTIAL BEARING RETAINER

THRUST WASHER (2)

DIFFERENTIAL COVER

RING GEAR

PINION SHAFT

THRUST WASHER (2)

SIDE GEAR (2)

SELECT SHIM

DIFFERENTIAL HOUSING

PINION GEAR (2)

85617019

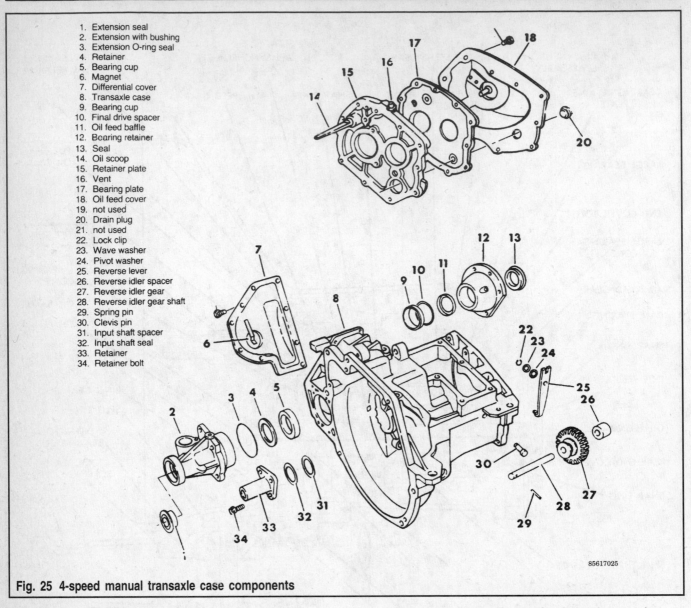

1. Extension seal
2. Extension with bushing
3. Extension O-ring seal
4. Retainer
5. Bearing cup
6. Magnet
7. Differential cover
8. Transaxle case
9. Bearing cup
10. Final drive spacer
11. Oil feed baffle
12. Bearing retainer
13. Seal
14. Oil scoop
15. Retainer plate
16. Vent
17. Bearing plate
18. Oil feed cover
19. not used
20. Drain plug
21. not used
22. Lock clip
23. Wave washer
24. Pivot washer
25. Reverse lever
26. Reverse idler spacer
27. Reverse idler gear
28. Reverse idler gear shaft
29. Spring pin
30. Clevis pin
31. Input shaft spacer
32. Input shaft seal
33. Retainer
34. Retainer bolt

85617025

Fig. 25 4-speed manual transaxle case components

18. Remove the intermediate shaft front bearing and oil feeder using a bearing puller.

19. Press the intermediate shaft front bearing with the oil feeder into the transaxle case. The bearing identification letters must be facing upward during installation.

20. Install the intermediate shaft front bearing retaining strap.

21. Press the input shaft front bearing cup into the transaxle case.

INTERMEDIATE SHAFT

▶ **See Figure 26**

➡**The 1st/2nd, the 3rd/4th shift forks are interchangeable, however, the synchronizer stop rings are not. The 1st and 2nd synchronizer stop rings have a larger diameter than the other stop rings.**

1. Remove the intermediate shaft rear bearing snapring.

2. Remove the intermediate shaft rear bearing with a bearing puller.

3. Remove the 3rd/4th synchronizer hub snapring.

4. Matchmark then remove the 3rd/4th synchronizer hub and the 3rd speed gear using a puller.

5. Install the 1st speed gear thrust washer, 1st speed gear, stop ring and 1-2 synchronizer assembly

6. Install the 1-2 synchronizer snapring.

7. Install the 2nd speed gear and stop ring.

8. Install the retaining ring and split thrust washer. Install the 3rd speed gear and the 3-4 synchronizer. Install the hub snapring.

9. Install the intermediate shaft rear bearing and retaining snapring.

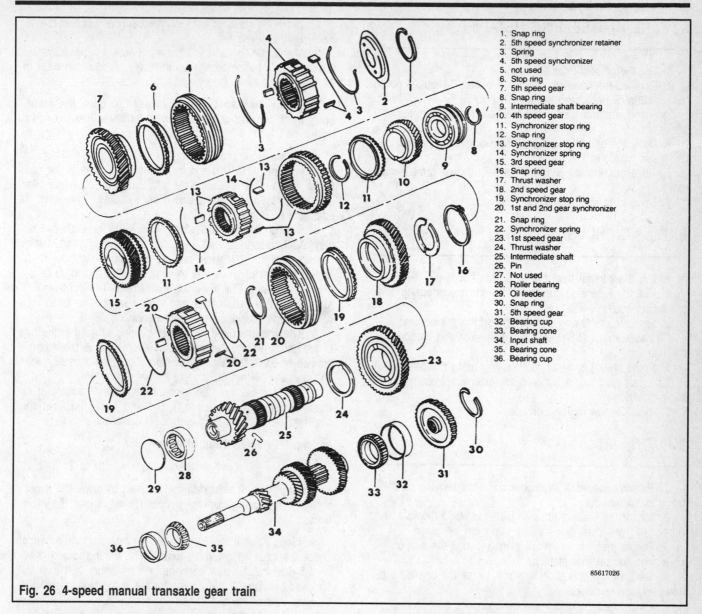

1. Snap ring
2. 5th speed synchronizer retainer
3. Spring
4. 5th speed synchronizer
5. not used
6. Stop ring
7. 5th speed gear
8. Snap ring
9. Intermediate shaft bearing
10. 4th speed gear
11. Synchronizer stop ring
12. Snap ring
13. Synchronizer stop ring
14. Synchronizer spring
15. 3rd speed gear
16. Snap ring
17. Thrust washer
18. 2nd speed gear
19. Synchronizer stop ring
20. 1st and 2nd gear synchronizer
21. Snap ring
22. Synchronizer spring
23. 1st speed gear
24. Thrust washer
25. Intermediate shaft
26. Pin
27. Not used
28. Roller bearing
29. Oil feeder
30. Snap ring
31. 5th speed gear
32. Bearing cup
33. Bearing cone
34. Input shaft
35. Bearing cone
36. Bearing cup

85617026

Fig. 26 4-speed manual transaxle gear train

10. Install the intermediate shaft front bearing.

➡️Pay attention to the following when servicing the intermediate shaft: When assembling the intermediate shaft, make sure the speed gears turn freely and have a minimum of 0.076mm endplay. When installing the 1st speed gear thrust washer make sure the chamfered edge is facing the pinion gear. When installing the 1st/2nd synchronizer make sure the relief faces the 2nd speed gear. Use an arbor press to install the intermediate shaft rear bearing, the 3rd/4th synchronizer hub and the 3rd speed gear. When installing the 3-4 synchronizer hub and 3rd speed gear, index the snapring 90° to the split washer. During the installation of synchronizer ring assemblies, make sure that all the matchmarks are aligned.

SELECTOR SHAFT HOUSING

1. Remove the snapring from the selector shaft boot and remove the boot.

2. Pry the shaft oil seal from the selector shaft housing.

3. With a small prybar positioned against the gearshift selector, compress the crossover and push the E-clip from the selector shaft. Remove the E-clip to release the selector shaft.

4. Withdraw the selector shaft from the selector housing.

5. Remove the plate stop retaining bolts and remove the stop.

6. Disassemble the selector shaft housing components.

7. Assemble the selector shaft housing components in the reverse order of removal. Use a new back-up lamp switch gasket if needed.

8. Install the plate stop with the retaining bolts.

9. Insert the selector shaft into the housing.

10. Compress the gearshift selector and install the E-clip.

11. Clean the bore and drive a new oil seal into the housing using the proper tool.

12. Place the boot onto the shaft and retain with the snapring.

DIFFERENTIAL BEARING RETAINER

1. Pry the oil seal from the retainer.
2. Remove the retainer cup with a puller. Be careful not to damage the oil baffle and the select shim .
3. Remove the oil baffle and the select shim from the retainer cup.
4. Drive the oil baffle and select shim into the retainer cup using the proper tool.
5. Drive the retainer cup into the retainer using the proper tool.
6. Drive in a new retainer oil seal.

EXTENSION HOUSING

1. Pry the oil seal from the extension housing.
2. Pull the extension cup from the extension housing using the proper tool.
3. Remove the O-ring and oil baffle from the housing.
4. Install a new O-ring into the groove on the outside of the housing.
5. Press the oil baffle in the housing using the proper tool.
6. Press the bearing cup into the extension housing using the proper tool.
7. Install a new housing oil seal.

INPUT SHAFT

1. Remove the input shaft rear and front bearing cones using a suitable puller.
2. Mount the bearing retainer plate on wood blocks and press the input shaft rear bearing cup from the plate.
3. Before pressing in the bearing cup, bolt the support plate onto the retainer plate.
4. With the support plate in place, press the bearing cup into the retainer plate.
5. Press the front and rear bearing cones onto the input shaft using the proper tool.

Bearing Endplay Adjustment

Shim thickness calculation and endplay adjustment need only be done if any of the following parts are replaced: transaxle case, input shaft seal retainer, bearing retainer plate, rear end cover, input shaft or input shaft bearings.

If any of the above components were replaced, use the following procedure to adjust the bearing preload and proper bearing turning torque.

1. Select a gauging shim which will give 0.025-0.250mm of endplay.

➡**Measure the original shim from the input shaft seal retainer and select a shim 0.25mm thinner than the original for the gauging shim.**

2. Install the gauging shim on the bearing cup and the input shaft seal retainer.
3. Alternately tighten the input shaft seal retainer bolts until the retainer is bottomed against the case. Torque the bolts to 21 ft. lbs.

➡**The input shaft seal retainer is used to draw the input shaft front bearing cup the proper distance into the case bore.**

4. Oil the input shaft bearings with A.T.F. (1984-87) or SAE 5W-30 engine oil (1988) and install the input shaft in the case. Install the bearing retainer plate with the input shaft rear bearing cup pressed in and the end cover installed. Torque all bolts and nuts to 21 ft. lbs.
5. Position the dial indicator to check the input shaft endplay. Apply moderate load, by hand, to the input shaft splines. Push toward the rear while rotating the input shaft back and forth a number of times and to settle out the bearings. Zero the dial indicator. Pull the input shaft toward the front while rotating the input shaft back and forth a number of times to settle out the bearings. Record the endplay.
6. The shim required for proper bearing preload is the total of the gauging shim thickness, plus endplay, plus (constant) preload of 0.050-0.076mm. Combine shims, if necessary, to obtain a shim within 0.04mm of the required shim.
7. Remove the input shaft seal retainer and gauging shim. Install the shim(s) selected in Step 6 and install the input shaft seal retainer with a 1/8 in. bead of RTV sealant.

➡**Keep RTV sealant out of the oil slot.**

8. Tighten the input shaft seal retainer bolts to 21 ft. lbs.

➡**The input shaft seal retainer is used to draw the input shaft front bearing cup the proper distance into the case bore.**

9. Using special tool L-4508 and an inch lb. torque wrench, check the input shaft turning torque. The turning torque should be 1-5 inch lbs. for new bearings or a minimum of 1 inch lb. for used bearings. If the turning torque is too high, install a 0.04mm thinner shim. If the turning torque is too low, install a 0.04mm thicker shim.
10. Check the input shaft turning torque. Repeat Step 9 until the proper bearing turning torque is obtained.

DIFFERENTIAL

▶ **See Figure 27**

1. Remove the bearing cone from the differential case.
2. Remove the ring gear bolts and separate the gear from the differential case. The ring gear bolts are epoxy patch type bolts and not to be reused.
3. Using a steel punch and hammer, knock the pinion shaft split pin from the ring gear and differential case.
4. Withdraw the pinion shaft(s) from the differential case.

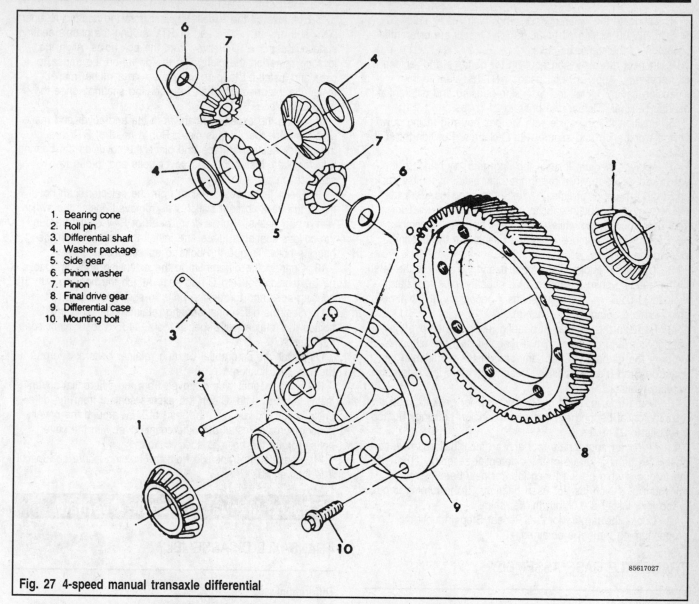

1. Bearing cone
2. Roll pin
3. Differential shaft
4. Washer package
5. Side gear
6. Pinion washer
7. Pinion
8. Final drive gear
9. Differential case
10. Mounting bolt

85617027

Fig. 27 4-speed manual transaxle differential

5. Rotate the side gears to align them with the case opening and remove the thrust washers, side gears and pinion gears.

➡**Shim thickness calculation and bearing preload adjustment need only be done if any of the following parts are replaced: transaxle case, input shaft seal retainer, bearing retainer plate, rear end cover, input shaft or input shaft bearings. If any of the those components were replaced, refer to the appropriate section to adjust the bearing preload, proper bearing turning torque or side gear endplay.**

6. In their original order, install the side gears, pinion gears and pinion gear washers.

7. Insert the pinion shaft(s) into the differential case making sure that the hole in the shaft is aligned with the roll pin opening in the case.

8. Insert the pinion shaft roll pin(s) into the notched opening(s) on the side of the differential case and drive them into place.

9. Connect the ring gear to the differential case using new bolts. Torque the bolts in a criss-cross pattern to the proper specification.

10. Attach special tool L-4410 to a suitable extension handle and press the bearing cone onto the differential case.

11. Refer to the appropriate section to check and adjust the bearing preload, if necessary.

Bearing Preload Adjustment Procedure

1. Remove the bearing cup and existing shim from the differential bearing retainer.

2. Select a gauging shim which will give 0.025-0.250mm endplay.

➡**Measure the original shim from the differential bearing retainer and select a shim 0.38mm thinner than the original for the gauging shim.**

3. Install the gauging shim in the differential bearing retainer and press in the bearing cup. Installation of the oil baffle is not necessary when checking differential assembly endplay.

4. Lubricate the differential bearings with A.T.F. (1984-87) or SAE 5W-30 engine oil (1988-89) and install the differential assembly in the transaxle case.

5. Inspect the extension housing for damage and replace it as necessary. Apply a 1/8 in. bead of RTV sealant to the extension flange. Install the extension housing and differential bearing retainer. Tighten the bolts to 21 ft. lbs.

6. Position the transaxle with the bell housing facing down on the workbench and secure with C-clamps. Position the dial indicator.

7. Apply a medium load to the ring gear, by hand, in the downward direction while rolling the differential assembly back and forth a number of times to settle the bearings. Zero the dial indicator. To obtain endplay readings, apply a medium load upward by hand while rolling the differential assembly back and forth a number of times to settle out the bearings. Record the endplay.

8. The shim required for proper bearing preload is the total of the gauging shim thickness, plus endplay, plus (constant) preload of 0.25mm. Combine shims if necessary, to obtain a shim within 0.05mm of the shim(s).

9. Remove the differential bearing retainer. Remove the bearing cup and gauging shim. Properly install the oil baffle. Be sure the oil baffle is not damaged. Install the shim(s) selected in Step 8 and press the bearing cup into the differential bearing retainer.

10. Using a 1/8 in. bead of RTV sealant for gaskets, install the differential bearing retainer and extension housing. Tighten the bolts to 21 ft. lbs.

11. Using an appropriate tool and an inch lb. torque wrench, check the turning torque of the differential assembly. The turning torque should be 9-14 inch lbs. for new bearings or a minimum of 6 inch lbs. for used bearings. If the turning torque is too low, install a 0.05mm thicker shim.

12. Check the turning torque. Repeat Step 11 until the proper turning torque is obtained.

TRANSAXLE CASE ASSEMBLY

1. Assemble the reverse shift lever components to the transaxle case and lock it in place with the E-clip.

2. Clean the input shaft bore and press in a new oil seal with special tool C-4674 or equivalent. Place the select shim into the retainer race and bolt the input shaft seal retainer onto the transaxle case. The drain hole on the retainer sleeve must be facing downward.

3. Assemble the clutch release shaft components in the reverse order of disassembly and secure the release lever with the E-clip. Insert the release shaft spline end through the bushing and engage it with the release shaft fork. Install the E-clip on the shaft groove to secure the shaft.

4. Install the shift fork and shift fork pads onto the intermediate shaft gear set. Install the intermediate and input shaft gear sets.

5. Install the reverse idler gear (with plastic stop) so that the roll pin on the end of the gear shaft aligns with the roll pin notch in the transaxle case. Lock the gear and engage the reverse shift lever. Make sure the plastic stop is firmly seated on the gear.

6. Install the 3-4 shift fork rail into the locating hole above the intermediate shaft assembly.

7. Remove all the excess sealant from the bearing retainer plate and run an 1/8 in. bead of RTV around the plate's seating surface. Keep the RTV away from the bolt holes. Align the locating dowel on the plate with the dowel on the transaxle case and install by tapping the plate with a rubber mallet. Install the intermediate shaft rear bearing snapring once the plate is in place.

8. Clean the excess sealant from the end cover and make sure the oil feeder hole is clear. Run a bead of RTV around the cover's seating surface and place the cover on the bearing retainer plate. Install the end cover bolts and torque to specification.

9. Clean the excess sealant from the selector shaft housing. If the back-up light switch was removed, install the switch with a new gasket. Run a 1/8 in. bead of RTV sealant around the cover's seating surface and install the housing with the housing bolts. Torque the bolts to specification.

10. Connect the differential to the extension housing. Use a new extension housing O-ring seal. Attach the housing with the housing bolts and torque the bolts to specification.

11. Seal the differential bearing retainer with RTV and tighten the retainer with special tool L-4435 or equivalent spanner wrench.

12. Install the differential bearing retainer bolts and torque them to specification.

13. If the magnet was removed from the differential cover, install it at this time. Clean the excess sealant from the differential cover and run a 1/8 in. bead of RTV around the cover's seating surface. Install the differential cover with the cover bolts. Torque the bolts to specification.

14. Remove the transaxle from the holding fixture and install it in the vehicle.

5-Speed Manual Transaxle Overhaul

TRANSAXLE DISASSEMBLY

Differential

▶ **See Figures 28, 29, 30, 31, 32, 33, 34, 35, 36 and 37**

1. Remove the transaxle from the vehicle and position on suitable holding fixture.

2. Remove the extension outer bolts.

3. Remove the differential retainer outer bolts.

4. Remove the differential assembly.

Transaxle

▶ **See Figures 38, 39, 40, 41, 42, 43, 44, 45, 46, 47, 48, 49, 50, 51, 52, 53, 54, 55, 56, 57, 58 and 59**

1. Remove the differential cover bolts and gently pry the cover from the extension.

2. Remove the extension housing bolts then separate the differential assembly and extension housing. Remove the O-ring seal and clean the RTV from extension housing. Discard the O-ring seal.

3. Unbolt and remove the differential retainer.

4. Remove the selector shaft housing assembly bolts and remove the selector shaft housing.

5. Unbolt and remove the rear end cover.

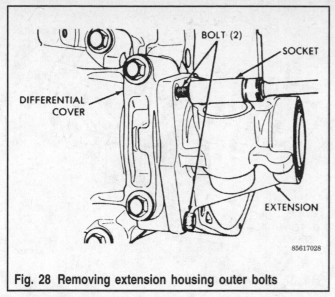

Fig. 28 Removing extension housing outer bolts

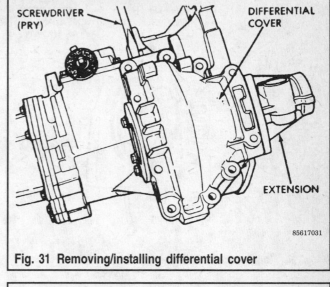

Fig. 31 Removing/installing differential cover

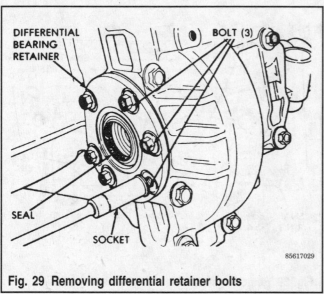

Fig. 29 Removing differential retainer bolts

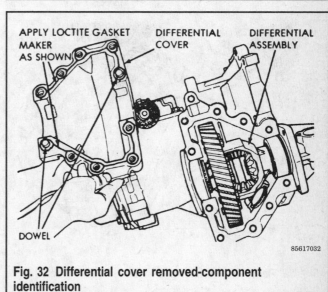

Fig. 32 Differential cover removed-component identification

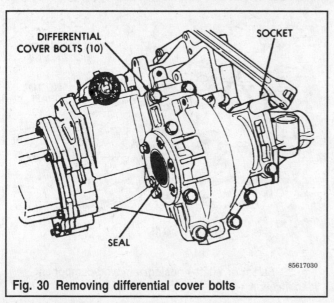

Fig. 30 Removing differential cover bolts

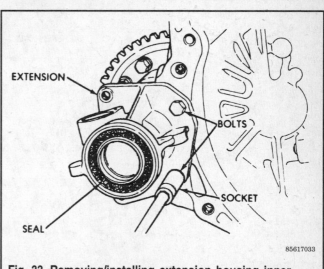

Fig. 33 Removing/installing extension housing inner bolts

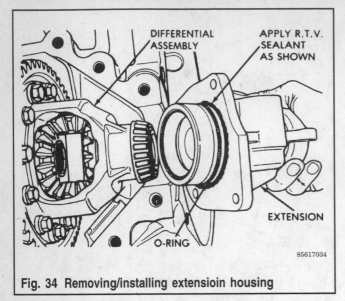

Fig. 34 Removing/installing extensioin housing

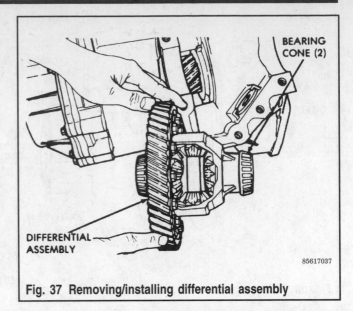

Fig. 37 Removing/installing differential assembly

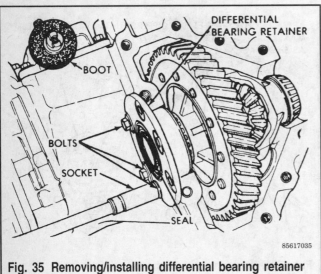

Fig. 35 Removing/installing differential bearing retainer bolts

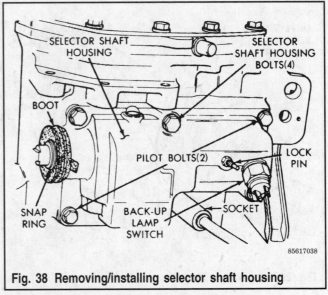

Fig. 38 Removing/installing selector shaft housing

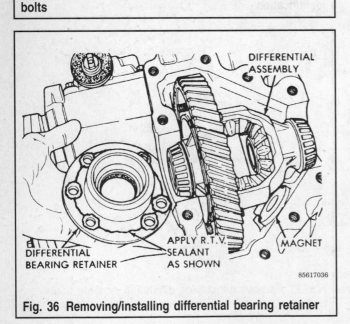

Fig. 36 Removing/installing differential bearing retainer

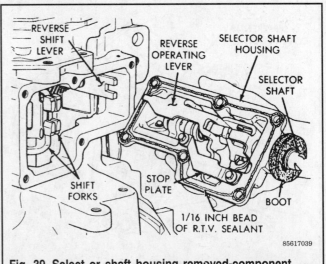

Fig. 39 Select or shaft housing removed-component identification

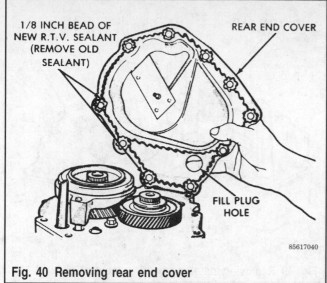

1/8 INCH BEAD OF NEW R.T.V. SEALANT (REMOVE OLD SEALANT)

REAR END COVER

FILL PLUG HOLE

85617040

Fig. 40 Removing rear end cover

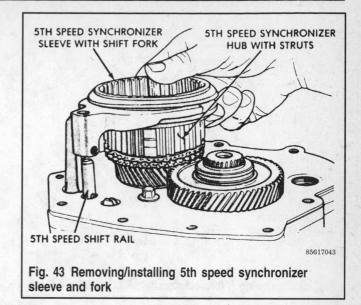

5TH SPEED SYNCHRONIZER SLEEVE WITH SHIFT FORK

5TH SPEED SYNCHRONIZER HUB WITH STRUTS

5TH SPEED SHIFT RAIL

85617043

Fig. 43 Removing/installing 5th speed synchronizer sleeve and fork

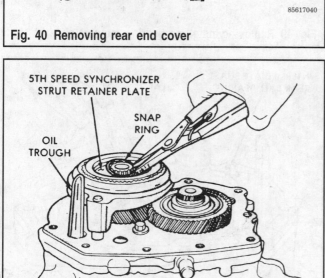

5TH SPEED SYNCHRONIZER STRUT RETAINER PLATE

SNAP RING

OIL TROUGH

85617041

Fig. 41 Fifth speed synchronizer plate and snap ring removal

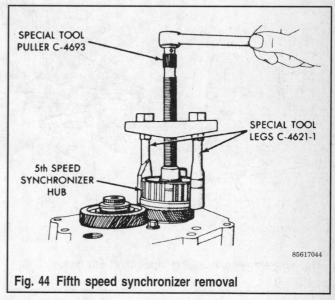

SPECIAL TOOL PULLER C-4693

SPECIAL TOOL LEGS C-4621-1

5th SPEED SYNCHRONIZER HUB

85617044

Fig. 44 Fifth speed synchronizer removal

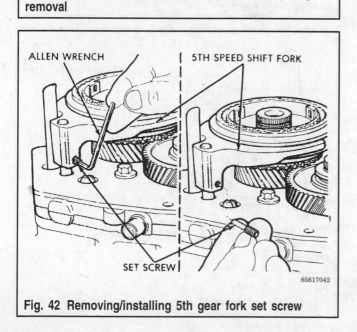

ALLEN WRENCH

5TH SPEED SHIFT FORK

SET SCREW

85617042

Fig. 42 Removing/installing 5th gear fork set screw

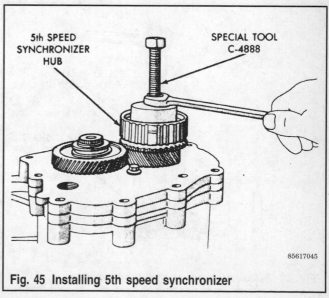

5th SPEED SYNCHRONIZER HUB

SPECIAL TOOL C-4888

85617045

Fig. 45 Installing 5th speed synchronizer

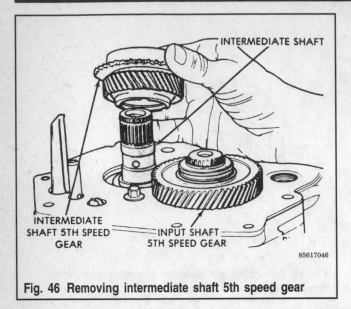

Fig. 46 Removing intermediate shaft 5th speed gear

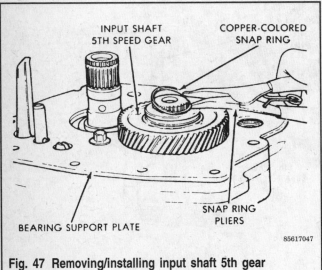

Fig. 47 Removing/installing input shaft 5th gear snapring

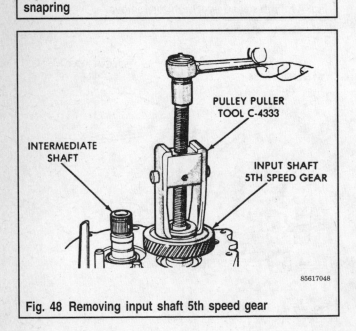

Fig. 48 Removing input shaft 5th speed gear

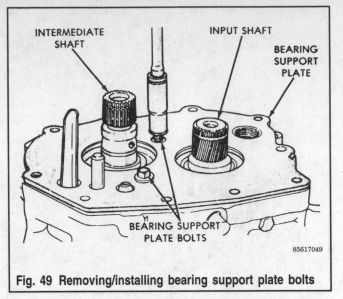

Fig. 49 Removing/installing bearing support plate bolts

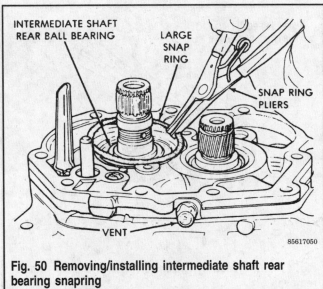

Fig. 50 Removing/installing intermediate shaft rear bearing snapring

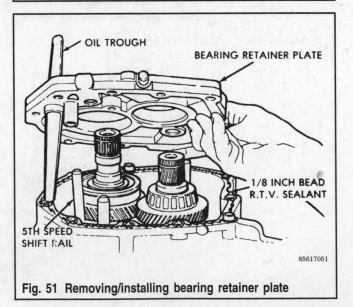

Fig. 51 Removing/installing bearing retainer plate

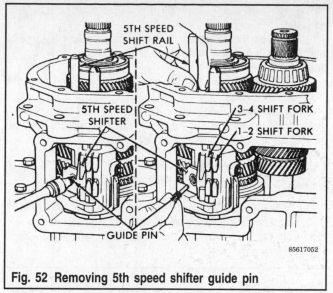

Fig. 52 Removing 5th speed shifter guide pin

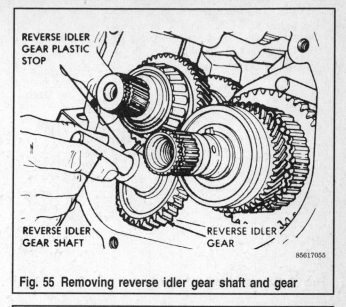

Fig. 55 Removing reverse idler gear shaft and gear

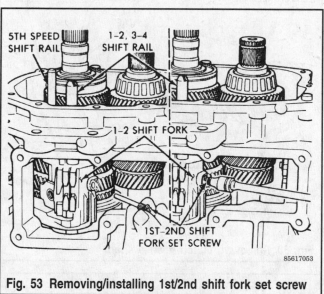

Fig. 53 Removing/installing 1st/2nd shift fork set screw

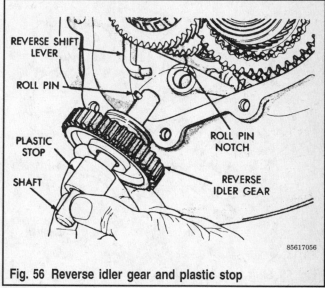

Fig. 56 Reverse idler gear and plastic stop

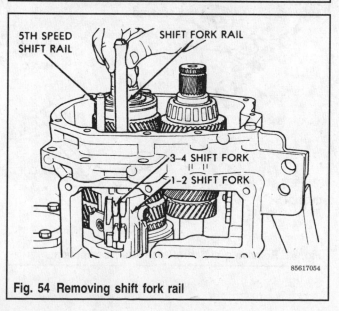

Fig. 54 Removing shift fork rail

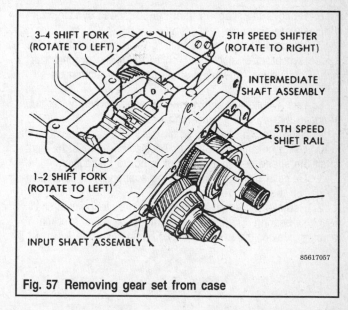

Fig. 57 Removing gear set from case

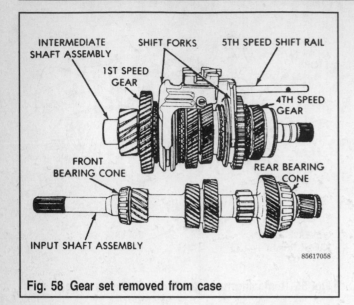

Fig. 58 Gear set removed from case

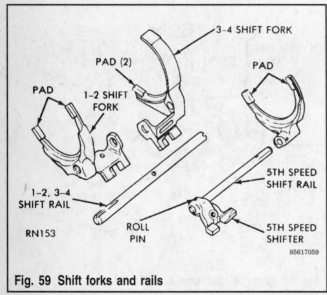

Fig. 59 Shift forks and rails

6. Remove the snapring from the 5th speed synchronizer strut retainer plate.

7. Unscrew the 5th speed shift fork set screw. Lift the 5th speed synchronizer sleeve and shift fork off the synchronizer hub. Retrieve the (3) winged struts and top synchronizer spring.

8. Use a puller to remove the 5th speed synchronizer hub. Retrieve the remaining synchronizer spring.

9. Slide the 5th speed gear off the intermediate shaft.

10. Using holding tool 6252 or equivalent, remove the input shaft 5th speed gear nut. This nut is not to be reused.

11. Remove the remaining bearing support plate bolts. Gently pry off the bearing support plate.

12. Remove the large snapring from the intermediate shaft rear ball bearing. Then, gently tap the lower surface of the bearing retainer plate with a plastic hammer to free it and lift it

off the transaxle case. Clean the RTV sealer from both surfaces.

13. Unscrew the 5th speed shifter guide pin. Do the same with the 1st/2nd shift fork setscrew. Withdraw the 1st/2nd, 3rd/4th shift fork rail.

14. Slide out the reverse idler gear shaft, gear, and plastic stop.

15. Rotate the 3rd/4th shift fork to the left, and the 5th gear shifter to the right. Pull out the 5th speed shift rail. Pull out the input shaft and intermediate shaft assemblies.

Clutch Release Bearing

▶ **See Figures 60 and 61**

1. Remove the 1st/2nd, 3rd/4th, and 5th speed shift forks.

2. To remove the clutch release bearing, remove the E-clips from the clutch release shaft, then disassemble the clutch shaft components.

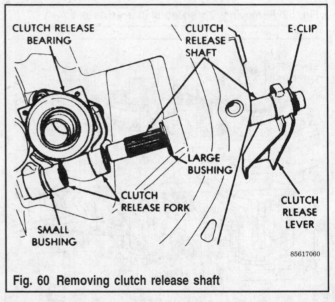

Fig. 60 Removing clutch release shaft

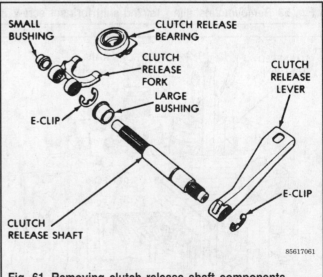

Fig. 61 Removing clutch release shaft components

Input Shaft Oil Seal

▶ **See Figures 62, 63, 64 and 65**

1. Remove the input shaft seal retainer bolts, the seal, the retainer assembly and the select shim.

Reverse Shift Lever

1. Remove the reverse shift lever E-clip and flat washer and disassemble the reverse shift lever components.

SUBASSEMBLY

▶ **See Figures 66, 67 and 68**

Transaxle Case

1. Press the input shaft front bearing cup from the transaxle case.
2. Unbolt and remove the intermediate shaft front bearing retaining strap.

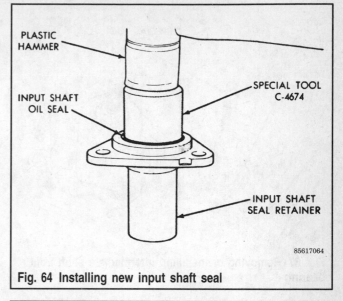

Fig. 64 Installing new input shaft seal

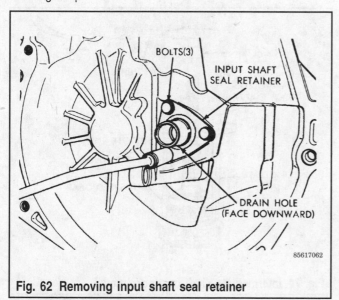

Fig. 62 Removing input shaft seal retainer

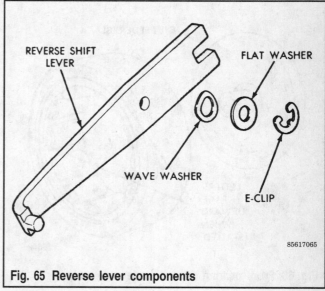

Fig. 65 Reverse lever components

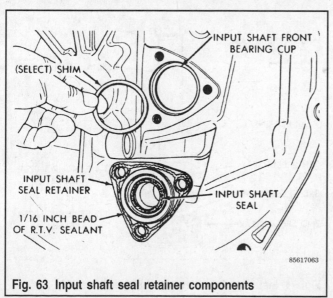

Fig. 63 Input shaft seal retainer components

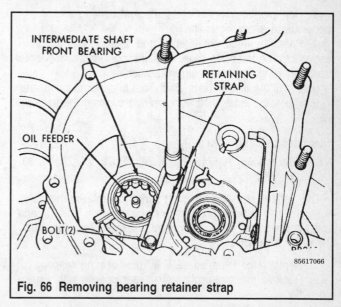

Fig. 66 Removing bearing retainer strap

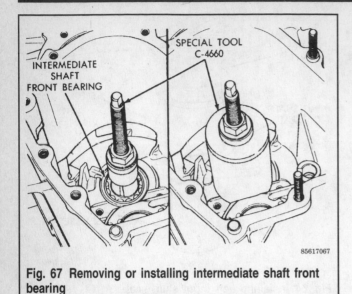

Fig. 67 Removing or installing intermediate shaft front bearing

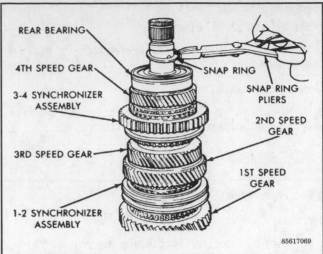

Fig. 69 Removing/installing intermediate shaft bearing snapring

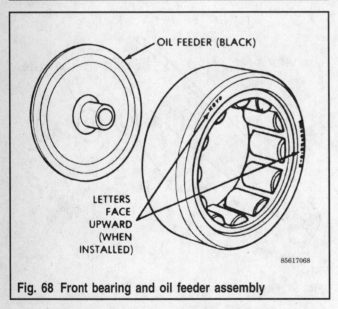

Fig. 68 Front bearing and oil feeder assembly

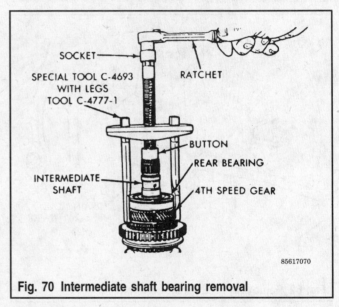

Fig. 70 Intermediate shaft bearing removal

3. Remove the intermediate shaft front bearing and oil feeder using a bearing puller.

4. Press the intermediate shaft front bearing with the oil feeder into the transaxle case. The bearing identification letters must be facing upward during installation.

5. Install the intermediate shaft front bearing retaining strap.

6. Press the input shaft front bearing cup into the transaxle case.

Intermediate Shaft Assembly

▶ See Figures 69, 70, 71, 72, 73, 74, 75, 76, 77, 78, 79, 80, 81, 83, 84 and 85

➡The 1st/2nd, the 3rd/4th shift forks are interchangeable, however, the synchronizer stop rings are not. The 1st and 2nd synchronizer stop rings have a larger diameter than the other stop rings.

1. Remove the intermediate shaft rear bearing snapring.

2. Remove the intermediate shaft rear bearing with a bearing puller.

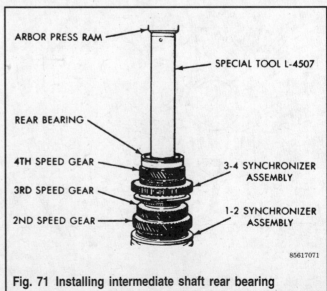

Fig. 71 Installing intermediate shaft rear bearing

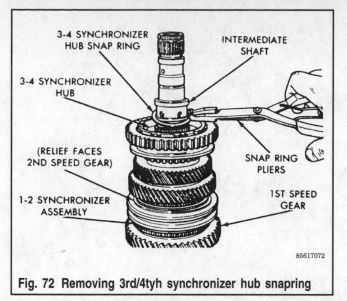

Fig. 72 Removing 3rd/4tyh synchronizer hub snapring

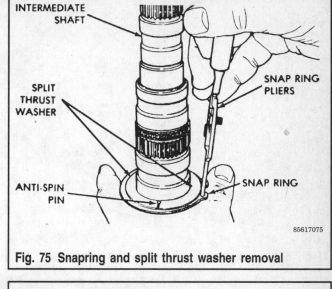

Fig. 75 Snapring and split thrust washer removal

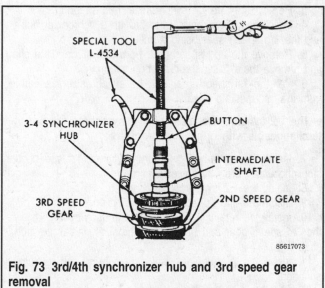

Fig. 73 3rd/4th synchronizer hub and 3rd speed gear removal

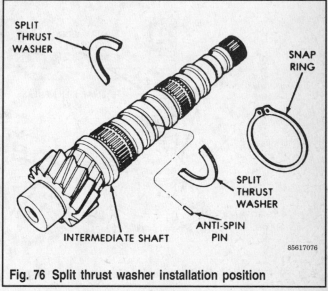

Fig. 76 Split thrust washer installation position

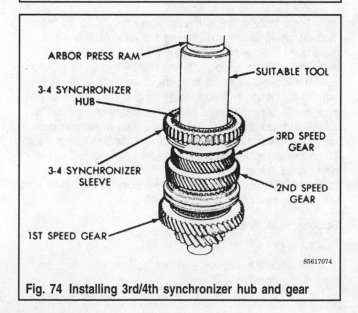

Fig. 74 Installing 3rd/4th synchronizer hub and gear

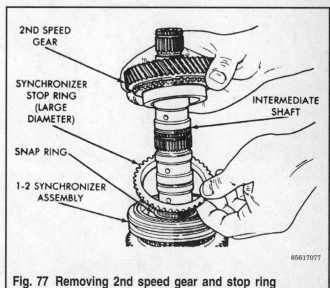

Fig. 77 Removing 2nd speed gear and stop ring

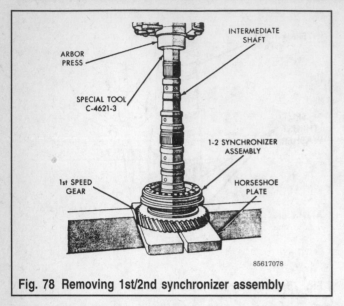

Fig. 78 Removing 1st/2nd synchronizer assembly

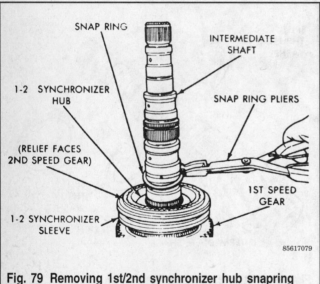

Fig. 79 Removing 1st/2nd synchronizer hub snapring

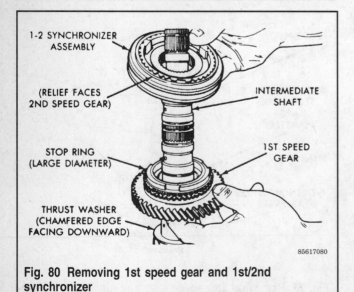

Fig. 80 Removing 1st speed gear and 1st/2nd synchronizer

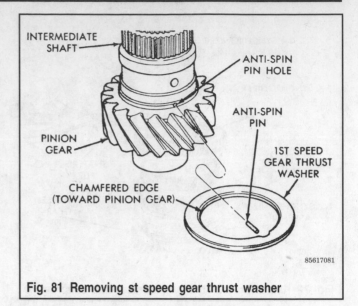

Fig. 81 Removing st speed gear thrust washer

3. Remove the 3rd/4th synchronizer hub snapring.

4. Matchmark then remove the 3rd/4th synchronizer hub and the 3rd speed gear using a puller.

5. Remove the 2nd speed gear from the intermediate shaft and remove the 1-2 synchronizer hub snapring.

6. Pull the 1st speed gear and 1-2 synchronizer assembly from the intermediate shaft.

➡The 1-2 synchronizer assembly components are not interchangeable with other synchronizers.

7. Install the 1st speed gear thrust washer, 1st speed gear, stop ring and 1-2 synchronizer assembly

8. Install the 1-2 synchronizer snapring.

9. Install the 2nd speed gear and stop ring.

10. Install the retaining ring and split thrust washer. Install the 3rd speed gear and the 3-4 synchronizer. Install the hub snapring.

11. Install the intermediate shaft rear bearing and retaining snapring.

12. Install the intermediate shaft front bearing.

➡Pay attention to the following when servicing the intermediate shaft: When assembling the intermediate shaft, make sure the speed gears turn freely and have a minimum of 0.076mm endplay. When installing the 1st speed gear thrust washer make sure the chamfered edge is facing the pinion gear. When installing the 1st/2nd synchronizer make sure the relief faces the 2nd speed gear. Use an arbor press to install the intermediate shaft rear bearing, the 3rd/4th synchronizer hub and the 3rd speed gear. When installing the 3-4 synchronizer hub and 3rd speed gear, index the snapring 90° to the split washer. During the installation of synchronizer ring assemblies, make sure that all he matchmarks are aligned.

Selector Shaft Housing
▶ See Figures 86, 87, 88, 89 and 90

1. Remove the snapring from the selector shaft boot and remove the boot.

2. Pry the shaft oil seal from the selector shaft housing.

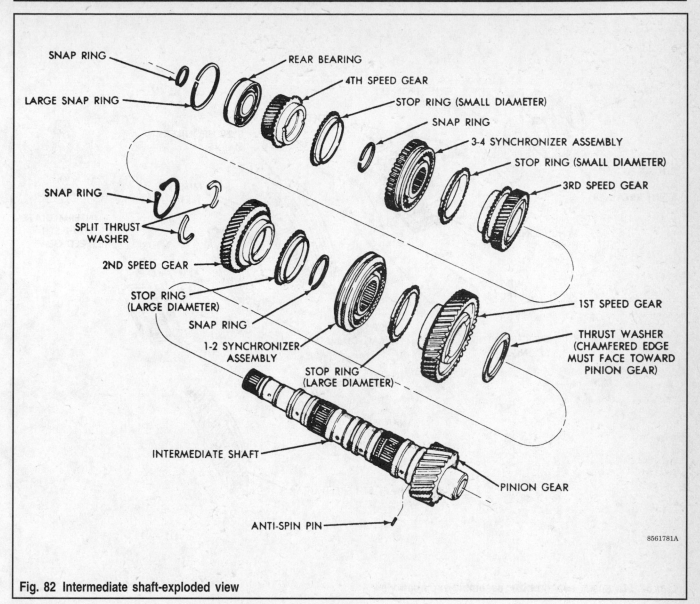

Fig. 82 Intermediate shaft-exploded view

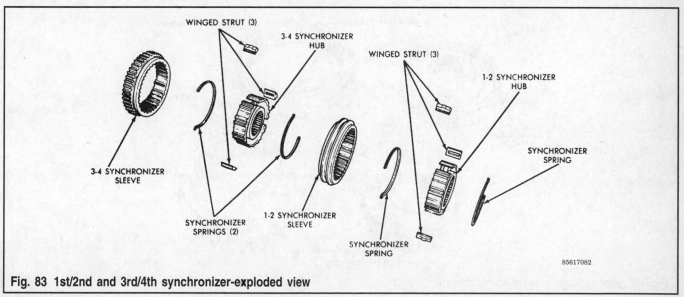

Fig. 83 1st/2nd and 3rd/4th synchronizer-exploded view

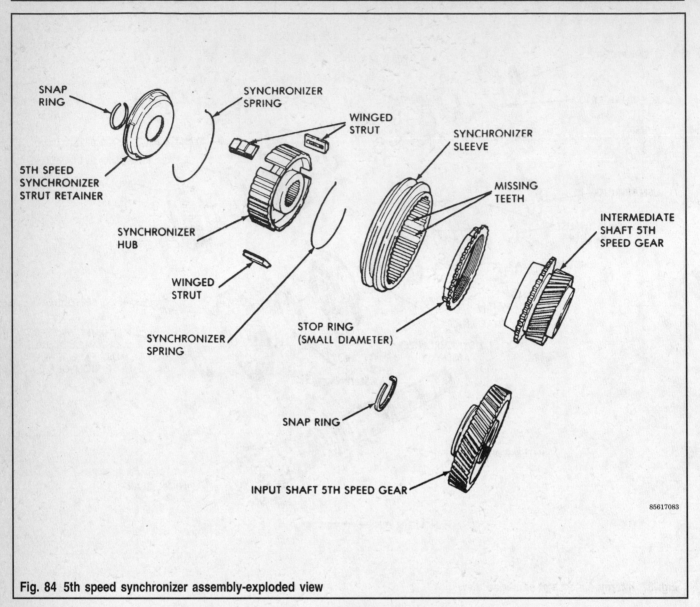

Fig. 84 5th speed synchronizer assembly-exploded view

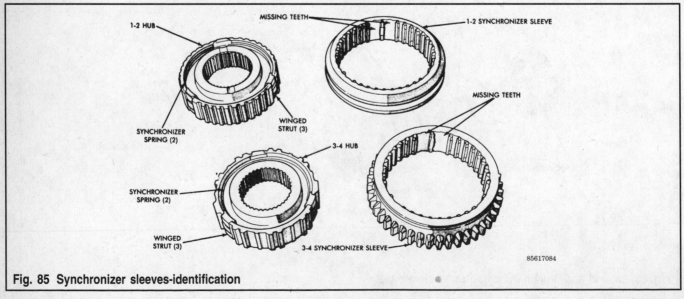

Fig. 85 Synchronizer sleeves-identification

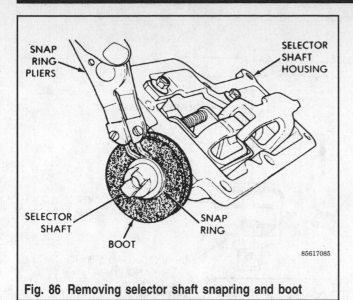

Fig. 86 Removing selector shaft snapring and boot

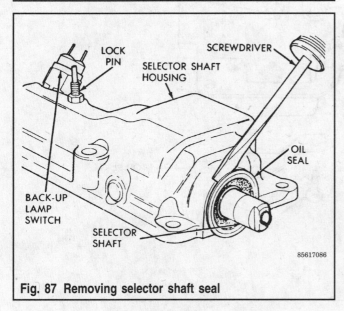

Fig. 87 Removing selector shaft seal

3. With a small prybar positioned against the gearshift selector, compress the crossover and 5th speed load spring and push the E-clip from the selector shaft. Remove the E-clip to release the selector shaft.

4. Withdraw the selector shaft from the selector housing.

5. Remove the plate stop retaining bolts and remove the stop.

6. Disassemble the selector shaft housing components.

7. Assemble the selector shaft housing components in the reverse order of removal. Use a new back-up lamp switch gasket if needed.

8. Install the plate stop with the retaining bolts.

9. Insert the selector shaft into the housing.

10. Compress the gearshift selector and install the E-clip.

11. Clean the bore and drive a new oil seal into the housing using the proper tool.

12. Place the boot onto the shaft and retain with the snapring.

Differential Bearing Retainer

▶ **See Figures 91, 92, 93, 94 and 95**

1. Pry the oil seal from the retainer.

2. Remove the retainer cup with a puller. Be careful not to damage the oil baffle and the select shim .

3. Remove the oil baffle and the select shim from the retainer cup.

4. Drive the oil baffle and select shim into the retainer cup using the proper tool.

5. Drive the retainer cup into the retainer using the proper tool.

6. Drive in a new retainer oil seal.

Extension Housing

▶ **See Figures 96, 97, 98, 99 and 100**

1. Pry the oil seal from the extension housing.

2. Pull the extension cup from the extension housing using the proper tool.

3. Remove the O-ring and oil baffle from the housing.

4. Install a new O-ring into the groove on the outside of the housing.

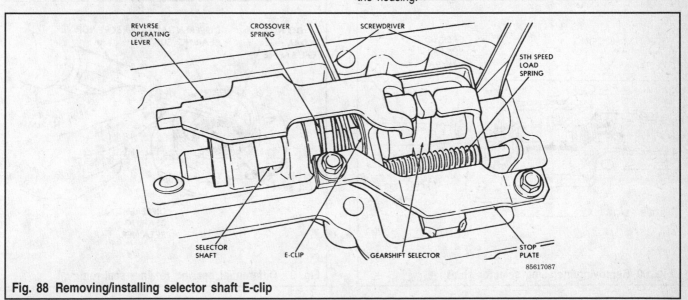

Fig. 88 Removing/installing selector shaft E-clip

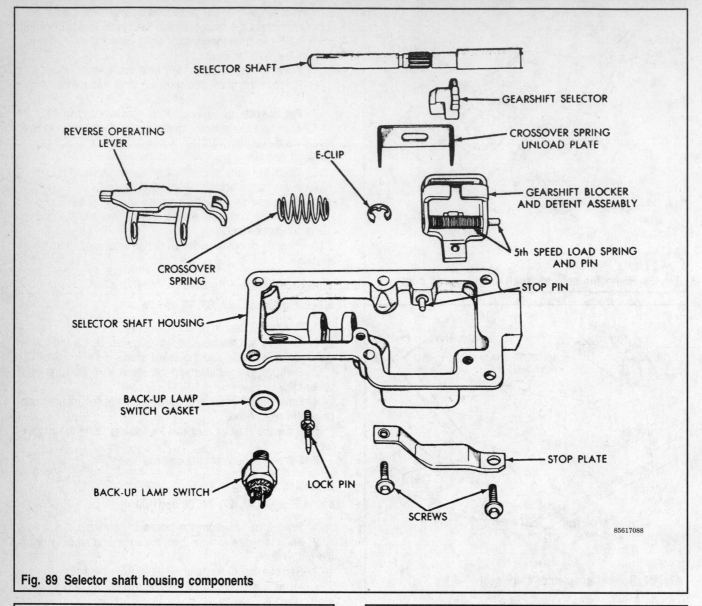

SELECTOR SHAFT

GEARSHIFT SELECTOR

REVERSE OPERATING LEVER

E-CLIP

CROSSOVER SPRING UNLOAD PLATE

GEARSHIFT BLOCKER AND DETENT ASSEMBLY

5th SPEED LOAD SPRING AND PIN

CROSSOVER SPRING

STOP PIN

SELECTOR SHAFT HOUSING

BACK-UP LAMP SWITCH GASKET

STOP PLATE

BACK-UP LAMP SWITCH

LOCK PIN

SCREWS

85617088

Fig. 89 Selector shaft housing components

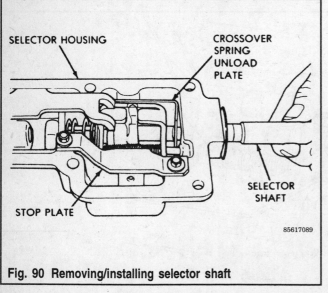

SELECTOR HOUSING

CROSSOVER SPRING UNLOAD PLATE

SELECTOR SHAFT

STOP PLATE

85617089

Fig. 90 Removing/installing selector shaft

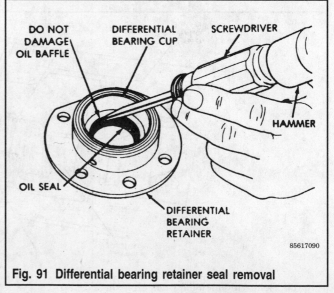

DO NOT DAMAGE OIL BAFFLE

DIFFERENTIAL BEARING CUP

SCREWDRIVER

HAMMER

OIL SEAL

DIFFERENTIAL BEARING RETAINER

85617090

Fig. 91 Differential bearing retainer seal removal

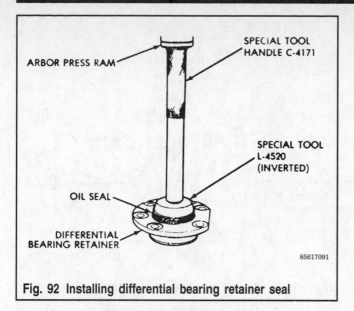

Fig. 92 Installing differential bearing retainer seal

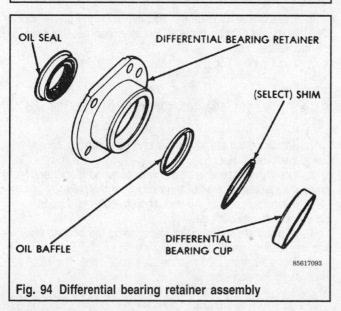

Fig. 93 Removing/installing differential bearing retainer

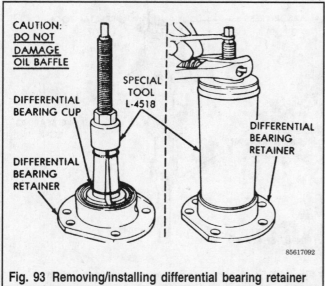

Fig. 94 Differential bearing retainer assembly

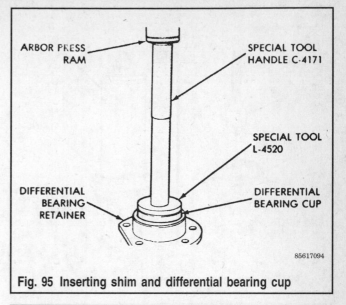

Fig. 95 Inserting shim and differential bearing cup

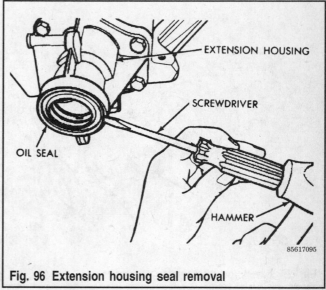

Fig. 96 Extension housing seal removal

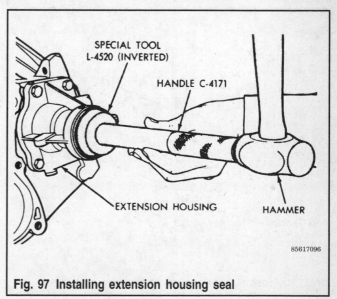

Fig. 97 Installing extension housing seal

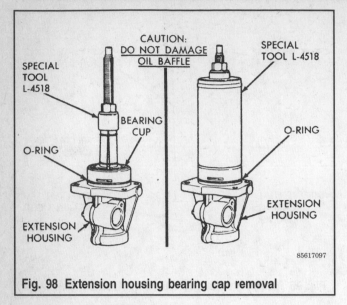

Fig. 98 Extension housing bearing cap removal

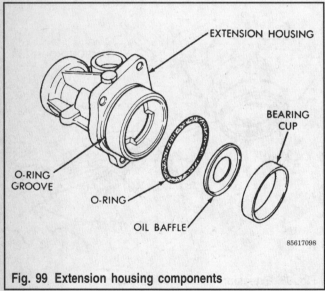

Fig. 99 Extension housing components

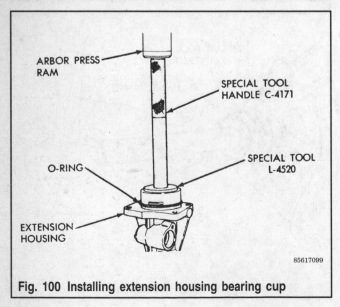

Fig. 100 Installing extension housing bearing cup

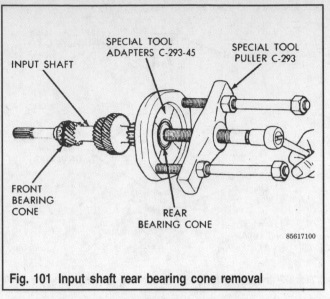

Fig. 101 Input shaft rear bearing cone removal

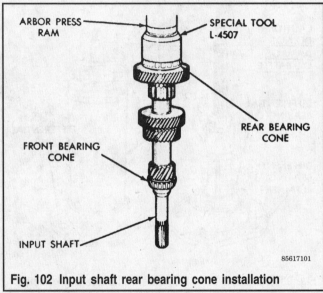

Fig. 102 Input shaft rear bearing cone installation

5. Press the oil baffle in the housing using the proper tool.

6. Press the bearing cup into the extension housing using the proper tool.

7. Install a new housing oil seal.

Input Shaft

▶ See Figures 101, 102, 103, 104, 105, 106, 107, 108 and 109

1. Remove the input shaft rear and front bearing cones using a suitable puller.

2. Mount the bearing retainer plate on wood blocks and press the input shaft rear bearing cup from the plate.

3. Before pressing in the bearing cup, bolt the support plate onto the retainer plate.

4. With the support plate in place, press the bearing cup into the retainer plate.

5. Press the front and rear bearing cones onto the input shaft using the proper tool.

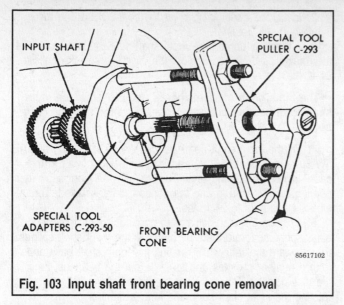

Fig. 103 Input shaft front bearing cone removal

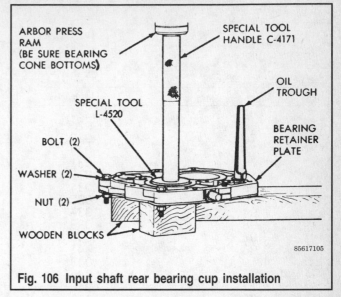

Fig. 106 Input shaft rear bearing cup installation

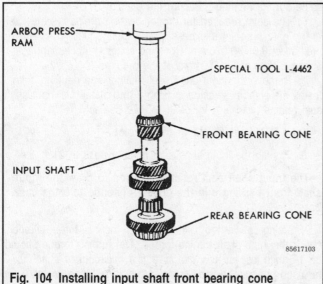

Fig. 104 Installing input shaft front bearing cone

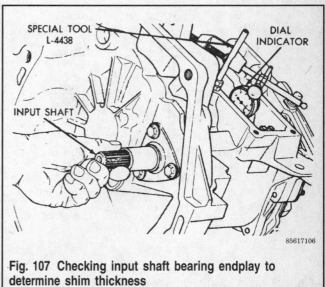

Fig. 107 Checking input shaft bearing endplay to determine shim thickness

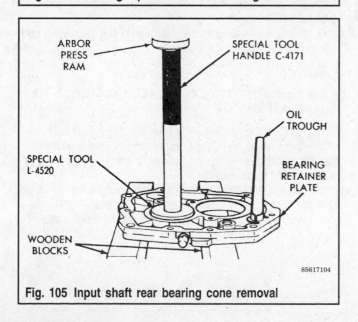

Fig. 105 Input shaft rear bearing cone removal

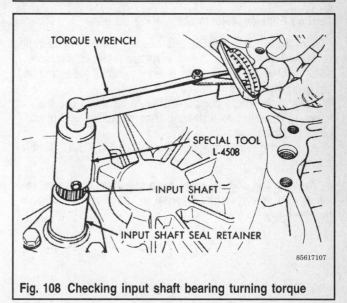

Fig. 108 Checking input shaft bearing turning torque

mm	mm	inch
.62		.024
.66		.026
.70		.028
.74		.029
.78		.031
.82		.032
.86		.034
.90		.035
.94		.037
.98		.039
1.02		.040
1.06		.042
1.10		.043
1.14		.045
1.18		.046
1.22		.048
1.26		.050
1.30		.051
1.34		.053
1.36	(.66 + .70)	.054
1.40	(.66 + .74)	.055
1.44	(.70 + .74)	.057
1.48	(.70 + .78)	.059
1.52	(.74 + .78)	.060
1.56	(.74 + .82)	.061
1.60	(.78 + .82)	.063
1.64	(.78 + .86)	.065
1.68	(.82 + .86)	.066
1.72	(.82 + .90)	.068
1.76	(.86 + .90)	.069

85617108

Fig. 109 Input shaft shim selection chart

Bearing Endplay Adjustment

Shim thickness calculation and endplay adjustment need only be done if any of the following parts are replaced: transaxle case, input shaft seal retainer, bearing retainer plate, rear end cover, input shaft or input shaft bearings.

If any of the above components were replaced, use the following procedure to adjust the bearing preload and proper bearing turning torque.

1. Select a gauging shim which will give 0.025-0.250mm of endplay.

➡**Measure the original shim from the input shaft seal retainer and select a shim 0.25mm thinner than the original for the gauging shim.**

2. Install the gauging shim on the bearing cup and the input shaft seal retainer.

3. Alternately tighten the input shaft seal retainer bolts until the retainer is bottomed against the case. Torque the bolts to 21 ft. lbs.

➡**The input shaft seal retainer is used to draw the input shaft front bearing cup the proper distance into the case bore.**

4. Oil the input shaft bearings with A.T.F. (1984-87) or SAE 5W-30 engine oil (1988-91) and install the input shaft in the case. Install the bearing retainer plate with the input shaft rear bearing cup pressed in and the support plate installed. Torque all bolts and nuts to 21 ft. lbs.

5. Position the dial indicator to check the input shaft endplay. Apply moderate load, by hand, to the input shaft splines. Push toward the rear while rotating the input shaft back and forth a number of times and to settle out the bearings. Zero the dial indicator. Pull the input shaft toward the front while rotating the input shaft back and forth a number of times to settle out the bearings. Record the endplay.

6. The shim required for proper bearing preload is the total of the gauging shim thickness, plus endplay, plus (constant) preload of 0.050-0.076mm. Combine shims, if necessary, to obtain a shim within 0.04mm of the required shim.

7. Remove the input shaft seal retainer and gauging shim. Install the shim(s) selected in Step 6 and install the input shaft seal retainer with a 1/8 in. bead of RTV sealant.

➡**Keep RTV sealant out of the oil slot.**

8. Tighten the input shaft seal retainer bolts to 21 ft. lbs.

➡**The input shaft seal retainer is used to draw the input shaft front bearing cup the proper distance into the case bore.**

9. Using special tool L-4508 and an inch lb. torque wrench, check the input shaft turning torque. The turning torque should be 1-5 inch lbs. for new bearings or a minimum of 1 inch lb. for used bearings. If the turning torque is too high, install a 0.04mm thinner shim. If the turning torque is too low, install a 0.04mm thicker shim.

10. Check the input shaft turning torque. Repeat Step 9 until the proper bearing turning torque is obtained.

Differential

▶ **See Figures 110, 111, 112, 113, 114, 115, 116, 117, 118, 119, 120 and 121**

1. Remove the bearing cone from the differential case.

2. Remove the ring gear bolts and separate the gear from the differential case. The ring gear bolts are epoxy patch type bolts and not to be reused.

3. Using a steel punch and hammer, knock the pinion shaft split pin from the ring gear and differential case.

4. Withdraw the pinion shaft(s) from the differential case.

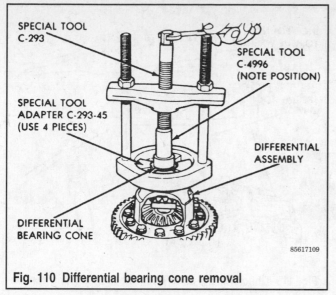

SPECIAL TOOL
C-293

SPECIAL TOOL
C-4996
(NOTE POSITION)

SPECIAL TOOL
ADAPTER C-293-45
(USE 4 PIECES)

DIFFERENTIAL
ASSEMBLY

DIFFERENTIAL
BEARING CONE

85617109

Fig. 110 Differential bearing cone removal

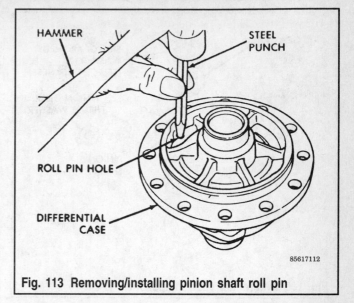

HAMMER

STEEL
PUNCH

ROLL PIN HOLE

DIFFERENTIAL
CASE

85617112

Fig. 113 Removing/installing pinion shaft roll pin

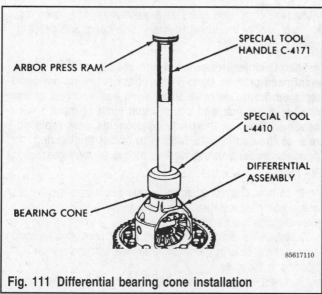

ARBOR PRESS RAM

SPECIAL TOOL
HANDLE C-4171

SPECIAL TOOL
L-4410

DIFFERENTIAL
ASSEMBLY

BEARING CONE

85617110

Fig. 111 Differential bearing cone installation

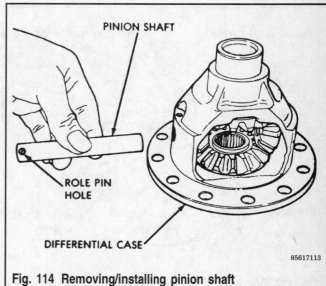

PINION SHAFT

ROLE PIN
HOLE

DIFFERENTIAL CASE

85617113

Fig. 114 Removing/installing pinion shaft

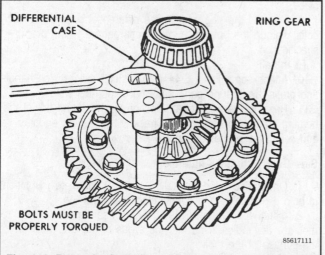

DIFFERENTIAL
CASE

RING GEAR

BOLTS MUST BE
PROPERLY TORQUED

85617111

Fig. 112 Removing/installing differential ring gear bolts
and ring gear

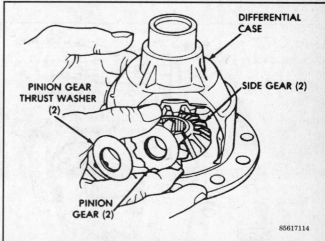

DIFFERENTIAL
CASE

PINION GEAR
THRUST WASHER
(2)

SIDE GEAR (2)

PINION
GEAR (2)

85617114

Fig. 115 Removing/installing pinion gears, side gears
and thrust washers by rotating pinion gears to opening
in differential case

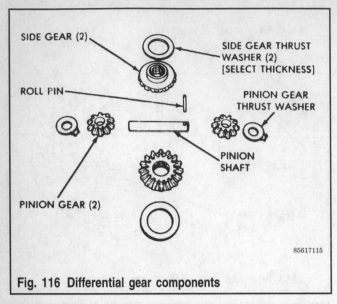

Fig. 116 Differential gear components

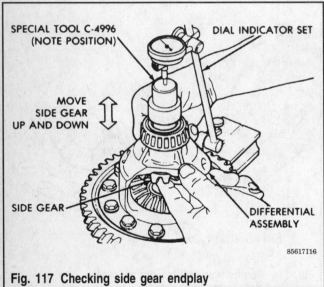

Fig. 117 Checking side gear endplay

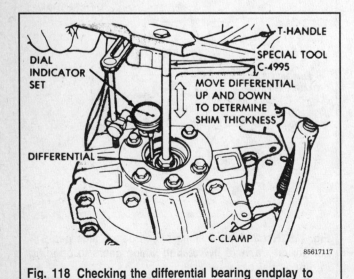

Fig. 118 Checking the differential bearing endplay to determine shim thickness

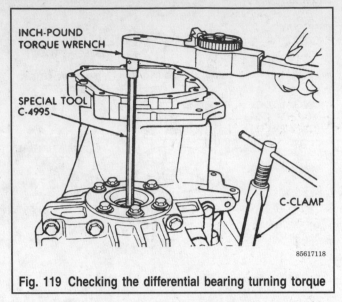

Fig. 119 Checking the differential bearing turning torque

5. Rotate the side gears to align them with the case opening and remove the thrust washers, side gears and pinion gears.

➡Shim thickness calculation and bearing preload adjustment need only be done if any of the following parts are replaced: transaxle case, input shaft seal retainer, bearing retainer plate, rear end cover, input shaft or input shaft bearings. If any of the those components were replaced, refer to the appropriate section to adjust the bearing preload, proper bearing turning torque or side gear endplay.

6. In their original order, install the side gears, pinion gears and pinion gear washers. Leave the thrust washer out until after the side gear endplay is adjusted.

7. Insert the pinion shaft(s) into the differential case making sure that the hole in the shaft is aligned with the roll pin opening in the case.

8. Insert the pinion shaft roll pin(s) into the notched opening(s) on the side of the differential case and drive them into place.

9. Connect the ring gear to the differential case using new bolts. Torque the bolts in a criss-cross pattern to the proper specification.

To install:

10. Attach special tool L-4410 to a suitable extension handle and press the bearing cone onto the differential case.

11. Refer to the appropriate section to check and adjust the bearing preload, if necessary. Check the side gear endplay and select the proper dimension thrust washer.

Side Gear Endplay Adjustment

1. Once assembled, rotate the gears 2 complete revolutions in both a clockwise and counterclockwise direction.

2. Install special tool C-4996 on the bearing cone and mount a dial indicator so that the stylus of the dial rests on the surface of the tool.

3. Move one of the side gears up and down by hand and record the endplay.

4. Zero the dial and rotate the side gear in 90° increments an repeat Step 3.

Required Shim Combination		Total Thickness			Required Shim Combination		Total Thickness			Required Shim Combination		Total Thickness	
mm		mm	Inch		mm		mm	Inch		mm		mm	Inch
.50		.50	.020		.50 + .70		1.20	.047		1.00 + .70		1.70	.067
.75		.75	.030		.50 + .75		1.25	.049		1.00 + .75		1.75	.069
.80		.80	.032		.50 + .80		1.30	.051		1.00 + .80		1.80	.071
.85		.85	.034		.50 + .85		1.35	.053		1.00 + .85		1.85	.073
.90		.90	.035		.50 + .90		1.40	.055		1.00 + .90		1.90	.075
.95		.95	.037		.50 + .95		1.45	.057		1.00 + .95		1.95	.077
1.00		1.00	.039		.50 + 1.00		1.50	.059		1.00 + 1.00		2.00	.079
1.05		1.05	.041		.50 + 1.05		1.55	.061		1.00 + 1.05		2.05	.081
.50 + .60		1.10	.043		1.00 + .60		1.60	.063		1.05 + 1.05		2.10	.083
.50 + .65		1.15	.045		1.00 + .65		1.65	.065					

85617119

Fig. 120 Differential bearing shim selection chart

5. Use the smallest endplay reading recorded and shim the side gear to within 0.025-0.330mm. For shimming, 4 select thrust washer sizes are available: 0.8mm, 0.9mm, 1.0mm, and 1.2mm.

6. Repeat Steps 1-4 for the other side gear.

Bearing Preload Adjustment Procedure

1. Remove the bearing cup and existing shim from the differential bearing retainer.

2. Select a gauging shim which will give 0.025-0.250mm endplay.

➡**Measure the original shim from the differential bearing retainer and select a shim 0.38mm thinner than the original for the gauging shim.**

3. Install the gauging shim in the differential bearing retainer and press in the bearing cup. Installation of the oil baffle is not necessary when checking differential assembly endplay.

4. Lubricate the differential bearings with A.T.F. (1984-87) or SAE 5W-30 engine oil (1988-91) and install the differential assembly in the transaxle case.

5. Inspect the extension housing for damage and replace it as necessary. Apply a ⅛ in. bead of RTV sealant to the extension flange. Install the extension housing and differential bearing retainer. Tighten the bolts to 21 ft. lbs.

6. Position the transaxle with the bell housing facing down on the workbench and secure with C-clamps. Position the dial indicator.

7. Apply a medium load to the ring gear, by hand, in the downward direction while rolling the differential assembly back and forth a number of times to settle the bearings. Zero the dial indicator. To obtain endplay readings, apply a medium load upward by hand while rolling the differential assembly back and forth a number of times to settle out the bearings. Record the endplay.

8. The shim required for proper bearing preload is the total of the gauging shim thickness, plus endplay, plus (constant) preload of 0.25mm. Combine shims if necessary, to obtain a shim within 0.05mm of the shim(s).

9. Remove the differential bearing retainer. Remove the bearing cup and gauging shim. Properly install the oil baffle.

Be sure the oil baffle is not damaged. Install the shim(s) selected in Step 8 and press the bearing cup into the differential bearing retainer.

10. Using a ⅛ in. bead of R.T.V. sealant for gaskets, install the differential bearing retainer and extension housing. Tighten the bolts to 21 ft. lbs.

11. Using an appropriate tool and an inch lb. torque wrench, check the turning torque of the differential assembly. The turning torque should be 9-14 inch lbs. for new bearings or a minimum of 6 inch lbs. for used bearings. If the turning torque is too low, install a 0.05mm thicker shim.

12. Check the turning torque. Repeat Step 11 until the proper turning torque is obtained.

TRANSAXLE ASSEMBLY

1. Assemble the reverse shift lever components to the transaxle case and lock it in place with the E-clip.

2. Clean the input shaft bore and press in a new oil seal with special tool C-4674 or equivalent. Place the select shim into the retainer race and bolt the input shaft seal retainer onto the transaxle case. The drain hole on the retainer sleeve must be facing downward.

3. Assemble the clutch release shaft components in the reverse order of disassembly and secure the release lever with the E-clip. Insert the release shaft spline end through the bushing and engage it with the release shaft fork. Install the E-clip on the shaft groove to secure the shaft.

4. Install the shift forks and shift rails onto the intermediate gear shaft assembly.

5. Install the intermediate and input shaft gear sets into the transaxle case and make sure that the gears are in proper mesh. Once the gear sets are in place, rotate the 5th speed shifter to the right and the 1-2 and 3-4 shift forks to the left.

6. Install the reverse idler gear (with plastic stop) so that the roll pin on the end of the gear shaft aligns with the roll pin notch in the transaxle case. Lock the gear and engage the reverse shift lever. Make sure the plastic stop is firmly seated on the gear.

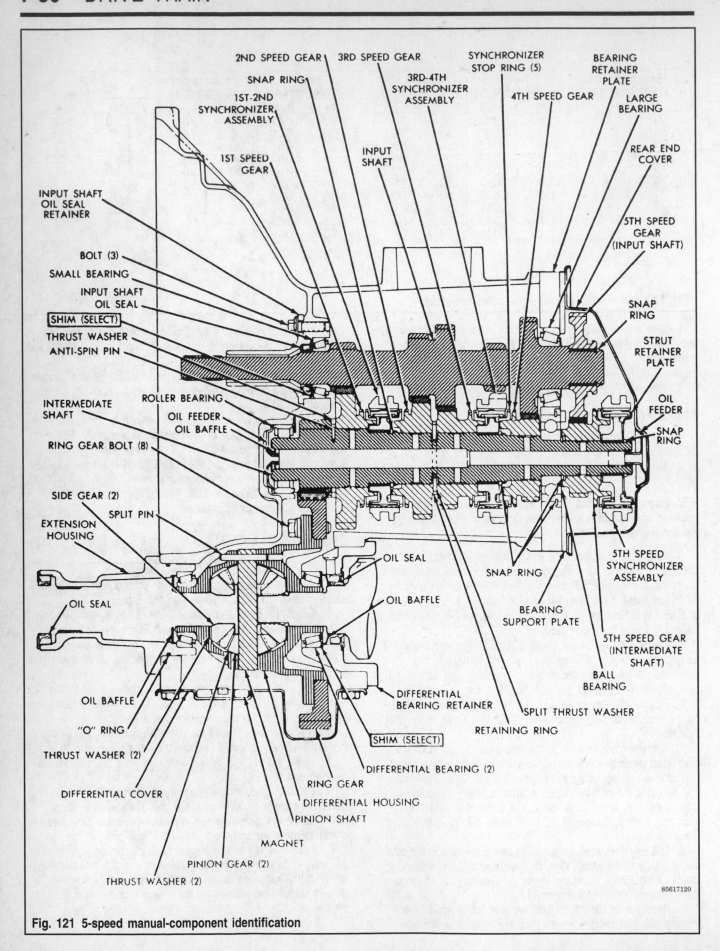

Fig. 121 5-speed manual-component identification

85617120

7. Install the 1-2, 3-4 and 5th speed shift fork rails into their respective locating holes.

8. Install and tighten the 1-2 shift fork set screw and 5th speed selector guide pin.

9. Remove all the excess sealant from the bearing retainer plate and run an 1/8 in. bead of RTV around the plate's seating surface. Keep the RTV away from the bolt holes. Align the plate with the transaxle case and install it. The plate will align with the oil trough and the 5th speed shift rail. Install the intermediate shaft rear bearing snapring once the plate is in place and seated.

10. Install the bearing support plate with the retaining bolts. Torque the bolts to specification.

11. Install the 5th speed gear onto the input shaft. Install a new gear nut with special holding tool 6252. The holding tool must be used to install the gear nut and the old nut must not be reused. Torque the nut to 190 ft. lbs. and remove the holding tool.

12. Install the intermediate shaft 5th speed gear, synchronizer hub and struts using special tool C-4888 or equivalent gear installer.

13. Position the 5th speed synchronizer sleeve and shift fork over the 5th speed shift rail and install it using the alignment marks for reference. Lock the fork to the rail with the set screw.

14. Install the 5th speed synchronizer strut retainer plate with the snapring.

15. Clean the excess sealant from the end cover and make sure the oil fill plug hole is clear. Run a bead of RTV around the cover's seating surface and place the cover on the bearing retainer plate. Install the end cover bolts and torque to specification.

16. Clean the excess sealant from the selector shaft housing. If the back-up light switch was removed, install the switch with a new gasket. Run a 1/8 in. bead of RTV sealant around the cover's seating surface and install the housing with the housing bolts. Torque the bolts to specification.

17. Apply RTV sealant to the portion of the differential bearing retainer that bolts to the ring gear to form a gasket.

18. Position the differential in the support saddles.

19. Connect the bearing retainer to the differential with the inner bolts and torque the bolts to specification.

20. Remove the O-ring seal from the extension housing and replace it with a new one. Remove the old sealant from the base of the extension and run a bead of new sealant.

21. Connect the extension to the other side of the differential with the outer bolts. Torque the bolts to specification.

22. Clean the excess sealant from the differential cover and run a 1/8 in. bead of RTV around the cover's seating surface. Install the differential cover with the cover bolts. Torque the bolts to specification.

23. Install the remaining extension and differential bearing retainer (outer) bolts and torque them to specification.

24. Remove the transaxle from the holding fixture and install it in the vehicle.

Halfshafts

The halfshafts used on your vehicle are of three piece construction, and are unequal in length and material composition. A short solid interconnecting shaft is used on the left side and a longer tubular interconnecting shaft is installed on the right side.

The halfshaft assemblies are three piece units. Each shaft has a Tripod joint on the transaxle side, an interconnecting shaft and a Rzeppa joint on the wheel side. The Rzeppa joint mounts a splined stub shaft that connects with the wheel hub. The inner Tripod joint mounts a spring that maintains constant spline engagement with the transaxle. The design enables the halfshaft to be removed without dismantling the transaxle.

Models equipped with a turbo charged engine incorporate an equal length halfshaft system. This system includes and extra, intermediate shaft installed on the right side. This helps to prevent torque steer induced by the power of the engine. The halfshaft removal procedure for all vehicles is the same.

REMOVAL & INSTALLATION

▶ **See Figures 122, 123, 124, 125, 126, 127, 128, 129, 130, 131, 132, 133, 134, 135, 136 and 137**

1. Remove the cotter pin, lock and spring washer from the front axle ends.

2. Have a helper apply the service brakes and loosen the front axle hub retaining nut.

3. Raise and support the front of the vehicle on jackstands.

4. Remove the hub nut, washer and wheel assembly. Drain transaxle fluid.

→**The speedometer drive pinion must be removed from the transaxle housing before the right side drive axle can be removed. Remove the retaining bolts and lift the pinion with cable connected from the housing.**

5. Remove the clamp bolt that secures the ball joint stud with the steering knuckle.

6. Separate the ball joint from the knuckle by prying downward against the knuckle connecting point and the control arm. Take care not to damage the rubber boot.

7. Separate the outer CV (constant velocity) joint splines from the steering knuckle hub by holding the CV housing and pushing the knuckle out and away. If resistance is encountered, use a brass drift and hammer to gently tap the outer hub end of the axle. Do not pry on the outer wear sleeve of the CV joint.

8. After the outboard end of the drive axle has been removed from the steering knuckle, support the assembly and pull outward on the inner CV joint housing to remove the assembly from the transaxle.

✳✳WARNING

Do not pull on the shaft or the assembly will disconnect. Pull only on the inner CV joint housing.

9. Remove the halfshaft from under the vehicle and service as necessary.

To install:

10. To install the halfshaft; Hold the inner joint assembly by its housing, align and guide the shaft into the transaxle or intermediate shaft assembly.

11. Lubricate the outer wear sleeve and seal with multi-purpose grease. Push the steering knuckle outward and install the splined outer shaft into the drive hub. Install the steering

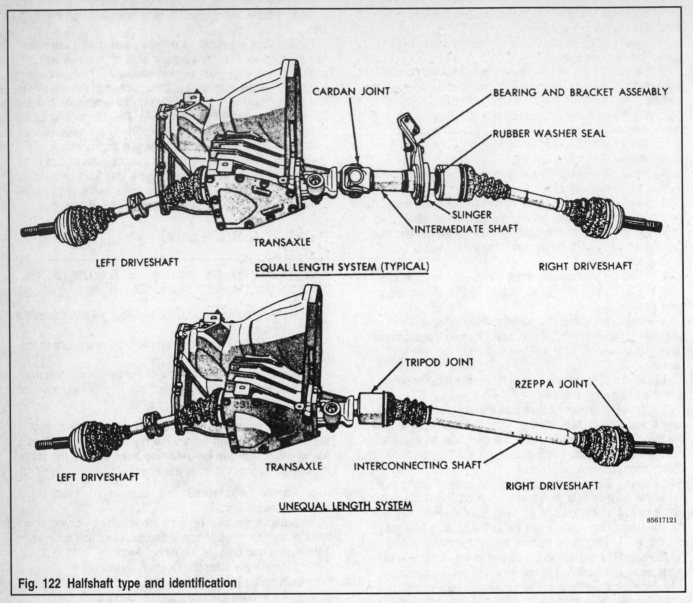

CARDAN JOINT

BEARING AND BRACKET ASSEMBLY

RUBBER WASHER SEAL

SLINGER

INTERMEDIATE SHAFT

TRANSAXLE

LEFT DRIVESHAFT

EQUAL LENGTH SYSTEM (TYPICAL)

RIGHT DRIVESHAFT

TRIPOD JOINT

RZEPPA JOINT

TRANSAXLE

INTERCONNECTING SHAFT

LEFT DRIVESHAFT

RIGHT DRIVESHAFT

UNEQUAL LENGTH SYSTEM

85617121

Fig. 122 Halfshaft type and identification

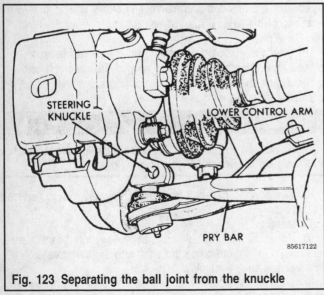

STEERING KNUCKLE

LOWER CONTROL ARM

PRY BAR

85617122

Fig. 123 Separating the ball joint from the knuckle

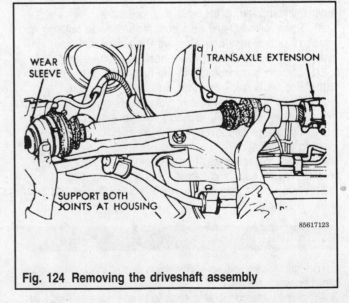

WEAR SLEEVE

TRANSAXLE EXTENSION

SUPPORT BOTH JOINTS AT HOUSING

85617123

Fig. 124 Removing the driveshaft assembly

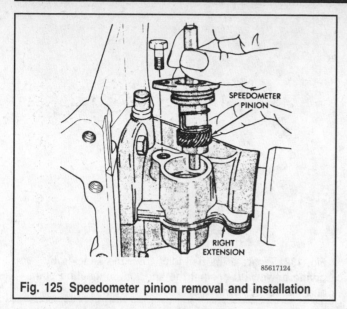

Fig. 125 Speedometer pinion removal and installation

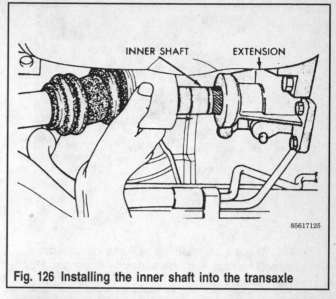

Fig. 126 Installing the inner shaft into the transaxle

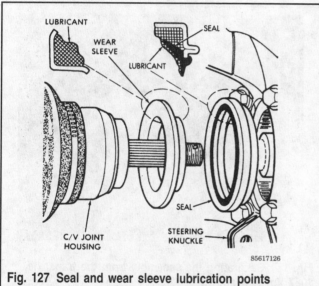

Fig. 127 Seal and wear sleeve lubrication points

Fig. 129 Removing the hub nut, 1987 Voyager shown

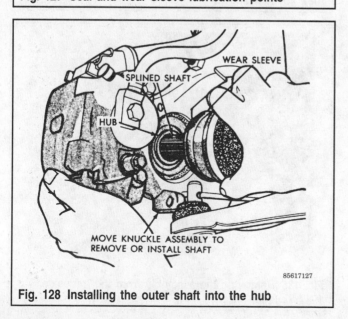

Fig. 128 Installing the outer shaft into the hub

Fig. 130 Removing the ball joint to steering knuckle clamp bolt, 1987 Voyager shown

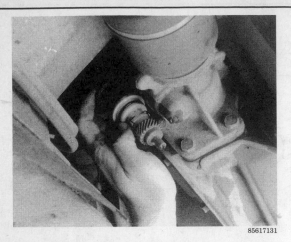

Fig. 131 Remove the retaining bolt and remove the speedometer pinion from the transaxle assembly, 1987 Voyager shown

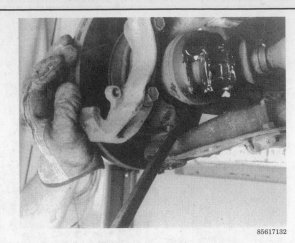

Fig. 132 Separate the ball joint from the knuckle by prying downward against the knuckle connecting point and the control arm, 1987 Voyager shown

Fig. 133 Separate the outer CV (constant velocity) joint splines from the steering knuckle hub by holding the CV housing and pushing the knuckle out and away, 1987 Voyager shown

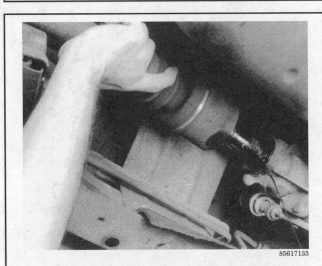

Fig. 135 Separating the assembly from the transaxle, 1987 Voyager shown

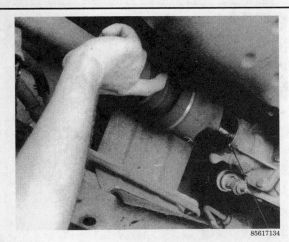

Fig. 134 Support the assembly and pull outward on the inner CV joint housing to remove the assembly from the transaxle, 1987 Voyager shown

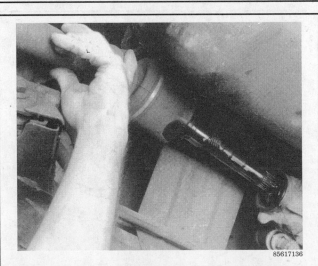

Fig. 136 Removing the assembly from the transaxle, 1987 Voyager shown

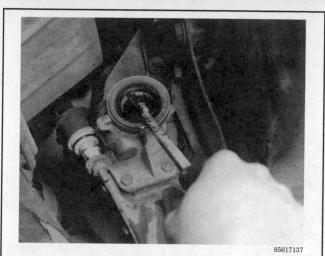

Fig. 137 Removing the seal from the housing using a suitable prying tool, 1987 Voyager shown

knuckle assembly. Torque the ball joint clamp bolt to 70 ft. lbs. Hub nut (splined shaft nut) torque to 180 ft. lbs. Refill the transaxle with the proper lubrication fluid.

➡If after installing the axle assembly, the inboard boot appears collapsed, vent the boot by inserting a thin round rod between the boot and the shaft. Massage the boot until is expands. Install a new clamp to prevent dirt from entering the boot.

CV-JOINT OVERHAUL

Inner Joint

▶ See Figures 138, 139, 140, 141, 142, 143, 144, 145, 146 and 147

1. With the halfshaft assembly removed from the vehicle, remove the clamps and boot.
2. Depending on the unit (GKN or Citroen) separate the tripod assembly from the housing as follows: Citroen type: Since the trunion ball rollers are not retained on bearing studs a retaining ring is used to prevent accidental tripod/housing separation, which would allow roller and needle bearings to fall away.

In the case of the spring loaded inner CV-joints, if it weren't for the retaining ring, the spring would automatically force the tripod out of the housing whenever the shaft was not installed in the vehicle.

Separate the tripod from the housing by slightly deforming the retaining ring in 3 places, with a suitable tool.

✳✳WARNING

Secure the rollers to the studs during separation. With the tripod out of the housing secure the assembly with tape.

3. GKN type: Spring loaded GKN inboard CV-joints have tabs on the can cover that prevent the spring from forcing the tripod out of the housing. These tabs must be bent back with a pair of pliers before the tripod can be removed. Under nor-

Fig. 139 Secure the rollers, then tap on the tripod retainer ring in 3 locations to separate the tripod from the housing, 1987 Voyager with Citroen type CV-joint

Fig. 140 Removing the spring and cup, 1987 Voyager with Citroen type CV-joint

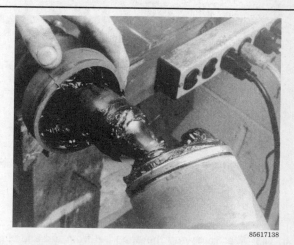

Fig. 138 After removing the boot clamps, pull back the boot to expose the tripod retention system, 1987 Voyager with Citroen type CV-joint

Fig. 141 Separating the cup from the spring, 1987 Voyager with Citroen type CV-joint

Fig. 142 Remove the snapring from the end of the shaft, 1987 Voyager with Citroen type CV-joint

Fig. 143 After removing the snapring from the end of the shaft remove the tripod, 1987 Voyager with Citroen type CV-joint

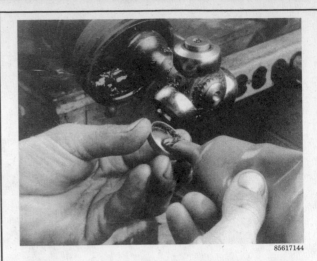

Fig. 144 Place a small amount of grease in the spring cup, 1987 Voyager with Citroen type CV-joint

mal conditions it is not necessary to secure the GKN rollers to their studs during separation due to the presence of a retainer ring on the end of each stud. This retention force can easily be overcome if the rollers are pulled or impacted. It is also possible to pull the rollers off by removing or installing the tripod with the connecting shaft at too high an angle, relative to the housing.

4. Remove the snapring from the shaft end groove, then remove the tripod with a brass punch.

To install:

5. Remove as much grease as possible from the assembly. Look at the ball housing races, and the components for excessive wear.

➡**DO NOT CLEAN THE INNER HOUSING WITH MINERAL SPIRITS OR SOLVENT. Solvents will destroy the rubber seals that are hidden in the housing and permit grease leakage. If wear is excessive, replace as necessary.**

6. Fasten the new boot onto the interconnecting shaft. Install the tripod on the shaft as follows: G.K.N. type: Slide the tripod onto the shaft with the non-chamfered end facing the tripod retaining ring groove. Citroen type: Slide the tripod onto the shaft (both sides are the same).

7. Install the retainer snapring into the groove on the interconnecting shaft locking the tripod in position.

8. On G.K.N. type: Put two of the three packets of grease into the boot and the remaining pack into the housing. On Citroen type: Put two thirds of the packet of grease into the boot and the remaining grease into the housing.

9. Position the spring into the housing spring pocket with the cup attached to the exposed end of the spring. Place a small amount of grease in the spring cup.

10. On G.K.N type: Slip the tripod into the housing and bend down the retaining tabs. Make sure the tabs are holding the housing firmly. On Citroen type: Remove the tape holding the rollers and needle bearings in place. Hold the rollers and needles in place and install the housing. Install the retaining ring into the machined groove in the housing with a punch and

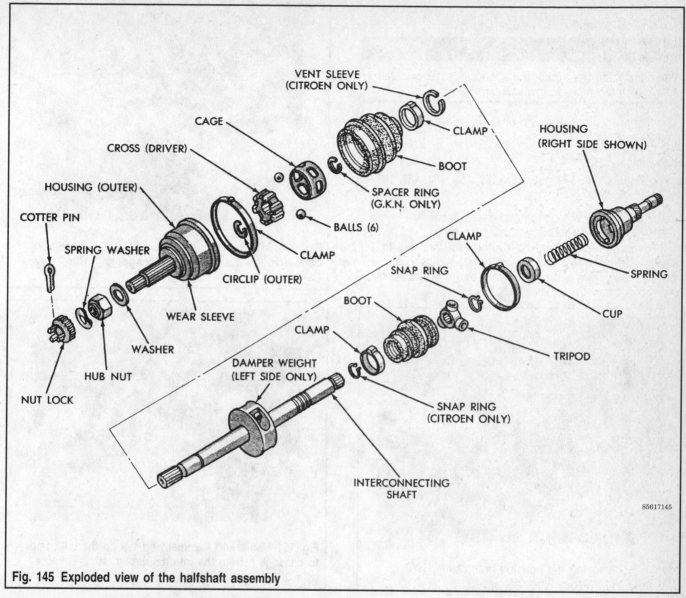

Fig. 145 Exploded view of the halfshaft assembly

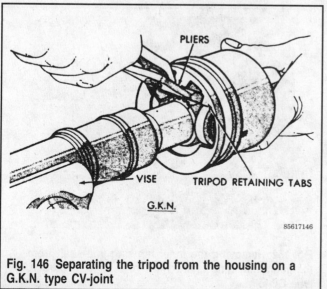

Fig. 146 Separating the tripod from the housing on a G.K.N. type CV-joint

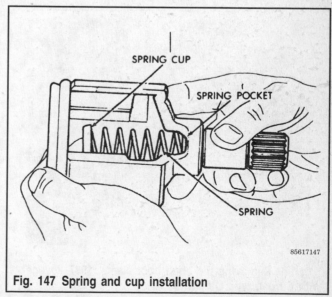

Fig. 147 Spring and cup installation

plastic hammer. Hold the retaining collar in position with two C-clamps while installing the retainer ring.

❊❊WARNING

When installing the tripod, the spring must be centered in the housing to insure proper positioning.

11. Position the boot over the retaining groove in the housing and clamp in position.

Outer Joint

◗ See Figures 148, 149, 150, 151, 152, 153, 154, 155, 156, 157, 158 and 159

1. Remove the boot clamps and discard them.
2. Wipe away the grease to expose the joint.
3. Support the shaft in a vise (Cushion the vise jaws to prevent shaft damage). Hold the outer joint, and using a plastic hammer, give a sharp tap to the top of the joint body to dislodge it from the internal circlip.

Fig. 150 After removing the clamps, pull the the boot back from the housing, 1987 Voyager with Citroen type CV-joint

Fig. 148 Removing the housing boot clamp, 1987 Voyager with Citroen type CV-joint

Fig. 151 Use a soft hammer and tap on the joint body to dislodge it from the internal circlip, 1987 Voyager with Citroen type CV-joint

Fig. 149 Removing the shaft boot clamp, 1987 Voyager with Citroen type CV-joint

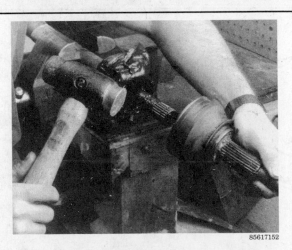

Fig. 152 Removing the inner housing and shaft from the interconnecting shaft, 1987 Voyager with Citroen type CV-joint

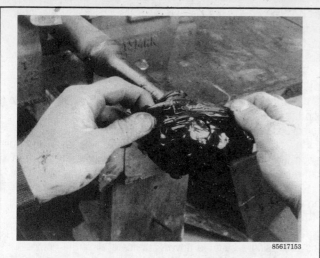

Fig. 153 Slide the boot and grease from the shaft, 1987 Voyager with Citroen type CV-joint

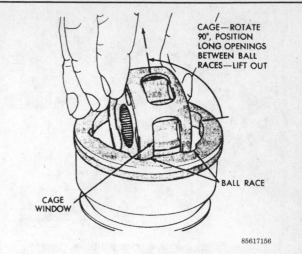

CAGE—ROTATE 90°, POSITION LONG OPENINGS BETWEEN BALL RACES—LIFT OUT

BALL RACE

CAGE WINDOW

Fig. 156 Removing the case and cross assembly from the housing

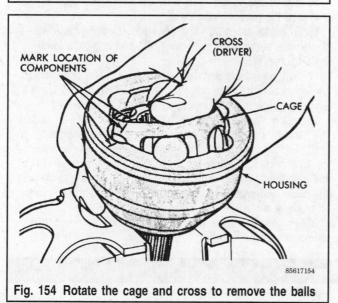

MARK LOCATION OF COMPONENTS

CROSS (DRIVER)

CAGE

HOUSING

Fig. 154 Rotate the cage and cross to remove the balls

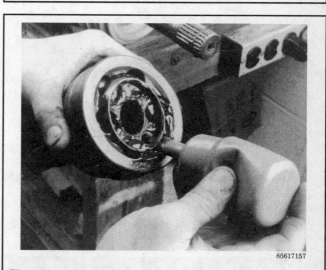

Fig. 157 Lubricate the ball races of the joint, 1987 Voyager with Citroen type CV-joint

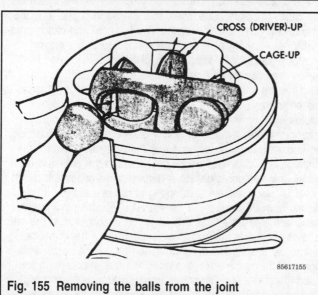

CROSS (DRIVER)-UP

CAGE-UP

Fig. 155 Removing the balls from the joint

Fig. 158 Gently tap the outer shaft and housing with a soft hammer onto the interconnecting shaft, 1987 Voyager with Citroen type CV-joint

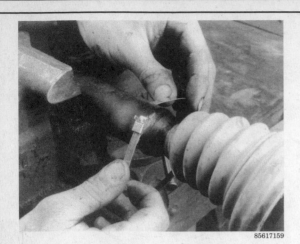

85617159

Fig. 159 After filling the new boot with the correct amount of grease install the boot retaining clamps, 1987 Voyager with Citroen type CV-joint

4. If the shaft is bent carefully pry the wear sleeve from the CV-joint machined ledge.

5. Remove the circlip from the shaft and discard it.

➡**Replacement boot kits will contain this circlip.**

6. Unless the shaft is damaged do not remove the heavy spacer ring from the shaft.

➡**If the shaft must be replaced, care must be taken that the new shaft is of the proper construction, depending on whether the inner joint is spring loaded or not. If the CV-joint was operating satisfactorily, and the grease down not appear contaminated, just replace the boot. If the outer joint is noisy or badly worn, replace the entire unit. The repair kit will include boot, clamps, retaining ring (circlip) and lubricant.**

7. Wipe off the grease and mark the position of the inner cross, cage and housing with a dab of paint.

8. Hold the joint vertically in a vise. Do not crush the splines on the shaft.

9. Press down on one side of the inner race to tilt the cage and remove the balls from the opposite side.

10. If the joint is tight, use a hammer and brass drift pin to tap the inner race. Repeat this step until all balls have been removed. DO NOT hit the cage.

11. Tilt the cage and inner race assembly vertically and position the two opposing, elongated cage windows in the area between the ball grooves. Pull the cage out of the housing.

12. Turn the inner cross 90° and align the race lands with an elongated hole in the cage. Remove the inner race.

To install:

13. Position a new wear sleeve on the joint housing and install it using a suitable driver. Lubricate all of the components before assembly.

14. Align the parts according to paint markings.

15. Install one of the inner race lands into the cage window and feed the race into the cage.

16. Turn the cross 90° and align the opposing cage windows with the land, pivot another 90° and complete land installation.

17. When properly installed, the cross counter bore should be facing outward from the joint on G.K.N. type. The cross and cage chamfers will be facing out on Citroen type.

18. Apply the grease to the ball races. Install the balls into the raceway by tilting the cage and inner race assembly.

19. Fasten the boot to the shaft. Install the new retainer circlip provided. Position the outer joint on the splined end of the stub shaft, engage the splines and tap sharply to engage the circlip. Attempt to pull the shafts apart to see if the circlip is properly seated.

20. Position the large end of the boot and secure with a clamp. Install the halfshaft.

CLUTCH

Understanding the Clutch

The purpose of the clutch is to disconnect and connect engine power from the transmission. A car at rest requires a lot of engine torque to get all that weight moving. An internal combustion engine does not develop a high starting torque, so it must be allowed to operate without any load until it builds up enough torque to move the car. Torque increases with engine rpm. The clutch allows the engine to build up torque by physically disconnecting the engine from the transmission, relieving the engine of any load or resistance. The transfer of engine power to the transmission (the load) must be smooth and gradual; if it weren't, drive line components would wear out or break quickly. This gradual power transfer is made possible by gradually releasing the clutch pedal. The clutch disc and pressure plate are the connecting link between the engine and transmission. When the clutch pedal is released, the disc and plate contact each other (clutch engagement), physically joining the engine and transmission. When the pedal is pushed in, the disc and plate separate (the clutch is disengaged), disconnecting the engine from the transmission.

The clutch assembly consists of the flywheel, the clutch disc, the clutch pressure plate, the throw out bearing and fork, the actuating linkage and the pedal. The flywheel and clutch pressure plate (driving members) are connected to the engine crankshaft and rotate with it. The clutch disc is located between the flywheel and pressure plate, and splined to the transmission shaft. A driving member is one that is attached to the engine and transfers engine power to a driven member (clutch disc) on the transmission shaft. A driving member (pressure plate) rotates (drives) a driven member (clutch disc) on contact and, in so doing, turns the transmission shaft. There is a circular diaphragm spring within the pressure plate cover (transmission side). In a relaxed state (when the clutch pedal is fully released), this spring is convex; that is, it is dished outward toward the transmission. Pushing in the clutch pedal actuates an attached linkage rod. Connected to the other end of this rod is the throw out bearing fork. The throw out bearing is attached to the fork. When the clutch pedal is depressed, the clutch linkage pushes the fork and bearing forward to contact the diaphragm spring of the pressure plate. The outer edges of the spring are secured to the pressure plate and are pivoted on rings so that when the center of the spring is compressed by the throw out bearing, the outer edges bow outward and, by so doing, pull the pressure plate in the same direction — away from the clutch disc. This action separates the disc from the plate, disengaging the clutch and allowing the transmission to be shifted into another gear. A coil type clutch return spring attached to the clutch pedal arm permits full release of the pedal. Releasing the pedal pulls the throw out bearing away from the diaphragm spring resulting in a reversal of spring position. As bearing pressure is gradually released from the spring center, the outer edges of the spring bow outward, pushing the pressure plate into closer contact with the clutch disc. As the disc and plate move closer together, friction between the two increases and slippage is reduced until, when full spring pressure is applied (by fully releasing the pedal), The speed of the disc and plate are the same. This stops all slipping, creating a direct connection between the plate and disc which results in the transfer of power from the engine to the transmission. The clutch disc is now rotating with the pressure plate at engine speed and, because it is splined to the transmission shaft, the shaft now turns at the same engine speed. Understanding clutch operation can be rather difficult at first; if you're still confused after reading this, consider the following analogy. The action of the diaphragm spring can be compared to that of an oil can bottom. The bottom of an oil can is shaped very much like the clutch diaphragm spring and pushing in on the can bottom and then releasing it produces a similar effect. As mentioned earlier, the clutch pedal return spring permits full release of the pedal and reduces linkage slack due to wear. As the linkage wears, clutch free-pedal travel will increase and free-travel will decrease as the clutch wears. Free-travel is actually throw out bearing lash.

The diaphragm spring type clutches used are available in two different designs: flat diaphragm springs or bent spring. The bent fingers are bent back to create a centrifugal boost ensuring quick re-engagement at higher engine speeds. This design enables pressure plate load to increase as the clutch disc wears and makes low pedal effort possible even with a heavy-duty clutch. The throw out bearing used with the bent finger design is 1¼ in. long and is shorter than the bearing used with the flat finger design. These bearings are not interchangeable. If the longer bearing is used with the bent finger clutch, free-pedal travel will not exist. This results in clutch slippage and rapid wear.

The transmission varies the gear ratio between the engine and drive wheels. It can be shifted to change engine speed as driving conditions and loads change. The transmission allows disengaging and reversing power from the engine to the wheels.

✳✳CAUTION

The clutch driven disc contains asbestos, which has been determined to be a cancer causing agent. Never clean clutch surfaces with compressed air! Avoid inhaling any dust from any clutch surface! When cleaning clutch surfaces, use a commercially available brake cleaning fluid.

All models are equipped with a self-adjusting clutch. No free-play adjustment is possible.

Driven Disc and Pressure Plate

➡**Chrysler recommends the use of special tool #C4676 for disc alignment.**

REMOVAL & INSTALLATION

▶ **See Figure 160**

1. Remove the transaxle.
2. Matchmark the clutch cover and flywheel for easy reinstallation.
3. Insert special tool C4676 or its equivalent to hold the clutch disc in place.
4. Loosen the cover attaching bolts. Do this procedure in a diagonal manner, a few turns at a time to prevent warping the cover.
5. Remove the cover assembly and disc from the flywheel.
6. Remove the clutch release shaft and slide the release bearing off the input shaft seal retainer.
7. Remove the fork from the release bearing thrust plate.
8. Inspect the components. Replace as necessary.
   To install:
9. Install the throw out bearing, fork and component parts.
10. Mount the clutch assembly on the flywheel (Mate the matchmarks if old unit is used). Install the clutch disc alignment tool. Hold the alignment tool in position and loosely install the pressure plate retaining bolts.
11. Tighten the bolts a few turns at a time in rotation. Tighten to 250 in. lbs.

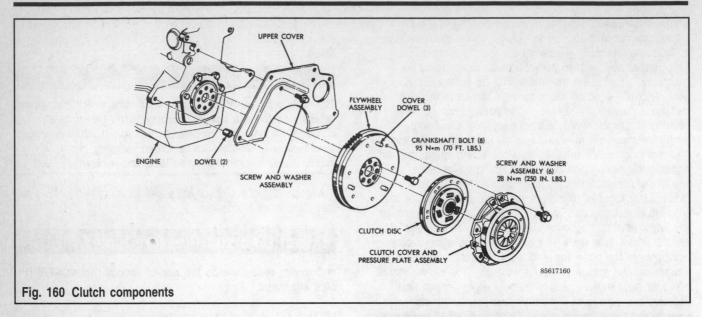

UPPER COVER

FLYWHEEL
ASSEMBLY

COVER
DOWEL (3)

CRANKSHAFT BOLT (8)
95 N•m (70 FT. LBS.)

SCREW AND WASHER
ASSEMBLY (6)
28 N•m (250 IN. LBS.)

ENGINE

DOWEL (2)

SCREW AND WASHER
ASSEMBLY

CLUTCH DISC

CLUTCH COVER AND
PRESSURE PLATE ASSEMBLY

85617160

Fig. 160 Clutch components

RELEASE CABLE ADJUSTMENT

The clutch release cable cannot be adjusted. When the cable is properly installed, a spring in the clutch pedal adjusts the cable to the proper position, regardless of clutch disc wear.

CLUTCH CABLE REPLACEMENT

▶ **See Figures 161 and 162**

1. Remove the clip from the cable mounting bracket on the shock tower.
2. Remove the retainer from the clutch release lever at the transaxle.
3. Pry the ball end of the cable from the positioner adjuster and remove the cable.
4. Installation is the reverse of removal.

Clutch Pedal

▶ **See Figures 161 and 162**

REMOVAL & INSTALLATION

1. Disconnect the negative battery cable.
2. Under the drivers side of the instrument panel, remove the clutch pedal return spring from the pedal and bracket.
3. Remove the retainer bolt from the clutch cable, at the top of the pedal arm. Release the cable from the pedal bracket.
4. Remove the lockring washers and bushing from the pedal pivot. Carefully slide the pedal assembly off of the pivot.
5. Install the pedal in position on the pivot and install the lockring. Reconnect the clutch release cable.
6. Check the operation of the pedal and make sure the clutch release is working.
7. Connect the negative battery cable.

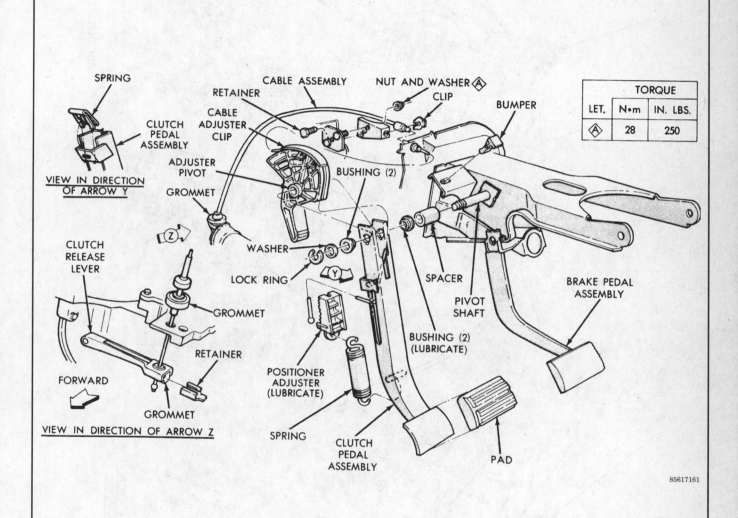

SPRING

CLUTCH PEDAL ASSEMBLY

VIEW IN DIRECTION OF ARROW Y

RETAINER

CABLE ASSEMBLY

CABLE ADJUSTER CLIP

ADJUSTER PIVOT

GROMMET

NUT AND WASHER⟨A⟩

CLIP

BUMPER

BUSHING (2)

TORQUE		
LET.	N•m	IN. LBS.
⟨A⟩	28	250

CLUTCH RELEASE LEVER

GROMMET

RETAINER

FORWARD

GROMMET

VIEW IN DIRECTION OF ARROW Z

WASHER

LOCK RING

POSITIONER ADJUSTER (LUBRICATE)

SPRING

CLUTCH PEDAL ASSEMBLY

SPACER

PIVOT SHAFT

BUSHING (2) (LUBRICATE)

BRAKE PEDAL ASSEMBLY

PAD

85617161

Fig. 161 Clutch pedal mechanism and components, 1984-90

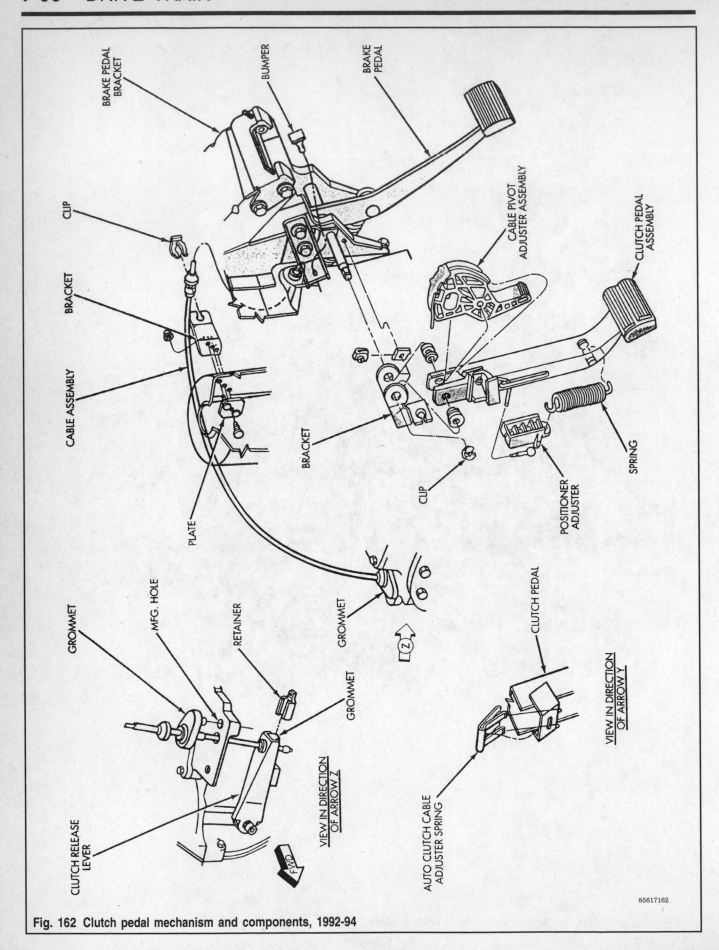

Fig. 162 Clutch pedal mechanism and components, 1992-94

BRAKE PEDAL BRACKET

BUMPER

BRAKE PEDAL

CLIP

BRACKET

CABLE ASSEMBLY

CABLE PIVOT ADJUSTER ASSEMBLY

CLUTCH PEDAL ASSEMBLY

BRACKET

CLIP

POSITIONER ADJUSTER

SPRING

PLATE

GROMMET

MFG. HOLE

RETAINER

GROMMET

GROMMET

CLUTCH PEDAL

VIEW IN DIRECTION OF ARROW Z

VIEW IN DIRECTION OF ARROW Y

CLUTCH RELEASE LEVER

AUTO CLUTCH CABLE ADJUSTER SPRING

FWD

85617162

AUTOMATIC TRANSAXLE

Understanding Automatic Transaxles

The automatic transaxle allows engine torque and power to be transmitted to the drive wheels within a narrow range of engine operating speeds. The transaxle will allow the engine to turn fast enough to produce plenty of power and torque at very low speeds, while keeping it at a sensible rpm at high vehicle speeds. The transaxle performs this job entirely without driver assistance. The transaxle uses a light fluid as the medium for the transaxle of power. This fluid also works in the operation of various hydraulic control circuits and as a lubricant. Because the transaxle fluid performs all of these three functions, trouble within the unit can easily travel from one part to another. For this reason, and because of the complexity and unusual operating principles of the transaxle, a very sound understanding of the basic principles of operation will simplify troubleshooting.

THE TORQUE CONVERTER

The torque converter replaces the conventional clutch. It has three functions:

1. It allows the engine to idle with the vehicle at a standstill, even with the transaxle in gear.

2. It allows the transaxle to shift from range to range smoothly, without requiring that the driver close the throttle during the shift.

3. It multiplies engine torque to an increasing extent as vehicle speed drops and throttle opening is increased. This has the effect of making the transaxle more responsive and reduces the amount of shifting required.

The torque converter is a metal case which is shaped like a sphere that has been flattened on opposite sides. It is bolted to the rear end of the engine's crankshaft. Generally, the entire metal case rotates at engine speed and serves as the engine's flywheel.

The case contains three sets of blades. One set is attached directly to the case. This set forms the torus or pump. Another set is directly connected to the output shaft, and forms the turbine. The third set is mounted on a hub which, in turn, is mounted on a stationary shaft through a one-way clutch. This third set is known as the stator.

A pump, which is driven by the converter hub at engine speed, keeps the torque converter full of transaxle fluid at all times. Fluid flows continuously through the unit to provide cooling.

Under low speed acceleration, the torque converter functions as follows:

The torus is turning faster than the turbine. It picks up fluid at the center of the converter and, through centrifugal force, slings it outward. Since the outer edge of the converter moves faster than the portions at the center, the fluid picks up speed.

The fluid then enters the outer edge of the turbine blades. It then travels back toward the center of the converter case along the turbine blades. In impinging upon the turbine blades, the fluid loses the energy picked up in the torus.

If the fluid were now to immediately be returned directly into the torus, both halves of the converter would have to turn at approximately the same speed at all times, and torque input and output would both be the same.

In flowing through the torus and turbine, the fluid picks up two types of flow, or flow in two separate directions. It flows through the turbine blades, and it spins with the engine. The stator, whose blades are stationary when the vehicle is being accelerated at low speeds, converts one type of flow into another. Instead of allowing the fluid to flow straight back into the torus, the stator's curved blades turn the fluid almost 90° toward the direction of rotation of the engine. Thus the fluid does not flow as fast toward the torus, but is already spinning when the torus picks it up. This has the effect of allowing the torus to turn much faster than the turbine. This difference in speed may be compared to the difference in speed between the smaller and larger gears in any gear train. The result is that engine power output is higher, and engine torque is multiplied.

As the speed of the turbine increases, the fluid spins faster and faster in the direction of engine rotation. As a result, the ability of the stator to redirect the fluid flow is reduced. Under cruising conditions, the stator is eventually forced to rotate on its one-way clutch in the direction of engine rotation. Under these conditions, the torque converter begins to behave almost like a solid shaft, with the torus and turbine speeds being almost equal.

THE PLANETARY GEARBOX

The ability of the torque converter to multiply engine torque is limited. Also, the unit tends to be more efficient when the turbine is rotating at relatively high speeds. Therefore, a planetary gearbox is used to carry the power output of the turbine to the halfshafts.

Planetary gears function very similarly to conventional transaxle gears. However, their construction is different in that three elements make up one gear system, and, in that all three elements are different from one another. The three elements are: an outer gear that is shaped like a hoop, with teeth cut into the inner surface; a sun gear, mounted on a shaft and located at the very center of the outer gear; and a set of three planet gears, held by pins in a ring-like planet carrier, meshing with both the sun gear and the outer gear. Either the outer gear or the sun gear may be held stationary, providing more than one possible torque multiplication factor for each set of gears. Also, if all three gears are forced to rotate at the same speed, the gear set forms, in effect, a solid shaft.

Most modern automatics use the planetary gears to provide either a single reduction ratio of about 1.8:1, or two reduction gears: a low of about 2.5:1, and an intermediate of about 1.5:1. Bands and clutches are used to hold various portions of the gear sets to the transaxle case or to the shaft on which they are mounted. Shifting is accomplished, then, by changing the portion of each planetary gear set which is held to the transaxle case or to the shaft.

THE SERVOS AND ACCUMULATORS

The servos are hydraulic pistons and cylinders. They resemble the hydraulic actuators used on many familiar machines, such as bulldozers. Hydraulic fluid enters the cylinder, under pressure, and forces the piston to move to engage the band or clutches.

The accumulators are used to cushion the engagement of the servos. The transaxle fluid must pass through the accumulator on the way to the servo. The accumulator housing contains a thin piston which is sprung away from the discharge passage of the accumulator. When fluid passes through the accumulator on the way to the servo, it must move the piston against spring pressure, and this action smooths out the action of the servo.

THE HYDRAULIC CONTROL SYSTEM

The hydraulic pressure used to operate the servos comes from the main transaxle oil pump. This fluid is channeled to the various servos through the shift valves. There is generally a manual shift valve which is operated by the transaxle selector lever and an automatic shift valve for each automatic upshift the transaxle provides: i.e., 2-speed automatics have a low/high shift valve, while 3-speeds have a 1-2 valve, and a 2-3 valve.

There are two pressures which effect the operation of these valves. One is the governor pressure which is affected by vehicle speed. The other is the modulator pressure which is affected by intake manifold vacuum or throttle position. Governor pressure rises with an increase in vehicle speed, and modulator pressure rises as the throttle is opened wider. By responding to these two pressures, the shift valves cause the upshift points to be delayed with increased throttle opening to make the best use of the engine's power output.

Most transaxles also make use of an auxiliary circuit for down shifting. This circuit may be actuated by the throttle linkage or the vacuum line which actuates the modulator, or by a cable or solenoid. It applies pressure to a special down shift surface on the shift valve or valves.

The transaxle modulator also governs the line pressure, used to actuate the servos. In this way, the clutches and bands will be actuated with a force matching the torque output of the engine.

The three speed automatic transaxle and differential are combined in a single housing and share the same Dexron®II type lubricant. Filter, fluid changes, and band adjustments are not require for average vehicle use. However, if the vehicle is used for constant heavy duty hauling, commercial use or more than 50 % operation in heavy traffic, the fluid and filter should be changed every 15,000 miles.

Fluid Pan and Filter

REMOVAL & INSTALLATION

▶ **See Figures 163, 164, 165, 166, 167, 168 and 169**

1. Raise and support the front of the vehicle on jackstands.
2. Remove the splash shield if it will interfere with the fluid pan removal.
3. Place a suitable container that will hold at least four quarts of fluid under the oil pan. Loosen all of the pan bolts slightly until the fluid stats to drain. Loosen the bolts around the point where the fluid is draining to increase the flow.
4. When the bulk of the fluid has drained, remove the oil pan. Clean the dirt from the pan and magnet. Remove RTV sealant or gasket material from the pan and case mounting surfaces.
5. Remove the filter from the bottom of the valve body.

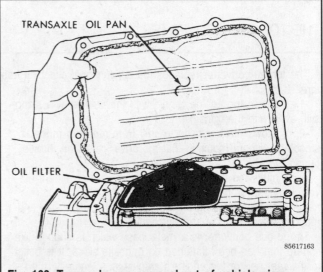

Fig. 163 Transaxle pan removal-out of vehicle view

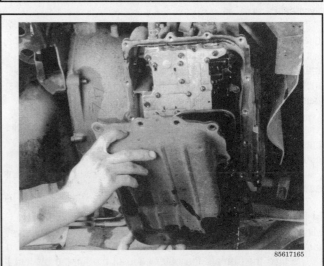

Fig. 164 Removing the transaxle oil pan, 1987 Voyager shown

Fig. 165 With the oil pan removed the transaxle valve body and filter are exposed, 1987 Voyager shown

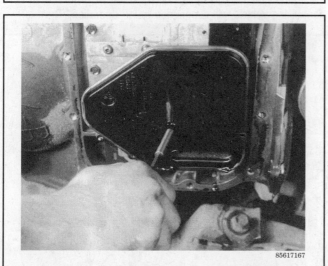

Fig. 166 Removing the transaxle oil filter retaining screws, 1987 Voyager shown

Fig. 167 Removing the transaxle oil filter retaining screws, 1987 Voyager shown

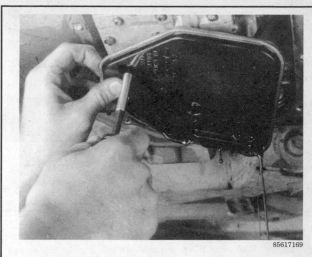

Fig. 168 Removing the transaxle oil filter retaining screws, 1987 Voyager shown

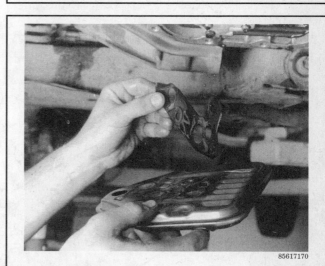

Fig. 169 Removing the transaxle oil filter and gasket, 1987 Voyager shown

To install:

6. Install a new filter and gasket. Tighten the mounting screw to 40 inch lbs.

7. Apply a unbroken bead of RTV sealant to the oil pan and install on case. Tighten the mounting bolts to 165 inch lbs.

8. Remove the differential cover. Use a clean cloth and wipe the cover and magnet to remove dirt. Clean the mounting surfaces of the cover and case.

9. Apply an unbroken bead of RTV sealant to the differential cover and reinstall. Tighten the mounting bolts to 165 inch lbs. Install the splash shield, etc. and lower the vehicle.

10. Pour four quarts of Dexron II type fluid through the dipstick fill tube. Start the engine, with the parking and service brakes applied, move the gear selector through the various positions ending up in Park.

11. Add sufficient fluid, if necessary, to bring the level to 1/8 in. below the Add mark.

12. Check the fluid level after engine and transaxle have reached the normal operating temperature. The level should be within the Hot range on the dipstick.

➡**Always make sure that the dipstick is fully seated in its tube to prevent dirt from entering the transaxle.**

Adjustments-Three Speed Torqueflite Transaxles

▶ **See Figure 170**

KICKDOWN CABLE

1. Run the engine until the normal operating temperature is reached. Be sure the choke is fully opened.
2. Loosen the adjustment bracket lock bolt mounted on transaxle to engine flange.
3. Be sure that the adjustment bracket can slide freely. Clean as necessary.

4. Slide the bracket toward the engine as far as possible. Release the bracket and move the throttle lever to the right as far as it will go. tighten the adjustment lock bolt to 105 inch lbs.

A-604 UPSHIFT AND KICKDOWN LEARNING PROCEDURE

A-604 Ultradrive Transaxle

In 1989, the A-604 4 speed, electronic transaxle was introduced; it is the first to use fully adaptive controls. The controls perform their functions based on real time feedback sensor information. Although, the transaxle is conventional in design, its functions are controlled by the ECM.

Since the A-604 is equipped with a learning function, each time the battery cable is disconnected, the ECM memory is lost. In operation, the transaxle must be shifted many times for the learned memory to be reinputed in the ECM; during this period, the vehicle will experience rough operation. The tran-

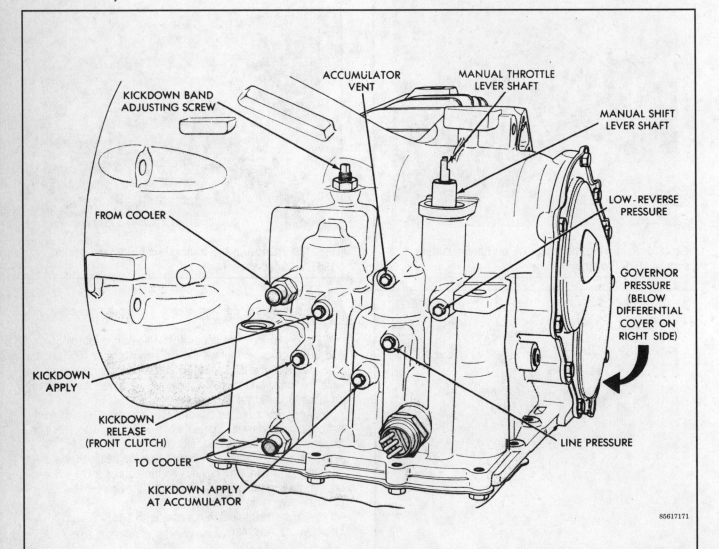

Fig. 170 Transaxle adjustment and maintenance points, 3-speed Torqueflite transaxle

85617171

saxle must be at normal operating temperature when learning occurs.

1. Maintain constant throttle opening during shifts. Do not move the accelerator pedal during upshifts.

2. Accelerate the vehicle with the throttle $\frac{1}{8}$-$\frac{1}{2}$ open.

3. Make 15 to 20 1/2, 2/3 and 3/4 upshifts. Accelerating from a full stop to 50 mph each time at the aforementioned throttle opening is sufficient.

4. With the vehicle speed below 25 mph, make 5 to 8 wide open throttle kick downs to 1st gear from either 2nd or 3rd gear. Allow at least 5 seconds of operation in 2nd or 3rd gear prior to each kickdown.

5. With the vehicle speed greater than 25 mph, make 5 to part throttle to wide open throttle kick downs to either 3rd or 2nd gear from 4th gear. Allow at least 5 seconds of operation in 4th gear, preferably at road load throttle prior to performing the kickdown.

THROTTLE PRESSURE CABLE ADJUSTMENT-4 CYL.

▶ See Figure 171

1. Run the engine until it reaches normal operating temperature.

2. Loosen the cable mounting bracket lock screw.

3. Position the bracket so that both alignment tabs are touching the transaxle case surface and tighten the lock screws.

4. Release the cross lock on the cable assembly by pulling the cross lock up.

5. To ensure proper adjustment, the cable must be free to slide all the way toward the engine against its stop after the cross lock is released.

6. Move the transaxle throttle control lever fully clockwise and press the cross lock down until it snaps into position.

7. Road test the vehicle and check the shift points.

THROTTLE PRESSURE ROD ADJUSTMENT-6 CYL.

1. Run the engine until it reaches normal operating temperature.

2. Loosen the adjustment swivel lock screw.

3. To ensure proper adjustment, the swivel must be free to slide along the flat end of the throttle rod. Disassembly, clean and lubricate as required.

4. Hold the transaxle throttle control lever firmly toward the engine and tighten the swivel screw.

5. Road test the vehicle and check the shift points.

Neutral Starting/Back-up Light Switch

▶ See Figure 172

The neutral starting/back-up light switch is screwed into the side of the automatic transaxle. If the vehicle fails to start in either the Park or Neutral positions, or starts in any of the drive gears a problem with the switch is indicated.

TESTING

1. The Neutral/Park sensing part of the switch is the center terminal, while the back-up lights are controlled by the outer two terminals.

2. Remove the wiring connector from the switch. Use an ohmmeter or continuity tester and connect the leads between the center switch terminal and the transaxle case to test the Neutral/Park circuit. Continuity should exist only when the gearshift is either in the Park or Neutral positions. Check the gearshift cable adjustment first before replacing the switch.

3. Connect an ohmmeter or continuity tester connected between the outer two terminals of the switch to check the back-up light. Continuity should be present when the gearshift selector is in the Reverse position.

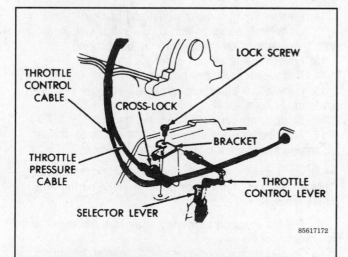

Fig. 171 Throttle pressure cable mounting, 3-speed transaxles

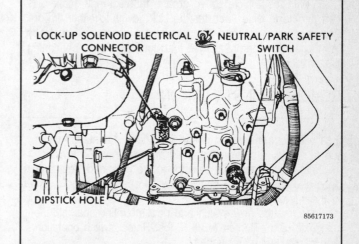

Fig. 172 Lock-up solenoid and neutral safety switch location, 3-speed transaxles

REMOVAL & INSTALLATION

1. Remove the wiring connector. Place a container under the switch to catch transaxle fluid and unscrew the switch.

2. Move the gearshift selector to the Park and Neutral positions and check to see that the switch operating fingers center in the case opening.

3. Screw the new switch and new mounting seal into the transaxle case. Tighten to 24 ft. lbs. Retest switch operation. Add transaxle fluid if needed.

A-604 4-Speed Upshift and Kickdown Learning Procedure

A-604 Ultradrive Transaxle

In 1989, the A-604 4 speed, electronic transaxle was introduced; it is the first to use fully adaptive controls. The controls perform their functions based on real time feedback sensor information. Although, the transaxle is conventional in design, its functions are controlled by the ECM.

Since the A-604 is equipped with a learning function, each time the battery cable is disconnected, the ECM memory is lost. In operation, the transaxle must be shifted many times for the learned memory to be reinputed in the ECM; during this period, the vehicle will experience rough operation. The transaxle must be at normal operating temperature when learning occurs.

1. Maintain constant throttle opening during shifts. Do not move the accelerator pedal during upshifts.

2. Accelerate the vehicle with the throttle 1/8-1/2 open.

3. Make 15 to 20 1/2, 2/3 and 3/4 upshifts. Accelerating from a full stop to 50 mph each time at the aforementioned throttle opening is sufficient.

4. With the vehicle speed below 25 mph, make 5 to 8 wide open throttle kick downs to 1st gear from either 2nd or 3rd gear. Allow at least 5 seconds of operation in 2nd or 3rd gear prior to each kickdown.

5. With the vehicle speed greater than 25 mph, make 5 to part throttle to wide open throttle kick downs to either 3rd or 2nd gear from 4th gear. Allow at least 5 seconds of operation in 4th gear, preferably at road load throttle prior to performing the kickdown.

REMOVAL & INSTALLATION

1. Remove the wiring connector. Place a container under the switch to catch transaxle fluid and unscrew the switch.

2. Move the gearshift selector to the Park and Neutral positions and check to see that the switch operating fingers center in the case opening.

3. Screw the new switch and new mounting seal into the transaxle case. Tighten to 24 ft. lbs. Retest switch operation. Add transaxle fluid if needed.

Automatic Transaxle

REMOVAL & INSTALLATION

➡If the vehicle is going to be rolled while the transaxle is out of the vehicle, obtain 2 outer CV joints to install to the hubs. If the vehicle is rolled without the proper torque applied to the front wheel bearings, the bearings will be destroyed.

1. Disconnect the negative battery cable. If equipped with 3.0L or 3.3L engine, drain the coolant. Remove the dipstick.

2. Install an engine support fixture.

3. Remove the air cleaner assembly if it is preventing access to the upper bell housing bolts. Remove the upper bell housing bolts and water tube, where applicable. Unplug all electrical connectors from the transaxle.

4. If equipped with a 2.2L or 2.5L engine, remove the starter attaching nut and bolt at the top of the bell housing.

5. Raise the vehicle and support safely. Remove the tire and wheel assemblies. Remove the axle end cotter pins, nut locks, spring washers and axle nuts.

6. Remove the ball joint retaining bolts and pry the control arm from the steering knuckle. Position a drain pan under the transaxle where the axles enter the differential or extension housing. Remove the axles from the transaxle or center bearing. Unbolt the center bearing and remove the intermediate axle from the transaxle, if equipped.

7. Drain the transaxle. Disconnect and plug the fluid cooler hoses. Disconnect the shifter and kickdown linkage from the transaxle, if equipped.

8. Remove the speedometer cable adaptor bolt and remove the adaptor from the transaxle.

9. Remove the starter. Remove the torque converter inspection cover, matchmark the torque converter to the flex plate and remove the torque converter bolts.

10. Using the proper equipment, support the weight of the engine.

11. Remove the front motor mount and bracket.

12. On vehicles equipped with D.I.S. ignition system, remove the crankshaft position sensor from the bell housing.

13. Position a suitable jack under the transaxle.

14. Remove the lower bell housing bolts.

15. Remove the left side splash shield. Remove the transaxle mount bolts.

16. Carefully pry the engine from the transaxle.

17. Slide the transaxle rearward until the locating dowels disengage from the mating holes in the transaxle.

➡Attach a small C-clamp to the edge of the bell housing. This will hold the torque converter in place during transaxle removal.

18. Pull the transaxle completely away from the engine and remove it from the vehicle.

19. To prepare the vehicle for rolling, support the engine with a suitable support or reinstall the front motor mount to the engine. Then reinstall the ball joints to the steering knuckle and install the retaining bolt. Install the obtained outer CV joints to the hubs, install the washers and torque the axle nuts to 180 ft. lbs. (244 Nm). The vehicle may now be safely rolled.

To install:

20. Install the transmission securely on the transmission jack. Rotate the converter so it will align with the positioning of the flex plate.

✳✳WARNING

If equipped with a 41TE Transaxle, and the torque converter has been replaced, a Torque Clutch Break-in Procedure must be performed. This procedure will reset the transaxle control module break-in statis. Failure to perform this procedure may cause transaxle shutter. To properly do this a DRB scan tool is required to read or reset the break-in statis.

21. Apply a coating of high temperature grease to the torque converter pilot hub.

22. Raise the transaxle into place and push it forward until the dowels engage and the bell housing is flush with the block.

23. Install the transaxle to bell housing bolts.

24. Jack the transaxle up and install the left side mount bolts. Install the torque converter bolts and torque to 55 ft. lbs. (74 Nm).

25. Install the front motor mount and bracket. Remove the engine and transaxle support fixtures.

26. Install the starter to the transaxle. Install the bolt finger tight if equipped with a 2.2L or 2.5L engine.

27. Install a new O-ring to the speedometer cable adaptor and install to the extension housing; make sure it snaps in place. Install the retaining bolt.

28. Connect the shifter and kickdown linkage to the transaxle, if equipped.

29. Install the axles and center bearing, if equipped. Install the ball joints to the steering knuckles. Torque the axle nuts to 180 ft. lbs. (244 Nm) and install new cotter pins. Install the splash shield and install the wheels. Lower the vehicle. Install the dipstick.

30. Install the upper bell housing bolts and water pipe, if removed.

31. If equipped with 2.2L or 2.5L engine, install the starter attaching nut and bolt at the top of the bell housing. Raise the vehicle again and tighten the starter bolt from underneath the vehicle. Lower the vehicle.

32. Connect all electrical wiring to the transaxle.

33. Install the air cleaner assembly, if it was removed. Fill the transaxle with the proper amount of Dexron®II.

34. Connect the negative battery cable and check the transaxle for proper operation. On the A-604 transaxle perform the upshift and kickdown learn procedure found earlier in this section.

POWER TRANSFER UNIT

▶ **See Figures 173 and 174**

Identification

For 1991-94 models, Chrysler made available an All Wheel Drive (AWD) version of the Caravan/Voyager. The AWD equipped vehicles use the same basic drivetrain layout as the front wheel drive versions, with the exception of the rear driveline module. To transfer the power from the engine and transaxle, to the rear driveline module, these vehicles use an Power Transfer Unit (PTU). The PTU is connected to the transaxle where the right halfshaft extension housing would be.

The PTU is a separate unit from the transaxle. It uses a standard hypoid type ring and pinion. The PTU is sealed from the transaxle and has its own oil sump. The unit uses SAE 85W-90 gear lube and holds 1.22 qts.

The PTU is not a repairable unit and can only be replaced. If you suspect the PTU has failed, take the vehicle to an authorized service center.

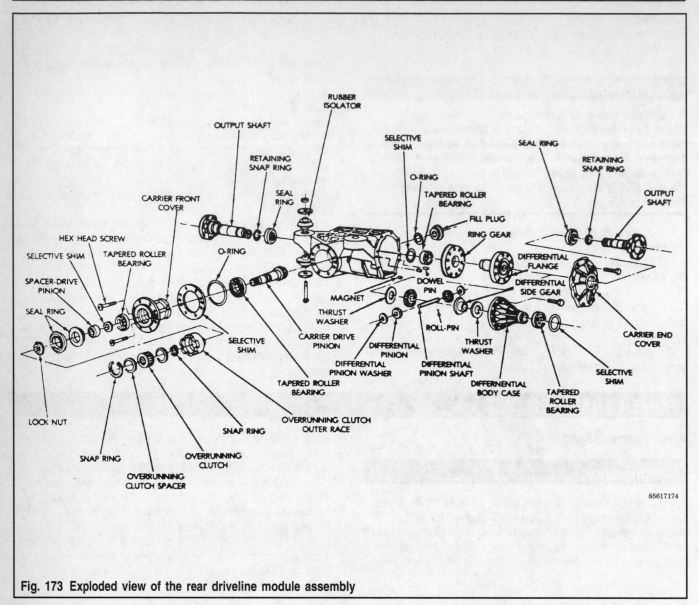

Fig. 173 Exploded view of the rear driveline module assembly

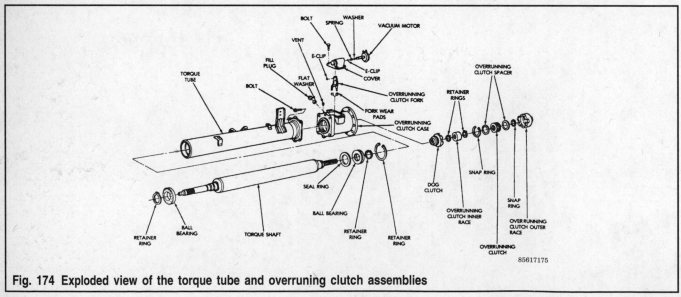

Fig. 174 Exploded view of the torque tube and overruning clutch assemblies

REAR DRIVE LINE MODULE

Identification

As an option in 1991, Chrysler offered All Wheel Drive (AWD) on Caravan/Voyager models. These models are basically the same as the front wheel drive versions, with the exception of the components needed for driving the rear wheels as well.

The power is transferred to the rear wheels through the Power Transfer Unit (PTU) attached to the transaxle. The power travels through the PTU to a torque tube that contains the center driveshaft. The power then enters an overrunning clutch assembly, attached to the front of the rear differential carrier.

The overrunning clutch assembly is separate from the rear carrier. The overrunning clutch assembly has an vacuum operated dog clutch, it is lubricated with Mopar ATF type 7176. The rear carrier is lubricated with SAE 85W-90 gear lube.

Rear Drive Line Assembly Module

▶ See Figure 175

REMOVAL &INSTALLATION

1. Raise and safely support the rear of the vehicle.
2. Remove the right and left inner halfshaft joint mounting bolts.
3. Support the inner side of the halfshaft, by hanging it from the frame using a piece of wire. Do not allow the shafts to hang freely or the joints will be damaged.
4. Remove the mounting bolts from the rear side of the propeller shaft at, the rear carrier.
5. Support the propeller shaft.
6. Remove the viscous coupling retaining nut and slide the viscous coupling off the rear driveline assembly.
7. Disconnect the vacuum line at the driveline module. Also disconnect the electrical lead from the assembly.
8. Support the rear of the driveline module with a jack.
9. Remove the rear driveline module front mounting bolts. Partially lower the unit from the vehicle.
10. Remove the rear driveline module from the vehicle.
    To install:
11. Position the driveline module in the vehicle. Install the front mounting bolts and tighten to 40 ft. lbs. (54 Nm).
12. Reconnect the vacuum line and electrical lead. Install the viscous coupling and nut. Tighten the nut to 120 ft. lbs. (162 Nm).
13. Connect the propeller shaft to the driveline module, tighten to 250 inch lbs. (28 Nm).
14. Connect the rear halfshafts to the rear driveline module. Tighten the bolt to 45 ft. lbs. (61 Nm).
15. Lower the vehicle. Check the operation of the drive train.

Rear Halfshaft

REMOVAL & INSTALLATION

1. Raise and safely support the rear of the vehicle.
2. Remove the rear wheel.
3. Remove the cotter pin, nut, lock and spring washer from the rear hub.
4. Remove the inner halfshaft retaining bolts.
5. The halfshaft is spring loaded, push it in slightly and then tilt it down to remove it. Pull it out from under the vehicle.
   To install:
6. Insert the end of the halfshaft into the rear hub assembly.
7. Position it on the rear carrier unit and install the retaining bolts.
8. Tighten the retaining bolts to 45 ft. lbs. (61 Nm).
9. Install the hub nut, spring and lock washers, and cotter pin.
10. Install the wheel and tire assembly.

Drive Pinion

▶ See Figures 176, 177, 178, 179, 180, 181 and 182

REMOVAL & INSTALLATION

1. Raise and safely support the vehicle.
2. Remove the rear driveline module from the vehicle.
3. Remove the overrunning clutch case-to-rear carrier bolts. Separate the overrunning clutch case from the rear carrier.
4. Remove the overrunning clutch outer race snapring and slide the clutch race off of the shaft.
5. Using a spline socket and a wrench, remove the pinion nut.
6. Remove the front carrier cover retaining bolts and remove the carrier cover.
7. Place a block of wood under the end of the pinion shaft. Tap the end of the pinion against the wood to remove the spacer from the shaft.
   To install:
8. Install the front carrier onto the case and tighten the retaining nuts to 105 inch lbs. (12 Nm).
9. Clean and inspect the seal area, apply a light coat of oil to the drive pinion seal. Install the seal using a seal installer. The seal must be installed with the spring towards the rear of the case.
10. Apply a light coat of oil onto the drive pinion spacer and slide it onto the pinion shaft with the tapered side facing out.
11. Apply a light coat of oil to the overrunning clutch seal and install with a seal installer, the seal must be installed with the spring facing outward.
12. Install the pinion nut and tighten to 150 ft. lbs. (203 Nm).

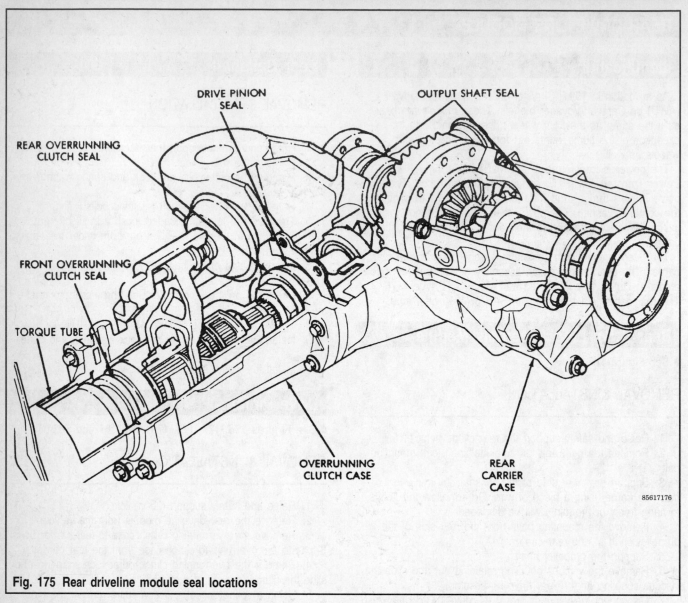

Fig. 175 Rear driveline module seal locations

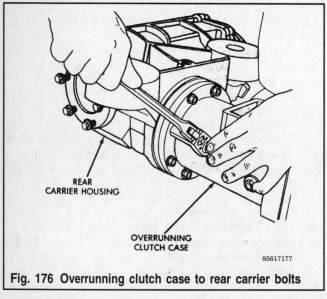

Fig. 176 Overrunning clutch case to rear carrier bolts

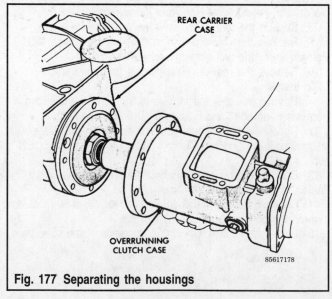

Fig. 177 Separating the housings

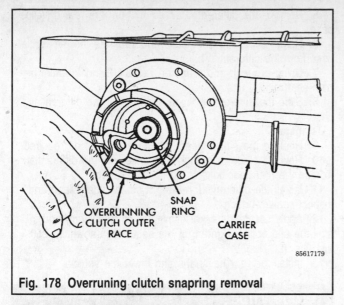

Fig. 178 Overruning clutch snapring removal

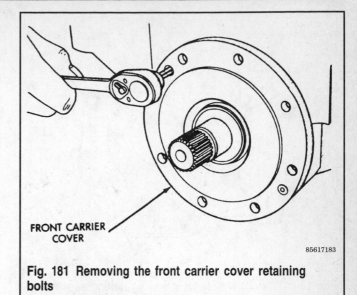

Fig. 181 Removing the front carrier cover retaining bolts

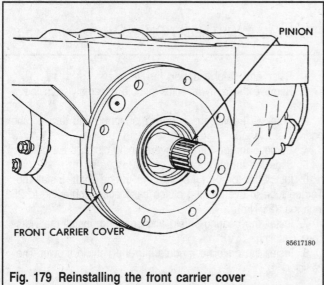

Fig. 179 Reinstalling the front carrier cover

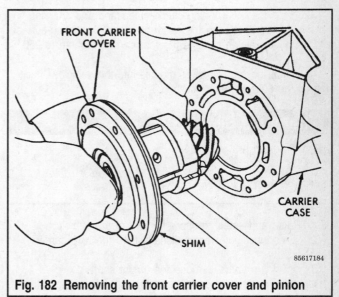

Fig. 182 Removing the front carrier cover and pinion

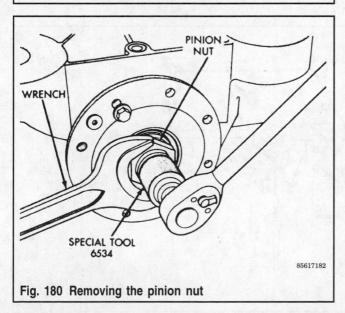

Fig. 180 Removing the pinion nut

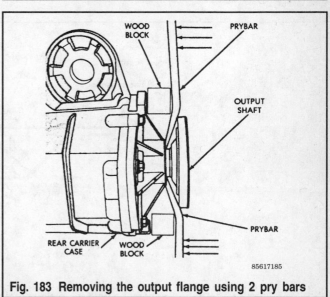

Fig. 183 Removing the output flange using 2 pry bars

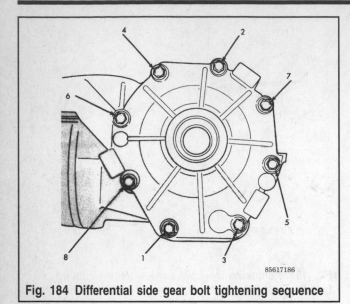

Fig. 184 Differential side gear bolt tightening sequence

13. Install the overrunning clutch outer race and snapring. Apply Loctite® sealer to the overrunning clutch sealing surface and install the clutch case to the rear carrier. Tighten to 250 inch lbs. (28 Nm).

14. Install the rear driveline module into the vehicle. Check and fill the fluid as required.

Differential Side Gears

▶ See Figures 183 and 184

REMOVAL & INSTALLATION

1. Raise and safely support the rear of the vehicle.
2. Disconnect both rear halfshafts from the axle carrier assembly.
3. Using 2 prybars, remove the output shaft.
4. Remove the end cover retaining bolts and remove the end cover.

5. Remove the differential assembly from the rear driveline case.
6. Remove the ring gear bolts and separate the differential case from the differential body.
7. Using a punch and hammer, remove the differential pinion shaft pin.
8. Slide the differential pinion shaft out of the differential case.

To install:
9. Replace the pinion gears, shaft or washers as required.
10. Reverse steps 8 through 5 to assemble the differential. Torque the ring gear bolts to 70 ft. lbs. (95 Nm).
11. Install the differential into the module case. Clean and inspect sealer surfaces.
12. Apply Loctite® gasket eliminator or equivalent, and install the end cover. Tighten, in the sequence shown, to 250 inch lbs. (28 Nm).
13. Install the rear halfshafts and lower the vehicle.

Torque Tube

REMOVAL & INSTALLATION

1. Raise and safely support the vehicle.
2. Remove the rear driveline module assembly from the vehicle.
3. Remove the viscous coupling, snapring and torque tube bearing shield.
4. Remove torque tube to overrunning clutch case bolts.
5. Slide the torque tube off of the torque shaft.
6. Install the torque tube onto the torque shaft. Install the Torque tube to overrunning clutch case bolts, tightening to 250 inch lbs. (28 Nm).
7. Install the bearing shield and snapring. Install the viscous coupling.
8. Install the driveline module into the vehicle. Lower The vehicle.

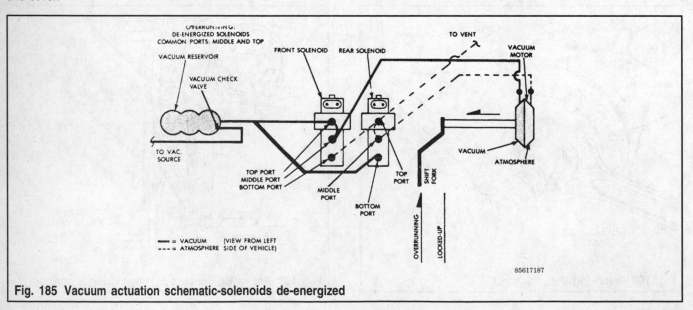

Fig. 185 Vacuum actuation schematic-solenoids de-energized

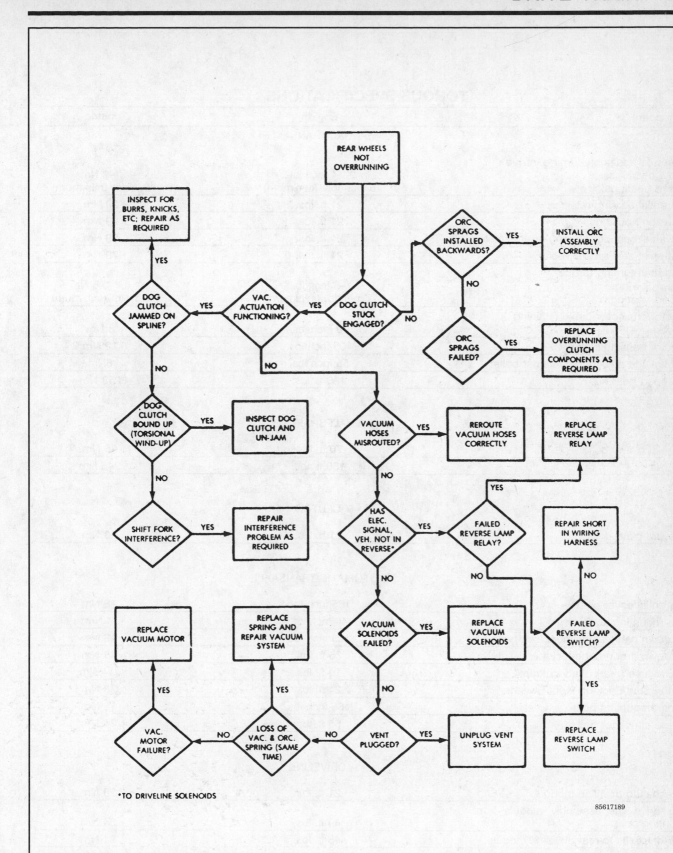

Fig. 186 Rear driveline vacuum shift motor diagnosis

*TO DRIVELINE SOLENOIDS

85617189

TORQUE SPECIFICATIONS

Component	English	Metric
MANUAL TRANSAXLE		
Differential assembly turning torque		
New bearings:	9–14 inch lbs.	1–2 Nm
Used bearings:	6 inch lbs. (minimum)	0.7 Nm (minimum)
Differential bearing retainer:	21 ft. lbs.	29 Nm
Extension housing:	21 ft. lbs.	29 Nm
Input shaft bearings bearing retainer plate:	21 ft. lbs.	29 Nm
Input shaft seal retainer bolts:	21 ft. lbs.	29 Nm
Input shaft turning torque		
New bearings:	1–5 inch lbs.	0.1–0.6 Nm
Used bearings:	1 inch lb. (minimum)	0.1 Nm (minimum)
Selector/crossover cable retaining screws:	70 inch lbs.	8 Nm
Selector housing lock pin:	105 inch lbs.	12 Nm
Shift linkage adjustment/retainer bolts:	55 inch lbs.	6Nm
5th speed gear nut:	190 ft. lbs.	258 Nm
HALFSHAFTS		
Ball joint clamp bolt:	70 ft. lbs.	95 Nm
Hub nut:	180 ft. lbs.	245 Nm
CLUTCH		
Pressure plate bolts:	21 ft. lbs.	29 Nm
AUTOMATIC TRANSAXLE		
Differential cover bolts:	165 inch lbs.	18 Nm
Filter mounting screw:	40 inch lbs.	4 Nm
Kickdown cable adjustment lock bolt:	105 inch lbs.	12 Nm
Kickdown (front) band locknut:	35 ft. lbs.	48 Nm
Low/reverse (rear) band locknut:	10 ft. lbs.	(14 Nm
Neutral Start/Back-up Light Switch:	24 ft. lbs.	33 Nm
Oil pan mounting bolts:	165 inch lbs.	18 Nm
Torque converter bolts:	55 ft. lbs.	74 Nm
DRIVELINE		
Driveshaft-to-driveline module:	21 ft. lbs.	28 Nm
Rear drive line assembly module front mounting bolts:	40 ft. lbs.	54 Nm
Rear halshafts-to-rear driveline module:	45 ft. lbs.	61 Nm
Viscous coupling nut:	120 ft. lbs.	162 Nm

85617C01

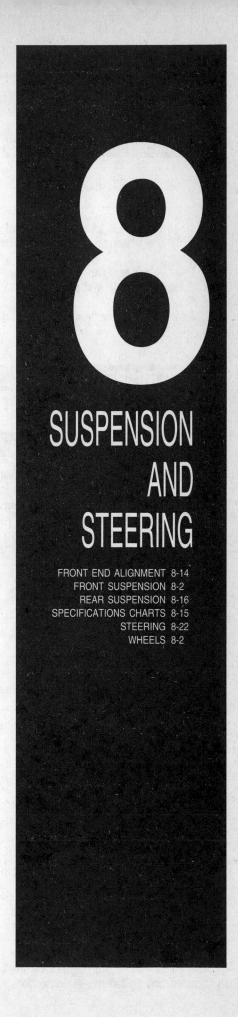

8

SUSPENSION AND STEERING

WHEELS

Front and Rear Wheel Assemblies

REMOVAL & INSTALLATION

1. Place the vehicle transmission in PARK.
2. Block the wheel diagonally from the wheel being removed.
3. Remove the hub cap and loosen the lug nuts.
4. Raise the vehicle and place a jackstand underneath it on the side being raised.
5. Remove the lug nuts and the tire and wheel assembly.

6. Install the wheel on the vehicle and install the lug nuts. The lug nuts should be tightened as much as possible, using a crossing or 'X' pattern.
7. Lower the vehicle and final torque the wheel nuts to 95 ft. lbs. (129 Nm).

INSPECTION

With the wheel and tire assembly removed from the vehicle, check the tire and rim for visible signs of damage. Check the rim for bends in its outer edge, or cracks and chunks missing on alloy type wheels. Check the tire for uneven wear or other signs of possible damage. Replace any damaged rim or excessively worn tire.

FRONT SUSPENSION

▶ **See Figures 1, 2 and 3**

MacPherson Struts

A MacPherson Type front suspension, with vertical shock absorbers attached to the upper fender reinforcement and the steering knuckle, is used. Lower control arms, attached inboard to a crossmember and outboard to the steering knuckle through a ball joint, provide lower steering knuckle position. During steering maneuvers, the upper strut and steering knuckle turn as an assembly.

REMOVAL & INSTALLATION

▶ **See Figures 4, 5, 6, 7, 8, 9, 10, 11, 12 and 13**

1. Loosen the front wheel lug nuts slightly. Raise and support the front of the vehicle on jackstands.
2. Remove the wheel and tire assemblies.

➡**If the original strut assemblies are to be installed, mark the camber eccentric bolt and strut for installment in same position.**

3. Remove the lower camber bolt and nut(at the steering knuckle), and the knuckle bolt and nut. Remove the brake hose to strut bracket mounting bolt.
4. Remove the upper mounting nuts and washers on the fender shield in the engine compartment. Remove the strut assembly from the vehicle.
   To install:
5. Inspect the strut assembly for signs of leakage. A slight amount of seepage is normal, fluid streaking down the side of the strut is not. Replacer the strut if leakage is evident. Service the strut and spring assembly as required.
6. Position the strut assembly under the fender well and loosely install the upper washers and nuts. Position the lower mount over the steering knuckle and loosely install the mounting and camber bolts and nuts. Attach the brake hose retaining bracket and tighten the mounting bolts to 10 ft. lbs.

7. Tighten the upper mount nuts to 20 ft. lbs. Index the camber bolt to reference mark and snug the nut. Install the nut on the mounting bolt and tighten slightly.
8. Mount a 4 in. (102mm) C-clamp over the inner edge of the strut and outer edge of the steering knuckle. Tighten the clamp just enough to eliminate any looseness between the knuckle and the strut. check the alignment of the camber bolt and strut reference marks. Tighten the mounting and camber nuts to 75 ft. lbs. plug 1/4 turn more. Remove the C-clamp.
9. Install the wheel and tire assembly and lower the vehicle.

Strut Spring

REMOVAL & INSTALLATION

▶ **See Figures 14, 15, 16, 17, 18, 19, 20, 21, 22 and 23**

➡**A coil spring compressor Chrysler Tool C-4838 or equivalent is required.**

1. Remove the strut and spring assembly from the vehicle.
2. Compress the coil spring with Chrysler Tool C-4838 or equivalent.

❋❋CAUTION

Make sure the compressor is mounted correctly and tighten jaws evenly. If the spring slips from the compressor, bodily injury could occur.

3. Hold the strut center rod from turning and remove the assembly nut.

➡**The coil springs on each are rated differently. Be sure to mark the spring for side identification.**

4. Remove the mount assembly and the coil spring. Inspect the assembly for rubber isolator deterioration, distortion, cracks and bonding failure. Replace as necessary. Check the mount

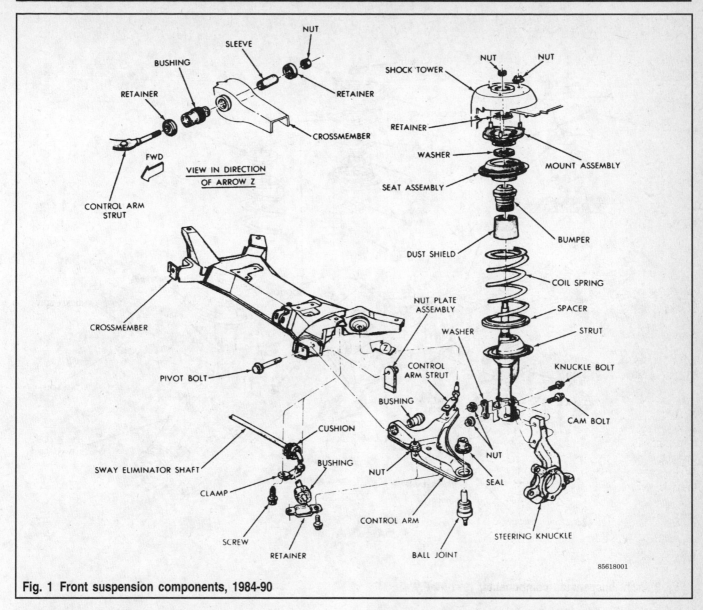

Fig. 1 Front suspension components, 1984-90

bearings for binding and the retainers for bends and cracks. Replace as necessary.

To install:

5. Install the spring on the strut in compressed mode. Install the upper mount assembly. The spring seat tab and the end of the coil spring must be aligned. install assembly nut and tighten while holding the center strut rod in position. Tighten the nut to 60 ft. lbs.

6. Release the coil spring compressor.

7. Install the strut assembly on the vehicle.

8. Misalignment of the upper coil spring seat can cause interference between the coil spring and the inside of the mounting tower. A scraping noise on turns will be an indication if the problem. To correct, raise and support the vehicle to take the weight off of the front wheels. Use two wrenches, one on the top of the center strut rod and one on the assembly nut. Turn both the strut rod and nut in the same direction. The

spring will wind up and snap into position. Check the torque on the assembly nut (60 ft. lbs.).

Lower Ball Joint

The lower front suspension ball joints operate with no free play. The ball joint housing is pressed into the lower control arm with the joint stud retained in the steering knuckle with a (clamp) bolt.

INSPECTION

With the weight of the vehicle resting on the ground, grasp the ball joint grease fitting, and attempt to move it. If the ball joint is worn the grease fitting will move easily. If movement is noted, replacement of the ball joint is recommended.

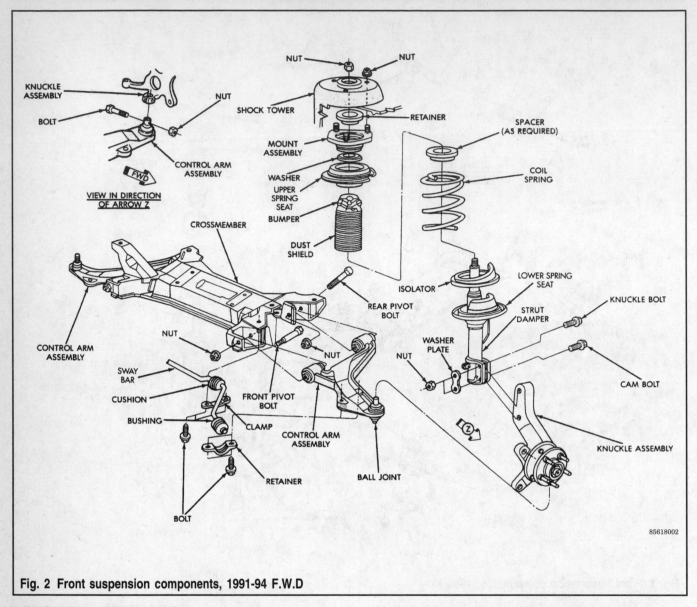

Fig. 2 Front suspension components, 1991-94 F.W.D

REMOVAL & INSTALLATION

▶ **See Figure 24**

➡**Special Chrysler Tools C-4699-1 and C-4699-2 or equivalents are required to remove and install the ball joint form the lower control arm. If the tools are not on hand, remove the control arm and have an automotive machine shop press the ball joint out and in. Refer to the Lower Control Arm Section.**

1. Remove the lower control arm. Pry off the seal from the ball joint.
2. Position a receiving cup, special tool C-4699-2 or its equivalent to support the lower control arm.
3. Install a 1⅛ in. deep socket over the stud and against the joint upper housing.
4. Press the joint assembly from the arm.
To install:
5. To install, position the ball joint housing into the control arm cavity.

6. Position the assembly in a press with special tool C-4699-1 or its equivalent, supporting the control arm.
7. Align the ball joint assembly, then press it until the housing ledge stops against the control arm cavity down flange.
8. To install a new seal, support the ball joint housing with tool #C-4699-2 and place a new seal over the stud, against the housing.
9. With a 1½ in. socket, press the seal onto the joint housing with the seat against the control arm. Install control arm.

Lower Control Arm

REMOVAL & INSTALLATION

▶ **See Figures 25 and 26**

1. Jack up the vehicle and support it with jackstands.
2. Remove the front inner pivot through bolt, the rear stub strut nut, retainer and bushing, and the ball joint-to-steering knuckle clamp bolts.

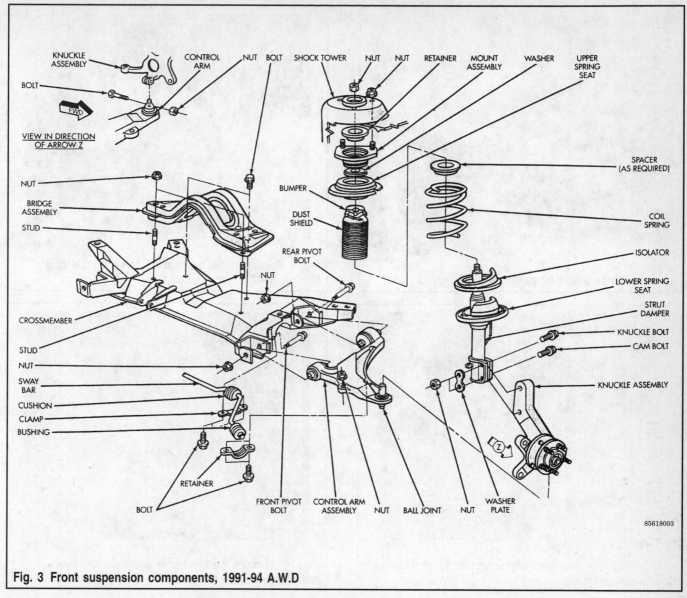

Fig. 3 Front suspension components, 1991-94 A.W.D

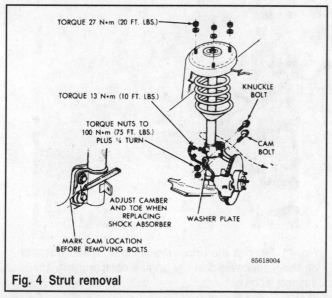

Fig. 4 Strut removal

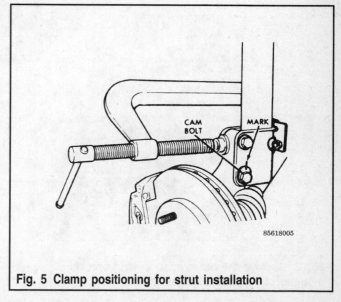

Fig. 5 Clamp positioning for strut installation

Fig. 6 Strut cam bolt location, 1987 Voyager shown

Fig. 7 Mark the strut cam adjusting bolt for installation, 1987 Voyager shown

Fig. 8 Remove the brake hose to strut bracket mounting bolt, 1987 Voyager shown

Fig. 9 Removing the brake hose to strut mounting bracket, 1987 Voyager shown

Fig. 10 Remove the strut cam and knuckle lower retaining nuts and washer, 1987 Voyager shown

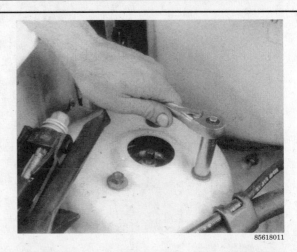

Fig. 11 Remove the upper mounting nuts and washers on the fender shield in the engine compartment, 1987 Voyager shown

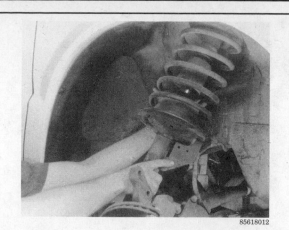

Fig. 12 After removing the upper mounting nuts and washers on the fender shield in the engine compartment lower the strut down and out, 1987 Voyager shown

Fig. 13 Removing the strut assembly from the vehicle, 1987 Voyager shown

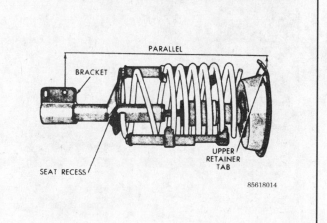

Fig. 14 A coil spring compressor Chrysler Tool C-4838 shown in the installed position

Fig. 15 An alternative coil spring compressor to the Chrysler Tool C-4838 is shown in the installed position

Fig. 16 With the the coil spring compressed, hold the strut center rod from turning and remove the assembly nut, 1987 Voyager shown

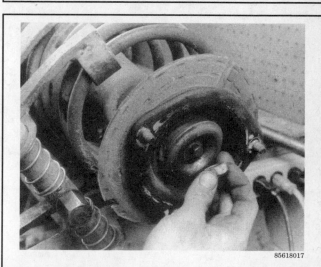

Fig. 17 Removing the nut from the shaft, 1987 Voyager shown

Fig. 18 Removing the washer from the shaft, 1987 Voyager shown

Fig. 21 After removing the upper strut mount, remove the washer from the shaft, 1987 Voyager shown

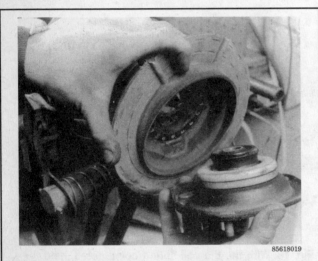

Fig. 19 Removing the upper strut mount from the shaft, 1987 Voyager shown

Fig. 22 Removing the rubber insulator, 1987 Voyager shown

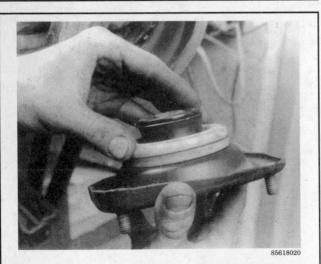

Fig. 20 The the upper strut mount shown removed from the shaft, 1987 Voyager shown

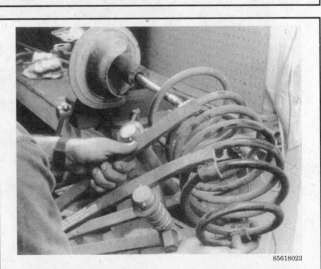

Fig. 23 Removing the coil spring from the strut, 1987 Voyager shown

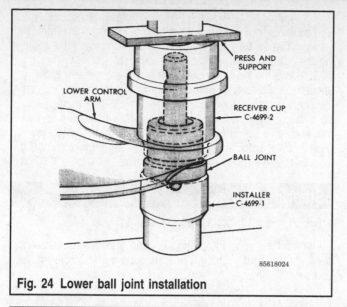

PRESS AND SUPPORT

LOWER CONTROL ARM

RECEIVER CUP C-4699-2

BALL JOINT

INSTALLER C-4699-1

85618024

Fig. 24 Lower ball joint installation

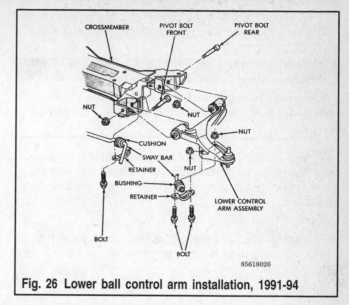

CROSSMEMBER

PIVOT BOLT FRONT

PIVOT BOLT REAR

NUT

NUT

NUT

CUSHION

SWAY BAR

RETAINER

NUT

BUSHING

RETAINER

LOWER CONTROL ARM ASSEMBLY

BOLT

BOLT

85618026

Fig. 26 Lower ball control arm installation, 1991-94

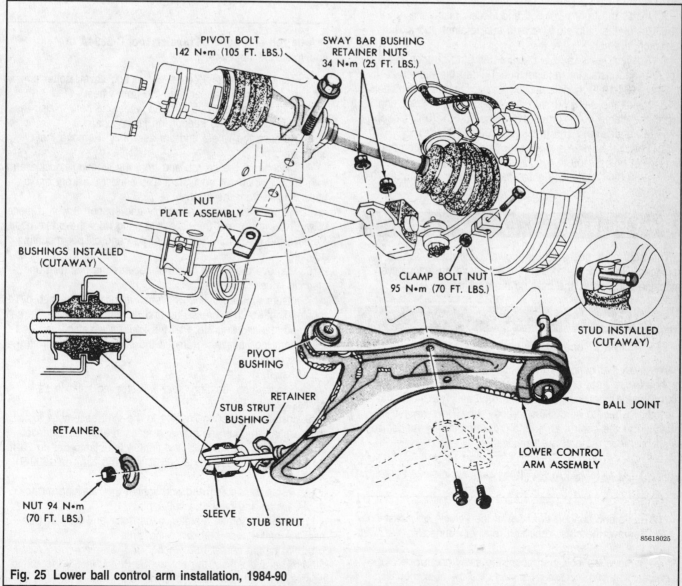

PIVOT BOLT
142 N•m (105 FT. LBS.)

SWAY BAR BUSHING
RETAINER NUTS
34 N•m (25 FT. LBS.)

NUT
PLATE ASSEMBLY

BUSHINGS INSTALLED
(CUTAWAY)

CLAMP BOLT NUT
95 N•m (70 FT. LBS.)

STUD INSTALLED
(CUTAWAY)

RETAINER

PIVOT
BUSHING

RETAINER

STUB STRUT
BUSHING

BALL JOINT

NUT 94 N•m
(70 FT. LBS.)

SLEEVE

STUB STRUT

LOWER CONTROL
ARM ASSEMBLY

85618025

Fig. 25 Lower ball control arm installation, 1984-90

3. Separate the ball joint stud from the steering knuckle by prying between the ball stud retainer on the knuckle and the lower control arm.

✳✳WARNING

Pulling the steering knuckle out from the vehicle after releasing it from the ball joint can separate the inner CV joint.

4. Remove the sway bar-to-control arm nut and reinforcement and rotate the control arm over the sway bar. Remove the rear stub strut bushing, sleeve and retainer. Remove the control arm.

To install:

➡The substitution of fasteners other than those of the grade originally used is not recommended.

5. Install the retainer, bushing and sleeve on the stub strut.
6. Position the control arm over the sway bar and install the rear stub strut and front pivot into the crossmember.
7. Install the front pivot bolt and loosely install the nut.
8. Install the stub strut bushing and retainer and loosely assembly the nut.
9. Position the sway bar bracket and stud through the control arm and install the retainer nut. Tighten the nuts to 25 ft. lbs. on 1984-1989 models and 50 ft. lbs. On 1990-94 models.
10. Install the ball joint stud into the steering knuckle and install the clamp bolt. Torque the clamp bolt to 70 ft. lbs. on 1984-89 models and 105 ft. lbs. on 1990-94 models.
11. Lower the vehicle, weight on wheels, and tighten the front pivot bolt to 105 ft. lbs. on 1984--89 models and 125 ft. lbs. on 1990-94 models. Tighten the rear stub strut nut to 70 ft. lbs.

Pivot Bushing

The front pivot bushing of the lower control arm can be replaced. Remove the control arm and have an automotive machine shop press the bushing out and in.

Sway Bar

▶ **See Figures 27 and 28**

The sway bar connects the control arms together and attaches to the front crossmember of the vehicle, Bumps, jounce and rebound affecting one wheel are partially transmitted to the other wheel to help stabilize body roll. The sway bar is attached to the control arms and crossmember by rubber-isolated bushings. All part are serviceable.

REMOVAL & INSTALLATION

1. Raise and support the front of the vehicle on jackstands.
2. Remove the nuts, bolts and retainer connecting the sway bar to the control arms.
3. Remove the bolt that mount the sway bar to the crossmember. Remove the sway bar and crossmember mounting clamps from the vehicle.

4. Inspect the bushings for wear. Replace as necessary. End bushings are replaced by cutting or driving them from the retainer. Center bushings are split and are removed by opening the split and sliding from the sway bar.
5. Force the new end bushings into the retainers, allow about ½ in. (13mm) to protrude. Install the sway bar. Tighten the center bracket bolts to 25 ft. lbs. on 1984-89 models and 50 ft. lbs. on 1990-94 models. Place a jack under the control arm and raise the arm to normal design height. Tighten the outer bracket bolts to 25 ft. lbs. on 1984-89 models and 50 ft. lbs. on 1990-94 models. Lower the vehicle.

Steering Knuckle

▶ **See Figures 29, 30, 31, 32, 33 and 34**

The front suspension steering knuckle provides for steering, braking, front end alignment and supports the front driving hub and axle assembly.

REMOVAL & INSTALLATION

➡**A tie rod end puller (Chrysler Tool C-3894A or equivalent) is necessary.**

1. Remove the wheel cover, center hub cover, cotter pin, nut lock and spring washer from the front wheel.
2. Loosen the front hub nut and wheel lug nuts. Raise the front of the vehicle and support on jackstands.
3. Remove the wheel and tire assembly. Remove the center hub nut.
4. Disconnect the tie rod end from the steering knuckle arm with Tool C-3894A or equivalent. Disconnect the front brake hose bracket from the strut.
5. Remove the caliper assembly and support it with a piece of wire. Do not permit the caliper to hang from the brake hose. Remove the disc brake rotor, inner pad and caliper mounting adapter.
6. Remove the clamp bolt that secures the ball joint and steering knuckle together.
7. Insure that the splined halfshaft is loose in the hub by tapping lightly with a brass drift and hammer. Separate the ball joint and steering knuckle. Pull the knuckle assembly out and away from the halfshaft. Remove the steering knuckle from the strut assembly.

To install:

8. Service hub, bearing, seal and steering knuckle as necessary.
9. Install the steering knuckle to the strut assembly. Install the halfshaft through the hub and steering knuckle. Connect the ball joint to the knuckle and tighten the clamp bolt to 70 ft. lbs. on 1984-89 models and 105 ft. lbs (145 Nm) on 1990-91 models.
10. Install the tie rod end and tighten the retaining nut to 35 ft. lbs. Install and bend the cotter pin.
11. Install the brake adapter, pads, rotor and caliper. Connect the brake hose bracket to the strut.
12. Install the center hub washer and retaining nut. Apply the brakes and tighten the nut to 180 ft. lbs. Install the spring washer, nut and new cotter pin. Install the wheel and tire assembly. Tighten the lug nuts to 95 ft. lbs. Lower the vehicle.

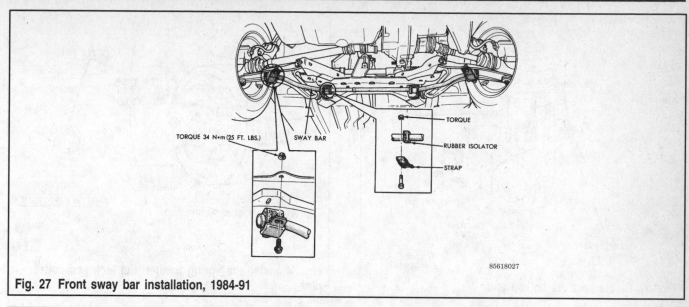

TORQUE 34 N•m (25 FT. LBS.)

SWAY BAR

TORQUE

RUBBER ISOLATOR

STRAP

85618027

Fig. 27 Front sway bar installation, 1984-91

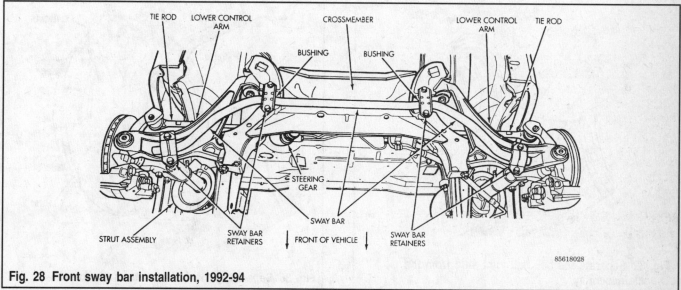

TIE ROD   LOWER CONTROL ARM   CROSSMEMBER   LOWER CONTROL ARM   TIE ROD

BUSHING   BUSHING

STEERING GEAR

STRUT ASSEMBLY   SWAY BAR RETAINERS   SWAY BAR   ↓ FRONT OF VEHICLE ↓   SWAY BAR RETAINERS

85618028

Fig. 28 Front sway bar installation, 1992-94

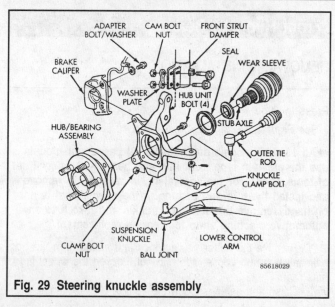

ADAPTER BOLT/WASHER   CAM BOLT NUT   FRONT STRUT DAMPER

SEAL   WEAR SLEEVE

BRAKE CALIPER

WASHER PLATE   HUB UNIT BOLT (4)   STUB AXLE

HUB/BEARING ASSEMBLY

OUTER TIE ROD

KNUCKLE CLAMP BOLT

SUSPENSION KNUCKLE

LOWER CONTROL ARM

CLAMP BOLT NUT   BALL JOINT

85618029

Fig. 29 Steering knuckle assembly

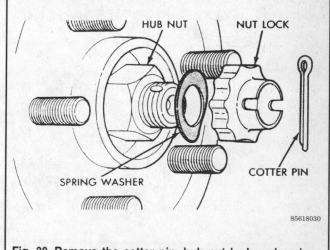

HUB NUT   NUT LOCK

SPRING WASHER   COTTER PIN

85618030

Fig. 30 Remove the cotter pin, hub nut lock and spring washer

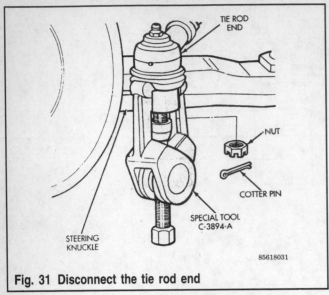

Fig. 31 Disconnect the tie rod end

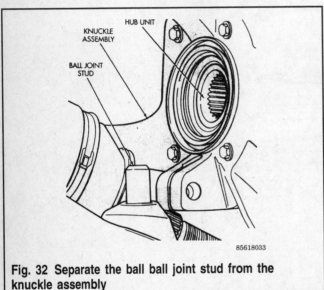

Fig. 32 Separate the ball ball joint stud from the knuckle assembly

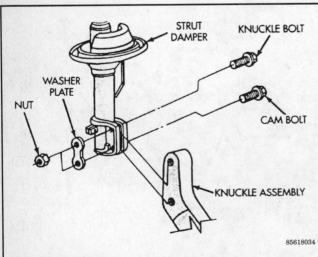

Fig. 33 Remove/install the steering knuckle from the strut assembly

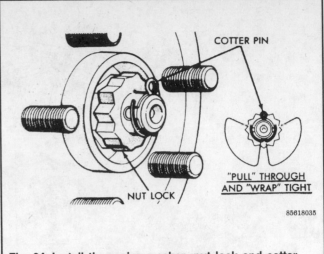

Fig. 34 Install the spring washer, nut lock and cotter pin

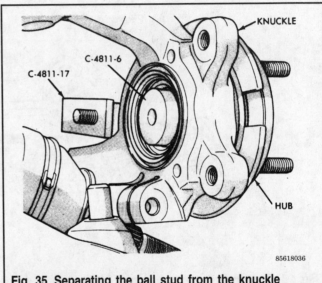

Fig. 35 Separating the ball stud from the knuckle

Front Hub and Bearing

REMOVAL & INSTALLATION

Press In Type

▶ See Figures 35, 36, 37, 38, 39 and 40

➡All 1984-88 models and 1989-90 (8) passenger models use the press-in type front hub and bearing. A special set of tools, C-4811 or the equivalent, is required to remove and install the hub and bearing. If the special tool is not on hand, remove the steering knuckle and take it to an automotive machine shop for bearing replacement.

1. Remove the cotter pin, nut lock and spring from the front halfshaft hub nut. Loosen the hub nut. Loosen the wheel lug nuts slightly.

2. Raise and safely support the vehicle on jackstands.

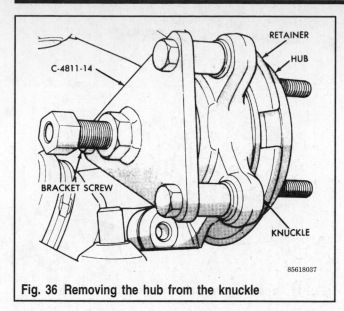

Fig. 36 Removing the hub from the knuckle

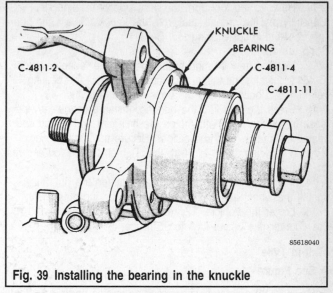

Fig. 39 Installing the bearing in the knuckle

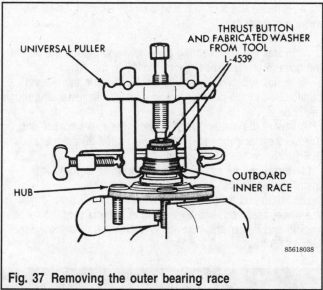

Fig. 37 Removing the outer bearing race

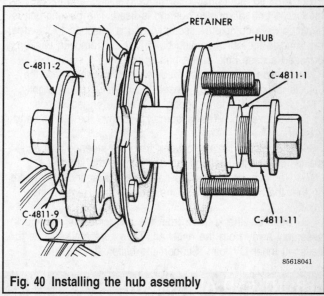

Fig. 40 Installing the hub assembly

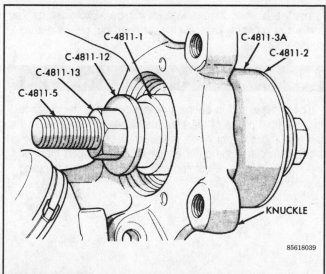

Fig. 38 Removing the bearing from the knuckle

3. Remove the wheel assembly. Remove the center hub nut.

4. Disconnect the tie rod end from the steering arm. Disconnect the brake hose from the strut retainer. Remove the ball joint clamp nut.

5. Remove the brake caliper, suspend it with wire so that no strain is put on the brake hose. Remove the disc rotor.

6. Separate the knuckle from the control arm ball joint.

7. Pull the knuckle from the halfshaft. Tap the halfshaft with a brass hammer to loosen it if necessary. Use care so that the inner CV joint does not separate. Support the halfshaft.

8. Using tool C-4811, or equivalent. Back out one of the bearing and install the tool adapter bolt into the retainer threads.

9. Position the tool at the back of the knuckle and install two mounting bolts in the brake caliper mounting holes. Center the tool and tighten the caliper adapter mounting bolts and the retainer bolt.

10. Tighten the center threaded driver on the tool and push the hub from the knuckle.

11. Remove the tool from the front side of the knuckle. Carefully pry the grease seal from the knuckle. Press the bearing from the knuckle using tool C-48ll.

To install:

12. Install a new bearing by using the puller adapter of tool C-4811. Install a new seal and lubricate. Install the bearing retainer and bolts, torque the bolts to 20 ft. lbs.

13. Press the hub into the bearing. Install a new wear/wipe seal. Install the halfshaft. Attach the ball joint and tie rod end. Install the brake rotor and caliper. Secure the brake hose. Tighten the clamp bolt to 70 ft. lbs. Tighten the tie rod end nut to 35 ft. lbs.

14. Install the washer and hub nut. Tighten the nut firmly. Install the wheel assemblies and tighten the lug nuts firmly.

15. Lower the vehicle. Tighten the center hub nut to 180 ft. lbs. Tighten the wheel lugs to 95 ft. lbs.

Bolt-In Type

▶ **See Figure 41**

On 1989-90 eight-passenger model vehicles and all 1991-94 models, a bolt in knuckle bearing is used. The bearing unit is serviced as a complete assembly. and is attached to the steering knuckle by four mounting bolts that are removed through a provided access hole in the hub flange.

1. Loosen the center splined retaining hub nut while the vehicle is on the ground. Loosen the wheel lug nuts slightly.

2. Raise and safely support the vehicle on jackstands.

3. Remove the wheel assembly. Remove the hub nut and washer.

4. Disconnect the tie rod end from the steering arm and the clamp bolt that retains the ball joint to the knuckle.

5. Remove the disc brake caliper and suspend it with wire so that there is no strain on the brake hose. Remove the rotor.

6. Separate the knuckle from the ball joint. Pull the knuckle assembly away from the halfshaft. Take care not separate the halfshaft inner CV joint. Support the halfshaft.

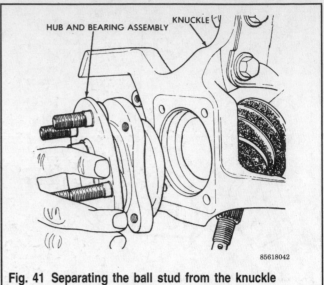

Fig. 41 Separating the ball stud from the knuckle

7. Remove the four hub and bearing retaining bolts. Remove the assembly.

To install:

8. Install the new bearing assembly and tighten the mounting bolts in a criss-cross manner to 45 ft. lbs.

9. Install a new wear sleeve seal. Lubricate the sealing surfaces with multi-purpose grease. Install the halfshaft through the hub.

10. Install the steering knuckle onto the lower control arm. Torque the clamp bolt to 70 ft. lbs. on 1984-89 models and 105 ft. lbs. on 1990-91 models.

11. Install the tie rod end. Tighten the nut to 35 ft. lbs. Install the brake disc rotor and caliper assembly.

12. Install and tighten the hub nut reasonably tight. Install the wheel assembly, tighten the lug nuts fairly tight. Lower the vehicle and tighten the hub nut to 180 ft. lbs. and the wheel lugs to 85 ft. lbs.

FRONT END ALIGNMENT

Front wheel alignment is the proper adjustment of all the interrelated suspension angles affecting the running and steering of the front wheels.

There are six basic factors which are the foundation of front wheel alignment, height, caster, camber, toe-in, steering axis inclination, and toe-out turns. of these basic factors, only camber and toe are mechanically adjustable. Any checks and required adjustments should be made to the camber first, then to the toe.

CAMBER

Camber is the number of degrees or inches the top of the wheel is tilted inward or outward from true vertical. Outward tilt is positive camber, inward-negative camber. Excessive camber (inward or outward) can cause poor handling, pulling and excessive tire wear.

Toe

Toe is measured in degrees or inches and is the distance that the front edges of the tires are closer or further apart then the rear edges. Front wheel drive vehicles usually have toe out which means that the outer edges are further apart than the inner. Incorrect toe adjustment will also cause poor handling and excessive tire wear.

WHEEL ALIGNMENT

Year	Model		Caster Range (deg.)	Caster Preferred Setting (deg.)	Camber Range (deg.)	Camber Preferred Setting (deg.)	Toe-in (in.)	Steering Axis Inclination (deg.)
1984	Caravan/Voyager	F	—	①	$1/4$N–$3/4$P	$5/16$P	$1/8$P	—
	Caravan/Voyager	R	—	—	$1 1/8$N–$1/8$N	$1/2$N	0	—
1985	Caravan/Voyager	F	—	①	$1/4$N–$3/4$P	$5/16$P	$1/8$P	—
	Caravan/Voyager	R	—	—	$1 1/8$N–$1/8$N	$1/2$N	0	—
1986	Caravan/Voyager	F	—	①	$1/4$N–$3/4$P	$5/16$P	$1/8$P	12.7
	Caravan/Voyager	R	—	—	$1 1/8$N–$1/8$N	$1/2$N	0	—
1987	Caravan/Voyager	F	—	①	$1/4$N–$3/4$P	$5/16$P	$1/8$P	12.7
	Caravan/Voyager	R	—	—	$1 1/8$N–$1/8$N	$1/2$N	0	—
1988	Caravan/Voyager	F	—	①	$1/4$N–$3/4$P	$5/16$P	$1/8$P	12.7
	Caravan/Voyager	R	—	—	1N–$1/2$P	0	0	—
1989	Caravan/Voyager	F	—	①	$1/4$N–$3/4$P	$5/16$P	$1/8$P	12.7
	Caravan/Voyager	R	—	—	1N–$1/2$P	0	0	—
1990	Caravan/Voyager	F	—	①	$1/4$N–$3/4$P	$5/16$P	$1/8$P	12.7
	Caravan/Voyager	R	—	—	1N–$1/2$P	0	0	—
1991	Caravan/Voyager/Town & Country	F	—	$1 1/16$P	$1/4$N–$3/4$P	$5/16$P	$1/8$P	12.2
	Caravan/Voyager/Town & Country	R	—	—	1N–$1/2$P	0	0	—
1992	Caravan/Voyager/Town & Country	F	—	$1 5/16$P	$1/8$N–$3/4$P	$5/16$P	$1/16$P	12.2
	Caravan/Voyager/Town & Country	R	—	—	$13/16$N–$7/16$P	$1/4$P	0	—
1993	Caravan/Voyager/Town & Country	F	—	$1 5/16$P	$1/4$N–1P	$3/4$P	$1/16$P	12.2
	Caravan/Voyager/Town & Country	R	—	—	$13/16$N–$7/16$P	$1/4$P	0	—
1994	Caravan/Voyager/Town & Country	F	—	$1 5/16$P	$1/4$N–$3/4$P	$5/16$P	$1/16$P	NA
	Caravan/Voyager/Town & Country	R	—	—	$13/16$N–$7/16$P	$1/4$P	0	NA

① Van: $7/16$P; Wagon: $1 11/16$P

85618C01

REAR SUSPENSION

◗ See Figures 42, 43 and 44

The rear suspension consists of a tube and casting axle, shock absorbers and leaf springs. Stub axles are mounted to the axle and spring by U-bolts. It is possible to align both the camber and toe of the rear wheels.

The rear leaf springs are mounted by shackles and a fixed end bushing. the shackle angles have been selected to provide increasing suspension rates as the vehicle is loaded. These angles provide a comfortable unloaded ride and ample suspension travel when the vehicle is loaded.

The rear shock absorbers are mounted at an angle, forward at the top and parallel to the springs. Greater stability and ride control are provided by this design.

✳✳WARNING

Do not install after market load leveling devices, air shocks or helper springs on your vehicle. These devices will cause the rear brake height sensing valve to adjust for a lighter lead than actually is contained.

Rear Springs

REMOVAL & INSTALLATION

Front Wheel Drive Models
◗ See Figures 42 and 43

1. Raise and support the rear of the vehicle on jackstands. Locate the jackstands under the frame contact points just ahead of the rear spring fixed ends.

2. Raise the rear axle just enough to relieve the weight on the springs and support on jackstands.

3. Disconnect the rear brake proportioning valve spring. Disconnect the lower ends of the shock absorbers at the rear axle bracket.

4. Loosen and remove the nuts from the U-bolts. Remove the washer and U-bolts.

5. Lower the rear axle assembly to permit the rear springs to hang free. Support the spring and remove the four bolts that mount the fixed end spring bracket. Remove the rear spring shackle nuts and plate. Remove the shackle from the spring.

6. Remove the sprlng. Remove the fixed end mounting bolts from the bracket and remove the bracket. Remove the front pivot bolt from the front spring hanger.

To install:

7. Install the spring on the rear shackle and hanger. Start the shackle nuts but do not tighten completely.

8. Assembly the front spring hanger on the spring. Raise the front of the spring and install the four mounting bolts. Tighten the mounting bolts to 45 ft. lbs.

9. Raise the axle assembly and align the spring center bolts in correct position. Install the mounting U-bolts. Tighten the nuts to 60 ft. lbs.

10. Install the rear shock absorber to the lower brackets.

11. Lower the vehicle to the ground so that the full weight is on the springs. Tighten the mounting components as follows: Front fixed end bolt; 95 ft. lbs. Shackle nuts; 35 ft. lbs. Shock absorber bolts; 50 ft. lbs.

12. Raise and support the vehicle. Connect the brake valve spring and adjust the valve.

All Wheel Drive Models
◗ See Figure 44

1. Raise and support the rear of the vehicle on jackstands. Locate the jackstands under the chassis, ahead of the springs.

2. Raise the rear axle just enough to relieve the weight on the springs and support on jackstands.

3. Disconnect the rear brake proportioning valve spring. Disconnect the lower ends of the shock absorbers at the rear axle bracket.

4. Loosen and remove the nuts from the U-bolts. Remove the washer and U-bolts.

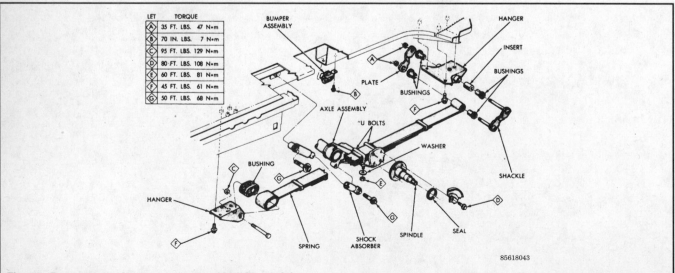

Fig. 42 Rear suspension components, 1984-88 models

85618043

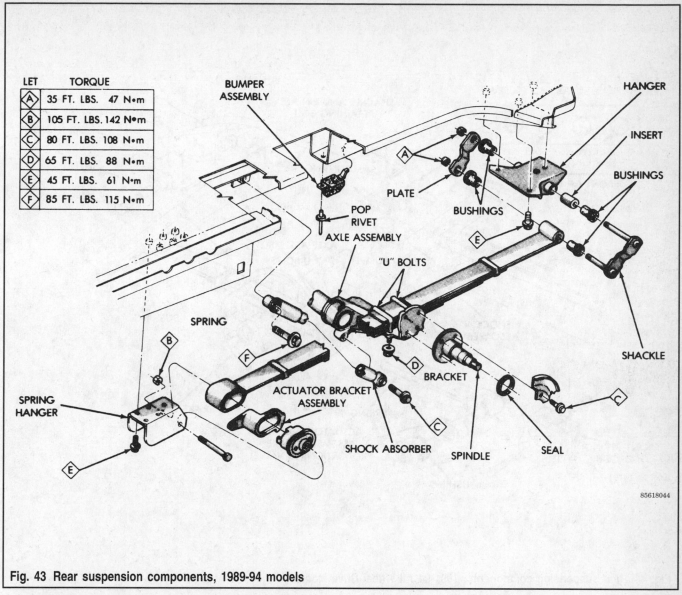

LET	TORQUE	
Ⓐ	35 FT. LBS.	47 N•m
Ⓑ	105 FT. LBS.	142 N•m
Ⓒ	80 FT. LBS.	108 N•m
Ⓓ	65 FT. LBS.	88 N•m
Ⓔ	45 FT. LBS.	61 N•m
Ⓕ	85 FT. LBS.	115 N•m

Fig. 43 Rear suspension components, 1989-94 models

5. Lower the rear axle assembly to permit the rear springs to hang free. Support the spring and remove the four bolts that mount the fixed end spring bracket. Remove the rear spring shackle nuts and plate. Remove the shackle from the spring.

6. Remove the spring. Remove the fixed end mounting bolts from the bracket and remove the bracket. Remove the front pivot bolt from the front spring hanger.

7. Separate the rear shackle plate from the shackle and pin assembly. Remove the shackle and pin assembly from the spring.

To install:

8. Assemble the shackle and pin assembly, bushing and shackle plate on rear of spring and spring hanger. Start the shackle and pin assembly through bolts, do not tighten.

9. Assemble the front spring hanger to the front of the spring eye and install pivot bolt and nut. Do not tighten.

➡**Pivot bolt must inboard to prevent structural damage during spring installation.**

10. Raise the front of the spring into position and install the 4 hanger bolts, tighten them to 45 ft. lbs. (61 Nm). Connect the actuator assembly for the proportioning valve.

11. Raise the axle assembly into position, centered under the spring center bolt.

12. Install the U-bolts, nuts and washers. Tighten the U-bolt nuts to 65 ft. lbs. (88 Nm).

13. Install the shock absorbers and start the bolts.

14. Lower the vehicle to the ground, with the full weight of the vehicle on the wheels. Tighten all of the fasteners in the following sequence and to the listed torques:

   a. Front pivot bolts — 105 ft. lbs. (142 Nm)

   b. Shackle and pin assembly through bolt nuts — 35 ft. lbs. (47 Nm)

   c. Shackle and pin assembly retaining bolts — 35 ft. lbs. (47 Nm)

   d. Shock absorber upper bolts — 85 ft. lbs. (115 Nm)

   e. Shock absorber lower bolts — 80 ft. lbs. (108 Nm)

15. Raise the vehicle and connect the proportioning valve.

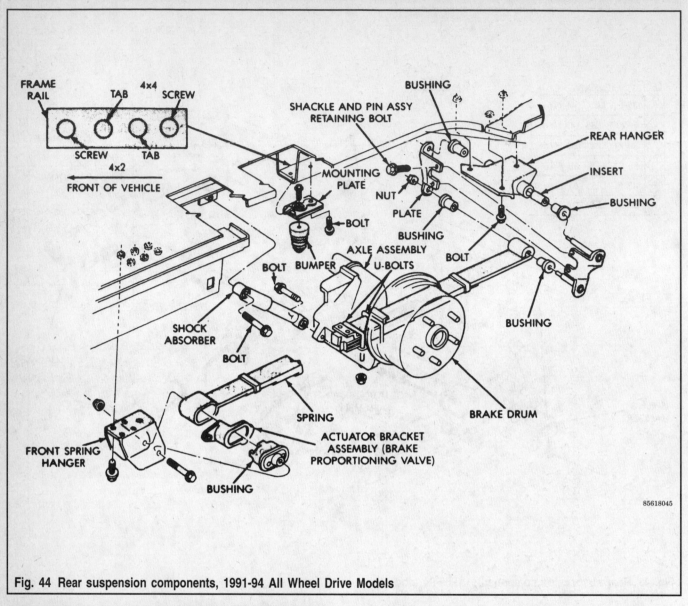

Fig. 44 Rear suspension components, 1991-94 All Wheel Drive Models

Shock Absorbers

TESTING

Shock absorbers require replacement if the car fails to recover quickly after hitting a large bump or if it sways excessively following a directional change.

A good way to test the shock absorbers is to intermittently apply downward pressure to the side of the vehicle until it is moving up and down for almost its full suspension travel. Release it and observe its recovery. If the vehicle bounces once or twice after having been released and then comes to a rest, the shocks are all right. If the vehicle continues to bounce, the shock will probably require replacement.

REMOVAL & INSTALLATION

▶ See Figures 45 and 46

1. Raise the vehicle and support it with jackstands.
2. Support the rear axle with a floor jack.
3. Remove the top and bottom shock absorber bolts.
4. Remove the shock absorbers.
5. Place the new shock in position and install the mounting bolts. Tighten to 80 ft. lbs. for the lower bolts and 85 ft. lbs for the upper bolts.

Fig. 45 Removing the top shock absorber retaining bolt

Fig. 46 Removing the bottom shock absorber retaining bolt

Sway Bar

REMOVAL & INSTALLATION

All Wheel Drive Models
▶ See Figures 47 and 48

The sway bar interconnects both sides of the rear axle and attaches to the rear frame rails using 2 rubber isolated link arms. It is attached to the rear axle through rubber isolated bushings.

1. Raise and support the vehicle.
2. Remove the 2 lower bolts which hold the sway bar to the link arm on each side of the vehicle.
3. Loosen the bolts that attach the sway bar bushings to the rear axle housing.
4. While holding the sway bar in place, remove the 4 bushing retaining bolts and remove the sway bar from the axle.

To install:
5. Inspect the bushings and replace any that appear damaged.
6. Install the sway bar to the rear axle. The slits in the bushing should face up in the installed position. Do not tighten the bolts.
7. Install the 2 lower link bolts, do not tighten these.
8. Lower the vehicle so that all the weight is on the wheels. Tighten all of the bolts to the following torques:
   a. Bushing-to-axle bracket — 45 ft. lbs. (61 Nm)
   b. Link arm-to-frame rail — 45 ft. lbs. (61 Nm)
   c. Sway bar-to-link arm — 45 ft. lbs. (61 Nm)
   d. Link arm bracket-to-frame rail 290 inch lbs. (33 Nm)

Rear Wheel Bearings

SERVICING

Front Wheel Drive Models
▶ See Figure 49

➡ Sodium-based grease is not compatible with lithium-based grease. Read the package labels and be careful not to mix the two types. If there is any doubt as to the type of grease used, completely clean the old grease from the bearing and hub before replacing.

Before handling the bearings, there are a few things that you should remember to do and not to do. **Remember to DO the following:**
- Remove all outside dirt from the housing before exposing the bearing.
- Treat a used bearing as gently as you would a new one.
- Work with clean tools in clean surroundings.
- Use clean, dry canvas gloves, or at least clean, dry hands.
- Clean solvents and flushing fluids are a must.
- Use clean paper when laying out the bearings to dry.
- Protect disassembled bearings from rust and dirt. Cover them up.
- Use clean rags to wipe bearings.
- Keep the bearings in oil-proof paper when they are to be stored or are not in use.
- Clean the inside of the housing before replacing the bearing. **Do NOT do the following:**
- Don't work in dirty surroundings.
- Don't use dirty, chipped or damaged tools.
- Try not to work on wooden work benches or use wooden mallets.
- Don't handle bearings with dirty or moist hands.
- Do not use gasoline for cleaning; use a safe solvent.
- Do not spin-dry bearings with compressed air. They will be damaged.
- Do not spin dirty bearings.
- Avoid using cotton waste or dirty cloths to wipe bearings.
- Try not to scratch or nick bearing surfaces.
- Do not allow the bearing to come in contact with dirt or rust at any time.

The rear wheel bearings should be inspected and lubricated whenever the rear brakes are serviced or at least every

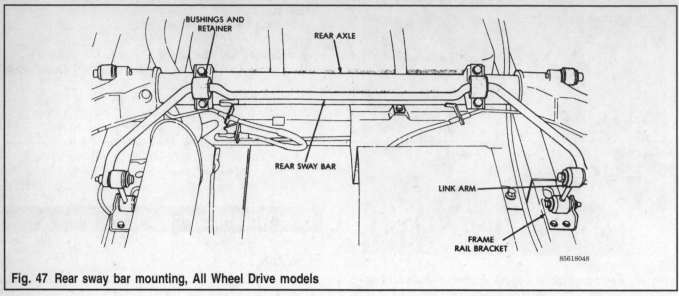

Fig. 47 Rear sway bar mounting, All Wheel Drive models

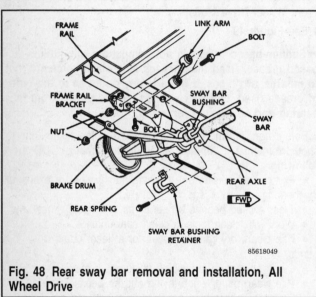

Fig. 48 Rear sway bar removal and installation, All Wheel Drive

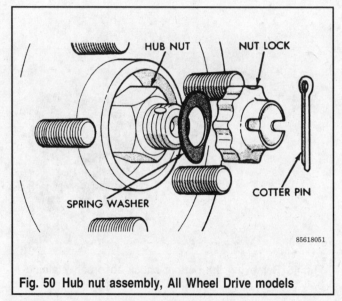

Fig. 50 Hub nut assembly, All Wheel Drive models

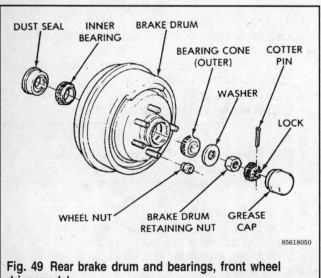

Fig. 49 Rear brake drum and bearings, front wheel drive models

30,000 miles. Repack the bearings with high temperature multi-purpose grease.

Check the lubricant to see if it is contaminated. If it contains dirt or has a milky appearance indicating the presence of water, the bearings should be cleaned and repacked.

Clean the bearings in kerosene, mineral spirits or other suitable cleaning fluid. Do not dry them by spinning the bearings. Allow them to air dry.

1. Raise and support the vehicle with the rear wheels off the floor.

2. Remove the wheel grease cap, cotter pin, nut-lock and bearing adjusting nut.

3. Remove the thrust washer and bearing.

4. Remove the drum from the spindle.

5. Thoroughly clean the old lubricant from the bearings and hub cavity. Inspect the bearing rollers for pitting or other signs of wear. Light discoloration is normal.

To install:

6. Repack the bearings with high temperature multi-purpose EP grease and add a small amount of new grease to the hub

cavity. Be sure to force the lubricant between all rollers in the bearing.

7. Install the drum on the spindle after coating the polished spindle surfaces with wheel bearing lubricant.

8. Install the outer bearing cone, thrust washer and adjusting nut.

9. Tighten the adjusting nut to 20-25 ft. lbs. while rotating the wheel.

10. Back off the adjusting nut to completely release the preload from the bearing.

11. Tighten the adjusting nut finger-tight.

12. Position the nut-lock with one pair of slots in line with the cotter pin hole. Install the cotter pin.

13. Clean and install the grease cap and wheel.

14. Lower the vehicle.

All Wheel Drive Vehicles

▶ **See Figures 50, 51, 52, 53 and 54**

The rear wheel bearings used on these models is a bolt in type unit, this is the same unit that is used on the front knuckle assembly.

1. Raise and support the vehicle.

2. Remove the wheel and tire assembly.

3. Remove the halfshaft flange retaining bolts and remove the halfshaft assembly.

4. Remove the wheel bearing mounting bolts and remove the wheel bearing and hub assembly.

To install:

5. Install the hub and bearing assembly, tighten the bolts to 96 ft. lbs (130 Nm) in a criss-cross pattern.

➡**Thoroughly clean the seal and wear sleeve, lubricate both before installation.**

6. Install the halfshaft.

7. Install the washer and hub nut, with the brakes applied tighten the nut to 180 ft. lbs. (244 Nm).

8. Install the spring washer, nut lock and new cotter pin.

9. Install the wheel and tire assembly.

Rear Axle Alignment

Camber and Toe adjustment are possible through the use of shims. Shims are added or subtracted between the spindle mounting surface and the axle mounting plate. Each shim equals a wheel angle change of 0.3 degrees.

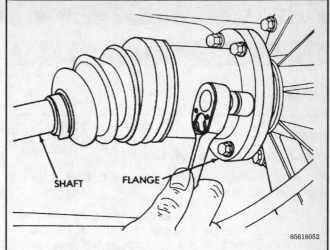

Fig. 51 Half shaft flange retaining bolts, All Wheel Drive models

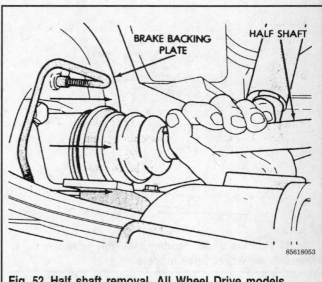

Fig. 52 Half shaft removal, All Wheel Drive models

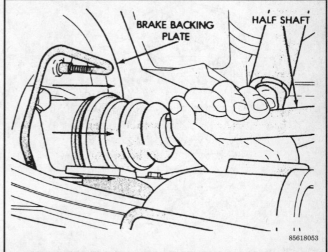

Fig. 53 Wheel bearing mounting bolts, All Wheel Drive models

STEERING

Steering Wheel

REMOVAL & INSTALLATION

1984-91

▶ See Figures 55, 56, 57, 58, 59 and 60

➡**A steering wheel puller (Chrysler tool C3428B or the equivalent) is required.**

1. Disconnect the negative battery cable at the battery.
2. Remove the center horn pad assembly. On standard steering wheels the horn pad is retained by two screws which are removed from underneath the wheel. Premium steering

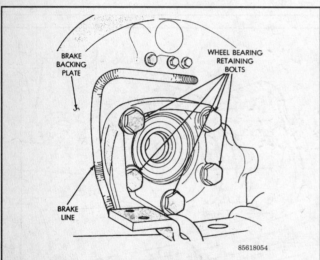

Fig. 54 Pull the wheel bearing assembly from the housing, All Wheel Drive models

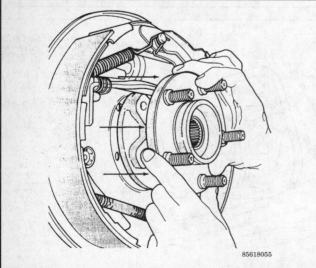

Fig. 55 Standard steering wheel horn pad and wiring

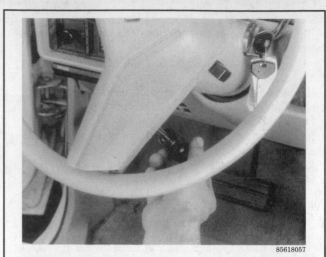

Fig. 56 From behind the steering wheel remove the cover retaining screws, 1987 Voyager shown

Fig. 57 Removing the horn pad from the steering wheel. The horn wires may be left connected, if desired, 1987 Voyager shown

wheels require that the horn pad be pried from internal retainers. Pry the horn pad up from the bottom edges of the steering wheel.

3. Disconnect the horn wires from the center pad, if necessary. Remove the pad.
4. Mark the column shaft and wheel for reinstallation reference and remove the steering wheel retaining nut.
5. Remove the steering wheel using a steering wheel puller (Chrysler Tool C3428B or the equivalent).

To install:

6. Line up the reference marks on the steering wheel and column shaft. Push wheel on to the shaft and draw into position with the mounting nut. Tighten the nut to 45 ft. lbs. Install the center horn pad after connecting the horn connectors. Connect the negative battery cable.

Fig. 58 Mark the column shaft and wheel for reinstallation reference and remove the steering wheel retaining nut, 1987 Voyager shown

Fig. 59 Remove the steering wheel using a steering wheel puller (Chrysler Tool C3428B or the equivalent), 1987 Voyager shown

Fig. 60 The steering wheel shown removed with the horn pad attached, 1987 Voyager shown

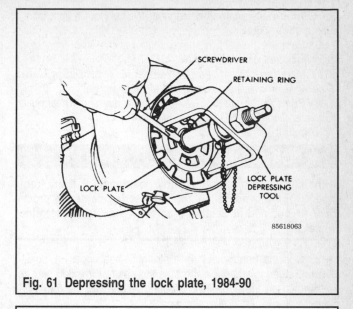

Fig. 61 Depressing the lock plate, 1984-90

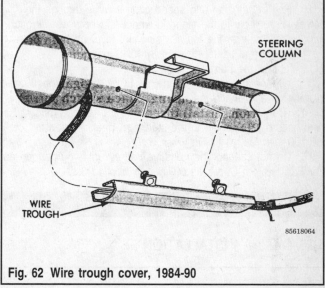

Fig. 62 Wire trough cover, 1984-90

1992-94

✳✳CAUTION

Disconnect and isolate the negative (ground) battery cable. This will disable the air bag system. Failure to disconnect the battery could result in accidental deployment and possible personal injury. Allow system capacitor to discharge for two minutes then begin air bag system component removal. Refer to Section 6 for additional air bag system precautions and information.

1. Make sure the front wheels are straight and the steering column is locked in place.
2. Disconnect the negative battery cable at the battery and isolate.
3. Wait 2 minutes for the reserve capacitor to discharge before removing non deployed module.
4. Remove the 4 nuts attaching the air bag module from the back side of the steering wheel.

5. Lift the module and disconnect the connector from the rear of the module.

6. Remove the vehicle speed control switch and connector, if so equipped or cover.

7. Mark the column shaft and wheel for reinstallation reference and remove the steering wheel retaining nut.

8. Remove the steering wheel using a steering wheel puller (Chrysler Tool C3428B or the equivalent).

To install:

❋❋CAUTION

If the clockspring is not properly positioned or if the front wheel were moved, follow the clockspring centering procedure as outlined in Section 6 before installing the steering wheel.

9. With the front wheels in a straight ahead position, position the steering wheel on the steering column, making sure to fit the flats on the hub of the steering wheel with the formations on the inside of the clockspring.

10. Pull the air bag and speed control wires through the lower, alrger hole in the steering wheel and horn wire through the smaller hole at the top. Be sure not to pinch the wires.

11. Install and tighten the nut to 45 ft. lbs.

12. Install the horn wire connector.

13. Connect the 4-way connector to the vehicle speed control switch and attach the switch to the steering wheel.

14. Connect the air bag lead wire to the air bag module and secure the module to the steering wheel. Tighten to 80-100 inch lbs. (9-11 Nm).

15. Do not connect the negative battery until you perform an Air Bag System Check as outlined in Section 6.

Turn Signal Switch

REMOVAL & INSTALLATION

1984-90

▶ See Figures 61, 62, 63 and 64

1. Disconnect the negative battery cable at the battery.

2. Remove the steering wheel. Remove the lower steering column cover, silencer panel and reinforcement.

3. The wiring harness is contained by a trough that is mounted on the side of the steering column. Remove the trough by prying the connectors from the column. New connectors may be required for installation.

4. Disconnect the turn signal wiring harness connector at the bottom of the steering column.

5. Disassemble the steering column for switch removal as follows:

6. On standard columns; remove the screw holding the wiper-washer switch to the turn signal switch. Allow the control stalk and switch to remain in position. Remove the three screws that attach the bearing retainer and turn signal switch to the upper bearing housing. Remove the turn signal and hazard warning switch assembly by gently pulling the switch up from the column while straightening the wires and guiding

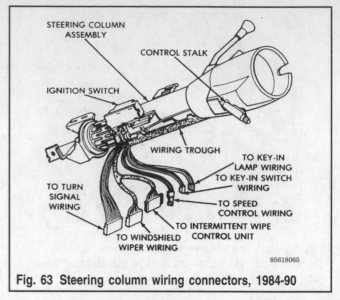

Fig. 63 Steering column wiring connectors, 1984-90

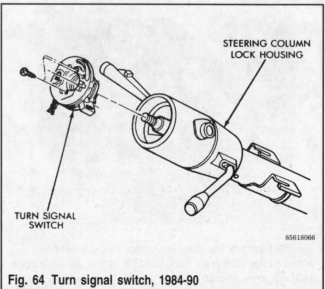

Fig. 64 Turn signal switch, 1984-90

them up through the column opening. Be sure to disconnect the ground connector.

7. On models with tilt wheel; remove the plastic cover (if equipped) from the lock plate. Depress the lock plate and pry the retaining ring form mounting groove. (Chrysler Tool C4156 or equivalent is used to compress the lock plate). Remove the lock plate, canceling cam and upper bearing spring. Place the turn signal switch in right turn position. Remove the screw that attaches the link between the turn signal and wiper-washer switches. Remove the screw that attaches the hazard warning switch knob. Remove the three screws attaching the turn signal switch to the steering column. Remove the turn signal and hazard warning switch assembly by gently pulling the switch up from the column while straightening and guiding the wires up through the column opening.

To install:

8. On models with the standard column; lubricate the turn signal switch pivot hole with a white lube (such as Lubriplate). Thread the connector and wires through the column hole carefully. Position the turn signal switch and bearing retainer in

place on the upper bearing housing and install the three mounting screws. Position the turn signal lever to turn signal pivot and secure with the mounting screws. Be sure the dimmer switch rod is in mounting pocket.

9. On models with tilt wheel; thread connector and wire harness through column hole. Position the turn signal switch in the upper column housing. Place the switch in the right turn position. Install the three mounting screws. Install the link between the turn signal switch and the wiper-washer switch pivot and secure mounting screw. Install the lock plate bearing spring, canceling cam and new retainer clip using Tool C4156 or equivalent. Install the hazard warning knob, screw.

10. Connect the wiring harness plug. Install the cover through wiring cover to the steering column.

11. Install the steering wheel and retaining nut. Connect battery cable and test the switch for operation.

Multi-Function Switch

REMOVAL & INSTALLATION

1991-94

On these models the turn signal switch is part of the multi-function switch.

1. Disconnect the negative battery cable.
2. With tilt column, remove the tilt lever.
3. Remove both upper and lower steering column covers.
4. Remove the multi-function switch tamper proof mounting screws.
5. Pull the switch away from the column and loosen the connector screw. The screw will remain in the connector.
6. Remove the wiring connector from the multi-function switch.

To install:

7. Install the wiring connector to the switch and tighten the connector retaining screw to 17 inch lbs.
8. Mount the multi-function switch to the column and tighten the retaining screws to 17 inch lbs.
9. With tilt column, install the tilt lever.
10. Connect the negative battery cable.

Ignition Lock Cylinder

REMOVAL & INSTALLATION

1984-90

▶ **See Figures 65 and 66**

1. Disconnect the negative battery cable.
2. Follow te turn signal switch removal removal procedures.
3. Unclip the horn and key light ground wires.
4. Remove the four screws that hold the bearing housing to the lock housing.
5. Remove the snap ring from the upper end of the steering shaft.
6. Remove the bearing housing from the shaft.

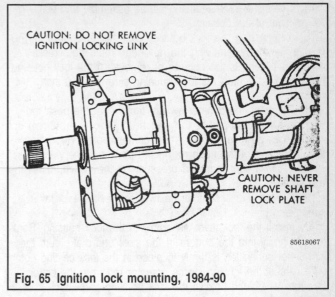

Fig. 65 Ignition lock mounting, 1984-90

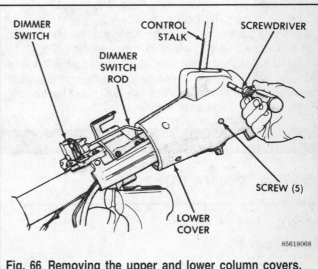

Fig. 66 Removing the upper and lower column covers, 1984-90

7. Remove the lock plate spring and lock plate from the steering shaft.
8. Remove the ignition key, then remove the screw and lift out the buzzer/chime switch.
9. Remove the two screws attaching the ignition switch to the column jacket.
10. Remove the ignition switch by rotating the switch 90 degrees on the rod then sliding off the rod.
11. Remove the two mounting screws from the dimmer switch and disengage the switch from the actuator rod.
12. Remove the two screws that mount the bellcrank and slide the bellcrank up in the lock housing until it can be disconnect from the ignition switch actuator rod.
13. To remove the lock cylinder and lock levers place the cylinder in the lock position and remove the key.
14. Insert a small diameter screwdriver or similar tool into the lock cylinder release holes and push into the release spring loaded lock retainers. At the same time pull the lock cylinder out of the housing bore.

15. Grasp the lock lever and spring assembly and pull straight out of the housing.

16. If necessary the lock housing may be removed from the column jacket by removing the hex head retaining screws.

17. Installation is the reverse of removal. If the lock housing was removed tighten the lock housing screws to 90 inch pounds.

18. To install the dimmer switch, firmly seat the push rod into the switch. Compress the switch until two ⅛ in. (3mm) drill shanks can be inserted into the alignment holes. Reposition the upper end of the push rod in the pocket of the wash/wipe switch. With a light rearward pressure on the switch, install the two screws.

19. Grease and assemble the two lock levers, lock lever spring and pin.

20. Install the lock lever assembly in the lock housing. Seat the pin firmly into the bottom of the slots and make sure the lock lever spring leg is firmly in place in the lock casting notch.

21. Install the ignition switch actuator rod from the bottom through the oblong hole in the lock housing and attach it to the bellcrank onto its mounting surface. The gearshift lever should be in the park position.

22. Place the ignition switch on the ignition switch actuator rod and rotate it 90 degrees to lock the rod into position.

23. To install the ignition lock, turn the key to the lock position and remove the key. Insert the cylinder far enough into the housing to contact the switch actuator. Insert the key and press inward and rotate the cylinder.

Ignition Switch

REMOVAL & INSTALLATION

1984-90

▶ **See Figure 67**

1. Disconnect the negative battery cable.
2. Remove the steering column cover.
3. If equipped with automatic transaxle, position the gear selector into DRIVE and disconnect the indicator cable.

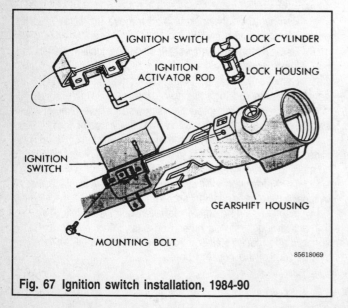

Fig. 67 Ignition switch installation, 1984-90

4. Remove the lower panel reinforcement.
5. Drop the steering column for switch replacement.
6. Disconnect the wiring connector from the ignition switch.
7. Position the ignition lock cylinder into the LOCK position.
8. Tape the ignition switch rod to the steering column to prevent the rod from falling out of the lock cylinder assembly.
9. Remove the screws attaching the ignition switch to the column jacket.
10. Remove the ignition switch by rotating the switch 90 degrees and pulling up to disengage from the rod.

To install:

11. Rotate the switch 90 degrees and push down to engage the rod.
12. Install the screws to the ignition switch mounting plate but do not tighten.
13. Remove the tape holding the rod to the column.
14. Adjust the switch by pushing up on the switch to take up rod system slack. This must be done with the key cylinder in the LOCK position and the key removed.
15. Tighten the screws attaching the switch to the column.
16. Connect the wiring connector to the ignition switch.
17. Install the steering column.
18. Install the steering column cover.
19. Connect the negative battery cable.

Ignition Switch And Lock Cylinder

REMOVAL & INSTALLATION

1991-94

▶ **See Figures 68, 69, 70, 71, 72 and 73**

1. Disconnect the negative battery cable.
2. If equipped with a tilt column, remove the tilt lever by turning it counterclockwise.
3. Remove the upper and lower covers from the column.
4. Remove the ignition switch mounting screws. Use a tamper proof torx bit Snap-on TTXR15A2, TTXR20A2 or equivalent to remove the screws.

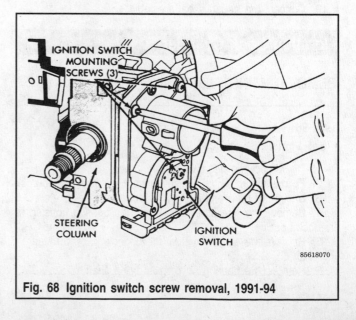

Fig. 68 Ignition switch screw removal, 1991-94

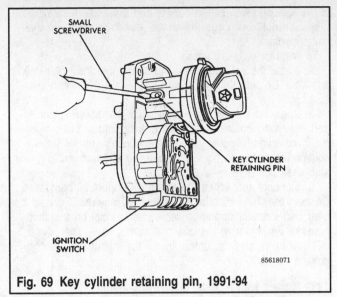

Fig. 69 Key cylinder retaining pin, 1991-94

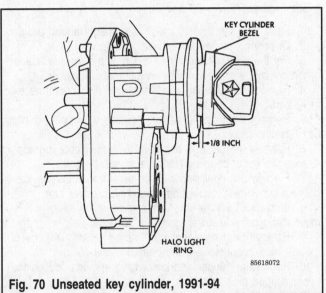

Fig. 70 Unseated key cylinder, 1991-94

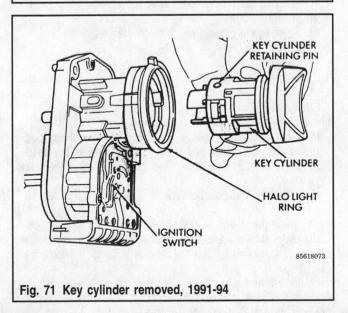

Fig. 71 Key cylinder removed, 1991-94

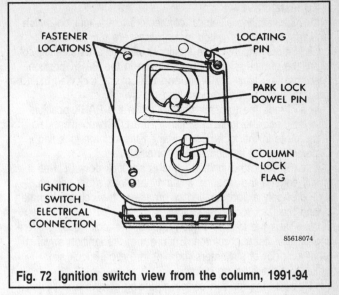

Fig. 72 Ignition switch view from the column, 1991-94

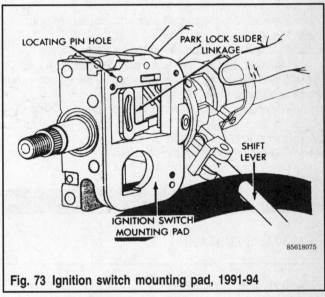

Fig. 73 Ignition switch mounting pad, 1991-94

5. Pull the switch away from the column, release the connector locks on the 7 terminal wiring connector, then remove the connector from the ignition switch.

6. Release the connector lock on the 4 terminal wiring connector, then remove the connector from the ignition switch.

7. To remove the key cylinder from the ignition switch:

a. Turn the key to the LOCK position. Using a small screwdriver, depress the key cylinder retaining pin until it is flush with the key cylinder surface.

b. Rotate the key clockwise to the OFF position. The key cylinder will unseat from the ignition switch. When the key cylinder is unseated, it will be approximately ⅛ inch away from the ignition switch halolight ring. DO NOT attempt to remove the key cylinder at this time.

c. With the key cylinder in the unseated position, rotate the key counterclockwise to the LOCK position and remove the key.

d. Remove the key cylinder from the ignition switch.

To install:

8. Connect the electrical connectors to the ignition switch and make sure the switch locking tabs are fully seated.

9. Before attaching the ignition switch to a tilt steering column, the transmission shifter must be in the PARK position. Also the park lock dowel pin and the column lock flag must be properly indexed before installing the switch.

a. Place the transmission shifter in the PARK position

b. Place the ignition switch in the LOCK position. The switch is in the lock position when the column lock flag is parallel to the ignition switch terminals.

c. Position the ignition switch park lock dowel pin so it will engage the steering column park lock slider linkage.

d. Apply a light coating of grease to the column lock flag and the park lock dowel pin.

10. Place the ignition switch against the lock housing opening on the steering column. Ensure that the ignition switch park lock dowel pin enters the slot in the park lock slider linkage in the steering column.

11. Install the ignition switch mounting screws and tighten the screws to 17 inch lbs. (2 Nm).

12. If the vehicle is equipped with a tilt steering column, install the tilt lever.

13. To install the ignition key in the lock cylinder:.

a. With the key cylinder and the ignition switch in the LOCK position, insert the key cylinder into the ignition switch until it bottoms.

b. Insert the ignition key into the lock cylinder. While pushing the key cylinder in toward the ignition switch, rotate the ignition key until the end of travel.

14. Connect the negative battery cable.

15. Check for proper operation.

Steering Column

REMOVAL & INSTALLATION

1984-90 Models
▶ **See Figures 74 and 75**

1. Disconnect the negative battery cable from the battery. If the vehicle is equipped with a column mounted shift, pry the shift cable rod from the lever grommet at the bottom of the steering column. Remove the cable clip and cable from lower bracket.

2. Disconnect the wiring harness connector at the bottom of the steering column.

3. Remove the instrument panel lower steering column cover and disconnect the bezel. On models with floor shift, unsnap and remove shroud cover extensions.

4. If automatic, remove the selector indicator set screw and pointer from the shift housing.

5. Remove the nuts that attach the steering column mounting bracket to the instrument panel support and lower the bracket.

➡**Do not remove the roll pin from the steering column assembly connector.**

6. Pull the steering column rearward, disconnecting the lower stub shaft from the steering gear connector. If the vehi-

cle is equipped with speed control and a manual transmission, take care not to damage the control switch mounted on the clutch pedal.

To install:

7. Install the anti-rattle coupling spring into the lower coupling tube. Be sure that the spring snaps into the slot in the coupling.

8. Align the column lower shaft stub with coupling and insert. Raise the column and place bracket into position on the mounting studs. Loosely install the mounting nuts. Pull the column rearward and tighten the nuts to 105 inch lbs. Tighten stub shaft connector.

9. Connect and adjust the linkage. Connect all harnesses. Connect the shift indicator and adjust as required. Connect the gear shift indicator operating cable into the slot on the shift housing. Slowly move the gearshift from 1 to P. The pointer will now be properly adjusted. Install the instrument steering column cover.

1991 Models with Acustar Steering Column
▶ **See Figures 76, 77, 78 and 79**

1. Make sure the wheels are in the straight ahead position.

2. Disconnect the negative battery cable.

3. Pry the shift link rod out of the grommet on the bottom of the column, if equipped with an automatic transaxle.

4. Remove the steering wheel pad and disconnect the electrical leads.

5. Remove the steering wheel. Remove the upper coupling bolt retaining pin.

6. Remove the nut and bolt from the upper coupling and remove the upper coupling from the lower coupling.

7. For vehicles equipped with an automatic transaxle, disconnect the PRNDL cable from the PRNDL driver arm.

8. If equipped with a tilt column, remove the tilt lever. Remove the upper and lower ignition shroud trim.

9. Remove the turn signal/multifunction switch. Disconnect the electrical connectors at the bottom of the column.

10. Remove the upper and lower fixed shrouds, loosen the upper support bracket bolts.

11. Remove the lower dash panel and column support standoff bracket bolts.

12. Remove the column out through the passenger compartment.

To install:

13. Install a replacement grommet on the shift rod arm and lubricate it.

14. Install the column in the vehicle, position it on the attaching studs and loosely assemble the upper bracket nuts.

15. Make sure the wheels are still in a straight ahead position and align the upper and lower coupling. Install the coupling nut and tighten to 250 inch lbs. (28 Nm). Install the retaining pin.

16. Install the multifunction switch and connect the column wiring.

17. Install the upper fixed shroud.

18. Make sure the 2 plastic retainer are fully seated on the column bracket and tighten the bracket bolts to 105 inch lbs. (12 Nm).

19. Install the lower shroud. Position the shift lever, if equipped with an automatic transaxle, in the farthest down position and install the PRNDL cable.

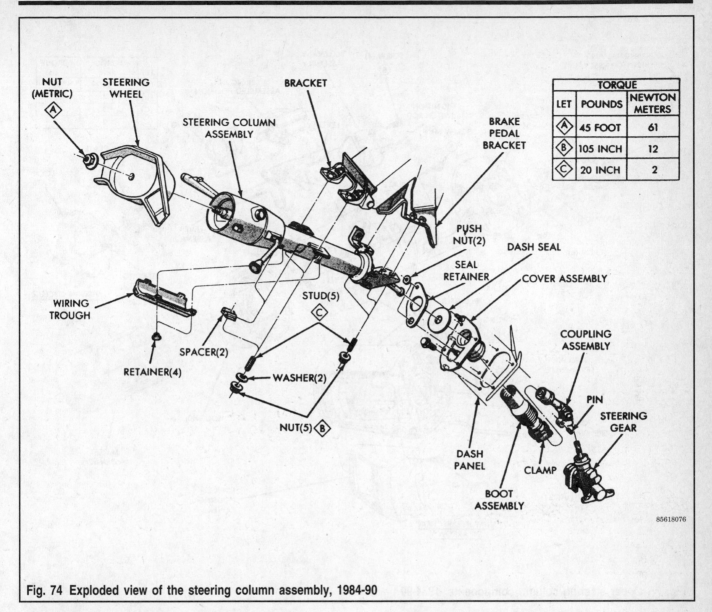

TORQUE		
LET	POUNDS	NEWTON METERS
Ⓐ	45 FOOT	61
Ⓑ	105 INCH	12
Ⓒ	20 INCH	2

Fig. 74 Exploded view of the steering column assembly, 1984-90

20. Install the tilt lever and the lower dash panel cover. Install the steering wheel. Connect the shift link rod.

21. Check the transaxle linkage adjustment through all of the gear positions.

22. Connect the negative battery cable.

1992-94 Models

▶ See Figures 80, 81, 82, 83, 84, 85, 86, 87, 88, 89, 90, 91, 92, 93, 94, 95, 96, 97, 98, 99, 100, 101 and 102

✳✳CAUTION

Disconnect and isolate the negative (ground) battery cable. This will disable the air bag system. Failure to disconnect the battery could result in accidental deployment and possible personal injury. Allow system capacitor to discharge for two minutes then begin air bag system component removal. Refer to Section 6 for additional air bag system precautions and information.

1. Make sure the front wheels are straight and the steering column is locked in place.

2. Disconnect the negative battery cable at the battery and isolate the cable from the battery terminal.

3. Remove the parking brake release rod, from the parking brake pedal assembly.

4. Remove the 5 screws attaching the steering column assembly cover.

5. Lower the steering column enough to disconnect the lift gate release switch connector.

6. Remove the fuse access/silencer panel assembly from the lower instrument panel.

7. Remove the nut from the stud, attaching the lower steering column bracket to the lower instrument panel reinforcement.

8. Remove the DRB diagnostic connector from its mounting bracket, on the lower instrument panel reinforcement.

9. Remove the 4 attaching bolts and lower instrument panel reinforcement from the lower instrument panel.

10. Position the steering wheel in the locked position and remove the key from the lock cylinder. Remove the 4 nuts

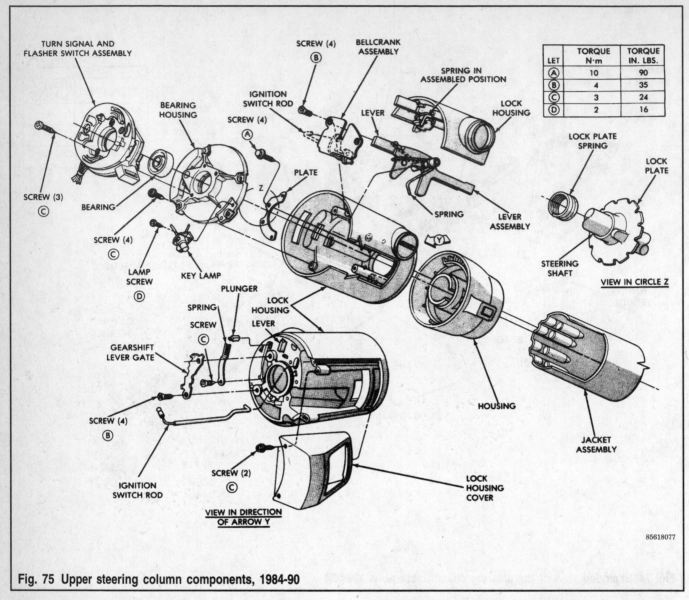

LET	TORQUE N·m	TORQUE IN. LBS.
Ⓐ	10	90
Ⓑ	4	35
Ⓒ	3	24
Ⓓ	2	16

TURN SIGNAL AND FLASHER SWITCH ASSEMBLY

SCREW (4) Ⓑ

BELLCRANK ASSEMBLY

SPRING IN ASSEMBLED POSITION

LOCK HOUSING

LOCK PLATE SPRING

LOCK PLATE

BEARING HOUSING

IGNITION SWITCH ROD

SCREW (4) Ⓐ

LEVER

SCREW (3) Ⓒ

BEARING

SCREW (4) Ⓒ

PLATE

SPRING

LEVER ASSEMBLY

STEERING SHAFT

VIEW IN CIRCLE Z

LAMP SCREW Ⓓ

KEY LAMP

PLUNGER

SPRING

LOCK HOUSING

SCREW Ⓒ

LEVER

GEARSHIFT LEVER GATE

SCREW (4) Ⓑ

IGNITION SWITCH ROD

SCREW (2) Ⓒ

HOUSING

JACKET ASSEMBLY

LOCK HOUSING COVER

VIEW IN DIRECTION OF ARROW Y

85618077

Fig. 75 Upper steering column components, 1984-90

attaching the air bag module from the steering wheel, then remove the air bag module from the steering wheel and disconnect the electrical lead at the air bag module.

11. Disconnect the steering wheel horn switch wiring connector from the steering wheel wiring harness.

12. Remove the steering column wiring harness connector from the speed control switch assembly.

13. Remove the steering wheel retaining nut and remove the steering wheel using a puller as outlined earlier.

14. Remove the 3 screws attaching the upper steering column shrouds to the steering column, then remove the upper and lower halves of the upper steering column shroud, from the steering column.

15. Remove the 3 screws attaching the lower steering column shrouds to the steering column, then remove the upper and lower steering column shroud, from the steering column.

16. Remove the wiring harness connectors from the clock spring and ignition switch, then remove the halo light and key in buzzer wiring harness connector from the ignition switch assembly.

17. Remove the 7 mm hex head bolt from the rear of the multi-function switch connector and disconnect the connector from the switch.

18. Remove the clock spring from the steering column assembly.

19. If the clock spring will not lift off the steering column do the following:.

a. Insert a screwdriver in the area of the clock spring's lower locking tab as shown.

b. Place the screwdriver against the locking tab of the clock spring assembly and push the locking tab back, and disengage the locking tab from the steering column.

c. Remove the clock spring from the column.

20. Remove the steering column assembly wiring harness from the column.

➡**The nut shown is part of the upper steering shift coupler and will remain on the coupler when removing the bolt. Do not attempt to remove the nut from the coupler.**

21. Remove the 3 nuts, attaching the lower mounting bracket of the steering column assembly to the dash panel

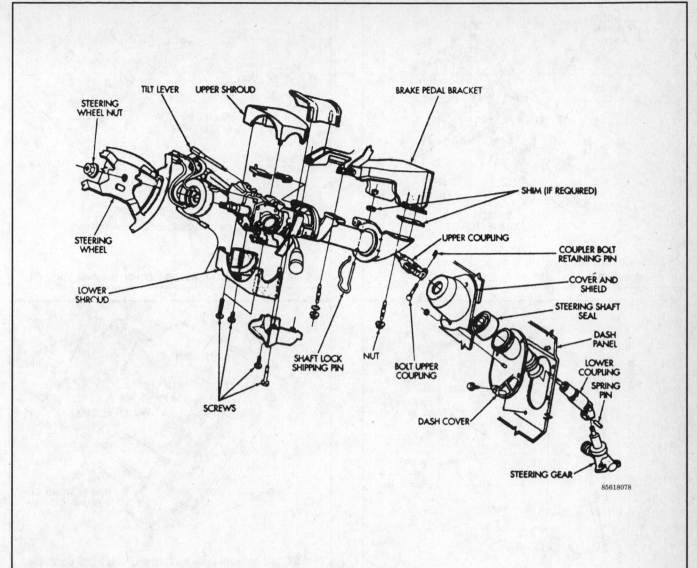

Fig. 76 Exploded view of the Acustar steering column assembly, 1991

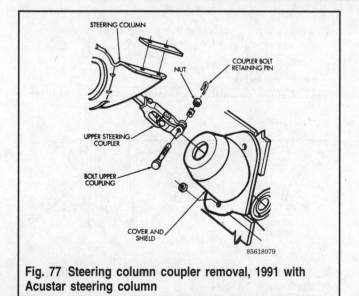

Fig. 77 Steering column coupler removal, 1991 with Acustar steering column

Fig. 78 PRNDL cable removal, 1991 with Acustar steering column

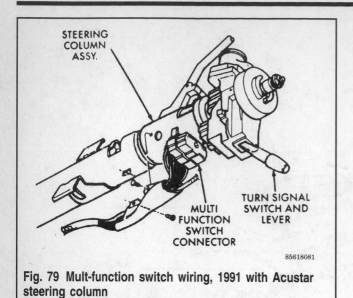

Fig. 79 Mult-function switch wiring, 1991 with Acustar steering column

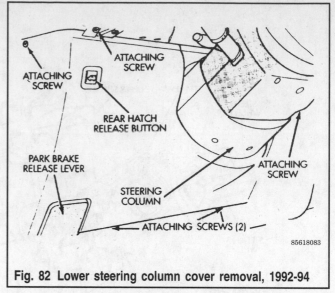

Fig. 82 Lower steering column cover removal, 1992-94

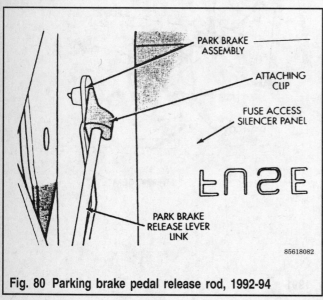

Fig. 80 Parking brake pedal release rod, 1992-94

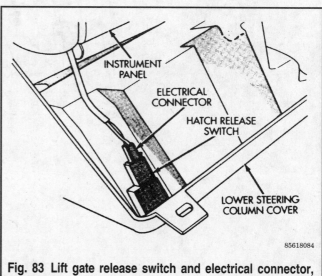

Fig. 83 Lift gate release switch and electrical connector, 1992-94

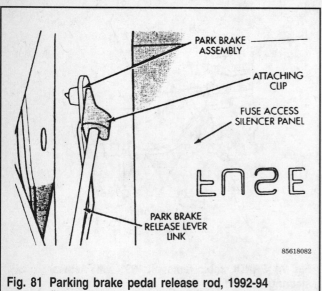

Fig. 81 Parking brake pedal release rod, 1992-94

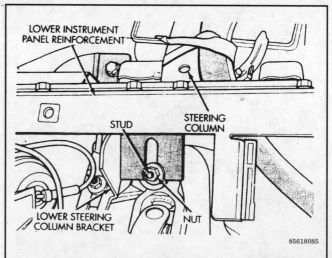

Fig. 84 Steering column attachment to instrument panel reinforcement, 1992-94

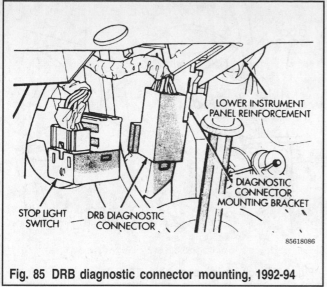

Fig. 85 DRB diagnostic connector mounting, 1992-94

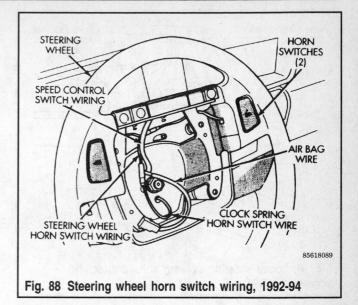

Fig. 88 Steering wheel horn switch wiring, 1992-94

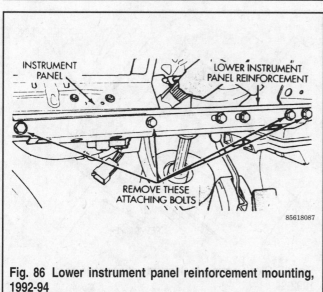

Fig. 86 Lower instrument panel reinforcement mounting, 1992-94

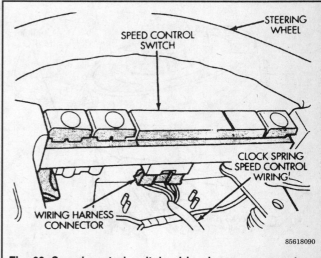

Fig. 89 Speed control switch wiring harness connector, 1992-94

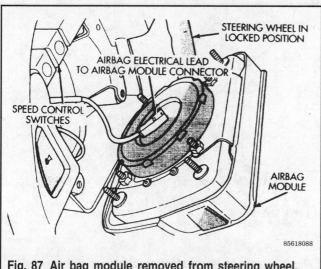

Fig. 87 Air bag module removed from steering wheel, 1992-94

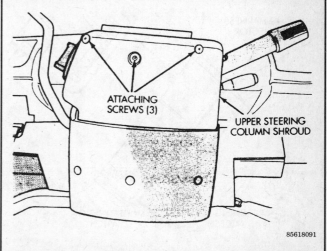

Fig. 90 Upper steering column shroud attaching screws, 1992-94

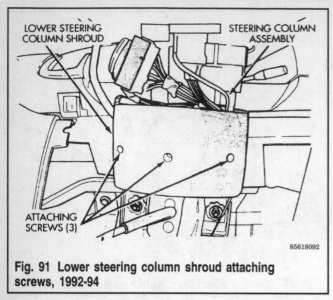

Fig. 91 Lower steering column shroud attaching screws, 1992-94

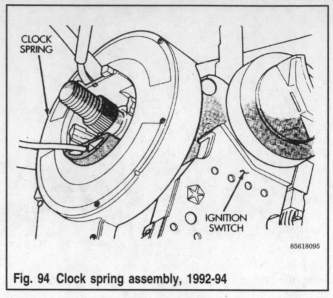

Fig. 94 Clock spring assembly, 1992-94

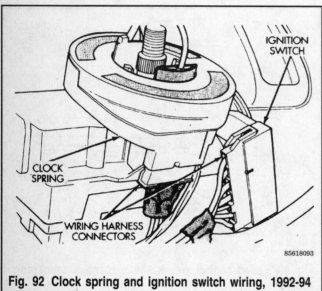

Fig. 92 Clock spring and ignition switch wiring, 1992-94

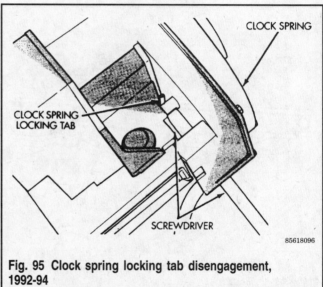

Fig. 95 Clock spring locking tab disengagement, 1992-94

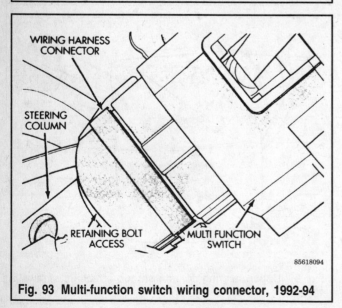

Fig. 93 Multi-function switch wiring connector, 1992-94

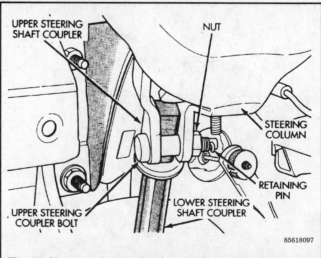

Fig. 96 Upper to lower steering shaft coupler removal, 1992-94

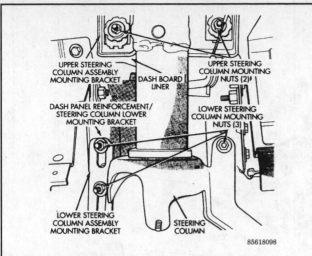

Fig. 97 Steering column upper and lower mounting brackets, 1992-94

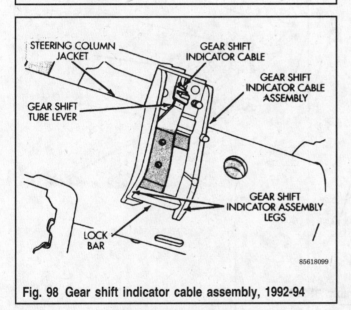

Fig. 98 Gear shift indicator cable assembly, 1992-94

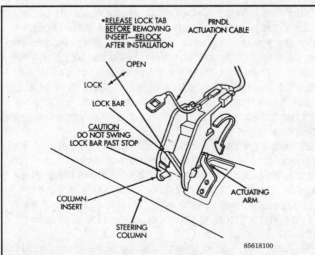

Fig. 99 Gear shift indicator cable removal from the steering column, 1992-94

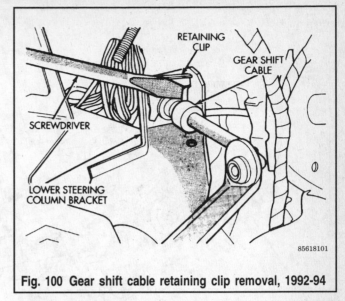

Fig. 100 Gear shift cable retaining clip removal, 1992-94

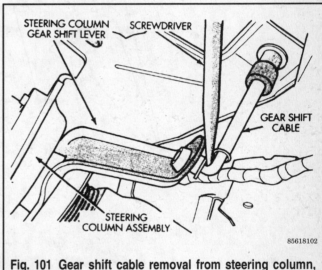

Fig. 101 Gear shift cable removal from steering column, 1992-94

reinforcement/steering column lower mounting bracket, then remove the 2 nuts attaching the upper mounting bracket of the steering column assembly to the dash board liner.

✳✳WARNING

During the following Step, do not allow the weight of the steering column assembly to be supported by the gear shift indicator cable.

22. Lower the steering column assembly from the dash board of the vehicle enough to access the gear shift indicator cable assembly, on the jacket of the steering column.

23. Position the gear shift lever on the steering column in the park position and remove the gear shift indicator assembly from the steering column jacket. Remove the indicator assembly, by first releasing the lock bar on the column insert and squeezing the legs of the column insert together and then lift the assembly from the column.

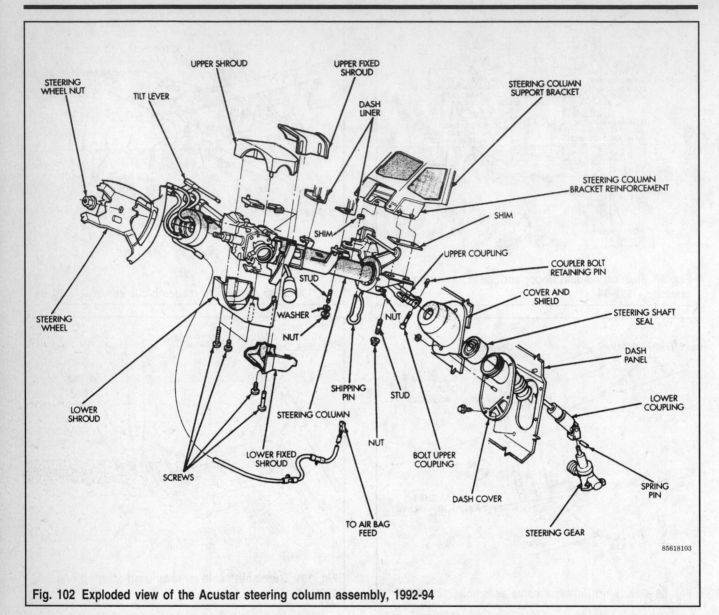

Fig. 102 Exploded view of the Acustar steering column assembly, 1992-94

24. Lower the steering column to the floor of the vehicle, then remove the clip attaching the gear shift cable to the lower bracket of the steering column assembly.

25. Remove the gear shift cable from the shift lever of the steering column

26. Carefully remove the steering column assembly from the vehicle.

To install:

27. Install a new gear shift cable attaching grommet into the steering column shift lever.

28. Prior to installing the steering column in the vehicle, install a ground clip on the left side capsule slot. The plastic capsules should be pre-assembled in the bracket slots. Remove the shipping lock pin, located on the lower column jacket when installing a new jacket. Place the steering column on the floor of the vehicle.

29. Install the gear shift cable on the lower mounting bracket of the steering column assembly. Install the gear shift cable into the new grommet on the steering column gear shift lever, then install the clip, attaching the shift cable to the steering column bracket.

30. Route the gear shift indicator assembly and its cable under the left upper mounting bracket of the steering column. Hook the eye of the gear shift indicator cable onto the lever of the steering column gear shift tube. Insert the flange of the gear shift indicator assembly into the steering column jacket. Squeeze the legs of the steering column insert together and install the tabs under the steering column jacket. Engage the lock bar to secure the shift indicator assembly into the steering column jacket.

31. Install the lower mounting bracket of the steering column assembly on the studs of the dash panel/reinforcement steering column mounting bracket then loosely install the 3 mounting nuts. Lift the steering column aligning studs in the dash board liner with insert in the upper mounting bracket of the steering steering column and loosely install the 2 mounting nuts.

32. Slide the steering column down until the lower bracket of the steering column assembly is against the studs in the dash panel reinforcement/steering column bracket. Center the steering column assembly assembly in the dash panel opening and tighten the mounting nuts at the upper bracket of the steering

column assembly, then torque all 5 steering column assembly mounting nuts to 105 inch lbs. (12 Nm).

33. Install the upper steering shaft coupler on the lower steering shaft coupler and install the upper coupler bolt. Torque the nut on the upper steering coupler bolt to 250 inch lbs. (28 Nm). Be sure to reinstall the retaining pin in the steering coupler retaining bolt.

34. Install the clock spring on the steering column assembly, making sure the locking tabs on the clock spring are engaged with the steering column assembly.

35. Install the wiring harness connector onto the multi-function switch. Torque the mult-function switch wiring harness connector retaining bolt to 17 inch lbs. (2 (Nm).

36. Install the wiring harness connectors onto the clock spring and ignition switch assembly.

37. Move the shift lever to the neutral position and check the pointer location in the PRNDL window on the instrument cluster. If the pointer does not indicate neutral, adjust the actuator assembly to center the pointer on N (neutral), and then check the pointer in other gear positions.

38. Install the clips attaching the steering column assembly wiring harness to the steering column assembly.

39. Install the upper and lower halves of the lower steering column shroud assembly on the steering column. Then install and securely tighten the 3 lower steering column shroud attaching screws.

40. Install the upper and lower halves of the upper steering column shroud assembly on the steering column. Then install and securely tighten the 3 upper steering column shroud attaching screws.

41. Install the tilt lever on the column.

42. Feed the speed control switch and air bag module wiring leads through the retangular hole in the steering wheel, then feed the horn switch wiring lead through the round hole in the steering wheel.

43. Install the steering wheel as outlined earlier in this Section.

44. Connect the horn switch wiring lead from the clock spring, onto the steering wheel horn switch wiring.

45. If equipped with speed control, connect the speed control wiring from the clock spring onto the speed control switch.

46. Install the wiring lead from the clock spring onto the air bag module. Make the wiring connection onto the air bag module, by pressing straight in on the connector. Make sure it is fully seated.

47. Install the air bag module into the steering wheel and then install the 4 air bag module attaching nuts. Torque all 4 air bag module attaching nuts to 100 inch lbs. (11 Nm).

48. Install the lower instrument panel reinforcement onto the instrument panel and tighten the 4 retaining bolts to 50 inch lbs. (6 Nm).

49. Install the nut on the stud attaching the lower steering column bracket to the lower instrument panel reinforcement and torque the nut to 100 inch lbs. (6 Nm).

50. Install the DRB diagnostic connector onto the instrument panel bracket on the lower instrument panel reinforcement.

51. Install the fuse access/silencer panel assembly on the lower instrument panel.

52. Position the lower steering column in the vehicle. Connect the lift gate release switch connector.

53. Install the steering column cover and 5 attaching screws.

54. Install the parking brake release rod, to the parking brake pedal assembly and lock attaching clip.

55. Redjust then test the transmission shift linkage.

56. When reconnecting the battery on a vehicle that has had the air bag removed, the following procedure should be used:

a. Connect the DRB to the ASDM diagnostic 6-way connector.

b. Turn the ignition key to the ON position. Exit the vehicle with the DRB, and install the latest version of the proper diagnostic cartridge into the DRB.

c. Make sure there are no occupants in the vehicle and connect the negative battery cable.

d. Using the DRB read and record active or stored fault codes and. Take appropriate actions to correct any faults.

e. Erase stored fault codes. If problems remain fault codes will not erase.

f. From the passenger side of the vehicle, turn the ignition key to OFF and then ON observing the instrument cluster air bag lamp. It should go on for 6 to 8 seconds, then go out. This will indicate that the air bag system is functioning normally.

❄❄WARNING

If the air bag warning lamp fails to light, blinks on and off or goes on and stays on, there is an air bag system malfunction.

g. Test the operation of any steering column functions such as the horn, lights or speed control system.

Steering Linkage

REMOVAL & INSTALLATION

Tie Rod Ends

1. Jack up the front of the vehicle and support on jackstands.

2. Loosen the jam nut which connects the tie rod end to the rack.

3. Mark the tie rod position on the threads.

4. Remove the tie rod cotter pin and nut.

5. Using a puller, remove the tie rod from the steering knuckle.

➡**Count the number of turns when removing tie rod end. Install the new end the same amount of turns.**

6. Unscrew the tie rod end from the rack.
To install:

7. Install a new tie rod end, screw in the same number of turns as removal. Tighten the jam nut to 55 ft. lbs..

8. Check the wheel alignment.

Steering Gear

The steering system (either manual or power) used on these vehicles is of the rack and pinion design.

The manual steering gear assembly consists of a tube which contains a toothed rack and a housing containing a straddle mounted, helical-cut pinion gear. Tie rods are connected to each end of the rack and an adjustable end (on each side) connects to the steering knuckles. A double universal joint attaches the pinion to the steering column shaft. Steering wheel movement is transmitted by the column shaft and the rack and pinion converts the rotational movement of the pinion to transverse movement of the rack. The manual steering gear is permanently lubricated at the factory and periodic lubrication is not necessary. The manual steering gear cannot be adjusted or serviced. If a malfunction occurs, the entire assembly must be replaced.

The power steering gear is similar to appearance, except for a rotary valve assembly and two fluid hose assemblies. The rotary valve assembly directs fluid from the power steering pump, through hoses, to either side of an internal rack piston. As steering wheel effort is applied, an internal torsion bar twists causing the rotary valve to direct the fluid behind an internal rack piston, which in turn builds up hydraulic pressure and assists in the turning effort.

Rubber boots seal the tie rods and rack assembly. Inspect the boots periodically for cuts, tears or leakage. Replace the boots as necessary.

REMOVAL & INSTALLATION

Front Wheel Drive Models

▶ **See Figures 103 and 104**

1. Loosen the wheel lugs slightly. Raise and support the front of the vehicle at the frame point below the front doors, not on the front crossmember. Use jackstands for supporting.
2. Remove the front wheels and tire assemblies.
3. Remove the tie rod ends from the steering knuckles.
4. Lower and disconnect the steering column from the steering gear pinion shaft.
5. If equipped, remove the anti-rotation link from the crossmember and the air diverter valve from the left side of the crossmember.
6. Place a transmission jack, or floor jack with a wide lifting flange, under the front suspension K-crossmember. Support the

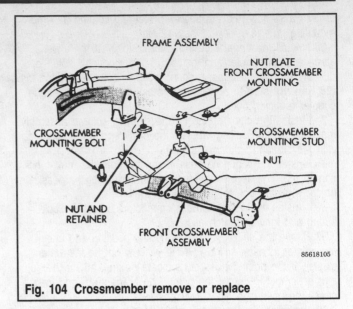

Fig. 104 Crossmember remove or replace

crossmember and remove the four crossmember to frame attaching bolts. Slowly lower the crossmember until enough room is gained to remove the steering gear assembly. Place stands under the crossmember, if available.

7. Remove the splash and boot shields. If equipped with power steering, disconnect the power steering hoses.
8. Remove the bolts that attach the steering gear assembly to the crossmember. Remove the assembly from the left side of the vehicle.

To install:

9. Line up the gear pinion with the column. Installation is in the reverse order of removal. On models with manual steering, be sure the master serration of the steering gear aligns with the steering column connector. the right rear crossmember bolt is the alignment pilot for reinstallation. Install first and tighten.
10. Attach the gear to the K-frame and secure the K-frame. Secure the anti-rotation link. Secure the K-frame. Torque all crossmember attaching bolts to 90 ft. lbs. Steering gear mounting bolts are tightened to 250 inch lbs.

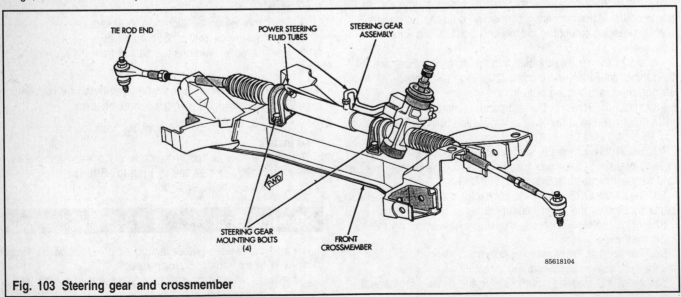

Fig. 103 Steering gear and crossmember

11. Connect the tie rod ends. Fill power steering reservoir (if equipped), start engine, turn the steering wheel from lock to lock and check for fluid leaks.

12. Check toe adjustment.

All Wheel Drive (AWD) Models

▶ See Figure 105

Before removing the steering gear on AWD models, the steering column must be removed to provide clearance for steering rack removal.

1. Raise and support the vehicle. Remove the wheel and tire assemblies.

2. Remove the steering column assembly from the vehicle.

3. Remove the tie rod ends from the steering knuckle using a suitable puller.

4. Remove the 2 bolts and the 2 nuts that attach the bridge assembly to the crossmember. The bolts and nuts can be reached through the access holes in the top of the bridge assembly.

5. Remove the crossmember to frame rail attaching bolts. Use a jack to lower the crossmember so that it is suspended

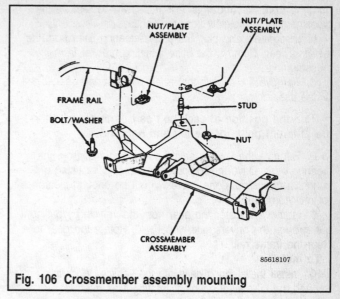

Fig. 106 Crossmember assembly mounting

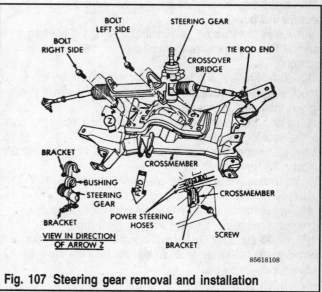

Fig. 107 Steering gear removal and installation

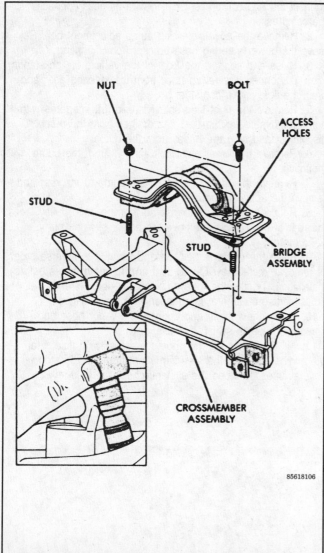

Fig. 105 Bridge assembly removal, All Wheel Drive vehicles

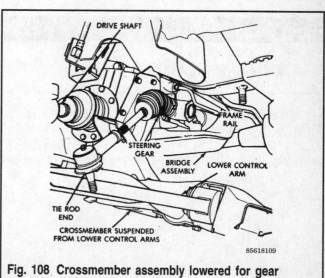

Fig. 108 Crossmember assembly lowered for gear removal

from the lower control arms. It is necessary to remove the crossmember completely from the vehicle.

6. Disconnect and plug the power steering lines from the steering gear. Remove the hose retaining bracket from the crossmember.

7. Remove the 4 bolts that retain the steering gear to the bridge assembly.

➡**Note the position of each bolt as it is removed, there are different bolts for the left and right sides.**

8. Remove the lower steering column coupler from the steering gear. Drive the roll pin from the coupler using a punch. If this is not done, there will not be enough clearance for rack removal.

9. Remove the steering gear from the vehicle by pulling it out through the drivers side wheel well. Rotate the gear to clear the frame rail.

To install:

10. Install the steering gear into the vehicle. Work it in through the left wheel opening, rotating it as needed.

11. Install the steering column coupler, make sure to fully seat the roll pin.

12. Install the steering gear mounting bolts. Do not torque them at this time, be sure to install them in the proper locations.

13. Install the steering hose bracket in position, tighten to 70 inch lbs. (8 Nm). Install the hoses on the steering rack and tighten them to 275 inch lbs. (31 Nm).

14. Raise the crossmember into position and install the bolts to the following torques:

   a. Crossmember-to-frame rail screw and washer — 90 ft. lbs. (122 Nm)

   b. Crossmember-to-frame rail stud nut — 90 ft. lbs. (122 Nm)

15. Install the bridge assembly onto the crossmember and tighten the mounting nuts to 50 ft. lbs. (68 Nm).

16. Install the outer tie rod ends on the steering knuckle and tighten the nuts, tighten to 38 ft. lbs. (52 Nm). Be sure to install a new cotter pin.

17. Install the wheel and tire assemblies. Lower the vehicle.

18. Connect the negative battery cable. Start the vehicle and check the power steering lines for leaks. Check the fluid level.

Boot Seals

REMOVAL & INSTALLATION

1. Raise and support the front of the vehicle on jackstands.

2. Disconnect the tie rod end from the steering knuckle. Loosen the jam nut and unscrew the end. Count the number of turns required when removing the end.

3. Cut the inner boot clamp, use pliers to expand the outer clamp and remove.

4. Locate and mark for reinstallation, the location of the breather tube.

5. Use a small tool to lift the boot from inner mounting groove and slide boot from the shaft.

6. Install the new boot and clamps. Locate breather tube to reference mark. Lubricate boot and mounting groove with silicone type lubricant. Install the tie rod end the same number of turns as counted when removing.

Power Steering Pump

REMOVAL & INSTALLATION

1. Disconnect the negative battery cable from the battery. Disconnect the vapor hose (canister) from the carburetor. Disconnect the A/C compressor clutch wire harness connector at the compressor.

2. Remove the power steering pump adjustment bolt. Remove the power steering hose bracket from mounting.

3. Raise and support the front of the vehicle on jackstands.

4. Disconnect the return hose from the steering gear and drain the fluid into a container.

5. Remove the right side splash shield if it interferes with pump removal. After the fluid has drained from the pump, disconnect and plug the hoses from the pump.

6. Remove the lower pivot bolt and nut from the pump mounting.

7. Remove the drive belt. Move the pump to the rear and remove the adjusting bracket.

8. Rotate the pump clockwise so that the drive pulley faces the rear of the vehicle. Remove the power steering pump.

To install:

9. Place the pump in position and install it in reverse order of removal. Install new O-ring seal on the pump hoses before installation. Tighten the tube nuts to 25 ft. lbs. Refer to belt adjustments in 'General Information and Maintenance'.

10. Lower the vehicle and connect the vapor hose and A/C compressor clutch switch harness..

11. Fill the power steering pump reservoir with fluid. Start the engine and turn the steering wheel from stop to stop, several times, to bleed the system. check the fluid level.

TORQUE SPECIFICATIONS

Component	English	Metric
WHEELS		
Wheel lug nuts	95 ft. lbs.	129 Nm
FRONT SUSPENSION		
Ball joint-to-knuckle clamp bolt		
1984–89	70 ft. lbs.	95 Nm
1990–91	105 ft. lbs.	145 Nm
Ball joint stud-to-steering knuckle clamp bolt		
1984–89	70 ft. lbs.	95 Nm
1990–91	105 ft. lbs.	143 Nm
1992–94	100 ft. lbs.	136 Nm
Brake hose retaining bracket	10 ft. lbs.	14 Nm
Coil spring assembly nut	60 ft. lbs.	82 Nm
Front Hub and Bearing		
Press-in-type		
Bearing retainer bolts	20 ft. lbs.	27 Nm
Bolt-in type		
Bearing mounting bolts	45 ft. lbs.	61 Nm
Hub retaining nut	180 ft. lbs.	245 Nm
Lower control arm front pivot bolt		
1984–89	105 ft. lbs.	143 Nm
1990–91	125 ft. lbs.	170 Nm
1992–94	95 ft. lbs.	129 Nm
MacPherson strut		
Upper mount nuts	20 ft. lbs.	27 Nm
Lower mounting and camber nuts	75 ft. lbs. + 1/4 turn	102 Nm + 1/4 turn
Rear stub strut nut	70 ft. lbs.	95 Nm
Steering knuckle-to-lower control arm clamp bolt		
1984–89	70 ft. lbs.	95 Nm
1990–94	105 ft. lbs.	143 Nm
Sway bar bracket stud nuts		
1984–89	25 ft. lbs.	34 Nm
1990–94	50 ft. lbs.	68 Nm
Sway bar center bracket bolts		
1984–89	25 ft. lbs.	34 Nm
1990–94	50 ft. lbs.	68 Nm
Sway bar outer bracket bolts		
1984–89	25 ft. lbs.	34 Nm
1990–94	50 ft. lbs.	68 Nm
Tie rod end nut	35 ft. lbs.	48 Nm
REAR SUSPENSION		
Hub and bearing assembly bolts		
All wheel drive	96 ft. lbs.	130 Nm
Shock absorber bolts		
Front wheel drive	50 ft. lbs.	68 Nm
All wheel drive		
Upper bolts	85 ft. lbs.	115 Nm
Lower bolts	80 ft. lbs.	108 Nm

85618C02

TORQUE SPECIFICATIONS

Component	English	Metric
Spring		
Front wheel drive models		
Hanger bolts	45 ft. lbs.	61 Nm
U-bolt nuts	60 ft. lbs.	82 Nm
Front fixed end bolt	95 ft. lbs.	129 Nm
Shackle nuts	35 ft. lbs.	48 Nm
All wheel drive models		
Hanger bolts	45 ft. lbs.	61 Nm
U-bolt nuts	65 ft. lbs.	88 Nm
Front pivot bolts	105 ft. lbs.	142 Nm
Shackle and pin assembly through-bolt nuts	35 ft. lbs.	47 Nm
Shackle and pin assembly retaining bolts	35 ft. lbs.	47 Nm
Sway Bar		
All Wheel Drive Models		
Bushing-to-axle bracket	45 ft. lbs.	61 Nm
Link arm-to-frame rail	45 ft. lbs.	61 Nm
Sway bar-to-link arm	45 ft. lbs.	61 Nm
Link arm bracket-to-frame rail	24 ft. lbs.	33 Nm
STEERING		
Crossmember-to-frame rail screw	90 ft. lbs.	122 Nm
Crossmember-to-frame rail stud nut	90 ft. lbs.	122 Nm
K-frame-to-crossmember attaching bolts	90 ft. lbs.	122 Nm
Outer tie rod ends-to-steering knuckle nuts	38 ft. lbs.	52 Nm
Power steering bridge assembly-to-crossmember	50 ft. lbs.	68 Nm
Power steering hose bracket	70 inch lbs.	8 Nm
Power steering hoses-to-steering rack	23 ft. lbs.	31 Nm
Power steering pump tube nuts	25 ft. lbs.	34 Nm
Steering column bracket mounting stud nuts	105 inch lbs.	12 Nm
Steering gear mounting bolts		
1984–90	21 ft. lbs.	28 Nm
1991–94	50 ft. lbs.	68 Nm
Steering wheel nut	45 ft. lbs.	61 Nm
Tie rod end jam nut	55 ft. lbs.	75 Nm
Upper and lower steering shaft coupling nut	21 ft. lbs.	28 Nm

85618C03

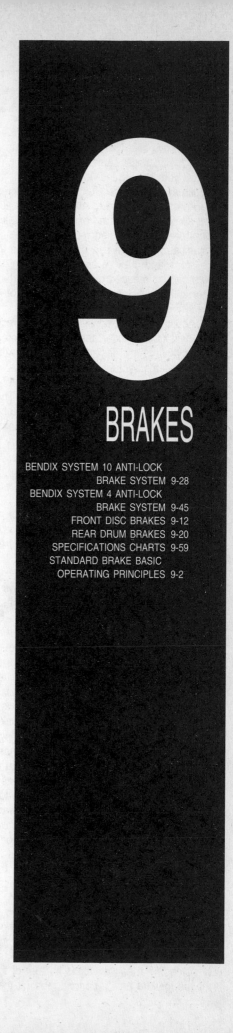

9

BRAKES

STANDARD BRAKE BASIC OPERATING PRINCIPLES

Hydraulic systems are used to actuate the brakes of all modern automobiles. The system transports the power required to force the frictional surfaces of the braking system together from the pedal to the individual brake units at each wheel. A hydraulic system is used for two reasons. First, fluid under pressure can be carried to all parts of an automobile by small hoses-some of which are flexible-without taking up a significant amount of room or posing routing problems. Second, a great mechanical advantage can be given to the brake pedal end of the system, and the foot pressure required to actuate the brakes can be reduced by making the surface area of the master cylinder pistons smaller than that of any of the pistons in the wheel cylinders or calipers.

The master cylinder consists of a fluid reservoir and either a single or double cylinder and piston assembly. Double type master cylinders are designed to separate the front and rear braking systems hydraulically in case of a leak.

Steel lines carry the brake fluid to a point on the vehicle's frame near each of the vehicle's wheels. The fluid is then carried to the wheel cylinders by flexible tubes in order to allow for suspension and steering movements.

Each wheel cylinder contains two pistons, one at either end, which push outward in opposite directions. In disc brake systems, the cylinders are part of the calipers. One or four cylinders are used to force the brake pads against the disc, but all cylinders contain one piston only. All pistons employ some type of seal, usually made of rubber, to minimize fluid leakage. A rubber dust boot seals the outer end of the cylinder against dust and dirt. The boot fits around the outer end of the piston on disc brake calipers, and around the brake actuating rod on wheel cylinders.

The hydraulic system operates as follows: When at rest, the entire system, from the piston(s) in the master cylinder to those in the wheel cylinders or calipers, is full of brake fluid. Upon application of the brake pedal, fluid trapped in front of the master cylinder piston(s) is forced through the lines to the wheel cylinders. Here, it forces the pistons outward, in the case of drum brakes, and inward toward the disc, in the case of disc brakes. The motion of the pistons is opposed by return springs mounted outside the cylinders in drum brakes, and by internal springs or spring seals, in disc brakes.

Upon release of the brake pedal, a spring located inside the master cylinder immediately returns the master cylinder pistons to the normal position. The pistons contain check valves and the master cylinder has compensating ports drilled in it. These are uncovered as the pistons reach their normal position. The piston check valves allow fluid to flow toward the wheel cylinders or calipers as the pistons withdraw. Then, as the return springs force the brake pads or shoes into the released position, the excess fluid reservoir through the compensating ports. It is during the time the pedal is in the released position that any fluid that has leaked out of the system will be replaced through the compensating ports.

Dual circuit master cylinders employ two pistons, located one behind the other, in the same cylinder. The primary piston is actuated directly by mechanical linkage from the brake pedal. The secondary piston is actuated by fluid trapped between the two pistons. If a leak develops in front of the secondary piston, it moves forward until it bottoms against the front of the master cylinder, and the fluid trapped between the pistons will operate the rear brakes. If the rear brakes develop a leak, the primary piston will move forward until direct contact with the secondary piston takes place, and it will force the secondary piston to actuate the front brakes. In either case, the brake pedal moves farther when the brakes are applied, and less braking power is available.

All dual-circuit systems use a switch to warn the driver when only half of the brake system is operational. This switch is located in a valve body which is mounted on the firewall or the frame below the master cylinder. A hydraulic piston receives pressure from both circuits, each circuit's pressure being applied to one end of the piston. When the pressures are in balance, the piston remains stationary. When one circuit has a leak, however, the greater pressure in that circuit during application of the brakes will push the piston to one side, closing the switch and activating the brake warning light.

In disc brake systems, this valve body also contains a metering valve and, in some cases, a proportioning valve. The metering valve keeps pressure from traveling to the disc brakes on the front wheels until the brake shoes on the rear wheels have contacted the drums, ensuring that the front brakes will never be used alone. The proportioning valve controls the pressure to the rear brakes to avoid rear wheel lock-up during very hard braking.

Warning lights may be tested by depressing the brake pedal and holding it while opening one of the wheel cylinder bleeder screws. If this does not cause the light to go on, substitute a new lamp, make continuity checks, and, finally, replace the switch as necessary.

The hydraulic system may be checked for leaks by applying pressure to the pedal gradually and steadily. If the pedal sinks very slowly to the floor, the system has a leak. This is not to be confused with a springy or spongy feel due to the compression of air within the lines. If the system leaks, there will be a gradual change in the position of the pedal with a constant pressure.

Check for leaks along all lines and at wheel cylinders. If no external leaks are apparent, the problem is inside the master cylinder.

Disc Brakes

BASIC OPERATING PRINCIPLES

Instead of the traditional expanding brakes that press outward against a circular drum, disc brake systems utilize a disc (rotor) with brake pads positioned on either side of it. Braking effect is achieved in a manner similar to the way you would squeeze a spinning phonograph record between your fingers. The disc (rotor) is a casting with cooling fins between the two braking surfaces. This enables air to circulate between the braking surfaces making them less sensitive to heat buildup and more resistant to fade. Dirt and water do not affect braking action since contaminants are thrown off by the centrifugal action of the rotor or scraped off the by the pads. Also, the equal clamping action of the two brake pads tends to ensure uniform, straight line stops. Disc brakes are inherently self-adjusting.

There are three general types of disc brake:
1. A fixed caliper.
2. A floating caliper.
3. A sliding caliper.

The fixed caliper design uses two pistons mounted on either side of the rotor (in each side of the caliper). The caliper is mounted rigidly and does not move.

The sliding and floating designs are quite similar. In fact, these two types are often lumped together. In both designs, the pad on the inside of the rotor is moved into contact with the rotor by hydraulic force. The caliper, which is not held in a fixed position, moves slightly, bringing the outside pad into contact with the rotor. There are various methods of attaching floating calipers. Some pivot at the bottom or top, and some slide on mounting bolts. In any event, the end result is the same.

Drum Brakes

BASIC OPERATING PRINCIPLES

Drum brakes employ two brake shoes mounted on a stationary backing plate. These shoes are positioned inside a circular drum which rotates with the wheel assembly. The shoes are held in place by springs; this allows them to slide toward the drums (when they are applied) while keeping the linings and drums in alignment. The shoes are actuated by a wheel cylinder which is mounted at the top of the backing plate. When the brakes are applied, hydraulic pressure forces the wheel cylinder's actuating links outward. Since these links bear directly against the top of the brake shoes, the tops of the shoes are then forced against the inner side of the drum. This action forces the bottoms of the two shoes to contact the brake drum by rotating the entire assembly slightly (known as servo action). When pressure within the wheel cylinder is relaxed, return springs pull the shoes back away from the drum.

Most modern drum brakes are designed to self-adjust themselves during application when the vehicle is moving in reverse. This motion causes both shoes to rotate very slightly with the drum, rocking an adjusting lever, thereby causing rotation of the adjusting screw.

Power Boosters

Power brakes operate just as standard brake systems except in the actuation of the master cylinder pistons. A vacuum diaphragm is located on the front of the master cylinder and assists the driver in applying the brakes, reducing both the effort and travel he must put into moving the brake pedal.

The vacuum diaphragm housing is connected to the intake manifold by a vacuum hose. A check valve is placed at the point where the hose enters the diaphragm housing, so that during periods of low manifold vacuum brake assist vacuum will not be lost.

Depressing the brake pedal closes off the vacuum source and allows atmospheric pressure to enter on one side of the diaphragm. This causes the master cylinder pistons to move and apply the brakes. When the brake pedal is released, vacuum is applied to both sides of the diaphragm, and return springs return the diaphragm and master cylinder pistons to the released position. If the vacuum fails, the brake pedal rod will butt against the end of the master cylinder actuating rod, and direct mechanical application will occur as the pedal is depressed.

The hydraulic and mechanical problems that apply to conventional brake systems also apply to power brakes, and should be checked for if the tests below do not reveal the problem.

Test for a system vacuum leak as described below:
1. Operate the engine at idle without touching the brake pedal for at least one minute.
2. Turn off the engine, and wait one minute.
3. Test for the presence of assist vacuum by depressing the brake pedal and releasing it several times. Light application will produce less and less pedal travel, if vacuum was present. If there is no vacuum, air is leaking into the system somewhere.

Test for system operation as follows:
4. Pump the brake pedal (with engine off) until the supply vacuum is entirely gone.
5. Put a light, steady pressure on the pedal.
6. Start the engine, and operate it at idle. If the system is operating, the brake pedal should fall toward the floor if constant pressure is maintained on the pedal.

Power brake systems may be tested for hydraulic leaks just as ordinary systems are tested.

Your vehicle is equipped with pin slider type caliper front disc brakes and automatic adjuster equipped rear drum brakes. The brake system is diagonally split, with the left front and right rear brakes on one hydraulic system and the right front and left rear on the other. Should one side of the split system fail, the other should provide enough braking power to bring the vehicle to a stop. Other components included in the brake system are: A brake warning switch, master cylinder, a lead sensing dual proportioning valve, a brake booster and the necessary hoses and lines.

Adjustments

Periodic brake adjustment is not necessary as the front calipers are inherently self-adjusting, and the rear brakes are equipped with self-adjusters. In the event of a brake reline or component service requiring brake shoe removal, initial manual adjustment of the rear brake shoes will speed up servicing time. Front brake pads adjust themselves as the brake pedal is applied. After installing new front brake pads pump the brake pedal several times until a firm feeling is obtained. The pads will be incorrect adjustment.

DRUM BRAKES

1. To make an initial rear brake shoe adjustment, raise and support the rear of the vehicle on jackstands, so that both wheels are off the ground and can turn freely.
2. Remove the adjusting hole cover at the back of the brake mounting plates.

3. Be sure the parking brake is fully released and that there is slack in the brake cables.

4. Insert a brake adjusting tool through the hole in the backing plate until the adjuster star wheel is engaged. move the adjusting tool upward to turn the star wheel. Continue until a slight drag is felt when the wheel is rotated.

5. Insert a thin screwdriver or piece of stiff rod through the backing plate slot and push the adjuster lock tab away from the star wheel. Move the adjusting tool down while holding the locking tab out of the way. Back off the star wheel until the wheel turns freely without any brake drag. Install the adjusting slot cover.

6. Repeat the procedure for the other rear wheel. Adjust the parking brake after initial rear brake adjustment is finished. Check parking brake adjustment after applying several times, insure freedom from brake drag.

Brake Light Switch

The brake light switch is a self adjusting unit installed on the brake pedal shaft pivot pin.

REMOVAL & INSTALLATION

1. Remove the old switch from the retaining bracket.
2. Install the new brake light switch into the bracket and push the switch as far forward as it will go.
3. The brake pedal will move forward slightly when the switch is pushed forward.
4. Pull back on the brake pedal gently. As the brake pedal is pulled back, the switch striker will move toward the switch. When the brake pedal can not be pull back any further, the switch will ratchet to the correct position. Very little movement is required, and no further adjustment is required.

Master Cylinder

The master cylinder is of tandem design, having an anodized aluminum body and a glass reinforced nylon reservoir. If the cylinder bore is pitted or scratched, the body must be replaced as honing will remove the anodized surface. The reservoir is indexed to prevent incorrect installation and the cap diaphragms are slotted to allow internal pressure to equalize. A secondary outlet tube leading from the master cylinder is connected to the differential valve mounted underneath the master cylinder. The front part of the valve supplied the right rear and left front brakes. The rear portion supplied the right rear and left front. The rear portion of the valve is connect to the primary outlet tube of the master cylinder.

REMOVAL & INSTALLATION

▶ See Figures 1, 2, 3 and 4

1. Disconnect the primary and secondary brake lines at the master cylinder. Tape or plug the ends of the lines.
2. Remove the nuts attaching the master cylinder to the power brake booster.

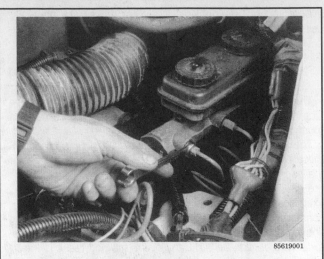
Fig. 1 Disconnecting the brake lines at the master cylinder, 1987 Voyager shown

Fig. 2 Removing the master cylinder attaching nuts, 1987 Voyager shown

Fig. 3 Removing the master cylinder away from the booster, 1987 Voyager shown

3. Wrap a rag around the brake line tilting holes, slide the master straight away from the booster and remove from the vehicle. take care not to spill any brake fluid on the finish. Flush off with water if any fluid is spilled.

To install:

4. Bench bleed the master cylinder. (See the Bleeding section). Install the master cylinder over the mounting studs. After aligning the master cylinder pushrod and mounting studs, hold the cylinder in position and start the attaching nuts but do not tighten completely. Install the brake lines but do not tighten completely.

5. After the brake lines are installed, tighten the cylinder mounting nuts fully and then the brake lines.

6. Finish bleeding the brake system.

OVERHAUL

▶ **See Figures 4, 5, 6 and 7**

The aluminum master cylinder cannot be rebuilt; service is limited to replacement.

Fluid Reservoir

REMOVAL & INSTALLATION

1. Remove the master cylinder from the vehicle. Clean the outside of the reservoir and cylinder.

2. Remove the reservoir caps and empty the brake fluid. Do not reuse the old fluid.

3. Position the master cylinder in a vise. Pad the vise jaws and do not over tighten.

4. Rock the reservoir from side to side to loosen and lift up to remove from the master cylinder. Do not pry the reservoir with an tools. Damage to the reservoir will result.

5. Remove the old housing to reservoir mounting grommets. Clean the cylinder and reservoir grommet mounting surfaces.

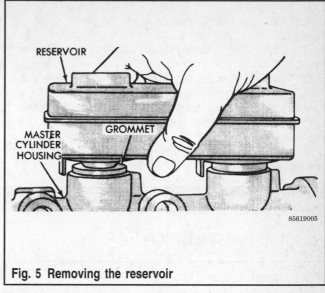

Fig. 5 Removing the reservoir

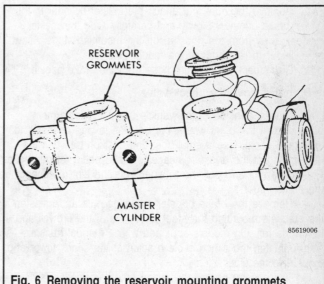

Fig. 6 Removing the reservoir mounting grommets

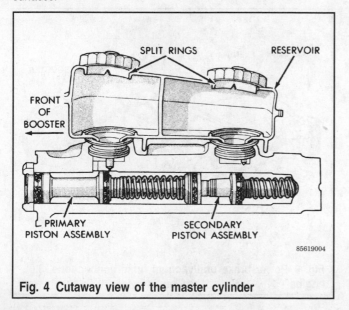

Fig. 4 Cutaway view of the master cylinder

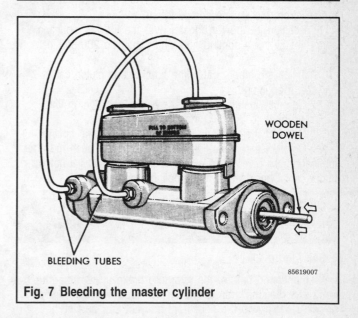

Fig. 7 Bleeding the master cylinder

To install:

6. Install new mounting grommets in the master cylinder housing.

7. Lubricate the mounting surfaces of the grommets with brake fluid.

8. Place the reservoir in position over the grommets and seat it into the grommets using a rocking motion.

9. Be sure that the reservoir is fully seated on the master cylinder and the bottom of the reservoir touches the top of the grommets.

10. Fill the reservoir with fresh brake fluid and bench bleed the master cylinder.

Power Brake Booster

REMOVAL & INSTALLATION

▶ **See Figures 8, 9 and 10**

1. Remove the nuts that attach the master cylinder to the power brake booster. Slowly and carefully slide the master cylinder away from the booster, off the mounting studs. Allow the cylinder to rest against the fender shield.

2. Disconnect the vacuum hose from the brake booster.

➡ **Do not remove the check valve.**

3. From the inside of the vehicle under the instrument panel, locate the point where the booster linkage connects to the brake pedal. Use a small tool and position between the center tang of the booster linkage to brake pedal retaining clip. Rotate the tool and pull the retainer from the pin. disconnect the brake pedal.

4. Remove the brake booster mounting nuts and unfasten the brackets mounting the steel water line at the firewall and left frame rail. On models equipped with a manual transmission, unfasten the clutch cable bracket at the shock tower and move it to the side.

5. The booster mounting bracket holes are slotted, slide the booster up and to the left. Tilt the booster inboard and up to remove from the engine compartment.

6. Position the power booster over the firewall mounting studs. Install the mounting nuts and tighten to 200-300 inch lbs.

7. install the steel heater line bracket and clutch cable bracket, if equipped.

8. Carefully install the master cylinder and tighten the mounting bolts to 200-300 inch lbs.

9. Connect the vacuum line to the power brake booster.

10. Connect the pedal linkage to the booster push rod after lubricating the pivot point with white grease. Install a new retainer clip. Check brake and stoplight operation.

Pressure Differential Switch/Warning Light

▶ **See Figure 11**

As mentioned before, the hydraulic brake system on your vehicle is diagonally split; the left front and right rear are part of one system and the right front and left rear part of the

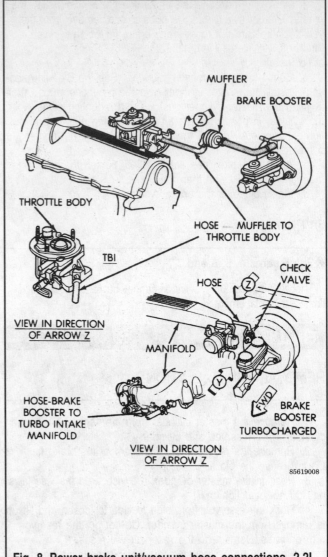

Fig. 8 Power brake unit/vacuum hose connections, 2.2L and 2.5L engines

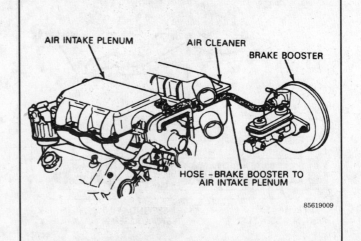

Fig. 9 Power brake unit/vacuum hose connections, 3.0L engine

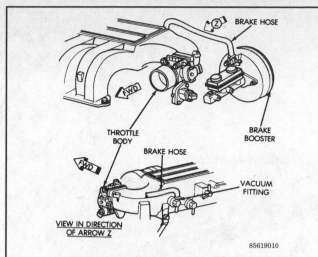

Fig. 10 Power brake unit/vacuum hose connections, 3.3L and 3.8L engines

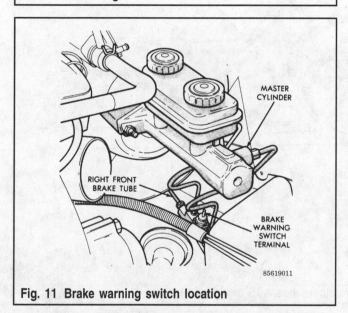

Fig. 11 Brake warning switch location

other. Both systems are routed through a pressure differential switch (located under the master cylinder) which is designed to warn the driver should a failure occur. If hydraulic pressure is lost in one side of the split system the switch will activate a warning light on the instrument panel, indicating that the brake system should be checked and repaired, if necessary. After repairs to the system have been made, the switch will automatically recenter itself and the light will go out.

TESTING

To test the warning switch system, raise the front or rear of the vehicle and safely support with jackstands. Open a caliper or wheel cylinder bleeder valve while a helper holds pressure on the brake pedal. As fluid is lost through the bleeder, the dash lamp should light. If the lamp fails to light, check for a burned out bulb, disconnected socket, or a broken or discon-

nected wire at the switch. Replace the warning switch if the rest of the circuit members check out. Be sure to fill the master cylinder and bleed the brakes after repairs have been completed.

Height Sensing Fuel Proportioning Valve

▶ See Figures 12 and 13

All vehicles are equipped with a height sensing dual proportioning valve. The valve is located under the rear floor pan just forward of the rear axle. The valve automatically provides the proper brake balance between the front and rear brakes regardless of the vehicle load condition. the valve modulates the rear brakes sensing the loading condition of the vehicle through relative height movement between the rear axle and load floor.

The valve is mounted on a crossmember and connected to an adjustable lever on the rear axle by a large spring. When the vehicle is unloaded or lightly leaded, the hydraulic line pressure is minimized. As the vehicle is more heavily loaded and the ride height lowers, the spring moves the valve control arm to allow higher rear brake pressure.

➡**Because ride height determines rear brake pressure, the use of after market load leveling or capacity increasing devices should be avoided.**

The proportioning section of the valve transmits full input pressure up to a certain point, called the split point. Beyond the split point the valve reduces the amount of pressure increase to the rear brakes according to a certain ratio. This means that on light brake pedal application equal pressure will be transmitted to the front and rear brakes. On harder pedal application, pressure transmitted to the rear brakes will be lower to prevent rear wheel lock-up and skid.

TESTING

➡**Two pressure gauges and adapter fittings (tool set C4007A or equivalent) are required of the following test.**

If premature rear wheel lock-up and skid is experienced frequently, it could be an indication that the fluid pressure to the rear brakes is excessive and that a malfunction has occurred in the proportioning valve or an adjustment is necessary.

1. If a pressure gauge and adapter fittings are on hand, proceed with the following test.
2. Disconnect the external spring at the valve lever.
3. Install one pressure gauge and T-fitting in line from either master cylinder port to the brake valve assembly.
4. Install the second gauge to either rear brake outlet port between the valve assembly and the rear brake line. Bleed the rear brakes.
5. Have a helper apply and hold pedal pressure to get a reading on the valve inlet gauge and outlet gauge. The inlet pressure should be 500 psi and the outlet pressure should be 100-200 psi. If the required pressures are not present, replace the valve. If the test pressures are all right, adjust the external spring and arm.

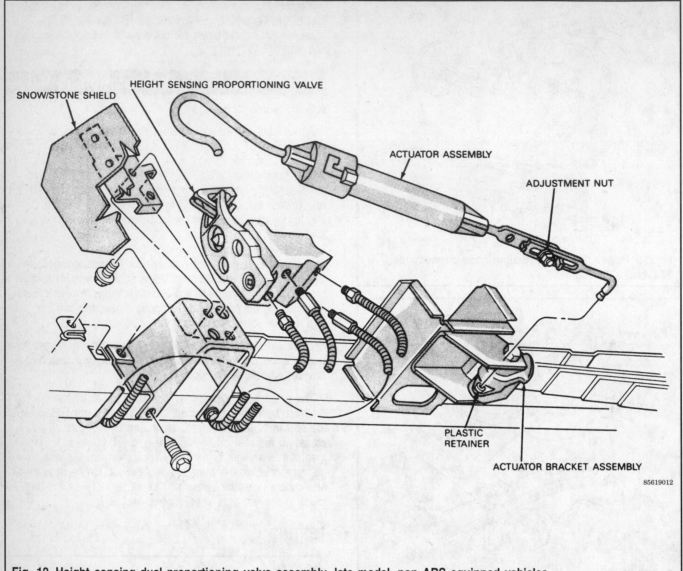

HEIGHT SENSING PROPORTIONING VALVE

SNOW/STONE SHIELD

ACTUATOR ASSEMBLY

ADJUSTMENT NUT

PLASTIC RETAINER

ACTUATOR BRACKET ASSEMBLY

85619012

Fig. 12 Height sensing dual proportioning valve assembly, late model, non ABS equipped vehicles

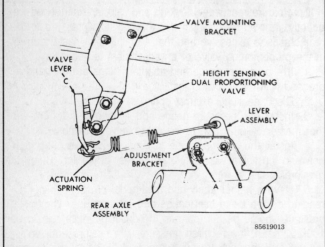

VALVE MOUNTING BRACKET

VALVE LEVER

HEIGHT SENSING DUAL PROPORTIONING VALVE

LEVER ASSEMBLY

ADJUSTMENT BRACKET

ACTUATION SPRING

REAR AXLE ASSEMBLY

85619013

Fig. 13 Height sensing dual proportioning valve and adjustment points, early models

VALVE REMOVAL, INSTALLATION AND ADJUSTMENT

1. Raise and support the rear of the vehicle. Position jack-stands at the rear contact pads so that the rear axle will hang free with the tires off the ground.

2. Loosen the rear axle mounted adjustable lever assembly and remove the actuating spring. Remove the brake lines from the proportioning valve and remove the valve.

3. Install the brake lines loosely in the proportioning valve and mount valve in position.

4. Tighten the brake lines, fill the master cylinder to the correct fluid level and bleed the brakes.

5. Confirm that the axle is hanging free and at full rebound position with the wheels and tires mounted.

6. Confirm that the actuating spring is connected between the proportioning valve and axle adjusting lever. the axle adjusting lever mounting bolts should be loose so that the bracket can be moved.

7. Push the control lever on the proportioning valve towards the valve until it is against the body and hold it in that position.

8. Move the axle lever up and away to apply tension to the spring. When all free play is taken out of the spring, but the spring is not stretched, tighten the mounting bolt that goes through the slotted side of the adjustment bracket. Tighten the anchor bolt. Both mounting bolts should be tightened to 150 inch lbs.

Brake Hoses

▶ **See Figures 14 and 15**

REMOVAL & INSTALLATION

1. Right and left brake hoses are not interchangeable. Remove the connector at the caliper, then remove the mounting bracket from the strut support and finally, remove the from the upper body mount and disconnect the hose from the steel line.

2. Always use a flare wrench to prevent rounding of the line fittings.

3. Install the new hose to the caliper first. Always use a new copper washer after making sure the mounting surfaces are clean. Tighten the caliper hose fitting. Install the strut bracket next, then attach the steel line fitting. Position the upper keyed end of the hose to the body bracket and secure it.

4. Rear brake hoses should be attached first to the trailing arm bracket and the to the floor pan tubes.

5. Keep the hose as straight as possible, avoid twisting.

6. Bleed the brake system.

Bleeding the Brake System

The purpose of bleeding the brakes is to expel air trapped in the hydraulic system. The system must be bled whenever the pedal feels spongy, indicating that compressible air has entered the system. It must also be bled whenever the system has been opened or repaired. You will need a helper to help bleed the system. Always use fresh brake fluid.

BENCH BLEEDING

Always bench bleed the master cylinder before installing it on the vehicle.

1. Place the master cylinder in a vise.

2. Connect two lines to the fluid outlet orifices, bend the lines upwards and insert the opened ends into the reservoir.

3. Fill the reservoir with brake fluid.

4. Using a wooden dowel, depress the pushrod slowly, allowing the pistons to return. do this several times until the air bubbles are all expelled.

5. Remove the bleeding tubes from the master cylinder, plug the outlets and install the caps.

➡**It is not necessary to bleed the entire system after replacing the master cylinder, provided that master cylinder has been bled and filled upon installation. However, if a soft pedal is experienced, bleed the entire system.**

SYSTEM BLEEDING

▶ **See Figures 16, 17, 18, 19, 20, 21 and 22**

❊❊CAUTION

Do not allow brake fluid to spill on the vehicle's finish; it will remove the paint. In case of a spill, flush the area with water.

1. The sequence for bleeding is right rear, left front, left rear and right front. If the vehicle is equipped with power brakes, remove the vacuum by applying the brakes several times. Do not run the engine while bleeding the brakes.

2. Clean all the bleeder screws. You may want to give each one a shot of penetrating solvent to help loosen the fitting. Seizure is a common problem with bleeder screws,

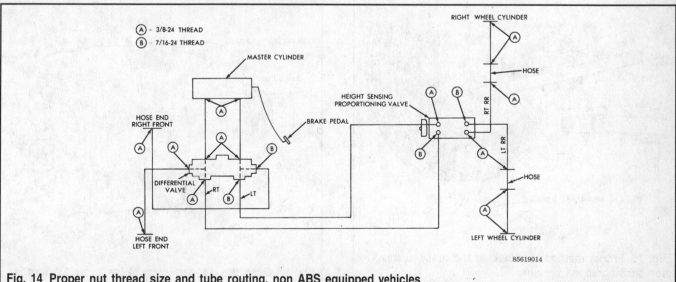

Fig. 14 Proper nut thread size and tube routing, non ABS equipped vehicles

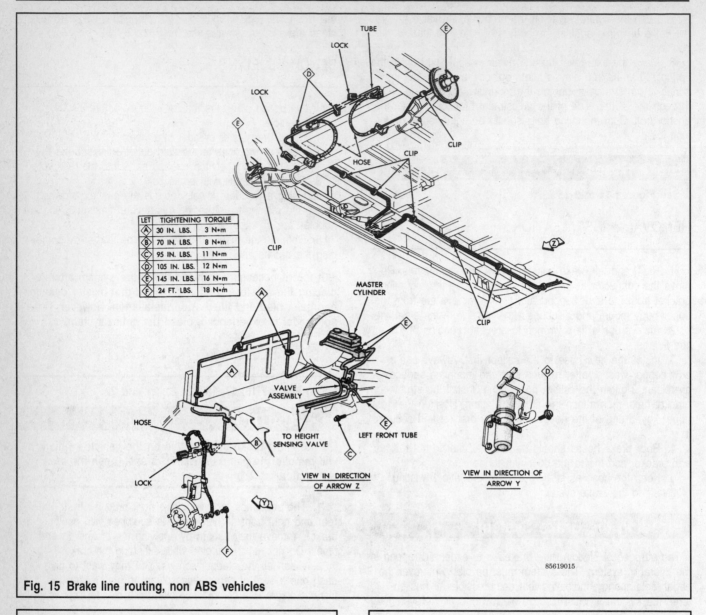

LET	TIGHTENING TORQUE	
A	30 IN. LBS.	3 N•m
B	70 IN. LBS.	8 N•m
C	95 IN. LBS.	11 N•m
D	105 IN. LBS.	12 N•m
E	145 IN. LBS.	16 N•m
F	24 FT. LBS.	18 N•m

Fig. 15 Brake line routing, non ABS vehicles

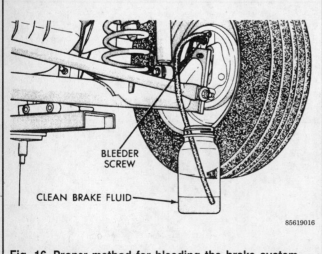

Fig. 16 Proper method for bleeding the brake system, non ABS equipped vehicles

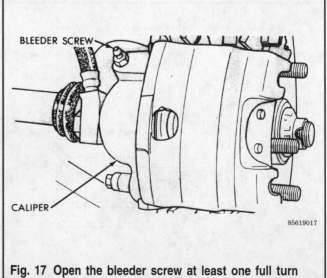

Fig. 17 Open the bleeder screw at least one full turn

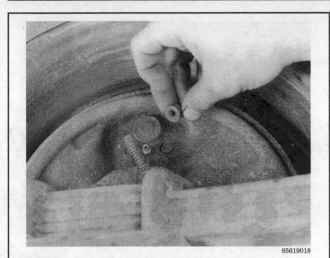

Fig. 18 Remove the bleeder screw cover plug from the brake drum backing plate, 1987 Voyager shown

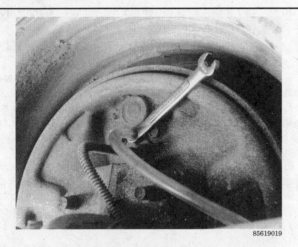

Fig. 19 Place a suitable size box wrench on the bleeder screw then attach a clear vinyl hose to the bleeder nipple, 1987 Voyager shown

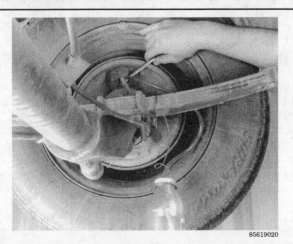

Fig. 20 Open the bleeder screw and bleed the fluid into a clean jar half filled with brake fluid, 1987 Voyager shown

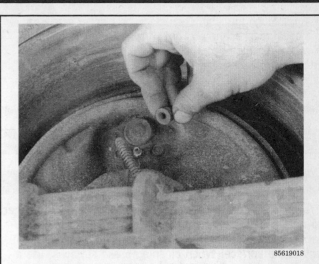

Fig. 21 Remove the bleeder screw cover plug from the brake caliper, 1987 Voyager shown

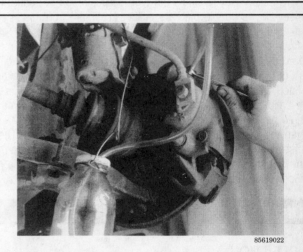

Fig. 22 Open the bleeder screw and bleed the fluid into a clean jar half filled with brake fluid, 1987 Voyager shown

which then brake off, sometimes requiring replacement of the part to which they are attached.

3. Check the fluid level in the master cylinder and fill with DOT 3 brake fluid, if necessary.

➡Brake fluid absorbs moisture from the air. Don't leave the master cylinder or the fluid container uncovered any longer than necessary. Be careful handling the brake fluid, it is a great paint remover. If any brake fluid spills on the vehicle's finish, flush off with water immediately. Check the level of the fluid often when bleeding, and refill the reservoirs as necessary. Don't let them run dry, or you will have to repeat the process.

4. Attach a length of clear vinyl tubing to the bleeder screw at the wheel cylinder or caliper. Insert the other end of the tube into a clear, clean jar half filled with brake fluid. Start at a rear cylinder first, then bleed the opposite side front cylinder.

5. Have your assistant slowly depress the brake pedal. As this is done, open the bleeder screw 1/3-1/2 of a turn on wheel cylinders and at least one turn on calipers, and allow the fluid

to run through the tube. Then close the bleeder screw before the pedal reaches the end of its travel. Have your assistant slowly release the pedal after the bleeder screw is closed. Repeat this process until no air bubbles appear in the expelled fluid.

6. Repeat the procedure on the other calipers and cylinders, checking the level of fluid in the master cylinder reservoir often. After you're done, there should be no sponginess in the brake pedal feel. If there is, either there is still air in the line, in which case the process should be repeated, or there is a leak somewhere, which of course must be corrected before moving the vehicle.

FRONT DISC BRAKES

✳✳CAUTION

Brake shoes contain asbestos, which has been determined to be a cancer causing agent. Never clean the brake surfaces with compressed air! Avoid inhaling any dust from any brake surface! When cleaning brake surfaces, use a commercially available brake cleaning fluid.

The Kelsey-Hayes single pin type caliper (1984-87) and the Kelsey-Hayes double pin type caliper (1987-94) front disc brakes are of the single position, floating caliper type. The caliper 'floats' through a rubber bushing, inserted into the inboard portion of the caliper, via a guide pin that is threaded into the mounting adapter. the mounting adapter for the caliper if fitted with two machined abutments that position and align the caliper. The guide pin and bushing, on the Kelsey-Hayes single pin type caliper, control the movement of the caliper when the brakes are applied, providing a clamping force. The Kelsey-Hayes double pin type caliper, uses two steel guide pins and mounting bushings to control the movement of the caliper upon brake application.

Disc Brake Pads

INSPECTION

1. Loosen the front wheel lug nuts slightly. Raise and support the front of the vehicle safely on jackstands. Remove the front wheel.
2. When the front wheels are off, the cutout built into the caliper housing will be exposed. Look through the opening and check the lining thickness of the inner and outer pads.
3. If a visual inspection does not give a clear picture of lining wear, a physical check will be necessary.
4. Refer to the following section covering pad removal and installation for instructions.

REMOVAL & INSTALLATION

Kelsey-Hayes Single Pin Type

▶ **See Figures 23, 24, 25, 26, 27, 28, 29 and 30**

➡**Three anti-rattle clips are provided on each brake caliper, take note of locations for installation purposes.**

1. The Kelsey Hayes caliper uses one mounting pin. Loosen the wheel lug nuts slightly. Raise and safely support the front of the vehicle on jackstands. Remove the front wheel and tire assemblies.
2. Siphon about one quarter of the brake fluid from the master cylinder and replace the cover caps.
3. Use the proper size socket wrench and remove the threaded caliper guide pin.
4. Insert a small prybar between the front edge of the caliper and the adapter rail. Apply steady upward pressure to loosen the adhesive seals.

➡**Do not use a C-clamp to retract the plastic composition piston or damage to the piston could result.**

5. Remove the caliper by slowly sliding it up and off the adapter and disc rotor.
6. Support the caliper by hanging it out of the way on wire. Do not allow the caliper to be supported by the brake hose.
7. Observe the location of the anti-rattle clips. One clip is on the top of the inboard (closes to axle) brake pad. Another clip is on the bottom of the outboard brake pad, and the third is installed on the top finger of the caliper.
8. Slide the outboard brake pad from the adapter. Remove the brake disc rotor if necessary, and remove the inboard pad.
9. Measure the brake lining and pad thickness. If the combined thickness at the thinnest point of the is $\frac{1}{8}$ in. (3mm) or less replace both front wheel brake pad assemblies.

To install:
10. Check around the caliper piston and boot for signs of brake fluid leakage. Inspect the dust boot around the caliper piston for cuts and breaks. If the boot is damaged or fluid leakage is visible, the caliper should be serviced. Check the adapter and caliper mounting surfaces for rust and dirt, clean them with a wire brush.
11. Remove the protective paper from the gaskets mounted on the metal part of the brake pads. Install the anti-rattle clips in position. Install inner brake pad on the adapter.
12. Install the brake disc rotor and outer brake pad.
13. Press the caliper back into the caliper until it bottoms. If may be necessary to place a small piece of wood on the piston and use a C-clamp to retract the piston. If so, tighten the clamp with slow steady pressure. Stop when resistance is felt.
14. Lower the caliper over the brake pads and disc rotor. Install the caliper guide pin and tighten to 25-35 ft. lbs. Take care not to cross thread the guide pin.
15. After both calipers have been installed, fill the master cylinder and bleed the brakes if the caliper were rebuilt. If the calipers were not serviced, pump the brakes until a firm brake pedal is obtained.
16. Install the front wheels and lower the vehicle. After the vehicle is lowered, check the lug nut torque and tighten to required specification to 95 ft. lbs. Road test the vehicle and

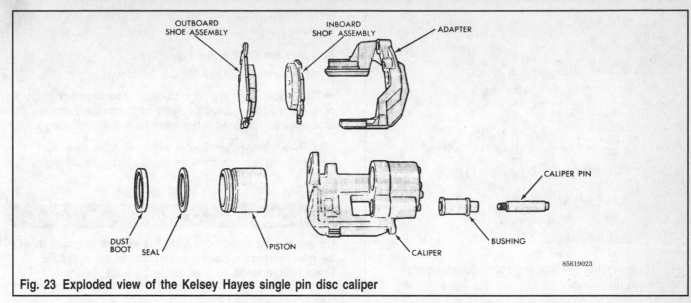

Fig. 23 Exploded view of the Kelsey Hayes single pin disc caliper

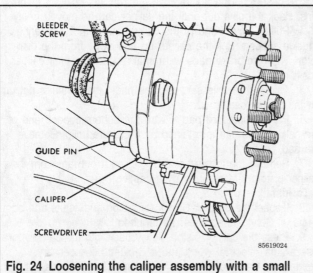

Fig. 24 Loosening the caliper assembly with a small prybar, Kelsey Hayes single pin disc caliper

Fig. 26 Remove the caliper and support it out of the way with a wire, Kelsey Hayes single pin disc caliper

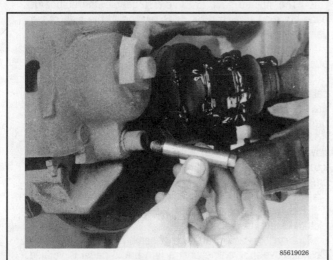

Fig. 25 Remove the single threaded caliper guide, Kelsey Hayes single pin disc caliper

Fig. 27 Slide the outboard shoe from the caliper, Kelsey Hayes single pin disc caliper

85619029

Fig. 28 Removing the inboard shoe, Kelsey Hayes single pin disc caliper

85619030

Fig. 29 Measure the brake lining and pad thickness, Kelsey Hayes single pin disc caliper

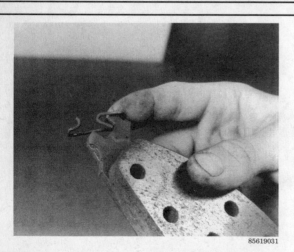

85619031

Fig. 30 Note one of the anti-rattle clips shown on the top of the inboard brake pad, Kelsey Hayes single pin disc caliper

make several firm but not hard stops to wear off any dirt from the pads or rotor.

Kelsey-Hayes Double Pin Type-1987-90

◗ See Figures 31, 32, 33, 34, 35, 36 and 37

➥The caliper is equipped with one holddown spring running across the outboard fingers of the caliper, and is also equipped with an inner shoe to piston mounting clip.

1. The Kelsey-Hayes double pin type caliper uses two mounting pins. Loosen the wheel lugs slightly. Raise and safely support the front of the vehicle.
2. Remove the wheel and tire assembly.

✳✳CAUTION

On models equipped with ABS, the system pressure must be released before disconnecting any of the hydraulic lines. Failure to do so, can cause personal injury.

3. Loosen, but do not remove the two steel caliper guide pins. Back the pins out until the caliper can be moved freely.
4. Pull the lower end of the caliper out from the steering knuckle support. Roll the caliper up and away from the disc rotor. The disc brake pads will remain located in their caliper positions.
5. Take care, while servicing the pads, that strain is not put on the brake hose.
6. Pry the outboard pad toward the bottom opened end of the caliper. The pad is retained by a captured clip. Remove the pad.
7. Remove the inboard pad by pulling it outward from the caliper piston. It is retained by a captive clip.
   To install:
8. Inspect the caliper. Check for piston seal leaks and boot damage. Service the caliper as required.
9. Press the caliper piston slowly back into the caliper bore. Use a small block of wood and a C-clamp, if necessary. Tighten the clamp slowly, and make sure the piston is not cocked. Gently bottom the piston in the caliper.
10. The inboard pads are interchangeable, the outboard pads are marked with an **L** or **R** relating to the side of the vehicle they are to be used on.
11. Place the inboard pad clip into the caliper piston and push into position on the piston.
12. Place the outboard pad retainer clip over the ears of the caliper and slide the pad into position. If the replacement pads are equipped with a noise suppression gasket, remove the protective paper from the gasket before installation.
13. Lower the caliper over the disc rotor and align the holddown spring under the machined surface of the steering knuckle. Install the caliper mounting pins, take care not to cross thread and tighten the pins to 18-26 ft. lbs. Pump the brake pedal several times to move the pads against the rotor. If the caliper has been rebuilt, or other system service completed, bleed the brake system.
14. Install the wheel and tire assembly. Lower the vehicle. Do not move the vehicle until a firm brake pedal is verified.

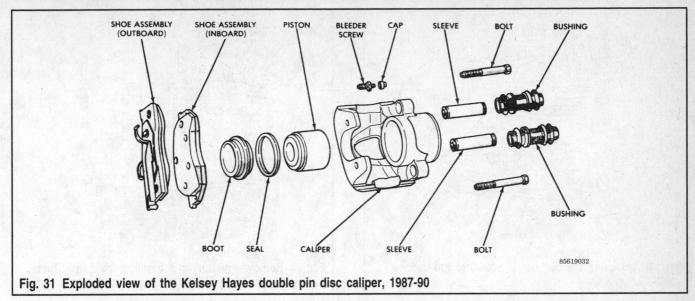

Fig. 31 Exploded view of the Kelsey Hayes double pin disc caliper, 1987-90

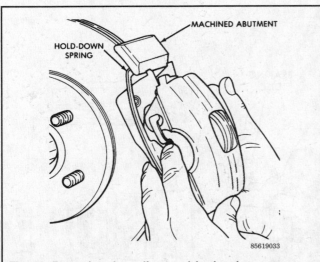

Fig. 32 Removing the caliper and brake shoes as an assembly, 1987-90

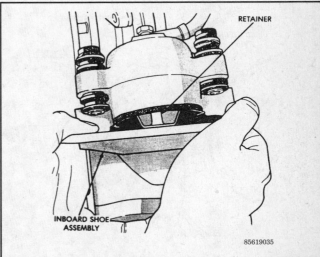

Fig. 34 Removing/installing the inboard shoe assembly, 1987-90

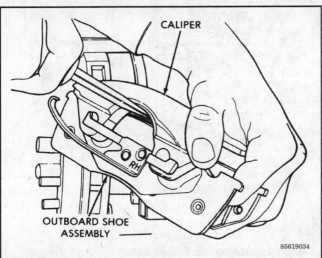

Fig. 33 Prying the outboard shoe away from the caliper, 1987-90

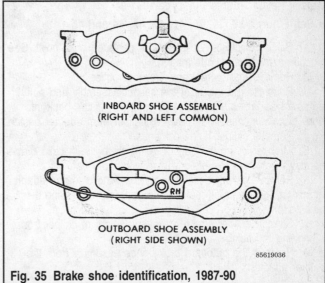

Fig. 35 Brake shoe identification, 1987-90

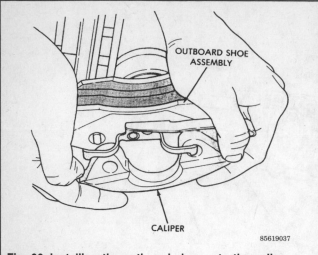

Fig. 36 Installing the outboard shoe onto the caliper, 1987-90

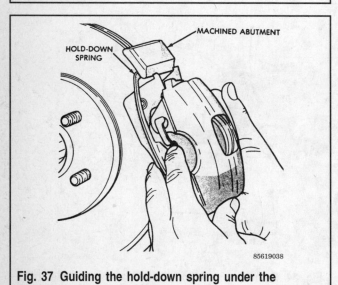

Fig. 37 Guiding the hold-down spring under the machined abutment, 1987-90

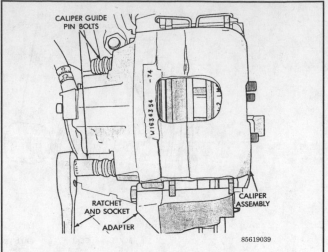

Fig. 38 Removing/installing the caliper guide pin bolts, Kelsey Hayes double pin disc caliper, 1991-94

Kelsey-Hayes Double Pin Type-1991-94

▶ See Figures 38, 39, 40, 41, 42, 43, 44 and 45

1. Raise vehicle on jackstands or centered on a hoist. See Section 1 for hoisting information.
2. Remove front wheel and tire assemblies.
3. Reach to the inside of the caliper assembly and pull it outboard as far as you can. This will push piston back into bore of caliper, making removal of caliper from adapter easier.
4. Remove caliper guide pin bolts.
5. After removing the caliper guide pin bolts lift caliper assembly away from the braking disc with a pry bar.
6. Remove caliper assembly from braking disc and adapter by sliding the assembly out and away from the braking disc and adapter.
7. Support caliper firmly to prevent weight of caliper from damaging the flexible brake hose.
8. Remove the outboard brake shoe assembly from the caliper adapter.

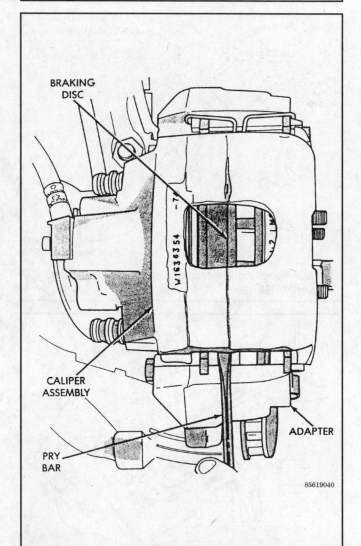

Fig. 39 Loosening the caliper assembly from the adapter and rotor, Kelsey Hayes double pin disc caliper, 1991-94

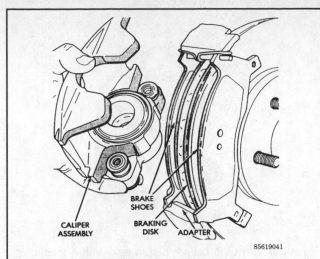

Fig. 40 Removing/installing the caliper assembly, Kelsey Hayes double pin disc caliper, 1991-94

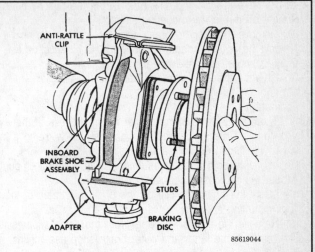

Fig. 43 Remove/install the braking disc (rotor), Kelsey Hayes double pin disc caliper, 1991-94

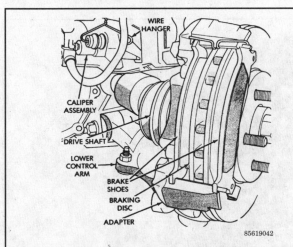

Fig. 41 Remove the tension from the brake hose by using a wire hanger to store the caliper out of the way, Kelsey Hayes double pin disc caliper, 1991-94

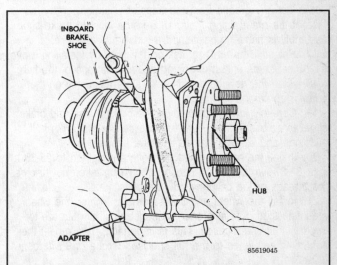

Fig. 44 Remove/install the inboard shoe assembly, Kelsey Hayes double pin disc caliper, 1991-94

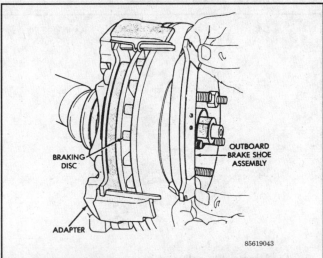

Fig. 42 Remove/install the outboard shoe assembly, Kelsey Hayes double pin disc caliper, 1991-94

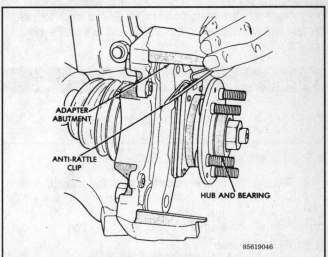

Fig. 45 Remove/replace the anti-rattle clip, Kelsey Hayes double pin disc caliper, 1991-94

9. Remove the braking disk (rotor) from the hub by pulling it straight off the wheel mounting studs.

10. Remove the inboard brake shoe assembly by sliding it out along the bottom adapter abutment until brake shoe assembly loosens from anti-rattle clip.

11. Remove the anti-rattle clip from the top adapter abutment.

To install:

12. Thoroughly clean both adapter abutment rails. If there is any build-up of rust on the adapter abutment rails, remove it using a wire brush do not sand rails.

13. Lubricate both adapter abutments with a liberal amount of Mopar Multipurpose Lubricant, or equivalent.

14. Install the anti-rattle clip on the upper abutment of the caliper mounting adapter.

15. Remove the protective paper from the noise suppression gasket on both the inner and outer brake shoe assemblies, if equipped.

16. Install the new inboard brake shoe assembly on the adapter by sliding it along the adapter abutments. Be careful not to get any grease from the adapter abutment on the surface of the brake lining material. Be sure inboard brake shoe assembly is correctly positioned against anti-rattle clip.

17. Reinstall the braking disk on the hub, by installing it over the wheel studs until it is seated against the face of the hub.

18. Slide the new outboard brake shoe assembly on the adapter abutment.

19. Carefully lower caliper over the braking disk and brake shoe assemblies. Make sure that the caliper guide pin bolt, bushings and sleeves are clear of the adapter.

20. Install the caliper guide pin bolts and tighten to 25-35 ft. lbs. (34-37 Nm). Extreme caution should be taken not to cross the threads of the caliper guide pin bolts.

21. Install the wheel and tire assembly. Tighten the wheel mounting stud nuts in proper sequence until all nuts are torqued to half specification. This is important. Then repeat the tightening sequence to the full specified torque of 95 ft. lbs. (129 Nm).

22. Remove jackstands or lower hoist. Before moving vehicle, pump the brake pedal several times to insure the vehicle has a firm brake pedal to adequately stop vehicle.

23. Road test the vehicle and make several stops to wear off any foreign material on the brakes and to seat the brake shoe linings.

Caliper

OVERHAUL

▶ **See Figures 46, 47, 48 and 49**

1. Remove the caliper as described in the previous section.
2. Place rags on the upper control arm and place the caliper on top of the rags. Take care not to put strain on the brake hose. Place a small block of wood between the caliper piston and outer fingers.
3. Have a helper slowly depress the brake pedal to push the piston from the caliper bore using hydraulic pressure. If both front caliper pistons are to be removed, disconnect the brake hose, to the first caliper, at the frame bracket; plug the

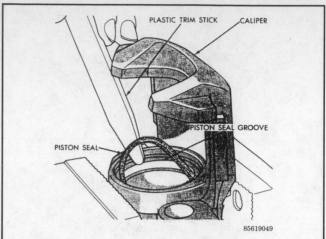

Fig. 48 Remove the caliper piston seal with a plastic tool, Kelsey Hayes single pin disc caliper shown, 1991-94

Fig. 46 Use a suitable prying tool to remove the caliper piston dust boot, Kelsey Hayes single pin disc caliper shown, 1991-94

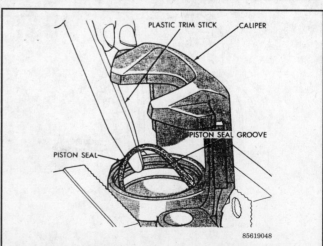

Fig. 47 Remove the caliper piston dust boot from the piston, Kelsey Hayes single pin disc caliper shown, 1991-94

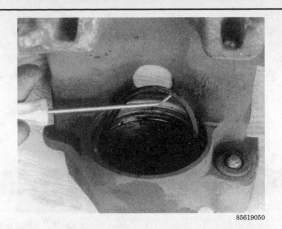

Fig. 49 Do not use a metal tool to remove the seal as shown. Even this tool could scratch the piston bore or burr the edges of the seal groove, Kelsey Hayes single pin disc caliper shown, 1991-94

brake tube and repeat Steps 2 and 3. Never use air pressure to blow the pistons from their bores. The pistons are made of a plastic composition and can damage easily, or can fly out and cause personal injury.

4. Disconnect the flexible brake line from the caliper and remove the caliper to work area.

5. Position the caliper between padded jaws of a bench vise. Do not overtighten since excessive pressure can distort the caliper bore. Remove the dust boot.

6. Use a plastic tool and work the piston seal from the mounting groove. Do not use a metal tool; damage can result to the bore or burrs can be created on the edges of the machined seal groove.

7. Remove the guide pin bushing from the caliper. A wooden dowel makes a good tool for this purpose.

To install:

8. Clean all parts using a safe solvent or alcohol and blow dry if compressed air is on hand.

9. Inspect the piston bore for pitting or scores. Light scratches or pitting can be cleaned with crocus cloth and brake fluid. Deep scratches or pitting require honing.

10. Caliper hones are available from an auto parts supplier. Do not remove more than 0.001 in. (0.025mm) of material from the bore. Deep scratches or pitting require caliper replacement.

11. After cleaning up the caliper bore with crocus cloth or hone, remove all the dirt and grit by flushing the caliper with brake fluid. After flushing, wipe dry with a lintless rag. Flush the caliper a second time and dry.

12. Carefully reclamp the caliper in the padded vise jaws. Dip the new piston seal in clean brake fluid and install in caliper bore mounting groove. Use your fingers to work the seal into the groove until properly seated.

13. Coat the caliper piston and piston boot with clean brake fluid. Install the boot on the caliper piston. Install the piston into the caliper bore. Push the piston past the seal until bottomed in the caliper bore. Use even pressure around the edges of the piston to avoid cocking when installing the piston.

14. Position the lip of the dust boot into the counter bore of the caliper. Use a seal driver or suitable tool to install the boot edge.

15. Compress the edges of the new guide pin bushing with your fingers and install into position on the caliper. Press in on the bushing while working it into the caliper until fully seated. Be sure the bushing flanges extend evenly over the caliper casting on both sides when installed.

16. Install the brake pads and the caliper. Bleed the brakes after caliper service.

Brake Disc (Rotor)

‣ **See Figures 50 and 51**

REMOVAL & INSTALLATION

1. Loosen the wheel lugs slightly. Raise and support the front of the vehicle on jackstands. Remove the front wheel and tire assembly. Relieve the brake system pressure if equipped with ABS.

2. Remove the disc brake caliper and outer brake pad.

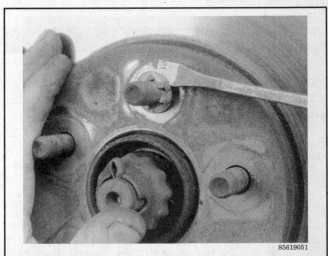

Fig. 50 Removing the rotor retaining clip from the wheel stud

Fig. 51 Removing the rotor from the studs

3. Remove the disc brake rotor.

4. Service as necessary. Place the rotor in position and install the caliper assembly. Refer to Brake Pad Removal and Installation for detailed procedures, if necessary.

INSPECTION

If excessive run out, wobble or thickness variation is present, feedback through the brake pedal will be felt when the brakes are applied. Pedal pulsation, chatter, surge and increased pedal travel can be caused when the disc rotor is worn unevenly or deeply scored. Remove the rotor and have an automotive machine shop measure the wear and check for run out. The machine shop can refinish the braking surfaces if replacement is not necessary.

REAR DRUM BRAKES

✳✳CAUTION

Brake shoes contain asbestos, which has been determined to be a cancer causing agent. Never clean the brake surfaces with compressed air! Avoid inhaling any dust from any brake surface! When cleaning brake surfaces, use a commercially available brake cleaning fluid.

Brake Drums

REMOVAL & INSTALLATION

▶ See Figures 52, 53, 54, 55, 56, 57, 58, 59, 60 and 61

Front Wheel Drive Vehicles

1. Raise and support the rear of the vehicle on jackstands. Remove the wheels and tire assemblies.

2. Remove the brake shoe adjusting slot cover from the rear of backing plate.

3. Insert a thin tool through the adjusting slot and hold the adjusting lever away from the star wheel. Insert an adjusting tool and back off the star wheel by prying downward with the tool.

4. Remove the center hub dust cover, nut, washer, brake drum, hub and wheel bearings.

Fig. 53 Backing off the adjuster star wheel

Fig. 54 Removing the dust cover from the axle stub

To install:

5. Inspect the brake lining and drum for wear. Inspect the wheel cylinder for leakage. Service as required.

6. Remove, clean, inspect and repack the wheel bearings. Install the brake drum. Tighten the hub nut to 240-300 inch lbs. and back off the nut until bearing pressure is released.

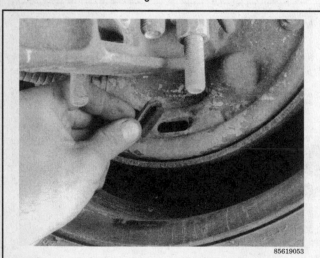
Fig. 52 Removing the rear drum adjusting hole cover plug

8561955B

Fig. 55 Removing the dust cover the washer from the axle stub

8561955E

Fig. 58 Removing the nut from the axle stub

85619555C

Fig. 56 Removing the cotter pin from the axle stub nut

85619055

Fig. 59 Removing the washer from the axle stub

8561955D

Fig. 57 Removing the nut lock from the axle stub

85619056

Fig. 60 Removing the bearing from the axle stub

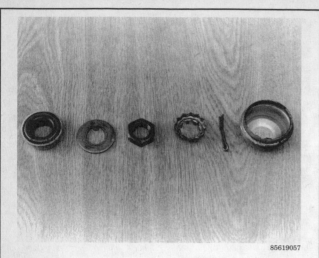

Fig. 61 All of these parts must be removed to remove the rear brake drum

Retighten the nut finger tight, align the cotter pin hole and install the cotter pin.

7. Adjust the rear brakes as described in the beginning of this section.

All Wheel Drive Vehicles

1. Raise and support the rear of the vehicle on jackstands. Remove the wheels and tire assemblies.

2. Remove the brake shoe adjusting slot cover from the front the of the brake drum.

3. Insert a thin tool through the adjusting slot and hold the adjusting lever away from the star wheel. Insert an adjusting tool and back off the star wheel by prying downward with the tool.

4. Remove the brake drum from the hub assembly. The rear hub and bearing does not come off with the brake drum on All Wheel Drive models.

To install:

5. Inspect the brake lining and drum for wear. Inspect the wheel cylinder for leakage. Service as required.

6. Install the brake drum on the hub. Tighten the wheel stud nuts to 95 ft. lbs. (129 Nm).

7. Adjust the rear brakes as described in the beginning of this section.

INSPECTION

Check the brake drum for any cracks, scores, grooves, or an out-of-round condition. Slight scores can be removed with Emory cloth, while extensive scoring or grooves will require machining. Have an automotive machine shop measure the wear and check the drum for run out. The shop will be able to turn the drum on a lathe, if necessary. Never have a drum turned more than 0.060 in. (1.5mm). If the drum is cracked, or worn more than the limit, replace.

Brake Shoes

REMOVAL & INSTALLATION

▶ **See Figures 62, 63, 64, 65, 66, 67, 68, 69, 70, 71, 72, 73, 74, 75, 76, 77, 78 and 79**

➡ **A pair of brake springs pliers or spring removal/installation tool and a retainer cap spring tool are good tools to have on hand for this job.**

1. Raise and support the rear of the vehicle on jackstands. Remove the rear wheels and brake drums.

➡ **Remove and install the brake shoes on one side at a time. Use the assembled side for reference.**

✳✳CAUTION

Brake shoes contain asbestos, which has been determined to be a cancer causing agent. Never clean the brake surfaces with compressed air! Avoid inhaling any dust from any brake surface! When cleaning brake surfaces, use a commercially available brake cleaning fluid.

2. Use a pair of brake spring pliers or appropriate tool and remove the shoe return springs from the top anchor. Take note that the secondary shoe spring is on top of the primary shoe spring. Install in the same position at installation time.

3. Slide the closed eye of the adjuster cable off of the anchor stud. Unhook the spring end and remove the cable, overload spring, cable guide and anchor plate.

4. Remove the adjusting lever from the spring by sliding forward to clear the pivot. Work the lever out from under the spring. Remove the spring from the pivot.

5. Unhook the bottom shoe-to-shoe spring from the secondary (back) shoe and disengage from the primary (front) shoe.

6. Spread the bottom of the brake shoes apart and remove the star wheel adjuster. Remove the parking brake strut and spring assembly.

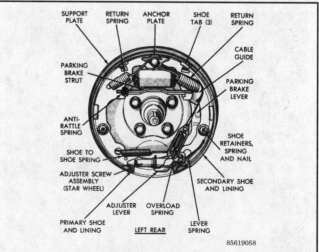

Fig. 62 Rear drum brake assembly components, front wheel drive models

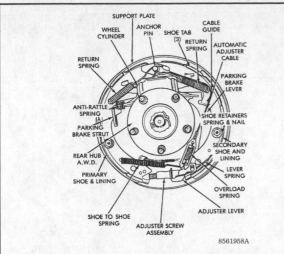

Fig. 63 Rear drum brake assembly components, all wheel drive models

Fig. 64 Rear drum brake assembly components

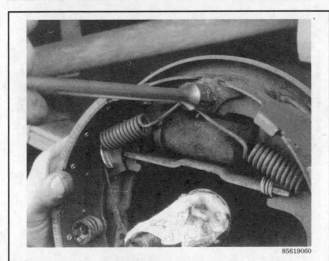

Fig. 65 Using a special brake tool to remove the return springs from the top anchor

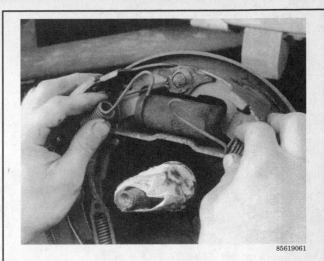

Fig. 66 The return springs shown removed from the top anchor

Fig. 67 Slide the closed eye of the adjuster cable from the top anchor

Fig. 68 Removing the anchor plate from the top anchor

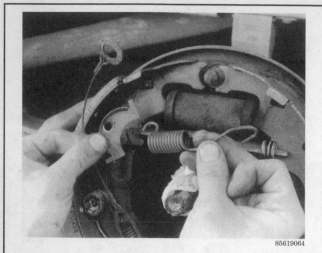

85619064

Fig. 69 The anchor plate, overload spring cable and return spring shown removed from the top anchor

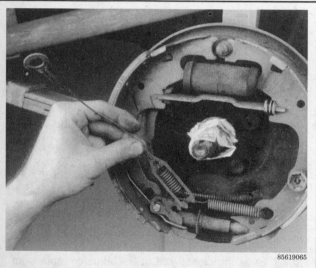

85619065

Fig. 70 Removing the overload spring

85619067

Fig. 72 The shoe to shoe spring shown removed

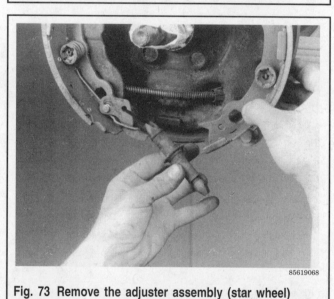

85619068

Fig. 73 Remove the adjuster assembly (star wheel)

Fig. 71 Unhook the shoe to shoe spring

85619066

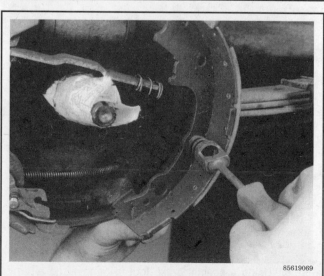

85619069

Fig. 74 Removing the shoe retainers, spring and nail

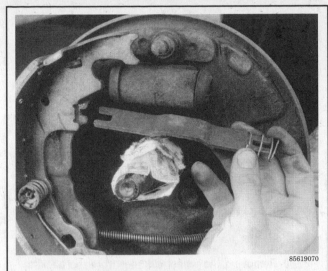

Fig. 75 Removing the parking brake strut

Fig. 76 Disengage the adjuster lever by sliding it forward to clear the pivot

Fig. 77 Removing the lever spring

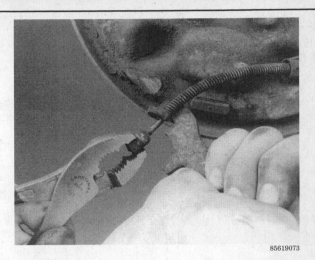

Fig. 78 Disengaging the parking brake cable from the parking brake lever

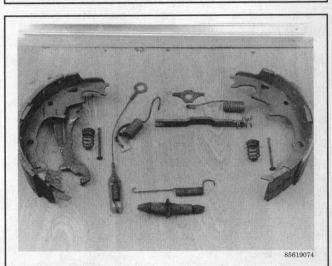

Fig. 79 Exploded view of the rear drum brakes, front wheel drive vehicle

7. Locate the shoe retainer nail head at the rear of the brake backing plate. Support the nail head with a finger, press in and twist the spring retainer washer with the special retainer tool or a pair of pliers. If you are using pliers, take care not to slip and pinch your fingers.

8. Remove the retainer, spring, inner washer and nail from both shoes. Remove the parking brake lever from the secondary brake shoe. Remove the shoes from the backing plate. Disconnect the parking brake lever from the brake cable.

To install:

9. Clean the backing plate with a safe solvent. Inspect the raised show support pads for rough or rusted contact areas. Clean and smooth as necessary. Clean and inspect the adjuster star wheels, apply a thin film of lubricant to the threads, socket and washer. Replace the star wheel if rust or threads show damage.

10. Inspect the holddown springs, return springs and adjuster spring. If the springs have been subjected to overheating or if their strength is questionable, replace the spring.

11. Inspect the wheel cylinder. If signs of leakage are present (a small amount of fluid inside the end boot is normal) rebuild or replace the cylinder.

12. Lubricate the shoe contact area pads on the backing plate with high temperature resistant white lube.

13. Engage the parking brake lever with the cable and install the lever on the secondary brake shoe. Engage the end of the brake shoe with the wheel cylinder piston and the top anchor. Install the retainer nail, washer, spring and retainer.

14. Position the primary shoe in like manner and install hold-down pin assembly. Install the top anchor plate.

15. Install the parking brake strut and spring in position, press the lower part of the brake.

16. Straighten the adjuster cable and install the eye end over the top anchor. Be sure the lower spring end hook is facing inward.

17. Install the primary (front) shoe return spring. Place the cable guide in position on the secondary (rear) shoe (keep cable out of the way) and install the return spring. Check the cable guide and ensure proper mounting position. Squeeze the anchor ends of the return springs with pliers until they are parallel.

18. Carefully install the star wheel between the brake shoes. The wheel end goes closest the secondary (back) shoe. Wind out the star wheel until snug contact between the brake shoes will hold it in position.

19. Install the adjusting lever spring over the pivot pin on the lower shoe web of the secondary shoe. Install the adjuster lever under the spring and over the pivot pin. Slide the lever rearward until it locks in position.

20. Thread the adjuster cable over the guide and hook the end of the overload spring on the adjuster lever. Make sure the cable is float on the guide and the eye end is against the anchor.

21. Check the operation of the adjuster by pulling the cable rearward. The star wheel should rotate upward as the adjuster lever engages the teeth.

22. Back off the star wheel, if necessary, and install the hub and drum. Adjust the brakes.

23. Repeat the procedures on the other rear wheel.

Wheel Cylinders

REMOVAL & INSTALLATION

▶ **See Figure 80**

1. Jack up the rear of the vehicle and support it with jackstands.

❋❋CAUTION

On models equipped with ABS, the system pressure must be released before disconnecting any of the hydraulic lines. Failure to do so, can cause personal injury.

2. Remove the brake drums as previously outlined.

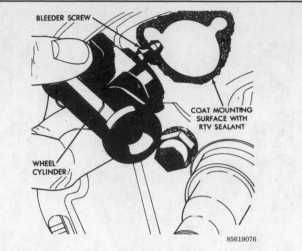

BLEEDER SCREW

COAT MOUNTING SURFACE WITH RTV SEALANT

WHEEL CYLINDER

85619076

Fig. 80 Removing the wheel cylinder from the backing plate

3. Visually inspect the wheel cylinder boots for signs of excessive leakage. Replace any boots that are torn or broken.

➡**A slight amount of fluid on the boots may not be a leak but may be a preservative fluid used at the factory.**

4. If a leak has been discovered, remove the brake shoes and check for contamination. Replace the linings if they are soaked with grease or brake fluid.

5. Disconnect the brake line from the wheel cylinder.

6. Remove the wheel cylinder attaching bolts, then pull the wheel cylinder out of its support.

7. Position the wheel cylinder onto the backing plate and loosely install the mounting bolts. Start the brake line into the cylinder. Tighten the mounting bolts and the brake line. Install the brake shoes and brake drum. Adjust the brake shoes.

8. Bleed the brake system.

OVERHAUL

▶ **See Figure 81**

1. Pry the boots away from the cylinder and remove the boots and pistons.

2. Disengage the boot from the piston.

3. Slide the piston into the cylinder bore and press inward to remove the other boot, piston and spring.

4. Wash all parts (except rubber parts) in clean brake fluid thoroughly. Do not use a rag; lint will adhere to the bore.

5. Inspect the cylinder bores. Light scoring can usually be cleaned up with crocus cloth. Heavier scores can be cleaned up with a cylinder hone. Black stains are caused by the piston cups and are no cause of concern. Bad scoring or pitting means that the wheel cylinder should be replaced.

6. Dip the pistons and new cups in clean brake fluid, or apply lubricant that is sometimes packaged in the rebuilding kit prior to assembly.

To install:

7. Coat the wheel cylinder bore with clean brake fluid.

8. Install the expansion spring with the cup expanders.

9. Install the cups in each end of the cylinder with the open ends facing each other.

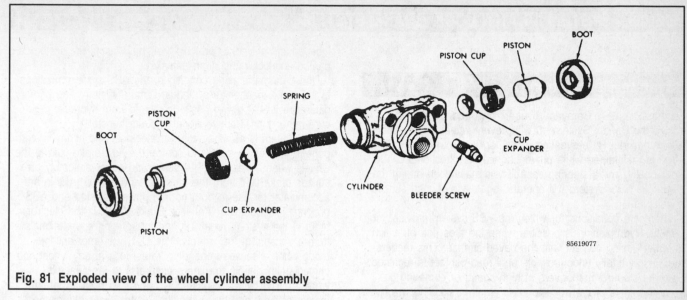

Fig. 81 Exploded view of the wheel cylinder assembly

10. Assemble new boots on the piston and slide them into the cylinder bore.

11. Press the boot over the wheel cylinder until seated.

12. Apply RTV on the mounting surface of the backing plate. Install the wheel cylinder, and connect brake lines.

13. Install brake shoes, and drum. Adjust and bleed brakes.

Parking Brake

ADJUSTMENT

1. Raise and support the rear of the vehicle on jackstands. Apply and release the parking brake several times.

2. Clean the parking park adjustment bolts with a wire brush and lubricate the threads. Back off the adjusting nut until there is slack in the cable.

3. Check the rear brake adjustment, adjust as necessary.

4. Tighten the parking brake cable adjuster until the slight drag is felt when turning the rear wheel.

5. Loosen the cable until no drag is felt on either rear wheel. Back off adjusting nut two full turns more.

6. Apply and release the parking brake several times to ensure there is not rear wheel drag. Lower the vehicle.

REMOVAL & INSTALLATION

▶ See Figure 82

Front Cable

1. Raise and support the front of the vehicle on jackstands.

2. Back off the adjuster nut until the cable can be released from the connectors.

3. Lift the floor mat for access to the floor pan. Force the seal surrounding the cable from the floor.

4. Pull the cable forward and disconnect from lever clevis. Remove the front cable from support bracket and vehicle.

5. Feed the new cable through the floor pan hole. Attach the front end of the cable to the parking brake lever clevis and support.

6. Engage intermediate cable and adjust.

Intermediate Cable

1. Back off the parking brake adjuster. Disengage the front cable and rear cables from the intermediate cable connector.

2. Remove the intermediate cable. Install the new cable and adjust.

Rear Cables

1. Raise and support the rear of the vehicle on jackstands.

2. Back off the cable adjustment and disconnect the rear cable (that is to be replaced) from the intermediate cable. Remove the rear cable from the mounting clips.

3. Remove the rear wheel and the brake shoes from the side requiring replacement.

4. Disconnect the cable from the rear brake apply lever. Compress the cable lock with a mini-hose clamp and pull the cable from the backing plate.

5. Install the new cable through the brake backing plate. Engage the locks. Attach the cable to the apply lever. Install the brake shoes, drum and wheel assembly.

6. Adjust the service brakes and parking brake.

BENDIX SYSTEM 10 ANTI-LOCK BRAKE SYSTEM

▶ See Figure 83

System Description

Found on 1991 Caravan/Voyager/Town and Country (AS body), the Bendix System 10 will prevent wheel locking under heavy braking. By preventing wheel lock-up, maximum braking effort is maintained while preventing loss of directional control. Additionally, some steering capability is maintained during the stop. The ABS system will operate regardless of road surface conditions.

There are conditions for which the ABS system provides no benefit. Hydroplaning is possible when the tires ride on a film of water, losing contact with the paved surface. This renders the vehicle totally uncontrollable until road contact is regained. Extreme steering maneuvers at high speed or cornering beyond the limits of tire adhesion can result in skidding which is independent of vehicle braking. For this reason, the system is named anti-lock rather than anti-skid.

Under normal braking conditions, the ABS system functions in the same manner as a standard brake system. The primary difference is that power assist is gained from hydraulic pressure rather than a conventional vacuum booster.

The system is a combination of electrical and hydraulic components, working together to control the flow brake fluid to the wheels when necessary. The pump and motor assembly pressurizes brake fluid from the reservoir and stores it within an accumulator for use in both normal power-assisted and ABS braking. The Controller Anti-lock Brake (CAB) is the electronic brain of the system, receiving and interpreting speed signals from 4 sensors at the wheels. The CAB will enter anti-lock mode when it senses impending wheel lock at any wheel and immediately controls the line pressure(s) to the affected wheel(s). The hydraulic assembly serves as both an integral master cylinder and the hydraulic booster assembly for the

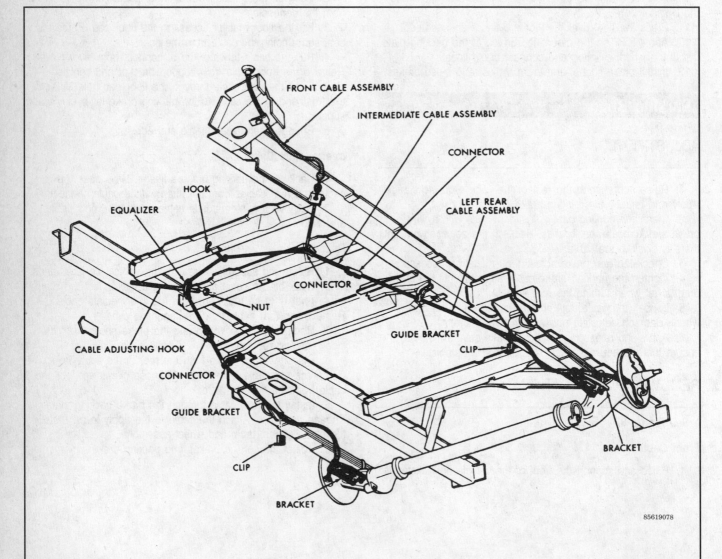

Fig. 82 Parking brake cable routing

85619078

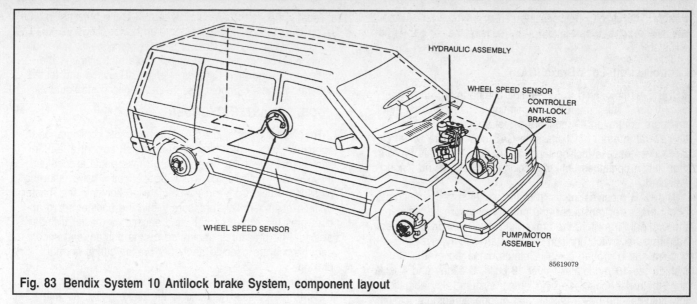

Fig. 83 Bendix System 10 Antilock brake System, component layout

brake system. It contains the wheel circuit valves used to control the brake fluid pressure to each wheel circuit.

During anti-lock braking, line pressures are controlled or modulated by the rapid cycling of electronic valves within the hydraulic assembly. These valves can allow pressures within the system to increase, remain constant or decrease depending on the needs of the moment as registered by the CAB. The front wheels are controlled individually while the rear wheels receive the same electrical signal, based on the wheel with the greatest locking tendency. Anti-lock function is available above 3-5 mph.

The operator may hear a popping or clicking sound as the pump and/or control valves cycle on and off during normal operation. The sounds are due to normal operation and are not indicative of a system problem; under most conditions, the sounds are only faintly audible. If ABS is engaged, the operator may notice some pulsation in the pedal. If additional force is applied to the pedal during an ABS-engaged stop, the operator will notice extremely hard pedal feel. This is due to isolation of the master cylinder during ABS operation. Some pulsing may also be felt in the body of the vehicle due to suspension movement as brake pressures apply and release at the individual wheels.

Although the ABS system prevents wheel lock-up under hard braking, as brake pressure increases, wheel slip is allowed to reach as high as 30%. This means that the rolling velocity of a given wheel is 30% less than that of a free-rolling wheel at a given speed. This slip will result in some tire chirp during ABS operation. The sound should not be interpreted as lock-up but rather as an indication of the system holding the wheel(s) just outside the point of lock-up. Additionally, since the ABS system turns off below 4 mph, the final few feet of an ABS-engaged stop may be completed with the wheels locked.

The Bendix system is equipped with built-in diagnostic capability. At every start-up, the CAB illuminates the dashboard warning lights and turns them off after checking the circuitry. When the vehicle reaches 3-5 mph, the CAB conducts a system check, briefly activating all the control valves to confirm their operation. This system check may be noticed by the operator as a series of rapid clicks during initial drive-off; the sound is normal and not indicative of a problem. Some fault

conditions will cause the CAB to set and retain a trouble code which may be retrieved for diagnostic purposes. Stored fault codes will remain stored until cleared by the DRB II.

The CAB will illuminate the appropriate dashboard warning lamp according to the fault detected. It is possible to have a fault affecting only the ABS function; in this case, the ABS system will be disabled but the vehicle will retain normal braking capability.

SYSTEM COMPONENTS

Wheel Speed Sensors
▶ See Figure 84

The speed of each wheel is monitored by a wheel speed sensor (WSS). A toothed tone wheel rotates in front of the sensor, generating a small AC voltage which is transmitted to the CAB. Each speed sensor is individually removable; the tone wheels are permanently mounted to either the front outer constant velocity joint assemblies or the rear wheel hub as-

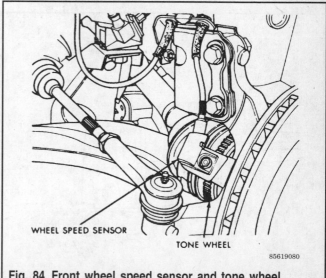

Fig. 84 Front wheel speed sensor and tone wheel

sembly. The air gap between the sensor and the tone wheel is set by the correct installation of the sensor; the air gap is not adjustable.

Controller Anti-Lock Brake (CAB)

The CAB is located in the engine compartment under the battery tray. This computer — operating separately from other on-board controllers — monitors wheel speed signals as well as several internal functions. The CAB controls the wheel circuit valves once a locking tendency is detected. This pressure modulation continues until the locking tendency is no longer detected.

The CAB receives inputs from the wheel speed sensors, the boost pressure transducer, the primary pressure transducer, the brake light switch, the brake fluid level sensor, the differential pressure switch, ignition switch, starter relay, system relay voltage and a ground signal. Outputs managed by the CAB include the 10 modulator valves (3 build, 3 decay and 4 isolation), both dashboard warning lamps, system relay actuation, low fluid/parking brake output, and diagnostic communication including transmitting fault codes.

➡ **The CAB found on 2wd Caravan, Voyager, and Town and Country vehicles is different from that on the 4wd versions. The controllers must not be interchanged.**

Pump and Motor Assembly
▶ **See Figure 85**

The integral motor and pump assembly is mounted on rubber isolators to a to a transaxle bracket below the hydraulic assembly. Fluid is taken from the master cylinder reservoir, pressurized and sent to storage in both the piston accumulator and the hydraulic bladder accumulator. The pump/motor assembly is serviceable only as a unit and should never be disassembled. Hoses running to and from the pump unit should never be repaired but replaced as an assembly.

Hydraulic Assembly
▶ **See Figure 86**

The integral hydraulic assembly is located on the firewall and provides the function of the power booster and master

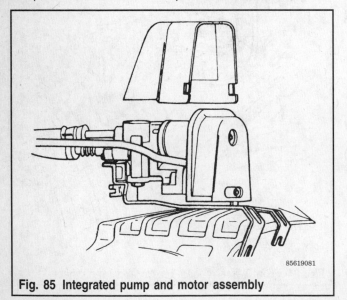

85619081
Fig. 85 Integrated pump and motor assembly

cylinder. Other components provide the brake pressure modulation and system monitoring required by the ABS system. The hydraulic assembly consists of several components with individual function as described below. Note that although the components and their function may be discussed and tested separately, most components are not serviced individually.

BOOSTER/MASTER CYLINDER

The master cylinder uses a diagonally split configuration in normal braking. The 2 circuits are isolated so that a leak in one will not affect the other. During brake pedal application, the pushrod applies force to the boost control valve, allowing pressurized fluid from the accumulator to flow into the master cylinder chamber. This pressure within the booster servo applies pressure to the primary and secondary master cylinder pistons. The pressures generated by the primary and secondary pistons are used to apply the brakes during normal braking.

The pressure within the hydraulic booster is directly proportional to the pressure applied to the brake pedal. As with vacuum operated boosters, brake efficiency depends on road surface and the force applied to the pedal.

HYDRAULIC ACCUMULATORS
▶ **See Figure 87**

The external or bladder accumulator stores brake fluid from the pump under very high pressure; the pressurized fluid is available for hydraulic assist (boost) and/or ABS braking. The accumulator uses a diaphragm and nitrogen pre-charge of about 1000 psi. Normally, the pump will charge the accumulator to a working pressure of 1600-2000 psi. For this reason, all safety precautions must be observed before working on the hydraulic system. The pressures within the accumulator are sufficient to cause serious personal injury or damage to the vehicle.

The piston accumulator is an integral part of the pump/motor assembly. It contains a pre-charge of approximately 460 psi nitrogen gas. This accumulator cannot be removed from the pump/motor assembly; component service is not possible.

DUAL FUNCTION PRESSURE SWITCH

This switch is located on the bottom of the hydraulic assembly and monitors the pressure within the accumulator. When accumulator pressure falls below 1600 psi, the dual function pressure switch causes the pump/motor to energize. When accumulator pressure reaches 2000 psi, the pump/motor is shut off.

The second purpose of this switch is to provide a signal to the CAB when accumulator pressure falls below the 1000 psi minimum. An internal warning pressure switch is normally closed at working pressures, grounding pin 17 at the controller. Should the accumulator pressure drop below minimum, the switch opens, a voltage signal is detected at the CAB and is read as low pressure. At this warning pressure, the CAB disables the ABS function and illuminates the dash warning lamps. After 2 minutes of continuous low pressure, a low accumulator fault code is stored in memory.

PRESSURE TRANSDUCERS

The boost pressure transducer is mounted on the bottom of the hydraulic assembly and monitors boost servo pressure.

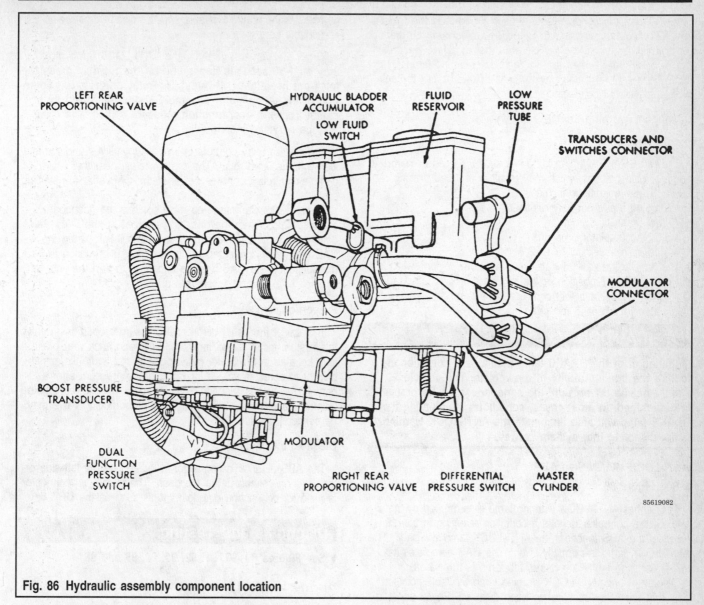

Fig. 86 Hydraulic assembly component location

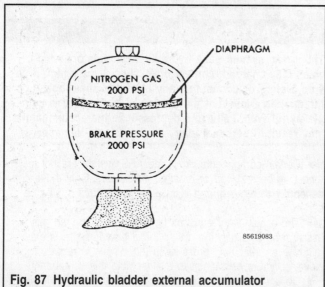

Fig. 87 Hydraulic bladder external accumulator

The primary pressure transducer is found on the left side of the hydraulic assembly and monitors the pressure within the primary master cylinder.

Both transducers generate a signal of 0.25-5.0 volts directly proportional to the fluid pressure. The CAB compares these signals and confirms proper operation. If either of the signals exceeds a pre-planned range, the CAB will disable the anti-lock system.

DIFFERENTIAL PRESSURE SWITCH

The differential pressure switch is used to detect a pressure differential between the primary and secondary master cylinder hydraulic circuits. When the pressure difference is 300 psi or more, this switch grounds the output of the primary pressure transducer. The CAB receives 0.0 volts from the transducer and reacts by shutting down the ABS function and illuminating the dash warning lights.

FLUID LEVEL SENSOR

A float and magnetic reed switch monitor the fluid level within the master cylinder hydraulic reservoir. Located in the reservoir cap, the sensor signal is used an input to the CAB. If low fluid level is detected, the BRAKE warning lamp on the dash is illuminated. If the vehicle is in motion above 3 mph, the ABS will be disabled and the anti-lock warning lamp will light. If the vehicle is not moving (or is below 3 mph) the anti-lock lamp will not come on.

Dashboard Warning Lamps

BRAKE WARNING LAMP

The red BRAKE warning lamp will be illuminated to warn the operator of conditions which may result in reduced braking ability. These conditions include:

- Parking brake not fully released.
- Low brake fluid.
- Low accumulator pressure.
- Hydraulic assembly or CAB

The lamp will also illuminate whenever the ignition switch is put in the **START** position or the ignition switch is turned to **ON**. Under these bulb test conditions, the lamp should stay illuminated for about 2 seconds.

❋❋CAUTION

Illumination of the BRAKE lamp indicates a condition affecting the braking ability of the vehicle. The vehicle should not be driven until the seriousness of the problem is determined. In most cases, conditions illuminating the BRAKE lamp will also illuminate the ANTI-LOCK warning lamp, disabling that system as well.

ANTI-LOCK WARNING LAMP

▶ See Figure 88

The amber ANTI-LOCK warning lamp is controlled by the CAB. If the controller detects a condition resulting in the shutdown of the ABS function, the ANTI-LOCK lamp will be lit. The ANTI-LOCK lamp is normally lit until the CAB completes its self-tests; if no faults are found, the lamp is turned off.

Display of the ANTI-LOCK warning lamp by itself indicates only that the ABS function has been disabled. Power-assisted

normal braking is still available and the car may be driven with reasonable care.

➡When starting the vehicle, the ANTI-LOCK lamp may stay on 1-30 seconds depending on the residual press the left front headlight (AS body) The relay controls the operation of the pump/motor assembly and is energized by a signal from the dual function pressure switch. The relay may be serviced individually.

The system relay controls the modulator valves and the anti-lock warning lamp relay. The system relay, near the pump/motor relay, controls power to the CAB after the start-up cycle.

The anti-lock warning lamp relay controls the dashboard warning lamp. When the relay is energized by the CAB, the dash lamp is held **OFF**. Thus, the lamp will light when the CAB fails, is disconnected or causes the ABS function to be discontinued. The CAB has the capability to turn the light on by itself by providing a separate ground.

Proportioning Valves

In place of the usual differential pressure proportioning valve, this system incorporates individual valves in each rear brake line. Located in the brake outlet ports of the hydraulic assembly, these screw-in valves limit rear brake pressure after a certain pressure is reached. This improves front-to-rear brake balance during normal braking. Each proportioning valve may be serviced individually.

Diagnostic Connector

The ABS diagnostic connector is located on the left side of the steering column under the dash. The blue 6-pin connector is used for connecting diagnostic tools such as the DRB II.

Diagnosis and Testing

▶ See Figures 89, 90, 91, 92, 93, 94, 95 and 96

SERVICE PRECAUTIONS

❋❋CAUTION

This brake system uses hydraulic accumulators which, when fully charged, contain brake fluid at very high pressure. Before disconnecting any hydraulic lines, hoses or fittings be certain that the accumulator pressure is completely relieved. Failure to depressurize the accumulators may result in personal injury and/or vehicle damage.

- Certain components within the ABS system are not intended to be serviced or repaired individually. Only those components with removal and installation procedures should be serviced.
- The accumulator contains high pressure nitrogen gas to assist in pressurizing the system. The gas pressure is maintained even after fluid pressure in the system is reduced. Never puncture or attempt to disassemble this component.
- Do not use rubber hoses or other parts not specifically specified for the ABS system. When using repair kits, replace all parts included in the kit. Partial or incorrect repair may lead

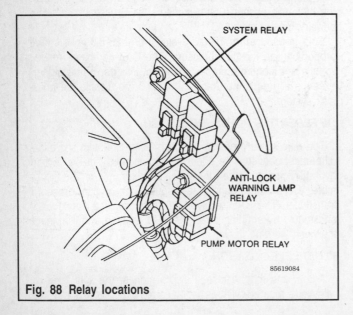

Fig. 88 Relay locations

85619084

DRB-II MESSAGE	WARNING LAMPS BRAKE	ANTI-LOCK	POSSIBLE CAUSES	DETECTED	LATCHING
CAB FAULT	—	ON	—Internal CAB fault	Anytime key on	YES
MODULATOR FAULT	—	ON	—Shorted or open solenoid or solenoid driver —Loose connector pin —Internal CAB fault	After drive-off until next ignition reset	YES
RIGHT REAR / LEFT REAR / RIGHT FRONT / LEFT FRONT } SENSOR	—	ON	—Missing sensor signal caused by defective wheel speed sensor —CAB fault	Vehicle speed above 15 mph	YES
RIGHT REAR / LEFT REAR / RIGHT FRONT / LEFT FRONT } CONTINUITY	—	ON	—Open or short in sensor, wiring or CAB	After start-up check, vehicle not in motion	YES
SYSTEM RELAY FAULT	—	ON	—System relay stuck on	During start-up check	YES
SOLENOID UNDERVOLTAGE FAULT		ON	—Low battery, low vehicle voltage —Open circuit on system relay output —System relay malfunction	During drive-off check	NO
ANTILOCK LAMP RELAY	—	—	—Open or stuck relay —Open wiring	During start-up check	NO
ANTILOCK LAMP	*	—	—Failed bulb or open wiring *If this code is set and a 2nd fault is detected, the brake lamp will light	During start-up check	—
LOW FLUID/PARK BRAKE FAULT	ON	ON ABOVE 3 MPH	—Low brake fluid —Parking brake engaged —Short to ground on low fluid wire	Anytime key on	NO
PRIMARY PRESSURE/ DIFFERENTIAL PRESSURE FAULT	ON DURING BRAKING	ON DURING BRAKING	—Hydraulic leak —Air in circuits —Malfunctioning pressure transducers	Anytime with brakes applied	NO
BOOST PRESSURE FAULT	ON DURING BRAKING	ON DURING BRAKING	—Malfunction in hydraulic booster or pressure transducers	Anytime with brakes applied	NO
EXCESS DECAY FAULT	—	ON	—Modulator fault —Incorrect tone wheels —Sensor fault —Hydroplaning —Long stop on ice	During ABS operation, if any 2 decay valves operate for more than 2 seconds	NO
LOW ACCUMULATOR FAULT	ON	ON	Malfunction in pump/motor system: —Dual function pressure switch —Pump/motor relay —Pump/motor assembly —Wiring faults	Anytime. Warning lamps light immed. Fault code sets after 2 min. of continuous detection	NO
NO RESPONSE	—	—	—Open circuit in diagnostic or data wiring or loose connectors —Defective CAB —Ignition off	Not a fault code. DRB-II cannot communicate with CAB.	—

85619085

Fig. 89 DRB-II Fault Messages, Bendix ABS System 10

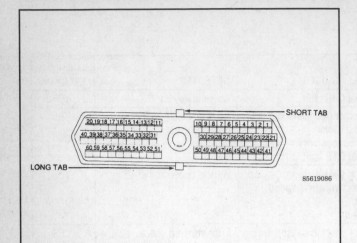

SHORT TAB

LONG TAB

85619086

Fig. 90 ABS controller-60 pin connector, pin identification

to functional problems and require the replacement of components.

• Lubricate rubber parts with clean, fresh brake fluid to ease assembly. Do not use lubricated shop air to clean parts; damage to rubber components may result.

• Use only DOT 3 brake fluid from an unopened container.

• If any hydraulic component or line is removed or replaced, it may be necessary to bleed the entire system.

• A clean repair area is essential. Always clean the reservoir and cap thoroughly before removing the cap. The slightest amount of dirt in the fluid may plug an orifice and impair the system function. Perform repairs after components have been thoroughly cleaned; use only denatured alcohol to clean components. Do not allow ABS components to come into contact with any substance containing mineral oil; this includes used shop rags.

• The Controller Anti-lock Brakes (CAB) is a microprocessor similar to other computer units in the vehicle. Insure that the ignition switch is **OFF** before removing or installing controller harnesses. Avoid static electricity discharge at or near the controller.

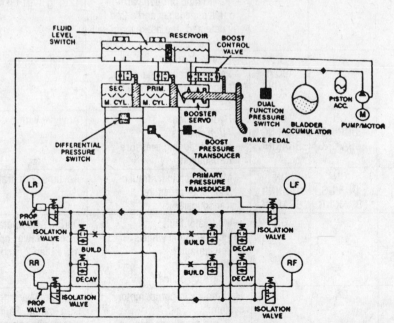

Isolation Valves—open, allowing fluid to flow from primary and secondary circuits to wheel brakes.

Decay and Build Valves—closed.

The brake pedal is in the released position, the booster servo circuit is closed to accumulator pressure. Booster servo circuit, primary and secondary circuits receive fluid from fluid reservoir. All brake circuits closed (check valves) to fluid from booster servo circuit.

85619087

Fig. 91 System schematic: Normal driving brakes off, Bendix ABS System 10

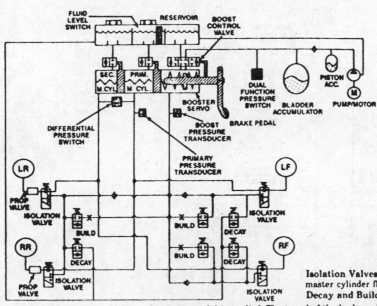

Isolation Valves—open to primary and secondary master cylinder fluid supply.
Decay and Build Valves—closed.

The brake pedal is applied. The travel of the brake pedal closes primary, secondary and booster servo circuits from fluid supply at the fluid reservoir. Brake fluid from the primary and secondary circuits flows through the open isolation valves and applies the wheel brakes. Fluid from the booster servo circuit does not flow to the wheel brakes. The fluid flow is blocked by the closed build valves and check valves.

Power Assist—The boost control valve shuttles between its three positions to provide power assisted braking

85619088

Fig. 92 System schematic: Normal driving brakes applied, Bendix ABS System 10

1. Turn the ignition switch **OFF** and leave it **OFF** during repairs unless specifically directed otherwise. Alternately, the negative battery cable may be disconnected; it must remain disconnected throughout the repairs.

2. Firmly apply and release the brake pedal a minimum of 40 times, using at least 50 lbs. of pedal force.

3. The pedal feel will become noticeably harder when the accumulator is completely discharged. Once this is felt, apply the brake pedal forcefully a few additional times. This will remove all hydraulic pressure from the system.

4. Do not turn the ignition switch **ON** or reconnect the battery cable after depressurizing the system unless service procedures specifically require it or all service operations have been performed.

→After the reserve pressure is depleted, the fluid level in the reservoir may rise above the MAX fill mark. This is normal; the reservoir will not overflow unless the system was over filled to begin with.

5. Always wear safety goggles when disconnecting lines and fittings.

DIAGNOSTIC PROCEDURE

Diagnosis of the ABS system consists of 3 general steps, performed in order. The visual or preliminary inspection is always required before any other steps are taken. A functional test drive is performed to confirm the existence of a problem. The functional test will indicate the need for specific diagnostic tests to be performed.

Some diagnostic tests will require the ignition being left **ON** for a period of time. This could lead to lowered battery voltage and erroneous voltage readings within the system. Unless the battery is known to be in sound condition, connect a slow-charger to the battery when performing extended testing.

Visual Inspection

Before diagnosing an apparent ABS problem, make absolutely certain that the normal braking system is in correct working order. Many common brake problems (dragging lining, seepage, etc.) will affect the ABS system. A visual check of specific system components may reveal problems creating an

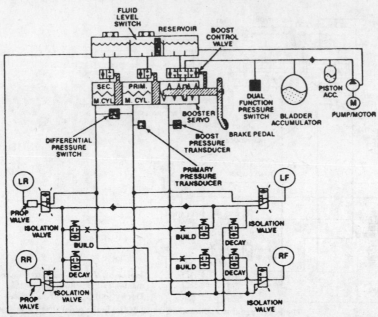

For explanation purposes, assume all speed sensors are sending the same wheel speed information, requiring the same modulation at the same rate.

Isolation Valves—closed, isolating the wheel brakes from master cylinder primary and secondary fluid supplies. Build and decay valves are closed preventing any fluid from reaching the open isolation valves.
Decay and Build Valves—closed.

85619089

Fig. 93 System schematic: ABS braking-hold pressure, Bendix ABS System 10

apparent ABS malfunction. Performing this inspection may reveal a simple failure, thus eliminating extended diagnostic time.

1. Depressurize the system.
2. Inspect the brake fluid level in the reservoir.
3. Inspect brake lines, hoses, master cylinder assembly, brake calipers and cylinders for leakage.
4. Visually check brake lines and hoses for excessive wear, heat damage, punctures, contact with other parts, missing clips or holders, blockage or crimping.
5. Check the calipers and wheel cylinders for rust or corrosion. Check for proper sliding action if applicable.
6. Check the caliper and wheel cylinder pistons for freedom of motion during application and release.
7. Inspect the wheel speed sensors for proper mounting and connections.
8. Inspect the tone wheels for broken teeth or poor mounting.
9. Inspect the wheels and tires on the vehicle. They must be of the same size and type to generate accurate speed signals. Check also for approximately equal tire pressures.

10. Confirm the fault occurrence with the operator. Certain driver induced faults, such as not releasing the parking brake fully, will set a fault code and trigger the dash warning light(s). Excessive wheel spin on low-traction surfaces, high speed acceleration or riding the brake pedal may also set fault codes and trigger a warning lamp. These induced faults are not system failures but examples of vehicle performance outside the parameters of the CAB.

11. The most common cause of intermittent faults is not a failed sensor but a loose, corroded or dirty connector. Incorrect installation of the wheel speed sensor will cause a loss of wheel speed signal. Check harness and component connectors carefully.

Functional Check

If the visual inspections do not lead to resolution of the problem, the test drive, or functional check must be preformed. Keep in mind that the vehicle driven, may have a problem affecting its braking ability; check the brakes at a very low speed in a safe location before beginning an extended drive. A

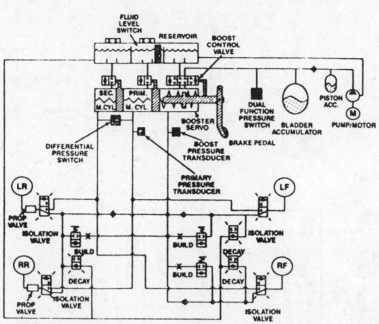

Isolation Valves—closed, isolating the wheel brakes from the master cylinder primary and secondary fluid supplies.

Decay Valves—open, allowing release of fluid through decay valve to the fluid reservoir.

Build Valves—closed, blocking booster servo circuit fluid to wheel brakes.

85619090

Fig. 94 System schematic: ABS braking-Decay pressure, Bendix ABS System 10

recommended method of testing and test driving for an ABS fault is:

1. Turn the ignition **ON** without starting the engine. Wait until both the BRAKE and ANTI-LOCK warning lights turn off. This will allow the pump to charge the system; if either or both warning lamps do not go off, proceed to Step 3.

2. Turn the ignition switch **OFF** for 15 seconds.

3. Start the engine. Wait for displays to achieve normal operation.

4. Place the shift lever in **P**. Using a full pedal stroke, slowly depress the brake pedal and release it.

5. Drive the vehicle carefully for a short distance. Achieve a speed of at least 20 mph; bring the vehicle to a full stop then accelerate to at least 20 mph.

6. If either the BRAKE or ANTI-LOCK warning lamps comes on, a fault has been detected by the CAB and, in most cases, a fault code has been entered into the memory.

Intermittent Faults

Most intermittent faults are caused by loose or faulty connections or wiring. Always check suspect circuits for poor mat-

ing of connector halves, improperly formed or damaged terminals. Any sign of corrosion or entry of foreign matter within a connector shell is cause for suspicion.

Most of the system faults will cause the ABS system to be disabled for the entire ignition on-off cycle. These are termed latching faults; in this case the warning lamp(s) will remain illuminated, even if the problem self-corrects during operation. There are some conditions which will allow the ABS function to be restored during a driving cycle; if one of these non-latching conditions exists and then ceases to exist, the warning lamp(s) will go off. When diagnosing a complaint of intermittent warning lamp illumination, investigate the following causes:

• Low system voltage. Once the CAB detects the correct voltage, the ABS function will be restored.

• Low brake fluid level. Once the fluid level sensor reads a normal level, system function is restored.

• Low accumulator pressure. May occur after long or hard stopping or as a result of riding the brake pedal. Once correct minimum pressure is achieved, the system is restored.

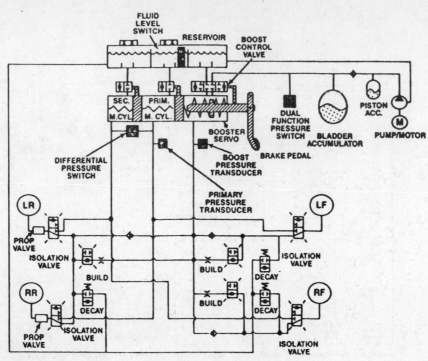

Isolation Valves—closed, isolating wheel brakes from master cylinder primary and secondary fluid supplies and open to booster servo circuit pressure through open build valves.

Decay Valves—closed.

Build Valves—open, allowing booster servo circuit pressure to flow to wheel brakes through the isolation valves.

Power Assist—The boost control valve shuttles between its three positions to provide power assisted braking.

85619091

Fig. 95 System schematic: ABS braking-Build pressure, Bendix ABS System 10

• Any interruption of power to either the CAB or the hydraulic assembly. Check the main power circuits, relays, fusible links and all related wiring.

Diagnostic Mode

Connect the DRB II or equivalent tester, according to instructions furnished with the tool. The system will enter diagnostic mode and prompt the operator through the assorted system checks and tests.

Component Replacement

✳✳CAUTION

This brake system uses a hydraulic accumulator which, when fully charged, contains brake fluid at very high pressure. Before disconnecting any hydraulic lines, hoses or fittings be certain that the accumulator pressure is completely relieved. Failure to depressurize the accumulator may result in personal injury and/or vehicle damage.

FILLING THE SYSTEM

1. Turn the ignition **OFF** and leave it **OFF** during inspection.
2. Depressurize the system.
3. Thoroughly clean the reservoir cap and the surrounding area.
4. Carefully remove reservoir cap, keeping all dirt out of the reservoir. Inspect the fluid level; fill to the top of the white screen in the front strainer if required. Do not overfill. Use only fresh DOT 3 brake fluid from unopened containers. Do not use any fluid containing a petroleum base. Do not use any fluid which has been exposed to water or moisture. Failure to use the correct fluid will affect system function and component life.
5. Replace the reservoir cap.

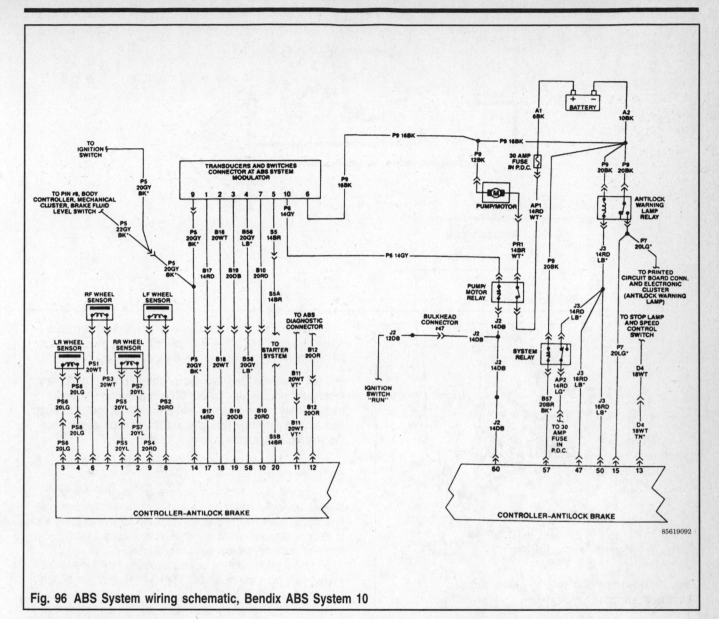

Fig. 96 ABS System wiring schematic, Bendix ABS System 10

BLEEDING THE SYSTEM

▶ **See Figures 97, 98 and 99**

The brake system must be bled any time air is permitted to enter the system, through loosened or disconnected lines. It is important to realize that air in the system, will cause a primary pressure fault to be set in the controller.

The system must be bled any time a hose or line is disconnected. Bleeding is also required after replacement of the hydraulic unit, caliper or wheel cylinder.

When bleeding any part of the system, the reservoir must remain close to FULL at all times. Check the level frequently and top off the fluid as needed. Do not allow the pump to run continuously for more than 60 seconds. If it becomes necessary to run the pump extensively, allow several minutes of cooling time between each 60 second operation period. Severe damage will occur to the pump if it is not allowed to cool. Never operate the pump with no fluid in the system.

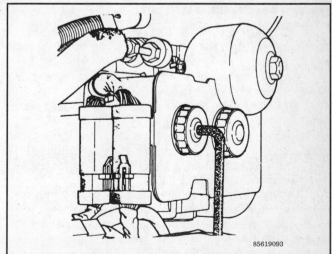

Fig. 97 The dummy cap must be installed when using pressure bleeding equipment

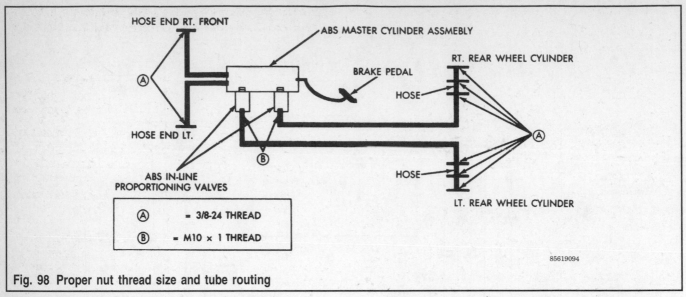

Fig. 98 Proper nut thread size and tube routing

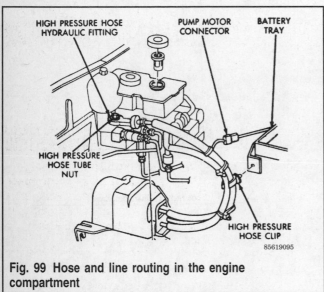

Fig. 99 Hose and line routing in the engine compartment

Pressure Bleeding the Brake Lines

Only diaphragm pressure bleeding equipment should be used. The diaphragm prevents the entry of dirt and moisture into the fluid.

1. Depressurize the system. The ignition must remain **OFF** throughout the bleeding procedure.

2. Thoroughly clean the reservoir caps and the surrounding area.

3. Remove both reservoir caps. Install the pressure bleeder adapter on one port and the dummy cap on the other port.

4. Attach pressure bleeding equipment. Charge the pressure bleeder to approximately 20 psi.

5. Brakes should be bled in the following order: Left rear, right rear, left front and right front. Connect a transparent hose to the caliper bleed screw. Submerge the other end of the hose in clean brake fluid in a clear glass container.

6. Turn the pressure bleeder on; open the caliper bleed screw $1/2$-$3/4$ turn and allow fluid into the container. Leave the bleeder open until the fluid is free of air bubbles.

➡ **If the reservoir was drained or the hydraulic assembly removed from the car before bleeding, pump the brake pedal slowly once or twice while the bleed screw is open and fluid is flowing. This will aid the escape of air from the hydraulic assembly.**

7. Close the bleeder screw, tightening it to 7.5 ft. lbs. (10 Nm).

8. Repeat the bleeding procedure at the other calipers. When bleeding is complete, close the pressure bleeder valve and slowly unscrew the adapter from the fluid reservoir. Failure to release reservoir pressure slowly will result in brake fluid spraying both the vehicle and those around it.

9. Use a clean syringe or similar device to remove the excess fluid from the reservoir. The system must not be left over filled.

10. Install the reservoir caps. Turn the ignition switch **ON**; the pump should charge the system, stopping after approximately 30 seconds or less.

Manual Bleeding of the Brake Lines

The individual lines may be bled manually at each wheel using the traditional 2 person method.

1. Depressurize the system. The ignition must remain **OFF** throughout the bleeding procedure.

2. Calipers should be bled in the following order: Left rear, right rear, left front and right front. Connect a transparent hose to the caliper bleed screw. Submerge the other end of the hose in clean brake fluid in a clear glass container.

3. Slowly pump the brake pedal several times. Use full strokes of the pedal and allow 5 seconds between strokes. After 2 or 3 strokes, hold pressure on the pedal keeping it at the bottom of its travel.

4. With pressure held on the pedal, open the bleed screw $1/2$-$3/4$ turn. Leave the bleed screw open until fluid stops flowing from the hose. Tighten the bleed screw and release the pedal.

5. Repeat Steps 3 and 4 until air-free fluid flows from the hose. Tighten the caliper bleed screw to 7.5 ft. lbs. (10 Nm).

6. Repeat the sequence at each remaining caliper.

➡**Check the fluid level in the reservoir frequently and maintain it near the full level.**

7. When the bleeding is complete, bring the fluid level in the reservoir to the correct level. Install the reservoir cap. Turn the ignition switch **ON** and allow the system to pressurize.

Pump/Motor Assembly

REMOVAL & INSTALLATION

❋❋CAUTION

This brake system uses a hydraulic accumulator which, when fully charged, contains brake fluid at very high pressure. Before disconnecting any hydraulic lines, hoses or fittings be certain that the accumulator pressure is completely relieved. Failure to depressurize the accumulator may result in personal injury and/or vehicle damage.

1. Disconnect the negative battery cable.
2. Depressurize the brake system.
3. Remove the fresh air intake ducts from the engine.
4. On Van/wagon vehicles, loosen the low pressure hose clamp at the hydraulic unit. Remove the clip holding the high pressure line to the battery tray.
5. Disconnect the electrical connectors running across the engine compartment in the vicinity of the pump/motor high and low pressure hoses. One of these connectors is the one for the pump/motor assembly.
6. Disconnect the high and low pressure hoses from the hydraulic assembly. Cap or plug the reservoir fitting.
7. Disconnect the pump/motor electrical connector from the engine mount.
8. Remove the heat shield bolt from the front of the pump bracket. Remove the heat shield.
9. Lift the pump/motor assembly from the bracket and out of the vehicle.
   To install:
10. Fit the pump motor assembly onto the bracket; install the heat shield and its retaining bolt.
11. Install the pump/motor electrical connector to the engine mount.
12. Connect the high and low pressure hose to the hydraulic assembly. Tighten the high pressure line to 145 inch lbs. (16 Nm). Tighten the hose clamp on the low pressure hose to 10 inch lbs (1 Nm).
13. Connect the electrical connectors which were removed for access.
14. Install the high pressure line retaining clip to the battery tray if it was removed.
15. Install the fresh air intake ducts.
16. Bleed the brake system.

High Pressure and Return Hoses

REMOVAL & INSTALLATION

▶ **See Figure 100**

1. Remove the pump/motor assembly.
2. Carefully cut the wire ties (Van/wagons, 4 ties; others, 2 ties)) holding the hoses and wiring harnesses.
3. Remove the banjo bolt from the pump/motor assembly and remove the hoses.
4. When installing, lubricate the rubber O-ring for the high and low pressure hoses with clean brake fluid before installation.
5. Place the hoses in position and install the banjo bolt.
6. Use care when routing the wiring along the hoses; install new wire ties in the proper locations. Noted that the wiring harness is not held within all the wire ties.
7. Install the pump/motor assembly.

Hydraulic Assembly

REMOVAL & INSTALLATION

▶ **See Figure 101**

❋❋CAUTION

This brake system uses a hydraulic accumulator which, when fully charged, contains brake fluid at very high pressure. Before disconnecting any hydraulic lines, hoses or fittings be certain that the accumulator pressure is completely relieved. Failure to depressurize the accumulator may result in personal injury and/or vehicle damage.

1. Depressurize the brake system.
2. Remove the air cleaner. Additionally, remove the windshield washer fluid bottle.
3. Disconnect all electrical connectors at the hydraulic assembly.
4. Use a syringe to remove as much fluid as possible from the reservoir.
5. Disconnect and remove the banjo bolt holding the high pressure hose to the hydraulic assembly.
6. Remove the hose from the steel tube and cap the tube.
7. Disconnect the brake lines from the hydraulic assembly.
8. Use a small flat tool to release the retainer clip on the brake pedal pin. The center tang on the clip must be moved back enough to allow the lock tab to clear the pin. Disconnect the pushrod from the pedal pin.
9. Under the dash at the firewall, remove the 4 bolts holding the hydraulic assembly.
10. Remove the hydraulic assembly from the engine compartment.
    To install:
11. Position the hydraulic assembly and install the retaining nuts. Tighten the nuts to 21 ft. lbs. (28 Nm).
12. Coat the contact surface of the pedal pin with all-purpose grease. Connect the pushrod to the pedal pin and install

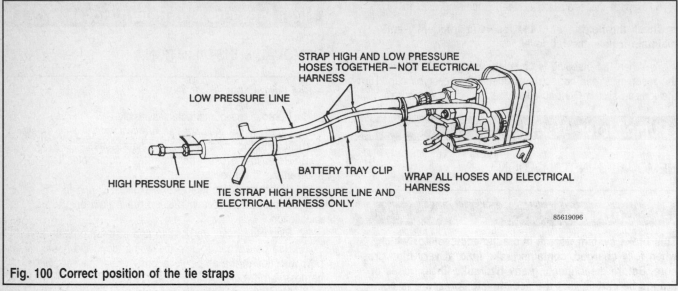

Fig. 100 Correct position of the tie straps

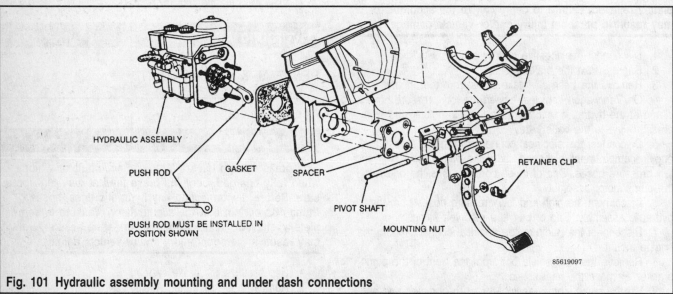

Fig. 101 Hydraulic assembly mounting and under dash connections

a new retainer clip. Make certain the lock tab on the retainer is firmly engaged.

✳✳WARNING

The hydraulic assembly pushrod must be in the correct position before assembly.

13. Install the brake lines and tighten them to 12 ft. lbs. (16 Nm). If the proportioning valves were removed, reinstall and tighten them to 30 ft. lbs. (40 Nm).

➡**Be certain the brake tubes are connected to the proper location.**

14. Install the return hose to the reservoir or the steel tube.

15. Before connecting the pressure hose to the hydraulic assembly, make certain the washers are in their correct positions. Install the hose and tighten the banjo bolt to 13. ft. lbs. (17 Nm).

16. Fill the reservoir to the top of the strainer screen.

17. Connect all the electrical connectors to the hydraulic assembly.

18. Bleed the entire brake system.

19. Install the air cleaner and washer bottle (Van/wagon) and the fresh air intake duct and clamps.

Hydraulic Reservoir

REMOVAL & INSTALLATION

✳✳CAUTION

This brake system uses a hydraulic accumulator which, when fully charged, contains brake fluid at very high pressure. Before disconnecting any hydraulic lines, hoses or fittings be certain that the accumulator pressure is completely relieved. Failure to depressurize the accumulator may result in personal injury and/or vehicle damage.

1. Depressurize the brake system.
2. Using a syringe or similar tool, remove as much brake fluid as possible from the reservoir.
3. Disconnect the high pressure hose banjo fitting and remove the hydraulic bladder accumulator from the hydraulic assembly.
4. Remove the 3 retaining pins holding the reservoir to the hydraulic assembly.
5. Use a blunt prying tool carefully installed between the reservoir and hydraulic assembly body to lift the reservoir. Use a rocking motion to gently lift the reservoir free of the grommets.

➡Be extremely careful to avoid damaging or puncturing the reservoir.

6. Remove the fluid level sensor switch from the reservoir.
7. Use fingers only to remove the grommets from the hydraulic assembly. Discard the grommets.

To install:
8. Lubricate new grommets with clean brake fluid and install them onto the hydraulic assembly. Always use new grommets.
9. Install the fluid level switch into the reservoir. Position the reservoir on the grommets and press it into place using hand pressure only. A rocking motion is helpful; make certain the reservoir is fully seated in all 3 grommets.

➡Do not attempt to pound the reservoir into place with a hammer or other tools. Damage will result.

10. Install the 3 locking pins to hold the reservoir in place.
11. Reinstall the high pressure hose banjo fitting onto the hydraulic assembly and torque the fitting to 10 ft. lbs. (13 Nm).
12. Install the hydraulic bladder accumulator onto the hydraulic assembly and tighten the fitting to 30 ft. lbs. (40 Nm).
13. Fill the reservoir to the top of the strainer screen with fresh clean fluid.
14. Bleed the entire brake system including the booster.

Proportioning Valves

REMOVAL & INSTALLATION

✳✳CAUTION

This brake system uses a hydraulic accumulator which, when fully charged, contains brake fluid at very high pressure. Before disconnecting any hydraulic lines, hoses or fittings be certain that the accumulator pressure is completely relieved. Failure to depressurize the accumulator may result in personal injury and/or vehicle damage.

1. Depressurize the brake system.
2. Remove the air cleaner and intake duct.
3. Disconnect the high pressure and return hoses from the hydraulic unit.
4. Remove the brake tube and fitting from the proportioning valve.
5. Remove the proportioning valve from the hydraulic assembly.

To install:
6. Install the valve to the hydraulic assembly and tighten it to 30 ft. lbs. (40 Nm).
7. Install the brake line and tighten to 12 ft. lbs. (16 Nm).
8. Install the high pressure and return hoses. Tighten the high pressure hose fitting to 145 inch lbs (16 Nm.).
9. Install the air cleaner and the ductwork.
10. Only the affected brake circuit needs bleeding.

Bladder Accumulator

REMOVAL & INSTALLATION

✳✳CAUTION

This brake system uses a hydraulic accumulator which, when fully charged, contains brake fluid at very high pressure. Before disconnecting any hydraulic lines, hoses or fittings be certain that the accumulator pressure is completely relieved. Failure to depressurize the accumulator may result in personal injury and/or vehicle damage.

1. Depressurize the brake system.
2. Loosen the accumulator fitting at the hydraulic assembly and remove the accumulator assembly.
3. Reinstall the accumulator and tighten the to 30 ft. lbs. (40 Nm).
4. Turn the ignition switch **ON**. Allow the pump to pressurize the system. Inspect the accumulator area carefully for any sign of leakage.
5. If any seepage or leaking is noted, turn the ignition **OFF** and fully depressurize the system before beginning any repairs.

Controller Anti-Lock Brakes (CAB)

REMOVAL & INSTALLATION

▶ **See Figure 102**

1. Turn the ignition switch to the **OFF** position or disconnect the negative battery cable.
2. Remove the speed control servo (cruise control).
3. Double check that the ignition switch is **OFF** or that the battery cable is disconnected.
4. Disconnect the 60-pin wiring connector at the CAB.
5. Remove the 3 CAB mounting bolts and remove the controller from the vehicle.

To install:
6. Install the CAB and tighten the mounting bolts.
7. After checking that the ignition is **OFF** or the battery disconnected, connect the 60-pin harness to the controller. Make certain that the connector is properly seated and locked in place. Do not force the connector into place.
8. Reinstall the speed control servo.
9. If the vehicle is elevated, lower it to the ground. Connect the negative battery cable if it was removed.
10. Drive the vehicle following the test drive procedures listed under Diagnosis and Testing. If a warning lamp is on

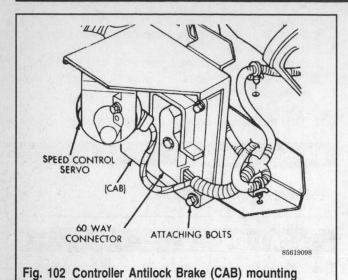

Fig. 102 Controller Antilock Brake (CAB) mounting location

and/or a fault code set (not previously present), closely inspect the 60-pin connector at the CAB for looseness or improper mating.

Wheel Speed Sensors

REMOVAL & INSTALLATION

Front Wheel
▶ **See Figure 103**

1. Elevate and safely support the vehicle. Remove the wheel and tire.
2. Remove the screw from the sensor retaining clip.
3. Carefully remove the sensor wiring grommet from the fender shield.
4. Disconnect the sensor wiring from the ABS harness.
5. Remove the screws holding the sensor wiring tube to the fender well.

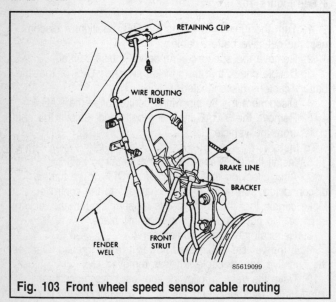

Fig. 103 Front wheel speed sensor cable routing

6. Remove the retainer grommets from the bracket on the strut.
7. Remove the fastener holding the sensor head.
8. Carefully remove the sensor head from the steering knuckle. Do not use pliers on the sensor head; if it is seized in place, use a hammer and small punch to tap the edge of the sensor ear. The tapping and side-to-side motion will free the unit.

To install:
9. Before installation, coat the sensor with high temperature multi-purpose grease.
10. Connect the speed sensor to the ABS harness.
11. Push the sensor assembly grommet into the hole in the fender shield. Install the retainer clip and screw.
12. Install the sensor grommets into the brackets on the fender shield and strut. Install the retainer clip at the strut.
13. On Van/wagons, install the sensor wiring tube and tighten the retaining bolts to 35 inch lbs. (4 Nm).
14. Install the sensor to the knuckle. Install the retaining screw and tighten it to 60 inch lbs. (7 Nm).

➡**Proper installation of the sensor and its wiring is critical to system function. Make certain that wiring is installed in all retainers and clips. Wiring must be protected from moving parts and not be stretched during suspension movements.**

15. Install the tire and wheel. Lower the vehicle to the ground.

Rear Wheel
▶ **See Figures 104 and 105**

1. Elevate and safely support the vehicle. Remove the wheel and tire.
2. Remove the sensor assembly grommet from the underbody and pull the harness through the hole in the body.
3. Disconnect the sensor wiring from the ABS harness.
4. Remove the 4 clips holding the sensor wiring along the underside.
5. Remove the attaching bracket holding the wiring to the frame rail.
6. On FWD Van/wagons, remove the nuts from the rear axle U-bolts. Remove the sensor mounting bracket.
7. Remove the fastener holding the sensor head.
8. Carefully remove the sensor head from the adapter assembly. Do not use pliers on the sensor head; if it is seized in place, use a hammer and small punch to tap the edge of the sensor ear. The tapping and side-to-side motion will free the unit.

To install:
9. Position the sensor bracket under the brake tube and start the outer attaching bolt by hand.
10. Align the brake tube clip and the bracket; install the retaining bolt.
11. Tighten both retaining bolts to 145 inch lbs. (17 Nm).
12. Before installation coat the sensor with high temperature, multi-purpose grease.
13. Install the sensor head into the rear axle and install the bolt. Tighten the bolt to 60 inch lbs. (7 Nm).
14. Carefully bend the rubber hose section of the sensor assembly toward the rear of the vehicle. Position the anti-

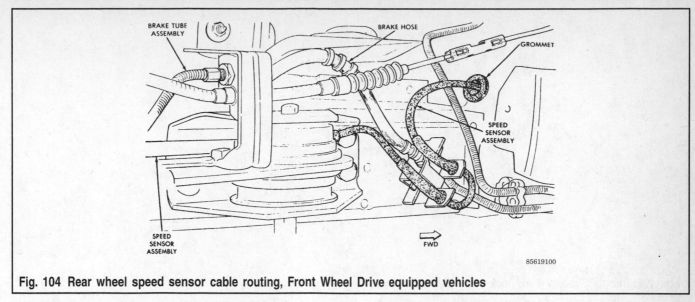

Fig. 104 Rear wheel speed sensor cable routing, Front Wheel Drive equipped vehicles

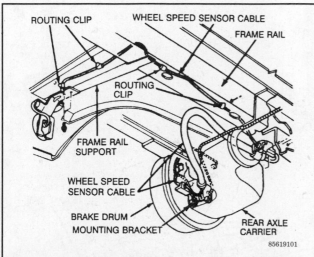

Fig. 105 Rear wheel speed sensor cable routing, All Wheel Drive equipped vehicles

rotation tab correctly and install the frame rail bracket. Tighten the bolt to 50 inch lbs. (5 Nm).

15. Connect the sensor wiring to the rear harness. Push the sensor assembly wiring grommet back into the hole.

16. Install the rear sensor grommet retaining bracket and tighten the 2 retaining bolts to 50 inch lbs. (5 Nm). Make certain the bracket does not pinch the sensor wiring.

17. Route the sensor wiring along the vehicle frame rail and install the 4 retaining clips.

18. install the rear wheel and tire; lower the vehicle to the ground.

Tone Rings

REMOVAL & INSTALLATION

The front toothed wheel or tone ring is an integral part of the outer Constant Velocity (CV) joint. Should the ring become unusable, the CV-joint must be replaced. Likewise, the rear tone ring is an integral part of the hub assembly and cannot be replaced individually.

The tone rings may be inspected in place on the vehicle. After gaining access, inspect for any evidence of contact between the speed sensor and the ring. If any contact occurred, the cause must be found and corrected before new parts are installed.

Teeth on the wheels should be unbroken and uncracked. The teeth and the valleys on the ring should be reasonably clean. Excessive run out of the tone ring can cause an erratic wheel speed signal. Replace the ring if run out exceeds 0.010 in. (0.25mm).

The air gap between the tone ring and the sensor is not adjustable. It is established by the correct installation of the wheel speed sensor.

BENDIX SYSTEM 4 ANTI-LOCK BRAKE SYSTEM

▶ See Figures 106, 107, 108 and 109

System Description

➡**The Bendix System 4 Antilock Brake system was introduced on 1994 models.**

The purpose of the antilock brake system is to prevent wheel lock-up under heavy braking conditions on virtually any type of road surface. Antilock braking is desirable because a vehicle which is stopped without locking its wheels will retain directional stability and some steering capability. This allows a driver to retain greater control of the vehicle during heavy braking.

Under normal braking conditions, the Bendix Antilock 4 Brake System functions the same as a standard non-Antilock brake system.

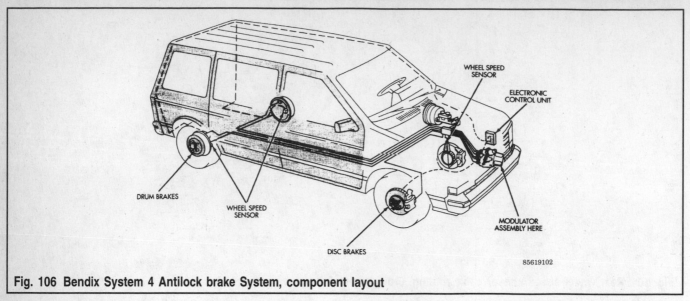

Fig. 106 Bendix System 4 Antilock brake System, component layout

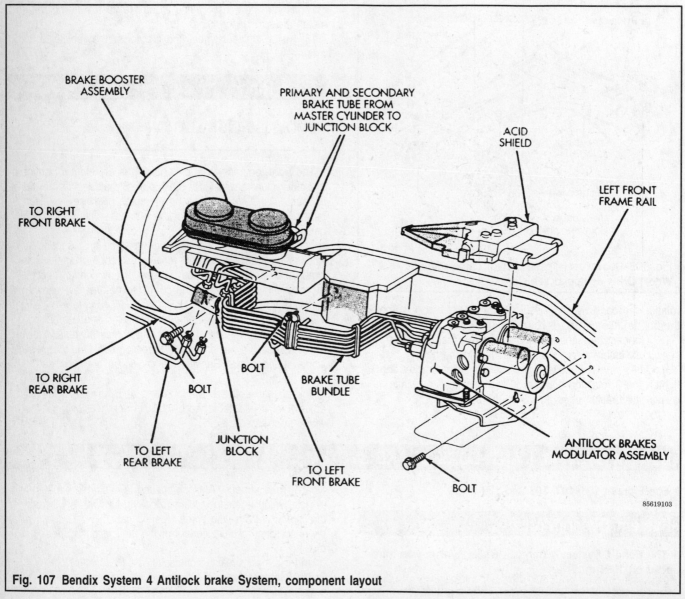

Fig. 107 Bendix System 4 Antilock brake System, component layout

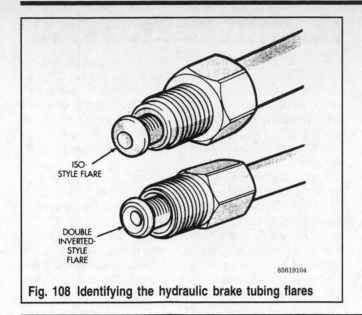

Fig. 108 Identifying the hydraulic brake tubing flares

ISO-STYLE FLARE

DOUBLE INVERTED-STYLE FLARE

85619104

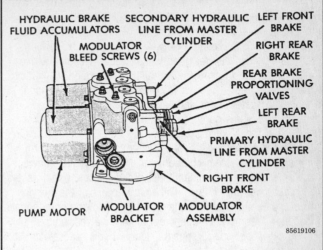

HYDRAULIC BRAKE FLUID ACCUMULATORS

SECONDARY HYDRAULIC LINE FROM MASTER CYLINDER

LEFT FRONT BRAKE

MODULATOR BLEED SCREWS (6)

RIGHT REAR BRAKE

REAR BRAKE PROPORTIONING VALVES

LEFT REAR BRAKE

PRIMARY HYDRAULIC LINE FROM MASTER CYLINDER

RIGHT FRONT BRAKE

PUMP MOTOR

MODULATOR BRACKET

MODULATOR ASSEMBLY

85619106

Fig. 110 Modulator assembly, Bendix System 4 Antilock brake System

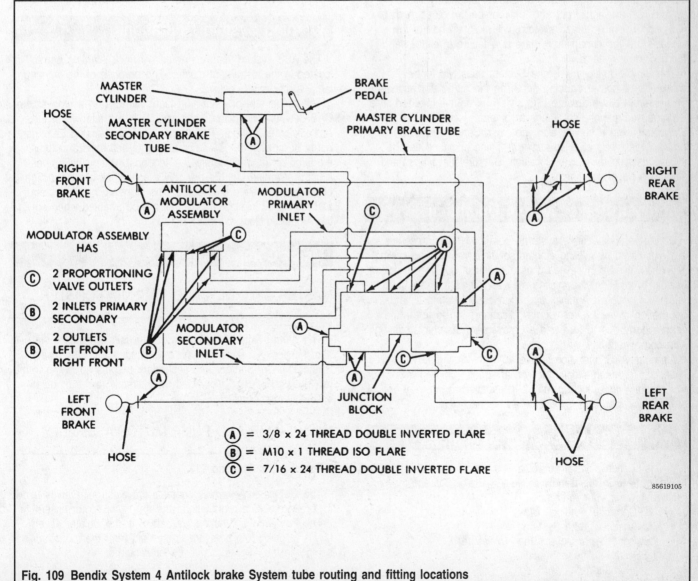

MASTER CYLINDER

BRAKE PEDAL

HOSE

MASTER CYLINDER SECONDARY BRAKE TUBE

MASTER CYLINDER PRIMARY BRAKE TUBE

HOSE

RIGHT FRONT BRAKE

ANTILOCK 4 MODULATOR ASSEMBLY

MODULATOR PRIMARY INLET

RIGHT REAR BRAKE

MODULATOR ASSEMBLY HAS

Ⓒ 2 PROPORTIONING VALVE OUTLETS

Ⓑ 2 INLETS PRIMARY SECONDARY

Ⓑ 2 OUTLETS LEFT FRONT RIGHT FRONT

MODULATOR SECONDARY INLET

JUNCTION BLOCK

LEFT FRONT BRAKE

HOSE

Ⓐ = 3/8 × 24 THREAD DOUBLE INVERTED FLARE

Ⓑ = M10 × 1 THREAD ISO FLARE

Ⓒ = 7/16 × 24 THREAD DOUBLE INVERTED FLARE

LEFT REAR BRAKE

HOSE

85619105

Fig. 109 Bendix System 4 Antilock brake System tube routing and fitting locations

When a wheel locking tendency is detected during a brake application, the vehicle brake system will enter the Antilock mode. During Antilock Braking, hydraulic pressure in the four wheel circuits is modulated to prevent wheels from locking. Each wheel circuit Is designed with a set of electrical valves and hydraulic line to provide modulation, although for vehicle stability, both rear wheel valves receive the same electrical signal. The system can modulate pressure at each wheel, depending on signals generated by the wheel speed sensors (WSS) and received at the CAB.

The Bendix Antilock 4 Brake System, uses the following standard brake system components. Master cylinder, power booster, brake caliper assemblies, braking discs, pedal assembly, brake lines and hoses. The unique parts of the Bendix Antilock 4 Brake System consists of the following components, modulator assembly, unique proportioning valves, unique junction block, wheel speed sensors, tone wheels, and electronic control unit.

The hydraulic system, on the Bendix Antilock 4 brake system is diagonally split. Diagonally split hydraulic brake systems, have the left front and right rear brakes on one hydraulic system and the right front and left rear on the other. A diagonally split hydraulic brake system, will maintain half of the vehicles braking capability if there is a failure in either half of the hydraulic system.

The Bendix Antilock 4 Brake System uses two types of brake line fittings and tubing flares on the modulator assembly. The different types are the ISO style and double inverted style with their corresponding fittings at different joint locations. When servicing a vehicle equipped with Bendix Antilock 4 Brake System, be sure correct tube fitting and tube flare is always used in the correct location. Be sure that fittings and flares are never mismatched.

Antilock Brake System Operation

During Antilock Brake system operation, brake pressures are modulated by cycling electric solenoid valves. The cycling of these valves can be heard as a series of popping or ticking noises. In addition, the cycling may be felt as a pulsation in the brake pedal. If Antilock operation occurs during a hard application of the brakes, some pulsation may be felt in the vehicle body due to fore and aft movement of vehicle suspension components.

Although ABS operation is available at virtually all vehicle speeds, it is automatically turn off at speeds below 7 mph. For this reason, wheel lockup may be perceived at the very end of an anti lock stop and is considered normal.

Antilock Brake System Definitions

In this section several abbreviations are used for the components that are in the Bendix Antilock 4 Brake System, they are listed below for your reference.
- CAB-Controller Antilock Brake
- ABS-Antilock Brake System
- PSI-Pounds per Square Inch (pressure)
- WSS-Wheel Speed Sensor
- AC-Alternating Current

System Self-Diagnostics

The Bendix Antilock 4 Brake System has been designed with the following self diagnostic capabilities. The self diagnostic ABS startup cycle begins when the ignition switch is turned to the on position. At this time an electrical check is completed on the ABS components such as Wheel Speed Sensor Continuity and System and other Relay continuity. During this check the Amber Antilock Light is on for approximately 1-2 seconds.

Further Antilock Brake System functional testIng is accomplished once the vehicle is set in motion, knows as drive-off.

1. The solenoid valves and the pump/motor are activated briefly to verity function.

2. The voltage output from each of the wheel speed sensors is verified to be within the correct operating range. If a vehicle is not set in motion within 3 minutes from the time the ignition switch is turned to the on position. The solenoid valve test is bypassed but the pump/motor is activated briefly to verify that it is operating correctly.

Warning System Operations

The ABS system uses an Amber Antilock Warning Lamp, located in the instrument cluster. The purpose of the warning lamp is discussed below.

The Amber Antilock Warning Light will turn on whenever the CAB detects a condition which results in a shutdown of the Antilock brake system. The Amber Antilock Warning Lamp is normally on until the CAB completes its self tests and turns the lamp off (approximately 1-2 seconds). When the Amber Antilock Warning Light is on, only the Antilock brake function of the brake system is affected. The standard brake system and the ability to stop the car will not be affected when only the Amber Antilock Warning Light is on.

Major Components

MASTER CYLINDER AND VACUUM BOOSTER

The Bendix Antilock 4 Brake System uses a vehicles standard Master Cylinder/Reservoir and Vacuum Booster. The master cylinder primary and secondary outputs go to the frame rail mounted junction block and then directly to the modulator assembly inlet ports.

MODULATOR AND PUMP MOTOR/ASSEMBLY

▶ **See Figures 110 and 111**

The Modulator Assembly contains the electronic valves used for brake pressure modulation, and the Pump/Motor assembly.

The Pump/Motor function, as part of the modulator assembly, is to pump low pressure brake fluid from the modulator sump into the ABS accumulator, as required.

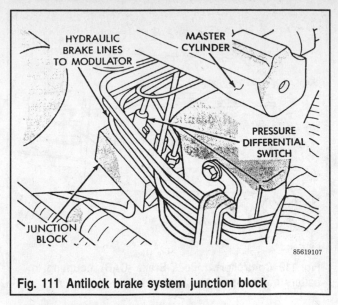

Fig. 111 Antilock brake system junction block

WHEEL SPEED SENSORS

▶ See Figures 112, 113, 114 and 115

A Wheel Speed Sensor is located at each wheel to transmit wheel speed information to the CAB.

CONTROLLER ANTILOCK BRAKE (CAB)

▶ See Figures 116, 117 and 118

The CAB is a small computer which receives wheel speed information, controls Antilock operation and monitors system operation.

ABS BRAKE SYSTEM ON VEHICLE SERVICE

The following are general precautions which should be observed whenever servicing and or diagnosing the ABS system

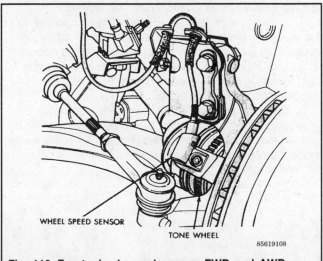

Fig. 112 Front wheel speed sensor, FWD and AWD vehicles

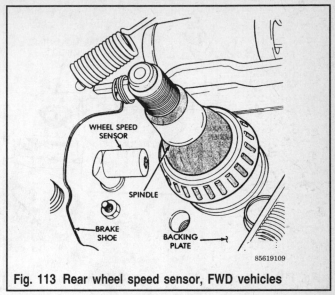

Fig. 113 Rear wheel speed sensor, FWD vehicles

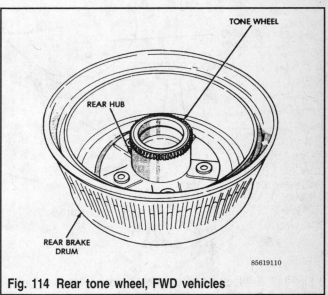

Fig. 114 Rear tone wheel, FWD vehicles

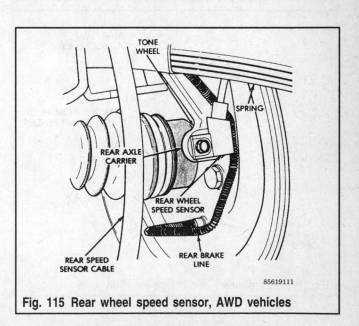

Fig. 115 Rear wheel speed sensor, AWD vehicles

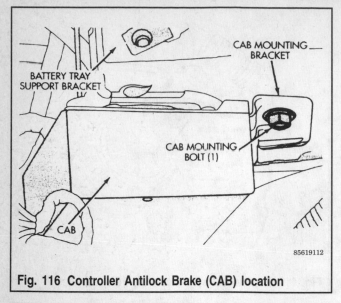

Fig. 116 Controller Antilock Brake (CAB) location

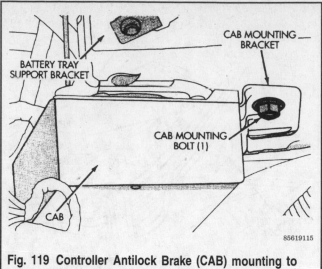

Fig. 119 Controller Antilock Brake (CAB) mounting to battery tray support bracket

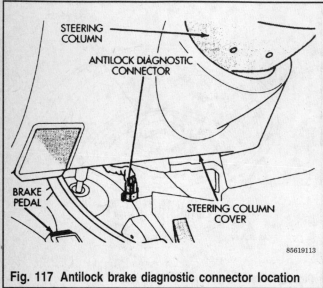

Fig. 117 Antilock brake diagnostic connector location

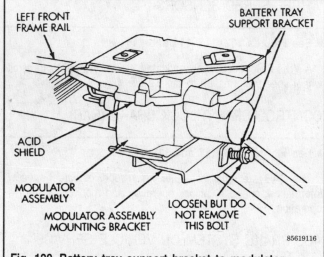

Fig. 120 Battery tray support bracket to modulator bracket attaching bolt

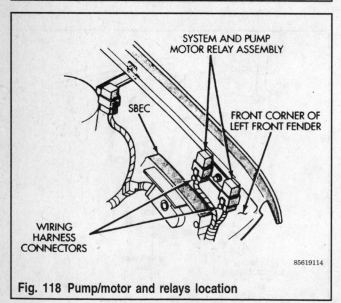

Fig. 118 Pump/motor and relays location

and other vehicle electronic systems. Failure to observe these precautions may result in ABS system damage.

1. If welding work is to be performed on a vehicle using an arc welder. The wiring harness connector should be disconnected from the CAB before beginning any welding operation.

2. The CAB 60 way connector and modulator assembly 10 way connector, should never be connected or disconnected with the ignition in the on position.

3. Some components of Bendix Antilock 4 Brake System assemblies can not be serviced separately from the assembly and will require replacement of the complete assembly for servicing. Do not disassemble any component which is designated as non-serviceable.

Modulator Assembly

REMOVAL

◗ See Figures 119, 120, 121, 122, 123, 124, 125, 126 and 127

1. Raise vehicle on jackstands or position vehicle centered on a frame contact hoist. See Hoisting in the Lubrication and Maintenance section of this manual.
2. Disconnect and remove both battery cables from battery.
3. Remove battery holddown clamp and battery from battery tray.
4. Remove the 2 bolts attaching battery tray to battery tray support bracket and frame rail. Remove battery tray from vehicle.

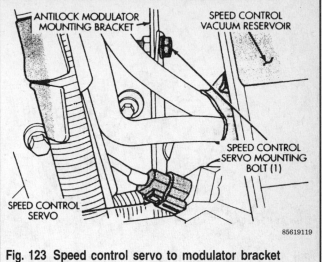

Fig. 123 Speed control servo to modulator bracket attaching bolt

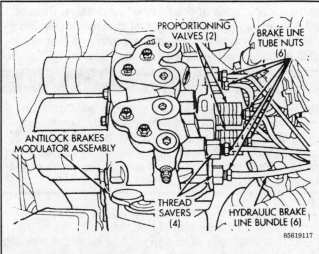

Fig. 121 Hydraulic brake line connections to the modulator assembly

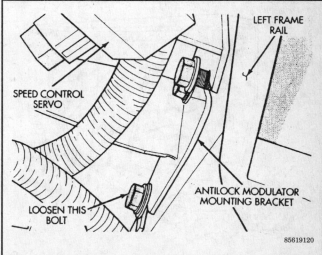

Fig. 124 Modulator bracket to frame rail rear mounting bolt

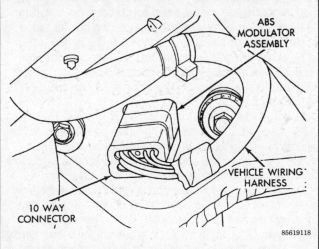

Fig. 122 Vehicle wiring harness connection to the modulator assembly

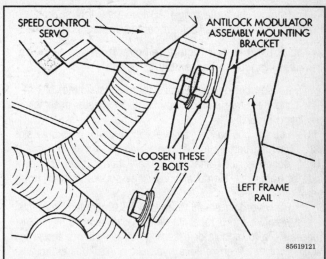

Fig. 125 Modulator bracket to frame rail front mounting bolt

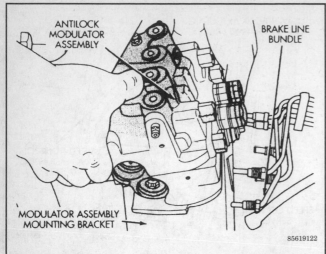

Fig. 126 Removing the modulator and bracket assembly from the vehicle

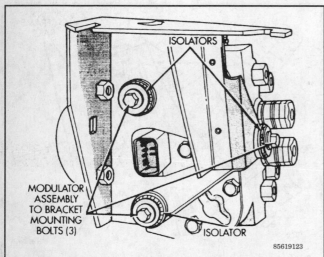

Fig. 127 Modulator assembly to mounting bracket attaching bolts

5. Remove bolt attaching CAB to battery tray support bracket, and remove CAB from battery tray support bracket.

➡The CAB does not require removal from vehicle when removing modulator assembly.

6. Loosen but do not remove (bracket is slotted) bolt attaching battery tray support bracket to modulator assembly mounting bracket.

7. Loosen but do not remove bottom bolt, (bracket is slotted) attaching battery tray support bracket to side of frame rail. Then loosen top bolt attaching battery tray support bracket to side of frame rail. Remove battery tray support bracket from vehicle.

8. Remove acid shield, from the ABS modulator assembly.

9. Remove the 6 tube nuts attaching hydraulic brake line tube bundle to modulator assembly, thread savers and proportioning valves. Then remove hydraulic brake lines as an assembly, from the modulator assembly. Brake lines do not need to be loosened at junction block.

10. Raise and safely support the vehicle.

11. Remove vehicle's wiring harness 10 way connector from modulator assembly.

12. If vehicle is equipped with speed control, remove bolt attaching speed control servo assembly to modulator assembly bracket.

13. Speed control servo does not need to be removed from vehicle, but should be moved out of the way.

14. Loosen but do not remove the 2 bolts at front of modulator assembly bracket, attaching it to frame rail.

15. Loosen, but do not remove bolt at rear of modulator bracket, attaching bracket to frame rail.

16. Lower the vehicle.

17. Remove modulator assembly and mounting bracket as an assembly from vehicle.

18. Remove modulator assembly from mounting bracket. Mounting bracket will need to be transferred to replacement modulator assembly, if a new modulator is to be installed.

To install:

➡Before installing modulator assembly back on mounting bracket, inspect the 3 modulator assembly to bracket isolators for any signs of deterioration or damage. Replace all 3 isolators if any show signs of damaged or deterioration, before mounting modulator assembly on bracket. Install modulator assembly on mounting bracket.

✱✱CAUTION

Be sure mounting isolators are correctly positioned on mounting bracket and modulator assembly, before installing and torquing modulator mounting bolts. Install the 3 bolts attaching antilock modulator assembly to mounting bracket. Then torque the 3 modulator assembly to mounting bracket bolts to 21 Ft. lbs. (28 Nm).

19. Mount modulator and mounting bracket assembly, on the 3 mounting bolts on the side of the frame rail.

20. Torque rear bolt attaching modulator assembly mounting bracket to frame rail to 125 inch lbs. (14 Nm)

21. Raise and safely support the vehicle.

22. Torque the 2 front modulator assembly to frame rail mounting bolts to 12 inch lbs. (14 Nm)

23. Mount speed control servo and bracket, on modulator assembly mounting bracket. Install mounting bolt for speed control servo and torque to 250 inch lbs. (28 Nm).

24. Install vehicle's wiring harness 10 way connector onto modulator assembly. Be sure lock on vehicle wiring harness connector is fully engaged with tab on modulator assembly electrical connector.

25. Lower the vehicle.

26. Align the 6 disconnected hydraulic brake lines with their appropriate fitting locations on modulator assembly. Then thread the 6 brake line tube nuts by hand into the proportioning valves and thread savers on modulator assembly.

27. Using a crow foot and torque wrench, torque the 6 hydraulic brake line tube nuts to 159 inch lbs. (18 Nm). When torquing tube nuts hold thread savers and +proportioning valves with an open end wrench to prevent them from turning.

28. Using approved battery jumper cables, attach battery, to the vehicles negative and positive battery cables.

29. Bleed the vehicles base brake and Antilock brake hydraulic systems. Refer to Bleeding Bendix Antilock 4 Brake.

30. System in this section for required bleeding procedure.

31. Install acid shield onto modulator assembly. Be sure acid shield is securely attached to modulator assembly before installing battery tray support bracket.

32. Install battery tray support bracket in vehicle. Then install the 1 bolt attaching support bracket to frame rail Then torque the 3 bolts attaching battery tray support bracket to frame rail and modulator bracket to 125 inch lbs. (14 Nm).

33. Install CAB module/mounting bracket assembly, on battery tray support bracket. Then install CAB assembly mounting bolt and torque to 14 inch lbs. (5.5 Nm).

34. Install battery tray. Then install the 2 bolts mounting battery tray to battery tray support bracket and fender shield.

35. Install battery on battery tray. Then install and securely tighten battery hold down clamp.

36. Install battery cables on battery. Securely tighten clamping bolts on battery cable terminals.

37. Reset any electrical components of the vehicle which were affected by the removal of the battery.

38. Road test vehicle to verify correct operation of the vehicles's base and Antilock brake systems.

Proportioning Valve

REMOVAL

➡**Screw-in proportioning valves can be identified by numbers stamped on the body of the valve. Be sure to replace with the correct numbered valve. Proportioning valves should never be disassembled.**

1. Raise vehicle on jackstands or position vehicle centered on a frame contact hoist. See Hoisting in the Lubrication and Maintenance section of this manual.

2. Disconnect and remove both battery cables from battery.

3. Remove battery holddown clamp and battery from battery tray.

4. Remove the 2 bolts attaching battery tray to battery tray support bracket and frame rail. Remove battery tray from vehicle.

5. Remove bolt attaching CAB to battery tray support bracket, and remove CAB from battery tray support bracket.

➡**The CAB does not require removal from vehicle when servicing the modulator assembly.**

6. Loosen but do not remove (bracket is slotted) bolt attaching battery tray support bracket to modulator assembly mounting bracket.

7. Loosen but do not remove bottom bolt, (bracket is slotted) attaching battery tray support bracket to side of frame rail. Then loosen top bolt attaching battery tray support bracket to side of frame rail. Remove battery tray support bracket from vehicle.

8. Remove acid shield, from the ABS modulator assembly.

9. Remove the brake tube from the proportioning valve.

10. Remove the proportioning valve from the modulator.

To install:

11. Lightly coat the proportioning valve to modulator sealing ring with fresh clean brake fluid.

12. Install the proportioning valve into the modulator assembly by hand, until the O-ring seal is fully seated against the modulator assembly, then using a crow foot, torque the proportioning valve to 26 ft. lbs. (35 Nm).

13. Install the hydraulic brake line on the proportioning valve and hand start the tube nut into the proportioning valve. Torque the tube nut to 159 inch lbs. (18 Nm).

14. Using approved jumper cables, attach the battery to the vehicles negative and positive battery cables.

15. Bleed the vehicles base brake and Antilock brake hydraulic systems as outlined in this Section.

16. Install acid shield onto modulator assembly. Be sure acid shield is securely attached to modulator assembly before installing battery tray support bracket.

17. Install battery tray support bracket in vehicle. Then install the 1 bolt attaching support bracket to frame rail Then torque the 3 bolts attaching battery tray support bracket to frame rail and modulator bracket to 125 inch lbs. (14 Nm).

18. Install CAB module/mounting bracket assembly, on battery tray support bracket. Then install CAB assembly mounting bolt and torque to 14 inch lbs. (5.5 Nm).

19. Install battery tray. Then install the 2 bolts mounting battery tray to battery tray support bracket and fender shield.

20. Install battery on battery tray. Then install and securely tighten battery hold down clamp.

21. Install battery cables on battery. Securely tighten clamping bolts on battery cable terminals.

22. Reset any electrical components of the vehicle which were affected by the removal of the battery.

23. Road test vehicle to verify correct operation of the vehicles's base and Antilock brake systems.

Controller Antilock Brake (CAB)

REMOVAL

▶ **See Figures 128 and 129**

1. Turn the ignition OFF.

2. Disconnect and remove both battery cables from battery.

3. Remove battery holddown clamp and battery from battery tray.

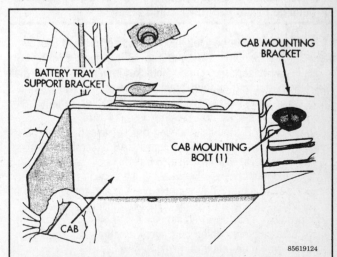

Fig. 128 Controller Antilock Brake (CAB) mounting to battery tray support bracket

85619124

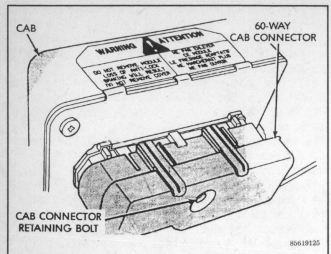

Fig. 129 Controller Antilock Brake (CAB) 60-way connector and retaining bolt

4. Remove the 2 bolts attaching battery tray to battery tray support bracket and frame rail. Remove battery tray from vehicle.

5. Remove bolt attaching CAB to battery tray support bracket, and remove CAB from battery tray support bracket.

❄❄WARNING

Before removing the 60-way connector from the CAB verify that the vehicle's ignition is in the OFF or LOCK position or damage to the controller could result.

6. Loosen the bolt retaining the wiring harness 60-way connector to the CAB, then disconnect the 60-way connector from the CAB by pulling it straight out without twisting.

7. Remove the CAB and mounting bracket from the vehicle.

To install:

❄❄WARNING

Before installing the 60-way connector from the CAB verify that the vehicle's ignition is in the OFF or LOCK position or damage to the controller could result.

8. Install the the bolt retaining the wiring harness 60-way connector to the CAB and tighten to 38 inch lbs. (4 Nm).

9. Install battery tray support bracket in vehicle. Then install the 1 bolt attaching support bracket to frame rail Then torque the 3 bolts attaching battery tray support bracket to frame rail and modulator bracket to 125 inch lbs. (14 Nm).

10. Install CAB module/mounting bracket assembly, on battery tray support bracket. Then install CAB assembly mounting bolt and torque to 14 inch lbs. (5.5 Nm).

11. Install battery tray. Then install the 2 bolts mounting battery tray to battery tray support bracket and fender shield.

12. Install battery on battery tray. Then install and securely tighten battery hold down clamp.

13. Install battery cables on battery. Securely tighten clamping bolts on battery cable terminals.

14. Reset any electrical components of the vehicle which were affected by the removal of the battery.

15. Road test vehicle to verify correct operation of the vehicles's base and Antilock brake systems.

Wheel Speed Sensors

REMOVAL & INSTALLATION

Front Wheel

▶ **See Figure 130**

1. Elevate and safely support the vehicle. Remove the wheel and tire.

2. Remove the screw from the sensor retaining clip.

3. Carefully remove the sensor wiring grommet from the fender shield.

4. Disconnect the sensor wiring from the ABS harness.

5. Remove the screws holding the sensor wiring tube to the fender well.

6. Remove the retainer grommets from the bracket on the strut.

7. Remove the fastener holding the sensor head.

8. Carefully remove the sensor head from the steering knuckle. Do not use pliers on the sensor head; if it is seized in place, use a hammer and small punch to tap the edge of the sensor ear. The tapping and side-to-side motion will free the unit.

To install:

9. Before installation, coat the sensor with high temperature multi-purpose grease.

10. Connect the speed sensor to the ABS harness.

11. Push the sensor assembly grommet into the hole in the fender shield. Install the retainer clip and screw.

12. Install the sensor grommets into the brackets on the fender shield and strut. Install the retainer clip at the strut.

13. On Van/wagons, install the sensor wiring tube and tighten the retaining bolts to 35 inch lbs. (4 Nm).

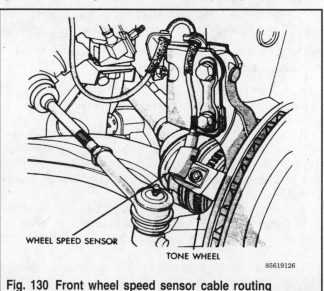

WHEEL SPEED SENSOR

TONE WHEEL

85619126

Fig. 130 Front wheel speed sensor cable routing

14. Install the sensor to the knuckle. Install the retaining screw and tighten it to 60 inch lbs. (7 Nm).

➡ **Proper installation of the sensor and its wiring is critical to system function. Make certain that wiring is installed in all retainers and clips. Wiring must be protected from moving parts and not be stretched during suspension movements.**

15. Install the tire and wheel. Lower the vehicle to the ground.

Rear Wheel
▶ **See Figures 131, 132 and 133**

1. Elevate and safely support the vehicle. Remove the wheel and tire.
2. Remove the sensor assembly grommet from the underbody and pull the harness through the hole in the body.
3. Disconnect the sensor wiring from the ABS harness.
4. Remove the 4 clips holding the sensor wiring along the underside.

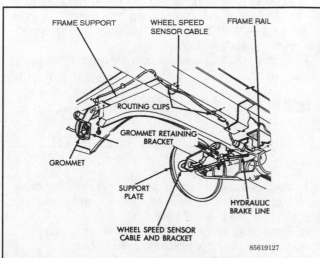

Fig. 131 Rear wheel speed sensor cable routing, front wheel drive equipped vehicles

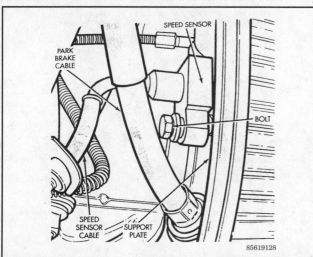

Fig. 132 Rear wheel speed sensor attaching bolt, front wheel drive equipped vehicles

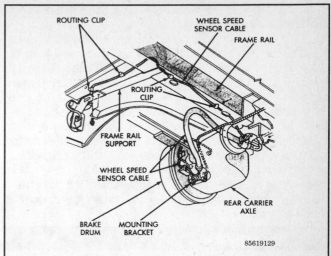

Fig. 133 Rear wheel speed sensor routing, All Wheel Drive equipped vehicles

5. Remove the attaching bracket holding the wiring to the frame rail.
6. On FWD Van/wagons, remove the nuts from the rear axle U-bolts. Remove the sensor mounting bracket.
7. Remove the fastener holding the sensor head.
8. Carefully remove the sensor head from the adapter assembly. Do not use pliers on the sensor head; if it is seized in place, use a hammer and small punch to tap the edge of the sensor ear. The tapping and side-to-side motion will free the unit.

To install:
9. Position the sensor bracket under the brake tube and start the outer attaching bolt by hand.
10. Align the brake tube clip and the bracket; install the retaining bolt.
11. Tighten both retaining bolts to 145 inch lbs. (17 Nm).
12. Before installation coat the sensor with high temperature, multi-purpose grease.
13. Install the sensor head into the rear axle and install the bolt. Tighten the bolt to 60 inch lbs. (7 Nm).
14. Carefully bend the rubber hose section of the sensor assembly toward the rear of the vehicle. Position the anti-rotation tab correctly and install the frame rail bracket. Tighten the bolt to 50 inch lbs. (5 Nm).
15. Connect the sensor wiring to the rear harness. Push the sensor assembly wiring grommet back into the hole.
16. Install the rear sensor grommet retaining bracket and tighten the 2 retaining bolts to 50 inch lbs. (5 Nm). Make certain the bracket does not pinch the sensor wiring.
17. Route the sensor wiring along the vehicle frame rail and install the 4 retaining clips.
18. install the rear wheel and tire; lower the vehicle to the ground.

Bendix Antilock 4 Modulator Bleeding Procedure

1. Assemble and install all brake system components on the vehicle, making sure all hydraulic fluid lines are installed and properly torqued.

2. Bleed the base brake system, using ONLY the bleeding procedure outlined in this section.

3. To perform the bleeding procedure on the ABS modulator assembly, the battery, battery tray and acid shield must be removed from vehicle. Then reconnect the vehicle's battery to vehicle's battery cables, using ONLY approved battery jumper cables.

4. Connect the DRB Diagnostics Tester to the vehicle's diagnostics connector. The vehicle diagnostic connector is located behind the fuse panel access cover on the lower section of the dash panel left of the steering column. The diagnostic connector is a blue 6 way connector.

5. Using the DRB check to make sure the CAB does not have any stored fault codes. If it does, remove them using the DRB..

✳✳WARNING

When bleeding the modulator assembly wear safety glasses. A clear bleed tube must be attached to the modulator bleed screws and submerged in a clear container filled part way with fresh clean brake fluid. Direct the flow of brake fluid away from the painted surfaces of the vehicle. Brake fluid at high pressure may come out of the bleeder screws, when opened.

6. When bleeding Antilock modulator assembly, the following bleeding sequence MUST be followed to insure a complete bleeding of all air from the Antilock brake, and base brake hydraulic systems. The modulator assembly can ONLY be bled using a manual bleeding procedure to pressurize the hydraulic system.

Modulator Assembly Circuit Bleeding Procedure And Sequence

1 MODULATOR PRIMARY CHECK VALVE CIRCUIT

▶ See Figure 134

➡To bleed hydraulic circuits of the Bendix Antilock 4 Brake System modulator assembly, the aid of a second mechanic or helper will be required to pump the brake pedal.

1. Install a clear bleed tube on the primary check valve circuit bleed screw. Then install bleed tube into a clear container partially filled with fresh clean brake fluid.

2. Pump brake pedal several times, then apply and hold a constant medium to heavy force on brake pedal.

3. Open primary check valve circuit bleed screw at least 1 full turn to ensure an adequate flow of brake fluid. Continue bleeding primary check valve circuit until brake pedal bottoms.

4. After brake pedal bottoms, close and tighten bleed screw. Then release brake pedal. Do not release brake pedal prior to closing and tightening bleed screw.

5. Continue bleeding modulator assembly, repeating Steps 2 through 4 until a clear, bubble free flow of brake fluid is evident.

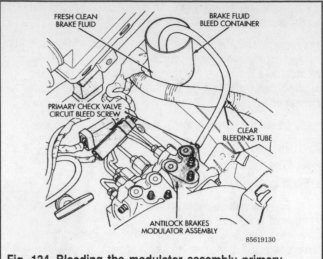

Fig. 134 Bleeding the modulator assembly primary check valve circuit

6. When all air is bled from primary check valve circuit, tighten bleed screw and remove bleed hose from bleed screw. Do not remove bleed hose before tightening bleed screw, air may re-enter modulator.

7. Torque modulator assembly primary bleed screw to 80 inch lbs. (9 Nm).

2 MODULATOR SECONDARY CHECK VALVE CIRCUIT

▶ See Figure 135

1. Move clear bleed tube to secondary check valve circuit bleed screw. Then install bleed tube into a container partially filled with fresh clean brake fluid.

2. Pump brake pedal several times, then apply and hold a constant medium to heavy force on brake pedal.

3. Open secondary check valve circuit bleeder screw, at least 1 full turn to ensure an adequate flow of brake fluid.

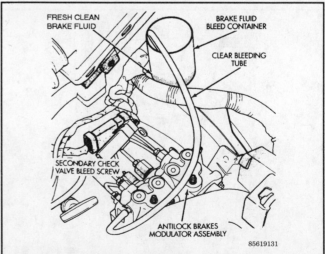

Fig. 135 Bleeding the modulator assembly secondary check valve circuit

Continue to bleed secondary check valve circuit until the brake pedal bottoms.

4. After brake pedal bottoms, close and tighten bleed screw and release brake pedal. Do not release brake pedal prior to closing and tightening bleed screw.

5. Continue bleeding secondary check valve circuit, repeating Steps 2 through 4, until a clear, bubble free flow of brake fluid is evident.

6. When air is bled from primary check valve circuit, tighten bleed screw and remove bleed hose from bleed screw. Do not remove bleed hose before tightening bleed screw, air may re-enter modulator.

7. Torque modulator assembly primary bleed screw to 80 inch lbs. (9 Nm).

3 MODULATOR ASSEMBLY PRIMARY SUMP CIRCUIT

▶ **See Figure 136**

1. Move clear bleed tube to primary sump bleed screw. Then install bleed tube into a container partially filled with fresh clean brake fluid.

2. Pump brake pedal several times, then apply and hold a constant medium to heavy force on brake pedal.

3. Open modulator assembly primary sump circuit bleed screw at least 1 full turn. This will ensure an adequate flow of brake fluid from the primary sump circuit.

4. Using the DRB, select the bleed ABS hydraulic unit mode. Then select the primary circuit. (The RF and LR solenoids will alternately fire for five seconds). Using the DRB, continue to select the primary circuit until an air-free flow of brake fluid from primary sump bleed screw is maintained or brake pedal bottoms. If an air-free flow is not maintained before brake pedal bottoms, close bleed screw and repeat Steps 2 to 4, until an air free flow is maintained.

5. After an air-free flow of brake fluid is maintained from primary sump bleed screw, close and lightly tighten bleeder screw. Then release brake pedal. Do not release brake pedal prior to closing and tightening bleeder screw.

6. After primary sump bleed screw is closed, remove bleed hose from primary sump bleed screw.

7. Torque modulator assembly primary sump bleed screw to 9 N.m (18 in. lbs.).

4 MODULATOR ASSEMBLY PRIMARY ACCUMULATOR CIRCUIT

▶ **See Figure 137**

1. Transfer clear bleed tube to primary accumulator bleed screw. Then install bleed tube into a container partially filled with fresh clean brake fluid.

2. Pump brake pedal several times, then apply a constant medium to heavy force on the brake pedal. Using the DRB, select the bleed ABS hydraulic unit mode. Then select the primary circuit valves. (The RF and LR modulator assembly solenoids will fire for 5 seconds).

3. Open the modulator assembly primary accumulator circuit bleed screw at least one full turn. This will ensure an adequate flow of brake fluid from the primary accumulator circuit. Continue bleeding primary accumulator circuit until an air-free flow of brake fluid from bleed screw is maintained or the brake pedal bottoms. If an air-free flow of brake fluid is not maintained before brake pedal bottoms, close bleed screw and repeat Steps 1 and 2 until an air free flow is maintained.

4. After an air-free flow of brake fluid is maintained from the primary accumulator bleed screw, close and lightly tighten bleed screw. Then release pressure from brake pedal. Do not release force from brake pedal prior to closing and tightening bleed screw.

➡ **For the next modulator assembly bleeding procedure, use of the DRB is not required. This step of the bleed procedure does not require modulator solenoids to be operated for bleeding to be performed.**

5. Pump brake pedal several times, then apply and hold a constant medium to heavy force on the brake pedal.

6. Again without firing modulator solenoids, open primary accumulator circuit bleed screw 1 full turn. This will ensure an

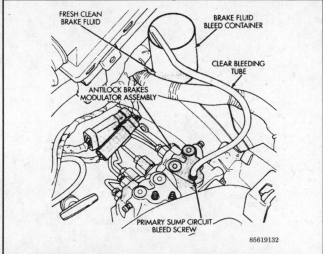

Fig. 136 Bleeding the modulator assembly primary sump circuit

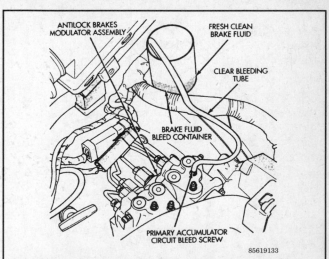

Fig. 137 Bleeding the modulator assembly primary accumulator circuit

adequate flow of brake fluid from the primary accumulator circuit.

7. Bleed primary accumulator circuit until a clear, air-free flow of brake fluid is maintained from the accumulator bleed screw or the brake pedal bottoms. If an air-free flow of brake fluid is not maintained from the bleed screw before the brake pedal bottoms. First, close bleed screw and then repeat Steps 4 and 5 of this bleeding procedure until an air-free flow is maintained.

8. After an air-free flow of brake fluid is maintained from the primary accumulator circuit bleed screw, close and lightly tighten bleed screw. Then release force from brake pedal. Do not release force from brake pedal prior to closing and tightening bleeder screw.

9. After primary accumulator bleed screw is closed, remove bleed hose from bleed screw.

10. Torque primary accumulator bleed screw to 9 N.m (80 in. lbs.).

5 MODULATOR ASSEMBLY SECONDARY SUMP CIRCUIT

▶ **See Figure 138**

1. Transfer clear bleed tube to secondary sump bleed screw on modulator assembly. Then install bleed tube into a container partially filled with fresh clean brake fluid.

2. Pump brake pedal several times, then apply and hold a constant medium to heavy force on brake pedal.

3. Open the secondary sump circuit bleed screw at least 1 full turn. This will ensure an adequate flow of brake fluid is expelled from the secondary sump circuit.

4. Using the DRB, select the bleed ABS hydraulic unit mode. Then select the secondary circuit valves. (The LF and RR solenoids will alternately fire for five seconds). Continue bleeding secondary sump circuit until an air-free flow of brake fluid from secondary sump bleed screw is maintained or brake pedal bottoms. If an air-free flow of brake fluid is not maintained before brake pedal bottoms, close bleed screw and repeat Steps 2 through 4 until an air-free flow is maintained.

5. After an air-free flow of brake fluid is maintained from secondary sump bleed screw, close and lightly tighten bleed screw. Then release force from brake pedal. Do not release brake pedal prior to closing and tightening bleeder screw.

6. After secondary sump bleed screw is closed, remove bleed hose from bleed screw.

7. Torque secondary sump bleed screw to 80 inch lbs. (9 Nm).

6 MODULATOR ASSEMBLY SECONDARY ACCUMULATOR CIRCUIT

▶ **See Figure 139**

1. Transfer bleed tube to secondary accumulator bleed screw. Then install bleed tube into a container partially filled with fresh clean brake fluid.

2. Apply constant, medium to heavy force on brake pedal. Then using the DRB, select the bleed ABS hydraulic unit mode,and then select the secondary circuit valves. (The LF and RR modulator assembly solenoids will fire for 5 seconds).

3. Open the secondary accumulator circuit bleed screw at least one full turn. This will ensure an adequate flow of brake fluid is expedded from the secondary accumulator circuit. Continue to bleed primary accumulator circuit, until an air-free flow of brake fluid from the bleed screw is maintained or brake pedal bottoms. If an air-free flow of brake fluid is not maintained from bleed screw before brake pedal bottoms, close bleed screw and then repeat Steps 1 and 2 until an air free flow is maintained.

4. After an air-free flow of brake fluid is maintained from the bleed screw, close and lightly tighten the bleed screw. Then release force from brake pedal.

5. Do not release force from brake pedal prior to closing and tightening bleeder screw.

➡ **For the next modulator assembly bleeding procedure, use of the DRB is not required. This step of the bleeding procedure does not require the modulator solenoids to be operated for bleeding to be performed.**

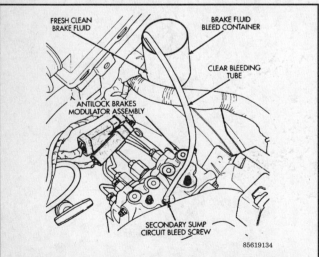

Fig. 138 Bleeding the modulator assembly secondary sump circuit

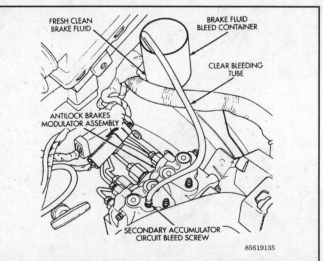

Fig. 139 Bleeding the modulator assembly secondary accumulator circuit

6. Pump brake pedal several times, then apply and hold constant medium to heavy force on brake pedal.

7. Again without firing modulator assembly solenoids, open secondary accumulator circuit bleed screw at least 1 full turn. This will ensure an adequate flow of brake fluid is expelled from the secondary accumulator circuit.

8. Bleed secondary accumulator circuit until a clear, air-free flow of brake fluid is maintained from the secondary accumulator bleed screw or the brake pedal bottoms. If an air-free flow of brake fluid is not maintained from secondary accumulator bleed screw before brake pedal bottoms. Repeat Steps 5 and

6 of this bleeding procedure until an air-free flow is maintained from the bleeder screw.

9. After an air free flow of brake fluid is maintained from secondary accumulator circuit bleed screw, close and lightly tighten bleed screw. Then release force from brake pedal. Do not release force from brake pedal prior to closing and tightening bleed screw.

10. After secondary accumulator bleed screw is closed, remove bleed hose from bleed screw.

11. Torque secondary accumulator bleed screw to 80 inch lbs. (9 Nm).

BRAKE SPECIFICATIONS
All measurements in inches unless noted.

Year	Model	Master Cylinder Bore	Brake Disc Original Thickness	Brake Disc Minimum Thickness	Brake Disc Maximum Runout	Brake Drum Diameter Original Inside Diameter	Brake Drum Diameter Max. Wear Limit	Brake Drum Diameter Maximum Machine Diameter	Minimum Lining Thickness Front	Minimum Lining Thickness Rear
1984	Caravan/Voyager	0.940	0.861	0.80	0.005	9.00	9.09	9.06	0.06	0.06
1985	Caravan/Voyager	0.940	0.861	0.80	0.005	9.00	9.09	9.06	0.06	0.06
1986	Caravan/Voyager	0.940	0.861	0.80	0.005	9.00	9.09	9.06	0.06	0.06
1987	Caravan/Voyager	0.940	0.861	0.80	0.005	9.00	9.09	9.06	0.06	0.06
1988	Caravan/Voyager	0.940	0.861	0.80	0.005	9.00	9.09	9.06	0.06	0.06
1989	Caravan/Voyager	0.940	0.861	0.80	0.005	9.00	9.09	9.06	0.06	0.06
1990	Caravan/Voyager	0.940	0.861	0.80	0.005	9.00	9.09	9.06	0.06	0.06
1991	Caravan/Voyager/Town & Country	0.940	0.861	0.80	0.005	9.00	9.09	9.06	0.06	0.06
1992	Caravan/Voyager/Town & Country	0.940	0.861	0.80	0.005	9.00	9.09	9.06	0.06	0.06
1993	Caravan/Voyager/Town & Country	0.940	0.940	0.88	0.005	9.00	9.09	9.06	0.06	0.06
1994	Caravan/Voyager/Town & Country	0.940	0.940	0.88	0.005	9.00	9.09	9.06	0.06	0.06

85619C01

TORQUE SPECIFICATIONS

Component	English	Metric
Accumulator pump/motor assembly		
High pressure hose-to-hydraulic assembly	12 ft. lbs.	16 Nm
Low pressure hose-to-hydraulic assembly	10 inch lbs.	1 Nm
Hydraulic assembly attaching nuts	21 ft. lbs.	28 Nm
Brake line to hydraulic assembly	12 ft. lbs.	16 Nm
Proportioning valve attaching nuts	30 ft. lbs.	40 Nm
Pressure line banjo bolt	13 ft. lbs.	17 Nm
Bleeder screws	8 ft. lbs.	10 Nm
Height sensing dual proportioning valve mounting bolts	13 ft. lbs.	18 Nm
Master cylinder mounting bolts	17–25 ft. lbs.	23–34 Nm
Power booster-to-firewall mounting stud nuts	17–25 ft. lbs.	23–34 Nm
Hydraulic reservoir high pressure hose banjo fitting	10 ft. lbs.	13 Nm
Hydraulic bladder accumulator-to-hydraulic assembly	30 ft. lbs.	40 Nm
Front wheel speed sensor wiring tube retaining bolts	35 inch lbs.	4 Nm
Front wheel sensor-to-knuckle retaining screw	60 inch lbs.	7 Nm
Rear wheel speed sensor retaining bolts	60 inch lbs.	7 Nm
Rear wheel speed sensor-to-rear axle	60 inch lbs.	7 Nm
Rear wheel speed sensor frame rail bracket bolt	50 inch lbs.	5 Nm
Caliper guide pins	25–35 ft. lbs.	34–48 Nm
Wheel lug nuts	95 ft. lbs.	129 Nm

85619C02

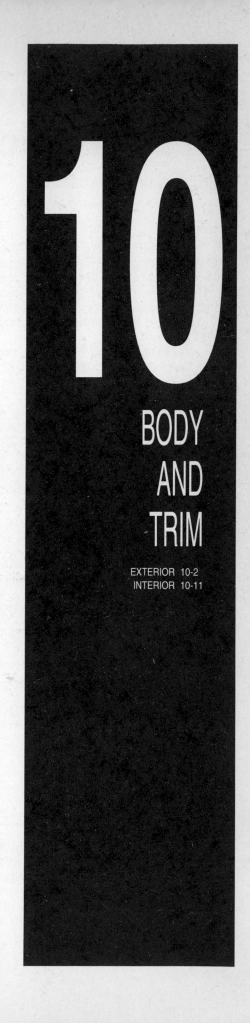

10

BODY AND TRIM

EXTERIOR

Front Doors

REMOVAL & INSTALLATION

1984-90

1. Open the front door and remove the inner door panel covering. Disconnect the interior light wiring harness and feed it through the access hole. Disconnect the door swing stop.
2. Open the door wide enough to gain access to the hinge bolts. Place a padded support under the door edge that will hold the door in a level position when the hinges have been unbolted from the frame.
3. Scribe around the door hinge on the door frame. Remove the hinge mounting bolts, lower hinge first, then the upper, from the door frame.
4. Remove the door.
5. Place the door on the padded support and install the hinge mounting bolts until they are snug enough to support the door, but not tight enough to prevent door adjustment. Adjust the door position until correctly aligned and tighten the hinge bolts. Adjust the striker as necessary. Connect the door stop and interior light harness. Install the inner trim panel.

1991-94

1. Remove the door trim panel, silencer pad and water shield.
2. Disconnect all wire connectors and wire harness hold downs inside of the door, and push the harness through the access hole in the front of the door.
3. Open the door and support it with a jack, an assistant should also be used to hold the door.
4. Using a hammer and punch, drive the bottom hinge pin upward and remove the pin from the hinge.
5. Drive the upper hinge pin from the hinge and remove it. Separate the door from the vehicle.
To install:
6. Install the door assembly on the hinges.
7. Install the hinge pins, by tapping them into position.
8. The door should not require any re-alignment. Install the wiring harness into the door.
9. Install the trim panel.

ALIGNMENT

The front doors should be adjusted so that there is a ¼ in. (6mm) gap between the edge of the front fender and the edge of the door, and a ¼ in. (6mm) gap between the back edge of the door and the lock pillar. Adjust the door to position and raise or lower it so that the stamped edge line matches the body panel line. Secure the door in proper position after necessary adjustments.

Front Door Hinge

REMOVAL & INSTALLATION

1991-94

1. Raise the front of the vehicle slightly.
2. Remove the wheel and tire assembly.
3. Remove the inner fender, plastic splash shield retaining screws and remove the shield.
4. Support the door assembly. Remove the door retaining pin on the hinge to be replaced.
5. Remove the hinge plate retaining bolts from inside the fender well.
6. Remove the hinge assembly.
To install:
7. Install the hinge plate in position and install the retaining bolts. Do not tighten them completely.
8. Install the hinge pin and check the door alignment, there should be a ¼ in. (6mm) gap around the sides of the door.
9. Tighten the hinge mounting bolts.
10. Install the inner fender splash shield and install the wheel.
11. Lower the vehicle.

Sliding Door

▶ **See Figures 1, 2 and 3**

REMOVAL & INSTALLATION

➡**When removing the sliding door as an assembly, it is not necessary to remove or loosen bolts that would change the doors alignment.**

1. Remove the sliding door upper track cover.

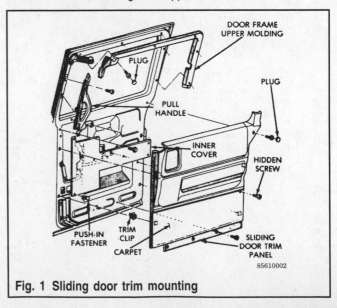

Fig. 1 Sliding door trim mounting

should be ¼ in. (6mm). The stamped edge line of the front door the sliding door and the quarter panel should be in line.

2. Remove the hinge trim panels and adjust the sliding door in the direction(s) required. Refer to the illustration provided for adjustment direction.

Liftgate

REMOVAL & INSTALLATION

▶ **See Figure 5**

1. Support the liftgate in the full opened position.
2. Scribe a mark on the liftgate to mark the hinge positions.
3. Place masking tape on the roof edge and liftgate edge to protect the paint surfaces during removal and installation.
4. Remove the liftgate prop fasteners and remove the props.
5. Have a helper on hand to support the liftgate. Remove the hinge mounting bolts and remove the liftgate.

To install:

6. Raise the liftgate into position and install the hinge mounting bolts. Tighten the bolts until they are snug, but not tight enough to prevent liftgate adjustment.
7. Shift the liftgate until the hinge scribe marks are in position and tighten the hinge mounting bolts.
8. Attach and secure the liftgate props.

Hood

REMOVAL & INSTALLATION

▶ **See Figures 6, 7, 8 and 9**

1. Raise the hood to its full open position.
2. Remove the cowl cover retaining screws, remove the wiper arms and remove the cowl cover.
3. Disconnect the under hood light connector.
4. Mark all bolt and hinge attachment points with a grease pencil or equivalent, to provide reference marks for installation.
5. Remove the top hood-to-hinge attaching bolts and loosen the bottom bolts until they can be removed by hand.
6. With the aid of a helper, support the hood and remove the hinge bolts.
7. Move the hood away from the vehicle and store it in a way to prevent it from being damaged.

To install:

8. With the aid of a helper, position the hood on the hinges and install the lower hinge bolt finger tight.
9. Install the remaining hinge bolts and align the hinge marks. Tighten the bolts.

➡**When the hood is properly aligned there should be a 4mm clearance at the fenders and the hood should be flush in height with the top of the fenders.**

10. Connect the under hood light and install the cowl cover. Install the wiper arms.
11. Check the hood latch operation.

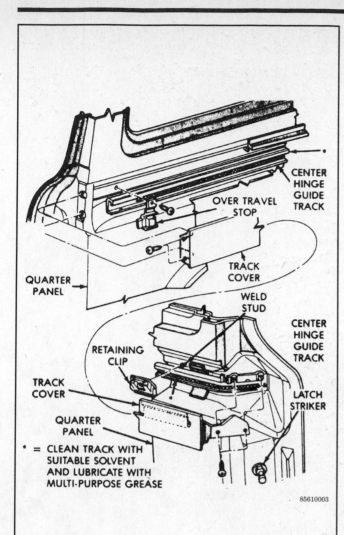

Fig. 2 Sliding door center track cover and over travel stop mounting

2. Remove the upper track over travel stop.
3. Remove the sill plate.
4. Remove the lower track over travel stop.
5. With the help of an assistant, roll the door back and out of its tracks.

To install:

6. Position the door carefully on its tracks and roll it into position.
7. Install the track over travel stops.
8. Install the sill plate.
9. Install the upper track cover.

ALIGNMENT

▶ **See Figure 4**

1. The gap between the back edge of the front door and the front edge of the sliding door should be ⁵⁄₁₆ in. (8mm). The gap between the sliding door edge and the quarter panel

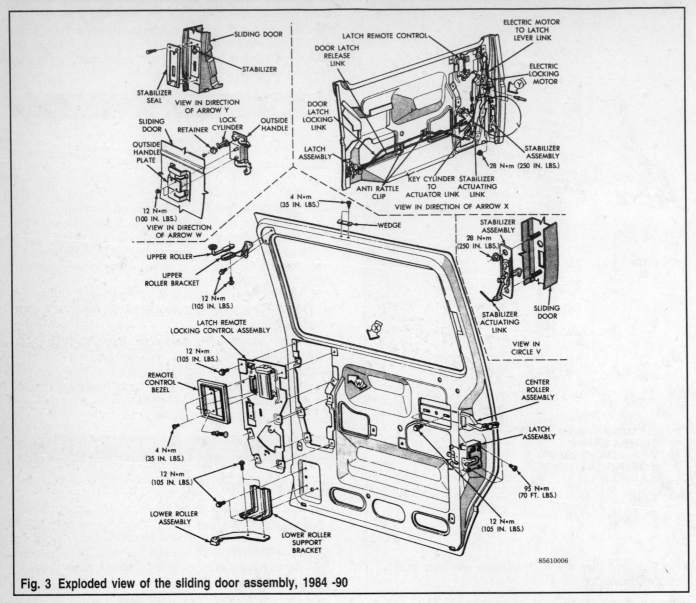

SLIDING DOOR

STABILIZER

STABILIZER SEAL

VIEW IN DIRECTION OF ARROW Y

LATCH REMOTE CONTROL

DOOR LATCH RELEASE LINK

ELECTRIC MOTOR TO LATCH LEVER LINK

ELECTRIC LOCKING MOTOR

SLIDING DOOR

RETAINER

LOCK CYLINDER

OUTSIDE HANDLE

OUTSIDE HANDLE PLATE

DOOR LATCH LOCKING LINK

LATCH ASSEMBLY

STABILIZER ASSEMBLY

28 N•m (250 IN. LBS.)

12 N•m (100 IN. LBS.)

VIEW IN DIRECTION OF ARROW W

ANTI RATTLE CLIP

KEY CYLINDER TO ACTUATOR LINK

STABILIZER ACTUATING LINK

4 N•m (35 IN. LBS.)

WEDGE

VIEW IN DIRECTION OF ARROW X

STABILIZER ASSEMBLY

28 N•m (250 IN. LBS.)

UPPER ROLLER

UPPER ROLLER BRACKET

12 N•m (105 IN. LBS.)

STABILIZER ACTUATING LINK

SLIDING DOOR

VIEW IN CIRCLE V

LATCH REMOTE LOCKING CONTROL ASSEMBLY

12 N•m (105 IN. LBS.)

REMOTE CONTROL BEZEL

CENTER ROLLER ASSEMBLY

LATCH ASSEMBLY

4 N•m (35 IN. LBS.)

12 N•m (105 IN. LBS.)

95 N•m (70 FT. LBS.)

LOWER ROLLER ASSEMBLY

LOWER ROLLER SUPPORT BRACKET

12 N•m (105 IN. LBS.)

85610006

Fig. 3 Exploded view of the sliding door assembly, 1984 -90

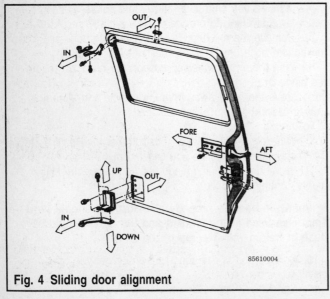

OUT

IN

FORE

AFT

UP

OUT

IN

DOWN

85610004

Fig. 4 Sliding door alignment

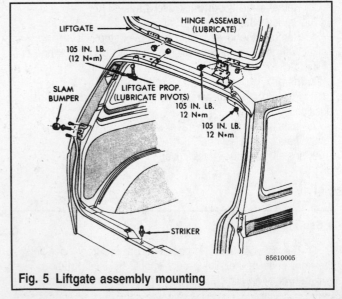

LIFTGATE

HINGE ASSEMBLY (LUBRICATE)

105 IN. LB. (12 N•m)

SLAM BUMPER

LIFTGATE PROP. (LUBRICATE PIVOTS)

105 IN. LB. 12 N•m

105 IN. LB. 12 N•m

STRIKER

85610005

Fig. 5 Liftgate assembly mounting

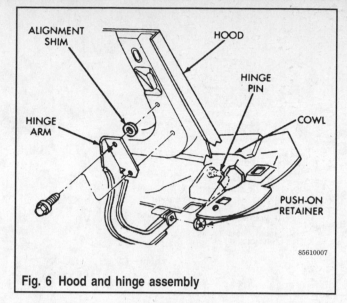

Fig. 6 Hood and hinge assembly

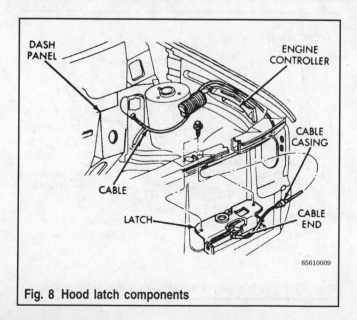

Fig. 7 Hood safety catch assembly

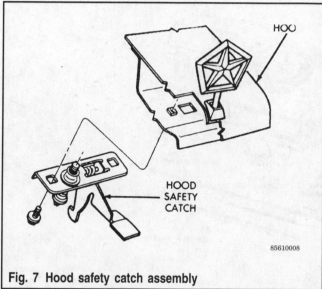

Fig. 8 Hood latch components

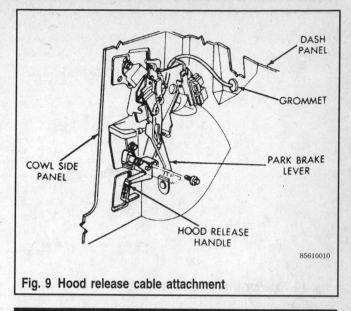

Fig. 9 Hood release cable attachment

Exterior Moldings and Body Side Appliques

REMOVAL & INSTALLATION

1991-94 Models
▶ See Figures 10 and 11

All of the 1991-94 models have various body moldings and applique panels, that are used to dress the appearance of the exterior of the vehicle. All of these trim pieces are either screwed or snapped in place.

1. Remove the screws that retain the trim piece being removed, these will be either under the edge of the trim or at the wheel openings. In some instances there will be clips holding the trim as well as screws. When removing front or rear bumper trim, be sure to remove all retaining bolts.

2. Once the screws are removed, lift the piece away from the vehicle, making sure no clips or screws are still in place.

3. When removing the side applique panels, they will need to be lifted slightly to release them from the tracks that retain them.

4. Install the replacement piece(s) in position and secure with screws or clips as needed. If replacing the trim piece, be sure to transfer any clips to the replacement. Install all front or rear bumper retaining bolts.

Bumpers

REMOVAL & INSTALLATION

▶ See Figures 12, 13, 14, 15, 16 and 17

1. Remove the end cap to bumper mounting screw and the two end cap to fender nuts from both ends of the bumper. On 1991 models, remove the necessary trim pieces from the vehicle.

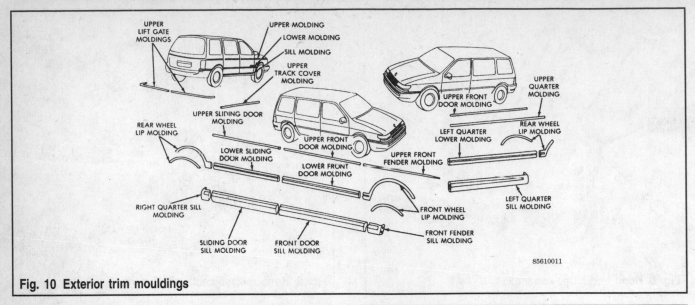

Fig. 10 Exterior trim mouldings

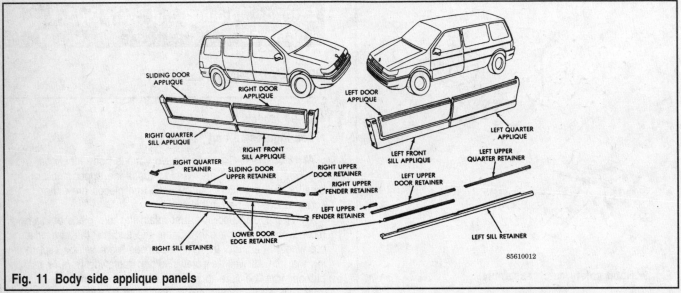

Fig. 11 Body side applique panels

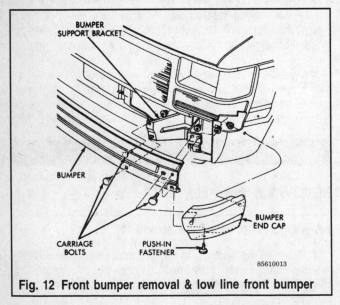

Fig. 12 Front bumper removal & low line front bumper

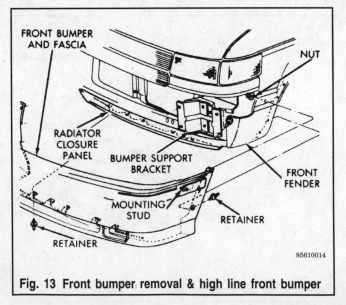

Fig. 13 Front bumper removal & high line front bumper

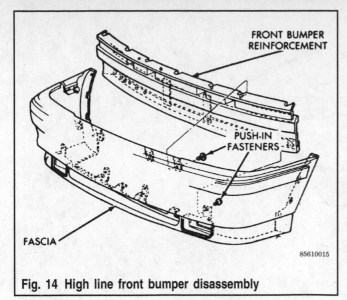

Fig. 14 High line front bumper disassembly

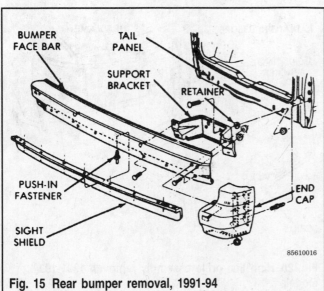

Fig. 15 Rear bumper removal, 1991-94

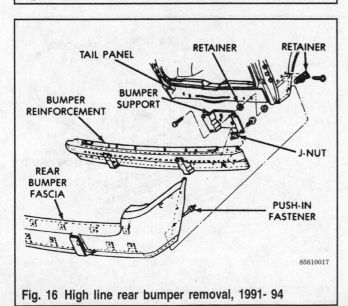

Fig. 16 High line rear bumper removal, 1991- 94

2. Remove the end cap to bumper nut and remove the end cap from both ends of the bumper.

3. Support the lower edge of the bumper on a padded jack.

4. Remove the bolts that mount the bumper to the body brackets and remove the bumper.

To install:

5. Place the bumper into the proper position, use a padded jack to support the bumper, and install the bracket to bumper mounting bolts. Tighten the bolts until they are snug. but not tight enough to prevent shifting of the bumper for proper centering.

6. Adjust bumper placement as required. Tighten the mounting bolts. Install the bumper end caps. On 1991 -94 models install the trim pieces.

Grille

REMOVAL & INSTALLATION

1984-1990 Models

◗ **See Figure 18**

1. Remove the screws from the headlamp bezels. Remove the screws from the sides of the grille.

2. Remove the screws from the grille to center support bracket.

3. Remove the grille.

4. Place the grille into position. Install the center support screws and the outer mounting screws. Center the grille and tighten the mounting screws.

5. Install the headlamp bezel screws.

1991-94 Models

◗ **See Figures 19 and 20**

There are 2 grille types used, one type incorporates the headlamp doors and the grille, the other is just the center grille assembly with separate headlamp doors.

1. Remove the bolt holding the grille to the radiator bracket, in front of the radiator.

2. On the one piece models, remove the headlight and turn signal lenses.

3. Remove the screws that retain the grille to the front headlight assemblies.

4. Remove the grille from the vehicle.

5. Install the grille in position, make sure it is positioned correctly.

Outside Mirrors

REMOVAL & INSTALLATION

◗ **See Figure 21**

1. Remove the door trim panel.

2. Remove the adjustment knob with an Allen wrench. Remove the screw cover plug and the mirror inner bezel mounting screws. Remove the bezel.

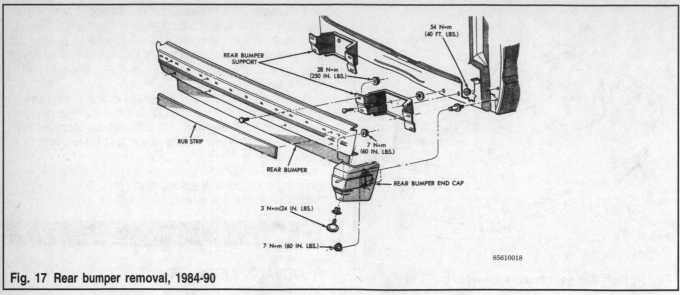

Fig. 17 Rear bumper removal, 1984-90

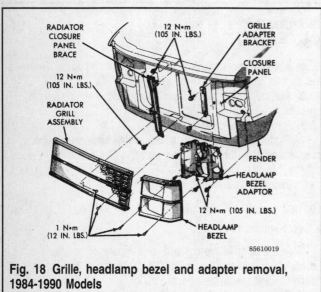

Fig. 18 Grille, headlamp bezel and adapter removal, 1984-1990 Models

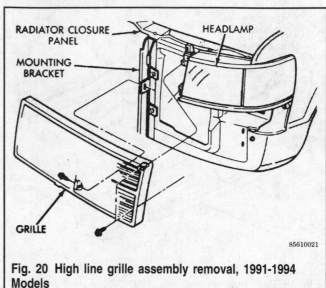

Fig. 20 High line grille assembly removal, 1991-1994 Models

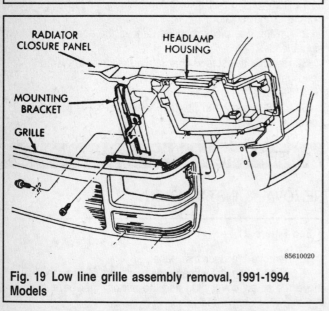

Fig. 19 Low line grille assembly removal, 1991-1994 Models

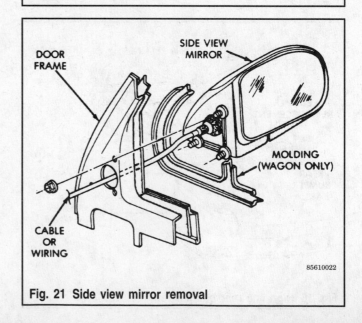

Fig. 21 Side view mirror removal

3. Remove the mirror mounting nuts and the mirror. If equipped with power mirrors, disconnect the electrical lead.

4. Place the mirror into position and install the mounting nuts. Connect the electrical lead, if equipped.

5. Place the bezel into position and install the mounting screws and cover plug.

6. Install the control knob and trim panel.

Antenna

Refer to Section 6 for antenna servicing under the Radio section.

Fenders and Splash Shields

REMOVAL & INSTALLATION

▶ **See Figures 22, 23, 24, 25, 26 and 27**

1. Remove the splash shields from the inner fender wells.

➡**Raising the vehicle slightly and removing the wheel and tire, will make splash shield removal easier.**

2. Remove the under vehicle splash shields where equipped, one will cover the transaxle and the other will be covering the accessory drive belts.

3. Remove the grille and headlamp assemblies.

4. Remove the bolts holding the vehicle jacking pad under the vehicle and remove the pad.

5. Remove the bolts holding the fender to the hinge pillar from inside the wheel opening.

6. Remove the bolts holding the fender to the rocker panel.

7. Remove the bolts holding the fender to the lower radiator panel.

8. Remove the remaining bolts along the top edge of the fender on the cowl side panel.

9. Remove the fender from the vehicle.

To install:

10. Install the fender in position on the vehicle.

11. Install the fender retaining bolts, but do not tighten.

12. Align the fender to $\frac{1}{4}$ in. (6mm) gap at the door and $\frac{5}{16}$ in. (8mm) at the edge of the hood.

13. Tighten all of the fender mounting bolts.

14. Install the splash shields, using new retainers.

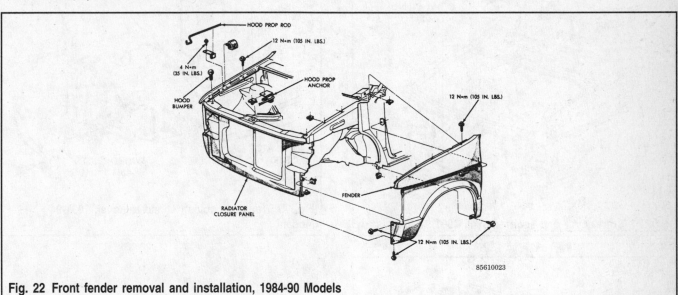

Fig. 22 Front fender removal and installation, 1984-90 Models

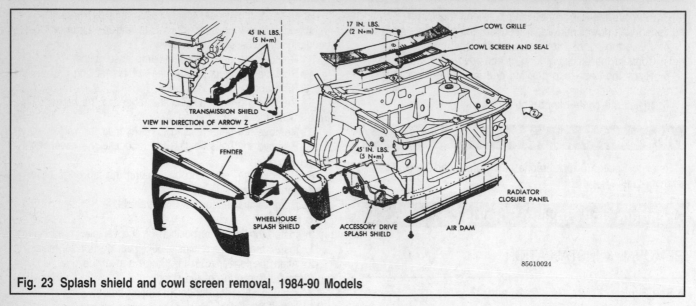

Fig. 23 Splash shield and cowl screen removal, 1984-90 Models

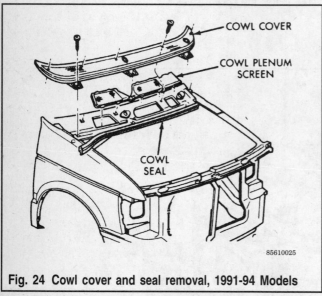

Fig. 24 Cowl cover and seal removal, 1991-94 Models

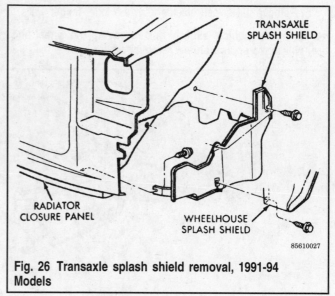

Fig. 26 Transaxle splash shield removal, 1991-94 Models

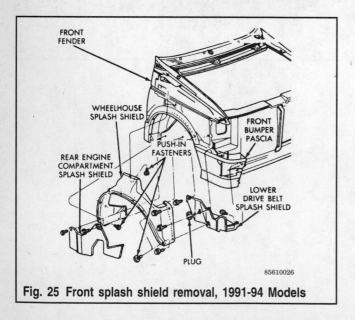

Fig. 25 Front splash shield removal, 1991-94 Models

INTERIOR

Door Panels

REMOVAL & INSTALLATION

▶ **See Figures 28 and 29**

1. Lower the door glass until it is 3 in. (76mm) from the full down position.

2. Unlock the door and remove the remote door latch control handle bezel by prying the front of the bezel out and rearward.

3. Remove the arrest mounting screw, and on models with electric controls, pry out the power window switch bezel.

4. Remove the window crank handle on models with manual window regulators.

5. Remove the two edge inserts that cover the mounting screws for the door pull strap, and remove the mounting screws and strap.

6. Insert a wide flat tool between the panel and door frame and carefully twist the tool to unfasten the retainer clips from the door.

7. If the vehicle is equipped with power locks, slide the switch bezel through the trim panel.

8. Disconnect the courtesy lamp connector. Remove the door trim panel.

9. Remove the inner plastic cover and service the components as required.

To install:

10. Place sealer along the edges of the plastic liner and put the liner onto the door frame.

11. Potion the trim panel, slide the power lock bezel through the panel, connect the courtesy lamp.

12. Potion the panel clips over their mounting holes and push the panel against the door frame to lock the clips.

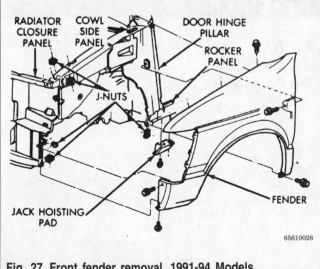

Fig. 27 Front fender removal, 1991-94 Models

RADIATOR CLOSURE PANEL
COWL SIDE PANEL
DOOR HINGE PILLAR
ROCKER PANEL
J-NUTS
JACK HOISTING PAD
FENDER
85610028

13. Install the pull strap, the arrest, widow handle/power switch, remote latch control/bezel.

Interior Trim Panels

REMOVAL & INSTALLATION

▶ **See Figures 30, 31, 32, 33 and 34**

All of the trim panels on the interior of the vehicle can be removed easily, by removing their retaining screws and separating them from each other. Almost all of the trim pieces are fastened with screws, most of the screws are visible, however a few have removable caps.

The interior trim panels can be removed without removing any of the interior components of the vehicle, such as seats, etc. Remove the panels carefully to avoid damaging them. In some cases, the trim may be attached with a hidden retaining clip. If the panel is fixed with a clip, remove it by gently prying it away from the clip.

The following is a recommended sequence for removing the trim pieces. Since the trim pieces overlap, this method of removal will avoid any damage.

1. Windshield surround trim and side garnish molding.

2. Front door scuff plate.

3. 'B' pillar trim, seat belt cover and seat belt assembly.

4. Sliding door upper track cover.

5. Sliding door scuff plate.

6. Liftgate scuff plate.

7. Quarter panel trim. On 1991 Models, remove the upper quarter panel trim, then the lower. If equipped with rear air conditioning, remove the vents from the trim panels.

Install the trim panels by reversing the order in which they were removed. Be sure to position the panels correctly, this will help to avoid squeaks and possible warpage.

Door Locks/Latch

REMOVAL & INSTALLATION

▶ **See Figures 35, 36 and 37**

This procedure can be used for both the front and sliding doors.

1. Remove the door trim panel and inner cover.

2. Raise the window to the full up position.

3. Disconnect all the locking clips from the remote linkage at the latch.

4. Remove the retaining screws at the door edge and remove the latch assembly.

5. Position the latch to the door frame and secure it with the retaining screws.

6. Connect all of the remote linkage to the latch levers.

7. Check latch operation. Install the inner cover and door trim panel.

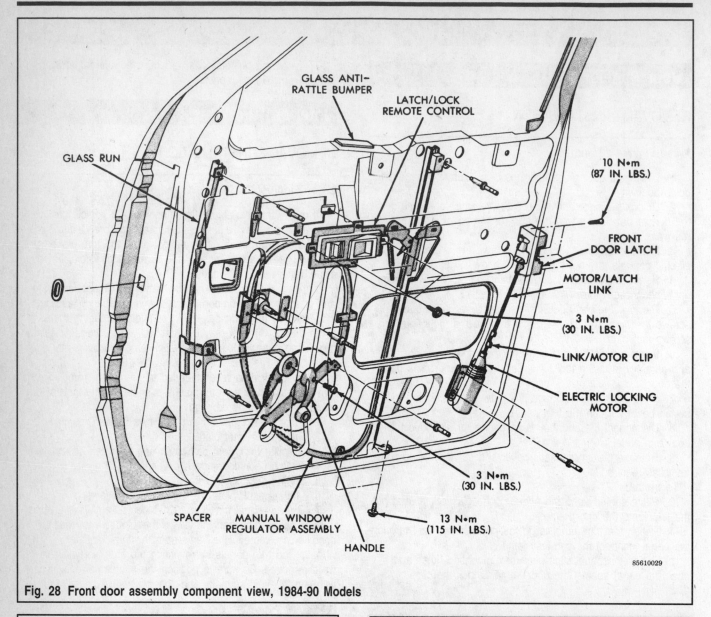

Fig. 28 Front door assembly component view, 1984-90 Models

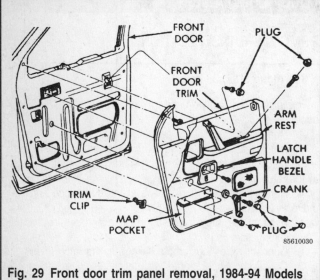

Fig. 29 Front door trim panel removal, 1984-94 Models

Door Glass Regulator

REMOVAL & INSTALLATION

▶ **See Figures 38, 39, 40 and 41**

1. Remove the door trim panel and inner liner.

2. Remove the window glass from the regulator and the door.

3. If equipped with power windows, disconnect the wiring harness and remove the retainer clip.

4. Drill out the regulator mounting rivets. Their are five on vehicles equipped with electric windows, and six if equipped with manual windows.

5. Remove the regulator through the larger access hole. Rotate the regulator through the hole as required for removal.

To install:

6. Install the regulator to the mounting holes using ¼-20 · ½ in. screws and nuts. Tighten the screws to 90 inch lbs.

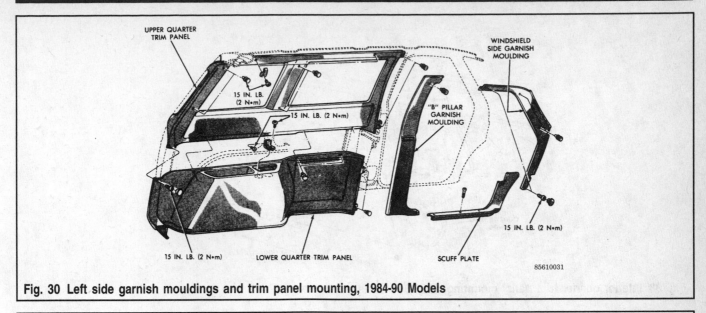

Fig. 30 Left side garnish mouldings and trim panel mounting, 1984-90 Models

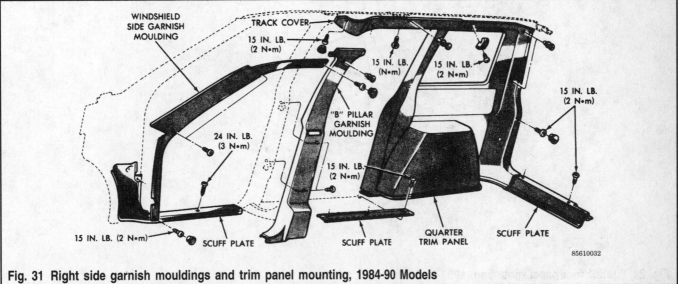

Fig. 31 Right side garnish mouldings and trim panel mounting, 1984-90 Models

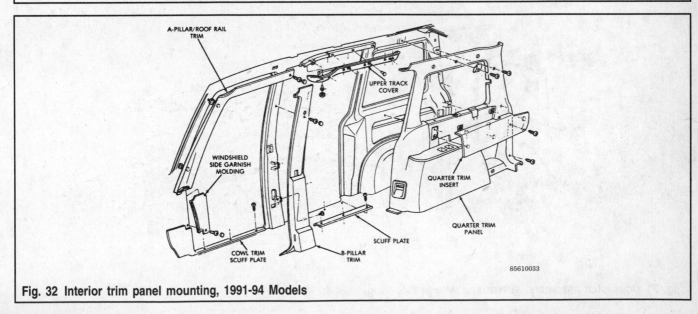

Fig. 32 Interior trim panel mounting, 1991-94 Models

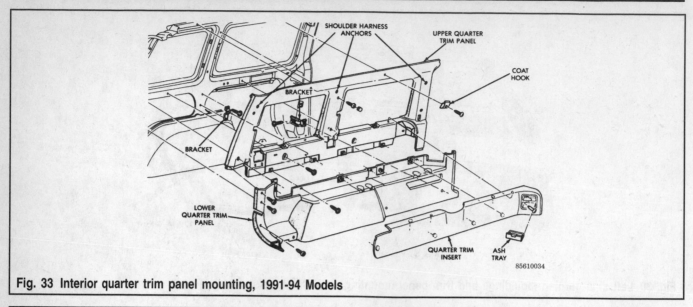

Fig. 33 Interior quarter trim panel mounting, 1991-94 Models

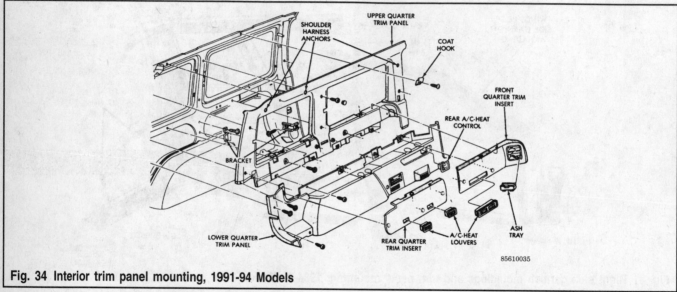

Fig. 34 Interior trim panel mounting, 1991-94 Models

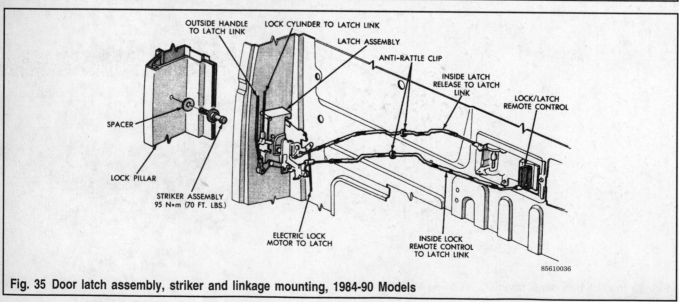

Fig. 35 Door latch assembly, striker and linkage mounting, 1984-90 Models

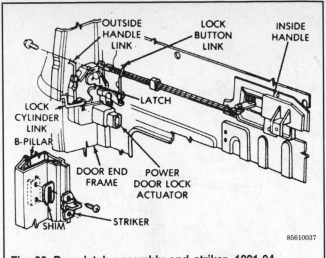

Fig. 36 Door latch assembly and striker, 1991-94 Models

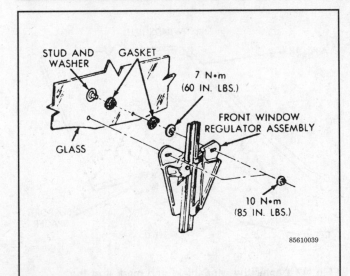

Fig. 37 sliding door latch and linkage

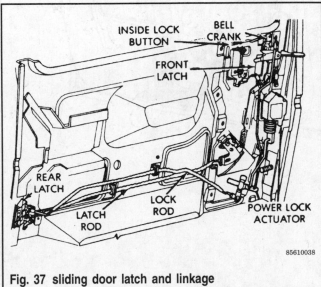

Fig. 38 Front door glass mounting, 1984-94 Models

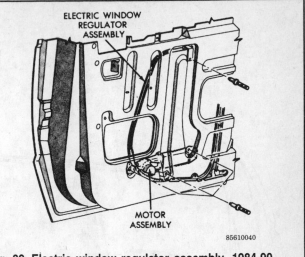

Fig. 39 Electric window regulator assembly, 1984-90 Models

7. Install the window glass, connect the motor wiring harness, and install the inner liner and door trim panel.

➡The window glass is mounted to the regulator by two mounting studs and nuts. Raise the glass until the mounting nuts align with the large access hole. Remove the nuts. Raise the glass up through the door frame. Rotate the glass so that the mounting studs pass through the notch at the rear of the door and remove the glass from the door.

Electric Window Motor

REMOVAL & INSTALLATION

1. Remove the window regulator. See procedure.
2. Remove the electric motor mounting screws and the motor.
3. Place the window motor into the door and secure the mounting screws.
4. Install the window regulator.

Inside Rear View Mirror

REMOVAL & INSTALLATION

1. Loosen the mounting set screw on the mounting arm.
2. Slide the mirror off of the windshield mounting button.
3. Slide the mirror mounting arm over the mounting button and secure the set screw.

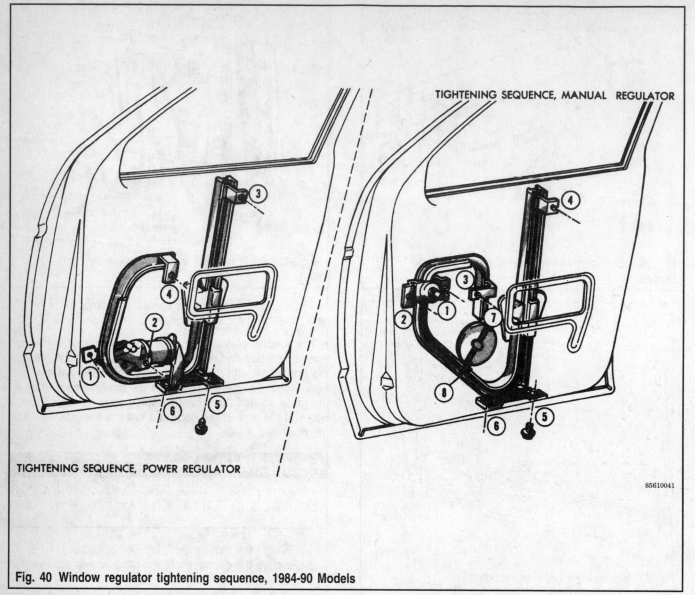

TIGHTENING SEQUENCE, MANUAL REGULATOR

TIGHTENING SEQUENCE, POWER REGULATOR

85610041

Fig. 40 Window regulator tightening sequence, 1984-90 Models

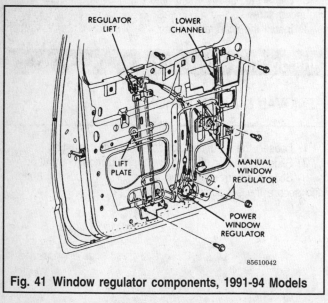

REGULATOR LIFT

LOWER CHANNEL

LIFT PLATE

MANUAL WINDOW REGULATOR

POWER WINDOW REGULATOR

85610042

Fig. 41 Window regulator components, 1991-94 Models

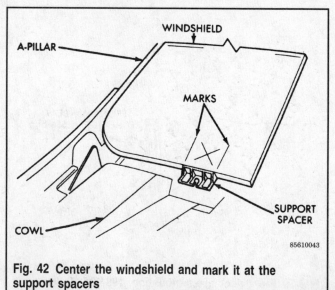

WINDSHIELD

A-PILLAR

MARKS

COWL

SUPPORT SPACER

85610043

Fig. 42 Center the windshield and mark it at the support spacers

Windshield Glass

REMOVAL & INSTALLATION

▶ **See Figures 42, 43 and 44**

➡**The removal and installation of the windshield must be done carefully, improper installation can cause the windshield to crack or shatter. An assistant must be used to insure that the windshield is positioned properly in the opening.**

1. Remove the inside rearview mirror.
2. Remove the cowl cover and the windshield moldings. The moldings can be removed by pulling them upward.
3. Cut the urethane bonding from around the windshield using a sharp knife. Separate the windshield from the vehicle.

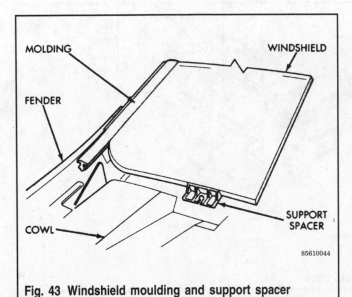

Fig. 43 Windshield moulding and support spacer

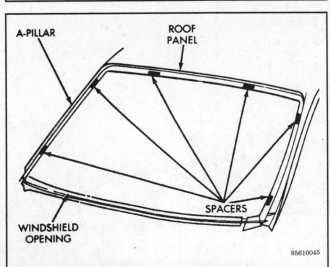

Fig. 44 Correct the positioning of the urethane compression spacers

To install:

4. Clean the windshield area of old urethane bonding that may be loose. Clean the support spacers and reposition them on the studs.
5. With the aid of a helper, place the replacement windshield in the opening and position it in the center of the opening. Mark the glass at the supports, once it is centered, using a grease pencil or masking tape. This will help position it properly.
6. Remove the windshield from the opening and place it on a suitable support, clean the inside of the glass. Apply clear glass primer in a 1 in. (25mm) path around the perimeter of the windshield and wipe with a clean cloth.
7. Apply a 15mm path of blackout primer around the top and sides of the windshield. Apply a 1 in. (25mm) path to the bottom of the windshield. Allow 3 minutes drying time.
8. Position the windshield bonding compression spacers around the opening for the windshield.
9. Apply a 10mm bead of urethane around the inside of the opening.
10. With the aid of a helper, install the windshield glass in position, aligning the reference marks made earlier. Push the windshield into position until it bottoms on the spacers and the top molding is flush with the roof line.
11. Clean excess urethane from the glass using a suitable solvent. Install the moldings.
12. Use pieces of masking tape around the windshield to hold the moulding until the urethane cures.
13. Install the cowl cover and the inside mirror.
14. When the urethane cures, remove the tape and water test the windshield for leaks.

Stationary Glass

REMOVAL & INSTALLATION

All of the fixed glass in the vehicle is removed and installed in the same manner as the windshield glass.

Front Seats

REMOVAL & INSTALLATION

▶ **See Figures 45, 46 and 47**

1. To remove the right front seat; raise and safely support the vehicle.
2. Remove the four nuts and washer that attach the seat to the floor pan.
3. Remove the seat.
4. Position the seat over and through the floor pan holes. Secure the seat with the nuts and washers.
5. To remove the left front seat: tilt the seat reward. Reach under the front of the seat and grab the cable near the clip that retains the cable to the lever. Pull the cable toward the driver's door until it is released from the lever assembly.
6. Turn the cable ninety degrees and push it inward to separate the cable from the lever assembly.

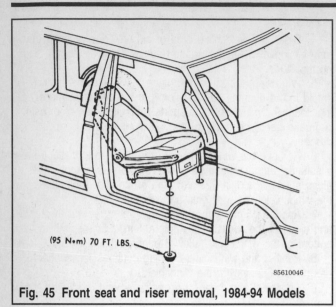

(95 N•m) 70 FT. LBS.

85610046

Fig. 45 Front seat and riser removal, 1984-94 Models

7. Disconnect the electrical connectors. Remove the mounting nuts and washers and remove the seat.

8. Position the seat over the mounting holes and lower through the holes. Secure the seat with the nuts and washers. Connect the electrical wiring and cable.

Rear Seat Assembly

▶ See Figures 48, 49, 50, 51 and 52

The rear seat assemblies can be removed without tools, they are of the quick release kind. To remove the assembly, pull the latch handle and tilt the seat assembly forward and lift it from its mounting. The seat can then be removed from the vehicle.

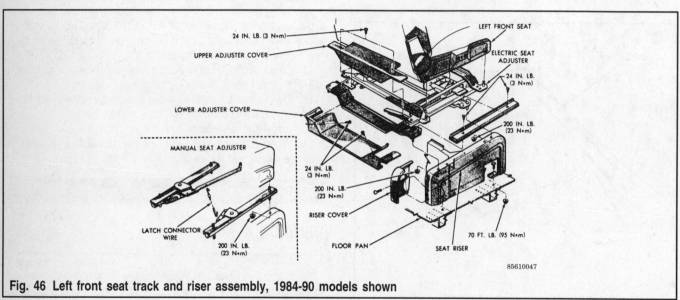

Fig. 46 Left front seat track and riser assembly, 1984-90 models shown

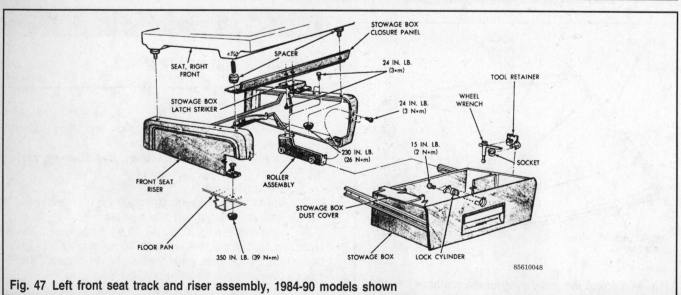

Fig. 47 Left front seat track and riser assembly, 1984-90 models shown

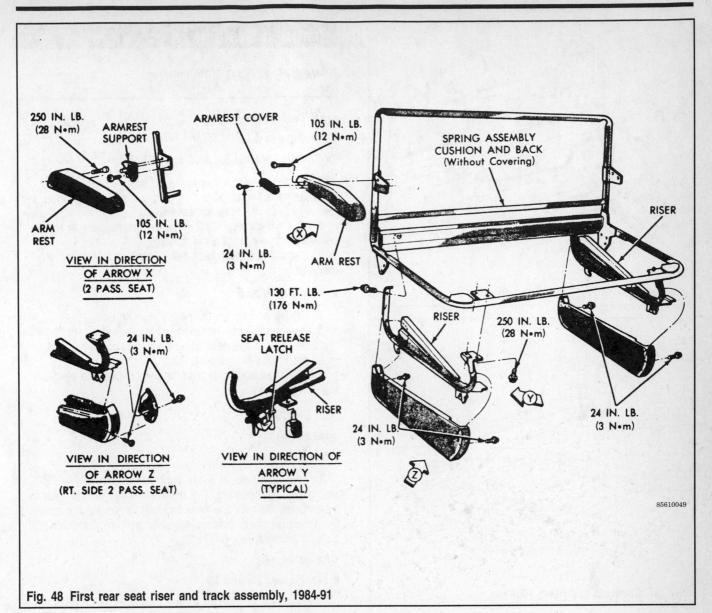

Fig. 48 First rear seat riser and track assembly, 1984-91

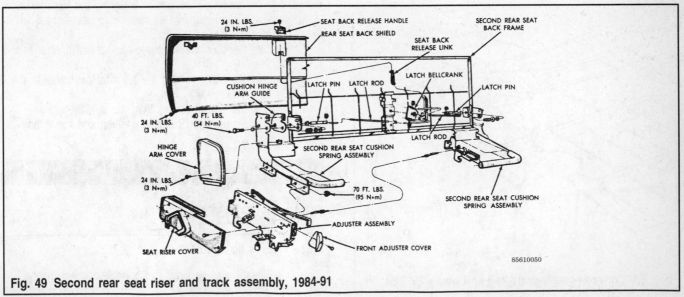

Fig. 49 Second rear seat riser and track assembly, 1984-91

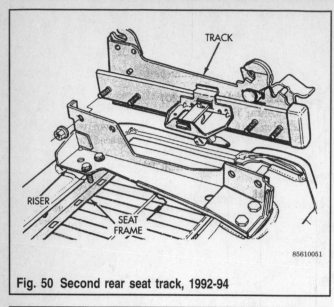

Fig. 50 Second rear seat track, 1992-94

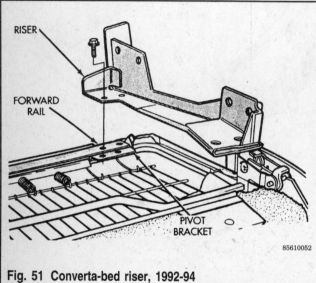

Fig. 51 Converta-bed riser, 1992-94

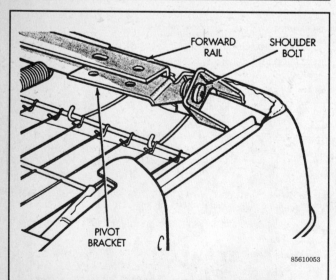

Fig. 52 Converta-bed forward rail and pivot, 1992-94

Seat Belt Systems

REMOVAL & INSTALLATION

Front Seat Belts
▶ **See Figures 53, 54, 55 and 56**

OUTBOARD HARNESS AND LAP BELT

1. Remove the shoulder harness turning loop.
2. Remove the 'B' pillar trim or quarter trim as needed, to gain access to the retractor assembly..
3. Remove the bolt holding the retractor assembly to the body and remove it from the vehicle.
4. Install the replacement belt in position and install any removed trim.

INBOARD BUCKLE

1. Lift the cover from over the mounting bolt.
2. Remove the bolt retaining the buckle to the seat riser.
3. Disconnect the seat belt sensor wire connector and remove the buckle from the vehicle.
4. Install the buckle in position and connect the electrical lead.

Rear Seat Belts

1984-90 MODELS
▶ **See Figure 57**

The rear seat belts in these vehicles are attached to the seat assembly mounting. The belt assemblies are retained by 1 bolt each. Remove the mounting bolt to remove the assembly. When installing replacement belts, tighten all mounting bolts to 350 inch lbs. (40 Nm).

1991-94 models
▶ **See Figures 58 and 59**

The seat belt assemblies in these vehicles are 3 point types mounted to the body in the same manner as the front belts.
1. Remove the interior trim as needed to gain access to the retractor assembly.
2. Remove the bolt holding the lower lap belt anchor to the floor bracket.
3. Remove the bolt retaining the retractor assembly to the inner quarter panel.
4. Remove the belt assembly from the vehicle.
5. Install the replacement belt in position and install any trim that was removed.

Headliner

REMOVAL & INSTALLATION

▶ **See Figures 60 and 61**

1. If equipped with an overhead console, disengage the sun visors from the console. Remove the screws retaining the

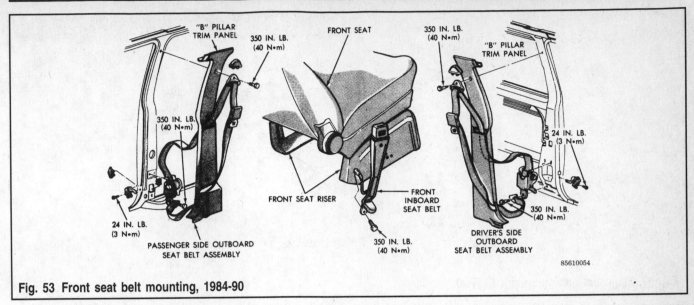

Fig. 53 Front seat belt mounting, 1984-90

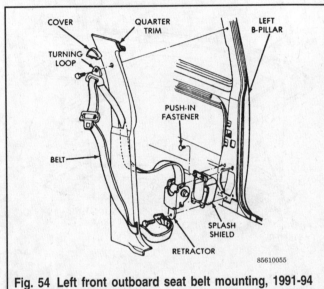

Fig. 54 Left front outboard seat belt mounting, 1991-94

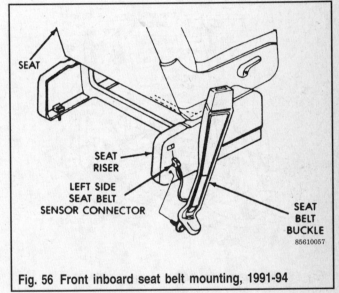

Fig. 56 Front inboard seat belt mounting, 1991-94

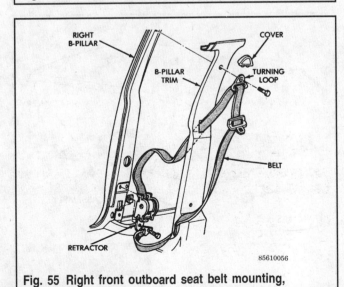

Fig. 55 Right front outboard seat belt mounting, 1991-94

console to the roof, disconnect the wiring and remove the console.

2. Remove the inboard sun visor clips, if not equipped with an overhead console. Remove the sun visors.

3. Remove the upper moldings as needed, to gain access to the headliner.

4. Remove the sliding door upper track cover.

5. Remove the right quarter trim panel.

6. Remove the dome lamp, if equipped.

7. Separate the lining from the vehicle and remove it from the vehicle.

To install:

8. Install the headliner in the vehicle, make sure it is positioned properly.

9. Install the dome lamp and install the right quarter trim panel.

10. Install the sliding door upper track cover.

11. Install any trim moulding that was removed.

12. Install the sun visor clips and the overhead console. Install he sun visors.

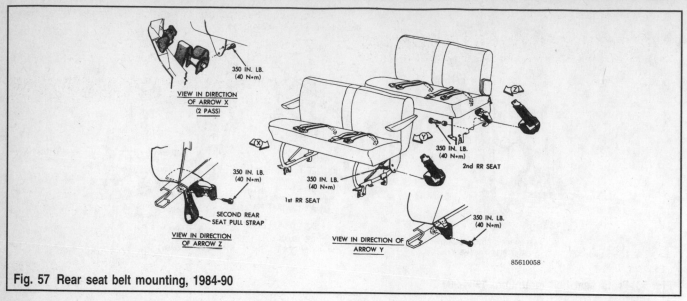

Fig. 57 Rear seat belt mounting, 1984-90

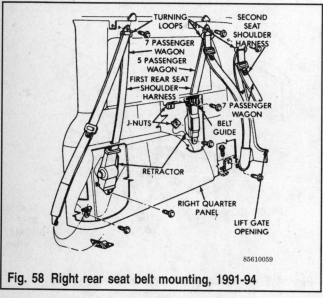

Fig. 58 Right rear seat belt mounting, 1991-94

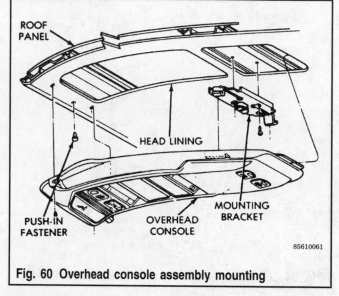

Fig. 60 Overhead console assembly mounting

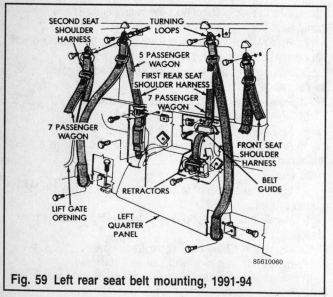

Fig. 59 Left rear seat belt mounting, 1991-94

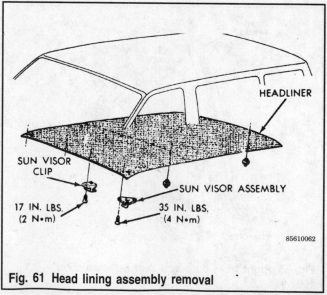

Fig. 61 Head lining assembly removal

13. Install the dome light, if equipped.

Floor Carpeting and Silencers

REMOVAL & INSTALLATION

▶ See Figure 62

1. Remove the front console, if equipped.
2. Remove all of the seat assemblies from the vehicle.
3. Remove the inboard seat belt buckle assemblies. Remove the door sill scuff plates.
4. Remove the rear seat anchor bezels.
5. Lift the carpeting and fold it toward the center of the vehicle, remove it through the sliding door.
6. Lift the silencer pads from the floor and remove them from the vehicle.

To install:

7. Install the silencer pads in position first, make sure they are positioned correctly.
8. Place the carpeting in the vehicle through the sliding door. Unfold and position it.
9. Pull the carpet so that it is straight and even throughout the vehicle.
10. Install the rear seat anchor bezels. Install the rear seat assemblies.

11. Install the front seat assemblies. Install the inboard buckle assemblies.
12. Install the door sill scuff plates.
13. Install the center console assembly, if equipped.

Roof Top Luggage Rack

REMOVAL & INSTALLATION

▶ See Figure 63

The center strips of the roof rack are stuck to the roof with an adhesive, they can be removed by heating them with a heat gun or lamp.

1. Slide the rail end covers from the side rails.
2. Remove the screws holding the rails to the roof.
3. Separate the luggage rack from the vehicle. Remove the center strips at this time, if they are to be removed.

To install:

4. Clean the area that the center strips mount to, if they were removed. All old adhesive must be removed.
5. Using new double sided trim tape, install the center strips.
6. Install the rack side rails to the roof. Make sure the gaskets are in position.
7. Install the rail end covers.

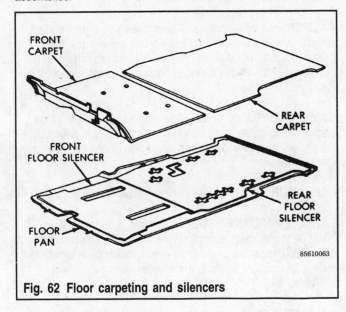

Fig. 62 Floor carpeting and silencers

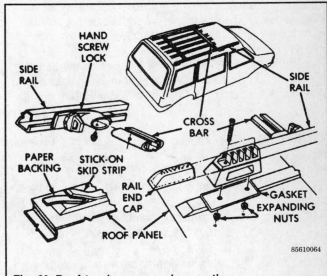

Fig. 63 Roof top luggage rack mounting

AIR/FUEL RATIO: The ratio of air to gasoline by weight in the fuel mixture drawn into the engine.

AIR INJECTION: One method of reducing harmful exhaust emissions by injecting air into each of the exhaust ports of an engine. The fresh air entering the hot exhaust manifold causes any remaining fuel to be burned before it can exit the tailpipe.

ALTERNATOR: A device used for converting mechanical energy into electrical energy.

AMMETER: An instrument, calibrated in amperes, used to measure the flow of an electrical current in a circuit. Ammeters are always connected in series with the circuit being tested.

AMPERE: The rate of flow of electrical current present when one volt of electrical pressure is applied against one ohm of electrical resistance.

ANALOG COMPUTER: Any microprocessor that uses similar (analogous) electrical signals to make its calculations.

ARMATURE: A laminated, soft iron core wrapped by a wire that converts electrical energy to mechanical energy as in a motor or relay. When rotated in a magnetic field, it changes mechanical energy into electrical energy as in a generator.

ATMOSPHERIC PRESSURE: The pressure on the Earth's surface caused by the weight of the air in the atmosphere. At sea level, this pressure is 14.7 psi at 32{248}F (101 kPa at 0{248}C).

ATOMIZATION: The breaking down of a liquid into a fine mist that can be suspended in air.

AXIAL PLAY: Movement parallel to a shaft or bearing bore.

BACKFIRE: The sudden combustion of gases in the intake or exhaust system that results in a loud explosion.

BACKLASH: The clearance or play between two parts, such as meshed gears.

BACKPRESSURE: Restrictions in the exhaust system that slow the exit of exhaust gases from the combustion chamber.

BAKELITE: A heat resistant, plastic insulator material commonly used in printed circuit boards and transistorized components.

BALL BEARING: A bearing made up of hardened inner and outer races between which hardened steel balls roll.

BALLAST RESISTOR: A resistor in the primary ignition circuit that lowers voltage after the engine is started to reduce wear on ignition components.

BEARING: A friction reducing, supportive device usually located between a stationary part and a moving part.

BIMETAL TEMPERATURE SENSOR: Any sensor or switch made of two dissimilar types of metal that bend when heated or cooled due to the different expansion rates of the alloys. These types of sensors usually function as an on/off switch.

BLOWBY: Combustion gases, composed of water vapor and unburned fuel, that leak past the piston rings into the crankcase during normal engine operation. These gases are removed by the PCV system to prevent the buildup of harmful acids in the crankcase.

BRAKE PAD: A brake shoe and lining assembly used with disc brakes.

BRAKE SHOE: The backing for the brake lining. The term is, however, usually applied to the assembly of the brake backing and lining.

BUSHING: A liner, usually removable, for a bearing; an anti-friction liner used in place of a bearing.

CALIPER: A hydraulically activated device in a disc brake system, which is mounted straddling the brake rotor (disc). The caliper contains at least one piston and two brake pads. Hydraulic pressure on the piston(s) forces the pads against the rotor.

CAMSHAFT: A shaft in the engine on which are the lobes (cams) which operate the valves. The camshaft is driven by the crankshaft, via a belt, chain or gears, at one half the crankshaft speed.

CAPACITOR: A device which stores an electrical charge.

CARBON MONOXIDE (CO): A colorless, odorless gas given off as a normal byproduct of combustion. It is poisonous and extremely dangerous in confined areas, building up slowly to toxic levels without warning if adequate ventilation is not available.

CARBURETOR: A device, usually mounted on the intake manifold of an engine, which mixes the air and fuel in the proper proportion to allow even combustion.

CATALYTIC CONVERTER: A device installed in the exhaust system, like a muffler, that converts harmful byproducts of combustion into carbon dioxide and water vapor by means of a heat-producing chemical reaction.

CENTRIFUGAL ADVANCE: A mechanical method of advancing the spark timing by using flyweights in the distributor that react to centrifugal force generated by the distributor shaft rotation.

CHECK VALVE: Any one-way valve installed to permit the flow of air, fuel or vacuum in one direction only.

CHOKE: A device, usually a moveable valve, placed in the intake path of a carburetor to restrict the flow of air.

CIRCUIT: Any unbroken path through which an electrical current can flow. Also used to describe fuel flow in some instances.

CIRCUIT BREAKER: A switch which protects an electrical circuit from overload by opening the circuit when the current flow exceeds a predetermined level. Some circuit breakers must be reset manually, while most reset automatically

COIL (IGNITION): A transformer in the ignition circuit which steps up the voltage provided to the spark plugs.

COMBINATION MANIFOLD: An assembly which includes both the intake and exhaust manifolds in one casting.

COMBINATION VALVE: A device used in some fuel systems that routes fuel vapors to a charcoal storage canister instead of venting them into the atmosphere. The valve relieves fuel tank pressure and allows fresh air into the tank as the fuel level drops to prevent a vapor lock situation.

COMPRESSION RATIO: The comparison of the total volume of the cylinder and combustion chamber with the piston at BDC and the piston at TDC.

CONDENSER: 1. An electrical device which acts to store an electrical charge, preventing voltage surges.
   2. A radiator-like device in the air conditioning system in which refrigerant gas condenses into a liquid, giving off heat.

CONDUCTOR: Any material through which an electrical current can be transmitted easily.

CONTINUITY: Continuous or complete circuit. Can be checked with an ohmmeter.

COUNTERSHAFT: An intermediate shaft which is rotated by a mainshaft and transmits, in turn, that rotation to a working part.

CRANKCASE: The lower part of an engine in which the crankshaft and related parts operate.

CRANKSHAFT: The main driving shaft of an engine which receives reciprocating motion from the pistons and converts it to rotary motion.

CYLINDER: In an engine, the round hole in the engine block in which the piston(s) ride.

CYLINDER BLOCK: The main structural member of an engine in which is found the cylinders, crankshaft and other principal parts.

CYLINDER HEAD: The detachable portion of the engine, fastened, usually, to the top of the cylinder block, containing all or most of the combustion chambers. On overhead valve engines, it contains the valves and their operating parts. On overhead cam engines, it contains the camshaft as well.

DEAD CENTER: The extreme top or bottom of the piston stroke.

DETONATION: An unwanted explosion of the air/fuel mixture in the combustion chamber caused by excess heat and compression, advanced timing, or an overly lean mixture. Also referred to as "ping".

DIAPHRAGM: A thin, flexible wall separating two cavities, such as in a vacuum advance unit.

DIESELING: A condition in which hot spots in the combustion chamber cause the engine to run on after the key is turned off.

DIFFERENTIAL: A geared assembly which allows the transmission of motion between drive axles, giving one axle the ability to turn faster than the other.

DIODE: An electrical device that will allow current to flow in one direction only.

DISC BRAKE: A hydraulic braking assembly consisting of a brake disc, or rotor, mounted on an axle, and a caliper assembly containing, usually two brake pads which are activated by hydraulic pressure. The pads are forced against the sides of the disc, creating friction which slows the vehicle.

DISTRIBUTOR: A mechanically driven device on an engine which is responsible for electrically firing the spark plug at a predetermined point of the piston stroke.

DOWEL PIN: A pin, inserted in mating holes in two different parts allowing those parts to maintain a fixed relationship.

DRUM BRAKE: A braking system which consists of two brake shoes and one or two wheel cylinders, mounted on a fixed backing plate, and a brake drum, mounted on an axle, which revolves around the assembly.

DWELL: The rate, measured in degrees of shaft rotation, at which an electrical circuit cycles on and off.

ELECTRONIC CONTROL UNIT (ECU): Ignition module, module, amplifier or igniter. See Module for definition.

ELECTRONIC IGNITION: A system in which the timing and firing of the spark plugs is controlled by an electronic control unit, usually called a module. These systems have no points or condenser.

ENDPLAY: The measured amount of axial movement in a shaft.

ENGINE: A device that converts heat into mechanical energy.

EXHAUST MANIFOLD: A set of cast passages or pipes which conduct exhaust gases from the engine.

FEELER GAUGE: A blade, usually metal, of precisely predetermined thickness, used to measure the clearance between two parts.

FIRING ORDER: The order in which combustion occurs in the cylinders of an engine. Also the order in which spark is distributed to the plugs by the distributor.

FLOODING: The presence of too much fuel in the intake manifold and combustion chamber which prevents the air/fuel mixture from firing, thereby causing a no-start situation.

FLYWHEEL: A disc shaped part bolted to the rear end of the crankshaft. Around the outer perimeter is affixed the ring gear. The starter drive engages the ring gear, turning the flywheel, which rotates the crankshaft, imparting the initial starting motion to the engine.

FOOT POUND (ft.lb. or sometimes, ft. lbs.): The amount of energy or work needed to raise an item weighing one pound, a distance of one foot.

FUSE: A protective device in a circuit which prevents circuit overload by breaking the circuit when a specific amperage is present. The device is constructed around a strip or wire of a lower amperage rating than the circuit it is designed to protect. When an amperage higher than that stamped on the fuse is present in the circuit, the strip or wire melts, opening the circuit.

GEAR RATIO: The ratio between the number of teeth on meshing gears.

GENERATOR: A device which converts mechanical energy into electrical energy.

HEAT RANGE: The measure of a spark plug's ability to dissipate heat from its firing end. The higher the heat range, the hotter the plug fires.

HUB: The center part of a wheel or gear.

HYDROCARBON (HC): Any chemical compound made up of hydrogen and carbon. A major pollutant formed by the engine as a byproduct of combustion.

HYDROMETER: An instrument used to measure the specific gravity of a solution.

INCH POUND (in.lb. or sometimes, in. lbs.): One twelfth of a foot pound.

INDUCTION: A means of transferring electrical energy in the form of a magnetic field. Principle used in the ignition coil to increase voltage.

INJECTOR: A device which receives metered fuel under relatively low pressure and is activated to inject the fuel into the engine under relatively high pressure at a predetermined time.

INPUT SHAFT: The shaft to which torque is applied, usually carrying the driving gear or gears.

INTAKE MANIFOLD: A casting of passages or pipes used to conduct air or a fuel/air mixture to the cylinders.

JOURNAL: The bearing surface within which a shaft operates.

KEY: A small block usually fitted in a notch between a shaft and a hub to prevent slippage of the two parts.

MANIFOLD: A casting of passages or set of pipes which connect the cylinders to an inlet or outlet source.

MANIFOLD VACUUM: Low pressure in an engine intake manifold formed just below the throttle plates. Manifold vacuum is highest at idle and drops under acceleration.

MASTER CYLINDER: The primary fluid pressurizing device in a hydraulic system. In automotive use, it is found in brake and hydraulic clutch systems and is pedal activated, either directly or, in a power brake system, through the power booster.

MODULE: Electronic control unit, amplifier or igniter of solid state or integrated design which controls the current flow in the ignition primary circuit based on input from the pick-up coil. When the module opens the primary circuit, the high secondary voltage is induced in the coil.

NEEDLE BEARING: A bearing which consists of a number (usually a large number) of long, thin rollers.

OHM:(Ω) The unit used to measure the resistance of conductor to electrical flow. One ohm is the amount of resistance that limits current flow to one ampere in a circuit with one volt of pressure.

OHMMETER: An instrument used for measuring the resistance, in ohms, in an electrical circuit.

OUTPUT SHAFT: The shaft which transmits torque from a device, such as a transmission.

OVERDRIVE: A gear assembly which produces more shaft revolutions than that transmitted to it.

OVERHEAD CAMSHAFT (OHC): An engine configuration in which the camshaft is mounted on top of the cylinder head and operates the valve either directly or by means of rocker arms.

OVERHEAD VALVE (OHV): An engine configuration in which all of the valves are located in the cylinder head and the camshaft is located in the cylinder block. The camshaft operates the valves via lifters and pushrods.

OXIDES OF NITROGEN (NOx): Chemical compounds of nitrogen produced as a byproduct of combustion. They combine with hydrocarbons to produce smog.

OXYGEN SENSOR: Used with the feedback system to sense the presence of oxygen in the exhaust gas and signal the computer which can reference the voltage signal to an air/fuel ratio.

PINION: The smaller of two meshing gears.

PISTON RING: An open ended ring which fits into a groove on the outer diameter of the piston. Its chief function is to form a seal between the piston and cylinder wall. Most automotive pistons have three rings: two for compression sealing; one for oil sealing.

PRELOAD: A predetermined load placed on a bearing during assembly or by adjustment.

PRIMARY CIRCUIT: Is the low voltage side of the ignition system which consists of the ignition switch, ballast resistor or resistance wire, bypass, coil, electronic control unit and pick-up coil as well as the connecting wires and harnesses.

PRESS FIT: The mating of two parts under pressure, due to the inner diameter of one being smaller than the outer diameter of the other, or vice versa; an interference fit.

RACE: The surface on the inner or outer ring of a bearing on which the balls, needles or rollers move.

REGULATOR: A device which maintains the amperage and/or voltage levels of a circuit at predetermined values.

RELAY: A switch which automatically opens and/or closes a circuit.

RESISTANCE: The opposition to the flow of current through a circuit or electrical device, and is measured in ohms. Resistance is equal to the voltage divided by the amperage.

RESISTOR: A device, usually made of wire, which offers a preset amount of resistance in an electrical circuit.

RING GEAR: The name given to a ring-shaped gear attached to a differential case, or affixed to a flywheel or as part a planetary gear set.

ROLLER BEARING: A bearing made up of hardened inner and outer races between which hardened steel rollers move.

ROTOR: 1. The disc-shaped part of a disc brake assembly, upon which the brake pads bear; also called, brake disc.
2. The device mounted atop the distributor shaft, which passes current to the distributor cap tower contacts.

SECONDARY CIRCUIT: The high voltage side of the ignition system, usually above 20,000 volts. The secondary includes the ignition coil, coil wire, distributor cap and rotor, spark plug wires and spark plugs.

SENDING UNIT: A mechanical, electrical, hydraulic or electromagnetic device which transmits information to a gauge.

SENSOR: Any device designed to measure engine operating conditions or ambient pressures and temperatures. Usually electronic in nature and designed to send a voltage signal to an on-board computer, some sensors may operate as a simple on/off switch or they may provide a variable voltage signal (like a potentiometer) as conditions or measured parameters change.

SHIM: Spacers of precise, predetermined thickness used between parts to establish a proper working relationship.

SLAVE CYLINDER: In automotive use, a device in the hydraulic clutch system which is activated by hydraulic force, disengaging the clutch.

SOLENOID: A coil used to produce a magnetic field, the effect of which is produce work.

SPARK PLUG: A device screwed into the combustion chamber of a spark ignition engine. The basic construction is a conductive core inside of a ceramic insulator, mounted in an outer conductive base. An electrical charge from the spark plug wire travels along the conductive core and jumps a preset air gap to a grounding point or points at the end of the conductive base. The resultant spark ignites the fuel/air mixture in the combustion chamber.

SPLINES: Ridges machined or cast onto the outer diameter of a shaft or inner diameter of a bore to enable parts to mate without rotation.

TACHOMETER: A device used to measure the rotary speed of an engine, shaft, gear, etc., usually in rotations per minute.

THERMOSTAT: A valve, located in the cooling system of an engine, which is closed when cold and opens gradually in response to engine heating, controlling the temperature of the coolant and rate of coolant flow.

TOP DEAD CENTER (TDC): The point at which the piston reaches the top of its travel on the compression stroke.

TORQUE: The twisting force applied to an object.

TORQUE CONVERTER: A turbine used to transmit power from a driving member to a driven member via hydraulic action, providing changes in drive ratio and torque. In automotive use, it links the driveplate at the rear of the engine to the automatic transmission.

TRANSDUCER: A device used to change a force into an electrical signal.

TRANSISTOR: A semi-conductor component which can be actuated by a small voltage to perform an electrical switching function.

TUNE-UP: A regular maintenance function, usually associated with the replacement and adjustment of parts and components in the electrical and fuel systems of a vehicle for the purpose of attaining optimum performance.

TURBOCHARGER: An exhaust driven pump which compresses intake air and forces it into the combustion chambers at higher than atmospheric pressures. The increased air pressure allows more fuel to be burned and results in increased horsepower being produced.

VACUUM ADVANCE: A device which advances the ignition timing in response to increased engine vacuum.

VACUUM GAUGE: An instrument used to measure the presence of vacuum in a chamber.

VALVE: A device which control the pressure, direction of flow or rate of flow of a liquid or gas.

VALVE CLEARANCE: The measured gap between the end of the valve stem and the rocker arm, cam lobe or follower that activates the valve.

VISCOSITY: The rating of a liquid's internal resistance to flow.

VOLTMETER: An instrument used for measuring electrical force in units called volts. Voltmeters are always connected parallel with the circuit being tested.

WHEEL CYLINDER: Found in the automotive drum brake assembly, it is a device, actuated by hydraulic pressure, which, through internal pistons, pushes the brake shoes outward against the drums.

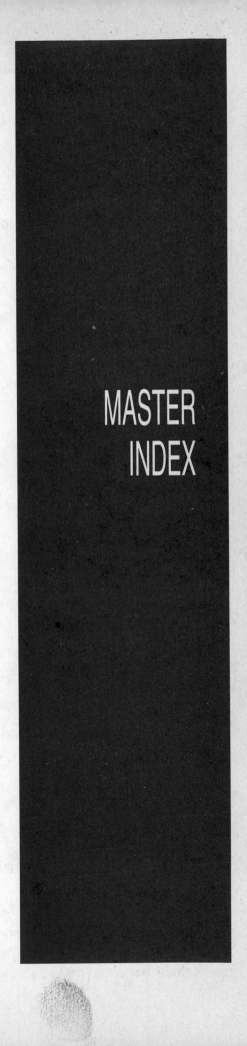

MASTER

INDEX